Praise for *Imperial Island*

"This is a terrific textbook that is destined to surpass anything extant in the field. It is beautifully written, clear and concise while also being miraculously comprehensive and wide-ranging ... Eighteenth century British historians have been waiting for a textbook like this for a long time."

Kathleen Wilson, SUNY Stony Brook

"A great introduction to the era. Paul Monod has brilliantly captured the vigorous, messy, complexity of eighteenth-century Britain in all its glory. This is where undergraduates need to start their encounter with Britain's first age of empire."

Daniel Szechi, University of Manchester

"An outstanding college textbook, *Imperial Island* reveals the character of the nation that ruled the world by the end of the eighteenth century. It takes advantage of new historical approaches to the period and includes descriptive accounts of Britain's military success and imperial expansion into North America, India, Africa, and the Pacific. Paul Monod's good-humored, unpretentious writing style makes this a delightful book to read."

Molly McClain, University of San Diego

"Paul Monod's new textbook is erudite yet easy to read. Deeply informed by the latest scholarship, it is also thematically focused, logically structured, nicely balanced, and engagingly written. *Imperial Island* will provide students with an excellent, up-to-date introduction to Britain and the British Empire in the 'long' eighteenth century."

Phil Harling, University of Kentucky

"This is a really excellent introduction to the history of the British Isles and the British Empire from the accession of Charles II to the accession of Queen Victoria. The strong political narrative is supported with excellent material on the economic, social and cultural contexts. The text is based on sound research and good judgement, but it is also written by an experienced scholar and well-regarded teacher in an accessible, even witty style. It is embellished with useful illustrations and relevant maps, as well as apt quotations that make it not only highly informative but a great pleasure to read. Paul Monod has put students and teachers in his debt."

H.T. Dickinson, University of Edinburgh

*To Jan, Evan,
and my students at Middlebury College.*

IMPERIAL ISLAND

A History of Britain and Its Empire, 1660–1837

PAUL KLÉBER MONOD

A John Wiley & Sons, Ltd., Publication

This edition first published 2009
© 2009 Paul Kléber Monod

Blackwell Publishing was acquired by John Wiley & Sons in February 2007. Blackwell's publishing
program has been merged with Wiley's global Scientific, Technical, and Medical business to form
Wiley-Blackwell.

Registered Office
John Wiley & Sons Ltd, The Atrium, Southern Gate, Chichester, West Sussex,
PO19 8SQ, United Kingdom

Editorial Offices
350 Main Street, Malden, MA 02148-5020, USA
9600 Garsington Road, Oxford, OX4 2DQ, UK
The Atrium, Southern Gate, Chichester, West Sussex, PO19 8SQ, UK

For details of our global editorial offices, for customer services, and for information about how
to apply for permission to reuse the copyright material in this book please see our website at
www.wiley.com/wiley-blackwell.

Library of Congress Cataloging-in-Publication Data

Monod, Paul Kléber.
Imperial Island : a history of Britain and its empire, 1688–1837 / Paul Monod.
p. cm.
Includes bibliographical references and index.
ISBN 978-1-4051-3444-6 (hardcover : alk. paper) – ISBN 978-1-4051-3445-3 (pbk. : alk. paper)
1. Great Britain–History–1689–1714. 2. Great Britain–History–1714–1837. 3. Great Britain–
Foreign relations–1689–1714. 4. Great Britain–Foreign relations–1714–1837. 5. Imperialism–
History–18th century. 6. Imperialism–History–19th century. I. Title.
DA480.M64 2009
909'.0971241–dc22
2008044267

A catalogue record for this book is available from the British Library.

Set in 10/12.5 pt Sabon
by SPi Publisher Services, Pondicherry, India

I 2009

Contents

Illustrations

Maps

Preface

More than 25 years ago, as a graduate teaching assistant at Yale University, I heard a celebrated professor pose an audacious question to a room full of under-graduates. In the first lecture of his course on eighteenth-century British history, he asked the members of his young audience what sort of semester they wanted. Would they prefer to hear a political narrative or an analysis of topics in social, economic, and cultural history? To my surprise, virtually all the students opted for a political narrative. Today, I suspect, a few more might be interested in a topical approach, but most undergraduates would probably still opt for a chrono-logical political survey. Almost 25 years of teaching at Middlebury College has convinced me that narrative history retains a strong appeal as a path to historical understanding. The challenge for teachers is how to incorporate important social, economic, and cultural issues into such a narrative.

This book tries to meet that challenge. It is essentially a political history of Britain and its empire from 1660 to 1837. Chapters that address social, economic, and cultural developments have been placed within the narrative, so as to relate them to the broad sequence of political events. An ideal text might integrate them fully, but it would be as complex and bewildering as the multiplicity of actual human experience. My overriding goal has been clarity. The book has been writ-ten for American and Canadian undergraduates, who are likely to use it in intro-ductory courses, although I hope that it will appeal to any reader who wants a basic comprehension of the subject.

This work was intended to be a sequel to the excellent *Early Modern England, 1485–1714*, by Robert Bucholz and Newton Key, but it differs from its predeces-sor in structure – it contains a larger number of shorter chapters – as well as in the amount of attention it gives to Scotland, Ireland, and the empire. These features represent responses to the growing diversification and increasing scope of under-graduate courses that deal with the late Stuart and Hanoverian periods. Courses on the British Atlantic world and on the British impact in South Asia or the Pacific have proliferated over the past 20 years. This book attempts to bring such topics together in a narrative that connects them with political developments in Great Britain. At the same time, attention has been paid to the unique characteristics of each area of study, so as to avoid merely subordinating them to the British political history that is at the heart of the book.

I have tried not to load down the text with names, especially the names of other historians. While I have often alluded to historical disagreements and conflicting interpretations, they are not usually explained in much detail. I believe they are better learned through lectures or supplemental readings, rather than in a textbook. At the same time, I have not hesitated to express my own opinions, which should provoke some readers to disagreement and others to wonder how my assumptions could possibly be correct. If this book stimulates students to question what they read, to debate the case, and perhaps to carry out further research, it will have achieved a much higher purpose than simply providing them with information.

The 21 chapters in the book are organized into seven chronological parts. Political events are discussed in ten of the chapters; social, economic, and cultural trends in five chapters; the arts and sciences in two chapters; and the empire in four chapters. No doubt every course, and every reader, will use the book in a different way. Each chapter has its own thematic unity, and many of the sections within chapters deal with discrete subjects, so they can be read in various combinations. A 14-week course on British history 1660–1837, in which students read one chapter a week, might stick to the ten political chapters, plus Chapters 2, 3, 11, and 15 for socio-economic trends. A course on the Atlantic world or British imperial history might use Chapters 6, 12, 13, 14, 17, and 21. A course that concentrated on British culture rather than politics might include Chapters 3, 4, 9, 11, 15, 18, 20, and 21.

A textbook should be useful, reliable, comprehensive, and versatile, but it should also be a pleasure to read. I enjoyed the process of writing this book, and I hope that some of that enjoyment will be conveyed to the reader.

Acknowledgments

My biggest debt in writing this textbook is to the students in my British history courses at Middlebury College, who over almost 25 years have provided me with the responses and reactions that have guided my thinking about Britain's past. Few undergraduates realize the impact that they have on the way their teachers approach the subjects they teach. While students may not always have the answers, they usually have the right questions. Parts of the text were read by a current student, Julia Whelan, and a former student, Ned Courtemanche. Their comments were of very great value to me, especially as neither of them seemed bored by what I had written. I cannot thank them enough for their efforts.

Next to the students, I am grateful to my wife, Jan Albers, who was initially supposed to write this book along with me, but who had to drop out of the project because of the demands of her job as a museum director. Nonetheless, she read the drafts and gave me constant encouragement. I hope my son Evan will some day read the book, too, and will laugh at the bits of humor that are scattered through it.

The three anonymous reviewers for Blackwell were exceptionally generous and helpful in their comments. In addition, 16 other scholars were kind enough to read parts of the initial draft of the book: Susan Amussen, Donna Andrews, Ian Barrow, Jim Epstein, Alison Games, Eliga Gould, Tim Harris, Bill Hart, Derek Hirst, Julian Hoppitt, Colin Kidd, Peter Mandler, David Monod, Daniel Szechi, Jacob Tropp, and Keith Wrightson. I am enormously grateful for their generosity, which saved me from a multitude of errors. The mistakes that remain (let them not be legion!) are entirely my own fault. Tessa Harvey of Blackwell has been an exemplary editor and I am happy that she persuaded me to take on this project. I must thank the whole Blackwell editorial team for their hard work and assistance. Finally, the influence of my own wonderfully diverse teachers in the British, American, and European history of this period – John Murrin, Jim Obelkevich, Ted Rabb, Lawrence Stone, John Brewer, Linda Colley, Peter Gay, John Merriman, Edmund Morgan, Conrad Russell, Jon Schneer, Frank Turner, David Underdown, and Robin Winks, among others – is evident on every page, at least to me. If a shadow of their learning and insight survives here, I am content.

Paul Monod
Middlebury, Vermont

A Note on Currency

According to the old system of British currency, 20 shillings (*s* for Latin solidarius) made a pound (£) and twelve pence (*d* for Latin denarius) made a shilling. A guinea was one pound one shilling.

Frequently Used Abbreviations

BCE   before the Common Era
CE   Common Era
MP   Member of Parliament
JP   justice of the peace
EIC   East India Company

Part I

Nations, Lands, Peoples

This is a history of the island of Great Britain and of its remarkable impact on the world in the century and a half after 1688. That may sound like a straightforward place to begin, but in fact it is not. In 1688, Great Britain was not a nation or a state – it was a geographical expression, identifying the biggest of a group of islands on the west coast of Europe. The island called Great Britain was made up of two kingdoms with one king, an awkward state of affairs. It encompassed many different regions and peoples. "Britishness," the national characteristics of a British people, did not yet exist. People thought of themselves as English or Welsh or Scots (not Scotch, which is the name of an alcoholic drink). To make matters more complicated, by the end of the period, the national state that we will be studying was no longer officially called Great Britain. After 1801, it was the United Kingdom of Great Britain and Ireland. These changes have left a legacy of linguistic confusion that persists today. People often say "British" when they mean "English," or mention "Britain" when they mean "the United Kingdom." Since there is no simple term for an inhabitant of the United Kingdom, some degree of confusion is probably inevitable; but it is worth sorting out, as much as we can, what Britain was, and what it became, in terms of nations, lands, and peoples.

If the British nation is a recent creation, as the first chapter of this part of the book will argue, the settlement of the land is not. The British Isles have been populated for thousands of years, and large sections of them have been under cultivation for twenty centuries or more. In the 1500s, however, a more intense type of land use began in some areas of southern England. This would lead to higher agricultural productivity and, eventually, lower food prices. New methods of farming also encouraged the creation of a labor force that could be employed, whether out of necessity or from choice, in spinning and weaving cloth, as well as in other industrial pursuits. English and Scottish towns, many of which had been in a state of decline in the fourteenth and fifteenth centuries, became commercially prosperous again, and trade expanded rapidly. The rich got richer, while the poor mostly had to wait until the late seventeenth century before they began to feel the beneficial effects of an expanding economy. These subjects are considered in the second chapter below.

The peoples of Great Britain are the subject of the third chapter. What were their numbers? How similar were they to us, in values or ideas? What differences existed between men and women, rich and poor? What did people do when they were not working? It is often hard to put the many answers to these questions into a broader pattern. Was life improving? Was it becoming more "modern," and if so, what do we mean by that term? Readers should understand that much of the material in the second and third chapters of this part of the book is generalized and that the interpretations are often controversial. Economic and social historians have engaged in almost as many arguments about this period as political ones. They are divided by when developments began, how they should be described, and how important they were. Almost everyone who has written on the period from 1500 to 1700, however, agrees that big changes were under way in every aspect of British life. What follows is an overview of how those changes came about, and what they meant.

1

Nations and Kingdoms

Nations are not natural formations: they are the products of historical processes. How were the nations of England and Scotland shaped in the centuries before 1660? In answering that question, we have to take some account of Ireland as well, because its history intersected with that of the other two kingdoms. The nations of the British Isles developed as a result of invasions, internal conflicts, the Protestant Reformation, and a bitter series of Civil Wars in the mid-1600s. From the eleventh century onwards, England was the most powerful and aggressive kingdom in the British Isles. Its imperial adventures in Wales, Scotland, Ireland, France, and the New World played a central role in nation-building. Constant wars against its neighbors built up a sense of English identity, as well as stimulating reactions from other peoples and kingdoms.

Ancient Invaders

The British Isles is an archipelago of islands on the northwest coast of Europe. The two biggest of them are Great Britain and Ireland, although it should not be forgotten that a number of smaller islands surround them – the Isle of Wight, Anglesey, the Isle of Man, the Hebrides, Orkneys, and Arran Islands, among others. Until the end of the last Ice Age, about 10,000 years ago, Great Britain was not an island at all, but an extension of the European continent. It was inhabited before the glaciers came down from the north for the last time, and as the great sheets of ice receded, the people came back. They established a series of Neolithic and Bronze Age cultures on the British Isles, whose most lasting achievements were the building of great stone circles and megalithic tombs. The stone circle at Stonehenge in England and the enormous chambered tomb at Newgrange in Ireland are the most famous. The early islanders did not live in isolation; they continued to have strong links with the rest of Europe, judging by the recent discovery at Stonehenge of the body of an archer who was identified as Swiss by the chemical composition of his teeth.

The *keltoi* or Celts (a Greek word for people who called themselves Gauls or Gaels) reached the islands around 600 BCE. They were migrants from Eastern Europe, who eventually settled in places across the continent, from Turkey to Spain. It is now generally believed that they infiltrated rather than invaded the British Isles, mixing with existing populations but not displacing them. People who claim today to be "pure Celts" may therefore be a little misled – leaving aside later additions, their ancestors were more likely a mixture of Celtic and pre-Celtic peoples. The Celtic priests, known as druids, were glamorized in the eighteenth century by historians, who embraced them, wrongly, as proto-Christians, although they actually worshipped a variety of gods. Much later, the druids were turned into nature worshippers by twentieth-century New Age believers who still gather yearly at Stonehenge (in fact, it is a pre-druidic shrine) to celebrate the summer solstice. The real Celts were fierce warriors and skilled metalworkers who traded tin to the Mediterranean, where they were known to Greek-speaking merchants as "Priteni" or Britons. In Ireland, they established a high kingship that lasted, with one major break, until the twelfth century CE, although it was not strong enough to unite the island.

The invasion of Great Britain by the Romans in 43 CE broke up the Celtic world of the British Isles. The province of Britannia, which remained under Roman rule for the next four centuries, was almost coterminous with the later English kingdom. Wales and Cornwall were never entirely subdued by the Roman legions, and the northern part of Great Britain, inhabited by a mysterious people known as the Picts, was conquered only briefly. Ireland remained outside the Roman Empire. The inhabitants of Scotland and Ireland nonetheless traded a great deal with the Romans, and were deeply affected by Roman culture, especially Roman Christianity, but it was only in England that the two cultures merged, at least among the upper classes. In time, Britannia was integrated into a Europe-wide Roman world based on commerce, cities, straight roads, and uniform imperial administration. Although that world eventually fell apart, its legacy would be revived among later inhabitants of the former province of Britannia. From then until the decline of Latin in the twentieth century, educated people in England and Scotland would tend to regard themselves as having more in common with classical civilization than with the "barbarism" of their Celtic neighbors.

The Romans withdrew from Britannia in 410 CE amidst a wave of invasions. Eventually, Germanic peoples from northern Europe, known today as "Anglo-Saxons" – actually, Angles, Saxons, Frisians, and Jutes – conquered the Romanized Britons, in spite of the resistance of the legendary military leader later celebrated as King Arthur. The Anglo-Saxons, like the Celts, did not wipe out the peoples that they had overcome, but they remained apart from the Britons in their laws and customs, and they drove the Celtic languages into Wales ("welsh" meant foreigner in Anglo-Saxon) and Cornwall. It took the invaders a long time to accept Christianity, which was already widespread among the native British population. The Christian religion had taken a firm hold in Ireland, and was reintroduced to northern Britain by Irish missionaries, while missionaries from Rome reconverted the south. Meanwhile, a line of Irish kings from Dalriada, which straddled northern Ireland and the Scottish islands, gained control over the northern Pictish lands,

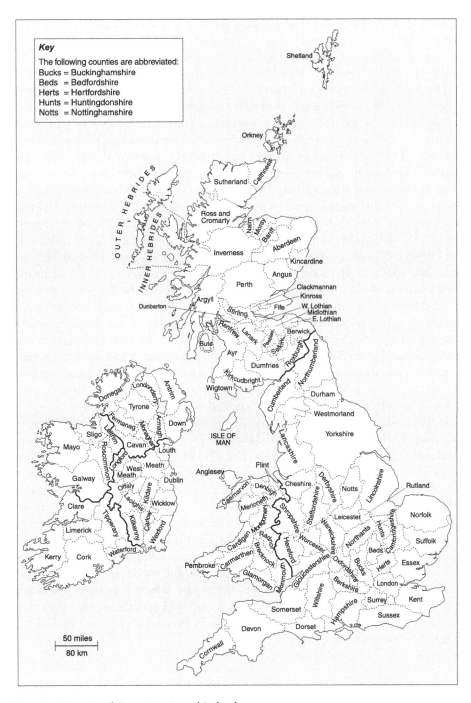

Map 1 *Counties of Great Britain and Ireland.*

which they renamed Scotia. The southern parts of Scotland fell under the sway of the kingdom of Northumbria, principal realm of the Angles, who would give their name to Angle-land or England. Here were the origins of a distinction between the Gaelic speaking Scottish Highlands and the English speaking Scottish Lowlands.

The Anglo-Saxons were followed by a second wave of invaders, this time from Scandinavia. The Vikings who sailed to the British Isles from Scandinavia between the ninth and the twelfth centuries are often remembered simply as murderous pirates, but they were also settlers and traders, who revitalized London and founded the city of Dublin. They landed in large numbers in the western islands of Scotland and set up a virtually independent lordship. Resistance to them rallied under Brian Boru in Ireland and King Alfred of Wessex in southwest England, both of whom became nationalist icons in modern times. The kingdom of England emerged in the tenth century through the unification, under Alfred's successors, of the Anglo-Saxon and Viking parts of the old Roman province of Britannia. Closely allied with the Catholic Church, the English monarch ruled over a violent land in which peasants were increasingly losing their freedom to powerful lords who offered them protection in return. To help recruit local military forces, the Anglo-Saxon kings divided their realm into shires or counties, which still exist. Each county would eventually have its own administrators and courts, set up on the same model throughout the kingdom. Such a degree of uniformity in local government was highly unusual in medieval Europe. Meanwhile, the Church had divided England and Wales into dioceses, each under the authority of a bishop, and parishes where priests held religious services for local people. The same hierarchical structure was not fully established in the Church of Scotland until the twelfth century.

It was a descendant of the Vikings, the French-speaking Duke William of Normandy, who crushed the Anglo-Saxons at the battle of Hastings in 1066 and established a dynasty of strong rulers that would keep England united. William's descendants (admittedly, not very direct ones) still hold the English throne today. The Norman knights rode on to subdue the eastern and southern parts of Wales, which were divided up into "marcher lordships," and to defeat repeated invasions by the King of Scotland. The Normans also moved into the southern parts of Scotland, where they were granted land by the King of Scots. Everywhere they went, the followers of Duke William built mighty castles and strengthened the authority of lords over peasants. The Normans did not invent the manor, the basic unit of territorial lordship, or serfdom, by which a peasant could not move off the land, and paid in hard work for a lord's protection. However, they extended the manorial system (often referred to by the misleading term "feudalism") wherever they made conquests.

The Medieval English Empire

Over the next two centuries, Norman-French Kings of England founded an empire whose heartland was actually in western and southern France, but which extended throughout the British Isles. The great King Henry II, who spent most of his time in France, extended this empire to its height. He made the King of Scotland his vassal, and in 1169 his "marcher lords" launched an invasion of Ireland. Henry's son King John suffered severe setbacks when he lost Normandy and had to grant the famous Magna Carta or Great Charter to his barons in 1215. It insured them certain legal and political rights, in terms vague enough to be interpreted much more broadly later. John's successors, however, never gave up the idea that they could only achieve greatness by putting back together the empire of Henry II. The independent kingdom of north Wales was conquered by King Edward I in the 1280s, a new principality of Wales was created, and huge castles were constructed to ensure that it would remain subdued. Scotland was also invaded and temporarily subjected, but its independence was re-established by the victory of Robert Bruce over an English army at Bannockburn in 1314. We should not interpret these wars in national terms: Robert Bruce was the descendant of Norman-French nobles, and he defeated a king whose dynasty was also Norman-French. Irish, Scottish, and Welsh peasants could hardly have cared much who their overlord happened to be, so long as he did not try to change their everyday lives. The Normans did in fact attempt to alter traditional laws in northern Wales and Ireland, but they were not very successful. Nevertheless, the fight to establish the hegemony of the King of England would give rise to the idea that there were fundamental national differences between the peoples that inhabited the British Isles. As in later times, empire and national identity went hand-in-hand.

After 1337, the Kings of England turned their attention to the restoration of their former domains in France. Thus began the so-called 100 Years' War, which lasted on and off until the English lost Calais, their final toehold in France, in 1558. In many ways, the war marked the flourishing of an English national consciousness, that is, awareness of being English rather than part of a Norman-French civilization. This may have started earlier among clerical chroniclers, but it now spread to the knights, who while mostly Norman-French in origin, were engaged in fighting the French, and began to see themselves as different from their enemies. They modeled themselves on the mythical British knights of King Arthur's Round Table. By the end of the 1300s, English rather than French was being taught in schools to the children of the upper classes. An English literature was emerging, whose greatest early figure was the poet Geoffrey Chaucer, author of the *Canterbury Tales*. Differences between the Scots and English went back further, but since the Scots were now allies of the French, the English upper classes saw themselves as separate from their northern neighbors as well, in spite of the fact that the Stewart kings who ruled Scotland after 1371 were descendants of Norman knights.

Another factor in creating national consciousness was Parliament. In seeking funds and support for making war against the Welsh, the Scots, and the French, the King of England found it useful to call a grand council of nobles, high ranking clergymen and representatives of counties and towns. The representatives were chosen by those who owned land, by town magistrates, and in some cases by wider groups of electors who enjoyed privileges in specific localities. Later, the nobles and clergy formed a House of Lords, while the representatives became a

House of Commons. The Parliament, or place to speak (*parler* in French), was not a democratic body, but it soon claimed that it spoke for the whole English nation, which supposed of course that such a nation existed.

At the same time, however, the power of the English nobles over the Welsh, the Irish, and the English peasantry was diminishing. This was partly due to a factor over which no noble and no king had any control: the bubonic plague or Black Death, which devastated the British Isles and most of Europe in 1348–50. It may have killed off one-third of the population of the islands. The sudden death of so many people was no doubt horrifying, but it meant that the remaining peasants were in short supply. It was no longer possible to keep them on the land as serfs; instead, they became free laborers. In fact, the old manorial system had probably been declining for some time before the Black Death, which merely gave it a final blow. As a result, attempts to reduce the Irish and Welsh peasantry to serfdom, or to colonize Ireland and Wales with English settlers, fizzled out. The Norman bid to control Ireland had been going awry in any case. With the attention of the English King focused on France, the Anglo-Norman lords of southern and western Ireland became like little kings within their domains. To safeguard their power, they were compelled to adapt to Irish conditions, rather than trying to force Norman-French culture on the Irish. The Irish Parliament, which was older than the English one but represented only the Norman and English settlers, became virtually independent. In Northern Ireland, the Gaelic lordships of the O'Neills and O'Donnells reconsolidated their power. A similar situation prevailed in the principality of Wales, where the "marcher lords" maintained an uneasy authority. In 1400, Owain Glyn Dŵr was proclaimed as Prince of Wales by some local nobles, and raised a rebellion against the King of England that went on for 14 years. Glyn Dŵr even called a Welsh Parliament. The effective beginnings of a Welsh national identity can be traced to the years of Glyn Dŵr's rebellion.

The Protestant Reformations

The long war against France weakened the internal government of England as well, because it made the King very dependent on the support of his nobles. This encouraged civil wars and usurpations. The crown was taken by force on five occasions: by Henry, Duke of Lancaster (Henry IV), in 1399; by Edward, Duke of York (Edward IV), in 1461 and again in 1470; by Richard, Duke of Gloucester (Richard III), who put aside and may have murdered his nephews, the lawful heirs, in 1483; and by Henry Tudor, Earl of Richmond (Henry VII), in 1485. This was a very bad record of usurpation by any standard, and it gained the English a reputation for having unsteady government. The last four of these incidents occurred during the baronial conflicts that were later known as the Wars of the Roses, which were sparked off by English defeats in France. The old Norman-French dream of an empire encompassing the British Isles and western France was now falling apart, externally and internally. Would the kingdom of England fall apart with it?

It might have, if the Scots had been strong enough to launch a successful invasion; but they were not strong enough, in spite of serious attempts in 1460, 1513, and 1542. The King of Scotland had his own worries at home, especially in controlling the Lords of the Isles, who governed the Hebrides and the west coast of Scotland, and who conspired with England to maintain their independence. King James IV finally forced the Lord of the Isles to forfeit his title in 1493. The Scots Parliament declared the Lord of the Isles a traitor, but the legislature was rarely so useful to the crown. It sat in a single chamber (not two as in England), and it was dominated by the great Scottish nobles. Such an assembly was not likely to give the King much financial support against his eternally feuding subjects. King James V began to strengthen royal control over money and justice, but he also had to fend off the English, which led him to depend heavily on an alliance with France. He died, like his father and his great-grandfather before him, in the midst of an unsuccessful war against England.

The Tudor dynasty came to the English throne in 1485, at the end of the Wars of the Roses. The Tudors did not exactly save the kingdom from ruin – it was already on the road to recovery – but they were able to rebuild English power and prestige after a century of disasters. More than any other line of monarchs, they are connected with the flowering of an English national identity. They were the first rulers since 1066 whose ancestors were not primarily Norman-French, which led them to describe themselves as natives, although the Tudor family was Welsh, not English, and it owed its questionable right to the throne to a tenuous link with the old Norman-French ruling house. The Tudors spoke of England as an empire, and they backed up their words by incorporating Wales into the kingdom (1536–43), converting the "marcher lordships" of the borderlands into English-style counties. They also intervened in Irish affairs, uniting that country to the English crown in 1541. From then until Ireland became a Republic in 1949, the King of England was also the King in Ireland. Seeking to restore English fortunes in France as well, Henry VII and his son Henry VIII fought wars against the French. These conflicts ended in defeat or bankruptcy, but they restored a sense of English prestige. In the mid-sixteenth century, the Tudors fought constant wars, usually successful, against the Scots. They used the English national Parliament to support their projects, which made the nation's representatives into their (mostly willing) partners. Most important of all, they created a separate English Protestant Church that claimed to be virtually the only true Christian church remaining on earth.

The English Protestant Reformation started because Henry VIII – the most fascinating, magnificent, and repulsive of Tudor monarchs – wanted to divorce the first of his six wives, but it soon went far beyond what the King had intended. Henry favored a conservative Reformation, one that would give him personal supremacy over the Church of England by removing the authority of the Pope, but would not change religious ceremonies and practices beyond what was necessary. By the time the King died in 1547, however, the Church and the government were full of Protestant reformers who wanted a religion in which salvation was based on faith in God alone and not linked to confession, communion, or any other works, no matter how good they might be. This was the essence of Protestantism, a movement that had recently begun in Germany. The reformers were encouraged by Henry's son, Edward VI (King 1547–53), but they were persecuted by his daughter, Mary I (Queen 1553–8), a Roman Catholic who was the first woman to rule England as Queen. The Protestants seemed finally to be victorious after Mary died in 1558, and was succeeded by Henry's younger daughter, Elizabeth I. The Elizabethan settlement of the Church was based on a Parliamentary Act of Uniformity, 52 Royal Injunctions, and a new Book of Common Prayer (all dating from 1559), but it did not fully satisfy the most zealous reformers, because it maintained certain religious practices that were associated by them with Catholicism. On the one hand, the strictly Protestant 39 Articles of Faith, accepted by an assembly of the Church in 1563, presented salvation as a matter of faith alone, and praised the "sweet and unspeakable comfort" of the Protestant doctrine of predestination, by which God determined in advance those who were to be saved. On the other hand, priestly robes or vestments were retained in the Church, as were some Catholic rituals like bowing before the communion table.

In spite of its internal contradictions, the founding of the Church of England was a turning point in the creation of national consciousness. From now on, English Protestants could see themselves as God's chosen people, unique among all the peoples of the world. The burning of Protestants by Elizabeth's sister and predecessor, Queen Mary, was now denounced as an act of horrible cruelty, and was to be remembered for centuries by avid readers of the *Book of Martyrs*, a lavishly illustrated compilation of Catholic crimes written by the clergyman John Foxe. The enemies of Protestantism – particularly, the Catholic Spaniards, French, and Irish – were seen as the enemies of God. They were labeled by Protestants as superstitious and cruel on account of their religious beliefs, which in the Irish case merely worsened an existing stereotype of barbarism and backwardness. Later, aspects of these descriptions would be transferred to peoples around the world whose cultures differed from those of the English. Not surprisingly, the great victory over the Spanish Armada in 1588, which was due as much to the weather as to English seamanship, was hailed by Protestants as a divine deliverance. So was the defeat of a rebellion by the Irish Gaelic chiefs, the O'Neills and O'Donnells, at the battle of Kinsale in 1601. It was evident to the Protestant English what nation God favored.

By the time the battle of Kinsale was won, Queen Elizabeth I was venerated by many of her Protestant subjects as the preserver of true religion. Many people even today consider her to have been the greatest of all English monarchs. Her reign had seen a flourishing of national literature, including the early career of the great playwright and poet, William Shakespeare. Elizabeth's rulership, however, had limits. She had more or less given up the idea of restoring an English empire in France, and the efforts of her subjects to colonize parts of the New World had ended in failure. The financial situation of the crown was far from secure, which had led to frequent confrontations with Parliament, especially in times of war. The Armada victory, however, bestowed an aura of divine approval on Elizabeth's final years.

If the Reformation created a new sense of what it meant to be English, it had much the same effect on Scottish identity. As in England, however, religious reform also became the source of deep divisions. The Scottish Reformation was promulgated not by the crown, but by the Parliament of 1560, which abolished the Catholic Mass and ended the authority of the Pope. This was largely a reaction against the crown's pro-French policies, but it quickly established a militant Protestant identity. Reform was promulgated by John Knox and other fiery preachers, who helped draw up the "Book of Discipline" in 1561, calling for the state to punish sins like blasphemy and idolatry with death. The reformers also wanted to set up schools in every parish and establish a national system to support the poor. The monarch, Mary, Queen of Scots, abhorred these men, and remained a Catholic. The hapless Mary was deposed in 1567 during a civil war – she fled to England, where, after twenty years of confinement, her cousin Elizabeth I had her executed for plotting against her. The Scottish throne was transferred to Mary's infant son, King James VI, who was raised as a Protestant. Reformers hoped that the Scottish Church or Kirk would adopt a form of church government by lay elders, or presbyters (hence Presbyterianism), but once he was grown up, James refused to comply, and started to appoint new bishops. As in England, the intentions of the radical reformers were thwarted.

It would be a huge mistake to imagine that everyone in Great Britain converted rapidly and easily to Protestantism. In England, the shift was slow, was marked by several reversals, and was never total. By the end of Elizabeth's reign, the clergy were officially entirely Protestants, but zealous reformers (called Puritans by their critics) remained a minority. The new religion also spread rapidly in towns, among merchants and tradesmen. The countryside was slower to convert. After a series of rural Catholic rebellions from the 1530s to the 1560s, most of the common people of England accepted Protestantism, without great enthusiasm. Among the aristocracy and landowning classes, especially in northern England, a substantial number of Catholics (called recusants) continued to adhere to the old faith. In Wales, the process of reformation was even slower, in part because most of the common people still spoke Welsh rather than English, and the borderlands remained home to a substantial Catholic community. The Scottish Reformation was most successful in the towns and farming communities of the Lowlands. The clan-based societies of the Highlands and islands mostly stuck to the old religion. As for Ireland, the Reformation made no headway among Gaelic-speakers or "Old Irish," as they were called, and very little among the Norman-French settlers or "Old English." Clearly, Protestantism was not likely to create a basis for unity throughout the British Isles.

Elizabeth I died, childless, in 1603, and was succeeded by her cousin James VI of Scotland, who became James I of England. He was the first English King of the house of Stuart, which was how his new subjects spelled the name Stewart. From now on, England and Scotland shared the same monarch; but they were not united in any other sense. James had wanted to bring about an administrative union, combining the two systems of government, but the English and Scottish Parliaments scuttled the project. He had other quarrels with his Parliaments, particularly concerning finances; and these contributed to his negative image in the memories of the English. In contrast to the great Elizabeth, James was unfairly remembered as a weakling with authoritarian tendencies, who dribbled when he spoke and had terrible hygiene. In fact, he was a cautious, intelligent man who had imposed royal authority on the factious Scottish nobles, while writing learned treatises in his spare time on subjects as diverse as monarchy, tobacco smoking, and witchcraft. Longing for a general settlement of religious issues in a divided Europe, he kept his kingdoms out of the brutal Thirty Years' War (1618–48). Unfortunately, his Puritan critics perceived James's peace policy as a sellout to Catholicism. James also had a weakness for handsome young men, whom he took as advisors and on whom he lavished great rewards. Whether or not he slept with them is a recurring subject for historical speculation. In any case, because of his favorites, James's court gained a terrible, and deserved, reputation for corruption.

It was under James's controversial rule that the first worldwide English empire was born. We should call it English rather than British, because the Scots were as yet excluded from English overseas trade and colonization. In south and east India, the English came to trade, not to settle or govern. The East India Company set up "factories" or trading posts in Indonesia, in Japan, and at Surat in India, within the territories of the Mughal emperor. The English merchants were challenging the Portuguese and the Dutch for control of the commerce in pepper, spices, silks, and the light Indian cotton cloth known as calico, all highly desirable commodities among the upper classes of Europe. In North America and the Caribbean, by contrast, the English came initially for gold, and later for land. Under James I, successful English colonies were founded at Jamestown, Virginia (1607), in Maine (1607), Newfoundland (1610), Bermuda (1612), and at Plymouth, Massachusetts (1621). Most of these colonies would not have survived without the help of native populations, although it soon became clear that one of their purposes was to eject native peoples and replace them with settlers.

The policy of colonization by settlement was not new. We have already seen it in the Norman-French Empire of the thirteenth century, applied to Wales, Ireland, and southern Scotland. It had been revived in the mid-sixteenth century, through the creation of "plantations" that were designed to draw new English settlers into previously "Old Irish" areas. As King of Scotland, James VI had set up similar plantations to bring Lowland colonists into the Gaelic-speaking Hebrides, Orkneys, and Shetland Islands. After 1609, Lowland Scots settlers began to arrive in the northern Irish province of Ulster, the most Gaelic part of Ireland and the seat of the recent insurrection of the Irish chiefs. The Catholic "Old Irish" were dispossessed of their lands, ostensibly because they had taken part in the rebellion. The Ulster plantation gradually became a predominantly Protestant society, strongly connected to Great Britain. It has survived to this day, with disturbing consequences for Irish unity as well as for British relations with Ireland.

The Civil Wars

The political and religious tensions that were building within the British Isles erupted in the reign of James's son, Charles I. A shy, quiet, family-oriented man who spoke with a mild stutter, Charles was confronted by three major problems at the very beginning of his reign: lack of money, religious disagreements, and a major European war. By seeking new forms of revenue, Charles irritated many of his subjects and a considerable number of Members of Parliament (MPs). By adopting a non-Calvinist, ritualistic form of Protestantism that seemed to smack of Catholicism, Charles infuriated radical reformers, meaning English Puritans as well as Scots Presbyterians. By dabbling disastrously in wars with France and Spain, Charles undermined the credibility of his government. He had an authoritarian disposition, but he always tried to stay within the boundaries of traditional kingly power. He was not a despot, and was never a Catholic. Yet many began to perceive him as both. In return, he imagined his critics as religious fanatics, bent on creating a republican government.

The result was a series of Civil Wars that overthrew the monarchy and created a short-lived English republic – so far, the only republic in English history. They began in 1637 with an uprising in Scotland, in protest against Charles's religious policies. The Scots drew up a National Covenant, a strong statement of Scotland's Protestant identity and national purpose. The uprising was soon taken over by Presbyterian Covenanters, who discarded the Scottish bishops and set about reforming the Church or Kirk. To confront them with a military force, King Charles needed money, and was compelled to call an English Parliament. When its members made demands on him, he dissolved it, but after the Scots beat him in battle, he was forced to call another. To his horror, it sided with the Scots! Deeply distrustful of the King, Parliament began to remove his control over his advisors and to treat Charles as if he were a minor or an incompetent. A reform of the English Church on Presbyterian lines appeared imminent.

The radical Protestants seemed to be victorious in both Scotland and England, which caused terrible fear in Ireland among the "Old Irish" (Gaelic) and "Old English" (Anglo-Norman) landowners. Both groups were Catholic. In November 1641, they raised a rebellion, not to overthrow the king, but to assist him against his radical Protestant antagonists. The rebels formed a Catholic Confederacy at Kilkenny that comprised the first self-proclaimed government of Ireland to be set up by the Irish themselves, at least since the old high kingship. In many respects, Irish national consciousness can be dated to the Confederacy; but as yet it existed only among the Catholic upper classes, and it did not override the longstanding ethnic conflict between the "Old Irish" and the "Old English." In the end, the latter were willing to make a settlement with Protestant royalists, while the "Old Irish," who felt they had more to lose, were not.

News of the Irish rebellion, and of massacres of Protestant settlers in Ulster by Irish peasants, inflamed the English political situation. London crowds demanded the abolition of bishops and a thorough reform of the Church. Charles I decided that he could not control the capital city; so he withdrew to the north, where he gathered military forces and, in August 1642, effectively declared war on his own Parliament. He received strong backing from moderate Protestants who were frightened by Puritanism, as well as from Catholics. In response, Parliament raised its own army and made war on the king, supposedly to bring him back to his senses. At the prompting of their Scottish allies, Puritan MPs also did away with bishops and adopted a Presbyterian settlement for the Church of England, vesting ecclesiastical government in lay elders or presbyters. The Civil War was eventually won by Parliament, but only after the creation of a New Model Army, based on up-to-date military principles and infused with Puritan zeal. The army imprisoned Charles I in 1646. Seeking to regain his power, the King began a series of devious negotiations with the Scots Covenanters and the moderate Presbyterians who dominated the English Parliament.

The New Model Army, however, was emerging as a political force in its own right. Its generals tended to be more radical than most Parliamentary leaders. Some of the generals wanted churches to be governed by their membership (Congregationalism) rather than by presbyters. A few wanted full freedom of worship for Protestants. Among the junior officers of the Army, there was considerable sympathy for the ideas of a republican group called the Levellers, who advocated voting rights for most adult males. The common ranks of the army contained many adherents of unorthodox religious beliefs. Later, they would join sects like the Fifth Monarchists, who believed rule by the saints was at hand, or the Baptists, who practiced adult baptism, or the Society of Friends, known as Quakers, who sought a divine light in everyone. Moderate Scottish and English politicians were horrified at the prospect of an army-led religious revolution; so they conspired with the King to start a second Civil War, in order to crush the radicals. The New Model Army quickly suppressed this attempt in the summer of 1648, and the generals took charge of political affairs. They purged the moderates from government, creating what was referred to insultingly as "the Rump Parliament." The King was put on trial before the new legislature and found guilty of conspiring against his people. On January 30, 1649, King Charles I was beheaded. To many observers, then and for decades afterwards, this was the most shocking event in all of English history.

What followed was the first and only British exercise in republican government. The new Commonwealth, as it was called, was dependent from the first on the New Model Army, and on its commander, Oliver Cromwell, a serious, well intentioned and pious man who was convinced that God was on his side. Cromwell and the Army throttled the Irish rebellion, perpetrating massacres that have scarred the Irish imagination to this day. Then they turned on the Scots, smashing the Covenanting army and defeating a Scottish-backed attempt by the late King's son, Charles II, to regain the throne. Ireland and Scotland were compelled to accept republican government, and for the first time, Scotland was incorporated into an English-dominated state. Always under the shadow of the military, the Commonwealth became a government by generals in 1653, when Oliver Cromwell overthrew "the Rump" because it was turning against the army and was close to passing a restrictive settlement for the Church. Cromwell became Lord Protector of the Commonwealth, an office halfway between a king and a president. His rule was characterized by freedom of religion for Protestants (but not for Catholics) and strong military rule over the entire British Isles. Cromwell's navies hammered the Dutch at sea and seized Jamaica from the Spaniards. For godly Protestants, this was the fulfillment of the English national dream, conceived during the Reformation and kept alive by Puritans for a century. For those who opposed Puritanism and republicanism, however, Cromwell's Protectorate was more like a nightmare.

The English republic did not long survive Lord Protector Cromwell's death in 1658. His son Richard was incapable of holding the office. Months of bickering among the generals and leaders of "the Rump" led to a *coup d'état* by General George Monck and his troops, stationed in Scotland. Monck called new elections, which he knew would result in a legislature favorable to the exiled King. Dominated by Presbyterian moderates who hated the army commanders and the sectarians, the Convention, as it was called, proclaimed Charles II in May 1660. Charles had been living in exile, and relative poverty, in France and the Dutch Republic. He came back to England with offers of peace and good will to virtually everyone, summed up in a declaration issued at Breda in Holland. His welcome home was deafeningly enthusiastic: after eleven years of unstable government, all but a determined minority of republicans wanted a monarchy again. Charles did not seek revenge against his enemies. Only a few individuals, including those who had signed his father's death warrant, were excluded from an Act of Indemnity and Oblivion that pardoned almost everything that had happened in the past twenty years. The King and his chief minister, the Earl of Clarendon, were also willing to make concessions to the Presbyterians, but the English Parliament elected in 1661 was led by old royalists who scorned such compromise. They drove out of the Church every clergyman who was not willing to swear to a renewed Act of Uniformity, upholding the old liturgy and condemning Presbyterianism. The expelled ministers and their followers – Presbyterians, Congregationalists, Baptists, and others – would collectively be known as Protestant Dissenters or Nonconformists. In Scotland, where a similar ejection took place, they would retain the name of Covenanters.

Charles II gave in to repression by his Parliament because, learning from his father's mistakes, he was cautious and wary. He kept his own religious opinions private, which was a good thing as they tended towards Roman Catholicism. Charles was an easy-going, pleasure-loving man who did not like to bother himself about the everyday tasks of government. He put his trust in powerful ministers: the Earl of Lauderdale in Scotland, the Duke of Ormonde in Ireland, the Earl of Clarendon in England. If he had not had a brother – James, Duke of York – and if his brother had not decided to convert to Catholicism, Charles might be remembered as a successful monarch. Unfortunately for the King, his brother's Catholicism became known. Worse still, for all his constant fornicating outside marriage, which brought him many illegitimate children, Charles II was not able to sire heirs by his wife, the Portuguese princess Catherine of Braganza, meaning that his Catholic brother would eventually succeed to the throne.

That story belongs to a later chapter. For now, we can ask what sort of nations England and Scotland were in the reign of Charles II. They were still very separate, with their own Parliaments and legal systems, their own established Churches and distinct cultures. The English, however, had established a dominant position within the British Isles with which the Scots could no longer compete. That dominance was derived not from a European empire, as in Norman times, nor even from military superiority within Britain. Increasingly, it was based on England's global importance, as a commercial center and as the hub of an empire. The empire now spread to the cod fisheries of Newfoundland, to Puritan New England and Dutch New York (the former New Netherlands, captured in 1664), to East and West Jersey (settled in the 1670s), to the tobacco colonies of Virginia and the Carolinas (chartered in 1669), to the sugar islands of Barbados and Jamaica, to Tangier in North Africa (acquired by Charles II as part of his marriage settlement), to James Fort on the Gambian coast of West Africa (where the Royal African Company was trading in slaves), to the Indian ports of Surat and Bombay (another Portuguese gift to Charles II on his marriage), and to "factories" in Java, Sumatra, South China, and Japan. The empire was bound together by the Navigation Acts (six of them in all, passed between 1651 and 1673), which stipulated that trade in the English colonies must be carried on in English ships, sailing from and to English ports. Commercial rivalries were responsible for three wars with the Dutch (1652–4, 1665–7, 1672–4), whose ships had until then carried a great deal of English colonial trade. The English did not win these wars, but the Dutch were not able to stop them either. English trade and empire continued to grow in North America, West Africa, and Asia, although not in North Africa, where Tangier, once the focus of grandiose plans for a plantation-like settlement, was abandoned in 1684.

The English in the late seventeenth century possessed a bounding self-confidence and a strong sense of national identity. Although they were bitterly divided among themselves by social, religious, and political issues, most English Protestants could subscribe to the idea of the nation's divinely appointed destiny. Protestant Scots had once shared the same view of themselves, but that self-image had been shattered by the defeat of the Covenanters and the humiliating annexation under the Protectorate. Only the most determined zealots could still believe that Scotland was intended to lead the world towards the millennium, the thousand years that would precede the end of the world. For the English, on the other hand, such an exalted view of themselves was not at all hard to accept, although after 1660 they tended to interpret God's blessings in terms of secular prosperity rather than Christian eschatology.

The period in which this book begins was a difficult one in English national history, but it was not a low point. In spite of the terrible troubles of the 1640s and 1650s, in spite of the long-term loss of a European empire, England remained a powerful nation, capable of pushing around its immediate neighbors in the British Isles, and of exerting its commercial influence on a global scale. It was already on its way towards creating the biggest empire that the world has ever seen. To understand how that happened, however, we have to know more about the land and peoples of Great Britain, on whom the wealth and success of the future empire would depend.

2

Landscapes in Motion

When you are flying over rural Britain today, and look down at what is below, you are likely to see a patchwork of relatively small, rectangular fields, surrounded by hedges and trees, stretching out in every direction. Many people assume that this is what the English and Scottish countryside has always looked like, but they are wrong. The farming patterns that we can see today were mostly shaped by enclosure between the seventeenth and nineteenth centuries. Those patterns were preceded by many different patterns, each of them a statement about how the inhabitants of Britain viewed the land, and how they chose to alter it.

The history of the British landscape, like that of the British economy, has often been told as one of steady, if not always even, progress towards what we see today. In the seventeenth century, people would have referred to "improvement" rather than progress, but they had in mind a similar idea. When we encounter this interpretation, we should always ask: "Progress of what sort, and for whom?" In fact, the history of land use in Britain is not as straightforwardly progressive as it may seem. It was characterized by changes in human activity that had complicated effects, both for the land itself and for those who worked it. On the one hand, the improvements of the sixteenth and seventeenth centuries – when they succeeded – would make it possible for Britain to raise the general level of prosperity and sustain a high level of population growth. This was a great achievement, one that only the Dutch could match. On the other hand, improvement created a higher level of exploitation of human beings, and of the land itself. In some cases, the conditions of work and the environment in which people lived seem to have deteriorated. These two aspects of improvement were connected, and we should try not to lose sight of either, or to exaggerate one at the expense of the other.

Farming

Great Britain can be divided into three main types of terrain: very hilly areas, that become mountainous only in the Scottish Highlands and north Wales; areas of rolling hills, suitable for pasturing, in the Scottish Lowlands, south Wales, the northwest and southwest of England; and more or less flat areas, along the coasts and through most of the eastern half of England, where arable crops can be grown. There are no high mountain ranges, no sprawling plains or prairies, no arid deserts, no big swamps, no great rivers (although the tidal river estuaries are often wide). By contrast, Ireland consists mostly of very hilly areas and peat bogs, with rolling hills and flatter lands in the eastern parts – the parts that were colonized by the Normans or settled in the Ulster plantation. For geographic and climatic as well as social reasons, it was much harder to spread improvement in Ireland than in Great Britain.

Of course, not all parts of Great Britain were equally open to improvement. The Scottish Highlands, like Ireland, had a rugged terrain, rocky and heavily wooded, that was more suited to grazing cattle than raising crops. Highland society, which was Gaelic-speaking, often Catholic, and relatively isolated, did not welcome improvement. Small Highland farmers or "cottars" (from "cottagers") looked to the local nobleman or laird for security and protection. In exchange, they might use his family name, pledge loyalty to him, and fight for him as members of his clan or kinship group. The cottars tended their cattle communally, in families or villages, paying little attention to boundaries – in fact, they were often accused of stealing cattle or using land to which they had no rights. Yet change was coming even to the Highlands. By the end of the seventeenth century, a middle group of landholders had emerged between the lairds and the cottars, called tacksmen. The landholdings of tacksmen were granted by the laird either through written leases (tacks), or through a hereditary lease, a *feu*, that gave the tenant almost complete control over a property. The small farmers looked for leadership to the local tacksmen, rather than to the distant laird, who often resided in Edinburgh. At the same time, some lairds and tacksmen began herding their cattle to market towns for sale, rather than keeping them on their estates. They also started to cut down the Highland forests for timber. These changes towards a market system of agriculture were as yet small, but they would gradually accelerate.

The pace of Scottish improvement outside the Highlands was faster, although it varied depending on the region and terrain. In the rural hamlets or "farmtouns" (farm towns) of Lowland Scotland, big, open fields were usually divided equally among tenants in what was known as "fixed runrig." In some cases, the farming strips within each field were actually exchanged every so often in what was known as "periodic runrig," which must have confused everybody. By the late seventeenth century, some combination of farming strips into larger units had taken place, but on nothing like the scale of what was happening in England. The Lowland Scots grew oats (which the English disdained as cattle feed) and barley, from which they brewed a malted beverage, "bear." A local court of "birlaymen," composed of farmers, determined how many animals each tenant could keep on the common land, an egalitarian procedure of a sort that was rare in England. For Scottish farmers, tenures were generally determined by custom, not by written lease, and rents were paid in kind, not in money. During the 1500s, however, an important shift took place in the ownership of land. The financially strapped Scottish crown and Kirk agreed to large numbers of hereditary leases or *feus*, made with tenants on church lands. "Feuing" in the Lowlands essentially gave the tenant control over the land, elevating some to the status of landlords, and allowing, in a few places at least, the sort of consolidation of holdings that was seen almost everywhere in England.

The foundation of English agricultural improvement was the disappearance of the old manorial system, under which peasants or serfs worked on the lord's personal land, or demesne, in exchange for the right to farm on the lord's manor. English peasants of the Middle Ages mostly lived in villages close to the big, open fields, which were typically three in number. Within each of these fields, a peasant would farm a strip, or several strips, of land. In one field, winter wheat would be planted; in the second, spring barley, while the third field would lie fallow so the soil could regain its fertility. Some of the fields, along with woods and undeveloped wastes, were common lands where anybody who lived in the village could gather firewood or graze animals. The land strips in the open fields were held by the custom of the manor, which spelled out the peasant's rights and responsibilities, and was copied out on a long piece of parchment known as the manor roll. This type of tenure, known as copyhold, continued in some cases down to the twentieth century.

Farming long strips in open fields was not very efficient, and the three-field rotation tended to exhaust the soil itself; so the breakdown of English manorial farming seems to have been an improvement from every perspective. The system was already faltering before the Black Death of 1348–50, which created a labor shortage and forced lords to make deals with their tenants. Serfdom gradually disappeared. The lords split up their demesne lands and began renting them out to tenants. Leases, which were short term and rested on a defined schedule of payments, began to replace the complexities of customary tenure. Farmers who survived the Black Death began to combine their strips with others into larger holdings, a process known as "engrossing." They also began to close their lands off with trees and hedges, splitting up the open fields and taking the first step in a very long series of changes that is collectively referred to as "enclosure."

The next stage in English enclosure, in the fifteenth and sixteenth centuries, was not so happy for the rural poor – in fact, it sometimes caused terrible suffering and gave rise to the mocking comment, made by Sir Thomas More in his book *Utopia* (1516), that in England, sheep "have become so voracious and fierce that they have even started eating men."[1] This stage of enclosure was caused by high wool prices, which increased the demand for sheep. Landlords threw tenants off the demesne lands, converting them from arable or crop farming to pastures where flocks of sheep would graze. Far fewer laborers were needed to tend sheep than to plant and harvest crops. In addition, the landlords began to claim common lands as their own property, so as to convert them to grass as well. The result was the disappearance of whole villages in certain parts of England, particularly the Midlands, where declining population was already causing settlements to be abandoned. The situation in the Midlands became so aggravated that a revolt against enclosures broke out among rural laborers in 1607. The government responded with an official inquiry, but like previous proclamations against enclosures, it had little impact.

In England, the seventeenth century tipped the balance against open fields. By the end of the century, most of the kingdom's farmland was enclosed, which delighted the agricultural writer John Worlidge. "Enclosing of lands," he maintained, in a book published in 1669, "is, and hath been ever esteemed a most principal way of Improvement, it ascertaineth every Man his just and due Propriety and Interest, and preventeth such infinite of Trespasses and Injuries, that Lands in common are subject unto, occasioning so much of Law, Strife, and Contention."[2] As Worlidge suggested, a great deal of enclosure was by consent, meaning that the landlords and tenant farmers of a village would agree among themselves to carve up the open fields and common lands into individual holdings. The process could take various forms: a squatter could enclose waste or woodland by building a cottage there, or a town could grow larger by enclosing common land outside its gates. Each case of enclosure had different consequences. Some caused distress and suffering among the poor, others did not. It is difficult, perhaps impossible, to judge the whole picture. It is equally difficult to understand its significance. Historians have seen enclosure as a big step towards rural capitalism, that is, a type of agriculture that was focused on increased profit rather than mere subsistence. Rural capitalism could exist without enclosure, however, and the enclosing of land did not necessarily lead to higher profits. Nevertheless, the burst of enclosure in the seventeenth century was a crucial consequence of the improving mindset that was transforming English agriculture.

In terms of profitability, the biggest improvement in English agriculture in the seventeenth century came from new methods of farming, which might be, but were not always, adopted as a consequence of enclosure. Many of these new methods were borrowed from the Dutch, who had to use their scarce farmland very carefully in order to feed a growing population. The most important of them was probably alternate husbandry (which has nothing to do with swapping marital partners), also known as convertible or (excitingly enough) up-and-down husbandry. This meant alternating the use of a field between arable farming and pasturing. Alternate husbandry worked on the principle that flocks and herds would leave behind plenty of manure to keep the crops growing on the next seasonal cycle. It seems a simple idea, but it made a profound change in farming, because it allowed farmers to respond to market conditions by switching from crop production to the raising of animals.

A second type of improvement that made a big difference to productivity was the regular flooding of pasture land by waters diverted from streams through water-wheels and irrigation channels – known, picturesquely, as the "floating of water meadows." John Worlidge recommended that on meadows "of a dry and hungry Soyl, and not frequently overflowed by Land-floods, may Artificial Works be made use of for the raising the water over the same to a very considerable advantage."[3] As English temperatures were seldom cold enough to freeze running water, "floating" kept frost off the grass during the winter, and the silt left behind by the water increased the fertility of the soil. More sheep could be fed on the same plot of land. If "floating" was not enough to increase the size of his flocks, a seventeenth-century farmer could turn to fodder crops, mainly turnips and various types of clover, fed to livestock in the winter months. These fodder crops had been brought into England and Scotland from the Low Countries. They grew easily and enriched the land, so they worked particularly well in hilly areas where light soils would not support other crops. Although some farmers continued to be wary of them, fearing that they impoverished the soil, their use spread rapidly after 1650, when a decline in the price of grain turned more farmers towards livestock raising. The main publicist for clover in the 1660s was the seed-agent and writer Andrew Yarranton, who even wrote a poem about his favorite plant:

> With what delight and pleasure have I seen
> The barren pastures cloathed all in green!
> Where neither Grass nor Corn would grow before
> It hath of Honey-suckles planted store ...
> But to conclude: thy purse will ne'er run over
> Till thou hast got the art of sowing *Clover*.[4]

Happily, Yarranton was a better farmer than he was a poet.

The seventeenth century was a golden age for new crops, including hops, another Dutch import, which were used in making beer. Older drinkers did not like the innovation, but one can only imagine how awful beer tasted before hops. English farmers also grew tobacco, and they might have competed with their own colonies in the New World if the government had not forced them to stop growing it. The selective breeding of livestock became highly advanced during this period, and it may suffice here to mention the famous ram breeders of Leicestershire without delving too deeply into their methods. New crops and better breeds of livestock led to increased specialization among farmers. Around the bigger towns of England, for example, market gardeners grew various types of fruits and vegetables to supply the urban public. In a society that preferred meat and bread, vegetables were considered to be cheap nourishment for the poor, although everybody ate some of them, as they were used in stews or to garnish meats and were understood to be beneficial to health.

One effect of agricultural improvement was that many of the great landowners had more money to spend on rebuilding their homes. Drafty old castles, with their military architecture, guardrooms, and huge dining halls, were replaced by "country houses." Most were framed in wood timbers and constructed around a central courtyard, but the largest were built in brick or stone, copying Italian or Dutch architectural designs, with stucco decoration, glass windows, elegant reception rooms, and long galleries for strolling or playing games. Around the English landlord's house spread carefully tended gardens and forested parks teeming with deer. Scottish landlords continued to build versions of medieval castles, with thick walls and turrets, but outside the Highlands, their interiors were now constructed for comfort, not for defense. Many English farmhouses were also reconstructed in this period. Tenant farmers who had made money from improvement wanted separate rooms in which to sleep, eat, and play. To fill these rooms, they purchased linens and table wares made of pottery or pewter, along with oak chests in which to store them.

To be sure, the sixteenth and seventeenth centuries saw periodic ups and downs in agricultural prosperity. The early seventeenth century marked a definite downturn, while the second half of the century experienced a slow, steady upturn. Overall, however, the two centuries before 1700 were characterized by the emergence of a remarkable, probably unprecedented, prosperity in English agriculture. Agricultural improvement was a long-term process, and it would be misleading to suggest that change was rapid or decisive. Nevertheless, we can state with some certainty that the English farmers of the eighteenth century had little or nothing to teach their fathers and grandfathers about how to make a profit. The great agricultural shift that allowed English farmers to feed more and more people, and to enrich themselves at the same time, had already occurred by 1700.

The positive aspects of this shift are easy enough to appreciate, but it also had its victims, in the many cottagers or laborers who gradually lost the use of common land, who were displaced by sheep, or who simply became poorer. These people comprised the majority of England's population. They tended to live with their families in makeshift mud-walled cottages, set up on unwanted land, with a single room where everyone slept on straw in front of the fireplace. They might keep a cow or a pig, grow vegetables in a garden plot, and plant crops on a tiny holding. They used the common lands for grazing and for gathering firewood. Those who lacked enough land to keep themselves and their families fed had to travel about the area in which they lived, looking for work. Some migrated to towns, to Irish plantations, or to the New World. In textile-producing regions of England or Scotland, the wives and children of rural laborers could take up domestic spinning. When employment was scarce, when they fell sick, or when they grew old, rural laborers might have to depend on charity or on poor relief, which was organized on a parish level throughout England, but was hardly adequate to support the indigent population. In England, the poor often went hungry, but at least they did not usually starve to death – unlike in Scotland, where famine struck on a national level as late as 1650, and locally into the 1690s.

Agricultural improvement brought mixed benefits and losses to the rural poor. It was not necessarily a beneficial process from an environmental point of view, either, as it could lead to changes in the land that could not easily be reversed, and might have unforeseen consequences. This was exemplified in the massive project of draining the Fens, the marshy lowlands of southeastern England. The big landowners of the area paid for the services of a Dutch engineer, who cut large drainage channels through the swampy terrain, at enormous cost. The local people, who were losing their rights to use the marshlands, responded with riots and uprisings. By the 1650s, resistance had been overcome, the drainage work had been completed, and the Fens seemed on the verge of a new prosperity; but then the dried peat began to shrink up and sink back into the ground. Deeper drains had to be dug, and windmills were built to provide power for carrying water up into the new channels. The drains and windmills, however, tended to shrink the peat even more. It took years before the situation stabilized.

Contemporaries were not usually aware of the environmental effects of their actions. The one ecological subject that did gain some attention was the constant decline of the English woodlands, which created alarm, although little was done to stop it. In the Middle Ages, England possessed substantial woodlands, including many royal forests where only the king and his retainers were allowed to hunt. After 1400, as the population expanded and more land was enclosed, woodlands began to disappear. Trees were cleared and used as fuel, as fertilizer (when reduced to potash), or as material for building houses. Even the royal forests began to shrink. James I and his son Charles I, always desperate for money, sold off many acres of forest land. In some areas, the depletion of woodland in royal forests was dramatic. Timber trees in the Hampshire New Forest, for example, were reduced by 90 percent over the course of the seventeenth century. The loss of English forests worried some observers, like John Evelyn. His work *Sylva*, published in 1664, avoided criticism of the King, but complained about landowners who "grub up, demolish, and raze, as it were, all those many goodly *Woods*, and *Forests*, which our more prudent *Ancestors* left standing for the Ornament, and service of their *Country*."[5] Evelyn wanted Charles II to preserve timber for use in building the navy. He was among the first to call for public awareness of ecology, but his plea was largely ignored for more than a century.

Industry and Manufacturing

Today, we tend to associate industry with urban areas. This is a misleading way to think about seventeenth-century Britain, where most large-scale industries were located in the countryside. One major exception was silk-weaving, which depended on raw materials initially imported from China, and was carried out in large workhouses around London. Other types of weaving and spinning – sheep's wool in England, linen made from flax in southern Scotland – took place mainly in country villages. The mining industry was also tied to rural life, since landowners had rights to the coal and iron and lead that lay underneath their properties. Metal ore, particularly iron, was smelted or purified on waste lands around forests, where wood charcoal could be obtained to fuel furnaces. Spinners, weavers, miners, and ironworkers often worked seasonally in farming as well, so that it can be hard to classify them as either industrial or agricultural laborers. Industry and manufacturing in seventeenth-century Britain was usually a supporting aspect of the rural economy, rather than belonging to a separate economic sphere.

England's leading industry was woolen textile production. Industrial statistics are not very reliable for this period, and they are subject to a variety of interpretations, but they suggest that wool manufacturing experienced a slow, uneven growth before the late seventeenth century. During the Middle Ages, southeastern England had become famous throughout Europe for producing a heavy, durable woolen cloth. Tastes changed, however, and lighter cloths became more desirable, especially in the hotter parts of Mediterranean Europe. By the mid-sixteenth century, the medieval expansion of the English woolen industry had ceased. Half a century of stagnation followed. Gradually, woolen merchants shifted production to the "New Draperies," as lighter woolen cloths were called. The new materials caught on with customers abroad, and villages in East Anglia (the counties of Norfolk, Suffolk, Cambridgeshire, and Essex) and the southwest (especially the counties of Devon, Somerset, and Gloucestershire) began to thrive on them. Wool-producing areas started to specialize in particular types of material – serges in Devon, kerseys in Norfolk. Lancashire in northwest England was known for a lightweight linen–wool mixture known as fustian. In the northeast county of Yorkshire, worsted or combed wool fabrics for the domestic market continued to be made. By the late seventeenth century, the wool trades were prospering again. Celia Fiennes, a female traveler from an aristocratic family, noted in the 1690s the "Increadible quantity" of serges displayed in the marketplace at Exeter in Devon. She recorded with wonderment how "the whole town and Country is Employ'd for at Least 20 mile round in spinning, weaveing, dressing and scouring, fulling and Drying of the serges. It turns the most money in a weeke of any thing in England."[6]

Wool was spun into thread by rural women, working at home and often assisted by children. Male weavers in both town and country, using looms and materials that were supplied for a fee by merchants, wove the thread into cloth. They then carried it from home to a market, where they were paid by the merchants and picked up more thread. The wages of textile workers were generally low, and when the costs of tools and materials were subtracted, it was hard to make a living from spinning or weaving alone. Usually, rural work in textile manufacture supplemented farm labor. Still, this meant extra income for small landholders and landless laborers. The wool industry had a big impact on settlement patterns, concentrating people in villages close to towns in which the wool merchants lived. Wool had to go through a number of specialized processes, in addition to spinning and weaving, in order to become cloth: it was brushed or "carded," soaked in urine, cleaned with soap, and plumped up or "fulled" in a large mill building. The grey-white wool fabric could then be dyed in various colors. In the sixteenth century, wool was mostly exported in an "undressed" state, and dyed in continental Europe, but by the late seventeenth century, dyeing was being done in England. Celia Fiennes was fascinated by the "the several ffats [i.e. vats] they were a Dying in" at Exeter, which were kept boiling by a furnace "made of Coal ffires."[7] The processes for finishing wool also required water, which was provided by the little streams and rivers that today run picturesquely through so many English villages. In wool-producing areas of the seventeenth century, the waters of these streams and rivers were used fairly intensively, and many of them were badly polluted. No wonder rural people preferred to drink beer rather than water!

Wool manufacturing probably had a less visible impact on the landscape than the mining of coal, lead, and tin, which was carried on without much regard for either human beings or the environment. Miners of the early seventeenth century could not get very deep down below the earth, because their mineshafts would fill up with water, so most mining was carried out relatively close to the surface. The curious remains of this method were "bell-pits," clusters of what look like giant ant-hills that can still be seen in parts of northern England. The increasing demand for coal, both as a domestic fuel and for use in industry, encouraged more intensive mining, especially in northeast England, around Newcastle upon Tyne. The coal trade of Newcastle was facilitated by access to river transport, and was entirely controlled by about two dozen wealthy merchants known as the Hostmen. Production from the Newcastle pits rose from half a million tons in 1650 to over a million tons in 1700. This may not seem like much compared to the 1 billion tons of coal now burned in the United States every year, but it represented a big step towards an age of massive coal use, with its accompanying pollution, grime, and, eventually, climate change. "Newcastle is Peru," declared one enthusiastic local writer, comparing the town's wealth to the gold of the Incas.[8] Shafts were driven deeper and deeper into the ground, with a complex network of tunnels connecting them. The engineering behind these mines was astonishing, as were their environmental effects. Already by the late seventeenth century, the Newcastle coal industry was leaving behind a residue of huge slag heaps along the river Tyne. Visitors to the area saw these massive piles of refuse as a sign of prosperity, although not surprisingly, nobody expressed a wish to live near them. The miners, of course, were obliged to live there, in conditions that were never far removed from dire poverty. Mining villages were often makeshift affairs, and their inhabitants were consequently regarded by many outside observers as "savages," lacking any contact with civilized society.

A third important industry was the production of iron. Used in nails, buckles, tools, cannons, small arms, and naval hardware, iron was mainly produced in the West Midlands (especially the counties of Worcestershire and Staffordshire), in the Weald, a hilly area of southeast England, and in North Wales. Making iron required a great deal of heat, supplied by burning wood, which is why the furnaces and forges were usually located on the edges of forests. Charcoal for use in the older type of furnaces, which were called "bloomeries," was provided by clearing a 20 or 30 foot circle of forest, then burning the wood in a heap formed around a central chimney. Heat from the fire separated the raw iron from rock and other minerals. It then had to be repeatedly heated and hammered in a forge to make refined iron. By the seventeenth century, the smelting process was usually done in a blast furnace, with a bellows to stoke the fire and a mechanical hammer to pound the raw metal. The bellows and hammer were powered by water-wheels, placed in artificially made "hammer ponds," which can still be seen in parts of the Weald. In the West Midlands, raw iron was refined and fashioned into bars, then sent to slitting mills to be rolled and cut into rods for making nails. Although John Evelyn held them partly responsible for the devastation of forests, the ironmasters may have been more careful conservators of woodlands than he

Map 2 *Regions and towns of Great Britain and Ireland, with battles of the Jacobite Wars.*

imagined. They tended to harvest undergrowth rather than felling large timbers. As a result, much of the forest of the Weald is still there, while the surrounding farming country has been almost entirely deforested by landowners.

Most ironworks, like those belonging to the Foley family in the West Midlands, operated on a relatively small scale, using local materials. In 1691, however, a West Midlands ironmaster named Ambrose Crowley started a much bigger operation on the river Tyne in northeast England, employing hundreds of skilled workers brought in from outside the area. The Crowley works imported large quantities of refined iron from Sweden, using it to make anchors, chains, hinges, locks, and other supplies for the Royal Navy. Crowley, who became Sir Ambrose after serving as sheriff of London, was a remarkable employer, who provided his workers with a doctor, a school, a minister, sickness and old age benefits, and funeral expenses. The workers paid for this social welfare system, however, through levies on their wages, and they had to accept the strict discipline of Crowley's works, which required them to pay fines for small infractions, like uttering blasphemous words. Nevertheless, Crowley provided a model for benevolent industrial employers of later generations. Most manufacturers did not imitate him. They sought quick profits, not the wellbeing of their workers.

They gave little thought to the environment either. The impact of their enterprises on the rural landscape shows that environmental change did not begin with modern industrialization. Already in the seventeenth century, the people of Britain were transforming the land in ways that were much more extensive than anything done by their ancestors. Only a few contemporary observers worried about this. Most regarded the land and whatever was found on it as having been given to them by divine Providence, to use in whatever way they wanted. This confident attitude of dominance over the earth would help to shape imperialism. In the seventeenth century, English and Scottish settlers had transplanted their ways of farming into parts of Ireland and the New World, replacing native systems of communal agriculture with private ownership and old techniques with new methods. The prosperity and air of "civilization" that accompanied such improvements served to attract new immigrants. In a sense, therefore, control over the environment of their own island was a first step towards control over larger parts of the globe.

Towns

So far, we have hardly mentioned larger towns and cities. The number of people who lived in them was rising. It has been estimated that 5.5 percent of the English population resided in towns of 5000 inhabitants or more in 1520. By 1600, this had reached 8 percent, and by 1670 it had risen to 13.5 percent. While the increase seems impressive, it should be noted that 86 percent of the population in 1670 lived in places that had fewer than 5000 people. The biggest urban center in the British Isles was London, which was approaching 500,000 people in the late seventeenth century (this includes the old walled City of London and its suburbs). Only two other English towns, Norwich and Bristol, were larger than 20,000. In Wales, there were no towns with more than a couple of thousand people. The capital of Scotland, Edinburgh, had about 25,000 inhabitants in the mid-seventeenth century. As yet, no other town in Scotland even approached this size. Judged by twenty-first century standards, Great Britain in the seventeenth century was an island of many very small towns, a handful of medium sized towns, and one small city.

This was not, of course, how contemporaries saw it. To them, London was a huge conglomeration, among the largest cities in Europe. It was also a hungry monster that greedily consumed massive resources, including people. In the seventeenth century, the capital needed about 8000 immigrants every year in order to grow, because so many of its inhabitants died of various diseases, and the natural rate of population increase was so low. The bustling city also provided an enormous market for wheat, butter, cheese, meat, and beer, carried into the town daily from the surrounding countryside. London's prosperity was based on trade, through its large, constantly busy riverside port. A German visitor in 1600 described the River Thames as "a center of trade for everything the world has to offer … it provides a perfectly safe – and at the same time beautiful – anchorage for shipping, and is so thick on all sides with the masts and sails of vessels that one might imagine it a closely entwined forest."[9] Textiles remained the most important single item of London's overseas trade, throughout the seventeenth century. English woolens were shipped out; Scottish linens, Chinese silks, and calicoes from India were shipped in, and often re-exported elsewhere. The merchants of the capital also imported large quantities of food and drink from overseas, especially wine, brandy, fruit, sugar, and molasses – obviously, English consumers of the seventeenth century had a craving for sweet things. London's main trading partners were in northern Europe (Scandinavia, Germany, France, and the Netherlands), but commerce with southern Europe (Spain, Portugal, and the Mediterranean) was also brisk, and trans-Atlantic exchanges with the Caribbean and North America were growing.

London had many small producers and a few large industries, like silk weaving, armaments making, and the naval dockyards, but its chief contribution to the economy of the nation was in trade and commerce. The capital was where mercantile adventures began, where deals were struck, where transportation networks converged, where trends and fashions were set. This made it a magnet for unskilled workers looking for a job, hauling or handling or perhaps hawking the goods that converged on the port. The environment in which they lived was dirty, smelly, noisy, and disease-ridden. If you had walked through London in the early 1660s, much of it would have looked like a decaying slum of run-down, overcrowded half-timbered buildings and dark, malodorous alleyways. During the last major outbreak of bubonic plague in 1665–6, an estimated 100,000 Londoners perished from disease in these fetid streets. After the Great Fire of 1666, the devastated center of the city was rebuilt with fine brick houses and the beautiful parish churches designed by Christopher Wren, but around them sprawled the same dingy inner suburbs as before. Only one bridge spanned the Thames. In order to cross at other places, you would ask a waterman to ferry you to the other side.

If you know the city today, you would have recognized the ancient Tower of London, but even by 1700, most modern public buildings did not yet exist. The monarch lived in the Palace of Whitehall, most of which burned down in 1698 and was never rebuilt. The only part of the Palace standing today is the elegant Banqueting House, in front of which Charles I mounted the scaffold in 1649. Old St Paul's Cathedral was destroyed by the Great Fire, and Wren's magnificent new version was not completed until 1710.

Other towns may not have been much cleaner or more sanitary than London, but they were less crowded and perhaps less impersonal places to live. They can be divided roughly into three categories: first, ports like Bristol and Liverpool, both of which looked out to the Atlantic; second, centers of manufacturing, like Norwich; and third, administrative centers built around law courts or a cathedral, like Perth in Scotland, or York, Chester, and Salisbury in England. The categories overlapped, of course, and the economic basis for a town could change over time. Glasgow in Scotland, for example, was primarily a market town, with an important university, until 1674, when the first tobacco imports began to arrive from North America. Eventually, Glasgow became the leading tobacco port in Britain. Although we tend to classify towns in terms of their economic activities, contemporaries often thought of them as legal entities or corporate bodies, enjoying certain rights and a limited amount of self-government. They were not designed to be open, competitive environments; on the contrary, they were supposed to be strictly regulated in all important ways. The structures of town governance, the rules of buying and selling, and even the timing of markets were spelled out in charters granted by the monarch. Townsfolk were fiercely proud of the privileges given to them in their charters, which distinguished them from their rural neighbors. Nevertheless, most urban dwellers played little role in their own government, which was usually restricted to narrow elites of leading merchants. Trade and industry in towns were also restricted by the charters and were controlled by local organizations of master craftsmen known as guilds.

By the early seventeenth century, many of these tightly regulated English towns seem to have been in a state of crisis, brought about by the decline of their medieval institutions and customs, as well as by an economic downturn related to population growth. An influx of unskilled labor from the countryside was undermining guild regulations in many sectors of manufacturing. In some places, Puritan factions challenged established elites for control of government. Town authorities were also noting an alarming increase in vagrants and beggars, who flocked to urban areas in hope of obtaining poor relief. One response, favored by those who had a Puritan religious disposition, was to tighten up moral ordinances against swearing, drinking, and fornication. Town magistrates also tried to deal with poverty by setting up workhouses where indigent people would perform menial labor in exchange for a place to live. They passed many ordinances to clean up the streets, for example by restricting the movement of pigs, which urban residents often kept in their gardens.

Economic conditions in most towns were improving in the late seventeenth century, while Puritan social legislation was grinding to a halt. Corporate feasts and celebrations were replacing the civic entertainments of former centuries. Celia Fiennes was in Norwich for the swearing-in of a new mayor in the late 1690s. She recorded how the town streets were decorated with the flags of the guild companies, and how the townspeople "dress up pageants and there are playes and all sorts of show that day. ... Then they have a great feast with fine flaggs and scenes hung out, musick and danceing."[10] Some towns were becoming fashionable places of leisure and consumption for the local landowners, who built fine brick houses in them, where they could mingle with others of their own social standing. The coach in which one rode about the streets, and the visiting card, left with a servant to announce one's arrival, became important signs of status for landowners who lived in town. They kept servants and employed all sorts of luxury tradesmen, from wig-makers and tailors to carriage painters and goldsmiths, which helped to stimulate the economic life of many small urban centers.

Still, most towns were probably not pleasant places to live. The fine houses of gentlefolk and merchants were built to keep out the disgusting smells and sounds of the streets. The more numerous houses of the poor tended to be cramped and poorly built. There were no public parks or amenities, few secular public buildings other than town halls, market halls and workhouses. Inns and alehouses were often the only non-religious centers of social life. Townsfolk lived in constant fear of fire, which could wipe out a whole community, and in periodic fear of plague, for which there was no effective remedy or treatment. So why did ordinary people increasingly choose to live in towns? Primarily, it was because they offered economic opportunities. For merchants, they were hubs of commerce, strategically placed for transporting goods by land, sea, coasts, and rivers; for tradesmen, they were markets in which to sell their wares; for craftsmen, they provided workshops where a skilled occupation could be learned and practiced; for ordinary laborers, they held out a chance of higher wages than were paid in agricultural work. Commercial and property transactions caused a proliferation of solicitors and scriveners. Lawyers flocked to the Assize courts, and clergymen vied for lucrative positions in the cathedral chapters.

The patterns of British urban life were carried overseas by immigrants, first to Ireland and then to the New World. With 45,000 inhabitants in the 1680s, and 62,000 by 1706, the Irish capital of Dublin was a boom town, due in part to the expansion of its trade, in part to its administrative importance. Dublin's law courts, cathedrals, and university would have seemed familiar to anyone who knew towns in England or Scotland. So would the religion of its people: seven out of ten of Dublin's inhabitants were Protestants. The port town of Cork, on the other hand, was predominantly Catholic, but was growing rapidly due to the trade in textiles and cattle, reaching 18,000 people by 1706. On the other side of the Atlantic, Boston was the biggest town in the English New World, with about 6700 inhabitants by the end of the seventeenth century. The brick buildings that began to appear in Boston around 1700 would enhance the impression that this was a new London, a center of English civilization, thriving amidst a wilderness.

The vast majority of information in this book, as in every book about British history, relates to people who lived in towns rather than to those who lived in the countryside. They produced far more written records; they participated more openly in politics; they were the main market for print culture; they were the major consumers of new commercial fashions; and they ran the commerce of an emerging empire. We have to keep reminding ourselves that they were only a minority of the population of Great Britain, even in 1837. We also have to remember that none of Britain's accomplishments after 1689 would have been possible without the enormous changes in the rural landscape that took place in the preceding two centuries. The industry and empire of the eighteenth century were largely built on the agriculture of the seventeenth century. Equally important, industry and empire were governed by the same idea or conviction that had gradually transformed English farming: namely, that constant improvement was necessary in all human endeavors. This idea, which may have been as much religious as economic in origin, seems to have spread from the countryside to the towns, and was then carried throughout the world.

3

Knowing One's Place

If you had met some of the people who lived in Great Britain in 1688, you might have had a shock. Perhaps it would not have surprised you to find that they were smaller on average than people today. You might have been taken aback, however, by their worn woolen and leather clothing, their badly damaged skin, their matted hair, and their terrible smell. Europeans gave up regular bathing in the Middle Ages (possibly because the Church found mixed public baths to be immoral). The English were thought to wash their face and hands more often than other Europeans, but this cannot have made much difference to their physical odor. Their bodies were covered with marks, boils, scabs, and scars. When women were accused of witchcraft in seventeenth-century Britain, midwives often searched their bodies to find "the devil's mark," usually a big pimple or boil. It was rarely hard to find! The people of Britain in 1688 did not wash their hair much either, although young women at least combed it out, for which they ran the risk of being accused of vanity. Clothes were worn for long periods of time, in all sorts of weather, without being cleaned. Richer people would have had finer and less worn garments, possibly made from silk, linen, or calico. The rich covered their body smells with perfume, and smothered their pockmarked faces with makeup. Their face paint often contained lead, which could melt and poison them if they sat too close to a fire. Wealthy men cut their hair short for fashion, and to control lice. They wore flowing wigs, while wealthy women sported elaborate coiffures capped with high lace headdresses. Everyone, rich and poor, educated and uneducated, would have spoken to you in thick, regional accents. Nobody yet used the "received standard pronunciation" that was later associated with being educated or upper class.

Seeing them in person would have reminded you that these people were in many respects different from us. It might have aroused feelings of sympathy or pity or revulsion, but it would not have told you very much about the broader society in which these individuals lived. To understand that topic better, we have to look beyond the physical appearance of seventeenth-century Britons, and consider broader questions. How were they affected by population increases? How did they relate to other social groups, or to the members of their own families? How differently were men and women treated? How were their lives shaped by the dominant features of their culture?

Population

As everyone who lives there will gladly tell you, Great Britain today is a very crowded island, with a population of 60 million; so it would be natural to assume that it has been crammed with people for a very long time. In fact, it has not. In 1520, England's population was around 2.4 million, more or less what it had been in the aftermath of the Black Death in the mid-fourteenth century. It had one of the lowest population densities of any major nation in western Europe. The number of people in England grew steadily for the next 130 years, to over four million by 1600 and over five million in 1650. After 1650, growth slowed down considerably, and the population was further thinned by emigration to North America, so that by the 1680s there were slightly fewer than five million people in England. The peak of 1650 was not reached again until around 1720. The population of Wales followed the English pattern, rising from a quarter million people in 1550 to around 400,000 in 1650, and remaining at more or less that level for most of the next century. Scottish population figures are harder to esti-mate, but the number of Scots probably rose from 700,000 in 1560 to about a million by 1650. Large numbers of Scots chose to emigrate in the early seven-teenth century, with 20,000–30,000 settlers leaving for Ulster and almost 50,000 young men departing for continental Europe to fight in wars. By the 1680s, there may have been around six million people in Great Britain, compared to 20 million Frenchmen, eight million Spaniards, or two million Dutchmen. By the standards of the late seventeenth century, Great Britain was not densely populated. Neither was Ireland, where about two million people lived in 1689.

Yet contemporaries felt the pressure of a growing population, even in seventeenth-century Britain. The major effect of population growth, in a society that could not increase production very fast or efficiently, was to create a situation of too many people seeking too few goods – and that situation, as every economist will assure you, must lead to inflation. The consequences of inflation in seventeenth-century Britain differed according to locality and social group, but for the poor, the steady yearly increase in prices was devastating, because it was not matched by a rise in wages. Some estimates place the drop in real wages from the mid-sixteenth to the mid-seventeenth century at 60 percent. According to one ingenious and frighten-ing calculation, in 1560 an unskilled building worker at Kingston-upon-Hull in northern England would have had to labor for 256 days in order to feed, clothe, and house his family. By 1630, to maintain the same standard of living, he had to work an impossible 459 days – meaning that, no matter how hard he worked, he was much poorer than his grandparents. Even if such figures are not very precise, they all point in the same direction: towards greater economic distress for those at the bottom end of the economic spectrum. Only the slowing down of population growth in the late seventeenth century eased the situation. By 1690, the Hull building worker was back to a manageable 251 days of labor. From the 1680s to the early eighteenth century, wages in the building trades may actually have risen by 20 percent.

Evidently, population levels made a big difference in everyday life, which explains why people tried to control them. It may seem incredible to think of millions of poor, uneducated people, with no access to effective contraceptive methods, reaching the same conclusions about how to deal with such a vague, imponderable variable as demography, but this seems to have been the case. To simplify a complex pattern: when economic conditions were bad, people began to marry later, and had fewer children. When conditions improved, they married earlier, and had more children. Most couples were wed in their mid- or late-twenties (in general, only rich people could afford to marry younger), and a delay in marriage of a few years could have a considerable effect on family size. Late marriage may have caused sexual frustration among young people. In the south-eastern village of Terling, for example, as many as one-third of brides went to the altar pregnant. On the other hand, by the mid-seventeenth century, a substantial number of people, perhaps one out of five, were not marrying at all.

Social Ranks in the Countryside

The effects of population growth and decline were shaped by the society in which these people lived. It was a very unequal and highly structured society, yet also remarkably fluid. We often try to understand social relations through categories, for example by dividing people into upper, middle, and working class. These generalizations can be misleading, because they fail to describe the ways in which people actually relate to one another, or how they experience their own place in society. At the same time, we cannot understand social groups without somehow categorizing them. England, Wales, and Scotland in the seventeenth century were societies composed of ranks, determined largely by status and partly by wealth. They were also, to a certain degree, societies stratified by type of income or labor (which we might call social class, if we chose to use that highly controversial term). In short, their social structure was as complicated as ours is today. However, it was held together by a fairly straightforward idea, shared by most of the wealthy and influential people in society: that the highest social rank should be derived from the ownership of land. "Authority," noted the seventeenth-century essayist Sir William Temple, "is much observed to follow land."[1] Wealth might be gained by trade, but land ownership bestowed superior status. This was, of course, an idea that went back to the Middle Ages, when valiant knights were rewarded for their service in battle by grants of land. It remained the defining principle of the landed classes in the late seventeenth century.

The landed classes of Great Britain had two main components. On the very top of the social hierarchy, just below the royal family, were the peers of the realm.

They numbered fewer than 200 in England and about 100 in Scotland. They held ancient titles (or at least titles that sounded ancient), and, for the most part, owned many broad acres of farmland. Both titles and land would be inherited by their eldest sons, with only minor portions doled out to daughters and untitled younger sons. Aristocrats married for financial and dynastic reasons, not for love; and their wives, however superior their status, suffered more than most women from the legal restrictions that made them, in medieval legal French, *femes coverte* or "covered women," preventing them from making contracts or owning property in their own right. Fathers sometimes tried to get around these restrictions by putting land or money into trusts for their daughters, but in response, aristocratic husbands might spend years trying to find legal ways to break the trust, and get their hands on all the assets of their wives.

Aristocrats maintained big country houses, as well as residences near London, and kept dozens of servants. Gregory King, who made his living tracing aristocratic families and spent his spare time working on statistics or "political arithmetic," estimated that the average aristocratic household in 1688 consisted of 40 persons, which seems a fair guess. Aristocrats rode around in coaches with their family coats of arms painted on the sides. They were patrons of writers, who often dedicated works to them, and they sat in their own boxes at the theater, or in special seats set up on the stage. They were trendsetters, whose likes and dislikes governed the fashionable world of London. Some of them led wild, debauched lives, like Robert Wilmot, Earl of Rochester, an accomplished poet whose writings included a set of verses chronicling the hilarious adventures of "Signior Dildo" among the ladies of Charles II's court. Others were highly moral and religious, like Daniel Finch, second Earl of Nottingham, a politician who strove to bring Dissenting Protestants back into the Church of England. Some aristocratic women were learned and accomplished, like Margaret Cavendish, Duchess of Newcastle, a scientist and philosopher and one of a small number of women who wrote works designed for publication.

As dukes and marquesses, earls and viscounts and barons, aristocrats were acutely sensitive to the tiny distinctions of rank among themselves, let alone the gulf that separated them from everybody else. Elevation into the aristocracy was possible, but was fairly rare, so it was not a very open group. The male heads of English aristocratic families enjoyed a right that was shared only by bishops: they sat in the upper chamber of Parliament, the House of Lords. Abolished under the republic of 1649, the English House of Lords had been reinstated at the Restoration of 1660, and among its members were the most powerful individuals in late seventeenth-century government. In Scotland, by contrast, aristocrats sat with the "barons" or town representatives in a single-chamber Parliament, but they arguably had even more influence than their English counterparts.

The other main component of the landowning classes was the gentry, meaning originally those who were of gentle blood and did not work with their hands, but did not hold noble titles. In Scotland, they were called lairds. Like the aristocracy, however, they bore coats of arms and were extremely proud of their ancestry. Gregory King thought that there were about 15,000 English gentlemen and "esquires" (that is, richer gentry) in 1688. To their ranks could be added 600 "knights," who enjoyed the title of "Sir" during their lifetimes, and 800 "baronets," who had the estimable privilege (often granted after a hefty payment to the crown) of bequeathing the title "Sir" to their male heirs. Knights and baronets are referred to by their full names or their first names – so, "Sir Clowdisley Shovell" or "Sir Clowdisley," but not (happily enough for this famous admiral, who died in a wreck on the Isles of Scilly) "Sir Shovell."

The aristocracy and gentry were often closely related by blood, which explains why they so often addressed each other as "Cousin." In Scotland in particular, the lesser lairds tended to be descended from the younger sons of peers. A significant number of English gentry families, however, had risen up from the ranks of rich farmers in the sixteenth century, when they bought up Church lands during the Protestant Reformation. In Yorkshire, 123 new families bearing coats of arms appeared between 1558 and 1679, while in Somerset, gentry families may have multiplied fourfold between 1502 and 1623. This social mobility slowed down during the seventeenth century, and in some counties the number of landed gentry families actually declined, making them a more exclusive group. Although a few of them could compete with the aristocracy in wealth, they were by no means all rich. The Welsh and Cornish gentry were particularly reputed to be poor, and an old proverb claimed that a Kentish farmer, with one year's rent, could buy out all the gentlemen of Wales.

Many gentry were pinched by the price rises of the late sixteenth and early seventeenth centuries, which cut deeply into revenues from land, causing rises in rents. After 1650, the gentry were hit again by price stagnation, which made it harder for tenants to pay what they owed. By the late seventeenth century, it was clear that, if a gentleman wanted to maximize his income, he would have not only to exploit the land that he owned – by enclosure, drainage, improvement, and renegotiation of leases with tenants – but also to invest in non-agricultural pursuits like mining, manufacturing, and trade. In other parts of Europe, this would have lessened the status of a landowner, but not in Great Britain. Some English gentlemen even became moneylenders, making mortgage loans to other gentlemen. It was not uncommon for the younger children of gentry families to go into commerce. "One must have some living now a days," wrote John Verney to his father, a Buckinghamshire baronet, in 1656, adding "I do verily think that I am a great deal fitter to be [in] some trade than to be a lawyer."[2] He became a London merchant, and made a fortune.

The gentry tended to define themselves by distinct cultural values. These were rooted in the social instrument by which land was transferred from generation to generation: that is, the family. Gentry families were strictly patriarchal. Wives and children were expected to submit to the authority of the father. A marital advice manual of 1591 instructed wives "to keep silence, and always speak the best of her head [i.e. her husband]. ... To her silence and patience she must add the acceptable obedience which makes a woman rule [over her children] while she is ruled. This is the wife's tribute to the husband, for she is not called his head, but he is called her head."[3] Marriages were carefully negotiated, and there are terrible stories from the seventeenth century about daughters who were beaten savagely or locked up by their parents for falling in love with the wrong man. Nevertheless, children were usually consulted in marriage negotiations, and could refuse a chosen partner. Aristocratic and gentry couples were not always happy, but plenty of evidence exists of real affection between husbands and wives, parents and children. In 1649, Sir Anthony Ashley Cooper, later Earl of Shaftesbury, fondly recalled his late wife as "a lovely beautiful fair woman, a religious devout Christian; of admirable wit and wisdom ... yet the most sweet, affectionate and observant wife in the world. ... She was in discourse and counsel far beyond any woman."[4]

Education was of great importance to the gentry. In early seventeenth-century England, the sons of the gentry were often educated at town grammar schools, alongside the children of merchants; but by the late seventeenth century, they were increasingly educated at home by tutors, or in the richly endowed "public schools" (so-called because they offered an alternative to domestic or private schooling), like Westminster, Winchester, or Eton. They then went on to university at Oxford or Cambridge, where they were trained in reading the classics of ancient literature. This allowed them to pepper their letters and conversation with Latin quotes that were incomprehensible to the unlearned multitude. It also inspired some of them to become notable scholars and writers, like John Dryden, the most celebrated poet of his age, or John Evelyn, who kept a fascinating diary chronicling his life. Girls were schooled at home in genteel feminine pursuits like drawing and needlework. They learned to read and write, but few of them were taught Latin.

Scottish lairds may have valued education even more highly. By the 1560s, only a tiny percentage of them were unable to read. They sent their sons to grammar schools, or to the parish schools established by an Act of Parliament in 1616. They had four universities to choose from: St. Andrew's, Glasgow, Aberdeen, and Edinburgh. Almost alone among European states, Scotland possessed a more or less national system of primary education by the late seventeenth century. It produced such notables as Sir Robert Sibbald, son of a laird from Fifeshire, who founded the Edinburgh Royal College of Physicians in 1681. Scottish universities would later become famous for scientific research and medical training.

The English gentry enjoyed many privileges in the countryside. They were often able to appoint a parish minister, and to enjoy some of the proceeds of Church revenues. They had a virtual monopoly on local government offices. They served as justices on the commissions of the peace, which were appointed on the recommendation of the lord lieutenant of each county. As justices of the peace (JPs), they heard criminal as well as civil cases, ordered repairs to roads and bridges, and carried out the commands of the central government. Justices could hold "petty sessions" in their own homes, and they met together four times a year to hold "quarter sessions" at the county courts. They were rarely trained in the fine points of the law, so they sent more serious criminal cases up to the traveling higher courts, known as Assizes. The judges of Assize courts were professionals, sent out from London. They met with great pomp and ceremony, twice a year in each county.

Members of the gentry also represented their counties in Parliament, where they were usually suspicious of efforts by royal ministers to increase taxes or alter the religious settlement. Each county elected two MPs, on a franchise that extended to all male owners of freehold land worth 40 shillings or more, which could encompass a substantial number of farmers, depending on how ownership was interpreted. More surprisingly, landed gentlemen were regularly chosen as Parliamentary representatives for incorporated boroughs or towns, both big and small. Because they were of higher status, better connected, and usually better educated than town merchants, the gentry were perceived by urban electors as having more potential influence on national affairs.

Scottish lairds also served in Parliament, as representatives of the "royal burghs," towns that had been granted the right to trade overseas ("burghs of barony" could only trade within Scotland). Unlike their English counterparts, however, they did not hold royal commissions as justices of the peace. Instead, Scottish landowners had their own baron courts, usually presided over by a baillie or estate manager rather than the laird himself. The Scottish baron court also had a jury of tenants, so it was not entirely dominated by the landlord. There are even examples of lairds being successfully sued by tenants in their own courts! In England, manorial courts had largely disappeared, although a few survived in towns that had no corporate charter of government.

The English gentry have often been seen as the most dynamic social group in seventeenth-century Britain: economically enterprising, socially ambitious, religiously divided, and politically discontented. They have been pictured as a kind of rising rural middle class, a threat to the domination of the nobility and the crown. This is an overstated picture. Most of the gentry were conservative in their tastes as well as in their views. They tended to follow the lead of the nobility in social as well as political matters, although aristocratic leadership broke down briefly during the Civil War period. Like the nobility, the gentry invested in agricultural improvement, mining, and manufacturing out of necessity, not because they had a premature capitalist mentality.

Below the gentry, rural society was characterized by a multitude of gradations of status and wealth. Tenant farmers or "yeomen" leased the land of the gentry and aristocracy, but they might also possess other land in freehold, meaning they were landowners themselves (in Scotland, they were called "bonnet-lairds"). Owning a freehold of 40 shillings gave a man the right to vote, along with a certain degree of independence. Wealthier farmers lived in big houses, which were divided up into separate rooms for privacy. They copied the manners and tastes of the gentry, especially in their dress. Not every village had a resident gentry family, so rich farmers might be the most important men in their locality, often referred to as "chief inhabitants" or even as "gentlemen." They owned pews in the parish church and often held parish offices, like churchwarden or vestryman in England, presbyter in Scotland. Their younger sons might be sent to town to be apprenticed to a trade, or educated to become clergymen. Sir Isaac Newton, the most famous scientist of his age, was the son of a prosperous farmer.

The big farmers headed a complex rural hierarchy that extended from substantial tenants and small landholders down to cottagers who might live in a shack set up on wasteland, keeping only a pig and a small garden. The most significant division among them may have been between those who subsisted on their own land and those who survived mainly by hiring out their labor. Those who did not own land, and even some of those who did, tended to move around a lot. The turnover of population in rural England was remarkably high – between one-half and two-thirds of the population moved within less than a decade, according to a study of two seventeenth-century villages. Farm laborers traveled around to hiring fairs, looking for work, while tenant farmers, even substantial ones, left in search of better opportunities. Most did not go far – they tended to stay within a ten or twelve mile radius of where they were born – but even so, the population of many localities was constantly changing. In one village, only two out of 63 family names recorded in the early seventeenth century could be found living there 100 years later.

The wives and families of laborers followed their husbands and fathers on these short migrations. Marriage among laboring folk created an economic unit, to which wives and children were expected to contribute. Spinning was a traditional rural female employment, just as weaving was for men. Women were also employed in dairying, raising chickens, harvesting, and haymaking. When they sold their labor, however, they were paid less than men – in Bedfordshire in the 1680s, for example, women were paid half of what male farm laborers earned. In some areas, poor women were given the privilege of gleaning, or clearing up the corn stubble after the harvest. We might consider this a small favor, but it was vital for people who lived on the edge of subsistence. For young women, service in the households of farmers or gentry was another employment option. Servants often performed farm labor as well as domestic duties. It was not uncommon for rural parishes to bind the female children of indigent families to contracts that made them apprentices in "husbandry" (farm labor) or "housewifery" (domestic service) for a certain number of years.

The prosperity of rural families usually followed a pattern linked to age and fertility. Families did well when both parents were young and working and there were few mouths to feed. Infants brought economic distress, but once they were a little older they could be put out to work, contributing to family income. Old age was devastating, because nobody enjoyed a pension and few people had any savings. Only the wealthy retired; most people worked as long as they were able. Dependence on children or on parish poor relief were the sole options for those who were too feeble to work. Wives tended to outlive their husbands, then as now, in spite of a high rate of mortality in childbirth. Widowhood could bring a certain amount of freedom, but it could also be economically disastrous for poor women who lacked grown children willing to support them. They might survive on meager earnings from taking in other people's laundry. Parish relief, in the form of small weekly payments, was often directed at impoverished widows, and charitable institutions, like village almshouses, were set up with them in mind, but many must have ended their solitary lives in terrible deprivation.

Rural workers who were skilled in non-agricultural labor earned higher wages and often enjoyed considerable autonomy. Miners in particular were thought of as "masterless men." Cornish tin miners preferred to work for "tribute," or a share of the yield, rather than a wage. Their profession was protected by the ancient Charter of the Stannaries, which set up a court whose officers, usually local gentlemen, were chosen by the miners. Coal miners around Newcastle upon Tyne worked their own hours, perhaps six to seven each day, and were given housing as well as domestic coal by their employers. We should remember, however, that brutal physical conditions, coal dust and damp usually shortened the working lives of these men. Moreover, not all miners were privileged with relative freedom. In Scotland, coal miners were bound to their work by restrictive contracts that virtually made them into serfs.

Social Rank in Towns

The structure of rural society was to some extent reflected in urban society as well. The local gentry formed the upper social level. Tradesmen who catered to their tastes and merchants who dealt in agricultural produce were dependent on the landed classes, and tended to imitate their habits, including religious worship in the Church of England. In places with a strong Puritan tradition, however, merchants and tradesmen of "the middling sort," as the middle ranks of urban society were called, sometimes inclined towards more independence. While they still chose gentlemen to represent them in Parliament, they resented direct interference from landowners in town affairs, and zealously guarded their civic privileges. Many Puritans of the middling sort became religious Dissenters after 1660, splitting with the Church of England. Even those who remained within the established Church tended to preserve a streak of godliness in their attitudes, which could set them apart from the local gentry.

To understand the social position of the middling sort in English and Scottish towns, we have to grasp the precariousness of their positions. Merchant families were rarely able to hang on to their wealth for more than a couple of generations. To reach the top of urban society and stay there, they had to make careful marriages, personal alliances, and loans that would establish a network of credit and financial dependency. Merchants aspired to dominate local affairs through family-based oligarchies, which required a generation or two to establish – just about as long as their family fortunes were likely to last. In larger towns, ambitious merchants joined the trading companies that enjoyed monopolies on specific types of commerce, like the Hostmen of Newcastle (known as the "Lords of Coal"). Together, they tried to fight off the crowd of small businessmen who wanted trade to be opened up to competition. They had to keep a careful eye on their assets and investments, which often depended on unpredictable factors like wars abroad or the sinking of ships in bad weather. They needed to know what was going on, both inside and outside Britain, which was why they were among the earliest readers of newspapers. Their desire to meet with one another for business, as well as to socialize, led to the appearance of Exchanges, where merchants could make deals, as well as coffee or chocolate houses where they could relax, drink exotic beverages, and peruse the newssheets. Ultimately, successful merchants wanted to get their money out of trade and into land, which was a safer investment. All of this led to a high degree of anxiety. "Abundance of Riches … Rob a Man of his Quiet," mused a Bristol merchant in the 1620s. "For what Care is there to be had of Rents?" he asked rhetorically, "What Caution and Wariness to be had of bad Debtors? What Fear of Losses and Casualties? What Distrust and Suspicion of our best Friends? What Vigilance and Diligence, that we be not over-charged in our Bargains? … To be brief, what Toil and Weriness throughout our whole Lives?"[5]

Town merchants could not afford to let toil and weariness overcome them. They were constantly seeking new outlets for investment, from company stocks to coal mines to the African slave trade. They became involved in industry through the so-called "putting out" system. Merchants bought raw materials, such as wool or iron bars, and sent them out to individual household producers in country villages, to be made into finished goods: cloth, iron nails, buckles, knives. The workers then delivered the finished goods to the merchants, who paid them a rate for every piece produced. Only a few merchants were daring enough to take the huge financial risk of establishing large scale industrial plants, as Sir Ambrose Crowley did when he set up his famous ironworks on the Tyne. Most merchants who became involved in manufacturing were eager to limit potential losses by passing them on to the workers, through reductions in what they paid for piece work.

The lives of urban tradesmen and skilled workers, or artisans, were even more precarious than those of the merchants. When trade was good, they might prosper; when it fell, they could be ruined. Tradesmen and artisans ranged considerably in status, from the goldsmiths who amassed great wealth acting as bankers for the merchant community, through the cabinet makers and printers and butchers, down to the lowliest joiners (carpenters), shoemakers, and weavers. In theory, they had all served apprenticeships for five to seven years, in order to gain mastery of their trade. In reality, an increasing number of them, especially in the larger towns, had just set themselves up in a business, without going through a full course of training. Town governments fined tradesmen for doing this, but the penalties were not severe enough to stop it, and in many places fines were no longer collected after the mid-seventeenth century. The wives of tradesmen and master artisans were often vital to the economic survival of a business, and they might run it themselves after the death of their husbands. However, it was rare for urban women to serve as apprentices, and almost unknown for them to join the town guilds that still protected skilled laborers. Some guilds imposed a limit of a single employee on businesses run by widows, so as to reduce competition with enterprises headed by men.

The principal aspiration of a tradesman or artisan was to avoid falling into the vast pool of unskilled labor that comprised the bottom level of urban society. These people, often immigrants from the countryside, had to take work wherever they could find it. They included servants, carriers of goods, street sellers, and rat catchers. They lived in dank tenements, slept on straw, dressed in second-hand clothing, and often ran into trouble with the law; but they also courted spouses, raised families, and participated in the religious and political life of the towns in which they lived. If skilled artisans were afraid of becoming like them, they in turn feared becoming indigent. Beggars and vagrants could be found everywhere in Britain, especially in the aftermath of wars, when soldiers and sailors were demobilized, and many fell directly into poverty. Poor relief might be available to them – in both England and Scotland, parishes were responsible for the support of the local poor – but if they wanted to claim it they would have to prove that they had a "settlement," that is, that they had been born in the parish.

Towns were also populated by professional people: clergymen, doctors, lawyers, army and naval officers, schoolteachers. Generally speaking, their numbers were increasing in the late seventeenth century, in spite of the efforts of some leading institutions to restrict their growth. To a limited extent, the professions offered a possibility of social mobility to people near the bottom end of the social scale. A lucky poor boy might still become a clergyman in England or (more likely) Scotland, if his talents were identified by a patron and he was able to attend one of the universities where ministers were trained. After 1660, the clergymen of the official churches had to compete with Dissenting ministers of other Protestant denominations, whose work was for the most part carried on illegally. Similarly, the English Royal College of Physicians complained bitterly about competition from doctors who were licensed to practice by other institutions – mainly by bishops of the Church of England, who had the authority to create medical doctors, or later by the Dutch university of Leiden. Even more abhorrent to the physicians were the surgeons and apothecaries who served the bulk of the population, and whose training consisted mainly of experience.

The legal profession was equally stratified. At the top of the English system were the barristers who were trained at the Inns of Court in London and held the right to plead in the high courts of King's Bench, Common Pleas, Exchequer and Chancery. The separate Scottish legal profession was headed by lawyers of the Court of Justiciary (established in 1672 for criminal cases) and the Court of Session, both located in Edinburgh. Beneath them buzzed a growing beehive of attorneys and solicitors who prepared cases, executed land deeds and conveyances, and registered wills. Naval and army officers were mostly drawn from the ranks of the landed elite, so there was not much chance for social mobility in the armed forces. Nonetheless, more officers were needed in the late seventeenth century, which created some opportunities for men of lower social origins. With the expansion of the armed forces came positions for civil servants drawn from the middling sort of people, men like the clerk at the Navy Board, Samuel Pepys, who left a fascinating diary of London life in the 1660s. Pepys was a hardworking bureaucrat, as his diary reveals: "At the office all morning. Dined at home at noon. And then to the office again in the afternoon to put things in order there, my mind being very busy in settling the office to ourselfs [himself and his two assistants]." Hard work was not enough to advance a career in administration. Pepys also needed an aristocratic patron, and he thought to have found one in the Earl of Sandwich. Patron–client relations, however, could be complicated.

When the Earl began to lose his influence at the royal court, Pepys boldly wrote to him, informing him that "I find a general coldness in all persons towards your Lordship."[6] Because he was viewed as talented and had other important protectors, Pepys was particularly sure of himself; most professional people would not have dared to address a patron in this way.

School teaching was the lowliest of the professions, and was heavily dependent on the goodwill of wealthy benefactors. It was also the only profession open to women, who generally instructed younger children and were paid less than men. The number of schoolteachers was growing throughout the seventeenth century. In England, alongside the old "public" schools for the sons of the landed classes, and the ancient town grammar schools for the sons of merchants, new private academies, some of them run by Dissenting ministers, had sprung up. Women taught mostly in charity schools for poor children and in "dame schools" where a mistress instructed students of various ages in reading, writing and arithmetic. In Scotland, a series of Parliamentary Acts of the early seventeenth centruy had established the financial basis for establishing a school in every parish, and by 1688 they existed in virtually every part of the Lowlands, teaching "godliness and gud manners." This made the Lowland Scots among the most literate people in Europe, although among their Highland compatriots schooling remained exceptional.

Professional training could provide financial rewards and a sense of belonging to a privileged group. It also encouraged association with other professional people, through clubs, societies, and regulatory organizations that resembled guilds. In status, professional people were associated with the higher levels of the middling sort, and shared many of their values. They tended to be more conservative than tradesmen or artisans, strongly attached to the monarchy, the Church of England, and the dominance of the landed elite. Nonetheless, because they mingled with the gentry, they were often more innovative than other middling groups in their cultural tastes. They went to the theater, commissioned portraits, and read poetry as well as writings on practical or scientific topics. They were among the first consumers of tea, coffee, and chocolate. They wore the latest fashions and copied the social graces of the landed classes. Just as the number of educated people was growing in England and Scotland, so too was the consumption of culture expanding.

Culture

Culture is a modern term that describes a variety of things: habits and customs, artistic production, and the values on which they are based. People of the seventeenth century would have recognized that all these things were related, but they would have seen religious and moral principles as what should tie them together. They already understood that culture could be purchased or consumed, just like any commodity, but they were still a little shocked by the idea. Most of them would have preferred that culture embody piety, obedience, and respect for authority rather than commercial values.

Within the image: Sold by H. Overton without Newgate; A Merry new Song; Les Chanteurs de Chansons; Cantarine & Strada; 13

Illustration 1 *Two London street vendors of the late seventeenth century, selling printed ballads with woodcut illustrations. Although poor, the woman has fancy ribbons on her shoes. ("A Merry New Song," engraved by John Savage from* The Cryes of London Drawne after the Life *by Marcellus Laroon, 1688. © City of London / Heritage-Images / Imagestate)*

Most educated people in England and Scotland were religiously observant, and religious works were the largest selling books of the seventeenth century. At the same time, a more secular culture of theater, music and print was available to the upper and middling sort of people, especially in larger towns. Samuel Pepys was addicted to music, not least because he loved to ogle at attractive women singers. "Here is the best company for Musique I ever was in in my life," he wrote of one concert, held at his house in 1665, "and wish I could live and die in it, both for music and the face of Mrs Pierce and my wife and [Mrs] Knipp, who is pretty enough, but the most excellent mad-hum[ou]rd thing; and sings the noblest that ever I heard in my life." He later admitted that his nature "will esteem pleasure above all things; ... music and women I cannot but give way to, whatever my business is."[7] Pepys also loved to attend plays, although he once took a vow to give them up. His conscience, raised in an atmosphere of Puritanism, was wrestling with the propriety of cultural delights that did not seem quite moral. His struggle may have been typical of many educated people in the late seventeenth century.

After the Restoration, Charles II wanted the royal court to dominate the culture of his kingdoms. Like many contemporary observers, he blamed the Civil Wars of the 1640s and 1650s on the promiscuous circulation of subversive ideas through pamphlets, newspapers, and other public media. Charles licensed only two theatres in London. An official *Gazette* was issued to give an acceptable version of the news. The King sponsored the Royal Society, which promoted discussion of scientific subjects, but its principal purpose was to come up with practical inventions that would benefit the regime, and its members, among them Samuel Pepys, declined to consider "speculative" subjects, like politics or religion. The most promising writer of the age, John Dryden, was made poet laureate by the King in 1670. Dryden had shed his earlier republican sympathies in order to write works praising the monarchy and the Church of England. In 1667, he published a long poem, *Annus Mirabilis* or *Year of Miracles*, praising Charles II and his brother, the Duke of York. Dryden pictured the citizens of London, their city destroyed by the Great Fire of 1666, looking to Charles II for comfort in their sorrows:

> No thought can ease them but their Sovereign's care
> Whose praise th'afflicted as their comfort sing;
> Ev'n those whom want might drive to just despair
> Think life a blessing under such a king.[8]

This was how the restored monarchy wanted to be seen, as the only guarantor of the nation's welfare.

However, it proved impossible for the court to control cultural expression. One of the most respected writers of the period, John Milton, was an unrepentant republican whose biblical verse epics, *Paradise Lost*, *Paradise Regained*, and *Samson Agonistes*, summed up his disillusionment with the restored monarchy. Because these long poems were based on the Scriptures, their political messages were effectively disguised, and what exactly they were supposed to mean remains the subject of much debate among critics today. *Paradise Lost* recounts the fall of Adam and Eve, who listened to a powerful tempter, perhaps in the same way that the English people had succumbed in 1660 to the seductions of Charles II. Satan is a monarch to his devils, and like King Charles, he aspires to divine power: "Towards him they bend/With awful reverence prone; and as a god/Extol him equal to the highest in heaven."[9] In *Paradise Regained*, Jesus fails to convince the people to follow him towards their own salvation, paralleling the failure of the godly Commonwealth to win over the common folk of England. In *Samson Agonistes*, the betrayed strongman, blind like Milton himself, takes revenge on the enemies of God by toppling their pagan temple. Milton meant these poems to be interpreted as commentaries on contemporary politics, from which he had separated himself after 1660. Other poets of the period were less circumspect in publicizing their political views. Andrew Marvell's *Last Instructions to a Painter* (1667) criticized Charles II's court, targeting especially the King's chief minister, Clarendon. The poem culminates with a warning to the monarch that his false courtiers may one day cut his throat, as they did his father's. In a poetic sequel, *Further Advice to a Painter* (1671), Marvell, or someone copying his style, represented the martyred King Charles I weeping at the bad behavior of his "degenerate" son.[10] This was dangerous stuff.

By the early 1670s, it was evident that Charles II's attempt to control English culture had not been successful. This was partly due to politics and to ineffective means of censorship, but it was also partly because cultural production was more responsive to market forces in England than in most other countries. Printers and publishers perceived that they could make money from selling works critical of the court, and many of them rushed to do so, especially those who had specific political or religious motivations for associating themselves with such materials. They saw no fundamental difference between political satires and the ballads or almanacs or reports of "marvels" that they also sold. This attitude may have originated in the Civil Wars, when censorship of the press had collapsed in England, and almost any type of work could find its way into print. Eventually, a lively and highly commercial sphere of political writing, printing, and publishing would emerge in both England and Scotland, churning out newspapers and pamphlets in large numbers.

If the government of Charles II sought to control English print culture, it also wanted to encourage the customary culture of the common people, to which Puritans had been fiercely hostile. In both town and country, customary culture rotated around a calendar of feast days and festivals that were marked by dancing, drinking, and carousing. These included planting and harvest festivals, as well as celebrations of Mayday, Whitsun, Christmas, Shrovetide, Easter, and parish saints' days. St Bartholomew's day in August, for example, was marked by a major fair held at Smithfield in London, with plays, puppet shows, music, and games. Celia Fiennes came across a Bartholomew's day fair near the town of Rye in Sussex: "Rightly Called beggarhill Faire being the saddest faire I ever sawe – ragged tatter'd booths and people – but the musick and danceing Could not be omitted."[11] Evidently, she did not much approve of what she witnessed.

She was not alone. Godly Protestant reformers had long tried to clean up or suppress such rowdy and "superstitious" festivities, which they saw as offences to religion. Under the republican government of the Commonwealth and Protectorate, it looked as if they might be successful, but in the end it proved impossible to stamp out popular customs, except in strongly Calvinist areas like the Scottish Lowlands. A Puritan minister in Cheshire was outraged when a "rabble of profane youths, and some doting fools" put up a maypole near his church, which he saw as "a relic of the shameful worship of the strumpet [and pagan goddess] Flora in Rome." The minister's wife cut it down, but another soon went up, where people began "drinking to debauchery in the evening."[12] This happened in 1661, by which time the maypole, a symbol of spring and renewal, was associated with political support for the Restoration of Charles II. Within a year, the Puritan minister had been ejected from his living, while the maypole presumably remained in its place. Meanwhile, the Duke of York had set up a huge maypole in the Strand, a street in central London. With the approval of the government, popular customs continued, much as they had for centuries. The Puritans had also railed against sports played on the Sabbath, like stoolball, a violent game that involved whole communities, sometimes including women. The spilling of blood in cock-fights, bull-baitings, or bear-baitings (where a chained animal was attacked by enraged dogs) caused furious excitement in English villages and small towns. Few people thought of blood sports as cruel, although reformers criticized them for encouraging sin and frivolity. Where the Puritan reformers did have some success was in removing official sponsorship from these events, which by the late seventeenth century were more likely to focus on an alehouse than on the parish church.

Village culture was also enlivened by gossip. Men gossiped in the fields and alehouses; women gossiped on their doorsteps. Gossip and rumor were not always benevolent; they could lead to accusations of name-calling or scandal-mongering, which were tried in church courts and punished by small fines. More seriously, rumor could be a source of witch accusations, which began in the mid-sixteenth century and were still being heard by the courts in the late seventeenth. "Witches" tended to be poor old women who depended on charity, although they might also be younger women or old men. They were accused of acts of malice, which by the end of the seventeenth century frequently meant involvement in the sudden deaths of children. Witches were also said to have had contact with Satan through a "familiar," usually an animal. Although the accusations originated with ordinary people, judges were to blame for giving credit to them. Witchcraft in England was punished by hanging, not by burning as in other parts of Europe, including Scotland. The prosecution of Scottish witchcraft was more systematic, and more brutal. Legal commissions of Scots gentlemen and clergy, fired up by Calvinist zeal, were empowered to bring charges against witches, and of course they generally found them wherever they looked. A notorious Scottish witch-hunt of 1661–2 led to accusations against 664 people, although fewer than half of them were brought to trial. By that point, in fact, many judges throughout Britain were growing skeptical about witch accusations, which they increasingly viewed as malicious and untrustworthy. Belief in witches did not die out, and trials continued until 1712 in England, until 1727 in Scotland. By then, the death-toll from witch cases had reached more than 500 in England, while in Scotland it may have exceeded 1000.

Historians of English rural society have sometimes argued that the widening gap between rich and poor was creating two distinct cultures in the seventeenth century. People at the upper end of the social spectrum developed a taste for private entertainment rather than public festivals, and ceased to believe in popular "superstitions" like witchcraft, while those at the lower end remained attached to traditional recreations and celebrations. The degree of cultural separation, however, can easily be exaggerated. Aristocrats and gentlemen of the Restoration period continued to sponsor bull-baitings, to dance around maypoles and to attend village feasts. They believed in spirits and feared devils, just as the common people did. Yet two factors were gradually drawing the culture of many privileged and educated people away from that of the majority. The first was fear of popular disorder, which in the wake of the Civil Wars was as strong among royalists as it was among Puritans. If customary observances led to riots, assaults, or breaches of the peace, then they would have to be controlled, if not suppressed. The second factor was the continuing criticism of "superstition" by clergymen and learned writers of all religious persuasions. Sustained attacks on false beliefs would undermine first witch accusations, then the public acceptability of magical practices like astrology and alchemy. This does not mean that educated people ceased to believe in such things, only that they were not able to display their beliefs in front of other educated people without embarrassment.

Already in the mid-seventeenth century, cultural divergence in Great Britain was clearly connected with politics. Royalists wanted religious unity, censorship of the press, and support for popular customs. Their Puritan or Dissenting opponents called for religious toleration, liberty of the press, and suppression of the immoral or impious traditions of the common people. The ways in which these divergent views were expressed, however, altered after 1660. The armed military confrontations of the Civil Wars gave way to a very different type of partisan conflict. Instead of killing each other, politicians and their supporters organized into parties and argued bitterly with one another, through public, commercial forms of discourse – chiefly through printed media that were widely published and could be purchased by anyone. Over time, this new type of politics would generate a transformation, not just in the governing institutions of England and Scotland, but in the political culture of the British Isles, and of the world.

Part II

Party Strife and Revolution, 1660–1689

In many parts of Europe, the first half of the seventeenth century was a terrifying time of violent political upheavals, rebellions, and revolutions. It was followed by a return to more stable, authoritarian government after 1660. In England and Scotland, however, the attempt to reconstruct a powerful monarchy following the Restoration was not successful, because political and religious divisions remained so intense. Between 1678 and 1689, the British kingdoms once again experienced serious turmoil. In Scotland, armed confrontation between radical and moderate Protestants flared up periodically. In England, a national scare over a Catholic successor, James, Duke of York, led to an unsuccessful attempt by the House of Commons to block him from the throne. After he became king, James II alienated his Protestant subjects by trying to extend toleration to Catholics. A Dutch invasion finally deposed the unpopular monarch in what became known as the Glorious Revolution of 1688, replacing him with William of Orange and his wife Mary, who was James's daughter.

The turmoil of this period comprised the last chapter of a story that stretched back to the Protestant Reformation. The story had three main themes. The first was religious conflict, between Protestants and Catholics as well as between different types of Protestants. Religion provided a path to personal salvation, but it was also seen as the foundation of the state. A second theme of the old story was the authority of the king over his Parliaments. In whose hands did sovereignty lie? Was the monarch a tyrant, or was Parliament leading the kingdom into anarchy? Disunity between the British kingdoms provided a third theme. Because the king ruled three separate kingdoms, religious and constitutional problems were often compounded by differences between them, as they had been during the Civil Wars of the 1640s and 1650s.

In other ways, however, the period between 1678 and 1689 was the first chapter of a new story. Politics was gradually changing from an era of armed confrontation to a period of more peaceful, although still aggressive, competition between organized party groups. A new political culture was developing, based less on religious ties than on self-interest and social interaction. A flood of information about politics became available, which made it easier for people outside the government to engage with political issues. This does not mean that the British kingdoms quickly settled down. The diarist John Evelyn desperately prayed after the Revolution of 1688 that God would "Compose these [things], that we may at last be a Nation and a church under some fixt and sober establishment."[1] Unfortunately, it took another three decades to move British politics from an era of rebellion and turmoil into one of less bloody conflict.

Political conflict spilled over into the English colonies in the Americas as well, dividing them internally and making them resist efforts at control from the home country. The last chapter of this part examines the colonial societies of the late seventeenth century, which had their own inner vitality but were not integrated into a unified English empire.

4

The Culture of Politics

Today, we are used to a political culture in which partisan groups, amply financed and organized at the local as well as national level, compete for popular support in order to take control of government. Divided by ideas, they use every variety of mass media (most recently, digital and electronic media) in order to spread their messages. Party politics rests on the assumption that government represents the will of the people. Surprisingly, this political culture emerged first in England, a kingdom that was decidedly *not* democratic, and in which the will of the people, while frequently invoked, was not in any straightforward sense the basis of government. It would be a mistake to call English politics in the late seventeenth century "modern," but it certainly pointed in the direction of what we know today. How was this possible in a system that retained a powerful monarch, a House of Lords, and an established religion? In addressing this question, we will consider four major elements that led to the emergence of political parties in England, and later in Scotland: religious tensions; the role of Parliament; the impact of print media; and the rise of a new sociability.

King-killers and Jesuitical Dogs

The first element in party politics was religious divisions, both between Protestants and Catholics and among Protestants themselves. These religious divisions began with the Reformations of the mid-sixteenth century. Waves of change in doctrine and practice swept over the Churches of England and Scotland, isolating a Roman Catholic minority that could not accept them. The Catholics comprised a small percentage of the total population of the two kingdoms in this period: less than 1.5 percent in England, about 2 percent in Scotland, mostly clustered in the north-west Highlands. Only in Ireland did Catholicism represent a majority of the people. Nevertheless, English and Scottish Catholics were prominent within the aristocracy and landed classes. Around 10 percent of English nobles and gentlemen stayed true to the old religion. In Scotland, Catholics were thought to be about a third of the landed classes. They included at least half a dozen clan leaders in the Highlands and a handful of Lowland peers. Catholic landed families throughout Britain offered protection to priests, but there were no resident bishops, so that by the late seventeenth century British Catholicism was a religion dominated by lay people rather than by religious leaders.

The English penal laws against Catholics, or more precisely against "recusants" who "recused" or failed to attend Protestant services, were first enacted in Elizabeth I's reign. They included heavy fines for non-attendance at the Anglican Church, and for saying or hearing the Mass. Catholic priests who entered England were guilty of high treason, and it was a capital offense to shelter one. Under James I, Catholics were forbidden to come within 10 miles of London, practice professions, hold government offices, or keep arms in their houses. They could be imprisoned and lose their property for refusing the oath of allegiance before a JP. In 1673, Parliament passed a Test Act that imposed a declaration condemning Catholic beliefs on all officeholders. It was extended in 1678 to members of the House of Lords. These laws were responses to real or perceived Catholic plots against the government. Outside government circles, the penal laws were not routinely enforced, so many Catholics lived without being molested by them. Nevertheless, they threatened anyone who adhered to the old religion. By contrast, although Scotland had a Test Act as early as 1573, and a stricter one after 1681, its anti-Catholic laws were generally milder. Ireland had no such laws before 1692.

The English obsession with the Catholic menace was as much political as it was religious. Catholics were seen as hostile to the growing power of the English state and as allies of its rivals, Spain and France. At the beginning of the Civil Wars, the unpopular policies of Charles I were blamed by Parliament on the malicious designs of "Jesuited Papists" who were thought (wrongly) to surround the king. Catholics were also blamed for igniting the Great Fire that incinerated central London in 1666, a false accusation that was inscribed on the Monument, a 202-foot tall column erected to commemorate the terrible conflagration. A few years later, an English satirist put the following wicked words into the mouth of an imaginary Jesuit priest, addressing his younger colleagues:

> Shame, faith, religion, honor, loyalty,
> Nature itself, whatever checks there be
> To loose and uncontroll'd impiety,
> Be all extinct in you – own no remorse
> But that you've balked a sin, have been no worse,
> Or too much pity shown.[1]

In other words, Catholics were capable of any kind of criminal behavior. Those who were most convinced of this tended to support the Whig party after 1678. "Whig" was originally an insult, meaning a Scottish cattle thief, but it endured as a party label for 200 years. The Whigs saw Parliament as the protector of Protestantism, and were suspicious of the Stuart monarchy because of its perceived softness towards Catholicism.

Yet there were those who felt that Dissenters or ultra-zealous Protestants were an even greater threat to the nation than Catholics. They pointed particularly to the history of Scotland, where fervent Presbyterians, a religious group that was opposed to the authority of bishops, rose in rebellion against Charles I in 1637. Named Covenanters for the Scottish National Covenant that contained their main demands, they later broke up into political and religious factions. Radical Covenanters opposed the Restoration of Charles II and the return of bishops. Although some moderate Presbyterian ministers were allowed to preach under license after 1669, the radicals, especially the so-called Cameronians led by the fiery Richard Cameron, rejected any compromise with the hated Episcopalians or supporters of bishops. The Cameronians preached illegally in private homes (house conventicles) or to large meetings in open fields (field conventicles), mainly in the southwest of Scotland.

The original Scottish Covenanters of the 1630s had allies in England among the "godly sort," known as Puritans. Like their Scottish counterparts, the Puritans later split into factions. The most moderate of them held to Presbyterianism. Bolder spirits might join the Independents or Congregationalists, who believed that individual congregations should control the choice of ministers. A few adopted even more radical views, like the Baptists, who practiced adult baptism, or the Society of Friends, known as Quakers, who preached that every human being bore an "inner light" of truth within. With the failure of the 1660 Savoy Conference, an attempt at reunifying the Church, the return of bishops, and the imposition of the Act of Uniformity in 1662, all of these groups became Dissenters from the Church of England (later, they were called Nonconformists). Those who were most zealous in driving them out of the Anglican communion, and who wanted no further changes to Church doctrine, were later called High Churchmen. Other Anglicans, however, defended the Dissenters, and wanted them to be brought back within the Church. They would become known as Low Churchmen.

From the start of the Restoration period, Dissenters rather than Catholics were seen by many Anglicans as the main enemies of the King and the Church of England. This view seemed to be confirmed in January 1661 by an uprising in London, when about 50 Fifth Monarchists led by a wine cooper named Thomas Venner took up arms and raised a panic for three days. Parliament responded with the Corporation Act of December 1661, an attempt to bar Dissenters from holding offices in town corporations by requiring them to swear oaths repudiating the rebellion against Charles I. The Act also stipulated that officeholders must take communion yearly within the Church of England. This was not a very effective measure, as many Dissenters were willing to meet the Act's stipulations in order to qualify for office. Dissenting meetings or conventicles were made illegal by Parliament in 1664. Having regained their monopoly on the rituals of baptism, marriage, and burial, Anglican ministers initiated a campaign to bring more people to weekly services, by compulsion if necessary. King Charles II tried in vain to interfere with the policy of religious uniformity, by proclaiming the suspension of penal laws against Dissenters (and Catholics too) in 1672. The declaration was met with howls of protest from Parliament, and was quickly cancelled. The persecution of Quakers was particularly intense during this period, because they refused to swear the oaths of allegiance. About 400 Friends, as the Quakers called themselves, died in prison under Charles II.

The Quakers were declared pacifists, and most Dissenters were peaceable people, not potential rebels. They were also a small minority. A 1676 parish census taken by the Church of England in the southern part of the country found Dissenters to be only 4.2 percent of the population. This was probably an underestimate, and their actual numbers may have been twice as large, but it is clear that they did not represent a big segment of the English people. They were influential nonetheless, because they were concentrated in urban areas and among the middling sort – merchants, tradesmen, shopkeepers, craft workers. In London, many leading merchants privately held on to Presbyterianism, although they often disguised their beliefs and attended Anglican services from time to time. This deceptiveness only inflamed their critics even further.

The Anglican enemies of the Dissenters usually ended up as Tories. The term "Tory," like "Whig," was at first derogatory – it meant an Irish wrecker, who lured ships onto the rocks and plundered them. It would endure as a party label, and is still used by some Conservatives in Britain today. Tory and High Churchman became virtually synonymous, as did Whig and Low Churchman. Strong upholders of monarchy, the Tories were convinced that the Dissenters remained the same republicans and subversives who had murdered Charles I in 1649. "The Phanaticks," declared a group of Tory jurymen in 1682, "with a High Hand raised a Rebellion, Murdered the Best of Kings, many of the Loyal Nobility and Gentry, Took away their Estates, Laid aside the Monarchy, Destroyed the Church, and for almost Twenty Yeares, exercised Arbitrary and Tyrannical Government against the Law."[2] The perception that the constitution, the social hierarchy, and the Church were in danger from Dissenters would be a mainstay of Tory and High Church rhetoric until the 1820s.

Religious animosities had the potential to mobilize large portions of the population. During the Exclusion Crisis of 1679–81, huge crowds of Londoners, perhaps as many as 200,000, appeared on November 17, the anniversary of Queen Elizabeth I's birthday, to burn effigies of the Pope and the devil. Whig supporters turned out at elections throughout England to chant anti-Catholic slogans and taunt their Tory rivals. Anglican ministers who cast votes for the Tories were denounced by jeering crowds as "Dumb Dogs, Jesuitical Dogs, Dark Lanthorns, Baal's Priests, Damned Rogues, Jacks and Villains, the Black Guard, the Black Regiment of Hell."[3] On the other side, Tories burned effigies of "Jack Presbyter" and drew up "Loyal Addresses," one of which was signed by 20,000 London apprentices.

Women were prevented from voting or serving in office, but this did not mean that they were totally excluded from politics. Whig writers often accused "weakminded" women of being more superstitious than men, and more susceptible to priests; therefore, they were seen as Tories. In reality, there were strong female advocates for both parties. Lady Anne Bland, for example, led the Whigs in

Manchester, while Mary Astell, an early feminist, wrote pamphlets in favor of the Tories. Religious issues crossed social barriers, stirring up passions in people who were normally excluded from the narrow, male power elite.

The Perils of Parliament

The second major element in political conflict was the role of Parliament, especially in England. Until the Civil Wars of the 1640s, the English Parliament had not been a permanent institution. It was summoned by the King at irregular intervals, for specific purposes, and dismissed by him when it had finished the business for which it had been called together. Between Parliaments, authority rested in the hands of the King's Privy Council, made up of leading aristocrats and members of his court. This changed dramatically in the early 1640s, when Parliament demanded the right to control King Charles I's appointments to his Council. Parliament also passed a Triennial Act stipulating that a legislature would assemble every three years, whether the king summoned it or not, and would continue to meet for 50 days even if the king tried to prorogue or dissolve it. The royalist members of the Restoration Parliament annulled this statute in 1664, replacing it with a weaker Act in which they "most humbly do beseech" the King to summon a Parliament every three years. The legislature continued to meet regularly until 1681, when Charles II angrily dissolved it over the Exclusion Bill. In 1684, after Parliament had not been summoned for three years, Charles chose to ignore the "humble beseeching" of the second Triennial Act, and continued to govern through his Privy Council, without a Parliament. This was the last episode of its kind in English history. When he became king in 1685, James II immediately called a Parliament.

The institutionalization of Parliament was only completed after 1688, but even under the Restoration the legislature seemed more of a fixed feature, which had a big impact on English political culture. It meant that there was a quasi-permanent arena for national political debate, such as existed in hardly any other European country. The Scottish Parliament was much more sporadic, and there was no Scottish equivalent to the Triennial Act. Moreover, the English Parliament, in spite of its undemocratic character, claimed to speak for the whole nation, a claim that could hardly be made by its Scottish counterpart. The electorate in Scotland was tiny, and the legislature was notoriously corrupt. It was chiefly a forum for working out the rivalries between members of the Scottish Privy Council. The power of the English Parliament, by contrast, was potentially greater than that of any other legislature in Europe, provided that the king was prepared to work with it rather than against it. As a result, Parliament became the main focus for English party rivalries. Although Whigs and Tories did compete on the local level for municipal offices, both parties were primarily fixated with the goal of controlling the two Houses of Parliament, which meant control over national legislation.

The English House of Lords contained groups of committed Whigs and Tories, but many Lords were willing to tilt in whatever direction the government was heading. The House of Commons, on the other hand, was elected by voters who had to be mobilized behind candidates, and might shift from one party to the other. Each county and each borough or town (with a few exceptions) elected two Members of Parliament (MPs). The county electorates were based on ownership of property. A freeholder who had 40 shillings of land could vote, which created a fairly large electorate in some counties. Yorkshire, the largest county, had about 8000 voters in county elections. The borough electorates were based on a bewildering variety of franchises. In some places, only members of a town corporation could vote; in others, the vote extended to those made "free" by the borough; in still others, virtually every male taxpayer was a voter. Borough electors, especially in small places, were notoriously open to being bribed, cajoled, or threatened into voting for a candidate. In addition, some boroughs were sadly decayed. One had fallen into the sea; another was populated only by sheep. To think of this system as representing the people seems ridiculous, but that was how MPs saw it at the time. They believed that they were acting on behalf of all their constituents, not just the electors. In fact, the competition between Whigs and Tories led to a growing number of voters, as each side tried to extend voting rights to its supporters.

In general, the men who were elected to the House of Commons were landed gentlemen. This was true not only in the county constituencies, but also in the boroughs. A few merchants and bankers did sit in the Commons, but they were usually owners of landed estates as well. Borough voters preferred to elect landed gentlemen because it was believed that they had more influence than men of lower social standing. An MP was expected to serve his constituents, by presenting their grievances and proposing legislation that would benefit them. If he failed to do this, all his influence and favors and treating of the voters to food and drink might not get him re-elected. While this was not a democratic system, it was one that could be responsive to the people.

MPs often spoke of the rights and liberties of the people, which they saw as rooted in the common law, the accumulation of procedures and precedents in cases brought before English courts. They did not usually seek to extend traditional rights, although that could be a consequence of defending them. A famous example is the Habeas Corpus Act of 1679, which gave the force of a Parliamentary statute to a long-standing custom of English law. The Act required prison officials to obey writs (that is, written orders) of *habeas corpus* (literally, "you have the body"), which any prisoner, or a person acting on behalf of a prisoner, could demand from a judge. The writ required that the prisoner be delivered to a court. In practice, this meant that the government could not imprison people without trial for lengthy periods. Although it was frequently suspended in times of national peril, *habeas corpus* would remain one of the most important rights in English law, and would later be enshrined in the American Constitution.

Spreading the News

The business of Parliament, unlike that of the King's Privy Council, could not be kept quiet. Even today, the records of British Cabinet meetings are secret, and are not made public until 30 years later. Debates in Parliament, on the other hand, can be watched on television. Even in the seventeenth century, Parliamentary business became almost immediately known through printed newssheets and handwritten newsletters. Although it was illegal to print or even to take notes of Parliamentary debates, publishers cheerfully broke the law, and newsletters often included details of votes and arguments.

This leads us to the third element in the emergence of party politics: the growth of the press. The use of printed books and pamphlets to spread opinions to a wide audience had begun with the Protestant Reformation. After 1586, government control over the press was exercised mainly through the Stationers' Company of London, the official guild of master printers. All printed material had to be licensed by the Company, which had the power to carry out searches and seize illicit materials. The system broke down during the Civil Wars, when Parliament was simply unable to regulate the publication of political and religious pamphlets. *Corrantos* or newssheets, carrying details of recent political events, proliferated in this tumultuous period, until Oliver Cromwell set up a commission to censor the press in the late 1650s. Under Charles II, the old licensing system, exercised by the Stationers' Company, was revived and strengthened by an Act of Parliament. Only members of the Company, or those given a special license, were allowed to sell books. In addition, the 1662 Act granted patents that conferred monopoly rights to print certain types of work, including newssheets.

The licensing system was rigid but not very effective, because it relied on prior censorship, meaning that works had to be seen *before* they were published. Many publishers simply ignored the restrictions and went ahead with publishing controversial pieces. They were taking a risk, because censorship was backed up, at least in theory, by the terrifying laws against treason. If a printed work was found to contain treason against the King, anyone who was associated with it, whether as writer, printer, or publisher, could be prosecuted and sentenced to a horrible death. A convicted offender was to be hanged until almost dead, then cut down, disemboweled, forced to watch his organs being burned, and finally beheaded. A printer was put to death in 1664 in this barbaric fashion. The punishment was so severe, however, that it may have dissuaded the government from using treason as an accusation against other printers and publishers. Most writers, in any case, were careful to avoid anything that could be clearly construed as treasonable. They could still be prosecuted for the lesser crime of seditious libel, so long as a jury was willing to bring in a guilty verdict, which was never a certainty.

The ramshackle English censorship system was already breaking down by the late 1660s, when a stream of satirical publications appeared, lampooning the administration of the Earl of Clarendon. Occasional newssheets or *corrantos* started to surface again, in spite of efforts to suppress them. Many aristocrats and country gentlemen received handwritten newsletters to keep them informed of what was happening in the capital. During the Exclusion Crisis of 1679–81, the censors simply could not cope with the explosion of political publications. A highly excited public in London and other towns eagerly purchased the latest reports of what was going on, which were usually presented on a couple of hastily printed sheets of paper with titles like *The Weekly Pacquet*, *The Loyal Protestant*, or *The London Mercury* (Mercury was the ancient god of news). These news-sheets were partisan, presenting either the Whig or the Tory interpretation of events. Once the Exclusion Crisis had cooled off, the newssheets declined, but they did not disappear. King James II was so convinced of their persuasive power that in 1688 he set one up to publicize his religious policy, employing a well known Whig printer to edit it.

The real explosion in newspapers would occur after the Glorious Revolution of 1688, especially after the lapsing of the Licensing Act, but the groundwork for it had been laid under the Restoration, and earlier. It would be hard to overstate the impact of an expanding press. The stream of printed political literature was constant. It informed, strengthened, and sometimes even created political points of view. Those who purchased and read this literature, most of them men of the landed classes and middling sort, were actively and instantly engaged in politics, whether they had ever voted or not. Perhaps we should not see the press as a democratizing force, since one had to be literate and even well educated to understand its productions, but it certainly widened the scope of political involvement in late seventeenth-century England.

Steam from the Coffeehouse

Sociability was the fourth element in the emergence of political parties. To form a party organization, people have to gather together, exchange views and come to some sort of agreement about what they believe. The place in which they choose to meet, and what they do there, can help to shape their political intentions. The mid-seventeenth century created new ways of being sociable, which in turn affected party politics. Prior to this period, social life was mostly centered either on the hospitality of individual households or on big public events, often with a religious focus, that were held outdoors and brought together whole communities. By 1700, however, there were many public spaces throughout Britain where small groups of people could pursue leisure, conversation, and other types of social interaction. Alehouses and taverns, which had long been places for drinking and carousing, were hosting other amusements as well: sports and games, music and dancing, clubs and societies of all sorts, including the lodges of Freemasons, a brotherhood with secret rites of membership. The royalists and republicans of the Civil Wars had gathered in separate taverns to discuss political affairs and plan strategy. During the Exclusion Crisis of 1679–81, the Whig Green Ribbon Club, which organized the popular processions that ended with the burning of an effigy of the Pope, met regularly at the King's Head Tavern in Chancery Lane in London.

The most innovative and fashionable type of public social space, however, was the coffeehouse. The first of them appeared in Oxford in 1650; two years later, there was one in London. Soon, they could be found in almost all the fashionable areas of the capital. They would spread gradually to English provincial towns, to Edinburgh, Dublin, Boston, and other North American ports. Coffee was an

Illustration 2   *A London coffeehouse around 1705. The clients are all male and well dressed. Some are reading newspapers or discussing business. The servers are boys, and the proprietress, in a high lace cap, surveys the scene from a wooden booth. ("Interior of a Coffeehouse," c.1705. © British Museum, London, UK, / The Bridgeman Art Library)*

exotic drink that came from Asia, and was imported into Britain by the East India Company, through dealers in the Arabian Peninsula. It could be sweetened with sugar that was grown by slaves in the English West Indian islands. Coffee's popularity was a sign of the global commerce of the big English trading companies. Coffee was expensive compared to beer, and its consumption became a status symbol. Its rapid spread was also, of course, helped by the fact that coffee-drinking was addictive.

Coffeehouses offered more than a strong dose of caffeine, however. You could have a meal there, smoke a pipe of tobacco, read the news, hold a conversation around a public table, or attend a meeting in a private room. Social fashions were passed on through coffeehouse contacts. Men of the middling sort could learned to dress and speak and behave properly – that is, more like the fashionable upper classes – by watching their social superiors in the coffeehouses. Most establishments offered patrons a selection of reading material, including newssheets and pamphlets. Some were linked to Turkish baths or "bagnios," where a bath and massage often led to further pleasures, so that the word "bagnio" came to mean a house of prostitution. Other coffeehouses provided the sites for public auctions. One coffeehouse in Chelsea housed both a barbershop and a museum of curiosities.

Politics, of course, was a major topic of conversation at coffeehouses, and they quickly became associated with one political group or the other. From the beginning, the government attempted to monitor them, regulate them and, if necessary, suppress them. It did not work. During the Exclusion Crisis, they became centers for political discussion and the circulation of news. On the eve of the Glorious Revolution, King James II complained that "men have assumed to themselves a liberty, not only in coffee houses, but in other places and meetings, ... to censure and defame the proceedings of state, by speaking evill of things they understand not."[4] The King might fume, but there was nothing much he could do about the spread of coffeehouses. Like the drink that they served, they had turned into an addiction.

5

Preserving the Constitution

Restored amidst boisterous scenes of popular enthusiasm in 1660, the Stuart monarchy eventually fell again in the Revolution of 1688. If you had asked a Whig politician to explain that Glorious Revolution, he might have summed it up as an act of Providence that prevented an absolute monarchy from taking root, rescued the nation from "Popery," saved the constitution, and preserved traditional English liberties. This worshipful, almost mythic view is in many ways misleading. It distorts the policies of the Restoration period, and does not fully address why the Revolution happened. It also fails to cast much light on a crucial development that began under the Stuarts and speeded up after their downfall: the emergence of a British state.

As we tell the complicated story of the Restoration and the Glorious Revolution, we have to pay attention to characters and situations. Because neither of the British kingdoms had a written constitution, English and Scottish politics depended a great deal on how key individuals, particularly monarchs and their chief ministers, made government work through their relations with Parliament, the Churches, and the public. In addition, we must keep in mind how the three kingdoms of England, Scotland, and Ireland interacted with one another, aggravating each other's problems and creating new tensions. Above all, however, we have to keep an eye on party politics.

How Charles II Managed to Die in His Bed

It could easily be argued that the Glorious Revolution *had* to happen in exactly the way it did, because the Stuarts were incorrigibly bad kings. The Stuart family had lost the throne before, between 1649 and 1660, and had never managed fully to restore confidence in its leadership. The Stuarts had not resolved the big issues, religious and constitutional, that had led to their first downfall, and they were to be caught up in a new maelstrom of party politics after 1678. This second bout with disaster was closely related to the foibles of King Charles II and the stubbornness of his brother James, Duke of York. No matter how imperfect a king he may have been, however, there is one fact about Charles II that prevents us from seeing him as a total disaster: unlike his father and brother, he died in his own bed. How did he manage to hold on to power for 25 years?

When Charles II returned to England in 1660, almost everybody was glad to see him arrive. He was greeted by huge, enthusiastic crowds everywhere he went. Most people were sick and tired of eleven years of republican rule by governments that were dominated by the army. Many were afraid that the breakup of the Church of England had opened the door for "fanatics" like the Quakers. The republicans had never managed to make a viable settlement for the Church. Instead, they had opted for Independency by default, allowing each congregation to decide on how to choose its minister. The Parliament elected in the spring of 1661, which was dominated by old supporters of King Charles I, called Cavaliers, quickly reversed that situation. Bishops were restored. Non-Anglicans were excluded from borough corporations. Ministers of the Church who would not conform to the 1662 Act of Uniformity were ejected from their livings. About 2000 ministers, or 10 percent of the English clergy, were deprived. Forced out of the Church, Dissenting ministers were further persecuted by laws against non-Anglican religious meetings. King Charles, who favored toleration, was displeased by the actions of his Parliament, and his chief minister, the Earl of Clarendon, had misgivings about them, but neither could control the fervently Anglican legislature.

Not surprisingly, Charles II did not really trust his Parliaments, but he went along with them because he needed their approval in order to raise money. Charles had received a seemingly adequate financial settlement after the Restoration, but Parliament had refused to pay off royal debts from before 1660, and Charles soon added to them by profligate spending. In 1664–7, England fought a humiliating and costly war against the United Provinces (the Dutch Republic), whose navy burned the docks at Chatham and captured the royal flagship. At the conclusion of this awful conflict, Charles dismissed his bossy chief minister Clarendon, who was promptly banished for life by a vindictive Parliament. By the end of the 1660s, King Charles owed his creditors about £2.5 million. He longed to have an income that did not depend on the consent of the squabbling politicians. In 1670, therefore, he negotiated the Treaty of Dover, a secret agreement with France that would give him French money in exchange for fighting the Dutch and promoting Catholicism. He did indeed make another war against the United Provinces in 1672, the third in 20 years, but he made peace two years later, and he forgot about the secret religious promises that he had made. The Treaty of Dover was very risky for Charles. It revealed him as an inveterate gambler, and a devious political player who was willing to act behind Parliament's back.

Charles lost a major gamble in 1672 when he tried to reverse the actions of Parliament by proclaiming a Declaration of Indulgence. This suspended the laws against non-Anglicans and allowed Dissenting congregations to obtain licenses to worship openly. Under heavy pressure from Parliament, the King was forced to withdraw the proclamation. The legislators feared, rightly, that the King, without asking their consent, was trying to give toleration to Catholics. He had lived among Catholics, his mother was one, and he seemed at times to favor them. His brother was less restrained. The first Test Act, keeping both Dissenters and Catholics out of political offices, was passed by Parliament in 1673 after reports began to circulate that James, Duke of York, had converted to Catholicism. The rumors turned out to be true, and they would soon rock the Restoration monarchy to its foundations.

Historians used to point to the Treaty of Dover and the Declaration of Indulgence as proof that Charles was trying to be an absolute monarch, like Louis XIV of France. Nowadays, Charles is seen as too lazy, pleasure-seeking, and unfocused to have been planning an absolute monarchy. It should also be remembered that absolute power is never really absolute; it has to be judged relative to the institutional restraints placed upon it, which in the English case were severe. What Charles may really have wanted was more freedom to make his own decisions on issues where he saw Parliament as hopelessly wrong, like toleration; but he did not have the stamina to stick to these decisions when they encountered resistance. On the other hand, he was a great promoter of his own divinely appointed power. For example, he frequently used the Royal Touch to cure scrofula, an inflammation of the lymph nodes that caused terrible skin lesions. Practiced by English kings since the Middle Ages, the Royal Touch was supposedly a direct gift from God. Charles II used it on almost 30,000 sufferers in his reign, and enough of them improved to make it seem as if he had a real knack for healing.

Unfortunately for him, by the 1670s, the royal healer had lost his magical touch with the public. Dissenters saw him as a harsh tyrant. Religious people of all sorts were scandalized by his gambling, drinking, and open flaunting of mistresses. The King liked beautiful, intelligent women, whom he rewarded handsomely, giving noble titles to them and to his many illegitimate children by them. Charles was accused in popular songs of thinking with his penis rather than his head, and of following the bad advice of his hated Catholic brother James:

> Let the Commons search for plots, with a hey, with a hey,
> And the Lords sit like sots, with a ho;
>   If my brother and my whore,
>   Say the word, they're no more,
> With a hey tronny nonny nonny no.[1]

Because he had no legitimate children by his Queen, Charles was determined that James would succeed him. This was worrisome to Protestants, but their worry was lessened somewhat by the fact that James himself had two Protestant offspring, Mary and Anne, born from his first marriage to Clarendon's daughter. Mary was wed in 1677 to Prince William of Orange, the hereditary captain-general or *stadholder* of the United Provinces, in order to secure peace after three Anglo-Dutch wars. With his typical crude humor, Charles ushered the couple into bed on their wedding night with the command, "Now, nephew, to your work!

Illustration 3 *Charles II riding to Parliament on the day before his coronation in April 1661, amidst enthusiastic crowds of people. To the right of the King are Lord Chancellor Clarendon in profile and James, Duke of York, wearing a small crown. (Richard Gaywood, "The Most Magnificent Riding of Charles the IId to the Parliament," 1661. © The Trustees of the British Museum)*

Hey! St George for England!"[2] The King knew, of course, that his brother James, who after being widowed had made a second marriage to an Italian Catholic princess, might have another child, a boy to carry on a Catholic line. What he thought of this prospect, he would not say.

Was England headed for a crisis in the mid-1670s? In fact, politics seem to have become unusually stable in this period, although the appearance of stability may have been an illusion. For seven years after Clarendon's fall, the King's main advisor had been the pliable Earl of Arlington, but Charles consulted with various courtiers, some of them Catholics. His greater freedom of action had led him into secret engagements, open mistakes like the Declaration of Indulgence, and another frustrating Dutch War. Between 1674 and 1678, however, Charles's leading minister was Thomas Osborne, Earl of Danby, a staunch defender of the Church of England who set out to manage Parliament by using appointments, pensions, and favors as well as personal contacts in order to win votes. It was a strategy that would be followed later by many successful chief ministers.

Under Danby, serious upheavals were felt not in England, but in the American colonies (see Chapter 6) and Scotland. Scottish affairs were in the hands of the King's trusted lieutenant, the Duke of Lauderdale, who was deeply hostile to radical Presbyterians, although he had once been a Covenanter himself and was far from intolerant. Nevertheless, Lauderdale supported the Episcopal Church settlement that had restored bishops to the Church of Scotland in 1662. The subsequent purge of the Church went even deeper than that in England: about 300 ministers, or one-third of the Scottish clergy, were driven out of their positions. The radical Presbyterians responded by staging an uprising in the western Lowlands in 1666. When it was suppressed, more than 100 Covenanters were executed, and many others transported into virtual slavery in the West Indies. Fears of a new uprising in 1678 led the government to send an army of northern clansmen, the so-called "Highland Host," marching into the Presbyterian southwest to stamp out open-air prayer meetings. The Highlanders gained a terrible reputation for pillage, plunder, and murder.

Meanwhile, in the English Parliament, opposition to Danby gradually emerged. It was composed of MPs who objected to his corrupt methods as well as those who simply did not profit from them. They saw Danby as pro-French, and feared that Louis XIV was aiming at a "universal monarchy." Their leader was the Earl of Shaftesbury, a small, highly ambitious man who had once been a royal advisor. The opposition called itself "the Country" because it claimed to represent the nation's interests against the corruption of "the Court." It won some minor victories in the House of Commons, which irritated the King, but Danby's control was not seriously shaken until the fall of 1678, when suddenly his whole system collapsed in an incredible avalanche of rumors and accusations known as the Popish Plot. Strangely enough, when the moment of truth arrived for Charles II's government, it was built on an enormous lie.

At the heart of the Popish Plot was an amazing and patently false story, told by an informer with a huge jaw and bull neck named Titus Oates. Born a Baptist, trained as a Church of England minister, expelled as a navy chaplain for acts of sodomy, Oates had made a phony conversion to Catholicism and had briefly studied at a Jesuit college in Spain. On his return to England, he concocted a wild set of lies about a Catholic plot to assassinate the King (with silver bullets, no less) and put his brother James on the throne, which he recounted before the Privy Council. Danby and the King were suspicious, but the story gained credibility after the London magistrate who heard Oates tell it under oath was mysteriously stabbed to death (he probably committed suicide). Parliament wanted to hear Oates, and when he appeared before them he was bold enough to name five Catholic noblemen as central to the plot. One of them was later put to death, to the disgust of John Evelyn, who wrote of Oates that "Such a mans Testimonie should not be taken against the life of a Dog."[3] Yet it was taken against the lives of men. In all, Oates was responsible for the execution of 35 innocent people, including Oliver Plunket, the Roman Catholic Archbishop of Armagh in Ireland.

Protestant England went wild over Oates's accusations, which were widely publicized in prints and newssheets. Oates spoke to longstanding fears of "Popery" that Danby's government had done nothing to allay. Worse was to follow. The English ambassador to France knew that Danby had been involved in secret negotiations with Louis XIV. The rakish young diplomat was having an affair with one of the King's former mistresses. When he foolishly seduced the lady's daughter as well, she complained to the King, who sacked the ambassador. Under threat of arrest, the ambassador showed the secret letters to the House of Commons. Danby was impeached, and the King hurriedly dissolved Parliament – the old Cavalier Parliament that had been in existence for 19 years. The elections to a new Parliament in January 1679 were no surprise: the King himself dryly commented that a dog would be elected if it stood against a courtier. The House of Commons was dominated by the "Country," led by a triumphant Shaftesbury, who had been appointed to the Privy Council. His supporters, soon to be known as Exclusionists or Whigs, drew up a bill to exclude James, Duke of York, from the succession, so that James's daughter Mary would come to the throne after the death of King Charles. The opponents of Exclusion, later called Tories, proposed instead that James should be allowed to succeed, but that his powers as king should be limited by law.

Underlying the party division was a religious one, between those who feared "Popery" more than Dissent, and those who mistrusted "King-killers" or Dissenters more than Catholics. The public was polarized between one side and the other through an intense pamphlet war. Some Whig writers were in fact quasi-republicans, who praised "the Voice of the People" as "the Voice of God," although by "the People" they usually meant those who owned property. They roused supporters with claims that "the People of *England* are ... Resolved to die *Protestant-Freemen*, rather than live as *Papists* and *Slaves*."[4] The Whigs organized huge Pope-burning processions in London to celebrate the anniversary of Elizabeth I's accession, and set up clubs in constituencies throughout England. The Guildhall, where the government of the City of London met, became a battleground between the two sides, with Dissenting merchants strongly backing the Whigs, while Anglican clergymen tried to turn out their congregations for the Tories. Both sides gathered thousands of signatures on petitions to Parliament from residents of London. Conflict in the capital was reflected in other English towns as well, and in parts of Scotland. Edinburgh University students, for example, imitated the London mob by holding their own Pope burning, which resulted in numerous arrests.

The King's tactic in response to this political earthquake was to buy time. He dissolved the Exclusionist Parliament and called new elections. By October 1679, when the results were known, it was clear that this approach had failed. Almost 40 percent of those who had voted against Exclusion had lost their seats. The king decided to stall again, by proroguing (that is, postponing) the first meeting of Parliament for over a year. In the meantime, he ditched Shaftesbury from the Council. When Parliament met at last in October 1680, and the House of Commons quickly passed another Exclusion Bill, Charles rallied his friends in the House of Lords to defeat it. He then dissolved Parliament again. A third election in February 1681 produced yet another heavy majority for the Exclusionists or Whigs. This time, Charles summoned them to meet in the hall of Christ Church College at Oxford, rather than in turbulent London. He wanted to avoid another situation like 1641, when the City of London had protected Parliament against his father's wrath. Charles II succeeded where his predecessor had failed. As the MPs began yet another debate on Exclusion, the King quietly arrived at Christ Church in a sedan chair, threw on his robes and crown, ran upstairs to the room where Parliament was meeting, and speedily dissolved it once again.

Charles had finally won, in part because his disaffected English subjects did not have the stomach for rebellion. They were not men of violent action like the Scots Covenanters, who assassinated the Archbishop of St Andrews early in 1679, then rose up in a fierce rebellion in the southwest of Scotland. The Covenanting rebels were defeated in July 1679 at Bothwell Bridge by the King's illegitimate son, James Scott, Duke of Monmouth. Ironically, this young man was soon to become a hero to the Whigs. After the failure of Exclusion, some Whig politicians in England looked to Monmouth as a possible Protestant savior, who could take the throne by force from his uncle James. They entered into vague conspiracies that ended in denunciations, trials, and executions. Some of these conspiracies were fabricated by informers, liars just as brazen as Titus Oates, while others, like the Rye House Plot, were blown out of all proportion. In the end, the Whig party was discredited, losing control even of the City of London, its stronghold. Shaftesbury fled to Holland, where he died. His physician and secretary, an Oxford lecturer named John Locke, followed him into exile, as did the thwarted Duke of Monmouth. The famous political writer Algernon Sidney, who had written that kings were bound by contracts with their people, was beheaded. The Whig party seemed to have died with a whimper, not a bang.

The King took his revenge on the Whigs by packing his Privy Council with Tories and giving them a free hand against their enemies. They upheld the laws against Dissenters with a vengeance, fining Presbyterians, locking up Quakers, closing down illegal religious meetings wherever they could be detected. Whigs were tossed out of local government bodies and replaced with Tories. The charters of towns were rewritten so as to increase the influence of Tory officeholders, and of the crown. This did not, however, represent a great personal victory for Charles II, who had begun his reign as a hopeful advocate of toleration, and a despiser of factions. Now he was virtually a tool of the Tory party, a political faction that was strongly opposed to toleration. Like his father, Charles had failed to control his Parliaments, and he now had to govern without them.

As he lay dying of kidney disease in February 1685 (some think he may have poisoned himself through alchemical experiments), Charles II finally agreed to be received into the Catholic Church by a priest who had once helped him during the Civil Wars. If his Protestant subjects had known about it, they would have been horrified. Although he would later be called "the Merry Monarch," the king was not remembered with much merriment by some of his subjects. The Whig Bishop Burnet compared him to the vicious Roman Emperor Tiberius, commenting on "his hatred of business, and his love of pleasure; his raising of favourites, and trusting them entirely; his pulling them down, and hating them excessively; his covering his revenge with an appearance of softness, his craft and artifice with a show of sincerity; and deceiving all who trusted him by fair words and artful insinuations."[5] While unduly harsh, this was not a false assessment. The king's traits were those, not of a brutal despot, but of a gifted survivor, who used all the arts of politics to maintain a hold on his throne in violent times. Cheating his critics to the end, he died in his bed.

The Second Downfall of the Stuarts

Charles II's brother was neither so gifted an actor, nor so lucky a king. James II was earnest, determined, and dull. At his accession, however, the British kingdoms were remarkably peaceful. The Scottish Covenanters had been crushed through executions, deportations, and torture, the last of which was legally acceptable north of the border. James, Duke of York, had presided over this repression as his brother's representative in the northern kingdom. The Irish Catholics were tranquil, due to the political skills of the viceroy, the Duke of Ormonde, one of the few politicians who had maintained a cool head during the Popish Plot. Mildly conciliatory towards the old Catholic landowning elite (he was related to many of them), Ormonde was also non-confrontational towards Presbyterians in the north. The start of James II's reign caused consternation to many Irish Protestants, but they kept quiet. Irish Catholics, of course, were delighted.

James felt secure enough at his accession to call Parliaments in both Scotland and England. The Scottish legislature, staunchly Episcopalian, declared in the preamble to an Act granting James revenue for life from the excise tax that the "Sacred Race" of Scotland's kings enjoyed "a solid, absolute authority."[6] This was about as strong a vote of confidence in James as a Parliament could give. In England, due to the removal of Whig officeholders and the rewriting of borough charters, Tories were returned to the House of Commons in overwhelming numbers. King James promised them that he would defend the Church of England. They rewarded him with a substantial subsidy, and stood by him in the summer of 1685, when the Duke of Monmouth made a bid for the throne. Returning from Holland, Monmouth gathered a small army in the southwest of England, made up of farmers and tradesmen, most of them Dissenters. They marched to a disastrous defeat at Sedgemoor in Somerset, where Monmouth was captured by the King's forces, hiding in a drainage ditch. The unfortunate young man was brought to London, where he pleaded in vain for his life before his impassive uncle. The subsequent beheading was bungled: the axe was not sharp enough, and it took several strokes to cut off Monmouth's handsome head. His followers were harshly treated by the notorious Judge Jeffreys, whose "Bloody Assizes" in the West Country sent about 300 of them to the gallows. Hundreds more were deported as convict laborers to the West Indies.

With the help of his Tory allies, James seemed to be doing well as King, but what he really wanted, they could not possibly support. James was not so foolish as to think that his kingdoms could be brought back to Catholicism, at least in the short term, but he did want Catholics to be included again in national politics, which meant they must be able to hold offices, in violation of the Test Acts.

No English or Scottish Parliament, Tory or Whig, could agree to this. The first sign of trouble came with James's decision to employ Catholic officers in his English army. A worried House of Commons tried to limit the king's revenue so as to discourage him from following this policy. James was furious. When the House of Lords took up the debate on Catholic officers, he prorogued Parliament in November 1685. It never met again in his short reign.

James now attempted to use the law courts to obtain his objectives. He ended the prosecution of Quakers and the harassing of other Dissenters. He had already told the Quaker leader William Penn "that he looked upon us [the Quakers] as a quiet industrious people and though he was not of our judgment, yet he liked our good lives."[7] Now he pressured the English high court judges to rule that the monarch could dispense with laws in particular cases – in other words, that he could ignore the Test Acts in appointing Catholics to military and civil offices. While most of the judges agreed with him, most of his Protestant subjects did not. They viewed with apprehension the behavior of the Earl of Tyrconnel, the king's lord deputy in Ireland and a Roman Catholic, who was busy filling up the Irish army and administration with his co-religionists. Protestants were disgusted when the King appointed Catholics as fellows at Oxford, and when he tried to force one into an Oxford College presidency. Even the normally quiet Isaac Newton took a stand against this last outrage. The worst insult to Anglican sensibilities, however, came in April 1687, when James issued a Declaration of Indulgence, granting "all our loving subjects" permission "to meet and serve God after their own way and manner," and suspending the laws against them "for not coming to church, or not receiving the sacrament, or for any other nonconformity to the religion established."[8]

Issued in all three British kingdoms, this was an incredibly broad act of toleration, extending to Catholics, Baptists, Quakers, all sorts of so-called heretics, even to non-Christians. As the Protestant sects did not much like one another, and none of them liked the Catholics, the Declaration must have bewildered people with its scope. The Tories were in agony over it: how could they continue to support a king who had done so much to undermine their beloved Church of England? James did not listen to them. He was now taking advice from a council of Catholic noblemen, some of whom wanted him to move faster. To find out what important people thought of his measures, James sent out a questionnaire to office holders, including justices of the peace, asking if they would favor a Parliamentary repeal of the Test Acts. He was encouraged by the results, although many answers were evasive, and only a small minority of Protestants replied that the Acts should be repealed. He set about turning those who opposed him out of local offices, rewriting borough charters, and canvassing potential candidates for election to Parliament. Clearly, he was planning to summon another legislature, one that would finally do away with the Test Acts.

He never had the chance. By April 1688, his son-in-law William of Orange was preparing to invade England. Although a Calvinist Protestant, William was not an opponent of toleration. In the urban, populous parts of the United Provinces, even Catholics could worship freely. What the Prince of Orange most feared was that James's pro-Catholic policies would throw him into the arms of Louis XIV of France, and into a war against the Dutch. To prevent this, William was willing to take an army to England and hold his father-in-law as a prisoner. He did not yet plan to seize the throne.

James played into William's hands with one last gigantic blunder. In May 1688, he ordered Church of England clergymen to read a reissued version of his Declaration of Indulgence from their pulpits. Archbishop Sancroft of Canterbury and six other bishops drew up a petition, explaining that "the great averseness they find in themselves to the distributing and publishing" of the Declaration proceeded not from want of obedience or disloyalty, "but amongst other considerations, from this especially, because that Declaration is founded upon such a Dispensing power, as hath been often declared illegal in parliament." The king, who received the bishops as he was preparing for bed, was stunned. "I did not expect this from you," he told them. "This is a Standard of Rebellion."[9] It was not intended to be, but in fact it was. Two weeks later, James made the momentously stupid decision of putting the bishops on trial for scandalous libel (later changed to the more serious charge of seditious libel). They decided to go to prison rather than accepting bail. When they came to trial in London, two of their four judges condemned the dispensing power, and only one, a Catholic, was hostile to the bishops. The jury acquitted them. The audience erupted into cries of joy. A huge throng of cheering people escorted the bishops through the capital. Bonfires were lit and church bells were rung in their honor. Engravings were made of their benign clerical faces, framed in glory. Outside the King's palace, a crowd set fire to an effigy of the Pope.

The next day, June 30, 1688, a group of seven men drew up a letter to William of Orange, assuring him that 95 percent of the English population was dissatisfied, and would rise up if given "protection" from abroad. One of the signers was the recently acquitted Bishop of London. The other six were a motley assortment of unemployed Whig and Tory politicians, including the Earl of Danby. No doubt they were terrified by the birth, on June 10, 1688, of a son to James II and his Queen. Rumors quickly spread that the baby was not genuine, and had been smuggled into the Queen's bed in a warming pan. They were evidently lies as dozens of witnesses had seen her give birth – although they did not include Princess Anne, who indignantly skipped the ceremony. Now there was a male heir, and Mary would not be first to inherit. The news, combined with the invitation, was all William of Orange needed. A Dutch invasion was imminent.

James would not at first believe it. Towards the end of August, he announced that he would call a Parliament, and even began canvassing candidates to run for it, among them many Dissenters. Then he realized that William was serious, and panic began to set in. He met privately with the Archbishop of Canterbury in September, and agreed to concede some Tory demands. He restored borough charters, brought back displaced Oxford fellows, and started to dismiss Catholic justices of the peace. William was not deterred; in October, he issued a manifesto blaming James's previous conduct on wicked advisors, and promising a "free" Parliament. After weeks of brutal storms, a sudden wind blew the Dutch fleet across the Channel, before the English fleet could catch them. William was carried ashore at Brixham in Devon on November 5, a day that celebrated the discovery of a Catholic plot to blow up Parliament in 1605. He had with him a large, well trained, and experienced Dutch army.

To godly Protestants, it all smacked of divine Providence. To James II, it was a nightmare. He was convinced that William was going to have him killed, his nose began to bleed profusely, and he could only sleep by taking opium. A trickle of defectors snuck over to William, Tories as well as Whigs, all of them claiming that they wanted only a free Parliament and were not aiming to depose the king. As the Dutch forces drew nearer to London, James was told that he could not count on the loyalty of his own army. He decided to flee. His wife and son left for France on December 9. James tried to join them two days later, but when he reached the coast, he was arrested and manhandled by some fishermen who thought he was a Jesuit. Meanwhile, Catholic chapels in London were burned, and a group of noblemen began to meet at the Guildhall to plan out a political strategy. The King returned to the capital, where he was greeted by happy crowds who were actually relieved to have him back. A few days later, however, he ran off a second time. Dutch guards were patrolling Whitehall palace, but William obligingly left a back door unguarded so that his father-in-law could escape. On December 24, James II landed in France. This strange, sad, misguided, and misunderstood man would never see England again.

In London, by the end of December, the politicians were already speaking of a "demise" or lapse in the government, and treating the Prince of Orange as if he were ruling the kingdom. The transfer of power would have to be made legal by Parliament, but for practical purposes, the Glorious Revolution, as it would be known, was over.

The Meaning of Revolution

When the three hundredth anniversary of the Glorious Revolution rolled around in 1988, British politicians were not quite sure what to do about it. The Conservative administration of Margaret Thatcher wanted to celebrate it as a triumph for liberty and the salvation of Parliament. Left-wing MPs criticized the Revolution as a coup by anti-Catholic bigots that eventually led to the Troubles in Northern Ireland. The public was largely indifferent. The anniversary passed without much fanfare.

Those who lived through the Glorious Revolution might have understood this ambivalence. They, too, were not at first quite sure what it meant. Within a short time, however, it had been blown up into the central event of recent English history. Historians were to a large extent responsible for this elevation of the Revolution, and they have been captivated by it ever since. Most of them have wanted to see it as a *real* revolution, a genuine change of direction in politics and society, even though it was orchestrated by an elite faction. They have argued that it was a constitutional watershed, the beginning of a strong state, and a turning point in the formation of English national identity. All of these are good arguments, but they relate to the consequences of 1688, which were not foreseen at the time. By December 1688, all that had happened was a Dutch invasion that had installed William of Orange as the effective ruler of England.

That event, however, carried with it three crucial implications. First, the legal foundation of English monarchy had been broken, and would have to be reconstructed. Parliament would have to provide a guarantee of the King's title, and whether he liked it or not, he would depend on it for his legitimacy. As a result, the legislature become a permanent institution of government, and a partner with the monarchy in uniting and guiding the nation, although no King would choose to regard it as an *equal* partner until much later. Second, England was now a Dutch ally, and would go to war with France, in the first of a series of conflicts that lasted, on and off, until 1815. The United Kingdom of Great Britain and Ireland would emerge from the long Anglo-French wars as the most powerful nation in the world, but that too could not be foreseen in 1688.

The third implication of the Revolution concerned Scotland, Ireland, and the American colonies. William of Orange had seized power only in England, but he could not possibly allow James and his supporters to retain control of the other two kingdoms. They would have to be brought into line with England, by their own choice or by force. Both Scotland and Ireland, however, were deeply divided by the Revolution. Scottish and Irish Protestants mostly chose to follow England, because they wanted to appropriate the Revolution for their own purposes. As for Scottish and Irish Catholics, they had to be beaten militarily before they would submit. In the Scottish case, military conflict went on intermittently until 1746. Ultimately, the protection of Protestantism in Scotland and Ireland subjected those kingdoms to English military and economic strength. The path to 1707 and 1801, when Scotland and Ireland gave up their independence, was becoming clear. Thus, the Glorious Revolution marked the beginning of a powerful, centralized, English-dominated state that would gradually absorb the other nations of the British Isles.

Some historians have argued that the Glorious Revolution also spelled a defeat for the Tories in England and Scotland, but that was not so clear. To understand what happened, we have to return to Parliamentary politics. Following the advice of peers and former MPs meeting in London, William of Orange had called a Convention, in other words a legislature that was not summoned by a king, to meet on January 22, 1689. At the elections, the Whig party, which had been moribund for almost seven years, rose up from the dead and captured a large number of seats in the House of Commons. Hundreds of Whig pamphlets appeared in the following months, arguing that, by his arbitrary actions, King James had violated an "Original Contract" with the people and deserved to be deposed. When Parliament met, the Whigs proposed a resolution to that effect, but after Tory objections it was changed to suggest that, while King James had in fact violated the Original Contract, he had also abdicated the throne by withdrawing from his kingdom. This would have been news to James, who had no intention of abdicating. The resolution also made no logical sense – was it a means of deposing James, or a recognition of his abdication? In fact, it was a device to satisfy everybody. The House of Lords, dominated by Tories, was not pleased, and changed the resolution to read that James had "deserted," not "abdicated," suggesting that he could come back if he chose. The Commons then rejected the Lords's amendments (although most Tories voted to uphold them), so the final wording continued to stipulate that King James had broken constitutional law *and* given up his throne.

Who then was to have it? That was obvious, at least. Mary had announced she would not rule alone, and William refused to be either a consort or a regent. So the Convention invented the bizarre device of a co-rulership, with both William and Mary as joint sovereigns, although in practice William did most of the ruling. Were they to hold the throne under any conditions? The answer to that question was the Declaration of Rights, drawn up by a committee of Whigs and Tories and passed by the Convention on February 12. The Declaration began with a long preamble, listing James II's crimes and concluding that he had abdicated the government. No mention was made of an Original Contract. The Declaration went on to make it illegal, among other things, to suspend or dispense with laws; to put clergymen on trial in a special ecclesiastical court (which James had indeed done); to prosecute subjects for petitioning the king, as in the Seven Bishops case; and to raise a standing army in peacetime without the consent of Parliament. Obviously, the Declaration was very specifically aimed at chastising James, not at creating new rights or even at providing a list of existing rights. Legal precedents existed for all the points mentioned in the Declaration, except possibly the abrogation of the dispensing power. The document was read out to William and Mary when they were offered the throne on February 13, but nobody can say how seriously they took it. They were not asked to swear to it at their coronation, although they did promise to govern according to the statutes of Parliament.

King William III now asked the Convention for a Toleration Act. What it gave him in the spring of 1689, after many disputes between Whigs and Tories, was partial and limited. It simply exempted from existing penalties those Dissenters from the Church of England who were willing to swear the oaths of allegiance and supremacy and who accepted the doctrine of the Trinity. Catholics refused to swear the oaths, and in any case they were specifically excluded from the Act. Radical Protestants who doubted the Trinity were also outside the Act, as were non-Christians. Quakers refused to take any oaths at all, but they were eventually allowed to make an affirmation instead. Church of England taxes or tithes would continue to be collected from all religious groups. The Test and Corporation Acts were to remain in force, blocking Dissenters from holding political office. This uncharitable Toleration Act contrasts starkly with James II's generous Declaration of Indulgence. It fell far short of the demands of Whig advocates of toleration like John Locke, who argued that a church "is a free and voluntary Society," and that "the Magistrate has no power to enforce by Law ... the use of any Rites or Ceremonies whatsoever in the Worship of God."[10] Nevertheless, the 1689 Act was backed by Parliament, which James's broad toleration was not. As in Holland, social conditions would encourage the further evolution of religious toleration, even for Catholics, in spite of the narrowness of existing legislation.

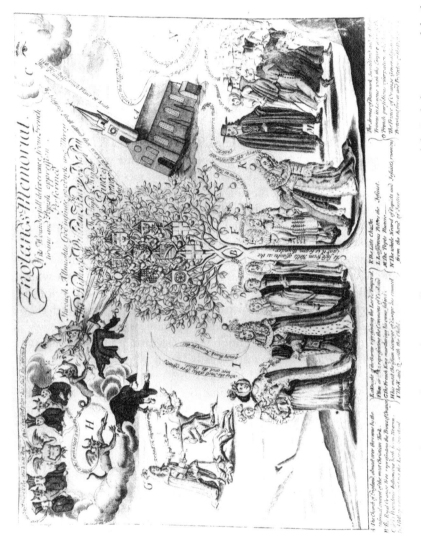

Illustration 4 *A cartoon summing up the events of 1688–9 from a Williamite perspective. At upper left, Catholic priests and devils conspire against England, while below them the French King massacres Protestants. King James II, Queen Mary of Modena, and their newborn son stand at bottom left, next to an orange tree symbolizing William of Orange. The tree protects the English bishops and Members of Parliament, but it drops fruit on Lord Chief Justice Jeffreys, knocking him out. Catholics flee at bottom right, while the eye of God looks with favor on the battered Church of England and the orange tree. ("England's Memorial," 1689. © Private Collection / The Bridgeman Art Library)*

By the end of the year, the Convention had strengthened the Declaration of Rights by making it a Bill of Rights, adding provisions that barred from the throne anyone who was or had been a Roman Catholic. This was by far the most original idea to come out of the Revolution settlement, and it was more significant than may at first appear. The Convention was effectively declaring who could be King – regardless of lineage or "divine sanction." England was to be a Protestant kingdom, with a Protestant ruler, forever. In this way, the Bill of Rights not only defined future kingship, subordinating it to Parliamentary statute, it also defined the nation's government and religion – for all time. That may have created a real revolution, in spite of the general conservatism of the revolutionaries. The Bill of Rights did not make Parliament a permanent institution, but this was ensured by the Mutiny Act of 1689, which set up a system of courts martial for the army. The Mutiny Act was to last for one year "and noe longer," meaning that the king had to have a Parliament every year to renew it or he would not be able to discipline his soldiers. While hardly radical, the Act led to a definite shift in political possibilities.

The brief, bloodless, and hence "Glorious" Revolution was supported by a majority of the English elite, but not by everyone. Whigs asserted that "There has been nothing done ... in this *great* and *wonderfull Revolution*, but is justifiable before *God* and the *World*, from *Scripture*, from *Reason*, and the *Constitution and Practice of this Kingdom*."[11] Many Tories, however, were unhappy with the change in monarchy, and were willing to accept William and Mary only as rulers in fact (*de facto*), not in law (*de jure*). Some of them would become Jacobites, supporters of the exiled James (*Iacobus* in Latin) and his family. A Jacobite poem of 1689 acidly commented on the illegality of the Revolution: "If People made their sov'reign Lord, / They ought to show it by Record. / The Law o' th' Land says no such Thing: / By Law Succession makes the King."[12] About 400 clergymen of the Church of England, including the highly principled Archbishop Sancroft and six other bishops, would refuse to swear oaths of loyalty to the new monarchs, and would be forced out of their positions in the Church. These men, who represented about 5 percent of the personnel of the Church, were known as Nonjurors. The degree of support for the Glorious Revolution in the general population of England is hard to judge, as it meant different things to different people. The Catholic religion was highly unpopular, but the Stuart monarchy was not. The issue of permanently changing the dynasty would cause much strife in later years. Still, as the saviors of Protestantism, William III and Mary II quickly became heroic figures in many minds. In London and other towns, they helped to generate a "moral revolution," spearheaded by religiously based Societies for the Reformation of Manners that attempted to clean the streets of drunkenness, blasphemy, and bad behavior. Puritanism was back, and the new co-sovereigns were its celebrity sponsors.

What about Scotland? There, the events of 1688–9 were not bloodless, and the consequences of the Revolution were more radical. The news of William of Orange's landing caused riots in Edinburgh and the burning of a Catholic abbey. Roaming bands of Covenanters carried out "rabblings" in the Lowlands, turning out Episcopalian ministers. The Scottish Convention met in March 1689, under the guard of 1000 Covenanters who protected it from the Jacobite troops still holding Edinburgh Castle. With only twelve votes against (seven of them bishops), the Convention decided that James II had "Forefaulted the right to the Croune" by "Inverting all the ends of Government," with the intention of changing Scotland from "a legall limited Monarchy, to ane Arbitrary Despotick power."[13] No matter how we interpret the legal term "forefault," this was stronger language than was used by the Convention's English counterpart. The Scottish Convention then went on to draw up a Claim of Right, stating that a Catholic could never become King of Scotland, denouncing the measures used by James to promote toleration, strengthening Parliament, and recommending the abolition of bishops. An additional thirteen Articles of Grievances removed certain rights of the Scottish crown, including the appointment of the Lords of the Articles, a steering committee that had controlled Scottish Parliamentary legislation.

King William III (or William I, as he was proclaimed in Scotland) did not like these conditions, and he struggled to reverse them, but in the end he gave in, because he needed money from the Scottish Parliament in order to conquer his Jacobite enemies. An army loyal to King James had been raised in the Highlands by Viscount Dundee. It defeated the Williamites in a bloody twenty-minute engagement at Killiekrankie in July 1689, but Dundee himself was killed. The Jacobite army failed to dislodge a Cameronian force at Dunkeld, and was finally defeated in the following year. By then, a broad revolution had taken place in the Scottish Kirk. Bishops were abolished in August 1689. The Assembly of the Church, under the leadership of Presbyterian ministers who had been expelled in 1661, took its revenge on those Episcopalians who declined to take oaths to William and Mary, or who opposed Presbyterian doctrines. By 1716, two-thirds of the parish ministers in Scotland had been ejected from their livings because they would not conform to the new Presbyterian settlement.

The Glorious Revolution led to an even bloodier civil war in Ireland. By 1689, about 20–25 percent of the two million people in Ireland were Protestants, many of them Presbyterians, almost all of them hostile to King James's pro-Catholic policies. James had maintained a sizable army there, under the command of his Catholic Lord Deputy, the Earl of Tyrconnel. In the crisis of December 1688, Catholic Ireland remained loyal to James. The most dramatic show of opposition to the king came at Londonderry (Derry to Catholics), where thirteen Protestant apprentice boys dramatically shut the town gates in the face of some of Tyrconnel's troops, initiating a long siege. The event is still celebrated today, to the joy of Protestants and the annoyance of Catholics. In the Irish countryside, poor rural Catholics responded to the Revolution in England by attacking the livestock of Protestant landowners, killing tens of thousands of cattle. Evidently, the situation was very tense. Showing his typical lack of good sense, James II decided to regain his throne by landing in Ireland in April 1689, further alienating his former Protestant subjects. He called a Parliament at Dublin, which not surprisingly turned out to be loaded with Roman Catholic gentry and peers. Most of them were "Old English," descendants of medieval English settlers, rather than "Old Irish" or Gaelic, but they had a clear Catholic agenda. They wanted to restore the lands that had been lost by Catholics after the great rebellion of the 1640s, which they partly achieved in spite of King James's objections. They also forced James to accept a Declaratory Act affirming that only Irish laws should apply in Ireland. In return, James was given a large sum of money to raise troops. If the legislation passed by the Irish Parliament of 1689 had endured, it would have created a largely independent kingdom under a Catholic ruling elite; but it did not endure.

Williamite forces had already relieved the city of Londonderry, where a Protestant garrison had held out for three months against a Jacobite siege, eating cats, dogs, and rats after their food supplies gave out. William himself landed in Ireland in June 1690, with an international army of veterans. One month later, he defeated James's troops at the famous battle of the River Boyne. Northern Irish Protestants still regard the battle as a triumph, while Irish Catholics see it as a tragedy. James abandoned Dublin and fled back to France, but the war was not yet over. The Jacobite army, led by Tyrconnel, was heavily defeated in July 1691 at Aughrim, where almost 10,000 men were killed. When the Jacobites finally surrendered at Limerick in October 1691, they negotiated a treaty that called for William and Mary to procure toleration for Catholics and to restore the estates of all Jacobite soldiers who were willing to swear allegiance to the new rulers. The Treaty of Limerick might have achieved a level of power-sharing between the Catholic and Protestant elites in Ireland, but it failed miserably, in spite of William's support. The English Parliament, acting with true colonizing zeal, had already declared that only Protestants could hold offices in Ireland. When an Irish Parliament met in 1692, it was a wholly Protestant body. Over the next five years, it would ban Catholic schools, banish Catholic priests, and forbid Protestants from marrying Catholics. When the Treaty of Limerick was ratified, the Irish Parliament left out the clauses seeking toleration for Catholics and restoring their estates if they swore loyalty to the new regime. This was a revolution, to be sure, but it benefited a religious minority at the expense of the majority. William III, a tolerant man at heart, might be disturbed to know that his name and image remain associated with anti-Catholicism in Ireland to this day.

If we consider its effects in all three kingdoms, however, the Glorious Revolution was more than just an anti-Catholic coup. By making a break in the succession, it weakened the legitimacy, and therefore the authority, of the King. The supporters of the Glorious Revolution did not seek to make the monarchy dependent on Parliament, but this was effectively what happened after 1689. Only one of the three Parliaments, however, would be strong enough to take full advantage of the situation.

6

A Disjointed Empire

In the seventeenth century, the term "empire" referred primarily to a type of rulership, based on the Roman concept of *imperium*, the highest governing power. To say that England was an empire, as King Henry VIII had declared in the 1530s, was to claim that its ruler had the same type of authority as a Roman emperor, and was the equal of emperors anywhere in the world. Most empires, like that of ancient Rome, were composed of different territories that had been conquered by the imperial state. Many writers and poets in the sixteenth and seventeenth centuries wanted England to be an empire of that sort. Their model was Rome, but they also aspired to imitate Spain, whose soldiers in the New World, the *conquistadores*, had carved a huge and enormously rich empire out of lands seized from native peoples. The Spanish empire was united under the crown of Castile. It used Castilian law, and was administered by a special royal council. Its primary aim was to fill the coffers of the Spanish king with silver.

The English empire (before 1707, it was not British and was closed to Scottish trade) did not develop exactly in this way. First of all, in spite of Henry VIII's bold words, it lacked a coherent structure of authority. Paradoxically, this may have been because England, unlike Spain, was a relatively centralized kingdom, with no semi-autonomous provincial governments. The English colonies overseas simply did not fit very well into the existing system of central administration, so in political affairs, they were usually left to themselves. Ireland provided a testing ground for English imperial government, but it fostered an ambivalent model. Neither a colonial dependency nor a fully self-governing kingdom, Ireland had its own Parliament, whose decisions needed approval from the English Privy Council to become laws. Although colonial legislatures in the New World were not subject to this provision, the English government always saw them as subordinate bodies, even if it had no effective way of exercising imperial control.

In economic terms, the English colonial system was driven by a trade in commodities rather than by the extraction of precious metals. This would later make the empire prosperous, but in the mid-seventeenth century, it was still a source of embarrassment that England's colonies had no silver or gold. What they did have was an abundance of enterprising colonists. Here again, the plantations in Ireland had provided prototypes for settlement by private enterprise schemes that enjoyed varying levels of government support. Like the Irish natives in Ulster, native peoples in the New World were dispossessed of their land by the settlers. The Irish moved to inferior land, or became tenant farmers, while the Indians simply died in great numbers. Mortality among native Indian peoples contributed to a growing labor problem in the Caribbean and southern mainland colonies, where planters produced profitable crops that required a lot of workers, particularly sugar and tobacco. Imitating the Spanish, Portuguese, and Dutch, the English colonists turned to slave labor. By the late seventeenth century, England enjoyed a lucrative trade to its colonies, but the mainland colonies were developing in some different directions from the home country.

Imperial Governance

Who governed the colonies in the New World? Ultimately, it was the King of England, who was sovereign over all English territories abroad, and who appointed their governors. Once the governor reached the New World, however, he was effectively out of the King's reach. It took about eight to ten weeks to sail across the Atlantic westward, from London to Boston or Barbados. No ruler could keep in close touch with a governor at that distance. The Spanish had addressed the problem by appointing viceroys, who actually replaced the king in his absence, but the English governors, for all the expensive finery with which they surrounded themselves, did not have such an exalted status. As colonial legislatures liked to remind them, they were merely officeholders.

The lack of strong direction in imperial government stemmed in part from the diversity of England's colonial possessions in the New World. Most of them were not under direct royal authority, and they all had different charters or constitutions. Newfoundland and Hudson's Bay were not officially colonies. The former consisted of a string of summer fishing ports, where fishermen landed to gut and salt their catch. The vast territory claimed by England in the far north of Canada was settled by only a few fur traders in scattered forts, working for the Hudson's Bay Company. Further south were the confederations of towns known as the New England colonies – Massachusetts, Rhode Island, and Connecticut. They elected their own governors, a horrible sign of democratic anarchy in the eyes of English politicians. New Hampshire became the only royal colony in the region in 1675. With the exception of Virginia, a royal colony since 1624, the rest of the mainland American possessions of Charles II (New York, East and West Jersey, Pennsylvania, Maryland, and the Carolinas) were proprietorial, meaning that the king had granted ownership to proprietors, usually aristocrats resident in England. The Bahamas was little more than a haven for pirates. The Atlantic outpost of Bermuda and the West Indian colonies, a multitude of little islands in the Caribbean Sea, were under direct royal authority, but even there, the colonists had succeeded in setting up legislatures. Within the Caribbean, Jamaica, Barbados, and the Leeward Islands were governed separately, with little attempt at coordination of policy.

The English possessions in the New World had been founded to promote trade and settlement, but before the late 1670s, the government in England was not quite sure what its role should be in bringing about these goals. A series of committees of the King's Privy Council were created to take charge of colonial affairs. They bore names like the Council of Trade, the Council of Plantations, or, imaginatively enough, the Committee of Trade and Plantations, and at first they did very little. Between 1675 and 1696, however, the chief colonial committee was the Lords of Trade and Plantations. The change in name was slight, but it revealed the beginning of a greater seriousness of purpose on the part of Charles II and his advisors. Above all, the Lords of Trade would bolster the governors against their legislatures. The English government also attempted to control colonial trade through the Navigation Acts, passed by Parliament between 1651 and 1673. They required all colonial goods to be carried in English (or colonial) ships, with crews that were at least three-quarters comprised of Englishmen. European goods were to be shipped first to England before re-export to the colonies, and intercolonial trade was subject to heavy duties. Enforcement of the Navigation Acts, however, was up to the customs service, which was not a highly efficient institution. While the Dutch were effectively excluded from English colonial trade, contraband commerce within the colonies continued.

Colonial opposition to the Navigation Acts and to royal governors boiled over in Bacon's Rebellion of 1676. Virginia tobacco planters who resented their high-handed governor's refusal to support a war against the Indians, and who were angered by the loss of Dutch trade, rose up and sacked the capital at Jamestown. Their charismatic leader, Nathaniel Bacon, forced himself onto the governor's council and took charge of the colony. The rebellion ran out of steam after Bacon's sudden death, however, and the governor retaliated by hanging two dozen rebels. King Charles II commented that he had hanged fewer men in England for killing his own father. Smaller insurrections broke out in Maryland against the Roman Catholic proprietor, Lord Baltimore, and in South Carolina, where the acting governor was imprisoned. The Carolina revolt was quietly settled by the Earl of Shaftesbury, chief proprietor of the colony and leader of the Country opposition in England. These uprisings pushed the court of Charles II towards a more interventionist policy in the New World.

For some time, one important English political figure had been promoting a stronger imperial government: James, Duke of York. He was proprietor of the New York colony, seized from the Dutch in 1663 (they took it back, briefly, ten years later). He set up no legislature in his colony, although he did establish religious toleration. Soon after, James separated New Jersey from New York, and granted it to proprietors, who divided it into East and West Jersey. Quakers eventually dominated among the proprietors of both colonies. East Jersey also saw a considerable influx of Scottish settlers, and has been called the first Scottish colony. They were backed by aristocratic Scottish proprietors with close ties to the Duke of York. Finally, William Penn, a close associate of James, established his colony of Pennsylvania in 1682, setting up a broad religious toleration. The Duke of York also sought to provide slaves to the New World, through the Royal African Company, of which he was governor and chief shareholder. In the 1670s and 1680s, the Company carried an average of 5600 African slaves every year to the English colonies in Virginia and the West Indies.

Even before he became king, therefore, James was deeply interested in colonial enterprise, and had developed a strategy for dealing with the colonies. He favored religious toleration, strong authority in the hands of governors, and trade relations that benefited merchants in England. James was not wholly opposed to legislatures – he allowed New York to have one in 1683, because the colony needed to raise more money – but he did not want them to have broad powers. At the end of the Exclusion Crisis, with the Tories in control at Charles II's court, some of the colonial objectives favored by the Duke of York were adopted – not including religious toleration. Strong-minded governors were dispatched to the West Indies and the southern mainland. The annulment of the Massachusetts Bay Company charter in 1684 was a crowning moment for the Tory colonial strategy. Now the Puritan colonies, those bastions of Dissenting religion, might be transformed.

James's biggest colonial experiment as king was the creation of the Dominion of New England, which united the three Puritan colonies with New York and the Jerseys under one consolidated regime. The Dominion resembled a Spanish vice-royalty, with a very powerful governor and no legislature. The governor, Sir Edmund Andros, was at first supported by merchants in the New England colonies who resented the old Puritan elite and wanted closer ties to the home country, but he eventually alienated his allies by imposing restrictions on foreign trade. Fear of Catholicism permeated the new Dominion, just as it did the Protestant elites of England and Scotland. In New England, anti-Catholic anxiety was focused on the threat of the colony of New France to the north. These factors combined to erode support for the Dominion.

When news of the Glorious Revolution arrived in the New World, Andros was quickly overthrown and imprisoned in Boston by officers of the old Massachusetts Bay chartered government. They went on to summon a Convention of representatives from Massachusetts towns, who voted to restore the old charter. Meanwhile, in New York, the merchant and militia captain Jacob Leisler evicted the lieutenant governor, and claimed authority for himself. Leisler had the support of the Dutch community, who had never much liked James II. A third uprising in Maryland, led by men calling themselves Protestant Associators, toppled the proprietorial government and banned all Catholics from holding office, a direct affront to the proprietor, Lord Baltimore, who was himself a Catholic. The Associators proceeded to call a Convention, which governed the colony until 1692. The colonies did not try to unite in their opposition to James II, however. Their only common effort came in 1690, when delegates from New England (minus Rhode Island) and New York agreed to launch an attack on the French colony at Quebec. It was a disaster. There would be no more close military cooperation between the colonies until the 1750s.

James II had not made himself quite as unpopular in the West Indies as he had in the mainland colonies, although there was resentment at the duty on sugar passed by Parliament in 1685, and at the high-handed behavior of the governors, who tended to side with the small planters against the big ones. As part of his reorganization of colonial affairs, James had considered the formation of a West India Company that would take over the whole sugar trade, but it was opposed by the planters and never materialized. The Glorious Revolution passed without notable incident in the West Indies, except in St Kitts, which was seized by Irish indentured servants, and handed over to the French, who held it for a short time.

The restoration of order under William and Mary brought about a compromise between imperial and local colonial governance. Massachusetts got its charter and legislature back, but not its elected governor. Leisler was hanged for refusing to recognize the authority of a new governor sent from England. This showed that William and Mary did not wish to be regarded as weak in handling the colonies. William would establish a new Board of Trade and Plantations in 1696, which at first took an active part in colonial governance. In particular, it pursued pirates, who had previously been used as instruments of English policy overseas. The celebrated Captain William Kidd was accused of robbing ships in the Indian Ocean. Although he had been commissioned by the government to attack French commerce, Kidd was hanged and his body suspended in iron chains until it rotted. Yet the government remained incapable of dealing with the Barbary pirates or corsairs of the North African coast, who routinely captured English vessels and enslaved their occupants. Between 1670 and 1734, at least 2200 Englishmen and women were ransomed out of captivity in North Africa.

Pirates might be hanged or paid off, but the empire was no better governed. The failure of James II's imperial experiment had severely impaired future attempts at restructuring the ramshackle colonial system. As long as trans-Atlantic commerce continued to thrive, why bother to meddle with so many diverse colonial interests? By the late 1690s, independent London merchants who had been excluded from monopolistic trading arrangements began to assert themselves. The Royal African Company and the East India Company lost their trading privileges. The American colonies would remain bound to the Navigation Acts, which were definitively codified in 1696, but until the 1760s, little further legislation was passed that significantly affected colonial trade. The English colonies remained an empire. By comparison with ancient Rome or modern Spain, however, there was hardly any imperial governance at all.

Life Beyond the Line: the West Indies

If government did not hold the English empire in the New World together, what did? To determine that point, we have to look in more detail at the colonies themselves. For all their social and economic diversity, common links of English culture and politics still united them. We will begin with the colonies that were most precious to the English: the West Indian islands. They were "beyond the line" because they lay on the Spanish side of an imaginary line drawn in 1494 to divide the territory of Spain from that of Portugal. Today, they are mostly poor and dependent on tourism, so it is difficult to imagine how important they once were to the Atlantic economy. In the seventeenth and eighteenth centuries, the lives of Europeans were sweetened up by West Indian brown sugar, white sugar, and molasses, the run-off from sugar production, which was usually distilled into rum. The sugar industry also produced a peculiar type of society, based on forced labor and severely divided between masters and slaves, white and black, big planters and small ones. Slavery, which had been of little importance in England since Anglo-Saxon times, became the basic institution of Caribbean society.

The beautiful West Indian islands were not a welcoming environment for the English. They found them to be unbearably hot and ridden with diseases. Many settlers were killed by malaria, yellow fever, dysentery, dropsy, and a mysterious "dry bellyache" which caused stomach cramps, paralysis, and death. White women tended to outlive white men, which was just as well as the gender ratio was heavily imbalanced in favor of males before the early eighteenth century. After that, the ratio was reversed on many islands, and females became the majority as men succumbed to disease. In the early years, the West Indian settlers also lived in fear of attack by the Spanish or the Dutch or the French, who occupied neighboring islands. The native peoples were not much of a threat to the English, as almost all of them, apart from the resilient Kalinagos of Dominica, had been conveniently wiped out through war, disease, and slavery.

Barbados was the model English colony in the West Indies, and in the late seventeenth century was reaching the height of its prosperity. First settling in 1627, its English inhabitants had turned from tobacco to sugar production, and a class of rich sugar planters quickly arose. By 1680, 175 big planters (about 7 percent of landowners) held 54 percent of the property and 60 percent of the slaves in Barbados. These men dominated the island's assembly and its social life. Sugar production expanded on the big plantations, but it depended on a constant influx of labor. At first, this was provided by indentured servants from England or Scotland, volunteers and convicts who were sold to masters just like slaves, and were required to work for up to seven years. As demand for labor rose, however, so did the price of servants. West African slaves, who were cheaper to buy, began to seem a better investment. Slaves served for life, and their children were born into the same condition. While they were looked down upon, they were seen as perfectly capable of carrying out the complicated, back-breaking tasks involved in sugar production: cutting down the cane, grinding it in a mill, boiling it in huge copper kettles, curing it in pots, and distilling the thick molasses syrup into rum. Richard Ligon, who lived on Barbados in the 1650s, thought that "slaves and their posterity, being subjects to their Masters for ever, are kept and preserv'd with greater care than the servants, who are theirs but five years," but high mortality rates among slaves do not support his claim.[1] Slaves died in shocking numbers in the islands, due to poor treatment as well as to diseases like yaws, skin ulcers that destroy bone and tissue, or hookworm, an insect that feeds on intestinal blood, leading to bloating and a ravenous desire to eat dirt. It only gradually

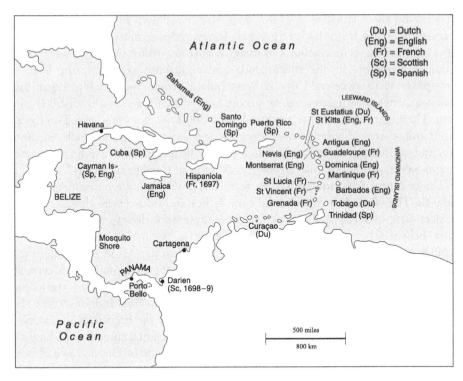

Map 3 *The Caribbean in the late seventeenth century. (Source: Nicholas Canny,* The Oxford History of the British Empire, *volume 1: The Origins of Empire,* Oxford, 1998, p. 220.)

dawned on their masters that more food and better working conditions might preserve them. In the meantime, they just bought more slaves. "One of the great Burdens of our Lives is the going to buy Negroes," complained a slave owner in 1689. "But we must have them: we cannot be without them."[2]

Although it created a society quite unlike that of England, slavery was constructed on the basis of opinions that were common among the English. African slaves were considered to be different from Europeans because of their black complexions and their "heathen" religions, as well as on account of their perceived "barbarism." The sense of separation, much stronger than the feelings that divided English settlers from the native Irish, was often backed up by the Bible, in which Noah's son Ham was cursed, a burden he supposedly passed on to his African descendants. Yet attitudes towards slaves were at first ambiguous. Richard Ligon, for example, thought African slaves "are as near beasts as may be, setting their souls aside," but he also found "there are as honest, faithful and conscionable people amongst them, as amongst those of *Europe*."[3] The idea that all black Africans were born inferior to white Europeans seems to have arisen from a desire to keep slaves in their place at the bottom of society. Inferiority was further bolstered by the Barbadian slave code of 1661, which allowed masters to punish slaves any way they wished, short of killing them. Slave rebellion was punishable by death. Sexual exploitation of slave women by masters was widespread, as was indicated by the growth of a mulatto or mixed race population.

Not all aspects of the Barbadian slaves' existence were miserable. They were not required to work on Sundays. As long as they had a ticket from their master, they were allowed to visit markets on neighboring plantations. The slave code even recognized them "as being created men," although they were also defined as chattels, that is, as possessions owned by their masters.[4] The law said nothing about making them Christians or changing their customs. In practice, West Indian slaves were allowed to preserve their religions, their music, and their family structures.

Between 1640 and 1700, about 135,000 Africans were brought to Barbados as slaves. By 1684, there were about 20,000 whites and 47,000 blacks on the island, which shows how quickly slaves died. The white population declined in subsequent decades, as the colony's prosperity was overtaken by Jamaica, and small planters left to make their fortunes in other places. Although the slave population slowly grew in these years, rebellion and escape remained rare on Barbados. There were always enough whites to keep control over blacks, and the small island offered few places to which slaves could run. On the other hand, suicide among slaves was a constant problem for masters. One of them addressed it cruelly by decapitating a slave and putting his head on a pole, so that others could see that he did not return to Africa after death, for "how was it possible, the body could go without a head?"[5]

If Barbados quickly became a stable planter oligarchy, Jamaica was at first the anarchic Wild West of the Caribbean. Conquered by England in 1655, the island became a center for contraband trade to the Spanish colonies, and a haven for the notorious pirates known as buccaneers. Port Royal, the capital, was a boisterous, rowdy town, full of drunken pirates, smugglers, and prostitutes. It was also home to Quaker merchants and Sephardic Jews from Portuguese Brazil. Its most famous citizen was Henry Morgan, a militia captain and pirate who carried on a private war against Spain in the late 1660s. After burning and looting several Spanish towns, including Panama, Morgan was recalled to England and imprisoned. Charles II pardoned him, making him a knight and lieutenant governor of Jamaica, with orders to clear out the buccaneers. In 1692, when a massive earthquake dropped most of Port Royal into the sea, pious observers felt that it must be a judgment of God on that wicked place.

Jamaica gradually followed Barbados in developing a planter oligarchy, based on sugar and slavery. Sir Henry Morgan, who never missed the main chance, was one of them. By 1694, about 10,000 whites and 30,000 blacks lived in Jamaica, and it was estimated that the island needed about 10,000 fresh slaves every year to replace those who died. A slave code had been adopted, based on that of Barbados. Jamaica, however, was a much larger island, with mountains and forests that provided plenty of places for escaped slaves to hide from the authorities. From the beginning, the English settlers were plagued by *marronage*, or armed resistance by runaway slaves, living in the interior. Distinct Maroon communities formed, with their own leaders and military organization. They raided plantations, often in search of women, and killed whites. Conflict with the Maroons would flare up periodically until becoming a small scale war in the 1730s.

Jamaica would eventually overtake Barbados as the richest sugar island in the Caribbean. By 1700, however, Barbados was averaging over £300,000 in annual sugar exports to England, compared to about £200,000 each for Jamaica and the Leeward Islands. Although the price of sugar was falling, the English producers were still in an enviable position, because as yet they had little competition. Thus, life in the West Indies became synonymous with easy wealth, although it was available only to a few. The big planters, who by that time included some Scots, imitated the gentry and aristocracy back in Great Britain, building huge brick houses, consuming profligately and entertaining lavishly. They even wore English fashions in spite of the Caribbean heat. They carefully preserved the social and gender differences of their homeland, and shared the political and religious views that divided their compatriots. The Glorious Revolution confirmed the authority of the big planters, by removing governors who had tried to control them. Eventually, many successful planters went back to Britain to live, visiting their West Indian estates only periodically. In a sense, the planters had never left home at all; instead, they had carried English values to a foreign land that they had exploited mercilessly, through the labor of servants and slaves for whom they had almost no regard.

The American Mainland

Like the West Indies, the English colonies of the American mainland were bound to the home country by ties of culture and politics. Their societies, however, were becoming more complex and diverse, which was beginning to set them apart from England. The loose structure of the empire also meant that the mainland colonies were not closely involved in the development of the English, and later British, state. Most of the colonists cheered the arrival of the Glorious Revolution, because it seemed to mean less direct interference from England. In this way, its results were quite different from those in Great Britain and Ireland, where it brought about an expansion of government. Moreover, unlike the big West Indian planters, few wealthy mainland colonists would choose to live in the home country, which meant that their views of it were often out of date. From an English perspective, the mainland colonists would remain stuck in a cultural and political time warp, fixed around 1689. As time passed, this would create serious issues of contention between the homeland and its colonies.

For its part, the English public cared little for most of the mainland colonies. If a contemporary English writer had been composing a history of the American mainland colonies in the late seventeenth century, his account would probably have concentrated on the Chesapeake Bay colonies of Virginia and Maryland, which were the only ones that aroused much interest among the English. The Carolinas were regarded as holding some promise, but the middle and northern colonies, with the exception of the port town of Boston, would not have been

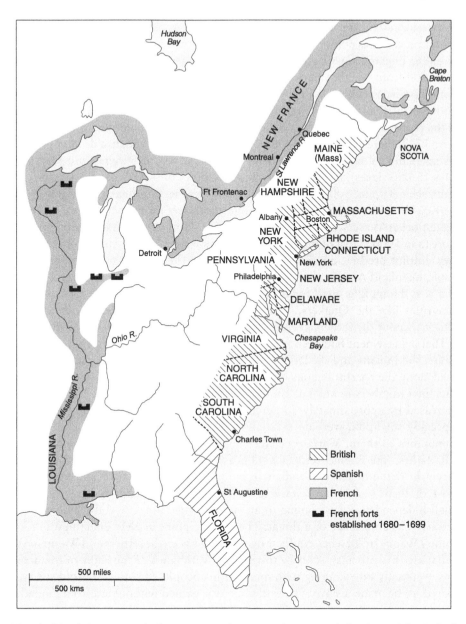

Map 4 *North America in the late seventeenth century. (Source: Nicholas Canny,* The Oxford History of the British Empire, *volume 1: The Origins of Empire, Oxford, 1998, p. 437.)*

given much attention. The tiny Caribbean islands were worth all of the mainland American colonies combined in terms of commercial profit for the home country. In 1686, England imported £675,000 of goods from the West Indies, but only £207,000 from North America, of which almost 70 percent consisted of tobacco from the Chesapeake. The rich West Indians also consumed more English goods. About as much in exports was sent to the 40,000 white islanders in 1686 as went to the North American settlers, who were five times as numerous.

By 1700, there were about 240,000 men and women of English descent living in the mainland colonies: 92,000 in New England, 85,000 in Virginia and Maryland (plus 13,000 slaves), 50,000 in the middle colonies of New York, the Jerseys, and Pennsylvania (plus 5000 slaves), and 12,000 in the Carolinas (plus 4000–5000 slaves). These inhabitants were spread out thinly over an enormous area, and their biggest urban centers were not very significant. Only Boston had a population of more than 5000. Most of the American settlers were farmers. Apart from tobacco, they did not produce anything that was sought after in the home country. As a result, mainland America beyond the Chesapeake seemed to be important chiefly as a vast dumping ground for the surplus English population, and for unwanted minorities like the Quakers. There was little appreciation back home for the achievement of the settlers in recreating English society in the New World.

That achievement had been made possible by controlling two great indigenous forces: the Indians and the land. We cannot know for certain how many Indians lived along the coastal regions of North America in this period, but one estimate puts their numbers in 1600 at about 500,000. By the end of the century, this had decreased by approximately 50 percent. The diseases carried by the Europeans, especially smallpox, were devastating to native peoples, who had developed no immunities to them. Warfare between Indians and Europeans had also taken a toll. At first, the English settlers were heavily dependent on Indian assistance for survival. Without learning Indian techniques of planting corn and vegetables, most of them would have starved. By the late seventeenth century, however, English dependence was coming to an end in settled areas, and the Indians were perceived as a nuisance or a threat. The turning point in New England was King Philip's War in 1676, when conflicts over land between the settlers and Wampanoag Indians led to raids against settler towns. The Wampanoag King Philip or Metacom was eventually killed, along with many of his people. His nine-year-old son was spared, to be made a slave. The settler victory, gained without aid from England, was won with the support of Christian Indians who had been converted in the "praying towns" set up along the frontier. Alliance with the English did not save "friendly" Indians from losing their land and being forced either to move or to live as paupers in English communities. On the frontier, however, more peaceable trading relations existed between the English and Indians. The leaders of the Iroquois Confederation, which had a highly organized military force, negotiated a series of agreements, known as the Covenant Chain, which would keep them at peace with the English colonies for generations.

The second great force that the settlers had to control was the land itself. The Indians had in fact cleared large areas of land long before the English arrived, using fires to create open fields for planting corn. The English, who believed that God had made the land for their use, were much more aggressive in sweeping back the forest to make farmland. They sometimes rooted out trees, a laborious process. More often, they "girdled" the trees by cutting into their bark, leaving them to die slowly, or simply burned them. The settlers also erected boundaries and fences around their properties, in imitation of the field systems they had known at home. Huge tracts of land were cleared in the Chesapeake, where tobacco farmers would exhaust the fertility of one part of their property, then simply start planting on another part. They did not appreciate how the destruction of the forest removed the source of nutrients in the soil and altered the pattern of water drainage. The result was a gradual depletion of fertility, and periodic flooding.

By 1700, each of the major areas of the Americas – the Carolinas, the Chesapeake, the middle colonies, and New England – was developing its own economy and society. The Carolinas were a sparsely populated frontier land, where enslaved black "cowboys" herded livestock and farmers burned huge numbers of trees to make pitch and tar for the Royal Navy. Rice was the main cultivated crop, planted and harvested by African slave labor. The Earl of Shaftesbury, the chief proprietor in the Carolinas, had wanted his "darling" colony to take shape as a sort of aristocracy, with a local nobility owning two-fifths of the land and dominating a unicameral assembly. He commissioned John Locke to write up the Fundamental Constitutions of this hierarchical society, and the result is disconcerting to anybody who wants to see Locke as a champion of representative government. The Carolina assembly was to be restricted to voting on legislation proposed by the governor's council; it could not make laws of its own. The colony's government, however, never worked as Shaftesbury had wished: instead, the turbulent Carolinians set up assemblies in the north and south of the colony, each of them separate from, and often hostile to, the governor's council.

The Chesapeake Bay area was the first to be permanently settled by English colonists. It remained in 1700 a place where young Englishmen went to get rich quick, although few of them succeeded. About three-quarters of the area's population arrived as indentured servants, most of them in their late teens or early twenties. They were recruited from the unskilled and semi-skilled laborers of southern England, and served for four or five years as laborers on tobacco farms, in order to pay off their passage to the colony. After that, they could acquire farms of their own. The immigrants were predominantly male, and there was a chronic shortage of English women in the colony. Apparently, the scarcity of white women did not raise their social status with respect to white men, although it sharpened the sense of superiority felt by married women towards servants and slaves.

Settlement in the two Chesapeake Bay colonies of Virginia and Maryland was centered not on towns, but on rivers, which connected the scattered tobacco farms to trans-Atlantic shipping routes. Lacking town government, rural areas of Virginia and Maryland were administered through parish vestries and county courts. The big tobacco planters ran both institutions, although they were never as exclusive or as controlling as the big sugar planters of the West Indies. Instead, they behaved like the English gentry, forming a class of privileged landowners who saw themselves as the natural leaders of the community. Most of them were members of the Church of England, which was the established religion in Virginia, and after 1692 in Maryland, in spite of the presence there of many Protestant Dissenters and Catholics. The numerous small planters of the Chesapeake continued to adhere to a vision of the New World as a land of liberty and prosperity, which it was for white people.

It was not so, of course, for African slaves, who were being transported to the Chesapeake in increasing numbers. As in Barbados, the Virginia assembly or House of Burgesses made ferocious laws to keep slaves under the control of their masters. A law of 1669 stated "if any slave resist his master … and by the extremity of the correction should chance to die, that his death shall not be accompted Felony, … since it cannot be presumed that prepensed malice (which alone makes murther Felony) should induce any man to destroy his own estate."[6] Clearly, slaves were considered property, not people. At first, such barbaric treatment adhered to the condition of slavery, rather than to African ancestry. Examples can be found in the Chesapeake Bay area of Africans who gained freedom, started farms, and even owned slaves themselves. After 1700, however, the West Indian attitude, that Africans were naturally barbarous and deserved to be kept in perpetual slavery, seems to have spread around the Chesapeake as well.

Slaves were also plentiful in the middle colonies of New York and Pennsylvania. In those places, however, they were household servants, often living in towns. The first voices against slavery were heard in the middle colonies towards the end of the seventeenth century, particularly among the Quaker followers of George Keith, who felt that slavery broke the divine command to do unto others as you would have them do unto you. Most of the white inhabitants of the middle colonies, including Quakers, did not accept this message, because so much of their economic prosperity was dependent on the West Indian sugar plantations. The wheat farmers of Pennsylvania supplied grain for the Caribbean islands, which was shipped south by Quaker merchants in the port of Philadelphia. If sugar production failed, so would they.

The four middle colonies had grown dramatically after 1660, as immigration to other mainland colonies had dried up. By 1700, they had ethnically and religiously diverse populations, and were not simply English colonial societies. Along the Hudson River and in the fur-trading town of Albany in New York could be found many Dutch settlers, who had moved to New Netherlands, as it was then called, before the English conquest. East and West Jersey contained a large number of Scots, while religious liberty had already attracted small German communities to William Penn's new colony. The patterns of land settlement in the middle colonies reflected the diverse origins of the settlers. The Hudson valley was divided into large estates or manors, established by the Dutch, who called them "patroonships." The English extended the system into Long Island. Farmers on the manors were tenants, who paid rents to proprietors. One of the biggest estates was the vast Rensselaerswyck manor along the Hudson, which had been acquired through marriage by the Scottish fur-trader Robert Livingston, a bitter enemy of Jacob Leisler and the New York revolutionaries of 1689.

The existence of similar large estates caused social tension in the Jerseys. The Scots proprietors of East Jersey had tried to set up big, independent estates that would imitate the "farmtouns" of their homeland, but this caused mounting resentment among small farmers who lived in the townships, modeled on those of New England. After the Glorious Revolution, when two leading Scottish proprietors went into exile with James II, the people of the Jersey townships began to take more aggressive action, including riots, to break what they saw as the "Scotch yoak." In response, the Board of Trade ended proprietary rule in 1702, and made the reunited New Jersey into a royal colony.

Pennsylvania was from the first a colony of small farms, but large manors did exist, and the proprietor William Penn reserved a great deal of land to himself. Penn had hoped to keep the settlers in his colony under control through a constitution known as the Frame of Government, which created an upper house that served as the governor's council and drew up all legislation. The constitution was rejected, however, by the first Pennsylvania assembly. Representatives from the western part of the colony, where most settlers were not Quakers, were particularly strident in opposing the interests of the proprietor, who clung tenaciously to his lands and rights. The western representatives saw themselves as continuing the same political struggle that had deposed William Penn's friend, King James II.

Small farms and strong town governments prevailed in the colonies of New England. Massachusetts had been settled originally by Separatists from the Church of England, and by Puritans who were opposed to the Church policies of Charles I. They had formed godly communities based on strict Calvinism. Souls were predestined to heaven or hell, and salvation was gained only by the freely given grace of God, which depended on no human action. An experience of grace, or "conversion," was necessary for membership in the Church. Male church members voted to elect parish ministers. After the Church of England was re-established in 1660, however, the New Englanders were more or less cut off from the mainstream of English Protestantism. At this point, they abandoned some of the rigor of their original beliefs, and accepted the "Halfway Covenant," allowing the offspring of Church members to have their children baptized in the Church, even if they had not had a "conversion." In this way, the Church was preserved for later generations. The original vision of founding the biblical "City on a Hill" was not wholly lost, and in 1689 the Puritan minister Increase Mather could still write of "the Almighty's most wonderful blessing and prospering *New England*, and his Gospel among the Heathen [i.e. the Indians] there, which to me looks like the Beginnings of the fulfilling [of] those many Prophecies in *Holy Writ*."[7] The Congregational Church in Massachusetts, however, moved only slowly towards toleration. Both Baptists and Quakers were persecuted. They could find more religious liberty in Rhode Island or Connecticut. Throughout New England, Puritans were traumatized by the presence of Catholics to the north in New France, a threat that was brought home to them by the bloody 1704 French and Indian attack on Deerfield, Massachusetts.

The family structure of the New England settlers was biblical and highly patriarchal, but it also called for benevolent rule by fathers and for loving relationships between husbands and wives. These ideas were not very different from those commonly held in England, but they may have been adhered to more piously. Couples married younger than in England, and women typically bore seven or eight children, which allowed the population of the colony to increase substantially without significant levels of immigration. Women also performed a variety of economic tasks, buying and selling household products with their neighbors. Divorce was made easier for wives in cases of adultery or desertion by a husband. The atmosphere of Puritanism, however, may have bred a suspicion of female sexuality and independence, which made older women vulnerable to accusations of witchcraft. The Salem witch trials of 1691 were the most famous examples of a phenomenon that was played out in many parts of New England. It should be noted that, while Puritan views may have heightened a fear of witchcraft, anxieties caused by minor social tensions within village communities lay at the heart of most witch accusations in the New World, as they did throughout Europe.

Unlike the southern colonists, most New Englanders lived in villages or small towns, from which they went out to work on farms each day. The towns were governed by "selectmen" and by annual meetings of adult male inhabitants. They maintained primary schools, which accounts for the high degree of literacy in New England. The social equality found in seventeenth-century New England towns was exceptional in the New World, and unknown in Great Britain. It was fading, however, in the booming port town of Boston, where the majority of the population was already non-Puritan by 1700. Boston thrived on shipping and shipbuilding, and had developed a social hierarchy of merchants, craftsmen, and unskilled laborers. However, in Boston as in all of New England and some parts of the middle colonies, the gentry were missing. The absence of a landowning elite would be important in the development of a separate American identity in New England.

In spite of this, an English visitor would have had no difficulty in identifying all the mainland colonies as English in 1700. They spoke the same language, read the same books, and shared many of the same habits as the inhabitants of the home country. The social and religious differences that set the colonial settlers apart were mostly matters of degree. Quakers and Congregationalists could be found in England, and as yet no non-British group of European immigrants was numerous enough to have much clout in the New World. What would change in the next 75 years were both the self-awareness of the American colonists themselves and the identity of the English. The politicians at Westminster would increasingly come to see themselves as patriotic subjects of a unified British state, whose purpose was to protect a far-flung empire. As it turned out, the mainland Americans could not entirely conform to that new identity.

The English in Africa and Asia

Whether the English empire extended to Africa and Asia in the seventeenth century is a moot point. If empire meant political dominance, then the English crown did not have an empire on either continent. Instead, two English trading companies and a host of interlopers did business with Africans and Asians, who usually had the upper hand in commercial relations. Attempts to turn trading connections into regional political influence were usually disastrous. The history of English imperialism in Asia and Africa, therefore, has to focus on commerce rather than settlement. Nonetheless, the presence of English trading forts in both West Africa and South Asia would provide the beachheads from which territorial dominance would later extend. Eventually, the trading companies would prove to be more reliable agents of the British state than the colonial governments in the Americas ever were.

English trade with Asia was officially monopolized by the East India Company (EIC), chartered by Queen Elizabeth in 1600. From the beginning, the EIC depended heavily on the English government in order to ward off potential competitors, and by the late seventeenth century it had become almost an extension of the administration. The main business of the Company was trade with East Asia, which initially catered to the European desire to liven up a bland diet with pepper and spices. By the late seventeenth century, the spice trade was slowing down, but the demand for other East Asian products was booming. The English simply could not have enough Chinese silks and porcelain or Indian dyed cotton textiles, known as calicoes. Between 1660 and 1690, the value of annual EIC imports from East Asia to England multiplied fivefold, to about £403,000. Asian merchants, however, were far less interested in English goods, so the EIC paid for these luxury imports in gold and silver bullion, obtained through English trade with Spanish America. Thus, the East Asian trade was linked to a worldwide system of commerce.

The EIC had a significant economic impact on East Asia, but its territorial impact was minor. After the Dutch and the local ruler closed down the EIC "factory" or trading post at Bantam (Banten) in 1682, the English lacked a fixed place to buy spices in the Indonesian islands, although they continued to trade through stations on the island of Sumatra. The Chinese emperor allowed the English to buy luxury goods through agents in one selected coastal town, first Amoy (Xiamen) and then, after 1699, Canton (Guangzhou), but the EIC did not own any property in China. The Company had a long-established "factory" at the port of Surat in western India, which sent out agents to towns in the interior. The principal territorial possessions of the EIC, however, were three fortified trading cities in India: Madras (now Chennai), Bombay (Mumbai), and Calcutta (Kolkota). Madras, on the Coromandel coast of southeast India, sprang up around Fort St George, a trading post constructed by the EIC in 1640. Madras was in fact *two* towns, as there was both a European settlement and a separate area called "Blacktown" by the English, where Indian merchants lived. Bombay or *Bom bahia* ("good bay"), an island on the western coast of India, was founded by the Portuguese, who gave it to Charles II as part of the dowry of his Queen, Catherine of Braganza. In turn, Charles granted it to the EIC in 1668, showing that he had no intention of directly ruling a place in distant India. Calcutta in Bengal was named after a local village, where the EIC in 1698 would start to build their most important settlement, the future capital of British India.

It would be a mistake to see the EIC as a dominant force in any part of India. Its trade depended on Indian merchants, who supplied the Company agents with goods, especially calicoes. The cotton industry around the three major forts was based on thousands of village spinners and weavers who worked at home, and on urban workshops where textiles were dyed, tie-dyed, or printed with wood blocks. It was a well organized industry, and it responded easily to huge increases in demand from English consumers. While relatively few Europeans profited from the calico trade, a large number of Indians did. It may have bothered the locals that some Company agents disdained them as "heathens," but many Englishmen chose to live like indigenous peoples, dressing like them, learning their language, and residing with Indian mistresses, who often assisted their business endeavors. Except in religious matters, the English felt no superiority to the peoples of Asia, whose arts and industries they greatly admired.

The political impact of the EIC in India was so far minor, although it may already have had predatory ambitions. An attempt was in fact made to extend the Company's influence by military means, in the late 1680s, when troops sent from England were used to make war against the Mughal Emperor Aurangzeb, who dominated northern India. The result was total defeat. The Emperor closed down the Surat "factory" and forced the Company to make peace. He must have wondered why this ridiculous gnat of a Company had been so foolish as to bite him. What he could not know was that the EIC would one day make his descendants into virtual puppets. This would have as much to do with the weakness of the Mughals as with the growing power of the English. The Mughals were a Muslim dynasty, ruling over mostly Hindu peoples. Aurangzeb was particularly devout in his religion, which alienated many Hindus and motivated them to break away from his rule. In the early eighteenth century, the Mughal empire began to fall apart, with provincial rulers acting virtually independently. The same disintegration was affecting the southern Indian kingdoms that had never been parts of the Mughal empire. The EIC would make itself a major player in this volatile political situation.

The equivalent to the EIC in African trade was the Royal African Company, whose charter was granted by Charles II in 1660. Although it is mainly known for supplying slaves to the Americas, in fact it also traded for gold, ivory, pepper, rare woods, and other African products. The west coast of Africa was divided into myriad small states that vied with one another through trade and constant warfare. By 1660, the rulers of these kingdoms were used to contact with Europeans, and they appointed official state merchants to deal with them. Militarily, the West Africans were already capable of making metal weapons, and their military leaders were eager to obtain muskets. Moreover, the Africans were not highly susceptible to European diseases, as American Indian peoples were; on the contrary, it was the Europeans who died in droves on the African coasts, afflicted with malaria, dysentery, and other sicknesses. The English had no chance of subjugating the peoples of West Africa, and probably little desire to do so. Instead, they settled into trading forts along the coasts that were granted to them by African rulers, like Cape Coast Castle and, after 1682, Whydah. There, they competed for commercial advantage with the Dutch, French, Danes, and Germans.

The Dutch dominated the gold trade, but the English emerged as the biggest slave traders in West Africa, carrying off 327,000 Africans between 1662 and 1700. English merchants did not seize slaves themselves; instead, they bought them from Africans, who had usually taken them as captives in war. Slavery was widespread in West Africa, where it took various forms. In some cases, slaves were like serfs, tied to the land on which they worked; in others, slaves were household servants. They were not normally transported far from their homes, or regarded as chattel, to be bought or sold. The European slave traders, by contrast, uprooted Africans and deprived them of their honor. They also treated them horribly, starving and abusing them, so that many slaves perished on the journey. The English surgeon Thomas Aubrey, who worked on slave ships, confessed that "my Heart hath been ready to bleed for those poor Wretches." After all, he wrote, "altho' they are Heathens, yet they have a rational soul, as well as us." According to Aubrey, slave captains often asked, *what a Devil makes these plaguy Toads dye so fast?* To which I answer: It's Inhumanity, Barbarity, and the greatest of Cruelty of their Commander, and his Crew."[8]

We tend to think of slave traders as carriers of European racism, but in fact their attitudes about African society were mixed, no matter how brutal they could be to slaves. Some took African wives; others identified dark skin with the devil. For their part, most African rulers did not think much of the Europeans, who seldom bathed, and whose skin color reminded Africans of dead people. On the other hand, West African monarchs were quite happy to exchange slaves for English knives or gunpowder or cooking pots. They believed that their people, not the English, reaped the biggest benefits of trade; otherwise, they would just have put a stop to it, as some rulers did.

After the Glorious Revolution, a political reaction set in against the monopolists who had profited from trading privileges during the reigns of Charles II and James II. In 1698, Parliament deprived the Royal African Company of its monopoly on West African trade, and even the venerable East India Company was forced to confront a rival, chartered as the New East India Company. Private merchants and ship captains now dominated the slave trade, while commerce with East Asia was thrown into confusion, as local Indian and Chinese merchants had to choose with which Company they wanted to deal. In the end, after nine years of conflict, the two East India Companies united. The anti-monopoly episode demonstrated that the English Parliament saw itself as responsible for regulating overseas trade, but it did nothing to advance an English territorial empire in Africa or Asia, which almost nobody in 1698 saw as desirable or even possible. It would take six decades for that attitude to change, and for a British Empire in South Asia to spring violently to life.

Part III

The Legacy of Revolution, 1689–1722

The three decades that followed the Glorious Revolution were among the most crucial in British history. They shaped the eighteenth-century state, which remained largely unchanged until the late 1820s. What were its main features?

First, the state became truly British, through the 1707 Act of Union between England, and Scotland. The Union, as we will see, was not a federal one, such as would later be adopted in the United States, Canada or Australia. It placed authority in the hands of a single central legislature, located in Westminster. Scottish national government simply ceased to exist. How the Union led to a new national identity for the English and Scots is an issue that will concern us throughout the rest of the book.

Second, Britain adopted a system of war finance that made it into what historians have called a "fiscal-military" state. The state's main task was to mobilize the nation's resources during two wars with France: the Nine Years' War (1689–97) and the War of the Spanish Succession (1702–13). The French wars required more men, more ships, more money, and more efficient revenue collection than England or Scotland had ever known before. Gradually, under the pressures of war, the state took a much bigger role for itself in the economy.

Third, power within the state came to depend on a competition for office between groups that were linked to organized political parties. A wide segment of the population was involved in this political jockeying, and became entwined in the doings of the state. The British system was not a democracy, but it was not a narrow oligarchy either.

Fourth, the state generally respected existing legal rights, even if it sometimes had impulses in an authoritarian direction. This can be attributed to the fact that no single group of politicians could count on controlling the government or Parliament for very long. Everybody might benefit at some point from the preservation of legal rights, which eventually became the pride of the British political system.

Fifth, while in theory a powerful executive authority remained in the hands of the King or Queen, in practice the post-Revolution monarchy was not strong enough to impose its will on the British state. This was partly because the ruling monarch had a rival overseas, in the exiled Stuart Pretenders, who created insecurity by claiming greater legitimacy. It was also partly due to the growth of a "Country" opposition in Parliament, which was mistrustful of any attempt to extend executive power.

Finally, although it was tolerant of other sects, the state continued to be based on religious affiliation. As some historians have put it, Britain remained a "confessional state." Everyone who was involved in government, at all levels, was supposed to conform, at least outwardly, to the established religion. Attempts were even made to tighten religious exclusions. As we will see, when the confessional basis of the state changed in the 1820s, fundamental political reform was quick to follow.

The next two chapters examine the emergence of the British state through an analysis of politics between 1689 and 1722. Chapter 9 is concerned with the cultural effects of the Glorious Revolution, in particular its impact on literature, the arts, and sciences. This was the greatest age of English writing since the reign of Elizabeth I, a fact that was not unrelated to political developments.

7

The Fortunes of War, 1689–1710

When William of Orange invaded England in 1688, he wanted to force his father-in-law to support the Dutch in their life-and-death struggle against Louis XIV of France. "His eagerness that way never ceased," wrote one of William's advisors, adding "it may be a question, whether that thought was not the greatest inducement to his undertaking [i.e. his coming to England]."[1] On May 5, 1689, William and Mary declared war against France, but they could hardly have foreseen what would come with it: decades of party strife, a persistent Jacobite menace, a stronger government but a weaker crown. They hoped for, but could not have foretold, the Union with Scotland and the great military victories that would finally be won in the first decade of the eighteenth century. The war brought about changes that were just as deep and consequential as those of the Revolution.

Kings, Queens, and Party Chiefs

If we want to understand the complex story of the French wars, we have to know its chief characters. Until he died in 1702, King William III was the central figure in English and Scottish politics. For many Protestants, he remained the godly hero who had saved the nation from Popery. His wife, Mary II, took his place in Council meetings when he was away on military campaigns, but she preferred to play a secondary part to that of her husband – as Bishop Burnet put it, "she meddled not in business."[2] They had no children, and there were rumors, but no clear evidence, of William's homosexuality. The King was clearly stricken with grief when his wife died, just after Christmas 1694. He ruled alone for the next seven years. William III was bold, intelligent, and a gifted negotiator, but he was also cold and manipulative. As a young man, he had regained his position as *stadholder* (supreme commander) of the United Provinces through the destruction of Dutch republicans, but he later promoted former enemies to office. He never personally supported religious persecution. He would use the same principles of compromise and moderation in his British kingdoms. He brought with him Dutch advisors, whom he continued to consult on key issues of policy, and whose influence was resented by English politicians. William preferred to govern through a small "Cabinet Council," made up of members of his larger Privy Council, so that he could make quicker decisions. On military matters, however, the King took nobody's advice but his own.

William was succeeded in 1702 by his sister-in-law, Anne. Unlike Mary, Queen Anne was determined to rule. Her husband, Prince George of Denmark, was a political non-entity, who had the good sense hardly ever to express an opinion on anything. Anne, by contrast, was highly opinionated. "I know my own heart to be entirely English," she announced in her first speech to Parliament, which was a slap in the face of her Dutch predecessor.[3] A convinced Anglican, she distrusted the Whigs, but was not willing to endorse the intolerant Tory religious platform. Unlike William III, who mocked it as a superstition, Anne was eager to use the Royal Touch, the monarch's traditional ability to cure the disease known as scrofula by the laying on of hands. Clearly, Anne believed in her royal powers, and was willing to use them. She was the last to do so, just as she was the last British ruler to veto a bill passed by Parliament. She was widely admired by her subjects, who put up an extraordinary number of statues to her, including one that stood in front of St Paul's Cathedral (the statue you see there now is a replica). She was much more corpulent than her statues show. Unlike William, Anne had close friends, to whom she wrote intimate letters, but she could reject them abruptly. Her family life was saddened by the deaths of all her 18 children. It is incredible that she lived through so many pregnancies. Only one of her offspring, the Duke of Gloucester, survived beyond the age of ten, but he too died in 1700. Even for a princess, this was a hard fate to bear.

Waiting in the wings were the exiled Stuarts, who had settled at the palace of St Germain-en-Laye outside Paris. There James II maintained a court, and continued to claim that he was the rightful King. Disgruntled English and Scottish politicians kept up his hopes with promises, and he was loyally supported by Catholics and Nonjuring Protestants in his former kingdoms. After James died in 1701, his son, James Francis Edward Stuart, a serious and pious young man, was proclaimed as King James III by the French. His opponents knew him as the Pretender. Many of his supporters in England and Scotland, the Jacobites, hoped that he would convert to Protestantism and reclaim his crown, but he never did. Queen Anne never admitted that her half-brother was legitimate. However, she also disliked the Protestant heirs to the throne, the Electors of Hanover, who had been chosen by Parliament in 1701 to succeed her.

Below the monarchs in the English political hierarchy were the Whig and Tory party leaders, almost all of them high-ranking aristocrats. Some of them were motivated more by personal ambition than by party ties, and would serve in any type of administration. Among the leading "time-servers" were John Churchill, Earl and then Duke of Marlborough, a brilliant general but a grasping and conniving man, married to Anne's close friend, Sarah; and Sidney, Earl of Godolphin, a highly competent money manager who rose to become Anne's Lord Treasurer.

Both were Tories, although they were willing to work with Whigs. Another Tory leader with much stronger religious principles was Daniel Finch, Earl of Nottingham. His chief opponents were the so-called Junto, a loosely organized group of Whig aristocrats. The Junto included men of great ability and judgment, such as John, Baron Somers, or the financial expert Charles Montagu, who became Earl of Halifax. William III worked closely with the Junto because they supported his war. Anne disliked most of them, but was forced to take them into her ministries because they were so influential.

The Junto's manager of Parliamentary elections was Thomas, Earl of Wharton, known as "Honest Tom," a belligerent, hard-drinking man who hated Tories. He was willing to go out among ordinary electors to convince them to vote for a party candidate, as the following story demonstrates. A Tory gentleman arrived in the town of High Wycombe to drum up support among the locals:

They found my Lord Wharton was got there before them, and was going up and down the town with his friends to secure votes on their side ... my Lord [Wharton] entering a shoemaker's shop, asked *where Dick was?* The good woman said, *her husband was gone two or three miles off with some shoes, but his Lordship need not fear him, she would keep him tight* [i.e. tied to the Whigs]. *I know that,* says my Lord, *but I want to see Dick, and drink a glass with him.* The wife was very sorry Dick was out of the way. *Well,* says his Lordship, *how does all thy children. Molly is a brave girl I warrant by this time. Yes, and thank you my Lord,* says the woman, and his Lordship continued, *Is not Jemmy breeched* [i.e. wearing trousers] *yet?* The [Tory] gentleman crossed over to his friend on the other side of the way and cried *Even take your horse and be gone. Whoever has my Lord Wharton on his side has enough for his election.*[4]

Elections could bring aristocrats face to face with the common people. Still, the shoemaker's wife had to maintain deference in the presence of "my Lord," and she may well have feared retribution if her husband did not "keep tight" with the Whigs.

Behind the great leaders in the House of Lords, and their spokesmen in the House of Commons, were the ordinary country gentlemen who made up the bulk of the Whig and Tory parties in Parliament. They were called "backbenchers" because they sat behind the ministers in the House of Commons. Some of them were elected by corrupt little boroughs, and were greedy for any promotion or pension that would benefit them or their relatives. Others would take no rewards or offices. Nevertheless, they all considered themselves to be the representatives of their localities, and they would fight for the interests of their constituents in Parliament. Whig country gentlemen spoke out loudly for "Revolution principles," meaning the Protestant succession and religious toleration. They suspected their opponents of being secret Jacobites. For their part, Tory country gentlemen feared that the Church and the monarchy were in danger from "sectaries" and "republicans." What country gentlemen on both sides could agree on was moral legislation, to combat blasphemy, drunkenness, and bad behavior.

One politician would emerge from the Parliamentary backbenches to lead the nation: Robert Harley. His family, from rural Herefordshire, were Puritans in religion, and opponents of the King in the Civil Wars. Harley entered Parliament as a Whig.

His strong moral principles, however, alienated him from the bribery and manipulation that were used by politicians of both sides. To limit the effects of such corruption, Harley endorsed a Triennial Bill to dissolve Parliament every three years, a measure that was reluctantly accepted by William III in 1694. Harley and his friends then formed a group of MPs, including both Whigs and Tories, that was called the "Country" to distinguish it from the ministers of the "Court." Their main objective was to gain Parliamentary control over wartime expenditures, whose growth was deeply resented by country gentlemen. For a while in the mid-1690s, the "Country" was successful, until the Whig Junto took over the public accounts committee. By then, Harley was the most important man in the House of Commons, respected by Tories as well as Whigs. In 1701, it was he who guided through the Commons the crucial Act of Settlement, which determined the succession after Queen Anne's death. Three years later, with Tory support, he became Secretary of State, guiding Queen Anne's ministry alongside Marlborough and Godolphin. Never loved by other politicians, Harley was a brilliant, manipulative and unscrupulous figure, a man who steered his own course in a frothing sea of party rage.

Partisans

Although few people liked to admit it, party conflict was at the heart of the political system after 1688. It altered everything, from reading matter and sociability to the electorate itself. The number of voters in England grew steadily in this period, as one side or the other sought to enfranchise its supporters. By the early eighteenth century, the voting population included perhaps one in four adult males, a proportion not reached again until after the Second Reform Act of 1867. These voters had to turn out for no fewer than 12 general elections between 1689 and 1715. Many non-voters also took part in the drinking, shouting, singing, fighting, and rioting that accompanied elections.

Party politics helped to create a vibrant, largely unshackled press. In 1695, under pressure from independent printers, Parliament refused to renew the Licensing Act, and from that point onwards, newspapers and pamphlets flourished in England. The first newspaper outside of the capital, the *Norwich Post*, appeared in 1701, followed a year later by the first successful London daily newspaper, *The Daily Courant*. By 1704, the *Post-Man*, a Whig paper, was selling 3800 copies, three times a week, while its rival, the Tory *Post-Boy*, sold about 3000 copies. This did not mean that complete liberty of the press existed. Treasonable or seditious libel could still be prosecuted in the courts; so could antireligious, blasphemous, or immoral works. Printers were put to death for issuing treasonable material in 1693 and 1719. Many others were pilloried, fined, or imprisoned. Restrictive taxes on the press might be levied, like the stamp duty on printed paper, imposed by Parliament in 1712. Queen Anne heartily approved of this measure, which she saw as a remedy to the "great license … taken in publishing false and scandalous libels such as are a reproach to any government."[5] The Stamp Act did not work very well, however, because it contained numerous loopholes.

What did people read in newspapers? By the early eighteenth century, most newspapers were printed in columns, on two to four large sheets of paper. On the first page was an engraved heading, showing the journal title and maybe a figure of Mercury, a postal rider, or Britannia, the female incarnation of Britain. The contents often included an opening essay on a social or political theme, followed by snippets of foreign and domestic news, reports of ships entering and leaving the port of London, the rise and fall of company stocks, births and deaths, and appointments at court, in the armed services, or in the administration. Advertisements, usually for books, pamphlets, or patent medicines, were placed at the end. Judging by the content, the readership of newspapers included government employees, landed gentlemen, clergymen, and merchants. A few periodicals targeted a female audience.

In addition to newspapers, readers of the early eighteenth century who were interested in politics could buy pamphlets, full-sized books, single broadsheets printed with a joke, a story or a song, and fairly crude graphic prints. Handwritten newsletters were also sent out from London to wealthy subscribers who lived in remote areas. William III was particularly irked by a newsletter issued by the Tory coffeehouse owner James Dyer, which was often critical of the government. Dyer was arrested three times, but his newsletter continued to appear. Printed works cost from a few pennies for a small pamphlet to a few pounds for a big volume of political theory. They were not cheap, relative to an average wage. Yet they reached far more people than had been possible in earlier centuries, drawing them directly into politics. "Thus fools turn statesmen, and blacksmiths and tinkers turn regulators and vindicators of the Church," complained one observer.[6] Ironically, he published this opinion in a pamphlet. By the early eighteenth century, London was home to a busy swarm of political writers, editors, printers, printing assistants, publishers, and street-hawkers.

Party politics also provided a focus for sociability. After the Glorious Revolution, a group of Whig politicians and writers set up an elegant dining club at the London pie-house belonging to Christopher Catling – the so-called Kit-Kat Club. A different type of Whig club was founded a few years later, when in order to fight Jacobite rioters in London, the government sponsored gangs who met in taverns called "Mughouses." Meanwhile, coffeehouses continued to proliferate. By 1734, 551 of them were licensed in the capital, and every important provincial town in England had at least a couple of them. The two political parties had latched onto their own coffeehouses, from which their opponents were excluded. In London, Ozinda's Chocolate House and the Cocoa Tree were havens for the Tories. The Whigs congregated at the St James's Coffeehouse and White's, where one could gamble as well. The proprietress of Old Man's Coffeehouse, Jenny Man, stood up to an attack by a Tory mob in 1710. A Whig newspaper sang her praises:

> She is no Friend to Right Divine
> Therefore she must not sell French Wine,
> But Tea and Coffee, very fine,
> And sure that is no Wrong, Sirs.[7]

Proprietresses and serving girls, however, were probably the only women to be seen in most coffeehouses. The smoky, noisy, raucous, highly political environment of the coffeehouse was a man's world. Women of the middling sort and upper classes preferred to drink tea, at home, with friends.

The whole of Britain did not wake up to the smell of coffee. While coffeehouses were common in larger towns, they were unknown to rural people throughout Britain. This reminds us that, while political culture did have a wide audience, large segments of the population were not much exposed to it. Rural laborers had no vote and were far removed from the national debates that raged in Parliament. They did not have access to newspapers, and for them, sociability meant a harvest dance or a drink and smoke at an alehouse. Still, they went to church or chapel, so they would know what a Whig or a Tory was. Occasionally, country folk were driven to riot by high prices or taxes. Beyond that, what their opinions of government may have been, we have no sure way to know.

King William's War, 1689–1702

One might have expected the Whigs to have held on to power after 1689. After all, they were the main upholders of the Glorious Revolution. They had framed the Declaration of Rights, and they had pushed for the Toleration Act. Unlike some Tories, who had qualms about the legitimacy of William and Mary, Whigs were willing to accept the new monarchs as rulers not just *de facto* (in fact) but also *de jure* (by law). So why did William III fail to keep them in office?

For a start, the new King did not call them Whigs. He used the term "commonwealthmen," meaning that he feared they were republicans. At heart, his sympathies, like those of Queen Mary, were with the Tories, whom they saw as upholders of monarchy. William did not want to drive the Tories into the arms of the Jacobites by keeping them out of office. Also, the Whigs began to cause serious dissension in the Convention Parliament, in a debate over restoring borough charters that had been surrendered under Charles II and James II. They wanted to exclude from local office anyone who had agreed to surrender a charter before 1686 (almost all Tories), but *not* those who had agreed to surrender them after 1686 (almost all Whigs). This partisan gambit was finally defeated in January 1690. Meanwhile, the Tories, meeting at the Devil's Tavern, promised to support the war against France. William obligingly dissolved Parliament and called an election.

The result was defeat for many extreme Whigs, as well as for a number of Tories who had voted against giving William and Mary the throne. The administration was largely handed over to the Tories, led by Nottingham and Thomas Osborne, Marquess of Carmarthen and former Earl of Danby, who had been Charles II's chief minister in the 1670s. Carmarthen tried to reconstruct the system of patronage that had kept his previous ministry afloat. He quickly made enemies, and was opposed from the first by Robert Harley's "Country" alliance. Meanwhile, the war went badly. In 1690, a combined Anglo-Dutch fleet was defeated by the

French at Beachy Head. This shocking blow opened up the whole south coast to a French attack. If Louis XIV had been prepared to invade England, his moment had arrived. Instead, the French King hesitated in order to build his forces. He opened secret negotiations with some angry Whigs, including Admiral Edward Russell, so as to win their support for a Jacobite restoration. They made vague promises, and quickly broke them. In December 1692, Russell himself was in command of an English fleet that wiped out the French invasion flotilla at Cape La Hogue. James II's plans to recover his kingdoms were wrecked.

The ailing Tory administration received little consolation from the Whig admiral's triumph. French privateers, sailing from Channel ports, continued to attack English shipping. A few months after La Hogue, a major English convoy was destroyed in the Mediterranean. William had had enough of his Tory ministers: they simply were not winning the war for him. Nottingham was dismissed in November 1693, and Carmarthen was kept out of further decision-making. The Junto Whigs were taken into office, and they would hold on to power for the next six years.

The Junto succeeded where the Tories had failed because they were willing to carry out sweeping changes in order to pay for the war. The most enduring change was the creation of the Bank of England in April 1694. Its purpose was to secure government loans, and if necessary to lend money directly to the state. The interest on the loans was paid by tax revenues, and the debt belonged to the nation, not to the King. Many of the investors in the Bank of England, however, were Dissenters or Dutchmen, which infuriated the Tories as it meant that non-Anglicans and non-Englishmen were upholding national finance. Country gentlemen were equally disgusted by a second Junto measure: the land tax, which leveled a whopping rate of 4 shillings to the pound (i.e. 20 percent) on the value of land. The tax was administered by local commissions, and was passed on to tenants, but the gentry never stopped resenting it. Further taxes on everything from leather and windows to salt and wine irritated even more of King William's subjects. For ordinary people, however, the most disturbing Junto measure was the recoinage of 1695–6. It was a necessary step, because too few silver coins were in circulation, and those that were often had parts clipped or shaved from them by dishonest dealers. Led by Charles Montagu, the Junto Whigs took the courageous decision to withdraw old coins and replace them with new ones. Damaged coins were declared worthless. Debtors were outraged as they had to pay back their creditors in higher value coinage. The recoinage, however, saved the English economy from a potential collapse.

In order to retain its control of Parliament, the Junto sometimes had to pacify the "Country." William III did not always agree with this, and he vetoed several measures that hedged royal power. Nevertheless, he accepted the Triennial Act, as well as the creation of a Land Bank that was supposed to raise the value of land (it eventually failed). When the Junto Whigs came out of the general elections of 1695 with a majority, they sought some way to undermine their "Country" critics. The answer was provided by Providence itself. In February 1696, a Jacobite plot to assassinate William III was announced to Parliament by the King. The details of the plot remain murky to this day, but apparently, William was to be killed while riding out in his carriage from Kensington Palace. The conspirators planned to lead an uprising, while a French invasion force was to be launched from Calais, with James II on board. Once the dreadful plot was discovered, the government wasted no time in suspending *habeas corpus* and proposing an Association in defense of the King, to be signed by all loyal subjects. Cleverly, the Junto included in the Association the words "rightful and lawful," referring to King William. More than 80 Tory Members of the House of Commons, most of them "Country" supporters, would not sign the Association, because they did not regard William as a "rightful and lawful" monarch. They were denounced by the government as Jacobites. The "Country" alliance seemed wrecked.

It reunited in the following year, during the trial of one of the Assassination Plot conspirators, Sir John Fenwick. A former MP, Fenwick was accused by only one witness (the other one disappeared), although two were needed in a treason trial. He threatened to spill the beans on Whig negotiations with the Jacobites in the early 1690s, about which the Junto, understandably, wanted him to keep his mouth shut. In the end, Fenwick went to the gallows without revealing too much, and the Junto ministers breathed more easily. Yet the government soon had to give way to "Country" demands for an Act instituting a yearly grant paid to the King for his personal expenses, known as the Civil List. An annual grant in place of customs duties had been voted by Parliament since 1689. It now became law, and has remained law ever since. King William was given £700,000, an amount that did not increase until the reign of George II.

By 1697, both England and France were exhausted by the war. It had cost England a staggering £50,000,000, of which £13,000,000 was borrowed. The Exchequer, the office that paid money out to the government's creditors, had lost track of its payments, which were registered according to medieval accounting methods, with wooden tallies. As a result, the government began issuing paper bills, which could be exchanged freely by anyone who held them. Few people trusted the first paper currency, because it had no intrinsic value, but it had come to stay. The Bank of England, meanwhile, had to cover the government's unsecured loans by issuing stock. This rescued the kingdom from financial ruin, although nobody was sure that it could be repeated as government debt mounted.

What was the purpose of all this debt? After nine years of war, neither William III nor Louis XIV had managed to gain a decisive victory. Louis had captured some Dutch fortresses; William had recaptured one of them, Namur. Most importantly, William had avoided an invasion of Great Britain and preserved his throne. Still, it was not a particularly inspiring record for either side. By 1697, both William and Louis had tired of the war. They were looking ahead to the next international crisis: the impending death of the childless King Carlos II of Spain, whose vast global inheritance was claimed both by Louis XIV's grandson Philip and by the son of the Holy Roman Emperor. The French King, who was running out of money, was prepared to hand back the territory he had conquered in the previous war in order to prepare his kingdom for the next one. The Peace of

Ryswick was duly signed in September 1697. In it, Louis recognized William as King of England, but he did not agree to expel his friend and client James II from France. No significant territory changed hands, and the issue of the Spanish Succession was not resolved.

The Junto's work was now effectively done. As it turned out, they had laid the fiscal foundations of the British state, but nobody could be sure of that as yet. William, who never much liked any of them except the charming Lord Somers, began to move away from them, towards a mixed ministry of Whigs and Tories. Most of the Junto ministers, however, held on to power through another general election in 1698 that was fought largely on "Court" versus "Country" lines. Now that peace had returned, and the Jacobite menace was removed, the "Country" latched onto the issue of disbanding the large standing army of 60,000 men. As in the 1680s, a peacetime army was viewed as a threat to English liberties. As one pamphlet put it, "we have enough to do to guard ourselves against the Power of the Court, without having an Army thrown into the Scale against us."[8] William wanted the army maintained for future service. Harley led the charge against it, and he was so successful that the disgruntled King actually considered retiring to Holland. By February 1699, however, William had to surrender, and accepted an army of no more than 10,000 men. He was further embarrassed when the "Country" began to investigate the grants of confiscated Irish land that he had made to his Dutch favorites. The traffic in Irish lands was a potential scandal that neither William nor the Junto wanted to have uncovered.

What good was the Junto doing the King now? Between May 1699 and June 1700, almost all of its members resigned or were dismissed. Somers was the last to go. They were mostly replaced with Tories, which encouraged the Tory back-benchers into thinking that the moment had come to impeach the rejected Whig leaders – that is, bring them to trial in Parliament for perceived misconduct, so that they could not be employed again by the King. The attempt failed, but it heightened tensions between the parties. The defeated Tories retaliated by trying to prosecute some smaller fry, the Whig judges and jurymen of Kent, who had sent a plucky but annoying petition to Parliament, complaining about disloyal Tory behavior. In this polarized situation, it seems almost miraculous that Harley was able to convince his Tory colleagues in the Commons, including some who had Jacobite sympathies, to pass the Act of Settlement in June 1701. It recognized the Protestant House of Hanover as the heirs to William and Anne. Tories with Jacobite inclinations probably thought they could ignore the Act later – for them, after all, the succession was determined by blood, not by Parliamentary statute.

Apart from the Act of Settlement, William had little to be happy about in dealing with his factious last Parliaments. His foreign policy was simultaneously deteriorating. The Peace of Ryswick had been followed by two secret Partition Treaties between Louis and William. They divided up the Spanish territories between the French and the Austrian claimants. The Austrians, however, were not consulted, and when the details of the second treaty became public, they denounced it. For his part, King Carlos rejected any partition of his empire, and made out a will naming Louis's grandson Philip as his sole heir. When Carlos died in November

Illustration 5   *A cartoon of 1690 showing King William III as the fulfillment of biblical prophecies. He tramples the Whore of Babylon from the Book of Revelations and stands between two columns symbolizing the Temple of Solomon. Queen Mary looks down on him from the upper left, and figures representing England, Scotland, and Ireland pay homage to him at right. The cartoon was controversial because it was based on an earlier picture of Oliver Cromwell as Lord Protector. ("The Embleme of Englands Distraction," Williamite Version, 1690. © The Trustees of the British Museum)*

1700, Louis XIV repudiated the Partition Treaties, and Philip became King of Spain. The Dutch, English, and Austrians entered into a Grand Alliance to prevent a future union of France and Spain. Another war seemed virtually inevitable.

A worried William turned again to his old allies, the Whigs, and reinstated some of the Junto ministers. His mounting political anxieties suddenly ended, however, in March 1702, when his horse was scared by a mole – a little gentleman in black velvet, according to the Jacobites – and threw him off its back. He died soon after. William III will always be remembered as the architect of the Glorious Revolution, although his last years revealed his authoritarian tendencies. Unlike his predecessors, he was always a skilled politician, willing to make compromises in order to obtain his greater goals: to secure the United Provinces, and hang on to his British throne.

A nasty, albeit clever, Jacobite poem of 1695 expresses a bitter, negative view of William III at a difficult moment in his reign:

> Rejoice you sots, your idol's come again,
> To pick your pockets and kidnap your men.
> Give him your moneys, and his Dutch your lands.
> Ring not your bells ye fools, but wring your hands.[9]

The poet accuses the English people of foolishly applauding a King who has plundered and abused the country. In reality, William did not pick anybody's pockets, but his war did put the nation under enormous financial and political strain, while producing no great benefits for England. Yet most of his English subjects continued to think of him as the savior of Protestantism and liberty. That image has given William a positive historical reputation, even today. His main legacy was a changed English state that his successor would preserve through another war.

Faction Displayed, 1702–1710

In 1704, the Tory William Shippen published a satirical poem entitled *Faction Display'd*, in which he drew a grim picture of the Whigs as the victims of mental disease:

> *Faction*, a restless and repining Fiend,
> Curdles their Blood, and gnaws upon their Mind;
> Off-spring of Chaos, Enemy to Form,
> By whose destructive Arts the World is torn.[10]

The Whigs would have agreed that faction was a terrible thing, but they saw the Tories as suffering from it, not themselves. Everybody thought that the nation should be united, and the way to achieve unity was to wipe out the other political party. Few were willing to give up their own attachments and beliefs in order to make an accommodation with their opponents. Factional strife would reach a height in Britain under Queen Anne, with jarring results for the state. It also reverberated in Ireland, where the Test Act of 1704 would exclude Presbyterians from holding office, making the biggest Irish Protestant group almost as disillusioned with government as Irish Catholics were.

When she came to the throne in March 1702, Anne's kingdoms were on the brink of a war with France, which was formally declared two months later. Yet the Queen was not convinced that the Whigs alone could be relied on to prosecute a war successfully. Her first ministry was overwhelmingly Tory, and included the pious Earl of Nottingham. The three men who would really run the government for the next six years were the Earl (later Duke) of Marlborough, Lord Godolphin, and Robert Harley, who by this time was widely considered to be a Tory. Like the Junto before them, their principal aim was to win the war. Marlborough took command of the Allied troops. Godolphin came up with the money to fund the war effort. Harley managed the House of Commons as Speaker, and after 1704 replaced Nottingham as one of the two Secretaries of State.

The Tory backbenchers, however, had no love for this war. Their main goal was domestic: as in the last years of William's reign, they simply wanted to ruin the Whigs. They were scandalized by the practice of "occasional conformity," which allowed Protestant Dissenters to serve in political office after they had taken communion in an Anglican church. "Is it not just and proper," fumed a Tory MP, "to keep those Men out of Offices and Places of Trust relating to the Government, either in Counties or Corporations, who have no other Way to come at them, but by acting contrary to their Original Principles?"[11] In 1703–4, the Tories proposed three Occasional Conformity Bills to end this obnoxious practice, by disqualifying anybody from holding office who dared to attend Dissenting services after taking Anglican communion The first two bills were defeated by Whig maneuvers in the House of Lords. The third, however, was "tacked" or added on to a land tax bill, meaning that, by Parliamentary precedent, the Lords were not supposed to vote on it. Harley had to work hard to defeat the "Tack" in the House of Commons. He succeeded, but the Tory backbenchers were furious that the supposedly Tory ministers, Marlborough and Godolphin, had betrayed them. The backbenchers did not care about the money that Dissenting merchants were lending to the government, and that might not be offered if the ministry supported a bill that penalized them. To the "Tackers," occasional conformity was a question of morality, not of finance.

The 1705 elections were fought mainly on the issue of the infamous Tack. The Tories lost a number of seats over this contentious question. Their losses made little difference to the ministry, which was already dependent on the Whigs. A number of high-ranking Tory office-holders had been jettisoned by Marlborough and Godolphin just before the elections. Some of them tried to get revenge afterwards by proposing a mischievous idea: that the Electress Sophia of Hanover, the heir to Queen Anne's throne, should be allowed to live in England. As Anne did not want her successor hanging around her court, waiting for her to die, it was not going to happen, but it took a lot of effort to defeat the measure. The ministry proposed instead that a Council of Regency be appointed after Anne's death from among the chief officers of state. It would smooth the transition from the last Stuart queen to her Hanoverian successor. During the transition period, all the major administrators in government were to retain their positions. The Regency Act was a blow directed at the Jacobites, who were becoming more numerous and vocal among discontented members of the Tory party.

It seems incredible that a nation in such a state of severe dissension and division could have successfully waged a major war, but such was the case. Wars in this period were fought by professional armies, and the winner was usually the nation that could best supply its forces over the course of a conflict. England was at a great advantage in this respect, because the Junto Whigs had created a system of war finance that was second to none in Europe. Lord Treasurer Godolphin revived the system during the War of the Spanish Succession, and he did so with even greater success, because he had so much influence with the bankers, both Whig and Tory. Godolphin used the Bank of England and the East India Company to cover the government's short-term loans. The Bank of England effectively treated the government like a private client, taking its tax revenues, paying itself what it was owed, and investing the rest. Of course, taxes had to go up as well, on many consumer items as well as land. By such methods, Godolphin was able to manage government expenditures that averaged £7.8 million every year, three-quarters of it in military expenses, and to service a debt that rose to £36 million over the course of the war. The economy suffered, however, as trade went into a recession.

Godolphin had one great advantage over his Junto predecessors in trying to raise money: Marlborough, who won a string of magnificent victories over his French opponents. Everybody wants to invest in a sure thing, and with Marlborough at its head, the English war effort soon looked like a very sure thing. His first big success was in August 1704 at Blenheim on the River Danube, where after a hard-fought battle his combined force of British, Dutch, and Imperial troops shattered a French and Bavarian army. For the first time, Louis XIV had experienced a major, irretrievable defeat on land. Marlborough scribbled down a note to his wife Sarah, using the back of a tavern bill: "I have no time to say more but to beg you will give my duty to the Queen and let her know the army has had a glorious victory."[12] It was indeed a glorious victory, one that would gain Marlborough a princely title from the Holy Roman Emperor, an English dukedom, a grant from Queen Anne of the royal manor of Woodstock, and £5000 per year, a huge sum of money, bestowed on him for life by Parliament. He and the duchess used the money to build a gigantic house near Oxford, named Blenheim after the battle. It cost far more than the initial estimate of £100,000 by the time it was finished, and with 187 rooms, it still looks very much like a royal palace.

Having saved Vienna, Marlborough returned to the Netherlands, where he faced the Franco-Bavarian army in a second major battle at Ramillies in May 1706. Carefully exploiting the mistakes of his opponent, the Duke gained another smashing victory, although at one point, showing more spirit than sense, he recklessly led a charge into the enemy lines and was thrown from his horse. Two years later, at Oudenarde, he demonstrated his tactical brilliance a third time, by hastily concocting a battle plan that defeated a French army under a divided command.

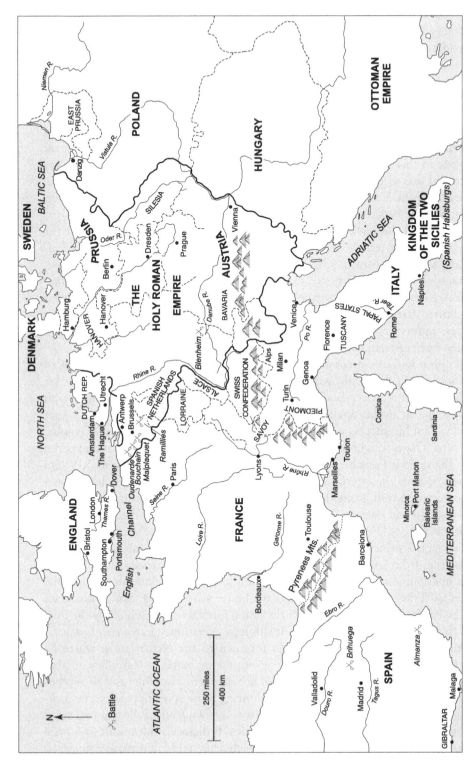

Map 5 *The War of the Spanish Succession in Europe, 1702–14.*

He followed up this victory by capturing the strategic fortress of Lille. Marlborough was well on his way to Paris, and he seemed unstoppable.

Many historians have been shocked at the lack of respect that Marlborough received from English politicians, and have concluded that they were simply petty, factious men who failed to appreciate a military genius. They were indeed petty and factious men, but they were preoccupied with a second theater of war, which they saw as equally important: namely, Spain itself. After all, if the war was to be won, and if England were to gain open trade with Spanish colonies in the New World, the Austrian claimant would have to be installed on the Spanish throne. This became less likely after April 1707, when a Franco-Spanish army under the command of the Duke of Berwick crushed an Allied army at Almanza. Berwick, curiously enough, was King James II's illegitimate son, and the Duke of Marlborough's illegitimate nephew. The war in Spain would see-saw back and forth for the next five years, but the Allies never managed to drive King Philip out of his central kingdom, Castile.

Marlborough's great victories could only erase Almanza if they forced Louis XIV to negotiate. The French King, however, was determined that his grandson would keep Spain, and he gambled everything to ensure it. He tried, unsuccessfully, to divide his enemies by offering a peace that would have left his family on the Spanish throne, which the English ministers could not accept. Louis also attempted an invasion of Scotland. In March 1708, the Stuart Pretender James III accompanied a French invasion force of 4000 troops that slipped past the Royal Navy and reached the Firth of Forth in Scotland. At that point, the British fleet caught up with it, and the French admiral fled northwards, refusing the Stuart prince's plea that he be put on shore.

The '08 rebellion had little chance of success, but it lent momentum to the political shift in England towards the Whigs. Harley had resigned in the previous month, to protest Godolphin's decision to admit Junto members into the ministry. Godolphin feared, rightly, that Harley planned to replace him as chief minister, so he was not sorry to see him go. In the elections of 1708, voters who had been panicked by the recent Jacobite rebellion threw their support to the Whigs, who re-established a secure grip on the government. Forced into opposition, Harley made friends again with the Tory backbenchers, and prepared himself for an opportunity.

It soon came. The year 1709 brought a terrible winter (by some accounts, the coldest of the eighteenth century), a severe economic downturn, high grain prices, and food riots. Many ordinary people were turning in favor of peace. A string of further events would throw the ministry into a crisis. The first was the battle of Malplaquet in September, when for the first time Marlborough mauled but did not destroy a French army, suffering heavy casualties in the process. Evidently, the war was going to continue. This was a disaster for the ministers. It came at a time when Queen Anne was turning away from the domineering Sarah, Duchess of Marlborough, towards a new Tory companion, Lady Masham. Worse still was the decision of the Whigs to impeach an obnoxious Tory preacher, Dr Henry Sacheverell. On November 5, 1709, the anniversary of the landing of William of

Orange, Sacheverell preached a sermon at St Paul's Cathedral before the lord mayor of London, in which he denounced the "false brethren," i.e. the Whigs, who were putting the Church of England in danger. By the end of the year, 60,000 printed copies of the sermon had been sold. With a strong majority in the House of Commons, the outraged Whigs resolved to put Sacheverell on trial before Parliament. It proved to be a horrendous mistake, that would catapult the nation into a decade of strife, as the next chapter will relate.

The British Union

The nation that faced a crisis in 1709–10 was neither English nor Scottish: it was British. The Union of 1707 between England and Scotland was the most important piece of legislation of Queen Anne's reign. It has endured to the present day, although the Scots regained a Parliament, with diminished powers, in 1999. The Union was not inevitable. It was the result of English security worries and Scottish economic weakness, which peaked in the two decades after 1688. Political maneuvering, not popular sentiment, created the Union, while economic success kept it alive.

After 1688, Scotland's one-chamber Parliament was bitterly divided into factions, but they had as much to do with personalities as with parties. The English terminology of Whig versus Tory did not fit Scottish politics very well before 1706. The "Court" party, which sought to carry out the monarch's business in Scotland, was a coalition of great Scottish aristocrats who had supported the Glorious Revolution. Its last leader was the indecisive James Douglas, Duke of Queensberry. Arrayed against the "Court" were groups of radical Presbyterians, who wanted to strengthen the Kirk, and Episcopalians, who sought religious toleration for their harassed co-religionists. Joining these groups were dissatisfied office seekers, like the wayward Duke of Hamilton. The opposition factions occasionally came together in a "Country" coalition, but more often, they bickered with one another as well as with the "Court." Almost all the Scottish factions had fallen in with Jacobitism at one period or another. In 1690, a Presbyterian group called "the Club" had offered to restore James II in return for guarantees of the right to *habeas corpus* and free speech in Parliament. In 1703, a Jacobite agent, Simon Fraser, Lord Lovat, tantalized Queensberry with promises of evidence about the negotiations of his political rivals, including the Duke of Hamilton, with the Stuart court. Five years later, Hamilton was briefly imprisoned for having encouraged the Jacobite invasion attempt of 1708. As for the Episcopalians, most of them, like the staunch Jacobite Sir George Lockhart of Carnwath, saw a Stuart restoration as the best way to protect their nation against England, and their persecuted Church against the Presbyterians.

In the Highlands, Jacobite sentiment ran very deep among Catholic and Episcopalian clansmen. It led to armed resistance to the Glorious Revolution that lasted until 1691. Those who had fought against William and Mary were then ordered to take an oath of allegiance to the new monarchs. When the Jacobite

Macdonalds of Glencoe were slow in taking the oath, the Lord Advocate of Scotland, Sir John Dalrymple, later Viscount Stair, ordered the massacre of every man in the glen under the age of 70. On a frosty morning in February 1692, more than 30 Macdonalds were murdered by soldiers. Although King William was not directly to blame for this, he tried to protect Stair by postponing an inquiry for three years. The massacre of Glencoe would provide the Jacobites with a huge fund of political ammunition against the Williamite regime.

The 1690s were a hard decade in Scotland. They saw the last significant outbreak of witch trials, the last use of torture in legal proceedings, and the execution of a university student for blasphemy. In 1695, a famine began that would starve thousands to death and send a wave of Scots immigrants into Ulster. In the same year, the Scottish government, attempting to imitate the imperial ventures of its southern neighbor, founded a colony at Darien on the Isthmus of Panama. The scheme was masterminded by the financier William Paterson, who had helped to found the Bank of England. Encouraged by the Scottish Parliament, investors placed £300,000 in the project, about a quarter of the cash in the whole kingdom. Beset by Spanish attacks and malaria-carrying mosquitoes, "New Edinburgh" was a dismal failure, and only 300 of the 2000 Darien colonists managed to return to Scotland. The financial impact was devastating.

In the wake of the Darien fiasco, William III proposed a union to the Scots. He was rebuffed. Instead, the Scots Parliament took measures to underline its independence. The voice of Scottish national sentiment was Andrew Fletcher of Saltoun, a radical Presbyterian who argued that, since 1603, Scotland had acted "more like a conquered province, than a free independent people."[13] He had plenty to aggravate him. The 1701 English Act of Settlement, granting the crown to the House of Hanover, had totally ignored the Scots. The Edinburgh Parliament responded in 1703 with the Act of Security, claiming the right to name the Scottish monarch. He or she was to be a descendant of the House of Stuart, and a Protestant (the Jacobites, of course, hoped to ignore that part), but was definitely *not* to be the same person who held the English throne, unless certain disputes between the two kingdoms had been satisfactorily resolved. Furious, the English Parliament took revenge with the Aliens Act of 1705, declaring that unless the Act of Security was withdrawn, Scots would be considered aliens in England. Queen Anne was also given the authority to name commissioners to negotiate a union with Scotland.

The two kingdoms were now in a state of hostility such as had not been seen since the 1650s. This time, however, the Scots did not fight. They were nudged into a compromise by several factors: first, the efforts of a *squadrone volante* or "flying squadron" of Scottish Whigs, who wanted union; second, the publicity of pro-union writers like William Paterson and Daniel Defoe, who concentrated on the economic benefits of free trade; and third, £20,000 handed out to Scottish politicians by the English ministers. No fewer than 530 pamphlets were published on both sides of the issue. "We do from our Hearts believe," wrote a group of Scottish merchants, "that this Union will bring Honor, Peace, Strength and Riches, to you as Men, and Moderation, Piety, Charity and Love amongst you as

Christians."[14] The result was clear by the end of 1705, when the Scottish Parliament suspended the Act of Security. The commissioners for union, hand-picked by the Queen, drew up an agreement in July 1706. It was passed without much debate by the English Parliament, with considerable reluctance by the Scottish one, and came into effect on May 1, 1707. The Anglo-Scottish Union included important economic enticements for Scotland: a lower land tax, exemption from certain other taxes for the duration of the war, and an "Equivalent" of almost £400,000, which would wipe out the debt from the Darien disaster. Interest groups that had supported the Union, like the salt manufacturers, also received lucrative favors. Whether the surrender of sovereignty was worth it is a question Scots have been asking themselves ever since.

This was an incorporating union, not a federal one, meaning that Scotland effectively disappeared as a self-governing entity. Technically, so did England: they were now the northern and southern parts of Great Britain. In fact, the English continued to think of themselves as the dominant partners, and to use "English" as if it meant "British." The Scots did maintain some differences: they kept their separate Presbyterian Kirk and their distinctive legal system. Their Parliament, however, was dissolved. They were entitled to send 45 Members from their counties and burghs (which voted in groups, except for Edinburgh) to join 513 English and Welsh Members in the House of Commons at Westminster. The Scottish peers, numbering about 150, would choose 16 representatives to sit in the House of Lords. As Scotland had about one-fifth of the population of the British Isles, this was a serious under-representation. It severely limited Scotland's impact on the British legislative process. However, Scotland in 1707 produced only one-fortieth of England's tax revenues. To the fiscally obsessed English ministers, the distribution of seats in Parliament seemed like a good deal for the Scots.

As will be seen in the next chapter, not all Scots accepted the Union. The '08 invasion scare was just a warning shot that presaged a volley of Scottish Jacobite uprisings and conspiracies over the next 40 years. Many Scots, however, *did* support the Union, because it brought them economic benefits and protection for the Presbyterian Kirk. As a result, the Jacobite uprisings were as much Scottish civil wars as they were Anglo-Scottish confrontations. Whatever one may think of it, the Union of 1707 created a powerful British nation state that would survive throughout the period covered by this book, and would only begin to fragment in the last decades of the twentieth century.

8

The Crisis of the Hanoverian Succession, 1710–1722

After 1710, the new British state was beset by a decade-long crisis that might have destroyed it. The crisis came in two stages. First, the Tory party took power and made peace. Some Tories considered a restoration of the Stuarts. Then, with the death of Queen Anne and the accession of George I, the Whigs returned to office. They clamped down on their enemies and drove many Tories into outright Jacobitism. A major rebellion, serious riots and numerous conspiracies shook the British state to its foundations. Adding to the crisis, the Whig ministers blundered into a major financial disaster. The whole system tottered, but it did not fall, which showed how strong the British state had become in only a few years. As the situation gradually settled down, one man came forward to claim the credit for saving the day: Sir Robert Walpole. He would be the kingpin in a more stable government that lasted for two decades.

Tory Resurgence, 1710–1715

Much of the blame for igniting the crisis of the Hanoverian succession can be placed on the arrogant Tory preacher Dr Henry Sacheverell. When he rose to harangue the lord mayor of London at St Paul's on November 5, 1709, he knew perfectly well that his sermon, "The Perils of False Brethren," would cause offense. In highly emotional tones, he condemned the Whigs, the Dissenters, "occasional conformity," and the present ministers. He drew a dire picture of a Church that was in mortal danger from heretics within its own ranks:

Her *Holy Communion* has been *Rent*, and *Divided by Factious, and Schismatical Impostors*; Her *Pure Doctrine* has been *Corrupted*, and *Defil'd*; … Her *Altars*, and *Sacraments Prostitut'd* to *Hypocrites, Deists, Socinians*, and *Atheists*; and this done, … not only by our *Profess'd Enemies*, but which is worse, by our *Pretended Friends*, and FALSE BRETHREN.[1]

Sacheverell also cast aspersions on the Whig doctrine of resistance, which he depicted as a threat to the monarchy. Most galling of all, he declined to mention King William III, on a day that was supposed to commemorate the Glorious Revolution.

Sacheverell uttered nothing that was overtly treasonable in his sermon. If he had, he could easily have been prosecuted for it before a judge and jury. Unsure of a conviction in a court of law, the angry Whigs impeached him instead, meaning that he would be prosecuted by the House of Commons and sentenced by the House of Lords, both of which had Whig majorities. Always a show-off, Sacheverell arrived for his trial in a glass coach, so that the crowd could see him. The managers of the trial planned it to be a showcase for defending the principle of resistance to tyranny, but they did not agree on what this meant. James Stanhope, the leading prosecutor, was willing to argue for John Locke's view, that all governments arose from contracts, and if a ruler violated the contract, he or she should be resisted. Most of the other Whigs timidly suggested that resistance was legal only in special circumstances. Sacheverell was also accused of maligning the Toleration Act, which he interpreted as an "indulgence" or exemption from penalties – exactly what its wording stipulated. One of his prosecutors conceded that "'tis true the word Toleration is not mentioned in that Act," but maintained that it was generally *understood* as granting a right to toleration.[2] The letter of the law was on Sacheverell's side; so was the London crowd. On the night of March 1, 1710, a mob stormed through central London, burning Dissenting chapels to cries of "High Church and Sacheverell!" The ministers, working late in the Whitehall office known as the Cockpit, were worried that their houses would be attacked next. The Queen ordered out the Horse and Foot Guards, who dispersed the crowds. The trial continued, under the shadow of popular violence. Sacheverell was convicted, but in an astounding decision, the House of Lords sentenced him only to a year's suspension from preaching. Effectively, this undermined the verdict and let him off with a slap on the wrist.

Queen Anne quickly responded. She hated the pompous windbag Sacheverell, but she had also come to despise her Whig ministers, and she wanted an end to the war. Soon after the trial, she began secretly to consult with Robert Harley. On his advice, she dismissed Godolphin, dissolved Parliament and called a general election. Buoyed by cries of "High Church and Sacheverell," the Tories won a smashing victory over the Whigs at the polls. Harley became the Queen's chief minister. In the process, he worsened his reputation for deviousness, although it may be wondered whether any politician who was not devious could have risen so high. Marlborough hung on as military commander until the end of 1711, but his fate was sealed. Although he had never been beaten in battle, Marlborough had failed to win the war. The destiny of Spain had already been decided, when General James Stanhope, the same man who had prosecuted Sacheverell, was defeated at Brihuega in December 1710.

Harley was not able to make peace at once. He had to fund one final year of campaigning in 1711, which meant diligent wooing of Tory financiers. The Whig bankers, angered by Godolphin's dismissal, threatened not to lend the government money, and fought off Harley's attempt to take control of the Bank of England. Harley created the South Sea Company as an alternative. In return for promises of future trade with the Spanish empire, the Company took over the interest payments on unfunded government debts, just as the Bank had under Whig ministries. Harley was able to finance a huge naval attempt on Quebec in the summer of 1711, with 69 ships and 11,000 men, but the fleet was wrecked by a storm in the Gulf of St Lawrence.

Secret peace negotiations had begun with France before the new government was even formed. The French tried hard to convince Harley to accept the Pretender as Anne's successor, which he agreed to consider if James would become a Protestant. Nobody knows how serious Harley was about this, but if James changed his religion, the main justification for the Act of Settlement would be removed, which might lead to its repeal by a Tory Parliament. All this turned out to be speculation. James refused to give up his Catholic faith, so Harley gave up on him, at least for the moment. The Stuart Prince may never have had a better chance of regaining his throne.

The preliminary peace negotiations with France were concluded in October 1711, but the Whigs still roared out "No Peace without Spain," meaning no end to the war if Philip V retained the Spanish empire. The Tory writer Jonathan Swift shot back at them in *The Conduct of the Allies*, a pamphlet that sold 11,000 copies in a month. It was better, Swift advised, "to accept such Terms as will secure our Trade … Rather than go on in a languishing way, upon the vain Expectation of some improbable Turn."[3] In order to overcome Whig resistance in the House of Lords, Harley, who had been made Earl of Oxford and Lord Treasurer, proposed a radical idea: the creation of 12 new Tory peers. In 1832 and 1911, governments would again threaten to "pack" the House of Lords, but the monarchs of later days balked at the consequences of devaluing a peerage. Only Queen Anne had the guts actually to do it. With Whig opposition in the Lords overcome, a peace conference opened at Utrecht in the United Provinces in January 1712. The British forces were ordered not to cooperate with the Allies in any new offensive. The restraining order looked like a betrayal to the Habsburg Emperor, whose army made one last unsuccessful attempt to advance on Paris. For Princess Sophia and her son, the Electoral Prince George of Hanover, heirs to the British throne by the Act of Settlement, the restraining order confirmed that the Tory ministers favored their Stuart rival.

In fact, the Treaty of Utrecht, signed in April 1713 after 15 months of negotiations, was not favorable to the Jacobites at all. It drove the Pretender out of France and obtained French recognition for the succession of the Hanoverian family. It also gave Britain trade concessions with Spain (known as the *asiento*) and recognized its possession of several territories: Newfoundland and Acadia (Nova Scotia) in North America, St Kitts in the Caribbean, Gibraltar and Minorca in the Mediterranean. The last two were strategic naval bases, and Newfoundland was the key to the rich cod fisheries of the Grand Banks. Overall, the Treaty of Utrecht was not a bad haul for Britain, especially compared to the Peace of Ryswick. Still, it did not alter the fact that Philip V remained King of Spain.

The Whigs denounced the Treaty as a disgrace, an opinion later echoed by many patriotic historians.

Harley had achieved his main goal, but it had taken a lot out of him. He had barely survived an assassination attempt in March 1711, when a French spy whom he was questioning pulled a knife from his clothes and stabbed him. Harley recovered within a couple of months, but his absence allowed the backbenchers in the Tory party to make their angry voices heard. Calling themselves the October Club after the month of the Tory electoral victory in 1710, they were committed to the "Country" principles that Harley himself had championed in the 1690s. They wanted to investigate government corruption, especially anything that embarrassed Marlborough; to put a Commons committee in charge of public accounts; and to promote the landed interest against the "moneyed men" who ran the Bank and the big companies. As High Churchmen, the October Club also dreamed of stamping out occasional conformity, and passed an Act to that effect in 1712. To irk the Presbyterians further, toleration was granted to the Scots Episcopalians. As Tories, the October Club longed to root out Whigs from every nook and cranny of government. Harley – or Oxford, as we should now call him – opposed these calls for revenge. He particularly resented it when some of the October Club actually joined the Whigs to defeat the commercial clauses of the Treaty of Utrecht, which would have opened up trade with France. By then, the October Club was splitting up into Hanoverian and Jacobite factions, as the issue of the succession loomed larger.

Although the elections of 1713 produced an even stronger Tory majority, the choice between Hanover and Stuart was badly straining party unity. Jacobite Tories, many of them Scots, hinted at a Stuart restoration and dissolution of the Union, a prospect that terrified their "whimsical" or Hanoverian Tory colleagues. Jacobite demonstrations were openly held in Edinburgh on the Pretender's birthday. The Whigs took advantage of the dissension among their enemies by proposing to invite George of Hanover's son to take up a seat in the House of Lords, and by supporting Parliamentary motions, which were narrowly defeated, that the Hanoverian Succession was in danger.

They were right: it was. The Northern Secretary of State, Henry St John, Viscount Bolingbroke, who sought to succeed Oxford as chief minister, was egging on the Jacobites, and corresponding secretly with James III. Strangely enough for a man who aspired to lead a High Church party, Bolingbroke was privately a libertine, who enjoyed drinking, swearing, and sex with prostitutes. Publicly, he made himself the darling of the pious Churchmen. A brilliant intellectual, yet inherently unreliable, Bolingbroke entranced the backbench Tories with visions of purging every last Whig from public office. He encouraged the backbenchers to pass the notorious Schism Act in 1714, which outlawed Dissenting schools. As for his colleague Robert Harley, Earl of Oxford, the prospect of choosing between Hanover and Stuart threw him into depression, worsened by rheumatism, gout, and the death of his favorite daughter. At first, the Queen sympathized, urging him to "lay everything open and hide nothing from me," and addressing him as "your very affectionate friend."[4] When he showed up drunk at cabinet meetings, however, the

Queen was disgusted. It was a sad ending to a productive career. Harley possessed characteristics unusual for a politician of his age: he was personally modest, he did not favor revenge or persecution, and he did not steal the public's money. Yet his double-dealing would be more remembered than his virtues.

Anne finally dismissed Oxford at the end of July 1714, but she did not name Bolingbroke as his successor. She mistrusted the Secretary, with good reason, as he was still fishing in the Jacobite pond. It was Anne's last intervention in politics. Two days later, the Queen fell sick. Her Privy Council met, and selected not Bolingbroke but a moderate Whig to take up Oxford's position as Lord Treasurer. On August 1, Queen Anne expired. London Dissenters rejoiced at her passing, while in Glasgow, Presbyterians attacked Episcopalian chapels. As Sophia of Hanover had recently died, the Regency Council proclaimed her son George as King. "The Earl of Oxford was removed on Tuesday, the Queen died on Sunday," Bolingbroke wrote to his friend, the writer Jonathan Swift. "What a world is this! And how does fortune banter us!"[5]

Fortune was not yet done with bantering Bolingbroke. He was dismissed from office even before George I arrived in England. The remaining Tory ministers knew that the King would not keep them long in power. Indeed, George was convinced that they were Jacobites to a man, and he wanted none of them in his new administration. General Stanhope took Bolingbroke's place as Northern Secretary of State, and the surviving members of the Junto received positions. In the counties, the government began to replace Tory local officeholders with Whigs, as it prepared for a general election.

The Tory party seemed finished. Many, including Bolingbroke, thought it was. What kept it alive was the popular support that Sacheverell had first tapped. Afraid of another war and mistrustful of the Whigs, the people reacted. On George I's coronation day in October 1714, Whigs gathered in towns throughout Britain to celebrate with triumphant bonfires, where effigies of Sacheverell and the Pretender were to be burned. The bonfires were attacked by Tory rioters who beat up the party-goers and rescued the effigies. It was the first sign of trouble for the Hanoverian King. When general elections were held in January 1715, a Tory manifesto was widely distributed throughout the country. Written anonymously by Bishop Francis Atterbury, it warned voters of "the Arbitrary Government of a Junto, that cannot bear to be controll'd even by the Regal Power," and of a King who "knows but little of our Constitution." It accused the Whigs of wanting another war, more troops to suppress mobs, the repeal of the Triennial Act, and an end to freedom of speech – in short, "an entire and thorough Revolution" in favor of despotic power.[6] The Tories, by contrast, were presented as the party of liberty, just as the Whigs had been in 1688. This reversal of rhetoric reflected a "Country" Tory mentality that saw the Whigs as corrupt, manipulative tyrants.

Atterbury's pamphlet rallied Tory support at the polls, but as in every general election in this period, the party favored by the King won a majority of seats. The Whigs were back in the saddle, determined to take revenge on their Tory adversaries. How far would they go? How would the Tories react?

Illustration 6 *Rioters supporting Dr Sacheverell and the Tories pull down a Presbyterian meeting house in London, March 1710. The wooden parts of the building are being burned in the background. The man in costume with AR (for Anna Regina or Queen Anne) on his back is a royal servant who took part in the riot. ("Dr Burgisses Theater," 1710. © The Trustees of the British Museum)*

Whig Vengeance, 1715–22

George I has a bad historical reputation that is not fully deserved. He was an intelligent and sophisticated man, interested in the ideas of philosophers and scientists. As he could not speak English, he communicated with his ministers in French and Latin. He was wise enough to leave most of the governing to them. Raised a Lutheran, he was generally indifferent to religion, and interfered little with the Church of England, of which he became the head. Yet George's poor image is also understandable. Unlike William III, he did not seek conciliation with his adversaries. He could be authoritarian and vindictive. Years before 1714, on learning that his wife had a lover, he had the man murdered and locked up his spouse for the rest of her life. His son, not unnaturally, hated him. George was unfairly pilloried for having fat German mistresses, and for keeping two Turkish servants with him at all times. The King was himself heavy, so the size of his mistresses was not disproportionate. As for the two Turks, it seems poignant rather than contemptible that, apart from a few Hanoverian advisors, they were the only human beings George could trust in his early years as King.

Whigs and Scots Presbyterians saw George I as another William of Orange, a Protestant hero-king who had saved the nation from Catholicism. "Their Popish Dragon now must lose his Sting," wrote a poet early in George's reign, "Because St George our Champion is, and King."[7] Unfortunately, a large number of George's Tory and Scottish Episcopalian subjects (not to mention Catholics) rejected him, almost from the first. Their dislike was registered in dozens of popular Jacobite songs and poems, like this ferocious one in which poor George was compared to the worst of Roman Emperors:

> Oh Free born Britons, since a Tyrant reigns,
> Assert your Liberty, shake off your Chains.
> Let us in justice rival antient Rome,
> Let Nero's vices meet with Nero's doom,
> And then call James your King from exile home.[8]

Britons might not have been so happy if James Stuart had actually been called home from exile, but some of them clearly were no more delighted with the prospect of keeping a Hanoverian on the throne.

The riotous fighting on George's coronation day was an insult suffered by no other monarch in British history. In the spring and summer of 1715, fresh riots broke out in London, the West Midlands, and Lancashire. As in the "night of fire" during Sacheverell's trial, the rioters sacked and burned Dissenting chapels, especially around the metal-working town of Birmingham and the textile center of Manchester. The government responded with the Riot Act. It imposed the death penalty on members of crowds who refused to disperse after a magistrate read out parts of the statute. "Reading the Riot Act" is an expression still used today. The riots fizzled out, but a rebellion was brewing. It was encouraged by Viscount Bolingbroke, who fled to France in March, just before he was impeached, and became the Pretender's chief advisor.

The Earl of Mar raised the rebellion at Braemar in the Highlands on September 15. Catholic and Episcopalian chiefs rallied to him, and he inspired them to fight with speeches about "the miserie and slaverie of our countrie ... being under a forreigne yoak."[9] By "our countrie," he meant Scotland. This was from the first a Scots nationalist as well as a Jacobite rising. It was also a Scottish civil war, with vigilante groups of Presbyterian "associators" fighting small Jacobite rebel forces throughout the Lowlands, and Hanoverian clans scrapping with Jacobite clans in the Highlands. The main Jacobite army, advancing from Perth towards Stirling with about 10,000 men, ran into the Duke of Argyll, commanding 3700 Hanoverian troops, on open ground at Sherrifmuir. The two armies fought to a standstill, taking heavy casualties, but the exhausted Jacobite troops refused Mar's order to advance again, forcing a withdrawal. Edinburgh was saved for King George. The arrival of King James in December gave some heart to the Jacobites, but he brought no French troops with him, and his army gradually frittered away in the course of a winter retreat. James himself soon fled back to France, with Mar in tow.

Would the Tory leaders in England have joined their Scottish colleagues in rebellion? We cannot really know, as they were mostly arrested at the end of September, before a planned uprising was to take place. When the moment came, a small army of mounted Catholic landowners in the north of England, supported by a few of their Protestant neighbors, rode out to support the exiled King. Joined by a substantial contingent of Lowland Scots, they marched to Preston in Lancashire, where they were attacked and surrendered after a fierce fight.

The rebels who were taken and imprisoned in Scotland were treated leniently. Only one was executed, and all the rest were eventually released. The rebels tried in England, however, were dealt with more harshly. Forty to fifty men, including two noblemen and a Church of England clergyman, were put to death, while about 640 others were transported to the colonies, to labor for seven years. The Jacobites were not discouraged. In 1716, they raised money to pay a Swedish army to invade Britain, hoping that a Protestant invader might be better received than the Catholic French. When that plot was discovered, they began to negotiate with Spain, which in 1719 was engaged in a brief conflict with Britain. The outcome of this conspiracy was another Jacobite rising in the Highlands, supported by a tiny Spanish force and joined by the famous Rob Roy MacGregor. They met defeat on the slopes of Glenshiel. None of the Jacobite plots after 1715 had a reasonable chance of success, but along with frequent Jacobite riots and the publication of Jacobite poems, pamphlets, and newspapers, the government was constantly preoccupied with the threat of sedition.

Faced with this persistent menace, the Whigs metamorphosed from a party of revolution to a party of order. The change had been developing since the 1690s, but it was fully accomplished under George I. The Triennial Act was repealed in 1716, and replaced with a Septennial Act, setting the maximum life of a Parliament at seven rather than three years. Clearly, the Whigs did not soon want to face another general contest. The effect on politics was immediate: fewer elections meant fewer occasions for popular involvement. *Habeas corpus*, the right to a swift trial, was suspended in 1715–16, and its further suspension in response to Jacobite scares became a bad habit for the government. The Riot Act was the first in a series of repressive legal measures that culminated in the notorious Black Act of 1723. A reaction to reports of organized gangs of deer stealers in the English forests, who may have had connections to Jacobitism, the Black Act made deer-poaching, cutting down young trees, breaking fishponds, or lurking in the woods with one's face painted black into offenses punishable by death.

On religious issues, however, the Whig administration remained a champion of liberty. The chief minister, James Stanhope, created Earl Stanhope in 1718, was committed to religious toleration, and he made sure that all the recent Tory legislation aimed against Dissenters – especially the Occasional Conformity Act and the Schism Act – was repealed. Dissenters who were elected to local office could be released from penalties if nobody sued them within six months. These measures, of course, were not just altruistic; they also strengthened the Whig party. Meanwhile, the Whig Bishop of Bangor, William Hoadly, outraged Tory clergymen by defending Dissenters and denying that the Church had any authority to punish unorthodox opinions. Scores of angry replies flew back at him in what became known as the Bangorian Controversy. The ministry stood by Hoadly. The lower house of Convocation, the Anglican Church assembly, which was full of High Churchmen, censured the Bishop, after which it was prorogued by the King, and not summoned again until the nineteenth century.

Stanhope and his colleague the Earl of Sunderland, who had become First Lord of the Treasury, planned to cap their legislative program with the Peerage Bill of 1719, which would have cemented Whig control of the House of Lords by forbidding any future monarch from creating new peerages. This extraordinary piece of proposed legislation was a direct insult to the Prince of Wales, the heir to the throne, who was then engaged in an embarrassing family feud with his father. At one point in their spat, the King actually had his son put under house arrest. The Peerage Bill, however, alarmed many country gentlemen in the House of Commons, who hoped that their families might some day be raised to the nobility. After a furious debate, the Bill was defeated by a combined opposition of Tories and opposition Whigs. The leaders of the opposition Whigs were Robert Walpole, a Norfolk gentleman who had served in Queen Anne's administrations, and his brother-in-law, Charles, Viscount Townshend. Both had been recently turned out of office, for which they blamed Sunderland. They had allied themselves with the Prince of Wales, and had angrily denounced the pointless war of 1719 with Spain.

After the debacle of the Peerage Bill, Walpole and Townshend were brought back into government, and the Whig party was, for the moment, reunited. Within a year, however, the ministry was almost ruined by the financial disaster that has been called the South Sea Bubble. Harley had created the South Sea Company to trade with the Spanish colonies, and to help fund the national debt. By 1720, the debt stood at around £50,000,000, which may seem unbelievable as the nation had not been involved in a major war for six years. The war debt had never been fully paid off. In addition, the constant Jacobite threat, and the cost of maintaining the fleet, meant that military expenditures had continued into peacetime. How could the debt be restructured so as to allow the government to borrow more money? Sunderland came up with an elegant solution: convert £31,000,000 of existing debt into South Sea stock. The government's creditors held annuities, on which they were paid 8 percent or more in interest every year. If those annuities were converted into stock certificates, or "privatized," then the investors could profit from the rise in the value of the stock, and the interest could be reduced to an annual dividend of 5 percent. The South Sea Company also stood to gain from a rise in the value of its stock, because it could sell stock to new investors at the current market value rather than the initial or "par" value. For its part, the government would receive a further £7,500,000 loan from the Company at the time of conversion. Of course, all these wonderful results depended on a rise in the value of Company stock.

Like an expanding water bubble, the price of South Sea Company stock rose and rose. At the beginning of 1720, the value of £100 of South Sea stock stood at £130. By July, it had risen to over £1000. Almost everybody who had money to spare imagined that investing in the scheme would make them rich. The government fuelled the stock-buying mania by issuing false claims about the potential profitability of the Company's trade, and by handing out South Sea stock as bribes to various well placed people, including the King's mistress. Then the bubble burst. By October, the value of £100 of stock had dropped to under £300. Fortunes were lost, and some investors committed suicide. James Stanhope became so overwrought during a speech defending himself from charges of fraud in the House of Lords that he burst a blood vessel and expired. The Chancellor of the Exchequer died mysteriously, probably by his own hand. The authors of "Cato's Letters," an opposition Whig newspaper column, cried out for vengeance: they hoped the hangman would soon "have the fingering of the throats of those traitors, who have fingered all the money in the nation."[10] They were disappointed. Sir Robert Walpole came forward not to punish his ministerial colleagues, but to protect or "screen" them from charges. He earned his nickname of "Screen-Master General" after he arranged for Sunderland's acquittal in March 1721, which was broadminded of him because Sunderland was his mortal enemy. In the same month, as a fitting reward, Walpole became Chancellor of the Exchequer and First Lord of the Treasury. He now held both the chief financial offices, and was the leading man in the ministry.

Walpole was still not trusted by the King, and he had to share power with the conniving Sunderland. The Jacobites solved the first problem for him; death solved the second. By 1720, the Jacobites were desperate for a restoration. The strongest voice among them was Bishop Atterbury, a veteran of the High Church struggles of Queen Anne's reign. In 1720–2, Atterbury was at the center of a confusing muddle of Jacobite plots, including one that involved an English insurrection and another that included an invasion by Irish troops in the Spanish army. The Earl of Sunderland, hoping to undermine Walpole, slyly promised to assist the Jacobites, although he was probably deceiving them. Atterbury, however, called off all plans for a rising just before the general elections of March 1722, because he feared the Tories were not ready. During the elections, Sunderland died suddenly of pleurisy, leaving Walpole in control but still on poor terms with King George. In August, Bishop Atterbury was suddenly arrested and imprisoned in the Tower of London on a charge of high treason. *Habeas corpus* was suspended again, and troops were stationed in the center of London. All the Bishop's possessions, including his toilet paper, were diligently searched, but no firm evidence could be found against him. As Walpole could not impeach Atterbury, he proposed instead a bill of pains and penalties that would exile him. Passage of the bill hinged on absurd scraps of evidence, such as whether the Bishop had received a little spotted dog named Harlequin as a gift from the Pretender. Spotted dog or no spotted dog, the bill passed, and the Bishop was sent into exile.

The Jacobites were left leaderless and rudderless. King George was delighted. Walpole was his man, from then until the day the King died. What nobody knew was that Walpole would remain the chief minister for two decades. His ministry established stability at home, and peace abroad, so that the British state, which had come so close to ruin, would be preserved, virtually intact, for the next century.

The Lineaments of Leviathan

In 1651, the philosopher Thomas Hobbes published a famous political treatise named *Leviathan*, in which he imagined a state that was composed of individuals who came together to protect their persons from harm by forming a single, unitary political body. He compared this body to the great sea-monster, Leviathan, mentioned in the Bible. Once they had agreed to form the sovereign body, individuals could not legitimately resist it, "because every Subject is by this Institution Author of all the Actions, and Judgments of the Soveraigne Instituted; it follows, that whatsoever he [the Sovereign] doth, it can be no injury to any of his Subjects; nor ought he to be by any of them accused of Injustice."[11] John Locke, writing in the 1680s, proposed a different view of the state. He argued that individuals formed social bonds and created property through their labor before they needed to create a government: "The great and *chief end*, therefore, of Mens uniting into Commonwealths, and putting themselves under Governments, *is the Preservation of their Property*." In exchange, individuals gave up some of their liberty, but not all of it, because "the Power of the Society, or *Legislative* constituted by them, *can never be suppos'd to extend farther than the common good*."[12] The original compact became null and void, and resistance was justified, if the government violated its terms.

Was the British state as it developed after 1689 more like Hobbes's Leviathan or Locke's contractual government? Virtually nobody approved of Hobbes in this period, while Locke was widely admired by Whigs, so it would seem obvious that Locke rather than Hobbes was the standard-bearer of the British state. Yet in several respects, the state as it was established in Britain by the 1720s resembled Hobbes's conception. First, it had a much broader social and economic impact than Locke wanted the state to have. Second, while criticism of the state was allowed, outright resistance to it was not. Nobody could claim a constitutional right to deny the legitimacy of the regime. A teenaged printer was put to death by hanging, drawing, and quartering in 1719 because he had worked on a pamphlet that called on the people to resist George I.

This does not mean that those who constructed the British state were hypocrites. They were simply building on the foundation of the Stuart monarchy, which put in place the groundwork of the state in the late seventeenth century, through increased spending and taxation, early financial experiments, the organization of the Navy, and attempts at religious toleration. The Stuart monarchy aimed to be strong, although in practice it was often weak. The politicians who guided the state after 1689 inherited this Stuart legacy. They added to it by uniting Britain, setting up a relatively secure fiscal system, and working out a viable toleration. They sacrificed the authoritarian rhetoric of the late Stuarts, although they turned to repressive measures at moments when they needed them. They did not write up a constitution conferring rights on individuals; nor did they formally bring any new social groups into the political process.

How significant was the British state in the early eighteenth century? Its size fluctuated, reaching a peak in wartime. During the War of the Spanish Succession, Britain kept employed about 40,000 sailors and 92,000 soldiers to fight its French enemies. By 1715, however, these numbers had been reduced to about 13,000 men in the Royal Navy and 19,000 in the army. George I used his army to control Ireland and the Scottish Highlands, as well as to intimidate Jacobites in the Scottish Lowlands and England. He employed about 6,000 additional Dutch troops to maintain order in Scotland during the 1715 rebellion. Soldiers made a considerable social impression, wherever they were. They drank, frequented prostitutes, eavesdropped on conversations, and got into fights with local people. The troops had to be supplied with arms, uniforms, food, and beer, which meant lucrative contracts for munitions and textile manufacturers, food provisioners, and brewers who had connections with the government.

The Royal Navy maintained its fighting strength even after the Treaty of Utrecht. In 1715, naval vessels weighed in at a total of 168,000 displaced tons, only slightly below their wartime peak. This was a formidable force, twice the size of the Dutch navy and about 60 percent larger than the French. The navy was to prove its worth repeatedly in the next 100 years. It could be used at any time, as in 1718 when it sunk a Spanish fleet at Cape Passaro off Sicily, before war was even declared. In war or peace, the sailors had to be fed, on huge helpings of meat, bread, and, of course, beer – no less than 60,000 hogsheads in 1703. Keeping the navy fighting-fit also required constant building and repairs, which in turn meant hiring a permanent workforce and negotiating with contractors. The naval dockyards at Deptford, Sheerness, Chatham, Portsmouth, Plymouth, and other towns employed 5800 workers in 1712. As the navy did not shrink in peacetime, the number of workers who were required to service it remained high. In the 1740s, 2000 men were working in the Portsmouth dockyards alone. The dockyards also required specialized parts like masts, wood planks, canvas sails, ropes, and iron fittings, which were obtained from private contractors, like the Crowley ironworks in Durham.

By comparison with the size of the army or the navy, the number of state-employed bureaucrats who collected and administered revenues was not very large, but it increased during the wars against France, and did not decrease for the next 30 years. About 2000 fiscal bureaucrats worked for James II. During the War of the Spanish Succession, with the addition of excise taxes and increases in customs duties, this number had grown to almost 4800. Astonishingly, there were *more* revenue collectors in Britain *after* the end of the war – almost 6000 in 1716, and close to 6500 in 1726. This was partly because the national debt continued to grow, partly because Whigs were trying to reward their supporters on the local level by giving them minor offices. The number of employees in the excise alone grew from 1200 in 1690 to almost 3500 in 1726. The excisemen were particularly resented, since at any time they could enter premises where goods were stored, to carry out searches. Excise taxes fell on a variety of common consumer items: beer, coal, salt, soap, leather. The tax had to be paid where these items were produced or imported, and before they were sold. The excise service was considered to be particularly efficient, honest, and well organized, qualities that were not generally admired by merchants and shopkeepers.

By contrast, the customs service was a ramshackle institution that depended on local officers who usually had connections with maritime trade. Some of them were notoriously corrupt. Customs duties were leveled on goods entering through British ports. Most of the duties were small, although some were high enough to discourage legal trade, like the tax on French wines and spirits. In 1698, the government had appointed Riding Officers, who rode along the coasts looking for smugglers. As there was no armed coastguard to support them, the Riding Officers were backed up by units of the army. This did not prevent smuggling, which occurred on a spectacular scale. In 1700, it was estimated that 150,000 packs of wool were smuggled out of Kent and Sussex alone. Almost 30 years later, a customs collector guessed that about 180,000 gallons of brandy was imported illegally every year along the east coast of England. Clearly, the British state had its limits: it could not control every taxable aspect of an expanding economy. Yet it did not give up trying.

The British were not a lightly taxed people. In the 1670s, the percentage of English national income that was claimed by the government in taxes amounted to about 3.5 percent. It was considerably lower in Scotland, at least before the Union. By 1714, taxation had reached over 9 percent of British national income. The French paid a lot less to King Louis XIV – by one estimate, only about half of what the British coughed up to their government. In addition, French taxes varied considerably between provinces and social groups. In Britain, Parliament was the only body that could levy a tax, and it did so for the entire nation – for the English, Scots, and Welsh of all social ranks. Louis XIV never enjoyed this sort of power. On the other hand, his tax collectors had armed paramilitary police at their disposal, while in Britain there was no such force, other than the army.

Relative to other European nations, British government was strikingly centralized, without intermediary bodies such as the local assemblies that existed in almost every other European state. The last regional governing body in the kingdom, the moribund Council of Wales, was abolished in 1689, and of course the Scottish Parliament went the same way after union in 1707, leaving only minor local survivals like the assemblies of the Isle of Man or the Channel Islands. The counties of Britain were administered by lord lieutenants, appointed by the central government. They drew up the commissions of the peace, containing the

Could Wisdom, Learning, Piety, & all
The gifts if Crowns to their afsistance call
Protect the Worthy in an impious Age,
From party Spleen & vile Fanatick Rage,

Then some if are Confin'd had been rever'd
And this unhappy Scene had ne'er appear'd,
But now! you may behold a second Laud,
Whose Christian Courage nothing fears but
                                        God.

Illustration 7 *A Tory print showing Bishop Atterbury in prison. He holds up a picture of Archbishop Laud, the advisor of King Charles I, who was put to death by Parliament in 1645. The print suggests that Atterbury may share Laud's unjust fate. (Anonymous engraving of Bishop Atterbury, 1723. © Ashmolean Museum, University of Oxford)*

names of justices of the peace (JPs) who presided over sessions courts. By the late seventeenth century, the central government was taking more and more interest in the naming of JPs. Each party, Whig and Tory, appointed JPs who were favorable to it. This meant that after 1714, the vast majority of the officers of local government were Whigs, although a few Tories were kept as JPs in areas where this was considered expedient.

It should be remembered that the British state did not exist in order to provide services to its people. The poor and unemployed, the old and the sick, were cared for by charity, or by a rate levied on property within each parish that was administered by local officers. The latter was a remarkable system, almost unique in Europe. The central government, however, did nothing for the indigent. Neither did it build roads and bridges, fund schools and universities, or give grants to the arts. All of that was done by local authorities, or by private initiatives. The purposes of the British state were minimal: basically, it existed to keep order and to protect the nation. In one of his first proclamations, George I announced that his overriding goal was to preserve property, just as Locke had recommended. "The good Effects of making Property secure are no where so clearly seen, and to so great a degree, as in this happy Kingdom," stated the King (or rather, his ministers, who wrote these words), "And I assure you there is not any among you shall more Earnestly endeavour the Preservation of it than Myself."[13] By 1714, however, the King's government also upheld Protestantism, maintained trade and suppressed crime, all of which fell within the domains of order and protection. By the mid-eighteenth century, the state would concern itself directly with stimulating the economy and expanding the empire. This went well beyond what John Locke had foreseen, but it does not mean that his ideas had become irrelevant. For its supporters, down to the 1830s, the British state *was* Lockean, because it embodied a benign, tolerant contractualism. However, to its opponents at home, and to those whom it dominated overseas, it sometimes wore the grim, controlling visage of Leviathan.

9

Art, Science, and Politics

The Glorious Revolution brought about a change that was more than political. It was also a cultural watershed. In two important ways, British culture changed after 1688. First, the patronage of the court became less central, so that artists had to look to patrons beyond the court, even to the general public. Second, political conflict created a broad public interest in works that related to current events. Not all of the literature of the period was politically inspired, but it tended to raise topical issues and was often deliberately controversial. At the same time, writers felt a great strain between the need to connect with current events and the belief that literature should relate to eternal questions of human existence. Literature benefited from this tension, and the period produced a number of writers whose works are still read and admired today. For various reasons, painting and music were less ready to adapt to the altered cultural scene, although portraiture flourished and opera had a brief period of glory. Strangely, the sciences also seem to have ossified in the post-Revolutionary milieu. This chapter attempts to explain a complicated, contradictory, and fluid cultural situation.

The New Augustans

The period after 1688 is sometimes called the "Augustan age" of English literature, by scholars who believe it was as great a period as the age of Augustus in Rome. Theater, poetry, and essay writing flourished, and the English novel was born. However, there was no figure in contemporary England who played the role of Augustus in encouraging and employing artists. King William and Queen Mary were certainly interested in the arts, but their patronage was much more limited than that of Charles I or Charles II. This was probably because they did not wish to appear extravagant in the eyes of their subjects. Queen Anne tried to be more like her ancestors in encouraging the arts, but she too was constrained by lack of money, and she does not seem to have had much interest in literature.

George I preferred to go to the public theaters, where he sat in a special royal box, rather than to have performances put on at his court. He did not speak English, so his name does not often appear in the dedications of literary works. He was not an uncultured boor, as historians used to suggest, but like his predecessors, in artistic terms, he was not much of an Augustus either.

In the early seventeenth century, most prominent writers had important connections at the royal court. By the early eighteenth century, almost none of them did. As a result, they had to turn to individual aristocratic patrons or to the general public if they wanted to make a living. Most of them chose to do both, dedicating their works to members of the nobility who would pay them a sum of money in return, but marketing them as broadly as was possible. Later in the eighteenth century, as aristocratic patronage began to dry up, writers began to use lists of subscribers to fund their works. Each subscriber contributed a limited sum of money to the publication. The first major work published by subscription, John Dryden's translations of the Roman poet Virgil, made £1200 for the author, but this level of profit was rare.

Authors usually sold their manuscripts to a publisher, who thereafter effectively owned the work outright. Most manuscripts were purchased for very small sums – in the early eighteenth century, it was estimated that the average novel cost the publisher less than half a guinea, or 10 shillings and six pence. A few well known authors could make good money from a single piece of writing: Jonathan Swift, for example, was paid £200 for the manuscript of *Gulliver's Travels* in 1726. Most, however, had to keep writing short works – poems, newspaper articles, pamphlets – at a furious pace in order to stay alive. The hack-writers of the back streets of London became known collectively as "Grub Street" from the area near St Paul's Cathedral where they congregated. As for the publishers, they too were overwhelmingly concentrated in London, although more and more booksellers were appearing in provincial towns. The average number of copies of books printed in the early eighteenth century was about 750, from which the publishers stood to make a small profit. However, they owned the rights to books over a long period of time, and could profit from further editions without paying anything more to the author. The Copyright Act of 1710 limited ownership (or copyright) to 14 years for a new work, 21 for works already in print, but this poorly written legislation did not resolve the problem of ownership. Publishers continued to claim perpetual rights until the 1770s. Pirated editions of popular works were very common, and were often published in Dublin, where it was difficult for the London publishers to sue.

In short, writing was becoming a business. It thrived because the audience for literature was growing, although its growth should not be exaggerated. Writers in the mid-eighteenth century still addressed their readers as if they were all landed gentlemen. In fact, many readers were from the middling sort of people in the towns, and quite a few were women. Specialized periodicals for women began to appear in the early eighteenth century, and they comprised a large segment of the readership for the fictional romance stories that appeared in considerable numbers in the late seventeenth century. Many of the writers of romance stories, like

Aphra Behn or Mary Delarivier Manley, were women. When the novel emerged in the early eighteenth century, it was heavily influenced by these amorous romances, and the writers of novels took it for granted that many of their readers would be female. This period also saw the appearance of a proto-feminist literature in the writings of Mary Astell. A Tory, Astell accepted that marriage was an unequal contract, but borrowed Whig arguments, or "modern Deduction" as she called it, to make a case against abusive husbands. She urged men to behave towards women "Not as an absolute Lord and Master, with an Arbitrary and Tyrannical sway, but as Reason Governs and Conducts a Man, by proposing what is Just and Fit."[1] She herself never married, and favored Protestant convents where women could retreat to study in isolation from men. She found an audience among female readers, and her works went through several editions. The rate of literacy for upper and middling class women was certainly increasing, although it is difficult to measure with precision.

Books were not cheap, and they were treated as prized commodities. They were consumed carefully and at leisure by individual readers. Richer folk bought books that were unbound, then had them put into expensive leather bindings, with ownership plates showing the family crest. Middling people purchased smaller, cheaper editions, keeping them unbound or in standardized covers. Lower class men and women who were literate could afford to buy chapbooks, little story booklets bound together with string, or poems printed on broadsheets, that is, large single pieces of paper. Although the expiration of the Licensing Act in 1695 allowed publishers much more freedom in what they could publish, censorship did not disappear, especially for treasonable, blasphemous, or pornographic works. Neither did the tastes of readers change very much after 1695. Throughout the late seventeenth and eighteenth centuries, the single largest category of books published in England was works of religion or divinity. They consistently accounted for about a third of all books in print. By the first decade of the eighteenth century, under the impact of the Tory "Church in danger" campaign, over 40 percent of new books were religious. The second biggest category was history, then law, mathematics (including guides to keeping business accounts), classics, and poetry. The hottest selling new type of printed matter, of course, was newspapers, which really took off after 1695. The number of newspapers sold in England reached 7.3 million in 1750, by which time many provincial towns had their own journals. Unlike books, the news might be read out loud to groups of listeners in coffeehouses.

Printed plays also sold very well. London had only two theaters in the late seventeenth century, in Drury Lane and Lincoln's Inn Fields, but the period is known for the brilliance of its plays. In part, this was because of numerous innovations that made the theater more exciting. Fantastic scenery and wild special effects were introduced, and women were allowed to act on the stage, instead of having their parts taken by young boys. The theater was expensive, and audiences consisted mainly of the nobility and gentry, with a sprinkling of merchants and wealthy professionals. They usually brought their servants with them, so there were always lower class members of the audience, but ordinary people would have preferred to go to the theatrical booths at Bartholomew Fair, where they could see puppet plays and bawdy comedies. Outside London, theaters were not very common, in part because they were expensive, in part because of religious objections from those who saw them as ungodly. Such views were not limited to Puritans; they were shared by the Nonjuring Jacobite Jeremy Collier, who wrote scathing attacks on the immorality of the stage in the 1690s. He railed against the "*Liberties*" taken by playwrights, including "Their *Smuttiness of Expression*; Their *Swearing*, *Profainness*, and *Lewd Application of Scripture*; Their *Abuse* of the *Clergy*; Their *making* their *Top Characters Libertines*, and giving them *Success* in their *Debauchery*."[2] In spite of Collier's criticisms, a new theater was opened in the Haymarket in London in 1705, built by the architect and writer John Vanbrugh.

No writer of the time could escape politics. The most celebrated and financially successful poet of the late seventeenth century was John Dryden, whose fame had been established at the Restoration court. His poem *Absalom and Achitophel* (1681) offered a biblical parallel to the struggle between Charles II and Whigs in the Exclusion Crisis. Dryden became a Roman Catholic under James II, and remained loyal to the exiled Stuarts after the Glorious Revolution, although he declined to live at their court. Instead, he stayed in London and wrote successful plays. In a poem of 1699, Dryden claimed that he longed only for peace and quiet:

> How bless'd is he who leads a country life,
> Unvex'd with anxious cares, and void of strife!
> Who studying peace and shunning civil rage
> Enjoy'd his youth and now enjoys his age.[3]

We can wonder whether retirement to the country was his true desire. Dryden was so admired when he died in 1700 that the Kit-Kat Club paid for his funeral, although they were Whigs and he was a known Jacobite.

In many ways, the early eighteenth-century successor to Dryden was Alexander Pope. He too was a Roman Catholic, a Tory, and an associate of dangerous people like Bishop Atterbury, but he was never involved directly in Jacobite plots. He kept a circle of Whig friends, among them the Earl of Burlington, who protected and supported him. Like Dryden, Pope wanted to imitate classical authors, and he was famous for translating Homer. His amusing "Heroi-Comical Poem" *The Rape of the Lock* (1712–17), in which the hair of the fair Belinda, a beautiful court lady, is cut off by a male admirer ("Oh hadst thou, Cruel! Been content to seize, / Hairs less in sight, or any Hairs but these!") contains deeply hidden political allusions which critics are still unraveling.[4] Pope himself would probably have preferred to be remembered for his philosophical poem *An Essay on Man* (1733), which is known today for the lines "Know then thyself, presume not God to scan; / The proper study of Mankind is Man." The *Essay* argued that self-interest was the foundation of social life, and proposed resigned acceptance of a divinely created Nature: "WHATEVER IS, IS RIGHT."[5] Although not overtly political, it bore a dedication to Viscount Bolingbroke, who was then leading the opposition to the Whig government. Pope despised Sir Robert Walpole, who had questioned him in 1722 during the Atterbury Plot. In a political sense, Pope did not really believe that whatever was, was right.

The other great Tory writer of the early eighteenth century was Jonathan Swift. Originally a Whig, Swift did not receive the patronage that he felt he deserved from the Junto, and switched to the Tories. As a clergyman of the Church of Ireland, he may also have found Toryism more congenial to his non-literary occupation. He published in 1704 a hilariously confusing (and today almost unreadable) satire in prose, entitled *A Tale of A Tub*, which is, among many other things, an attack on the Dissenters. With Pope, Bolingbroke, John Gay, and other Tory writers, he formed the Scriblerus Club, a convivial society that maintained ties with both the literary and political spheres. Swift was close to Robert Harley, the first politician to orchestrate a government publicity campaign. Sadly for him, however, Swift received few rewards for his attacks on the Whigs. He was named Dean of St Patrick's Cathedral, Dublin, where he returned to live "like a rat in a hole" when the Whigs returned to power in 1714. In the bitterness of political exile, Swift wrote *Gulliver's Travels* (1726), the work for which he is best known. Like Swift's friend Bolingbroke, Lemuel Gulliver encounters party conflict in the miniature kingdom of Lilliput. Accused of high treason, he flees to neighboring Blefescu. He later admires the balanced constitution of the giants of Brobdingnag, which is a kind of perfect version of Great Britain. Gulliver ends up thoroughly disgusted with human nature, and unable to bear even the smell of other human beings. He laments that "when I behold a Lump of Deformity, and Diseases both in Body and Mind, smitten with *Pride*, it immediately breaks all the Measures of my Patience."[6]

Swift's Gulliver is opposed to setting up colonies in other parts of the world: "those Countries which I have described do not appear to have a Desire of being conquered, or enslaved, murdered or driven out by Colonies."[7] This attitude was not shared by the other famous fictional traveler of the period, Robinson Crusoe. Daniel Defoe's 1719 novel shows its hero constructing a little civilized world after being shipwrecked on an island in the Caribbean. He builds a hut, herds goats, and even gains a native servant. Central to the Crusoe story, however, is religion. The turning point for the despairing castaway is when he sees a vision of an angel "as Bright as a Flame," who tells him "Seeing all these Things have not brought thee to Repentance, now thou shalt die."[8] Crusoe repents, and with God in his heart, sets out to make a new world on his island. Defoe was himself a Protestant Dissenter, and a strict moralist. He landed in the pillory in 1703 for a satire in which he suggested that Tories wanted to put Dissenters to death for "occasional conformity," a practice of which he did not actually approve. He later attached himself to Robert Harley, supporting the Union of 1707 and the Treaty of Utrecht, although he cannot have been comfortable with the Tory government's religious policy. Out of favor after the Hanoverian Succession, Defoe had to live from his writings, and he produced an incredible number of publications on every subject, including several novels. Because he praised commerce and industry, he is often described as a "middle class" writer, but his main concerns were moral rather than economic.

Defoe's Puritanism may seem a little old-fashioned in comparison to the "politeness" of the two leading Whig writers of the early eighteenth century, Joseph Addison and Richard Steele. Both were committed to the Whig cause, but the periodical essays that they wrote several times a week for *The Tatler* (1710–11) and *The Spectator* (1711–12, 1714) were designed for a mixed audience, and they did not discuss politics. Instead, in a gently satirical tone, Addison and Steele set down the rules for living as a civilized and polite gentleman. These consisted mainly of honesty, openness, good fellowship, a disdain for showy, pretentious things, like fine clothes or the opera, an admiration for the classical Romans, and an adherence to simple maxims about human nature, like this one: "There is Nothing which gives one so pleasing a prospect of human Nature, as the Contemplation of Wisdom and Beauty."[9] The essays of Addison and Steele were addressed to the sort of landed gentlemen who frequented London coffeehouses, went to the theater, and enjoyed the company of other gentlemen. By contrast, fashionable women were not held in much esteem; instead, they were condemned as "a very injudicious silly Animal."[10] The influence of these essays on polite culture was enormous. They struck a moral tone that was markedly different from either Dissenting Puritanism or High Church anxiety. That confident, tolerant, somewhat secular tone would permeate the British ruling classes later in the eighteenth century.

This section has concentrated on English literature. Scotland had its own literary tradition, one that found expression in the dialect known as "Scots English." The leading Scottish writer of the early eighteenth century was the humorous poet Allan Ramsay, best known for his comic play *The Gentle Shepherd* (1725). Today, most English-speaking readers would require a Scots dictionary to understand lines like these: "But ablins, Nibour, ye have not a Heart, / And downa eithly wi' yer Cunzie part."[11] Ramsay was a critic of the Union, and the Edinburgh publisher of *The Gentle Shepherd* was a Jacobite. By the mid-eighteenth century, however, works written in local dialect were considered vulgar by the upper classes in Scotland as well as England. Almost nothing was printed in Welsh or Scots Gaelic in this period. Songs and stories in those languages were transmitted orally or, occasionally, written in manuscripts. In most of rural England, few people owned any books other than a Bible or a Book of Common Prayer for use at Sunday services. If Britain had a national print culture after 1707, it was an English language culture, based in London and other towns.

Come Ye Sons of Art

The flowering of English literature after 1688 was not matched in the other arts. To some extent, this was due to the unavailability of artistic training in the British Isles. Neither England nor Scotland had academies to educate painters, sculptors, architects, or musicians, as was the case in many other parts of Europe. After 1688, these continental academies of art, which were mostly funded by royalty and princes, came to be associated with French "despotism" and were soundly rejected by "free-born Englishmen." In addition, the visual arts themselves were often viewed with suspicion by Britons who had been brought up in a strict Protestant tradition, because they seemed to smack of Roman Catholicism and "idolatry." Painted portraits and landscapes were acceptable, but there were doubts about the supposedly highest form of visual art, "history" paintings of biblical or classical themes. An attractive representation of the saints or of the Virgin Mary might lead an unwary spectator into "Papist" veneration, while classical scenes were pagan, often immoral, and usually full of naked bodies. Added to this, the court did not provide much cultural leadership after 1688. Although efforts were made to improve and decorate royal palaces like Kensington or Hampton Court, no new royal residences were constructed, even after the monarch's main palace at Whitehall burned down in 1698. George I spent much of his reign living in the cramped, ugly, and old-fashioned London palace of St James.

Under such circumstances, it is not surprising that England produced few great architects and only one prominent "history" painter in this period. The most renowned English architect was Sir Christopher Wren. The son of a bishop, trained as a scientist, Wren was employed to rebuild the churches of London after the Great Fire of 1666. He is particularly known for his ornate steeples, which were imitated on many later American churches, as well as for the precise mathematical perspectives of his interiors. His masterpiece was the rebuilt St Paul's Cathedral, surmounted by an enormous dome and faced with double rows of huge columns. As Surveyor General of the King's Works from 1669 to 1718, Wren had a hand in the construction or renovation of virtually every royal building. He was not much interested in contemporary aesthetics, however, and by 1718 he looked like a relic of the past to the young Whig aristocrats who were beginning to dominate English taste. They were inspired by the philosophical writings of the third Earl of Shaftesbury, grandson of the first Whig leader, who had argued in favor of restoring the cultural and moral standards of the ancient Romans, so that England might become the artistic center of Europe. Young aristocrats who had made a Grand Tour to Italy, like the Earl of Burlington, came back to England with visions of imitating the classical-based style of the Renaissance architect Palladio. Burlington hated Wren's buildings, with their elaborate and fussy decoration. The old Surveyor General was forced into retirement, and the Palladian style of "classical" (in reality, Venetian Renaissance) architecture became all the rage among the landed classes.

The leading "history" painter in England, Sir James Thornhill, experienced a similar humiliation at the end of his long and productive career. Trained in England, Thornhill worked for Queen Anne at Hampton Court and at the Hospital for Royal Navy veterans at Greenwich, where he painted an apotheosis of William and Mary on the ceiling of the dining hall. They are shown seated in the heavens, looking like Jupiter and Juno, the rulers of the gods. Thornhill was also responsible for the uncolored religious paintings that adorn the interior of Sir Christopher Wren's dome at St Paul's Cathedral. He founded a painting academy in London, but it failed. As a Whig, he might have expected to prosper under George I, but the young aristocrats who guided English taste after 1714 found his

Illustration 8 *A mid-eighteenth century engraving of Christopher Wren's masterpiece, the Cathedral of St Paul's in London. In front of the Cathedral is a statue of Queen Anne. ("A Perspective View of the Cathedral Church of St Paul's in London," engraved by J. Maurer, 1747. © City of London/Heritage-Images / Imagestate)*

style to be outdated and not Italian enough. He lost commissions to foreigners and to Burlington's favorite artist, William Kent, who was a gifted garden designer but an awful painter.

Thornhill's resentment at his treatment was passed on to his son-in-law, William Hogarth, the most celebrated English painter of the mid-eighteenth century. Throughout his long and successful career, Hogarth made fun of the Palladians and of foreign artists. He rejected, at least outwardly, French or Italian styles. Although, like Thornhill, he was a Whig, Hogarth was never close to the party establishment. His first great print, in fact, was a satire on the South Sea Bubble. Hogarth longed to be a "history" painter, but he ended up making a living from portraits and the series of satirical prints, based on painted originals, for which he is still famous.

At least he had a good income, which was more than most painters could hope for, especially if they worked outside London. Painters in Scotland may have been more receptive to continental European influence than Hogarth, but the most ambitious of them could not make a living in their home country, so they had to move. The Scots artist John Smibert, a friend of Allan Ramsay, lived for some time in Rome, hanging around the fringes of the Stuart court. He later emigrated to Boston, where he became the first professional painter in the American colonies.

The lack of academic training in England and Scotland also affected music. In the sixteenth century, England had been renowned for its musicians, but most of them were Roman Catholics, and they primarily composed religious music. After 1660, Charles II tried to revive music at the royal court, employing the greatest of late seventeenth-century English composers, Henry Purcell. Today, Purcell's most famous work is probably an opera written during the Exclusion Crisis, *Dido and Aeneas*. He also wrote anthems for James II, of which "Come Ye Sons of Art" is perhaps the best known. Purcell continued to compose music for the court through the Glorious Revolution, and one of his last pieces was an anthem for the funeral of Queen Mary II. However, he left no school of composers behind him, and after his death, English music languished.

It received a boost in 1710, with the arrival of the German composer George Frederick Handel, court musician to the Elector of Hanover. Handel, who had lived many years in Italy, wrote operas in a fashionable new style, and brought over Italian singers to appear in them, including castratos whose high voices and lack of testicles fascinated the English public. Opera productions were expensive, however, and only the very wealthy could afford to attend them. They were also un-English and highly ridiculous, according to Joseph Addison, who stated as a rule "That nothing is capable of being well set to Musick, that is not Nonsense."[12] Nonetheless, the aristocracy loved operas, and their money founded the Royal Academy of Music in 1720. In spite of its name, the Academy did not promote music in all its forms; essentially, it existed to fund Handel's operas. It failed financially in 1728. Handel also received support from George I, who eventually forgave him for running away from Hanover, but he wrote little for the English court. Even his famous "Water Music" of 1715 was composed for a prominent aristocrat, although it was performed for the King. Later, Handel faced competition from an "Opera of the Nobility," founded to combat the composer's supposedly "despotic" influence over the musical stage. After he went bankrupt in the 1730s, Handel turned from operas to oratorios, but that story belongs to a later period.

It is not likely that many people went about the streets of London humming Handel's opera arias. For ordinary people, music meant traditional songs and airs whose tunes everybody knew. New words to these songs, often with a political twist, could be purchased from street-vendors in London, from whence they spread to provincial towns. The most popular composer of new songs in this period was Henry Carey, whose charming ditty "Sally in Our Alley" is still known today. Its words are very simple:

> Of all the girls that are so smart
> There's none like pretty Sally.
> She is the darling of my heart,
> And she lives in our alley.

Carey's songs were recycled in musical stage plays, performed impromptu in taverns and alehouses, and used as a repertoire by street musicians. They were a far cry from Italian opera, but were what the general public thought of as English music: commercial, without classical allusions, and easy to sing. In this sense, music was not actually declining in England; it had just moved, like Sally, into the alley.

Nature Revealed by Science

According to many historians, the late seventeenth century saw the birth of modern science in England. If so, then modern science had an exciting childhood and a dull adolescence. The extraordinary work of the chemist Robert Boyle, his lab assistant Robert Hooke, the astronomers John Flamsteed and Edmond Halley, and above all the mathematician Sir Isaac Newton led to the formulation, not of mere hypotheses, but of what were called "the laws of nature." The founding of the Royal Society in 1662, an international club devoted to the pursuit of natural knowledge, seemed to foretell that science would have a glowing future in England. Yet the great discoveries of the late seventeenth century were not followed up for another century. Those who were interested in science in the early eighteenth century generally took the view that Newton had solved most of the big problems, and all that was left was to refine his work.

Boyle, Hooke, Flamsteed, Halley, and Newton were men of strong views who did not get along well with each other. Boyle came from a wealthy aristocratic family (he was a great-uncle of the Palladian Earl of Burlington), and his experiments at Oxford with air pumps and "compressed air" or gases were carried on at his own expense. In his book *The Sceptical Chymist* (1661) he expressed concern "that even Eminent Writers, both Physitians and Philosophers ... have of late suffer'd themselves to be so far impos'd upon, as to Publish and Build upon Chymical Experiments, which questionless they never try'd; for if they had, they would, as well as I, have found them not to be true."[13] His famous law, that the volume of "compressed air" expands in inverse proportion to the pressure put on it, was published in 1662. His friend Robert Hooke, the prime mover behind the Royal Society, was one of the first to view creatures and objects through a microscope, from which he derived a cell theory of matter and a wave theory of light. He probably gave Newton the idea that led to the mathematical formula for gravity, although Newton never admitted it. The theory also relied on the minute astronomical calculations of John Flamsteed. Edmond Halley was best known for tracking the path of the comet named after him. He actually traveled to the remote island of St Helena in the South Atlantic in order to chart the southern skies.

On all their giant shoulders perched the moody, obsessive, quarrelsome, and brilliant figure of Isaac Newton. A mathematics professor at Cambridge University, he developed a form of differential calculus in the mid-1660s, although the calculus used today is derived from a simpler version invented by Gottfried Leibnitz. Newton went on to consider the problem of gravity, which he claimed to have solved by watching an apple fall to the ground. In fact, Newton's theory of gravity grew out of many discussions and calculations, especially about the force of the earth's attraction on the moon, and was based on Johann Kepler's observation that the planets receded from the sun in inverse proportion to the squares of their distance from it. Newton's genius lay in proving mathematically that this was a universal rule of gravitational attraction. He published his findings in *Principia Mathematica* (1687), and instantly became the most celebrated scientist in the

THE OLD OBSERVING-ROOM, GREENWICH.

Illustration 9 *The Great Room of the Royal observatory at Greenwich in 1676. It was built by Sir Christopher Wren to a design by John Flamsteed, who was appointed the first Astronomer Royal. The scientists are making precise measurements of time and the movement of stars, in order to calculate geographic longitude. On the wall behind them are three clocks and portraits of Charles II and James, Duke of York. ("The Greenwich Observatory: Interior of the Camera Stellata," engraved by Francis Place, 1676. © Mary Evans Picture Library)*

world. His later work on optics confirmed his reputation. Newton's vision of "the System of the World" was cosmic and universal: he was convinced that the phenomena of nature "all depend upon certain forces by which the particles of bodies, by some causes hitherto unknown, are either mutually impelled towards each other and cohere in figures, or are repelled and recede from each other."[14]

The great scientists of the late seventeenth century were not conventional men. Newton and Boyle never married; Hooke had a long-term relationship with his niece. Flamsteed had paranoid tendencies, while Halley was a Tory in politics who held Whig religious views. Newton hated Hooke and fell out with Flamsteed, who in turn disliked and distrusted Halley. Newton was secretly attracted to the Arian religious doctrine that Jesus Christ was entirely human during his life on earth, and only became divine after death. Boyle described himself as a "Christian Virtuoso," open to various religious opinions, and he refused to swear the Test Act oaths. Newton was an enthusiastic alchemist, who carried out many experiments to find the philosopher's stone that would convert base metals into gold. Boyle practiced alchemy too, in hope of seeing angels through the use of a "red powder." When Boyle died in 1691, Newton gave his alchemy apparatus, including the red powder, to their mutual friend, John Locke.

After 1688, science gradually became more detached from such unorthodox views, which made it much less lively. Part of Boyle's vast fortune was used to endow an annual lecture at Oxford, in which the truth of the Christian religion was to be upheld against doubters and infidels. The Boyle lecturers, mostly Whig clergymen, tended to argue for the perfect compatibility of Anglicanism with Newtonian science. Newton himself became a politician. As an opponent of James II, he was rewarded by the Junto Whigs with the offices of Warden (1696), then Master (1699), of the Mint, meaning that he oversaw the making of money, an important office during the period of recoinage, and a fitting one for an alchemist. After the death of his enemy Hooke in 1703, Newton became Secretary of the Royal Society. He spent the rest of his life figuring out the chronologies of ancient history, which tied in with his religious preoccupations. He also forced poor Flamsteed, by royal order, to hand over his astronomical calculations. The meetings of the Royal Society, however, turned into dull discussions of private experiments carried out by over-enthusiastic amateurs. Flamsteed died in 1719, Newton in 1727. Halley continued to work on the earth's magnetism, and lived until 1742, not long enough to see the return of his comet in 1758.

These great scientific theorists and observers were not much interested in practical inventions or technology (although Boyle invented the match). There were plenty of practical innovations after 1688, as the Royal Society transactions show, but few of them were widely adopted. Perhaps the most important was the steam engine. The military engineer Thomas Savery demonstrated a "model Fire Engine" before William III in 1698, and obtained a patent for it the following year. He later showed it off to the Royal Society. Savery's engines, however, had an unhappy tendency to explode. Around 1710, a blacksmith named Thomas Newcomen built an "Atmospheric Steam Engine," based on Savery's designs and on those of the French inventor Denys Papin. In Newcomen's engine, steam from a boiler raised a piston, which then fell back again through air pressure. The resulting motion could be used to pump water out of an underground mine. Within a few years, Newcomen's engine had been widely adopted in the tin mines of Cornwall. Surprisingly, it took decades for other uses to be thought of for it. New technology could catch on in early eighteenth-century England, but usually on a limited scale.

Historians of science may be disappointed by what failed to happen in the early eighteenth century, but contemporaries were not. For them, Newton had explained almost everything of importance in nature, and he had done it without openly questioning Christian beliefs. John Locke's philosophy of empiricism, which maintained that all knowledge was derived from experience and "the internal operations of our minds," rather than from innate ideas, provided the scientists of the eighteenth century with what they saw as a foolproof method for investigating the world around them.[15] What remained to be done was to record and classify all the aspects of divine creation, a worldwide scientific enterprise that happened to coincide with the imperial expansion of the later eighteenth century.

Part IV

State and Empire, 1722–1760

After 1722, the British state was secured, but it did not immediately enter into a period of expansion. Instead, for 17 years, the government of Sir Robert Walpole avoided alterations at home or adventures overseas. War, which had brought such upheavals to the state in its early days, was avoided. The Whigs ruled without rocking the constitutional boat, and without driving the Tories into another rebellion. Walpole's system was highly successful in creating what some historians have described as "political stability." This might be better described as a dynamic equilibrium, in which the political forces that had previously shaken the state were balanced or neutralized, without being totally eliminated.

In social terms, Britain was not static. It continued to change, towards a society in which money had as much impact, although not as much prestige, as land. The return of better economic times and the availability of consumer goods encouraged the view that owning more things meant higher status even for those who did not have high birth. Social commentators became alarmed by what they saw as the effects of luxury, including crime and irregular marital unions. The perceived lack of spiritual values in this worldly society set off a reaction, with the preaching of the first evangelical ministers in Wales and England.

Walpole's peace policy collapsed after 1739, with the outbreak of new wars against Spain and France. Patriotism, focused on the protection of British commerce and the defeat of Britain's traditional Catholic enemies, began to have a jarring effect within the British state. The stability of the government was temporarily sacrificed, and the early 1740s saw a brief return to the factionalism and power grabbing of earlier periods. Walpole's protégé Henry Pelham emerged as the victor from these squabbles, and managed to reinstate his mentor's system of Whig control. In the 1750s, however, war with France began again, leading to a struggle for colonial domination in North America and India. Patriotism rapidly re-emerged as the central theme in British political discourse, and the empire, for so long taken for granted, became a manifestation of the patriotic sentiments that bound Britons together within the state. Empire and state were finally linked by a patriotic zeal that had a wide popular audience.

10

Whigs and Patriots

Although Sir Robert Walpole is usually seen as the man who achieved "political stability" in the early 1720s, he was not solely responsible for it. The calmer mood of British politics depended on the efforts of many office holders, both local and national, who had tired of constant shifts and tumults. Stable government was also a reflection of a quieter society. The dramatic economic ups and downs of the period 1690–1710, which had caused so much hardship to ordinary people, largely ended with the Treaty of Utrecht. The mechanisms of power – the army, the navy, the tax-collecting bureaucracy – were all in place and functioning smoothly by 1722. Learning from past successes and mistakes, Walpole simply made the existing system work.

We can admire him for this, but we should keep a critical perspective concerning his motivations and methods. Walpole was an able and intelligent man, especially in financial matters. Always a moderate, in his early years he avoided the extreme politics of the Junto Whigs, and served in Harley's administration until the Tory backbenchers had him imprisoned in the Tower of London on charges of corruption. The charges were false, but not unbelievable. As chief minister, Walpole certainly enriched himself from the proceeds of his offices. He built a huge Palladian mansion on his family estate at Houghton, filling it with classical sculptures and works by the most fashionable contemporary artists. Fat and flamboyant, Walpole spent over £1000 per year on food and drink. "I am no saint, no Spartan, no reformer," he declared, and he made little attempt to impose moral limits on himself or others.[1] He once said of his Whig critics that "all those men have their price," and he knew what the price was for each one.[2] Bluff, blunt and straightforward, he had many enemies and many insulting nicknames: Bob Booty, Sir Robert Brass, Robin of Norfolk, the Great Man. Whatever we think of him, he governed longer than any of his successors as chief minister to the crown. Although the formal title did not exist until 1907, many historians hail him as the first British prime minister.

Walpole's System

Walpole developed a system for governing Great Britain that was referred to by his critics as "Robinocracy," since it centered on him as chief minister. The system emerged through experience, and it changed over time, but it had several key elements that remained constant: first and foremost, retaining the support of the monarch; second, controlling Parliament and the Whig party; third, keeping the Church of England and the Tories quiet; and fourth, imposing Parliamentary authority on Scotland and Ireland. The success of Walpole's system also depended on careful decisions in foreign and domestic policy. In particular, war was to be avoided, the financial burden on the landed classes was to be reduced, and domestic reforms were to be limited.

The first and most necessary element in Walpole's system was to retain the support of the King. Although the first two Hanoverian monarchs were less engaged than their predecessors in the business of government, they nonetheless had formidable authority at their disposal. The ministers were responsible to them, not to Parliament. Walpole kept the monarchs happy by avoiding situations that might endanger the Electorate of Hanover, and by allowing them to determine promotions in the army. He enjoyed George I's complete confidence after 1722, but when the King died on the road to Hanover in June 1727, Walpole faced dismissal. The new King, George II, called Walpole "a great rogue" and his brother-in-law Lord Townshend "a choleric blockhead." The chief minister was ordered, "Go to Chiswick, and take your directions from Sir Spencer Compton," the royal favorite.[3] The canny Walpole outmaneuvered Compton by obtaining for the King a salary or Civil List grant that was about £200,000 greater than what George I had received, adding a further sweetener of £100,000 for the Queen. This demonstrated the minister's control of Parliament, and cemented his relationship with George II for the next 15 years.

George II was an affable man, but he was greedy, lazy, and devoted to his army. While he could make his power felt, especially on matters of foreign policy, the real boss in the royal family after 1727 was Queen Caroline, a woman of much greater intellect than her husband. She exercised considerable influence on the appointment of bishops, preferring High Churchmen in spite of their connections with Toryism. Caroline ruled as regent when her husband was away in Hanover, so her support was crucial for Walpole. The King was stricken with grief when she died in 1737, as was the chief minister. On her deathbed, she told her husband to marry again, but he replied between sobs, *"Non – j'aurai – des – maitresses"* ("No, I will have mistresses"), a good example of the "mixture of brutality and tenderness" with which he treated his wife.[4] He did take mistresses, but none of them interfered with politics, as Walpole feared they might.

The House of Commons was harder to manage than the King, but Walpole was able to do it through a combination of rewards (or bribes, depending on your point of view), appeals to Whig party unity, and careful management. The rewards were given out as public offices (or "places," as they were called), pensions, and payments. Offices and pensions were usually given through the King; payments could be arranged surreptitiously, through the Secret Service funds. The number of officeholders or "placemen" in the House of Commons rose from about 125 under Queen Anne to 185 under Walpole. He could not always count on these men to support him in Parliamentary votes, but if they failed him too often, they would lose their positions. As long as they did not oppose him, Walpole interfered little with his sticky-fingered subordinates. Not surprisingly, his government gained a reputation for corruption and graft. The Lord Chancellor, chief legal officer to the crown, was convicted on embezzlement charges in 1725. Financial scandals rocked government connected institutions, like the South Sea Company, the Charitable Corporation (which was supposed to provide loans to the poor), the York Building Company, and the Commission for administering the forfeited estates of executed Jacobite rebels. Walpole was not seriously implicated in these frauds, but it was widely believed that he had allowed them to happen.

To combat such insinuations, Walpole often called on the Whigs to rally behind his government, which he presented as the only protection for peace, prosperity, and the Hanoverian Succession. He put a particular emphasis on party unity after 1733, when his government ran into increasing political difficulties from Whig "patriots" who had gone into opposition. In a 1739 speech to the House of Commons, Walpole characterized his opponents as Jacobites bent on subversion, Tories who "contend for Party Prevalence and Power," and "patriots" who "from discontent & disappointment would change the ministry and themselves succeed. ... Does not a Whig Administration as well deserve the support of the Whigs as the contrary?"[5] An effective speaker, Walpole often used his good memory for figures and the plain speaking style of a country gentleman to unite his Whig colleagues. He never ignored Parliament, although the government's business was normally conducted through a small Cabinet Council of ministers.

Walpole was the first chief minister to govern from the House of Commons rather than the Lords. This did not mean that the upper house had lost importance; in fact, no government could last long without its support. Walpole had to rely on trusted colleagues to manage the Lords. The first of them was his brother-in-law, Viscount Townshend, who became Secretary of State for the Northern Department (there were two Secretaries in charge of foreign policy, dealing ostensibly with Northern and Southern Europe). In 1730, after Walpole negotiated a treaty with Spain behind his brother-in-law's back, an offended Townshend chose to resign. He was replaced by Thomas Pelham-Holles, Duke of Newcastle, an obsessive, almost paranoid man who feared damp sheets and Jacobite invasions, but who was nonetheless an excellent administrator. Newcastle became elections manager and chief dispenser of government patronage.

Walpole's attitude towards religion was much more cautious than that of his Whig predecessors. He left the privileges of the Church of England intact, and did not try to gain further concessions for the Dissenters. He allied himself with the influential Bishop of London, Edmund Gibson, who was satirized as "Walpole's Pope." Gibson was a High Churchman, but was willing to work with the Whigs, setting a trend among ambitious clergymen that would last for decades. In the mid-1730s, as he fell back on the support of Whig backbenchers in the Commons, Walpole allowed several measures to reach the floor of the House that angered Gibson, including a bill to repeal the Test and Corporation Acts, another to relieve Quakers from paying Church tithes, and a third to make it more difficult for landowners to give land to the Church. The first was defeated in the Commons, the second in the Lords, and only the last became law. Nevertheless, Gibson was outraged, and he broke off his alliance with Walpole. The pious Duke of Newcastle replaced him as the government's arbiter of ecclesiastical patronage.

By not antagonizing the Church too much, Walpole hoped to keep the Tories quiet. The number of Tories in the House of Commons declined from around 195 after the 1715 elections to around 136 in the elections of 1741, but they held many of the prestigious county seats and represented a large proportion of voters. They could also look to the support of a few important peers in the House of Lords. Luckily for Walpole, however, the Tories remained divided, both by the issue of Jacobitism and by the question of whether or not to ally with the opposition Whigs in a "Country" opposition. Walpole kept close tabs on the Jacobites, by planting agents at the Stuart court and by opening the letters of suspected adherents. At one point, he even convinced a gullible Jacobite organizer that he was willing to work for the Stuart cause – which allowed him to gain further information that he could use to tarnish his enemies. At the same time, he made every effort to break up the "Country" alliance, by playing up the differences between Whigs and Tories.

Walpole did not often concern himself directly with the affairs of Scotland and Ireland, but they were important parts of his system, because trouble in either place could lead to difficulties in Parliament. The management of Scottish politics was placed in the hands of the Campbell brothers, the Duke of Argyll and the Earl of Islay. They made sure that reliable Whigs were returned from the Scottish constituencies. The Highlands were dominated by loyal Hanoverian clans and by the British army, which constructed excellent roads so that its troops could be moved around more easily. No new Jacobite uprising broke out, although the impact of the British state remained deeply resented by many Scots. In 1725, violent riots erupted in Glasgow against a new excise on malt, which seemed to violate the Act of Union. Worse still was the 1736 Porteous riot in Edinburgh. When a crowd of sympathizers gathered at the public hanging of a smuggler, Captain Porteous ordered the city guard to fire into them, killing six people. He was imprisoned, tried, and condemned, but when Queen Caroline postponed his execution, a furious mob of 4000 people broke into the Tollbooth prison and lynched him. Lord Islay ruefully observed that "All the lower rank of the people … speak of this murder as the hand of God doing justice."[6] Realizing that prosecutions in Scotland would "end in nothing," Walpole agreed to a Parliamentary bill that punished the residents of Edinburgh for the outrage, by imposing a £2000 fine and other humiliating conditions on the city. Furious at the insult to his leadership in Scotland, the Duke of Argyll went into opposition. Overall, Scotland was not particularly well managed by Walpole, and the government's treatment of it may remind us of how it would deal with the rebellious Americans 30 years later.

Ireland was a more complicated situation, because it had a separate Parliament, representing Protestant landowners of the Church of Ireland, later nicknamed "the Ascendancy." They maintained a tight rein on Catholics through the Penal Acts, and kept Presbyterians out of government through the 1704 Test Act. Whether the rule of the Ascendancy was harsh or benevolent is a matter still debated by historians. It was certainly resented by the Catholic elite, which had forfeited most of its land but still dreamed of a return to a happier past. The nostalgic views of the deprived Catholic upper classes were summed up in Gaelic poetry, notably the *aisling* ballads that extolled the days of freedom before William III's cursed invasion, and called wistfully for a restoration of the Stuarts.

With the Irish economy expanding through cattle, linen, and wool exports, the Protestant Ascendancy was able to indulge in big houses and expensive fashions, while developing its own sense of national pride. Protestant Irishness was deeply offended in 1720 when the British Parliament declared that it had the authority to make laws for Ireland. Two years later, a patent for minting Irish coins was granted to William Wood, an English ironmaster, who had obtained it by giving a bribe of £10,000 to the king's mistress. "Wood's halfpenny," as it was called, was denounced by the Irish Parliament and mocked by the Dean of St Patrick's Cathedral, Jonathan Swift, who under the pseudonym "M. B. Drapier" published a series of inflammatory letters attacking the patent. "Drapier's" fourth letter was addressed to "The Whole People of Ireland," and it assured them "that by the Laws of GOD, of NATURE, of NATIONS, and of your own Country, you ARE and OUGHT to be as FREE a People as your Brethren in *England*."[7] Was this rousing rhetoric of freedom designed to appeal to the Catholic majority as well as to Protestants? Perhaps not, but the British government was threatened enough to launch an unsuccessful prosecution of Swift's printer.

Meanwhile, boycott associations were formed, an effigy of Wood was paraded through Dublin, and a flotilla of small boats prevented the hated coinage from being landed at Cork. Even Irish Jacobites took up the cause. On the Pretender's birthday in 1724, Catholics in Dublin marched around St Stephen's Green, behind "a thing like a woman dressed in white on horseback" – an incarnation of Hibernia, symbol of Ireland.[8] In the face of such resistance, the patent for "Wood's halfpenny" was finally revoked in 1725, but it left a bad taste in Ireland that did not soon dissipate. From then on, Walpole relied on political "undertakers" in the Irish Parliament to carry out government business, rewarding them with offices and pensions as he did his British cronies. The most successful of them was the Speaker of the Irish House of Commons, William Connolly, a lawyer who made a huge fortune from "undertaking."

Sir Robert Walpole would not have wanted the success of his government to be judged on the basis of the "Wood's halfpenny" affair or the Porteous riot or even the occasional mob violence that broke out in England over elections, taxes, enclosures, or the construction of turnpike roads. Instead, he would have pointed to the preservation of the Protestant succession and the avoidance of Jacobite rebellions as his greatest achievements. He prided himself on the complicated set of alliances with other European powers, including France, that kept Britain out of war for 17 years. "My politics," he once wrote to Townshend, "are to keep free from all engagements [i.e. commitments to fight], as long as we possibly can."[9] He prevented George II from embroiling his kingdom into the War of the Polish Succession in 1734–5, at which point he boasted to the Queen, "Madam, there are fifty thousand men slain this year in Europe, and not one Englishman."[10] He reduced the interest paid on the national debt from 5 to 4 percent, and between 1729 and 1732 brought the land tax down from 3 shillings to 1 shilling in the pound, while maintaining an army of 18,000 men. In short, his system, whatever its faults, put the British state on a more secure footing, fiscally and internationally. If the British state was often viewed with suspicion in England, unloved in Scotland, and treated as an outside force in Ireland, it was nonetheless supported by the majority of the ruling elite throughout the British Isles, because it guaranteed Protestantism and prosperity. What Walpole's administration could *not* provide was patriotic fervor, and in the end, that failing would be fatal.

Walpole's Enemies

Sir Robert Walpole made a lot of enemies in his 20 years as prime minister. Among them were most of the best writers of the period. Alexander Pope savagely satirized the government's lack of literary taste in his mock-epic poem, *The Dunciad* (1726–42), which was an attack on "the Dunces" or hack writers, many of whom worked for the government. In the last part of the *Dunciad*, Pope took aim at Walpole himself, when he had the Queen of the Dunces pronounce:

> Princes are but things,
> Born for First Ministers, as Slaves for Kings,
> Tyrant Supreme! Shall three Estates [Parliament] command,
> And MAKE ONE MIGHTY DUNCIAD OF THE LAND!"[11]

Pope's friend John Gay, who had once held a minor office in Walpole's administration, mocked Walpole more crudely in his popular play *The Beggar's Opera* (1727), where the prime minister was associated with the arch-criminal Macheath (who became "Mack the Knife" in a twentieth-century musical version of the play, *The Threepenny Opera*, by Bertolt Brecht and Kurt Weill). The opposition Whig dramatist Henry Fielding made a name for himself in the 1730s by lampooning the government in a series of successful comedies. These attacks struck home. Walpole was so upset by them that he pushed a Licensing Act through Parliament in 1737, stipulating that all plays were to be approved in advance of production by the Lord Chamberlain. The Act silenced his critics on the stage, although poets and pamphleteers continued to represent him as a sinister political force.

More threatening than "the Wits," as the anti-Walpole writers were called, was the "Country" opposition. It had formed in the late 1720s through the efforts of two of Walpole's political enemies. The first was William Pulteney, a Whig and a

Illustration 10   *An anti-Walpole print of 1740, sarcastically comparing the "Great Man" to the Colossus of Rhodes, a gigantic statue that was one of the seven wonders of the ancient world. (George Bickham, "The Stature of a Great Man or the English Colossus," 1740. © The Trustees of the British Museum)*

former officeholder, who had become disaffected when Walpole recommended the Duke of Newcastle, not Pulteney, as Secretary of State in 1724. The other "Country" leader was none other than Viscount Bolingbroke, the former Tory minister. After renouncing Jacobitism in 1723, he had been pardoned and allowed to return to England, although not to take his seat in the Lords. He soon quarreled with Walpole. By the late 1720s, he and Pulteney wanted the Whigs and Tories to give up their old animosities and unite in a single "Country" alliance whose purpose would be the welfare of the nation, not the enrichment of a few rapacious ministers. The Tories must turn their backs on Jacobitism and intolerance; the Whigs must learn to put the common good before self-interest. Bolingbroke and Pulteney argued that the old factional labels were obsolete (which they were not), and that the "Country" was not a party at all, but a collection of independent gentlemen whose mission was to restore the constitution, in order to save Britain from the vile minions serving the ministry.

Bolingbroke, Pulteney, and their supporters made these arguments in a remarkable periodical known as *The Craftsman*. Every week, readers of *The Craftsman* were addressed by its fictional author, Caleb D'Anvers, on subjects like the need for frequent elections, the unlawfulness of excise taxes, the dangers of a standing army, and the blessings of free speech. Bolingbroke's essays in the *Craftsman* tended to be more philosophical than those of his colleagues, and would have a lasting impact on political thought, especially in the American colonies, where they were later read and absorbed by Thomas Jefferson. To understand what Jefferson saw in Bolingbroke, consider the following passage about the difference between a constitution and a government:

By *Constitution* we mean … that Assemblage of Laws, Institutions and Customs, derived from certain fix'd Principles of Reason, directed to certain fix'd Objects of publick Good, that compose the general System, according to which the Community hath agreed to be governed. By *Government* we mean … that particular Tenor of Conduct, which a chief Magistrate, and inferior Magistrates, under his Direction and Influence, hold in the Administration of publick Affairs. This is a *good Government*, when … the whole Administration of publick Affairs is wisely pursued, and with a strict Conformity to the Principles and Objects of the *Constitution … Constitution* is the Rule, by which our Princes ought to govern, at all Times.[12]

The insistence on strict adherence to the somewhat vague ideals of a quasi-mythical constitution would be typical of British opposition groups for the next century.

The "Country" party was at first an uneasy alliance that gained no success against the ministry. Then in 1733, Walpole handed it a big issue. As part of his general plan to reduce the land tax by substituting indirect duties on goods, he proposed an excise on wine and tobacco. Tea, coffee, and cocoa had been added to the excise a decade earlier, and prior to the new proposal, Walpole had brought the land tax down to 1 shilling in the pound through an excise on salt, a commodity that was widely used to preserve and flavor food. The excise on wine and tobacco would raise £200,000–300,000, and virtually eliminate the land tax, so Sir Robert was convinced it would give great satisfaction to landed gentlemen of all political persuasions. In addition, in the prime minister's view, an excise would eliminate customs fraud and the illegal importation of wine and tobacco. He reckoned, however, without the merchants, or *The Craftsman*. Merchants dealing in wine or in American tobacco were furious at the prospect of being subjected to the excise officers, who had the right to carry out searches and seizures at will. Complaints against the officers were heard by the excise commissioners, not by common law courts. *The Craftsman*, meanwhile, stirred up fears that this was only the first step towards a general excise, such as had been imposed under Oliver Cromwell. As in the 1650s, *The Craftsman* warned, general excise would be backed up by military force.

The threat was taken seriously, and there were riots against the excise bill in many provincial towns. The City of London sent a petition to Parliament against it on April 10, and when the ministry called on the House of Commons to reject the petition, its majority sank to 17 votes. The next day in the Commons, Sir Robert effectively withdrew the measure by postponing debate until a date when the House would not be in session. As he left Parliament, however, Walpole and his son were manhandled and abused by an angry mob of tradesmen, or "Sturdy Beggars" as he insultingly called them. Bonfires and fireworks in London and other towns celebrated the death of the bill, and *The Craftsman* was exultant: "We have the Pleasure to observe that the Spirit of Liberty is not yet extinct in this Kingdom, and that the original Power of the People, in their Collective Body, is still of some Weight."[13]

The Excise Crisis was not yet done. At the height of the agitation, Sir Robert had been abandoned by several leading aristocrats at court, who had tried to turn King George against him. This was as worrisome to him as the attacks of his enemies in Parliament or his critics in the press. He ruthlessly purged the renegade courtiers from office. In revenge, they would use all their influence against him in the general elections of 1734, when the government lost ground to the opposition in large constituencies throughout Britain, and became even more reliant on the tiny "rotten" boroughs. When Parliament reassembled after the elections, Walpole immediately had to fight off a "Country" attempt to repeal the Septennial Act, which would have severely weakened the Whig grip on power by requiring more frequent elections. He gained another, greater victory in May 1735, when his nemesis Bolingbroke, who had begun corresponding secretly with the French government and possibly with the Pretender, went into a second, voluntary exile in France.

Walpole had saved himself from ruin in the Excise Crisis by deft political maneuvering, of which he was a master. By 1735, however, he had run out of political steam. He had no more big ideas for domestic or financial policy, and concerned himself mostly with foreign policy and court intrigues. For a time in 1736, he would even allow the Whig backbenchers to determine the business of the House of Commons. They proposed the religious legislation that mortified Bishop Gibson. Full of moral zeal, they also rallied to support a Gin Act that imposed licensing on the sellers of the mind-numbing drink known as "Madam Geneva." This measure would be greeted with considerable grumbling and some riotous incidents in the streets of London.

After 1737, Walpole faced an enemy even more formidable than Bolingbroke or the London mob: Frederick, Prince of Wales. The prince considered himself a "patriot," an expression being used by Whig supporters of the opposition to describe their heart-felt attachment to the nation rather than to a party. He also aspired to be a great collector and patron of the arts, in the image of Charles I. Frederick fell out with his parents, as many children do, over the amount of his allowance, which was subject to Parliamentary approval. He began to consult with William Pulteney, and attended opposition dinners where he drank healths to "Liberty and Property." His mother was disgusted: "My God," she was heard to exclaim, "popularity always makes me sick; but Fretz [i.e. Fritz]'s popularity makes me vomit."[14] After a series of angry scenes, the Prince stormed out of St James's Palace with his wife and newborn daughter in September 1737, to take up residence at Leicester House. He never returned to his father's court. Instead, he placed himself behind the opposition to Walpole, hoping to be seen as its leader. Leicester House became a magnet to ambitious politicians who hated Walpole and were waiting eagerly for George II to die.

In 1738–9, the patriot opposition clamored for war with Spain. Walpole had negotiated a series of treaties with Spain that were designed to protect the trade clauses of the Treaty of Utrecht, while preventing a repetition of the brief war of 1719. However, the Treaty had granted Britain very limited trading rights. Under the *asiento*, the South Sea Company was to supply Spanish America with 4800 African slaves every year; and one British ship was allowed to bring general goods to the colonists annually. The Spanish had continued to crack down on illegal trade by boarding British ships and arresting their crews. In a notorious incident, a brig commanded by Captain Robert Jenkins was boarded by Spanish coast-guards near Havana. Jenkins supposedly insulted the coastguard commander, who cut off one of his ears. In 1738, Jenkins was summoned before the House of Commons, where he showed his severed ear in a box and called for retribution. Walpole tried to forestall further trouble by renegotiating a convention with the Spanish, but merchants in the City of London, Bristol, Liverpool, and other trading towns were baying for war. Their real reason for wanting to fight was not Jenkins's famous ear. They were convinced that the Spanish empire was weak and would soon collapse, leaving Britain with rich pickings in the Caribbean. At the very least, they could force the Spanish into accepting more open trade. "The general Cry is War, Revenge on the Spaniards, Restitution for our past Losses, Satisfaction to our National Honour, and above all, Ample Security to our Future Trade and Navigation," declared *The Craftsman*.[15] The desire for war, and for Walpole's downfall, was so strong among the opposition in Parliament that some of them stopped attending its sessions as a protest, a rather pointless gesture that was soon abandoned.

Walpole gave in to his critics in October 1739, and war was declared. He had been pressured into this course of action by the Duke of Newcastle, who was worried that violent anti-ministerial riots might break out. Sir Robert probably should have resigned, as he had lost control over both domestic and foreign policy, but he loved power too much to give it up. He held on for more than two years, fighting off an opposition motion in January 1741 that blamed him alone, as "sole minister," for all the misgovernment of the past 20 years, and called for his removal from the King's councils forever. The Tories, furious because they had not been consulted on the motion by the opposition Whigs, voted for Walpole. The leading Jacobite in the House of Commons, William Shippen, declared that "he would not pull down Robin upon republican principles," meaning that the King should be free to choose his ministers, even if they were villains.[16] Walpole's Parliamentary skills had saved him for the last time. He faced a general election in the spring of 1741 in which the Prince, the patriot Whigs, and the Tories were united against him. He could not hope to win against such odds.

In fact, the war had doomed him. At first, it seemed to go well, with the capture in November 1739 of the fortified town of Puerto Bello ("Portobello" to the British) in Panama by Admiral Edward Vernon, who had with him only six ships. Vernon, a supporter of the opposition, was nicknamed "Old Grog" because he had invented a potent mixture of rum and water that would remain the staple drink of the Royal Navy for more than two centuries. He immediately became a popular political icon, with his face and name emblazoned on medals, tavern signs, and drinking mugs. His victory was celebrated by opposition supporters throughout Britain. His later battles, at Cartagena, Santiago de Cuba, and Panama, were all disastrous defeats, but this did not affect his popularity, because they were blamed on lack of sufficient support for the war from the ministry. In the general elections of May 1741, Vernon ran as a candidate in Westminster, where the ministry had never faced any opposition. The ministerial candidates resorted to wholesale buying of votes, using Secret Service money. Vernon lost, but when the House of Commons met at the end of the year, it declared the election void by reason of bribery, and called for a new one. This time, the patriot candidates, bolstered by a club of Independent Electors, ran unopposed.

This humiliation should have been the end of the fight for Walpole, but still he held on, until February 1742, by which point his wafer-thin majority of votes in the House of Commons had disappeared. In a sense, he had "lost" the general election of 1741, because his supporters had not gained enough seats to keep him safely in power. For the first time, a chief minister had to resign because of the results of an election. Most ministerial changes, down to 1837 and beyond, took place *before* elections, so that the voters simply ratified what the King had already decided. That did not happen in 1741–2; instead, the electorate delivered a rebuke to a sitting ministry. Walpole was not going to let it appear that he was responsible to Parliament rather than to George II, so he clung on desperately to power until the King was willing to let him resign his offices. He was raised to the House of Lords as Earl of Orford. To the bitter end, Walpole was the King's man, always ready to defend his policies before the House of Commons, which he did with great skill, but never willing to allow Parliament to run the country.

Walpole's Successors

The political history of the period 1742–54 can be summed up quickly: four years of weak and muddling ministries, followed by the re-establishment of Walpole's system under his former lieutenant, Henry Pelham. The period deserves more attention than this, however. The British state under Pelham and his brother, the Duke of Newcastle, would weather the next, inconclusive round of war against France, and survive the last Jacobite rebellion. This was an era of transition between an administration that was still focused on the policies and aims set by the Junto in the 1690s, to one that foreshadowed the reforming politics of the 1780s.

The ministries that followed Walpole's fall were handicapped by the King's personal meddling, as well as by disputes between the so-called "Old Corps" of Whigs under Henry Pelham and the Whig opposition. George II refused to employ the Tories as a party, although he would take individual Tories into his employment. He also hated one particular patriot Whig, William Pitt, because Pitt claimed, with some reason, that British interests were being subordinated to those of Hanover, which he called a "despicable Electorate." Unfortunately, the King's preferences could not maintain a stable government. Walpole's ministry was replaced by one led by opposition figures like William Pulteney. It quickly became dependent on the votes of Pelham's "Old Corps," who had stood by Sir Robert to the end. This ruled out any effective prosecution of Walpole or his henchmen for their misdeeds. The King did not much like either Pulteney or Pelham; he put his trust in Lord Carteret, a Whig aristocrat who happened to speak German and supported George's foreign policy aims. Although the King looked to him as a chief advisor, Carteret (or Lord Granville, as he became after his mother died) lacked influence in Parliament, and was forced to resign his offices in November 1744. The distressed King then considered a "Broad-Bottom" ministry that would include some Tories, but not Pitt. He continued to consult privately with Granville, which infuriated his ministers. In February 1746, the Pelham brothers and their friends took the bold step of resigning their offices in protest. George tried in vain to put Granville back in power, but the London financiers stuck to the Pelhams and threatened to withdraw a government loan of £300,000. George swallowed his pride, recalled the Pelhams, and even agreed to give Pitt a minor office. The constitutional message was clear: the King could choose his own ministers, but they had to have the backing of Parliament and the financiers.

This political infighting took place against the background of war, not just with Spain, but with France. The French war was undeclared until 1744, but became an open conflict thereafter. The main cause of war was once again an issue of dynastic succession. Under an agreement known as the Pragmatic Sanction, Maria Theresa of Austria had inherited the Habsburg domains in central Europe, parts of which had been invaded by Frederick the Great of Prussia. Maria Theresa's husband Francis claimed the title of Holy Roman Emperor against a rival, the Elector of Bavaria. The French government backed Prussia and Bavaria against the Austrians. George II stood by Maria Theresa, but he also wanted to prevent Hanover from being invaded, so he made a secret deal with the French to that effect. Against strong Parliamentary opposition, his ministers had arranged that Britain should pay for the employment of Hanoverian troops against France. Meanwhile, Britain was providing heavy military subsidies to the Austrians.

Hostilities broke out without a formal declaration of war. The fighting started well for Britain, with an Allied victory over the French at Dettingen in 1743, a battle in which King George himself commanded. This was the last time a British monarch personally led troops in battle, and the King was delighted to be doing what he loved best. Early in the following year, however, Britain was alarmed by a French invasion scare, which led to a formal declaration of war. Against King George's wishes, Pelham insisted that command of the Allied army be given to the King's lumpish second son, William, Duke of Cumberland. In May 1745, Cumberland was hammered by the French at the battle of Fontenoy in the Austrian Netherlands (now Belgium). Irish Catholic troops played a large role in the French victory. Then, in the summer of 1745, shocking news reached London: the Pretender's 25-year-old son, Prince Charles Edward Stuart, who had been waiting idly in France since the aborted invasion attempt of the previous year, had crossed into northwest Scotland with a handful of followers, and was marching on Edinburgh with a Highland army.

Charles Edward had been encouraged to take this incredible gamble by Tory politicians, who had made promises to the Stuart court that they would back up a French invasion attempt with a national insurrection. Whether the Tories were serious or just blowing off steam in the wake of their failure to dislodge the "Old Corps" of Whigs is debatable. In any case, the headstrong Charles Edward called their bluff. His "Manifesto" promised "a free Parliament, wherein no Corruption, nor undue Influence whatsoever shall be used to byass the Votes of the Electors." His father, King James, would protect the established Churches, and guarantee toleration, "he being utterly averse to all Persecution and Oppression whatsoever."[17] To everyone's surprise, Charles Edward took Edinburgh, defeated a Hanoverian army at Prestonpans, and invaded England. His Scottish troops marched through Carlisle and Manchester, slipped past the Duke of Cumberland's Hanoverian forces in the Midlands, and reached Derby, about 150 miles from London, in the first week of December 1745. There was a brief financial panic in the English capital, where patriotic theater managers played "God Save the King" before performances, to rally public sentiment in favor of George II. The English Jacobites, however, quaked in their riding boots and made no attempt to join the Stuart Prince. Disappointed, the Scottish military leaders informed Charles Edward they were not willing to advance further across open terrain, so he reluctantly ordered a retreat to the north. The Jacobites beat a second Hanoverian army at Falkirk in January, and withdrew into the northwest Highlands. They were finally cut to pieces by Cumberland's forces at Culloden Moor in April 1746. Charles Edward went into hiding before escaping back to France in September.

In Scotland, the '45 rebellion was yet another civil war. Although it has the reputation of a Highland uprising, in fact many Highlanders fought on the government side, and by early 1746, the Jacobite army was full of Lowlanders. The real divisions were religious and political: the Jacobites were generally Episcopalians and Catholics, while those who fought against them were mostly Presbyterians. "Bonnie Prince Charlie," as he was later nicknamed, was greeted with cheers in

Episcopalian Edinburgh, with boos in Presbyterian Glasgow. The '45 was also a Scottish nationalist uprising. Charles Edward did not formally dissolve the Union, but it was understood that he would do so as soon as he conquered England. Many people also hoped, or feared, that he would repudiate the national debt. Clearly, his rebellion was a direct threat to the British state, which responded to it with some vehemence. Villages were burned in the Highlands; Episcopalians were forced to swear loyalty oaths; hereditary judges lost their legal positions; and the wearing of the long plaid cloak known as a tartan was forbidden. The famous short tartan or "kilt" was not part of traditional Highland dress, and in fact it may have been invented in England.

The response of the English Jacobites to the rising was anemic, which was understandable as they were scared out of their wits. English Hanoverian supporters, by contrast, launched a vigorous campaign, forming loyal associations and raising money for the support of the ruling dynasty. Pamphlets and prints condemned the Scots "banditti" for their disloyalty, painting a grim picture of what would happen if a Roman Catholic returned to the throne – it would mean tyranny, French domination, a Spanish Inquisition. Clergymen throughout the land condemned "the present unnatural Rebellion ... in favour of an abjur'd *Popish* Pretender," which threatened an "excellent Constitution and Government." Was not the uprising, they asked, "an open Defiance of the living GOD, and the pure Religion with which he has blessed us?"[18] Even the writer Henry Fielding, once an opposition supporter, returned to the government camp during the '45. He later published a hilarious account of the rising in his comic novel *Tom Jones* (1749). In that work, however, he also noted the ambivalence or outright Jacobitism of many ordinary people in England, and the incompetence of the forces that were sent to counter the rebellion. In one very funny passage, when it seems that the Jacobite army has broken through to London, Fielding puts these self-interested words in the mouth of a Puppet-Show-Man: "I don't care what Religion comes, provided the Presbyterians are not uppermost, for they are Enemies to Puppet-shows."[19] Like others who had lived through it, Fielding knew that the '45 was a close call for the unloved Hanoverians.

The rebellion did not extinguish English Jacobitism, which went through a small-scale revival after 1746. In the northwest and Midlands, Tory gentlemen drank to the Pretender; Tory ladies wore Highland plaid garters and danced to Jacobite airs; and anti-Hanoverian crowds hanged King George in effigy. Charles Edward Stuart was hailed as a patriot hero, the "Great Genius of Britain." These effusive demonstrations did little good for the Tories in the Parliamentary elections of 1747, when a united Whig party reduced them to about 115 seats. The beaten Tory leaders began to warm up to the Hanoverian Prince of Wales. In 1750, Charles Edward himself visited London, hoping to incite an uprising, but at a meeting with Tory politicians, he was dissuaded from another rash attempt. Within a few years, he had become a bitter alcoholic. He continued to plot with the Prussians and the French, but as a political force, Jacobitism was finished.

The war did not go much better for Britain after the rebellion. The trading city of Madras in India was captured by the French. Cumberland was defeated again at Lauffeld in 1747, and the Austrian Netherlands were lost. The only bright spots were naval successes. After sailing around the world, sacking Spanish towns, and seizing their ships, Admiral George Anson went on to win a naval victory over the French off Cape Finisterre, while Admiral Edward Hawke defeated a French squadron near La Rochelle. Britain's 150 years of predominance as a sea power had begun. The land war in Europe, however, was what counted, and the Treaty of Aix-la-Chapelle put an end to it in 1748. Prussia gained territory, which left Maria Theresa fuming at her British allies. France exchanged Madras for the vital fortress of Louisbourg, which controlled the strategic gulf of the St Lawrence River. The British government accepted the Treaty as the best way of terminating a conflict that had lost its initial popularity and was putting an increasing strain on the economy. The war had added about £31,000,000 to the national debt, and in its last year, had cost the nation a staggering £12,000,000. A large part of the debt was borrowed from private investors rather than the big Companies, which complicated the government's task of reducing its financial obligations.

Henry Pelham was now in charge. More honest and less self-serving than Walpole, he nonetheless shared his mentor's ideas about how to put the affairs of the British state in order. He kept his seat in the House of Commons, where he rallied the Whig party with rousing speeches. He used his brother Newcastle to control the Lords; and he made use of patronage as the basic glue of his administration. Like Walpole, Pelham paid careful attention to finance, reducing the army from 50,000 men to 19,000, and the navy from 51,000 sailors to 10,000. In a series of brilliant financial moves between 1749 and 1751, he converted the securities held by private individuals on the national debt from an interest rate of 4 down to 3.5 percent, which annoyed wealthy City merchants but saved the government a great deal of money. He also simplified national debt stocks, creating the famous 3 percent consols that would be the mainstay of British public finance for the rest of the century.

Pelham was a lucky politician, because the Tories were in decline and the Whigs were more or less unified. To be sure, Frederick, Prince of Wales, continued to see himself as a potential "patriot king" who would revive and unite the nation through suppressing faction. He was inspired by a visionary essay written by the ageing Lord Bolingbroke, entitled "The Idea of a Patriot King," that circulated in manuscript among his circle. Echoing Bolingbroke, Frederick announced his intention "to abolish those unhappy distinctions [of Whig and Tory] which have so long subsisted, and are productive of every mischief that can attend a divided state.... Let my faithful people then unite in enabling me to execute an honest plan of Government."[20] The Prince also promoted popular manifestations of patriotism. At a theatrical event sponsored by Frederick in 1740, an audience first heard the song "Rule Britannia," which would later become the anthem of British imperial power. However, the threat represented by the Prince of Wales to Pelham's ministry was suddenly removed in 1751, when Frederick died unexpectedly after an accident on a tennis court. His son George would later uphold the image of a "patriot king," with catastrophic results.

Some of the most strident voices of patriotism in this period were actually heard in Dublin, where an apothecary and town councilman named Charles Lucas made himself a hero to the Protestant middling sort through publishing an anti-government newspaper, *The Censor*. Lucas argued that Ireland was a distinct kingdom and should determine its own trade policies. He also hinted that previous Irish rebellions against the English might have been justified. When he ran for the Irish Parliament in 1749, these views were condemned as sedition by the House of Commons, and Lucas fled to England. At first fiercely anti-Catholic, Lucas later moderated his opinions to gain the support of Catholic tradesmen and shopkeepers. As a radical patriot who appealed to middling people, he would be imitated by many later politicians in Britain and America.

Henry Pelham's regime survived Prince Frederick and paid little attention to Charles Lucas. Because his government was so secure, Pelham was able to reach beyond financial reform, and introduce social measures that would have bewildered Sir Robert Walpole. These reforms were motivated by practicality and paternalism, combined with a vestige of Puritan morality and a strong dash of upper class moral indignation. Their aim was the preservation of good order, not the welfare of ordinary people. Yet they represented an important shift in government priorities, towards greater intervention in social issues. The most important of them was probably the calendar reform of 1751, when Britain adopted the Gregorian calendar that was used by the rest of Europe. As a result, New Year's Day, which formerly fell on March 25, became January 1. The calendar changed at midnight on September 2, 1752, so that the next day was September 14. Eleven days of wages were lost by laborers, who were highly disgruntled but utterly powerless to prevent it.

Most of Pelham's other reforms were connected with morality. A government campaign was initiated against blasphemous and pornographic literature, which nabbed John Cleland, author of the classic sex novel *Fanny Hill*. Pelham then turned to the suppression of cheap alcohol. The Gin Act of 1751 reduced the number of establishments that could sell the potent, gut-rotting distilled liquor. The next target for reform was the criminal law. Responding to a perceived increase in crime, the Murder Act of 1752 declared that the bodies of executed murderers would be handed over to the surgeons for dissection, which was a way of dishonoring a criminal's corpse. Finally, the Marriage Act of 1753, whose author was Lord Chancellor Hardwicke, stipulated that minors had to obtain the consent of their parents in order to be married. Adopted in order to stamp out irregular marriages, the Marriage Act was a particularly far-reaching attempt at social control.

Pelham's biggest failure concerned religious toleration. Having already extended to displaced German Protestants the privilege of naturalization as British subjects, Pelham tried to do the same for Jews. According to the Jewish Naturalization Act of 1753, foreign-born Jews could become British by having a private bill passed by Parliament. Needless to say, only very wealthy people could aspire to this. In fact, the Act was designed specifically to benefit the Jewish financier Sampson Gideon, who had loaned a great deal of money to the government. Most Jews in Britain were poor; they worked in the rag trades, or held other low-status positions. In spite of this, the Naturalization Act generated paranoid fears, especially among Tories, that the nation would be overrun by Jewish immigrants. Every anti-Semitic stereotype was dredged up by the opposition in its publicity. "As trade now stands with us," warned one pamphleteer, "our Merchants are obliged to use all their Abilities to guard against the Craft and undermining Artifice of the *Jews*: What then may be expected from them, when admitted to the same Privileges and Protection of your Majesty's natural born Subjects?"[21] Afraid of its possible effects on the upcoming elections of 1754, Pelham repealed the legislation.

Henry Pelham died suddenly in March 1754. As prime minister for eight years, he had entrenched Walpole's system of management, while adding a reformist twist that was partly modernizing, partly coercive. His administration had been less aggressive in foreign affairs. His brother vainly strove to keep peace in Europe, and to maintain the unsatisfactory alliance with Austria. Pelham did not seek expansion of the British empire, and he may have assumed that the effervescent patriot impulse of the 1730s had dissipated. Instead, it was about to emerge again, with much greater strength. Within a few years of Pelham's death, patriotism, with William Pitt as its voluble spokesman, was overshadowing cautious reform and offering promises of dramatic political change.

Mr Pitt's War, 1754–1760

It seems ironic that the transition to a new type of politics was initially presided over by the fretful, uninspiring figure of the Duke of Newcastle, who succeeded his brother as the King's chief minister. A long-time master of political management, the Duke had no trouble with the general elections held a month later. The triumphant Whigs even took away two of the most secure Tory seats in England, representing Oxfordshire. In this symbolic contest, both sides disbursed enormous sums in favors and treats for voters – the Tories alone were said to have spent £20,000. William Hogarth engraved a series of satirical prints on the Oxfordshire election, including a mocking depiction of a fat candidate being paraded victoriously on a chair, led by a blind fiddler, while angry mobs fight around him. As he passes a churchyard gate, the candidate is shocked by the sight of a death's head, carved in stone. It is a sign that he must one day pay for the violence and corruption that he has caused, but it also indicates something that Hogarth could not have predicted: the death of the old party system.

Newcastle himself wanted to end that system, by wooing or crushing the opposition, so that the government's business could be carried out without substantive criticism in Parliament. The opposition Whigs and leading Tories would be absorbed, and everyone of importance would become a ministerial supporter. This was not a patriotic vision; instead, it was the culmination of traditional Whig politics. One of the Duke's colleagues compared the Whigs "to an Alliance of different Clans, fighting in the same Cause, professing the same Principles, but influenced, and guided by their different Chieftains."[22] Newcastle wanted them all in the same camp. To show how broad and inclusive his ministry would be, he selected as his two chief spokesmen in the House of Commons William Mansfield,

Illustration 11   *After a corrupt campaign, a successful Parliamentary candidate is carried in a chair around the town in this print by William Hogarth. We can tell he is a Tory by the crowd behind him, carrying signs saying "TRUE BLUE." Blue was the Tory color. Two men symbolizing the Whig and Tory parties fight it out beneath him, while at the right, rich Whigs jeer at him while they enjoy an election feast. As the candidate topples in his chair, disaster is obviously about to happen. (William Hogarth, "Chairing the Member," Plate 4 of Four Prints of an Election, 1758.)*

a reformed Scottish Jacobite, and the ambitious, scheming Henry Fox, who came from an old Tory family.

The Duke's plans for political dominance ran into a major snag however, when Anglo-French hostility boiled over in the forests of North America. Newcastle was not particularly concerned by the early string of British defeats along the American frontier, but he was panicked at the thought that George II's beloved Electorate of Hanover would be lost to the French, which would of course put his own job in jeopardy. Early in 1756, therefore, he concocted an agreement with Frederick II of Prussia, called the Convention of Westminster, according to which the Prussian King guaranteed the neutrality of Germany, and promised to defend Hanover in the event of its invasion. This set in motion the so-called "diplomatic revolution," an exchange of allies by the two leading powers. An angry Maria Theresa of Austria, Frederick's mortal enemy, signed a treaty with the French against the Prussians. Open warfare between Britain and France began in May 1756.

Frederick II, fearing encirclement by the Russians, Austrians, and French, invaded Saxony the following year, igniting a wider European conflagration.

The Seven Years' War, as it was later known, began with a horrendous setback for the British. The French attacked the island of Minorca, a strategic naval base in the Mediterranean Sea. Admiral John Byng was sent with a British fleet to save the garrison, but after an indecisive engagement with the enemy, he turned back to Gibraltar, and the island was taken by France in June 1756. The public response to the loss of Minorca was fast and furious. Counties and towns petitioned the King, demanding an inquiry. An effigy of Byng was hanged before a crowd of 10,000 people, who exhibited "the greatest contempt by firing of Musketts, throwing stones, Mud, &c."[23] The admiral was court-martialed, found guilty of failing to do enough to defeat the French, and shot by firing squad, *"pour encourager les autres"* ("to encourage the others") in the immortal words of the French writer Voltaire. Many people thought that Byng was simply a scapegoat, sacrificed to protect the real culprits – Newcastle and maybe even the King himself. A popular ballad summed up the suspicion of foul play behind the scenes:

> Then Councils are call'd, and dark Factions engag'd,
> To screen the true Objects from popular rage;
> Now all with Clamour, they press on to the K[ing]
> With Thirst for the Blood of poor Admiral Byng.[24]

In fact, the political pressure placed on Newcastle's "dark Faction" by the Byng affair was intense. Mansfield chose to avoid it by accepting the position of Lord Chief Justice. Fox, who had alienated everyone by his deviousness, resigned as Secretary of State. Unable to carry out business in the House of Commons, Newcastle soon delivered his own resignation to the King. Now George II would have to turn to the politician he hated above all others: Mr Pitt.

Who was William Pitt, and why was he so loathsome to King George? He was the grandson of an East India merchant who had made a fortune from a 410-carat diamond that he bought while serving in Madras. William Pitt became the leader of a small group of Whig politicians, most of them his cousins, who opposed the ministry of Sir Robert Walpole. In the early 1740s, Pitt was the most vocal Parliamentary critic of a pro-Hanoverian foreign policy. The King never really forgave him for these attacks. Although he had taken a position in Pelham's administration as Paymaster of the Army, Pitt had refused to take financial kickbacks from the office, which enhanced his reputation as a disinterested patriot. Pitt wrote of himself in exalted terms, "as a gentleman, and as a member of the commonwealth, who is to answer for all he does to the laws of his country, to his own breast and conscience, and at the tribunal of good fame."[25] In keeping with these views, he continued to criticize whatever he saw as serving Hanoverian rather than British interests. Pitt was a brilliant speaker in the House of Commons (his nickname was "the Great Commoner"), and he particularly impressed the back-benchers. Tories admired him, and one of his closest allies was the Tory William Beckford, a rich West Indian planter. Beckford financed a newspaper,

The Monitor, that portrayed his friend as "peerless Pitt," to whom "the faction [i.e. the Whigs] must submit."[26] Pitt had hoped to become the chief government spokesman in the Commons after the death of Henry Pelham, but Henry Fox had outmaneuvered him. By October 1756, however, Pitt was poised to become the leader of a new administration, built on patriot principles.

George II simply would not have it. He agreed to make Pitt Secretary of State, so long as "Old Corps" Whigs held all the other positions in the ministry. By April 1757, the King had changed his mind even about this arrangement, and dismissed the offensive Secretary. The ministry collapsed. Pitt turned to his old allies in the opposition, especially to the Tories. They obtained for him the "freedom" of several important English towns, an honor symbolized by a giant key contained in a golden box. This "rain of gold boxes" was intended to show Pitt's popularity, and it was backed up by a newspaper campaign in his favor, orchestrated by Beckford. Meanwhile, the Duke of Newcastle was sending the most extraordinary letters to the king, refusing to serve in a new ministry without Pitt. "I can't come in without bringing in my enemy, Mr Pitt," wrote the nervous Duke. "He turned me out. But I can't serve without my enemy."[27] By late June, 1757, George II gave in at last. Pitt was brought back as Secretary of State, with Newcastle as First Lord of the Treasury and Henry Fox as Paymaster of the Forces (unlike Pitt, he happily lined his pockets with the perquisites of office). Pitt told one of his colleagues, "I am sure I can save this country, and nobody else can."[28] For the next four years, he was the leading minister in fact, although not in title.

Anyone who is astonished by this complicated political wrangling in time of war should glance back at the even more lamentable in-fighting of the early eighteenth century. Unlike in that period, however, the pig-headedness of George II had serious consequences, because Britain in the summer of 1757 had no Duke of Marlborough to lead its forces into battle and save the day. Instead, it had the Duke of Cumberland, who was well past his prime. Beaten by the French at Hastenbeck, Cumberland was permitted by his royal father to negotiate a convention with the enemy, which essentially handed most of Hanover over to them. Poor King George was dumbfounded! His dear Electorate had been given away – by his darling boy! Worse was to come, as the French occupied the Austrian Netherlands, the Russians marched into Berlin, and Pitt's first military brainstorm, a raid on the French coast, ended in total failure. The minister's other big initiative of 1757 was a Militia Act, requiring each English parish to choose, from a list of adult male inhabitants, a certain number of men to serve in county defense regiments. The rumor that the plan would lead to compulsory military service abroad set off riots throughout small towns in eastern England. "We will not fight for what does not concern us, and belongs to our landlords," declared the rioters in Lincolnshire.[29] Clearly, Pitt's war was not popular with everybody. In fact, in his first months of office, he had been an almost complete disaster.

It is not easy to determine how much credit Pitt himself should receive for turning this dire situation around. He has often been compared to Winston Churchill, the great British prime minister of the Second World War. Like Churchill, Pitt was determined, hard-working, egotistical, occasionally rash, always unwilling to admit defeat. Both men were hard drinkers and prone to mental depression. In contrast to Churchill, however, Pitt had no global strategy for defeating his nation's enemies. He gave most of his attention to the war in Europe, and to the defense of Britain's coasts against invasion. The North American conflict was secondary to him, and until 1759 his government played almost no role in the struggles that were taking place in India. Pitt has been credited with the "blue water" policy of naval supremacy, but in fact he kept most of the Royal Navy in European waters. In the end, this proved a sound approach, because the eventual defeat of the French navy in Europe prevented Britain's enemies from recovering their losses abroad. Pitt also pressed for the employment of greater numbers of Scottish Highlanders to serve in the British armies. "I sought for merit wherever it was to be found," he later stated, "it is my boast that I was the first minister who looked for it and found it in the mountains of the north."[30]

Pitt was well supported by Frederick II of Prussia, who received £670,000 every year in British subsidies. Frederick's disciplined army defeated the French, turned back the Russians, and kept the Austrians at bay. The Prussian King became a Protestant hero to the British, who fixed his likeness on everything from teapots to inn signs. Credit for victory should also go to the Duke of Newcastle, who ably managed the government's finances through a period of spiraling expenditures. Between 1756 and 1763, the national debt almost doubled, from about £74 million to over £130 million. Most of this was issued in the form of short-term securities, covered by revenues raised from excise taxes. Thus, the financial system created by the Junto, Lord Godolphin, and Walpole stood up remarkably well to the strain of a protracted and expensive global war. By comparison, the French were virtually bankrupted by the conflict.

The conquest of Louisbourg in 1758, and the defeat of the French at Crefeld in Germany the same year, were the first signs of a military turnaround, but it was 1759 that was to be remembered as the *annus mirabilis*, the year of miracles. To the mind of George II, always fixed on Germany, the biggest miracle was the battle of Minden in August, where the British and Hanoverian infantry under the command of Prince Ferdinand of Brunswick withstood a series of tremendous French attacks, without breaking. In the end, the demoralized enemy cracked and retreated. Minden was a serious defeat for the French – their army more or less disintegrated in the following weeks – but it did not restore Hanover to George II.

Britons exulted in the other triumphs of 1759. French slave-trading forts in Gambia, along the Senegal river, and on the West African island of Gorée surrendered to a small British naval expedition. The French West Indian sugar island of Guadeloupe was seized in a bold amphibious landing. Above all, British patriots rejoiced at the victory of General James Wolfe at Quebec, which opened French Canada to conquest. None of the African or American gains of 1759, however, would have been secure if the British fleet had not won two great naval engagements in that year. The first was fought in August near Lagos Bay off the coast of Portugal, where Admiral Edward Boscawen surprised the French Mediterranean squadron on its way north to join the main fleet. Five French ships were lost, including a magnificent 80-gun vessel that was blown to smithereens to prevent its capture. At Quiberon Bay near the coast of Brittany in November, Admiral Sir Edward Hawke broke all the rules of naval warfare by attacking the enemy in a howling gale, and driving his ships into battle towards a rocky coastline. The attack was not an unqualified success – Hawke lost two ships to the enemy's five – but it severely damaged and demoralized the French fleet.

These victories removed the possibility of a French counterattack in North America or India. They also ended the threat of a French invasion of Britain, which had been looming for most of the year. The French ministry had toyed with the idea of another Jacobite uprising in Scotland, and had even tried to drag Prince Charles Edward out of the alcoholic stupor into which he had fallen. When he turned up drunk for a meeting with the French ministers, however, they knew he was useless to them. Still, they kept up the hope of an invasion until the disaster at Quiberon.

The French invasion plan did not revive Scottish Jacobitism, but it had serious repercussions in Ireland, where rural gangs calling themselves Whiteboys began to appear in 1759. They carried out violent raids against landowners who practiced enclosure, as well as against tithe collectors for the Protestant Church of Ireland. The Whiteboys reportedly sang Jacobite songs as they marched through the countryside. A small French force actually landed in northern Ireland in 1760, but it was quickly forced to surrender. The Protestant militia was mobilized to suppress the Whiteboys, and in 1766 a Catholic priest who had supposedly incited them was hanged on a trumped-up charge of murder.

Although Irish Protestants feared a French invasion and celebrated British victories as their own, Protestant patriots in Ireland were not particularly attached to the aims of the British government. They detested the chief "undertaker" in the Dublin Parliament, George Stone, Archbishop of Armagh, who was viciously satirized in the Irish patriot press for alleged sodomy with an English army officer. When a rumor reached Dublin in December 1759 that a union was being contemplated between Ireland and Britain, it sparked off riots. Mr Pitt's measures were not loved across the Irish Sea.

His reputation was flying high in Britain, however, throughout 1760. Pitt had by then more or less patched up his differences with George II, although he could still irritate the old man, by demanding, for example, that the Order of the Garter be conferred on his brother-in-law, Lord Temple, whom the King particularly disliked. Pitt had an even more stormy relationship with the headstrong young heir to the throne, Prince George, and his influential tutor, Lord Bute. The patriot minister hoped that the 76-year-old George II would live to the end of the war, but he was to be disappointed. At 6 a.m. on October 25, 1760, King George rose, took his morning chocolate, and retired to his close-stool, a little portable toilet, for a bowel movement. He burst a ventricle and died instantly, if inelegantly. William Beckford's *Monitor* lamented "The loss of such a Patriot-King," during whose reign "this nation, from a distracted, rebellious people, is become all of one mind."[31] In fact, George II had never wanted to be a patriot king, or to court popularity. He was a good-natured, stiff man, with few interests or talents. "Everything in his composition was little," sniffed the aristocratic essayist Lord Chesterfield, "and he had all the weaknesses of a little mind, without any of the virtues, or even the vices, of a great one."[32] At least he had the good sense to give in when he knew the leaders of Parliament were against him, as in the case of Mr Pitt.

George's 21-year-old grandson was now king: and he *did* see himself as a patriot, who would become the beloved leader of his people. "Born and educated in this country, I glory in the name of Briton," he announced in his first speech to Parliament as King.[33] He hated "faction" (i.e. the Whig party) and he held grudges; for example, he complained to Lord Bute that Pitt treated the two of them "with no more regard than he would a parcel of children, he seems to forget that the day will come, when he must expect to be treated according to his deserts."[34] Now the day *had* come. Nothing in British politics would ever be the same again.

11

Polite Society and Its Discontents

In the mid-seventeenth century, many observers of English society had been worried that it would fall apart through the effects of civil strife. A century later, few people thought that social anarchy threatened to ruin the British state. What worried mid-eighteenth-century social critics was change. They were concerned that money was replacing land as the basis for status. They were anxious about the spread of luxury goods, which they saw as corrupting morals. They fretted about the rise in crime and the number of clandestine marriages. Finally, they perceived with trepidation a society in which religious participation was voluntary and the Church of England seemed unable to meet the spiritual needs of the people. These worries were caused by the gradual transformation of British society, which was moving away from a hierarchy of ranks in which everybody's place was obvious, towards a more complex structure in which individual status had to be constantly renegotiated by anyone who stood outside the uppermost levels of wealth and prestige. People in Britain were certainly not more equal in the mid-eighteenth century than they had been a century earlier, but their inequality was determined as much by circumstances and shifting values as by fixed assumptions.

Landed Men and Moneyed Men

Viscount Bolingbroke was one of the sharpest observers of a changing society, and one of the most pessimistic. In his political writings, Bolingbroke repeatedly contrasted the condition of "the moneyed men," that is, investors in the Bank of England, the East India Company, and the South Sea Company, with that of the landed interest and honest merchants. By 1713, according to Bolingbroke, "the proprietors of the land, and the merchants who brought riches home by the returns of foreign trade, had during two wars bore the whole immense load of the national expenses; whilst the lender of money, who added nothing to the common stock, throve by the public calamity, and contributed not a mite to the public charge."[1] In other words, gentlemen and merchants had grown poor, while low-born "stock-jobbers" grew rich.

Bolingbroke was not completely wrong about this. During wartime, the higher rate of land tax and the reduction of overseas trade did indeed hurt landowners and merchants, while rising rates of interest benefited those who owned government securities. At the height of the War of the Spanish Succession, the land tax accounted for 17.3 percent of income from rents, a figure not exceeded before the twentieth century. However, Bolingbroke's comment was partly misleading. The biggest investors in the public securities that were issued by the Bank or the great Companies were in fact British merchants. A lot of landowners also owned stock in the public funds. When the South Sea Bubble burst in 1720, the names of many Tory gentlemen appeared among the lists of subscribers to South Sea Company stock, which is hardly surprising as it had been founded by a Tory government. Daniel Defoe acknowledged that stock-jobbing had "once bewitched the nation almost to its ruin," but felt that "almost all the men of substance in England are more or less concerned in it."[2]

By the 1720s, in fact, a link had developed between investment in securities and land values. When the rate of interest on the public funds was high, as in wartime, landowners preferred not to purchase property, so that the price of land fell. "I know what my estate produces and have calculated what I should recover from £8,800 vested in 3 per cent annuities," wrote a landowner who was offering to sell property in 1753. He concluded that "[I] cannot make an abatement in my price set upon the estate without doing myself injustice. If peace continues two or three years longer I am persuaded I shall make more of the estate than I asked of you for it."[3] Obviously, he saw no contradiction between investment in land or in the public funds.

Contrary to what Bolingbroke suggested, landowners were not becoming poorer, despite the long wars and a nagging agricultural depression in the 1730s and 1740s. They kept their wealth by a variety of means, apart from investment in public funds. The most important was careful estate management, usually by professional agents. Good management meant improvement. Because rents remained stable through the first half of the eighteenth century, the only way to increase revenue from land was to improve it. The enclosure of land, usually by agreement among property owners, continued at a brisk pace throughout this period, as did the drainage of marshy land and the development of coal mines. Landowners came to favor long leases of 21 years that would allow tenants security and encourage them to make their own improvements. In Scotland, land improvement meant cattle droving, combining the scattered fields of the older "runrig" divisions into single tenant farms and merging isolated "farmtouns" into consolidated villages. After 1720, an enterprising Scottish landlord could join the Honorable Society of Improvers at Edinburgh in order to promote such changes.

A second way to retain landed wealth was the strict settlement or entail, by which an estate was bequeathed intact by a landowner to a grandson, whether living or not yet born. The parents of the heir were not allowed to sell or alienate any of the property, making them into mere guardians of the land. Provisions were written into strict settlements for younger children, dowries and marriage portions, but daughters usually lost out from arrangements that favored a single male heir. In the 1760s, it was estimated that half the land in England lay under strict settlement. Large landowners, however, tended to use the device more often than small ones, and the entail could often be broken by a lawsuit or a private Act of Parliament. Overall, strict settlement was just one factor that encouraged the consolidation of large landholdings in the eighteenth century.

The landed classes remained exclusive. Although it was not uncommon for a rich young woman of middling origins to marry into a landed family, it was rare for a family of the middling sort to work its way into landed status. Unlike in the sixteenth century, when there was a big infusion of wealthy farmers into the gentry, the landed classes did not grow in the period 1688–1760. At the top, the English peerage remained stable at about 180 families, while the Scottish aristocracy actually shrank from 135 to 82 families. Two-thirds of marriages in the English peerage during this period were made into other families of peers, or the close relatives of peers. This practice of endogamy, or marriage within one's own social group, seems to have been the general rule among the highest levels of the landed classes. While a merchant might be able to buy an estate in the country, he would remain a merchant, not a member of the gentry, until his heirs married into established gentry families, which could take several generations. At the same time, however, the younger sons of the gentry were moving into the higher echelons of the middling sort, especially into the professions: the law, the army, the navy, the clergy. By 1750, about a third of English landowners had some family connection to the professions. A few had merchants or bankers in the family. The social mobility of the British elite was differentiated by gender, and was mainly unidirectional: the younger sons of landowners could choose to move into the upper ranks of the middling sort, while a few of the daughters of rich middling families were lucky enough to marry into the landed classes. The sons of people of the middling sort had little hope of being accepted as the equals of the sons of gentlemen.

This does not mean that the two groups never mixed – they did, especially in public spaces like town assembly rooms, where fashionable dances were held. Any landowner who could afford it would keep a house in London to attend the "season" of balls, masquerades, operas, and plays. Edinburgh and Dublin had their own scaled-down seasons. Furthermore, by the mid-eighteenth century, it was typical for the English upper classes to rent a house in the spa town of Bath for part of the year, where they would drink or bathe in the sulfurous waters, and attend yet more rounds of dancing and card-playing. Defoe commented of Bath that "the bathing is made more a sport and diversion, than a physical prescription for health; and the town is taken up in raffling [gambling with dice], gameing, visiting, and in a word, all sorts of gallantry and levity."[4] By the mid-eighteenth century, wealthy people of the middling sort might be encountered at any public event in Bath. For men and especially women of the upper classes, however, the season also meant private visits: dropping in on each other's houses, sipping tea, playing card games, and exchanging visiting cards. These were occasions for show as well as sociability. The carriage in which one arrived, the magnificent livery in which one's servants were dressed, the opulence of drawing rooms, and the degree of hospitality that was extended all counted as signs of status. Visits in the country were even more elaborate affairs, in which a guest might stay for days or weeks of hunting, feasting, and card-playing. A gentry family would have been shocked by a country visit from anyone who was of the middling sort, unless it was for business reasons, or to arrange a marriage.

It disturbed the gentry that, in the larger towns at least, people of middling status and polite manners – professional men, merchants, and their families – chose to use the term "gentleman" to describe themselves. These pseudo-gentlemen also dressed like the gentry and imitated their tastes or habits. Not all outward distinctions had lapsed: for example, it was uncommon for people who were not *real* gentry to wear swords. Members of Parliament still wore them – Henry Pelham is supposed to have used his to fend off a mob during the Excise Crisis – and they frequently fought duels with one another, to uphold their honor. Pseudo-gentlemen were not likely to fight duels.

If the upper classes were consolidating themselves financially in the first half of the eighteenth century, so too were the middling sort. In economic terms, merchants and shopkeepers fared particularly well. English overseas commodity trade expanded steadily, from a gross total value (imports, exports, and re-exports) of £12 million in 1699–1701 to about £20 million in 1752–4, with re-exports growing faster than any other sector. Internal trade was burgeoning as well, mostly along the coasts and internal waterways, but also along turnpike roads, which were improved toll-paying highways. The increase in commerce in the first half of the eighteenth century may not have been as great as during the late seventeenth century, but it was more far-reaching. Even small English ports and market towns, which had been in a state of economic decline for much of the seventeenth century, and were hard-hit by war between 1689 and 1714, were recovering by 1750, as they became linked to a national system of transportation and distribution. Shops appeared throughout England. By 1759, it was estimated that the kingdom had 141,700 retailers, of which 120,000 were outside London. The Scottish situation was more mixed, however, with many small ports falling into further decline, while Glasgow boomed through the American tobacco trade. In 1715, 2 million pounds of tobacco entered Glasgow. By 1743, this had rise to 9 million pounds, much of it destined for re-export to Europe.

The middling sort who handled this commerce were not united as a single social or cultural group, as might be said of the upper classes. Although most of them prospered through business or commerce, they did not all share the same habits. Small tradesmen, with accumulated wealth of £500–5000, lived in or near their places of work, and married into other families engaged in similar types of business. They loaned money to relatives and other small tradesmen, took leases on urban shops or houses, and if they had cash left over, put it into government securities. While they did not reject the amenities of upper class living, they usually valued frugality and were not given to conspicuous displays of wealth. On the other hand, big merchants who were worth more than £5000 lived in fashionable areas of town, loaned money to the gentry and aristocracy, took leases on suburban villas or farmland, speculated on the development of urban properties, and invested heavily in shipping and Company stocks. The wealthy trans-Atlantic merchants of London, many of them Scottish immigrants, developed distinct patterns of opulent living. Heavily engaged in the slave trade, they sought to marry West Indian plantation heiresses. They bought land in the English countryside, built great houses and filled them with furniture and pictures – just like the gentry.

Social barriers among the middling sort of people may have been hardening. The big London merchants, who were able to copy the expensive tastes of the gentry, were less likely to fraternize with small tradesmen than they had been in the seventeenth century. Among those small London tradesmen, however, and among manufacturers, merchants, and shopkeepers in provincial towns, the sense of being different from the gentry, and perhaps morally superior to them, may have been growing. A woolen manufacturer of Halifax in northern England wrote in 1749 about a trip to the spa town of Buxton, where he had been humiliated for wearing unfashionable clothing: "I did not come to Buxton in fine gay clothing as some people might do to make their fortunes; perhaps I look upon [a] man's character before clothing. ... A man ought not to be despised that has not land for the same God rules over the poor as well as the rich landed men."[5] In comments like these, we can detect the beginnings of a middle class consciousness that was not always deferential to the landed elite. Although there was no outright conflict between landed and moneyed men, the potential for tension between them was not just a product of Viscount Bolingbroke's imagination.

Luxury

Like many other social commentators, Bolingbroke was convinced that the advance of luxury was sapping the potential greatness of Britain. "[E]very Nation has made either a great or inconsiderable Figure in the World," he advised, "as it has fallen into Luxury or resisted its Temptations." He therefore warned his countrymen to "be wise in time, before *Luxury* has made too great a progress among us."[6] Historians have tended to take the opposite view, agreeing with the Dutch-born philosopher Bernard Mandeville, who argued that "with a wise Administration all People may swim in as much Foreign Luxury as their Product can purchase."[7] The private desire for pleasure, according to Mandeville, led to public economic benefits. Mandeville's unorthodox approach was widely condemned, especially by clergymen, but it reflected an economic reality. Luxury commodities, streaming into Britain in the early eighteenth century, encouraged consumption, which in turn generated demand for more items. The desire for luxuries can also be linked to the spread of British power around the globe after 1750. The lust for empire was partly fuelled by the desire for luxuries.

Britain's eighteenth-century taste for luxuries was shaped by cultural factors that date to the previous century or earlier. The first was a fascination with Asian goods. Carpets from Turkey, calicoes from India, silk, porcelain, and tea from China, fascinated English consumers who knew little about their origins. Asian goods seemed to possess exotic or mysterious qualities, redolent of the supposedly sybaritic lifestyles of eastern rulers, and were imported in huge quantities. During the eighteenth century, a million pieces of Chinese porcelain were shipped to Britain every year. Imports of Chinese tea to Britain multiplied sixfold between 1700 and 1750, as tea-drinking became a typical British custom. Trade with the eastern Mediterranean was controlled by the Levant Company, while the East India Company had a monopoly on trade to India and China, but there was competition from foreign companies and interlopers whose goods were often smuggled into Britain.

A second important factor in British taste was the ambivalent, love-hate relationship with France. In the seventeenth century, the French were the arbiters of European fashion in luxury goods, although in many respects they simply copied the Italians. The wars against France from 1689 to 1714 put an embargo on British imports from that country, and placed a negative image on many French products. High tariff barriers remained in place for most of the eighteenth century. In spite of this, French taste would gradually filter into Britain, to be adapted by British designers. For example, the ornate, swirling French rococo style of the 1720s and 1730s was imitated a little later by fashionable furniture makers, dressmakers, metalworkers, and engravers in Britain, but in ways that made their goods seem distinctly British.

A third important factor that affected British consumption of luxuries was the willingness of British manufacturers to alter their production in accordance with changing demand. By 1700, Britain had a number of well established industries catering to luxury tastes. Furniture was constructed in London and other major towns. Flint-glass drinking vessels, which contained a quantity of lead, were blown in London, Bristol, and Newcastle. Pottery was fired in Staffordshire, in west central England. Buttons, buckles, and small ornamented metal goods (called "toys") were cast around Birmingham. Knives, forks, and spoons ("cutlery" to the English, "silverware" to Americans) were made in the northern town of Sheffield. All these luxury industries experienced rapid change in the first half of the eighteenth century. The heavy oak furniture of the Stuart era gave way to lighter forms in exotic imported woods like mahogany, often with rococo decoration. Glassware with thick "baluster" stems swelling in bulbous knops was replaced by thinner stemmed vessels with delicate twists of air or colored glass worked into the stem. Pottery shapes imitated Chinese, French, or classical Roman designs, and in 1751 an Irishman living in Birmingham figured out how to transfer engraved prints or etchings onto pottery. Ceramics manufacturers tried to reproduce Chinese porcelain, which unlike pottery was highly resistant to hot liquids. Since they had no access to the kaolin clay from which hard porcelain was made, the English manufacturers came up with various types of soft porcelain, which often cracked when boiling water was poured into it. A bewildering variety of metal buttons and buckles and "toys" was designed, for every taste and almost every budget. In 1742, a Sheffield manufacturer came up with the idea of fusing thin layers of silver onto copper cutlery, which gave birth to the famous "Sheffield plate" industry.

A fourth and final factor in the success of the luxury trades in Britain was that new consumer habits quickly became associated with respectability or politeness. To drink tea out of a porcelain cup – or to pour it into the saucer if it was too hot – became a mark of gentility and correct behavior. To wear elaborate, decorated buckles, made from expensive metals, was a sign of distinction. To display luxury objects in one's house, on the mantelpiece, or better yet, in a curio cabinet, enhanced one's social status. Moreover, the association of luxury consumption and respectability was carried throughout Britain and Ireland, and abroad to the British colonies. Through sharing similar consumer habits, the landed classes and the upper levels of the middling sort were integrated into a national market, governed by a set of polite cultural values. Wealthy West Indian and American colonists were partially integrated into the same system, which gave a significant boost to British manufacturers, since consumer goods were not supposed to be made in the colonies. The social effects of this integration should not be exaggerated. Whigs and Tories did not love each other any better just because they drank from the same type of glasses, and all the tea exported from China could not prevent the American Revolution. Nevertheless, among privileged groups, luxury consumption became an important aspect of British national identity as well as of imperial unity.

British women of the upper classes and middling sort were important consumers of luxuries, but how they were affected by such consumption has been a matter of debate. Some historians have argued that privileged women gained social and economic clout from increased consumption, because they were making more and more decisions about how to spend family money on luxury goods. Others have denied that they gained any status from buying, because their choices as consumers were seen by men as frivolous and irrational. What seems clear is that eighteenth-century women often attached special meanings to luxury purchases, associating them with particular events or people. Men also did a lot of buying of luxury items, and were probably just as influenced as women by early forms of advertising, like engraved trade cards, painted shop signs, items placed in newspapers, and descriptive pamphlets. For the first time in history, children became consumers, with the proliferation of toys, books, and games designed for them.

To a large extent, consumption was an urban trend. It flourished amidst what has been called an "urban renaissance," the commercial and social revival of English towns in the early eighteenth century. The "urban renaissance" entailed the construction of new public buildings, such as town halls and assembly rooms, as well as privately owned shops. It also saw the installation of amenities like street lights or water conduits in many places, often paid for by private subscribers. Facilities for consumers were particularly concentrated in spa towns like Bath and genteel resorts like York, where customers were catered to by a wide variety of artisans and tradesmen, from coach-painters and clock-makers to goldsmiths and barbers who shaped and powdered men's wigs. In the 1720s, Daniel Defoe compiled a book of travels through England and Wales, in which he frequently remarked on the politeness of small towns. He described Bideford in Devon as "a pleasant, clean, well-built town ... with considerable and wealthy merchants," and a church "large, spacious and well-filled too, and that with people of the best fashion." Lichfield in Staffordshire had "a great many very well-built houses, and well inhabited too; which makes [the town] a place of good conversation, and good company." Ripon in Yorkshire was "a very neat, pleasant well built town," where "the market place is the finest and most beautiful square that is to be seen of its kind in England."[8] Defoe saw decay and overcrowding as well, especially in larger towns like Bristol, but he tended to blame this on narrow-minded local authorities, who rejected the benefits of free and open trade. Even this most optimistic traveler, however, had to admit that Newcastle upon Tyne, with its close, old buildings and "the smoke of the coals," was "not the pleasantest place on earth to live in."[9]

Should we call early eighteenth-century Britain a consumer society? If we use that expression, as many historians have, we should remember that most people in Britain were outside the urban world of luxury consumption. Towns with more than 5000 inhabitants were home to about 20 percent of England's population in 1750, and about 13 percent of Scotland's. Three-quarters of the people in Great Britain belonged to families of landless laborers or small tenant farmers, who did not have a great deal of disposable income. They were largely ignored by Defoe in his famous tour. For them, luxury might mean wearing clothes purchased from a peddler, instead of home-made leather or coarse wool garments. Even poor rural people might smoke a little tobacco from long pipes with tiny bowls, or drink weak tea made with a few leaves in earthenware mugs. They might long for sugar to sweeten it with, but this was an expensive commodity that they could not often afford. The tea drunk by poor people was often smuggled into Britain to avoid customs duties, a criminal practice that caused immense concern to the government. As for tobacco and sugar, they were raised in the British colonies of North America and the West Indies, by slave labor. Even the simple private desires of the common people, it seems, could lead to public vices.

Crime and Social Disorder

"The great Increase of Robberies within these few Years," wrote the novelist Henry Fielding in 1751, "is an Evil which to me appears to deserve some attention." His perception that theft was increasing was based on his own experience as a London magistrate. Fielding blamed this on "the vast Torrent of Luxury which of late Years has poured itself into this Nation," which had seduced the common people into expensive diversions, gambling, drinking, and immorality.[10] Like many contemporary observers, he felt that crime was on the increase, and had to be stopped.

Historians have no reliable way to measure the level of crime in eighteenth-century Britain. We can count the number of prosecutions for theft that came before the law courts, which in many places did spike upwards around 1750, but that does not tell us how they relate to the total number of robberies. No national police force existed to which such crimes could be reported. London, however, was developing a rudimentary system of policing in the early eighteenth century, with constables making arrests and night watchmen patrolling the City wards. Magistrates became concerned with deterring rather than simply punishing offenders. A Street Lighting Act was passed by Parliament in 1736, to bring urban crime out of the darkness. Thief-takers proliferated in the capital. They made a business out of the detection and prosecution of criminals in order to gain rewards offered by the state. Henry Fielding had satirized the most famous thief-taker, Jonathan Wild, accusing him of being a criminal operator who made false accusations, but in fact the legal system often depended on such shady characters. In sum, while we cannot accurately assess whether robbery was increasing in London, Fielding had sound reasons for making his claim.

His explanation for this phenomenon, however, was not very convincing. It rested on the old conviction that luxury bred immorality. A better explanation can be provided for why crimes against property may have been increasing in 1751. After the end of every major war, soldiers and sailors were released from service into the general population. It was often difficult for them to find honest employment, so they might take to theft instead. Consequently, criminal prosecutions in English courts tended to rise at the conclusion of wars, as they did after the Treaty of Aix-la-Chapelle in 1748.

People commit crimes for many reasons: poverty, peer pressure, greed, anger, malevolence. The majority of property crime in England involved relative deprivation, which is to say that the criminals, mostly unskilled laborers and artisans in the textile or building trades, were poor, and of slightly lower social status than the people who accused them. Some types of criminal behavior, like poaching or smuggling, were tolerated or even supported by ordinary people, and can be interpreted as forms of protest against unfair conditions, like the Game Acts, which restricted hunting to property owners. As a result, such behavior has been labeled "social crime" by historians. It is hard to determine the boundaries of "social crime," however, as we know so little about the motivations of criminals. In addition, a "social crime" that enjoyed wide acceptance, like smuggling, could easily turn into common theft, assault, or murder, which everybody condemned.

By the eighteenth century, England and Wales had a well developed and uniform national system of criminal justice. In every county, justices of the peace tried minor criminal cases in local sessions courts, which usually met four times a year (hence the name "quarter sessions"). The principal sessions court for London assembled in the famous courthouse known as the Old Bailey. Many English towns, including London, had their own magistrate's courts, presided over by members of the civic government. Henry Fielding was a JP at the magistrate's court of the City of Westminster in Bow Street. Above these sessions courts in the hierarchy of the law were the Assize courts, whose judges were directly appointed by the monarch. Twice every year, the Assize judges rode on circuits through the English and Welsh counties, holding criminal courts in the chief market towns.

They heard serious accusations that might result in a hanging. Finally, cases in which the crown itself was involved, or that were considered particularly complex, were brought to the Court of King's Bench in Westminster. All these courts operated according to English common law, based on previous legal precedents. They had similar procedures. The initial accusation was written into a bill of indictment that was presented to a grand jury. If found to be a "true bill," the indictment was then heard by a petty jury of twelve members that decided the guilt or innocence of the accused. Trial by a jury of one's peers was central to the unique system of English justice, and was seen as a basic right. The judge, however, had the power to question witnesses, advise the jury, and pronounce the sentence.

By contrast with England and Wales, Scottish criminal justice was far from uniform. The highest courts, the Court of Justiciary and Court of Sessions, had fixed procedures, but throughout the countryside, the sheriff's courts tended to follow their own rules. The judges in 21 out of 33 sheriff's courts held their office by inheritance, rather than by royal appointment, which made them resistant to any efforts at standardization. Parliament abolished hereditary jurisdictions in sheriffs' courts in 1747, although judgeships in the lesser baron's courts, in which minor civil suits were tried, remained hereditary. After that momentous change, the lawyers gradually constructed a more regular system of criminal law in Scotland. An English legal structure had been imposed on Ireland in the seventeenth century, to replace traditional Gaelic *brehon* law, although it is hard to know how well it operated as most of its records have been destroyed.

It usually shocks modern readers to learn that, under English law, a man or woman accused of stealing 2 shillings and 6 pence worth of goods – about the value of a couple of silver teaspoons – could be sentenced to hang. The number of offenses for which capital punishment could be imposed increased in the eighteenth century, to include everything from deer-stealing to forging a signature. However, most people accused of crimes did not hang. About one in eight indictments for capital crimes against property were found to be "not true bills" by the grand jury, and of the offenders who went before a petty jury, only half were found guilty. Even the guilty could still be pardoned by the King, as about 40 percent of men and two-thirds of women were. A person accused of a capital crime faced odds of about one in four of being hanged. Of course, this may not have been very comforting. Following the Transportation Act of 1718, a convicted criminal stood a high chance of being deported to the colonies in North America and the Caribbean. Those who had been pardoned for capital offences were transported for 14 years, while those who were found guilty of petty larceny, which had previously been punished by a whipping, were sent out of England for seven years. Mortality on convict ships was very high. Prisons housed debtors, and those awaiting trial, but they were not favored for long-term punishment, which was just as well as most were damp, disgusting, unhealthy places where inmates suffered from disease and neglect.

Were the English courts fair? This is a difficult question to answer. Trial by jury was a fundamental protection for defendants, and judges generally stuck to the rules, taking great pains to hear both sides of a case. They were particularly careful in recommending pardons. However, judges were also able to influence juries in ways that would now be seen as improper. The presumption that an accused person was innocent until proven guilty was not generally accepted until the end of the eighteenth century. Although lawyers were becoming more common in courtrooms, nobody thought that a defendant had a right to be advised by one, except in treason cases. The ceremonies and procedures of courts were supposed to awe and frighten the accused, not to protect them from injustice. At the same time, anyone who knew how a court worked could use its rules to communicate directly with the judge. This is why some historians see courtroom trials as a kind of negotiation between two sides rather than as the authoritarian imposition of law on helpless defendants.

Like Henry Fielding, many upper class observers in mid-eighteenth century England felt that the law was too soft rather than too harsh. Fielding was also worried that crime could spill over into popular riots and disorders. He was particularly angered by the case of Bosavern Penlez, a gentleman's servant who had been hanged in 1749 for taking part in a riot against houses of prostitution in Westminster. The destruction and looting were led by sailors who claimed that some prostitutes had robbed them. The riot was only suppressed when Justice Fielding himself requested troops to be sent. Many people felt sorry for Penlez, but in a pamphlet defending his own behavior, Fielding asked them whether "a licentious Rabble" should have been allowed to take justice into its own hands, as "Accuser, Judge, Jury and Executioner; to inflict corporal Punishment, break open Men's Doors, plunder their Houses, and burn their Goods?"[11]

He knew, of course, that mobs had often inflicted punishment on the property of those who were seen as violating traditional rules of behavior. This was what tended to happen in food riots, when mobs would break into the mills and warehouses of merchants and distribute grain, in order to prevent it from being shipped out of an area. Food riots were responses to rises in the price of grain, which often occurred in wartime. Their cause was deprivation, or relative shortage, rather than starvation. From the 1690s until the 1790s, in fact, Britain did not face a serious threat of famine. Food riots on a regional scale, however, broke out in 1709–10, during the bitterly cold winter of 1740, and in 1756–7. If local magistrates were not willing to control prices or prevent the export of grain, crowds took it upon themselves to protect what historians have called a "moral economy," the idea that economic relationships should be governed by moral concepts rather than by a desire for profit. "Moral economy" motivated other forms of protest as well. Turnpike roads, which charged tolls and raised the cost of transporting commodities, were regularly attacked by crowds of coal miners and farmers in the west of England. In 1724, tenant farmers in Galloway, a county of southeast Scotland, went about the countryside destroying stone walls that were used by landowners to enclose land for cattle grazing. The Galloway Levellers' revolt, as it was called, was a response to rent rises and evictions stemming from the transition to cattle ranching. It was a particularly vigorous example of the defense of "moral economy."

Henry Fielding's preoccupation with crime and disorder should warn us against seeing eighteenth-century society as perfectly stable or harmonious. Of course, we cannot measure the social problems of the period, but their effects obviously made a deep impact on many minds. The damage done to British society, however, was limited by a combination of force and leniency. On the one hand, magistrates used the threat of hanging, the mobilization of troops, and the implementation of new types of policing; on the other hand, they lessened criminal sentences and were willing to tolerate a certain amount of popular protest. By these seemingly contradictory means, the social peace of the British state was, more or less, maintained.

Marriage à la Mode

William Hogarth became famous by depicting the vices of his day in series of engraved prints that could be followed like the scenes of a play. He began in the 1730s with "The Harlot's Progress," showing the sad life of a London prostitute, and "The Rake's Progress," chronicling the moral descent of a fashionable man-about-town, whose drinking, gambling, and whoring land him first in debtor's prison, then in the Bedlam madhouse. In 1745, Hogarth published a new series of prints, devoted to upper class marriage. Entitled "Marriage à la Mode," it told the story of an arranged union between a worthless young aristocrat and the rich daughter of a London merchant, who quickly become bored with one another. The husband infects a teenage prostitute with venereal disease, while the wife flirts with a young clergyman. Surprising his wife with her lover in a dingy flophouse, the husband is stabbed to death. In the last print, the wife has poisoned herself, and we can see that her infant daughter already has syphilis. The greed, vanity, ostentation, lechery, and foolishness of the couple are mercilessly exposed.

Was eighteenth-century marriage really like this? Many historians have argued that it was not, and have pointed to changes in the ways such unions were contracted. Although upper class parents continued to arrange matches for their offspring, young men and women were usually able to veto the choices of their parents if they did not like their prospective spouses. A few even made love matches, although these were still generally disapproved of as unstable. Although it was a rare occurrence, enough heiresses were being carried off by unacceptable young men, to be married without the consent of their parents, that the government saw fit to pass Lord Hardwicke's Marriage Act of 1753, outlawing clandestine or irregular weddings.

In spite of the Marriage Act, the traditions of upper class marriage were probably not in deep jeopardy in the mid-eighteenth century. Marriages in landed families were typically negotiated so as to reach agreement between parents, the couple themselves, relatives, and even friends. These negotiations were centered, as they always had been, on money and land, although mutual compatibility usually counted as well. Negotiations might be cancelled if one partner objected strongly enough – but there are plenty of examples where the marriage went ahead over the objections of the prospective bride. The marriages of the upper classes could be

Illustration 12 *After staying up all night, an unhappy aristocratic couple take an early afternoon breakfast in Scene 2 of William Hogarth's print series,* Marriage à la Mode. *Hanging from the pocket of the Earl of Squanderfield is the handkerchief of his mistress. His wife has been giving a party at home, and stares at him slyly. Their steward, who manages the couple's finances, holds up his hand in horror at the pile of bills. The crowded room, with its Oriental curios and French ornaments, mocks the contemporary taste for luxuries. (William Hogarth, "The Breakfast Scene," Plate 2 of* Marriage à la Mode, 1745.)

happy and harmonious, unlike the miserable one in Hogarth's prints. Instead of boredom, married women of the landed elite could find pleasure and fulfillment in the management of a household and the leisurely pursuits of a genteel social life. They might devote themselves to new ideas of child-rearing, derived from John Locke, who recommended breast-feeding, kindness, and rational persuasion rather than severity. Yet we can also find examples of upper class wives who were physically abused by their husbands, who ignored their children, or who took no joy in dancing or the theater. No matter what their situation, women tended to accept their lot with resignation. Marriage remained a sacrament: separations were rare among the landed classes, and divorce was almost impossible, as it had to be granted through an Act of Parliament. Between 1670 and 1875, a mere 325 divorces were granted in England, and only four of them were initiated by women.

Britain remained a patriarchal society. Wives were still legally considered *femes coverte*, meaning that their identity was subsumed for legal purposes in that of their husbands. They could not sign contracts or hold separate property. Everything they owned belonged to their husbands, although they often benefited from trusts set up by their families, which their spouses did not control. Whether or not female legal inferiority interfered with marital life depended on circumstances, but for most landed couples it seems to have been only a minor irritant, if it mattered at all. Women in the landed ranks of society were not expected to work at anything except domestic management, which in a big house could be a considerable task. If a husband died, however, his wife might have to manage his estate. Among the middling sort, cooperation between spouses in business affairs was more common, and dowries could be vital in setting up businesses, but it was generally accepted that respectable wives should not be seen at work in a public place.

During the first half of the eighteenth century, a few writers, like Mary Wortley Montagu or the novelist Sarah Robinson Scott, were critical of patriarchal domination and arranged marriages, but they did not inspire a protest movement. It may seem strange that a higher literacy rate among women, and the tendency of contemporary literature to emphasize the importance of love matches, did not lead to greater female dissatisfaction with patriarchal values. Evidently, there was a disjunction between what women liked to read and how they lived their lives. Two of the most popular novels of the period, Samuel Richardson's *Pamela* (1740) and *Clarissa* (1747–8), are both concerned with women who are sexually victimized by powerful male figures. Pamela is a servant, relentlessly pursued by her lecherous employer, whom she eventually tames and marries. Clarissa is attracted to the dashing Robert Lovelace, who drugs and rapes her. She dies of shame. Richardson's stories, intimately told in the form of letters that record every emotional nuance, may have attracted female readers because their heroines experienced not the muddled everyday reality, but a fantasy of patriarchy, full of sexual danger, righteous resistance, the lure of submission, and the eternal hope of romantic love.

The lower classes of society inhabited a different marital universe. They chose their own spouses, usually for reasons of mutual affection, although a couple was expected to have the approval of family and friends before marriage. In rural areas, courtships were long and elaborate, and betrothal ceremonies, called "handfastings" in the north of England, were observed solemnly, with the drawing up of a contract, gift-giving, and an exchange of rings. If a betrothal was broken after the couple had kissed, a man could recover only half of the gifts he had given to his betrothed, while a woman could recover all of them, kiss or no kiss. Formal weddings could be held only after having been announced in church for three Sundays, in a process known as "reading the banns." By the eighteenth century, however, many ordinary people who lived in towns were dispensing with the expensive customs of betrothal, and with waiting for the banns. They were married by license, which required only a small payment to a minister, the signing or marking of a document alleging that there was no impediment to marriage, and a quick exchange of vows, usually in private. If a couple wanted to dispense even with these simple procedures, they could be married clandestinely or irregularly, by a minister who was ordained but had no salaried position. Within the "Rules" of the Fleet Prison for debtors in London, the area where prisoners were allowed to roam, clergymen could sell marriages cheaply to anyone who wanted one. Passers-by were accosted with cries of "Madam, you want a parson? ... Sir, will you be pleased to walk in and be married?"[12] In the "marriage houses" of the Fleet, a couple could be wed for as little as 2 shillings and 6 pence, and the parson might even rent them a ring and a bed for the honeymoon.

They did not necessarily live happily ever after. Marriages were economic as well as emotional unions, designed to create a self-sufficient household in which children could be raised. To marry without secure financial support could mean years of misery and struggle, with an increasing number of mouths to feed. This explains why most people in Britain put off marriage until an age when they had established themselves in a trade or occupation: mid to late twenties for men, early to mid-twenties for women. It also explains why so many safeguards were placed on marriage, from parental approval to the reading of banns. Clandestine marriages were more likely to unite people who were too young or too insolvent to support themselves.

The Hardwick Marriage Act was designed to stamp out clandestine unions and strengthen parental authority over marrying couples. It made illegal any wedding ceremony except those performed in Anglican Churches, Quaker meetings, or Jewish synagogues. Ministers of other Protestant Dissenting sects were vexed by their exclusion, but went along with the law, because they supported the principles on which it was based. The Marriage Act outlawed cheap marriages for poor people, which meant that in the future, many of them would choose to live together without being married at all. However, the Act applied only to England and Wales. If an eloping couple could afford to ride up to Gretna Green on the Scottish border, they could still be married privately, at a reasonable rate, with no questions asked.

The Evangelicals

Bolingbroke, Fielding, and Hogarth were among many writers and artists who complained about the moral decay of British society in the first half of the eighteenth century. While their fears of the effects of luxury, vice, and disorder were often exaggerated, they were widely held. From the 1730s onward, such fears helped to generate a number of religious movements that were aimed at reviving the moral and spiritual basis of the established Churches of England and Scotland. They were called "evangelical" because they sought to spread the word of God to new audiences. Evangelical preaching emphasized a message of God's presence in everyday life, which starkly contrasted with the worldly, rationalist trends in mainstream thought and society.

Evangelicalism was a response to a perceived lethargy within religion, but it was not the result of an immediate crisis. In fact, by the mid-eighteenth century, the established Churches were more secure than they had been since before the Reformation. The Presbyterian Church of Scotland had defeated its Episcopalian rival, and it had no other serious competitors for the religious allegiance of most of the Scottish people. Yet it was divided within itself by the issue of lay patronage. After 1712, lay patrons or "heritors" gained the right to name parish ministers and to choose the masters of parish primary schools. In 1751–2, the "heritors" even gained control of poor relief funds, including charitable bequests. The General Assembly of the Kirk was dominated by a group of ministers, known as Moderates, who supported the lay patrons, but they were strongly opposed by those who looked back to the old Covenanting tradition of an independent ministry. In 1733, four clergymen who wanted to eliminate lay patronage broke from the Kirk and formed the Seceding Church. By 1760, the Seceders had almost 100 congregations in Scotland, and they were spreading among the Presbyterians of Ulster. The Seceders would later fracture into smaller groups, but they retained a strong appeal to people of the middling sort as well as to tenant farmers.

Similarly, the Church of England was not in any danger in the early eighteenth century, in spite of what High Church alarmists had predicted. It maintained its privileged position as the state religion, and kept the members of other denominations out of political office through the Test and Corporation Acts. Its long-time antagonists, the Protestant Dissenters, were declining in numbers and splintered by theological divisions. Latitudinarian Whig clergymen like Bishop Hoadly, who wanted a broad toleration for diverse religious opinions, never succeeded in dominating the bench of bishops in the House of Lords. Instead, Queen Caroline and then the Duke of Newcastle had preferred to nominate episcopal candidates who held High Church religious views, but who were willing to accept Whig government and the necessity of the Toleration Act. The English bishops, whether High Church or Latitudinarian, were mostly conscientious and hard-working men. They were not, however, willing to tamper with the structure of the Church of England, which allowed what some saw as scandalous abuses. The parish clergy, increasingly drawn from the younger sons of landowners, were sometimes lacking in spiritual dedication. In most parishes in England, landowners held the right to choose a minister, so that pleasing a lay patron could be more important for a successful career than serving a congregation. A clergyman did not have to reside in a parish, and could hold multiple salaried positions or benefices, a practice known as pluralism.

In spite of these problems, the Church of England was remarkably successful in ministering to the everyday needs of its flock, through baptisms, marriages, the provision of Holy Communion, and burials. Church attendance at Easter services remained high. Church courts were still active in prosecuting scandalous words, fornication, and irregular marriage, for which offenders could be excommunicated. What the clergy lacked was dynamism and a connection with the thoughts and feelings of ordinary people.

Voluntary lay activities made up for this, at least in part. Lay people were very active in the Church of England in the first half of the eighteenth century, forming religious societies, donating money to repair church buildings, and making philanthropic bequests, especially to charity schools. In London and other towns, Societies for the Reformation of Manners targeted swearing, Sabbath breaking, drunkenness, and prostitution, sending volunteers and paid informers out into the wicked streets with blank warrants in order to prosecute offenders. In 1699, the Society for the Propagation of Christian Knowledge (SPCK) was founded, to spread the Gospel in foreign lands and to found catechism schools for children in England and Wales. Only one of the five founding members of the SPCK was a clergyman; the rest were landowners. By 1716, there were 1221 charity schools in Britain and Ireland, educating 30,000 boys and girls in the rudiments of reading and religion. Boys were instructed in arithmetic, while girls were trained in spinning and sewing. The momentum of the charity school movement declined under the Hanoverians, in part because many of its leaders were Tories, but in 1734 there were still 134 charity schools in London, with 5000 pupils.

The charity school movement fed into evangelicalism, especially in Wales, where the SPCK had been very active. The Anglican Church in Wales was severely out of touch with the majority of its Welsh-speaking members. No bishop of a Welsh diocese spoke Welsh between 1716 and 1870. Ignorance of Welsh did not bar one clergyman from appointment to a parish in Anglesey where only 5 out of 500 parishioners understood English, although in 1766 a Church court ruled that it should have. The early SPCK charity schools aggravated the situation, because they taught only in English. In 1731, however, an Anglican clergyman in southwest Wales named Griffith Jones had the bright idea of starting charity schools that actually taught children in Welsh. The schoolmasters were to move from place to place, teaching for about three months at each location. Between 1737 and 1761, Jones's itinerant school movement claimed to have given instruction to 158,000 people, both children and adults.

Griffith Jones often preached in open fields, outside his own parish. He denied that he had enouraged others to imitate him, but he was certainly friendly with the leaders of the evangelical revival in Wales. The most important of them was a layman and son of a carpenter, Howell Harris. At Sunday communion in 1735, Harris had felt divine grace enter his heart, and took up a mission of spreading the Gospel. Without theological training, Harris saw himself as an "exhorter" rather than a preacher. He went about the Welsh countryside, traveling about 6000 miles a year, calling on listeners to repent their sins and accept "conversion," as he had, through an emotional infusion of grace. Harris's belief that some were predestined to heaven, others to hell, was derived from Calvinism. The doctrine was rejected by the other great Welsh evangelical, Daniel Rowland, an ordained Anglican clergyman. "God's mercy," Rowland maintained, "knows neither measure nor end. O let us call upon him with eager importunity, and he will hear us. Let us seek for grace to repent, and he will pardon us."[13] Like Harris, Rowland preached in Welsh to large open air gatherings, and founded religious societies among his listeners. His message of salvation by divine mercy was similar to that of Harris, but he gave greater importance to free will, and he did not share Harris's belief in ecstatic visions or prophetic dreams. In spite of their bitter public disagreements, by 1750 there were about 400 evangelical societies in Wales, with an organized structure of superintendants and regular meetings.

The English evangelical awakening had very different origins. It was born out of an Oxford University society, the Holy Club, founded in the early 1730s by a group of pious undergraduates, including John and Charles Wesley. They practiced a spiritual "method," consisting of self-denial, visits to the sick, examinations of conscience, and meditations on the afterlife. As a result, they were nicknamed Methodists. Almost all of them went on to become Anglican clergymen. In February 1739, a former member of the Holy Club, George Whitefield, who had corresponded with Howell Harris, began to preach in the open air to crowds of coal miners near Bristol. He told his hearers that "They must be REGENERATE, they must be BORN AGAIN, they must be renewed in the very *Spirit*, *i.e.* in the *inmost* Faculties of their Mind, ere they can truly call Christ *Lord*, *Lord*, or have any Share in the Merits of his Precious Blood."[14] When he left a month later for a hugely successful preaching tour of the American colonies, Whitefield asked John Wesley to replace him at the open air meetings. The two men would soon quarrel, however, over precisely the same issue that divided Harris and Rowland: the Calvinist doctrine that human beings were predestined to heaven or hell, and could do nothing themselves to obtain divine grace. Whitefield accepted predestination; Wesley advocated free will. They eventually built competing chapels, close to one another in London. Whitefield went on to preach to excited crowds in Scotland and Wales, where he married Howell Harris's fiancé, to the chagrin of the disappointed Welsh evangelist. While preaching, Whitefield spoke without notes, frequently shedding tears, and at the end of a sermon might put on a black cap like a judge giving sentence. He would then condemn unrepentant members of his audience to hell. Although he despised the theater as an idle amusement, no clergyman was more theatrical than George Whitefield.

His former friend John Wesley was the son of a High Church clergyman. As a missionary in Georgia, Wesley had been strongly influenced by an evangelical German Protestant sect, the Moravians. In May 1738, after his return to London, he experienced a sense of grace in his heart, or conversion, at a religious society meeting. After that, he was ready to take up an evangelical ministry. Wesley shared Whitefield's abhorrence of recreations like dancing and drinking, and urged his listeners to abandon them. He counseled Methodists "to abstain from fashionable *Diversions*, from *reading* Plays, Romances, or Books of Humour, from *singing* innocent Songs, or *talking* in a merry, gay, diverting Manner."[15] Nevertheless, he was sympathetic to many popular beliefs, and objected to the 1736 Act abolishing witch trials, because he thought that the devil could operate in the world. He saw celibacy as more perfect than marriage, and regarded sexual desire as diabolical, although he eventually entered into an unhappy marital union. After 1739, Wesley traveled through England, Wales, Ireland, and Scotland on preaching tours, following an annual circuit from London to Newcastle and Bristol. His listeners, most of them poor laboring folk, reacted to his words by crying, shouting, fainting, and, occasionally, going into fits. He tried to organize his hearers into regular societies, which held annual conferences after 1744, but many more people came

Illustration 13 *Entitled "Credulity, Superstition, Fanaticism," this print by William Hogarth makes a strong attack on the evangelical preacher George Whitefield. Hogarth depicts him as a Catholic monk in disguise, using puppets to terrify an ignorant and near hysterical congregation. (William Hogarth, "Credulity, Superstition and Fanaticism," Second State, 1762.)*

to his sermons than joined his societies. Until the end of his life, Wesley refused to separate from the Church of England and form a separate denomination, as his brother Charles advised.

In contrast to Whitefield, John Wesley rejected predestination and argued that *anyone* could be saved by God's grace. However, sinners did not have an indefinite number of chances of salvation. God, according to Wesley, "calls us to himself, and shines upon our hearts. But if we do not then love him who first loved us, if we will not harken to his voice ... his Spirit will not always strive; he will gradually withdraw, and leave us to the darkness of our own hearts."[16] Wesley's God practiced very tough love, demanding total submission and causing his followers deep depression as well as great joy. Women, for whom submission was already a key virtue, were particularly attracted to teachings that incited them to wrestle constantly with the demons of disobedience within their own minds.

In spite of their theological differences, the evangelical preachers were lumped together as "Methodists" by critics, who denounced them as hysterical enthusiasts, preaching superstitious nonsense to uneducated laborers and gullible women. Fielding mocked them in prose, while Hogarth satirized them in a terrifying print. Evangelical laymen like Howell Harris were denounced by Anglican clergymen who thought that only ordained ministers should preach. Physical attacks on the evangelicals were frequent: Wesley himself was assaulted in 1748 by a mob instigated by a local Anglican clergyman. Yet the movement continued, and grew. It was reproduced on a small scale in many Anglican parishes, where evangelical ministers, who might not feel any connection to the Methodists, confronted their congregations with a stark choice between salvation through grace and eternal damnation. In 1742, Presbyterian Scotland witnessed its first indigenous evangelical revival, the enormous prayer meetings around Glasgow known as the "Cambuslang Wark."

Historians are often unsure of what to make of the evangelicals. Their elevation of emotion over reason, their opposition to modern trends in thought, their condemnation of human pleasure, and their embrace of the supernatural are difficult for many historians to fathom. We tend to identify modernity with the skepticism of a theologian like Reverend Conyers Middleton, who in 1749 denied that miracles had occurred since the days of the Apostles. In so doing, we overlook the complexity of the modern world, in which heart-felt religion remains widespread, and carries a variety of social implications. Early evangelicalism reached out to people who were marginalized by the established Church, validating their primary beliefs and allowing them to release their emotions publicly. Wesley told them that they might *all* be saved by grace, a remarkably hopeful message. The promise of salvation, however, was always accompanied by fear and self-denial. As Daniel Rowland put it, "a sense of pardoning mercy in our souls is a most delicious feast; yet ... there must be a rending of the heart, a deadness to the world, a renewal of nature, a love of holiness, and an earnest desire to mortify every hidden as well as open corruption."[17] Ultimately, the severe moral strictures that were advocated by the evangelicals may have provided just as much social control as Justice Fielding could have wished.

12

An Empire Emerging

In the mid-1750s, shortly after Henry Pelham's death, the empire leaped to the forefront of British politics. Another war against France, the fourth since the Glorious Revolution, was beginning on the American frontiers. It would become a European war, and as always, military events in Europe would take precedence over those in the rest of the world in the minds of politicians. For the public, however, the war in North America had a powerful significance, as a struggle for the preservation of a divinely supported Protestant British empire against its malevolent, tyrannical French Catholic nemesis. "They want *America*, and then the world beside!" fumed a poet calling himself "Antigallican" (that is, anti-French) in 1754. He exhorted his readers to smash the "tawdry," "unclean," and "obscene" French at once: "BRITAIN, *strike home*!"[1] Over the next six years, British losses and gains in the New World continually fired up such patriotic sentiments. To a lesser extent, so did the war in far-off India, where the East India Company was successful in virtually eliminating its French rival. India suddenly became not simply a place for trade, but an essential contributor to the well-being of the British state. A writer in 1754 who wished to promote British intervention in East Asia argued that trade "has now become so important, that it is the Basis of our Liberty and Happiness, the Support of the State, the Bulwark of our Religion, and the Source of our Wealth."[2]

The public attention shown to the empire was not new. It had flared up before, in the 1730s over the war with Spain. Merchants who traded with the New World or with East Asia had an obvious interest in imperial affairs, and a public that was increasingly addicted to American or Asian goods – sugar, tobacco, tea – could hardly ignore the places where they originated. Never before, however, had the welfare of British territorial possessions overseas been so closely identified with the security and prosperity of the home country. The new concern with its preservation was accompanied by a gradual rethinking of imperial government. Britain's relations with South Asia altered dramatically, although this was due more to decisions taken in India than to imperial planners in Britain. As for North America, the war revived attempts to integrate the colonies more fully into the British state, in a military and fiscal sense. Such attempts took for granted that the colonies existed for the benefit of Britain, a point of view not shared by the colonists themselves. "Antigallican" might portray Britain and America as "sisters," but the older sister felt that she held all the power in their relationship, and she did not much care what her younger sibling thought about it.

Atlantic Worlds

The British North American colonies in 1755 were not the same places that we left in 1700. They were bigger, more prosperous, more aggressive, more socially stratified. The British West Indies, however, were not affected by change in the same way as their mainland counterparts. Slave economies as well as racial hierarchies were already well established in the Caribbean. The island legislatures were relatively weak, and the great wave of evangelical revival never came ashore on the Caribbean beaches.

In the West Indies, an incredible amount of wealth was produced by relatively few people – unless we count the hundreds of thousands of dead Africans who did not long survive the transition into slavery. In 1700, there were about 31,000 whites and 114,000 blacks in the English-speaking islands of the West Indies. Fifty years later, there were 41,000 whites and 258,000 blacks – barely one-quarter of the total population of the North American colonies. The largest increase in the number of slaves had come in Jamaica and the Leeward Islands, which by 1720 had overtaken Barbados as the main sugar producers, but it was an increase due to continual importation of Africans. Slaves still died like flies from disease, malnutrition, and neglect, while slave women bore few children, perhaps because they had little desire to bring offspring into such an awful environment. Due to the labor of slaves, the West Indies remained Britain's most profitable colonies. Exports of sugar and rum to the home country almost doubled in the first half of the eighteenth century, reaching an annual average of about £1.6 million by 1750. The human misery that brought such sweetness into the world had not lessened. A few people in Britain were beginning to find this embarrassing. "The negroes in our colonies," one writer noted in 1757, "endure a slavery more compleat, and attended with far worse circumstances, than what any people in their condition suffer in any other part of the world, or have suffered at any other period of time." He recommended "allowing a more moderate labour, and some other indulgences," so that more slaves could be kept alive.[3] It was not a very satisfactory solution to a massive injustice.

The strongest resistance to the slave system came from the Maroons, the runaway slaves of Jamaica. From their stronghold at Nanny Town in the Blue Mountains, named after a legendary Queen of the Maroons, they waged a long-running guerilla war against the planters and the army. The Maroons tried to reconstruct an African warrior society in the Jamaican interior, from fighting rituals to polygamous marriages. When threatened with danger, they responded to the sound of the *abeng* or cow-horn, just as their ancestors had in West Africa. After Nanny Town was sacked (or abandoned, depending on which account you believe) in 1734, the Maroons divided into different groups, but continued to attack plantations and harass British troops. Finally, in January 1739, the leader of one Maroon group, King Cudjoe, or Captain Cudjoe as his enemies called him, agreed to make a treaty with the British officers who were pursuing him. The Maroons received 15,000 acres of land on which to farm and hunt; in exchange, they would fight against the enemies of the British, and "if any Negroes shall hereafter run away from their Masters or Owners, and fall into Captain Cudjoe's Hands, they shall immediately be sent back to the Chief Magistrate of the next Parish where they are taken."[4] In the 1760s, when slaves rose up in revolt in Jamaica, Maroons assisted the planters in suppressing them.

As they needed British troops to keep down the slaves, the big West Indian planters were divided as to how much autonomy they desired from the home country. They could all agree, however, on the necessity of protecting themselves against competition from the booming French colonies in the Caribbean, especially Saint-Domingue (Haiti). This was the purpose of the Molasses Act of 1733, which put heavy tariffs on sugar products imported from outside the British colonies, and pitted the islands against the mainland for the first time. Passage of the Act was assisted by heavy lobbying from the big planters, several of whom sat in the British House of Commons. The planters were embittered by the South Sea Company's monopoly on trade with the Spanish New World, and were delighted when this was lost in 1750. The influence of the West Indians on Parliament seemed enormous and corrosive to many British observers.

The development of the mainland colonies of North America in the period 1700–55 differed from that of the islands in several ways. First, the mainland settlers experienced rapid growth in population and territory. Second, slave economies were still consolidating on the mainland. Third, a distinct pattern of mainland American politics emerged, setting "Country" oppositions in conflict with colonial governors. Finally, North American evangelicalism flowered in what was known as the "Great Awakening." Although the effects of these developments were complex, they can be seen as setting the Americans apart from the British. On the other hand, Americans of the upper and middling sort were increasingly influenced by British tastes and fashions, just as the big planters of the islands were. This seemed to be shaping the British Atlantic into a unified consumer market, bound together by a common set of cultural values.

The growth of British North America can be summed up in population figures. In 1700, the colonies contained about 240,000 white settlers and perhaps 18,000 slaves. By 1750, there were about 957,000 whites and 247,000 slaves. Settler numbers had quadrupled, mostly through natural increase. Another round of steady immigration, primarily from Scotland and Ireland, was about to begin. Altogether, from 1700 until the American Revolutionary War in 1775, 217,000 British and Irish emigrants crossed the Atlantic to North America, of whom 35,000 were Scots, 42,000 were Southern Irish and 66,000 were what Americans call "Scotch-Irish," meaning Ulster Presbyterians. Clearly, North America was changing from a cluster of English colonies into much more diverse societies, made up of Britons and Irish of all religious and ethnic varieties. This did not translate into a stronger allegiance to Great Britain, as so many of the immigrants were from parts of the British Isles where the state was not held in high regard. Also among the newcomers were many German speaking Protestants: Moravians, Baptists, Lutherans from Salzburg, and others. The British and Irish generally crossed the Atlantic as indentured servants, whose labor had been contracted to an employer. The Germans tended to be "redemptioners," meaning they came without labor contracts and had to pay their passage by finding work after they arrived.

Many emigrants stayed in the cities, which had reached the size of substantial British urban centers. Boston contained 16,000 people, New York about 12,000, but the boom town of Philadelphia had swollen to 20,000. It remained the chief port for agricultural goods bound for the West Indies. Social inequality characterized the American cities, as merchants, grown rich from overseas trade, built big houses and bought fine household items to imitate their wealthy counterparts in Britain, while the poor clustered around the harbors, looking for work. Through the ports of British North America, about £1 million of goods were sent annually to the mother country – still far less than the value of sugar exports from the West Indies, but a substantial sum nonetheless. Almost half of the value of North American exports to Britain was in tobacco. The Americans also traded directly with the Caribbean and with Europe, in violation of the Navigation Acts. While the West Indians still consumed British goods at an astonishing per capita rate, the Americans were more abstemious, although their appetite for British commodities was growing.

The expansion of the North American population would lead to pressure on the frontiers, where settlers wanted land. To get it, they were willing to displace Indians by any means necessary. In areas where the settlers felt threatened, and were not restrained, as on the borders of the Carolinas, they killed and enslaved Indians with virtual impunity. The colonial governors and the British government, however, resisted pleas for a more aggressive policy towards native peoples, because they wanted to preserve peace, especially with the Iroquois Confederation. War was costly and might create allies for the French. Peace, on the other hand, allowed commercial relationships to spring up, especially the lucrative fur trade, which brought to Indian peoples the benefits of European metal goods like axes and knives. By the 1750s, however, the Iroquois were losing control over many of the Indian nations with which they were allied in the Covenant Chain, a situation that would fuel the outburst of a great imperial war.

The territorial expansion of the mainland settlers in the first half of the eighteenth century was mainly westward, and did not involve the creation of new colonies. Only two were founded in this period, both in special circumstances. Nova Scotia – the southeastern part of the present Canadian province – was ceded to Britain in 1713. Its inhabitants were French-speaking Catholic farmers, called Acadians, and Micmac (pronounced Migmaw) Indians. The British made no attempt to form a settlement until 1749, when the port of Halifax was founded.

Germans arrived soon after to settle the fishing town of Lunenburg. The forced deportation of the Acadians in 1755 made their land available to New England "planters," several thousand of whom moved to Nova Scotia. They did not establish New England town governments, but they were granted an assembly in 1758 – the first legislature in Canadian history. The other new colony was Georgia, which started as a philanthropic experiment. Chartered in 1732, the proprietors of Georgia were trustees who were not allowed to profit in any way from their venture. The settlers were supposed to be poor debtors released from English prisons. They were to raise hemp and silk, and form a militia to protect themselves from the Indians as well as from the Spanish to the south in Florida. Rum and slavery, those two icons of West Indian wickedness, were forbidden. The religiously tolerant colony became a haven for German Protestant sects, and for Jews. It also attracted young ministers with evangelical aspirations, like Wesley and Whitefield. Socially and economically, however, Georgia was a total failure. The settlers thirsted for hard drink, and they wanted slaves to do the work for them. By 1752, they had been granted both, and the despondent trustees sadly handed over the charter to a royal governor.

The victory of slavery in Georgia was predictable. Throughout the southern colonies, the system seemed to be irresistible. By 1750, slaves on the mainland were bound by legal codes that governed every aspect of their lives. As in the islands, their status was defined as inherited through their mothers – hence, the illegitimate offspring of a slave owner and a slave were not born free. Except in the rugged Carolinas, life for North American slaves was generally better than in the West Indies: they lived longer, were able to form stronger families, and had more offspring. On the other hand, West Indian slaves could often raise their own livestock and crops when they were not working for a master, and sell their produce for small profits. This was not allowed to slaves in the Chesapeake, although it did occur in the Carolinas. Throughout the British colonies, slaves showed remarkable resourcefulness in terrible conditions. They invented "creole" languages to overcome the linguistic barriers among themselves, preserved African traditions of music, and quietly adhered to African religious beliefs. They did not become Christians, in part because their masters opposed it. The law throughout the southern colonies (and in New Jersey) stated that Christ would not make black people free. A few evangelical ministers were beginning to assert that slaves should be "brought to Christ," although George Whitefield, who owned land in the southern colonies, gave sermons justifying slavery on biblical grounds.

Slavery was not confined to the southern colonies. There were thousands of slaves in Pennsylvania, New Jersey, New York, and Rhode Island, and they were not just household servants. Many of them worked as skilled craftsmen, and they were often put out to hire by their masters. The laws restricting them were no more humane than anywhere else in British America. In 1712 and again in 1741, slave conspiracies were discovered in New York, involving plans, real or imagined, to burn down the city. The 1741 incident led to the execution of four whites and 31 slaves, several of whom were burned alive in order to make them confess. The War of Jenkins's Ear was then raging, and the Spanish had promised to free any slaves who fled to Florida (35 years later, the British used the same tactic against the American revolutionaries). The Spanish offer had already inspired an uprising in 1739 by slaves in South Carolina, known as the Stono Rebellion, which had resulted in the killings of several whites before it was suppressed. Fear of slave rebellion was rampant among whites. The reality, however, was that open revolts among slaves were very rare.

The South Carolina assembly answered the Stono Rebellion with an Act forbidding slaves from assembling in groups, learning to read, or earning any money from their own crops. Assemblymen throughout the colonies were united in their abhorrence of slave uprisings, but this may have been one of the few points on which they could agree. Politics in the mainland colonies remained lively and factious. The assemblies of the mainland colonies were not democracies: women, slaves (even free blacks, in many cases), and men who owned no property could not vote. Still, the franchise was fairly widely spread among rural white adult males, because so many of them owned land. They elected men who saw themselves as representatives of the people, who read John Locke and *Cato's Letters*, and who strongly defended the liberties of free-born Englishmen, even when they denied any liberty at all to slaves. Organized political opposition may have been more acceptable in the colonies than in Britain, where few wanted to admit that they supported a "faction" or party. "Opposition is the life and soul of public zeal, which, without it, would flag and decay for want of an opportunity to exert itself," opined the *New York Gazette*.[5] Governors did not always share this view, and might take extraordinary steps to suppress their critics. In 1735, the governor of New York tried to stifle the *Weekly Gazette*, an opposition newspaper, by putting the printer, John Peter Zenger, on trial for seditious libel. In such cases, the jury was asked only to determine the involvement of the accused, not whether the publication was in fact seditious, but Zenger's jury rejected instructions from the judge and found the printer innocent. A similar case, involving John Wilkes and the *North Briton*, would arouse political passions in Britain 30 years later.

Governors often clashed with colonial assemblies, whose members accused them of setting up mechanisms of "tyrannical" control and corruption similar to Sir Robert Walpole's system in Britain. In fact, the colonial governors did not have much patronage at their disposal, and were not able to establish secure administrations in the face of opposition from the assemblies. Pennsylvania was an extreme case, where the "Country" opposition, led by the fiery Welsh Quaker David Lloyd, launched sharp attacks on the proprietary interest that tied up all government business. Lloyd pressured William Penn into removing the legislative power of the governor's council in 1701, and for the next three decades, he continued to defy the will of the governor and the Board of Trade. In the 1740s, Quaker pacifists in the Pennsylvania assembly went so far as to block the colony's participation in the war effort.

The actions of the "Quaker party" indicate the continuing strength of religion in American life. Yet the perception of many New England Congregational ministers around 1740 was that religious belief was declining in America, and along with it was fading the dream of a godly outpost in the wilderness.

Presbyterian ministers in the middle colonies were not so pessimistic, but they too were convinced that Christian faith needed a new stimulus. Then George Whitefield descended upon them like a whirlwind. He made his first preaching tour in the middle colonies and New England in 1739–41. Whitefield thrilled audiences throughout the colonies, motivating an outburst of evangelicalism that was known as "the Great Awakening." Congregational and Presbyterian ministers threatened their parishioners with imminent damnation if they did not accept Christ as their savior and change their worldly ways. Thousands experienced shuddering conversions after hearing such terrifying sermons. The Congregational minister Jonathan Edwards marveled at the effects of evangelical preaching on listeners: "Very often they have a lively idea of the horrible pit of eternal misery; and at the same time it appears to them, that the great God who has them in his hands, is exceedingly angry, and his wrath appears amazingly terrible to them." The "glorious reformation" that followed such fears filled Edwards with wonder. He worried that those who scoffed at the evangelists "will fail of any share of so great a blessing, and will miss the most precious opportunity of obtaining divine light, grace, and comfort, heavenly and eternal benefits, that God ever gave in New England."[6]

Although the words used by evangelicals might be similar on both sides of the Atlantic, their effects were not. The Great Awakening was a highly divisive force in American society. It split congregations into "New Lights" who were open to the evangelical message, and "Old Lights" who rejected it. The minority party often stormed out of the church, to found a separate meeting. In some places, ministers who truly abhorred the Awakening defected to the Church of England. While in Britain the evangelicals appealed mainly to the downtrodden, and remained a minority tendency within the established Churches, in America they had listeners in every social category, and battled for control of whole denominations. Whether the Awakening prepared the way for the American Revolution is debatable, but it certainly revived the sense among Americans that they were more godly than their rulers in the home country, and it spread this conviction of spiritual superiority to a wide audience.

The feeling of being specially designated by God did not make white Americans unreceptive to British culture, especially in the upper levels of society. The gentry of Virginia and the rich merchants of Philadelphia, New York, and Boston wanted to dress in the latest fashions, drink tea, and ride in elegant coaches. They bought sophisticated furniture, constructed in America but designed according to the latest British styles. Voluntary societies and institutions flourished in America as they did in Britain, and several colonial universities were founded, so that neither aspiring clergy nor the sons of the privileged would have to travel overseas in order to gain a higher education. The Americans worshiped in churches that were copies of Christopher Wren's originals, and in countless country houses or assembly rooms they practiced the rules of politeness. A young Virginia gentleman named George Washington carefully copied out "Rules for Civility and Decent Behaviour" from an English courtesy book. He did not write down all the recommendations for dealing with social inferiors, many of which would have been ridiculous in America, even in Virginia, the most hierarchical of mainland colonies. He did, however, record this guiding principle: "Let thy ceremonies in Courtesie be proper to the Dignity of his place with whom thou conversest for it is absurd to act the same with a Clown and a Prince."[7] This advice would have served Washington as well in London as in Williamsburg.

Yet Washington never set foot in London, and Americans who did often felt that they were not quite refined enough, not quite deferential enough, to fit into British high society. Like many people of middling status in Britain itself, wealthy Americans wanted to imitate the British upper classes, but felt distanced from them. They often inclined towards the plain-spoken frankness espoused by the famous Benjamin Franklin of Philadelphia, a printer, writer, and inventor. Franklin opined that one became "an agreeable and entertaining Companion" by "seasonably introducing into Conversation useful Subjects on human Life and Characters, by making solid and practical Reflexions thereon, and engaging the Attention by a polite, an easy and lively Manner."[8] This was a practical, didactic, American sort of politeness, and it bored British sophisticates. It would be going too far to claim that such attitudes inclined the Americans towards independence – after all, the West Indian planters were also treated as outsiders by the British elite, although they bought estates in Britain and married into established landed families. The West Indies was definitely not moving towards independence. The North American experience, however, can be seen as pointing, if not towards a break with Britain, at least towards a rising degree of distinction between two similar societies on either side of the Atlantic. The renewal of war with France would accelerate this process.

The Struggle for North America

In North America, the Seven Years' War was known as the French and Indian War. It began earlier than in Europe, and was carried on by the colonists without much regard for what was happening across the Atlantic. Although the involvement of the Royal Navy and the regular British army was linked to a grand strategy whose main focus was Europe, the war in North America took on a character of its own, mobilizing colonial fighting forces on a scale never seen before, and encouraging the first tenuous links between the colonial legislatures. It would also open up a rift between the mainland colonists and the home country that would never be healed.

For British North Americans, the war meant above all a confrontation with the French, who had been established in the St Lawrence Valley since the early seventeenth century. The terror inspired by the French is hard to understand – after all, there were only 55,000 settlers in New France, most of them peaceable farmers. To the British colonists, however, they represented the threat of Catholicism, whose supposedly insidious influence seemed to be spreading. French fur traders were active throughout the interior of the continent. French forts were appearing around the Great Lakes and on the Ohio River, and French settlements were springing up in the Mississippi valley. The French and their Indian allies were blocking the westward expansion of Protestantism and British dominion. Evidently, God wanted them to disappear.

However, the colonial elites were not united in their response to the French menace. They longed for war, but they did not necessarily want to pay for it. Colonial assemblies were incredibly stingy in financing military efforts. Above all, they resented paying for the defense of other colonies, and they refused to cooperate in a common defense, to the disgust of the British government. For their part, the colonists felt that previous military experience had not left them with much confidence in the home country. Colonial troops had died in droves, mostly of disease, during the badly planned British attack on Cartagena in 1740. Five years later, a New England expedition had captured Louisbourg, the strategic French fort on Cape Breton Island. It was returned to France by British peace negotiators in 1748, in spite of howls of betrayal from New England.

The immediate cause of the renewal of war in North America was the breakdown of the Covenant Chain, the set of agreements between New York and the Iroquois Confederacy that guarded the western frontiers of British America. In 1753, the spokesman of the Mohawk nation, Chief Theyanoguin, known to the British as Hendrick, told the governor of New York, "So brother you are not to expect to hear from me any more, and brother we desire to hear no more of you."[9] The alarmed governor called a conference at Albany the following year, to discuss a common colonial strategy towards the Indians. Virginia failed to send delegates, as it had already dispatched a militia force under George Washington to attack Fort Duquesne, at what is now Pittsburgh. The inexperienced young officer was instead forced to surrender. Meanwhile, the Albany congress had failed too, demonstrating to the Board of Trade a pathetic lack of cooperation among the colonies. Now Britain would have to take over the war that young Washington had started.

One of the first decisions made by the British was to deport the Acadians from Nova Scotia. The Acadian leaders had promised not to assist their French compatriots, but they would not swear an oath of allegiance to the British crown. As a result, about 6000 Acadians, along with many Micmac Indians, were loaded into ships and sent to New England ports, from whence they were dispatched to France, New France, or the Mississippi. Some of them escaped the roundup, while others secretly returned. Their descendants have not forgotten what they still see as "ethnic cleansing" by the British.

The first two years of war in North America were marked by disaster after disaster for Great Britain. In spite of the warnings of George Washington, who was learning from experience, a major expedition to the Ohio valley of British regular troops was ambushed by a small force of French and Indians in July 1755. Its commander General Braddock was killed, and the badly mauled force retreated. French and Indian troops, under the command of the Marquis de Montcalm, captured Fort Oswego and Fort William Henry on the frontiers of New York. Montcalm's Indian allies, furious at being denied war prizes, massacred part of the garrison at Fort William Henry, which caused panic at Albany, less than 100 miles away. Faced with these severe defeats, Secretary of State William Pitt, who was in charge of the war effort, decided in 1757 to change British policy towards the colonies. First, he removed the British commander-in-chief's authority to compel colonial governments to assist him, and instead offered subsidies. Second, he ended the system of military discrimination by which colonial officers were considered subordinate to regular British officers holding the same rank. In these ways, Pitt hoped to win the support of the colonial assemblies for a renewed war effort.

The campaign season of 1758 did not begin well for the British. A major assault on the defenses of Fort Carillon (Ticonderoga) on Lake Champlain was beaten back by Montcalm's army. Advancing through woods towards the French trenches, the British regulars were mowed down like wheat, and had to abandon the hope of attacking Montreal through the Champlain valley. On the same day as this defeat, however, General Jeffrey Amherst made a rash decision to throw his soldiers into the roaring surf near Louisbourg. They landed successfully, and after a three-week siege the fort surrendered. The St Lawrence River was now open to British attack.

Pitt decided to exploit the Louisbourg victory by sending a detachment of the Royal Navy down the river, accompanied by an army under the ambitious and neurotic General James Wolfe. Its aim was to capture the French colonial capital at Quebec. A veteran of the '45 Rebellion, Wolfe treated the French colonists along the St Lawrence just as brutally as Cumberland had treated the Scots Highlanders, burning their villages and destroying their crops. After an initial landing above the fortified city failed, Wolfe made a second attempt below it. His troops boldly scaled a high cliff by night, to appear on a plain in front of Quebec as day broke on September 13, 1759. Surprised, Montcalm hastily ordered an attack, which was repulsed by the solid line of redcoats. The French army retreated back to the city in chaos, along with their mortally wounded commander. Meanwhile, struck by bullets in the wrist, the intestines, and the chest, General Wolfe died on the battlefield. Quebec surrendered the next day.

The battle of the Plains of Abraham was seen by the British as nothing less than miraculous, their greatest victory in the *annus mirabilis* or year of miracles. The news of Quebec's fall was celebrated by the colonists with fireworks and concerts, and their clergymen predicted that this glorious victory would be followed by the Second Coming of Christ. Preaching before the government of Massachusetts on the theme of Wolfe's victory, a Congregational minister hoped that God would "advance the Cause of Liberty, and pure Religion, till every Nation shall be happy under the Government of the Prince of Peace."[10] The American artist Benjamin West later painted a famous depiction of Wolfe's heroic death, in which the general appears like a dying Christ, surrounded by admiring officers and a pensive Indian. Yet the battle was not decisive. A French army advanced from Montreal in the following year, and defeated the British outside Quebec. The city was rescued only by the arrival of the Royal Navy. It was in fact British naval power that had made Wolfe's victory possible, and that prevented the French from mounting a counter-offensive in Canada. With Quebec secured, the British advanced on

Illustration 14 *An engraving of Benjamin West's famous painting, "The Death of General Wolfe." Like the worshipful figures around him, we are meant to admire the death of the British general as a kind of patriotic martyrdom. (Auguste Le Grand, after William Woollett, engraving of "The Death of General Wolfe" by Benjamin West, 1776. © Private Collection,/The Bridgeman Art Library)*

Montreal from the north, along the valley of the St Lawrence, and from the south through the Champlain and Richelieu valleys. The surrender of Montreal in August 1760 marked the end of New France, and of military operations in mainland North America.

It was not the end of the war, however. British naval supremacy was now complete, and prizes of far greater value than Quebec could be seized. The French West Indian islands of Guadeloupe and Martinique fell to the British, as did the Spanish colonial city of Havana in Cuba, captured at a cost of 6500 British lives, most of them taken by disease. The collapse of Britain's imperial enemies, France and Spain, seemed to be total. By the time Havana fell in 1762, however, Pitt had resigned, and the new King, George III, was determined to end this exhausting, expensive war. By the Peace of Paris in 1763, the British would retain Canada, but the conquests in the Caribbean would be returned to France and Spain, so as to prevent future attempts to regain them.

The French and Indian War witnessed the biggest mobilization of colonial resources that had ever been seen in the Americas. Every British colony was asked to provide troops and money for the war effort. The British government saw this as a common effort in support of imperial interests, but the colonists were more likely to interpret it as self-defense. Many of them believed that they had carried a disproportionate burden. Their militia forces, used to egalitarian relationships and a casual enforcement of regulations, were not pleased at having to serve under the command of British officers, whose social views were hierarchical, and who exercised a ferocious discipline, based on the threat of corporal punishment.

Worst of all to the Americans, however, were the disappointing results of the war. The Peace of Paris had actually guaranteed the preservation of Catholicism in Canada, to the horror of godly Protestants. Shortly after it was signed, an uprising broke out among the Indian nations of the Great Lakes region, who resented the incursions of British settlers and chafed at the continuing influence of the Iroquois. They rallied around Chief Pontiac, whose goal was to restore French power in North America. Although Pontiac ultimately had to make peace with the British, his insurrection alarmed the government of George III. A Royal Proclamation of 1763 forbade colonial expansion beyond the Appalachian Mountains. The colonists were outraged: what had they fought for, if not Indian lands? Even the conquest of French Canada seemed to be in jeopardy. Although the 1763 Proclamation established English law in the new colony of Quebec, the military governor permitted French law to be used in lower courts, and did not remove Catholics from juries. New England merchants who had streamed into Montreal were horrified by the thought that "Papists" would be allowed to make judgments on them.

The great war for empire had not ended as the Americans had wished, with a triumph for Protestantism and British commerce that might herald the end of the world. God had given total victory to Britain, but the King and his ministers seemed to have thrown it away. For how long would the colonists accept this?

War in India and the *Diwani*

The war for empire was a world war. It was fought in West Africa, where the Royal Navy in 1758 seized major slave-trading forts from the French. It was fought in East Asia, where a 1762 British expedition captured the Spanish town of Manila in the Philippines, only to find that its trade was negligible and most of its population poor. The West African forts were kept by Britain in the Peace of Paris, while Manila was given back to Spain. The most important center of warfare outside Europe and North America, however, was India, where the East India Company crushed its French competitor and in 1765 made itself a territorial ruler for the first time.

This was not, as some historians used to insist, a war for control of India; instead, it was a limited conflict for commercial and territorial advantage between two trading companies. To a large extent, the British and French companies were responding to actions by Indian princes; they were not following a blueprint for conquest and dominion. The war was fought almost entirely by Indian troops, called sepoys, who served both the British and the French, and it involved little expense for the European powers. Yet it was also the outcome of a deepening British economic involvement in India, due to what was called country trade, meaning the personal commercial activities carried on by employees of the EIC, often in territories far beyond the trading forts. The disintegration of the Mughal empire had given local rulers more independent authority, creating new regimes throughout India. Company officials who were involved in country trade had an interest in expanding British influence over these local rulers, and they used the imperial mindset of the British public to gain support for their initiatives.

In the south, Britain and France clashed over the issue of who should rule as Nawab, or ruler, of the state of Arcot. The British backed one candidate, the French another. The superior ability of the Royal Navy to bring troops and supplies to India proved decisive in this confrontation. In 1760, a tiny EIC army, commanded by an Irish Protestant general, defeated an equally tiny French army, commanded by an Irish Catholic general, that was besieging the fort of Wandiwash (Vandivas), near Madras. The French trading fort of Pondicherry fell to the British early in the following year. The EIC had now eliminated its French competition in southern India, and the British-backed Nawab of Arcot was secure. He would use British troops to expand his territory, making Arcot into a formidable power in southern India.

In the northern state of Bengal, the Nawab Siraj-ud-daula wanted more control over the British, whose trading fort at Calcutta had become enormously profitable. When they refused to negotiate, Siraj-ud-daula seized the city, locking up its British residents in a prison that became known as the Black Hole. About 50 people died there of suffocation. The EIC sent Robert Clive to the north with a force of British troops and sepoys. After reoccupying Calcutta, Clive with 3000 men confronted Siraj-ud-daula's 50,000 troops, encamped in a mango grove near a village named Plassey. Clive had already convinced the Nawab's chief lieutenant,

Mir Jafar, to desert to the British side, and the Bengali ruler's troops had been bribed to throw down their arms. The result, predictably enough, was a great British victory. Siraj-ud-daula was murdered, and Mir Jafar became Nawab. He quickly signed a treaty advantageous to the Company, and reimbursed its employees for their losses. "The Interests of the Company, and the Country Government, are declared to be the same," a British writer enthusiastically observed. "This stupendous Revolution," he continued, "may be also considered as equally glorious and advantageous to the *British* Nation ... it is a signal Proof of the Utility of Maritime Empire."[11] It did not long benefit Mir Jafar, however. When he refused to grant more territory to the EIC, the Nawab was deposed. His successor tried to regulate the Company, and was overthrown by Clive, now an English lord and governor of the EIC possessions in Bengal.

At this point, Lord Clive had a clever idea that would change the nature of British involvement in India. The EIC was already enjoying tax revenues from lands that had been given to it by Indian rulers. Why not give the Company the taxing rights of a Nawab of Bengal, which would put all the revenues of that wealthy state into British hands? The long-suffering peasant farmers, who were forced to turn over one-third or more of their produce in taxation, would have to pay to support the forts and sepoys and salaried clerks of the EIC. The trading concerns of the Company and its employees would be carried on without the massive fixed costs associated with running a huge monopoly business. Admittedly, the Company would also have to provide law courts and protection for the Bengalis, but this would not involve great expense. The manifest injustice of making Indians pay so that the Company, and the Company alone, could trade with them did not occur to Clive or to the Company directors or to the British ministers, although a few opposition Members of Parliament raised their eyebrows at what they saw as typical EIC corruption. Clive forecast an initial annual profit of £1.5 million from the revenues of Bengal, which was roughly equivalent to the whole sugar trade of the West Indies. That was all the British government needed to know.

Clive had no intention of bringing British settlers out to India. He envisaged a government in which a few Europeans would reap the benefits from a system run largely by Indians. Company officials tended to look down on the Indians, especially Hindus, and did not want them to have any authority over Britons. However, the Company officials typically had ambivalent feelings about life in India. They enjoyed the easy-going splendor of an EIC employee's existence, which they could not afford in Britain. William Hickey, an attorney who lived in Calcutta, wrote that "everybody dressed splendidly, being covered with lace, spangles and foil. I ... gave in to the fashion with much goodwill, no person appearing in richer suits of velvet and lace than myself. I kept a phaeton [a sleek carriage] and beautiful saddle horses, ... my whole establishment being of the best and most expensive kind."[12] Britons in India were not above adopting Indian customs, like smoking the hookah, and many EIC officials kept Indian mistresses. Theirs was a privileged, adventurous, male world, although it contained a handful of intrepid British women, like Lady Clive, who had come to India as the wives of officials.

Very few Britons wanted to stay in India permanently. Some, like Clive, returned as wealthy "Nabobs" to Britain, where they purchased big country houses and Parliamentary seats, to the disgust of the old landed gentry.

In 1765, by the Treaty of Allahabad, the Mughal Emperor granted to the East India Company the *diwani* or right to draw revenues from the state of Bengal. From then on, the Company acted like an Indian ruler. Like other rulers, it was dependent on armies of Indian troops, on Indian merchants, and on the Indian landlords, called *zamindars*, who collected the revenues from their estates. Unlike other rulers, the Company was a monopolistic British trading concern that used tax revenues to increase its business profits. As for the British government, it was alternately dazzled by and suspicious of the success of the EIC. To control the results of the Company's actions, it would have to involve itself increasingly in Indian affairs. One of the most complex and tortured imperial relationships in history had begun.

Part V

The Fall of the First British Empire, 1760–1784

If you were looking for the beginning of "the modern age" of world history, then Britain after 1760 might be a good place to start. Many of the characteristics that we think of as modern – democratic politics, secular ways of thinking, industrialization, opportunities for social advancement – seemed to get off the ground in the last 40 years of the eighteenth century, and all of them profoundly affected British history. However, these modern traits are not very precise characteristics, and if we try to make them more definite, we may disagree about what exactly makes an age modern. Furthermore, "the modern age" did not jump up out of nothing. The characteristics mentioned above can all be found before 1760, and they were not fully established until long after that date. On the surface, the British constitution and social hierarchy hardly altered at all until the nineteenth century. It might be more accurate to suggest that the path towards a modern society, as it is commonly understood, became more clearly defined in the late eighteenth century, but the British ruling elite did not choose to follow that path very quickly. Other parts of the world were transformed in much more dramatic ways. For example, the decades 1760–1800 saw the birth of the pre-eminent global power of the modern age, the United States of America, and the violent emergence of the first modern democracy in France.

In spite of such qualifications, it remains clear that this period of British history did mark a break of some sort with the past – not a sudden, sharp, revolutionary break, as in North America or France, but a definite change in political, social, and economic life nonetheless. The old system of political control that had been established by the Junto Whigs after the Glorious Revolution was faltering, and in its place, new ideologies were emerging, based less on the defense of Protestantism than on patriotic attachment to the state. At the same time, the expanding economy of the early eighteenth century was shifting into a higher gear, as landowners and businessmen were tempted towards unprecedented levels of innovation. The landscapes and peoples of Britain would be transformed in ways that nobody could have predicted. These changes took place against the background of the traumatic loss of Britain's first empire. The American crisis helped to generate the first serious demands for reform of the British political system, but the government chose not to satisfy them. Instead, it relied on the continuing financial strength of the state to ward off attempts at constitutional change. It would take another 50 years before the British state began to alter its own course.

13

The Patriot King, 1760–1770

After the death of Henry Pelham, the system of control that had been perfected by the ministerial Whigs began to fall apart. The Seven Years' War (actually, a nine years' conflict for Britain) hastened its demise. The Whig system was finally killed off by two men who saw themselves as acting purely in the interests of the nation, without thought of personal or party gain. The first was the patriot minister, William Pitt; the second was the idealistic young king, George III. Between them, they fomented more than a decade of political mayhem in which factional groups competed for power, forming and dissolving coalitions and bringing one government after another crashing down in ruin. The "Old Corps" Whigs, the party of Walpole and Pelham, gradually lost their grip on power, and stability was not found again until the "King's Friends" coalesced around a set of ministers who claimed to have no party affiliations.

No wonder the American colonists were alienated! They were faced by a British political system that seemed to be in constant disarray, and in which the Whigs, the party of the Glorious Revolution and religious toleration, had been thrown out of office. To many Americans, the reign of George III was a return to the monarchical tyranny of the Stuarts. Their fears were upheld by radical voices in Britain itself, particularly that of the brash, rude and charismatic patriot, John Wilkes. By making patriotism into a way of criticizing the system, Wilkes and his supporters foreshadowed both the American Revolution and the later reform movement in Britain. They added a riotous sideshow to the chaotic carnival of British politics in the 1760s.

Patriot Culture

Where did this upsurge of patriotism come from? We have already noticed its roots in the 1730s and 1740s. The merchants who wanted war with Spain called themselves patriots, as did the politicians who hung around Frederick, Prince of

Wales, and even the rebels who backed the Stuart Pretender. By 1775, the writer and lexicographer Samuel Johnson was so sick and tired of politicians who declared themselves to be patriots that he denounced all of them with a famous definition: "Patriotism is the last refuge of a scoundrel." Johnson's friend and biographer, James Boswell, was quick to add that "he did not mean a real and generous love of our country, but that pretended patriotism which so many, in all ages and countries, have made a cloak for self-interest." However this may be, Johnson was unable to agree with Boswell in identifying *any* patriot politician who was not a scoundrel (the only close contender was Edmund Burke).[1]

Most people were not as skeptical as Dr Johnson. They believed in patriotism, for reasons that were religious as well as secular. They accepted that Britain was a nation destined by Providence for greatness in the world. Since the Reformation, English Protestants had seen themselves as the "new Israel," the people specially chosen by God to lead all of humanity towards the fulfillment of Scripture, the Second Coming of Christ. In the seventeenth century, godly Protestants expected the end of the world to happen any day, and saw signs of it in events like the downfall of the monarchy, the Restoration, or the Glorious Revolution. Speculation about the Second Coming did not by any means cease after 1700. Minor earthquakes in London, followed by a major tremor that destroyed the city of Lisbon in 1755, convinced many people that divine judgment was at hand, and a pastoral letter on the subject by the Bishop of London sold 100,000 copies in a month. The biblical foundation of British patriotism remained strong. The Hanoverian dynasty was praised as the triumphant house of King David, picked by God over the house of King Saul, or the Stuarts. Audiences in the 1740s and 1750s were thrilled by the music of the great religious oratorios composed by George Frederick Handel – *Messiah*, *Sampson*, *Saul*, *Israel in Egypt*, and others. Listeners were convinced that the history of the people of Israel was *their* story, and that God's promises to the Israelites had in fact been transferred to them. It helped that Handel's oratorios were sung in English, and that the words were familiar to anyone who knew the Bible.

Religiously based patriotism, however, had become secondary to the more worldly concern of promoting national interests. The formation of the British state had given patriotism a less spiritual tone. The older patriotism was attached to a geographical homeland, England or Wales or Scotland. The newer patriotism was attached to an administrative entity, Great Britain, that tied together diverse peoples in a common national enterprise. The older form of patriotism survived, but British patriotism surpassed it in impact. This was an aggressive, masculine, and populist patriotism that drew on classical Roman models of virtue in defense of the nation. Patriot heroes like William Pitt were depicted wearing Roman togas, their faces shown in stark, realistic profile, as on ancient coins and medals. British patriotism was also closely intertwined with polite entertainments and genteel culture. At Vauxhall Gardens in London, where Frederick, Prince of Wales, was the landlord, respectable citizens could wander through the "pleasure grounds," listening to music by British composers like Thomas Arne, or admiring paintings by British artists like Francis Hayman. Patriots hailed William Shakespeare as the great national writer, and in 1769 the theatre producer David

Garrick organized an elaborate celebration of the 200th anniversary of his birth. Fittingly for England, it rained.

British patriotism took as its particular enemies the supposedly effete, enslaved, and effeminate French. "Surely the infamous Figure they have made upon the Continent, both of Europe, and America, must draw the Contempt of all mankind upon them," maintained one British politician, who described war against them as "truly national, pure and unmix'd with any other Interest or Consideration."[2] We can see this anti-French feeling in William Hogarth's caricatures of the 1750s, showing starving Frenchmen hungering for English beef. We can hear anti-French patriotism in popular tunes like the rousing naval anthem "Hearts of Oak," written by David Garrick amidst fears of an invasion in 1759:

> They talk to invade us, these terrible foes,
> They frighten our women, our children, and beaux [effeminate men],
> But if their flat bottoms in darkness come o'er,
> Sure Britons they'll find to receive them on shore.
> Heart of oak are our ships, hearts of oak are our men,
> We always are ready, steddy, boys, steddy,
> We'll fight and we'll conquer again and again.

It might be argued that "Britons" here really meant "Englishmen," and that British patriotism was essentially English. Anti-French sentiment, however, was just as strong in Glasgow or Cardiff as it was in Bristol or Liverpool. Anti-Gallican Societies were formed throughout Britain during the Seven Years' War.

Patriot culture was crucial in generating the concept of a British public, a national audience that included not just the upper classes but every respectable member of society. The dimensions and limits of the British public were always amorphous. It was often perceived as being made up of independent country gentlemen and men of the middling sort, artisans and tradesmen and shopkeepers, but it might also include women. "Britannia," the personification of the British state, was portrayed as an armored female warrior, and women could take part in public displays of patriotism. They were usually expected merely to support male "warriors," or to be nurturing mothers to future patriots. The lower classes were usually seen as too dependent and "self-interested" to be real patriots, although at times their boisterous behavior was described as the essence of patriotism. Whatever its parameters, the British public was clearly much bigger than the elite that governed or the property owners who were allowed to vote. Patriotism pushed British politics in the direction of greater participation, although democracy, meaning voting rights for both men and women, lay more than a century in the future.

Lord Bute's Peace, 1760–1763

The first decade of George III's reign reveals two important features about the British state, one of which can be regarded as positive and one as negative. On the positive side, in spite of the dire predictions of many seasoned political observers, the state was able to survive without its creator, the Whig party. George III kicked them out, and while his monarchy tottered, it did not fall. By 1770 the King's ministers had even found ways to manage Parliament without a strong party organization at all, through a combination of patronage and appeals to loyalty to the crown. However, this was not, as some historians used to think, the "normal" situation of eighteenth-century government; instead, it was a transitional phase, generated by the King's obstinate refusal to deal with "factions." The main opposition group, the self-labeled "Old Corps" of Whigs, continued to identify itself as a coherent party, with a clear ideological position, and by the 1780s, a two-party system had largely re-established itself.

The negative point about the British state that emerged after 1760 was that it was more lacking in constitutional safeguards than most politicians had believed. The power of Parliament since the Glorious Revolution had depended on royal restraint, not on written guarantees. Because he was a native born monarch and the first King in 70 years who was unafraid of a Jacobite rival, George III was more willing to challenge the wishes of the majority party in Parliament. Yet as he bludgeoned his way through his first decade of rule, King George denied that he was claiming any authority that had not been enjoyed by his grandfather. He was right. The main constitutional power exercised by the King was the ability to appoint and dismiss ministers at will. He was not obliged to choose his ministers from among the politicians who dominated Parliament – he could pick anybody he wanted. George II had held the same authority, and he had twice thrown the political system into crisis by using it: in the early 1740s, when he supported Lord Granville, and in 1756–7, when he tried to keep William Pitt out of office. On both occasions, the King had been defeated by pressure from the Whig party. What George III learned from his grandfather's experience was that rulers should not accept "a state of bondage." Instead, the new King resolved "to rely on the hearts of my subjects, the only true support of the Crown."[3] Because party organization was weakening, the young monarch could not be reined in by Parliament as easily as his grandfather had been.

George III was not, as many Americans still believe, a tyrant. He acted according to what he saw as traditional British constitutional principles, and with a few notable exceptions, he did not overstep them. He governed on the advice of his ministers, not by his own will, and he tried to act with the support of Parliament. On the other hand, he was not the paragon of modern kingship that some admiring British historians have made him out to be. Like James II, he was a King with a plan. His good intentions were precisely what made him dangerous to the balance of the political system. If he had succeeded in ridding Britain of parties or "factions," he might have ruled without any serious Parliamentary resistance to his authority, as no monarch had done since the reign of Henry VIII. The only remaining check on royal power might then have been popular revolution – the option chosen by the American patriots.

King George was later perceived as mad, a diagnosis that was upheld by his doctors and led to his physical confinement in old age. He suffered seven bouts of "madness" between 1762 and 1809 before he was finally hidden from public view. They involved uncontrolled conversations, inappropriate behavior, and hallucinations. Medical historians have persuasively argued that he suffered from a hereditary genetic condition known as porphyria, which affects the nervous system and causes delirium. His contemporaries, however, were convinced that he was insane, and treated him accordingly.

King George's condition seems all the more tragic in light of his intellectual interests, which were more developed than those of any other Hanoverian monarch. Like his mother Princess Augusta, he liked botany, and assembled a magnificent collection of plant specimens in the garden of his house at Kew, outside London. Like his father Prince Frederick, he enjoyed music, and was proud to own Handel's own harpsichord. He patronized the German astronomer F. W. (William) Herschel, who together with his sister Caroline discovered the motion of the solar system (towards the star Lambda Herculis, apparently). He liked studying the mechanisms of clocks and watches. In 1768, George III founded the Royal Academy of Arts, which remains the most prestigious society of British painters and sculptors. He collected 65,000 books for the Royal Library, and made them available to scholars. The American John Adams described it in 1783: "the King's Library struck me with admiration. … [The books] were chosen with perfect taste and judgment; every book that a king ought always to have at hand, and as far as I could examine, and could be supposed of judging, none others."[4]

George III had better judgment in books than in chief ministers. Political historians, who like to divide periods into administrations, point to at least eight of them in the first decade of this reign, each identified by its leading ministers: Pitt-Newcastle (1760–1); Bute (1761–3); Grenville (1763–5); Rockingham (1765–6); Chatham (1766–8); Grafton (1768–70); and North (1770–82). In reality, the shift from one ministry to another was not always clearly defined, and the same cast of minor characters served in many of these administrations. The impression of constant political change, however, was acute. The man who was generally blamed for this instability was the King's tutor, mentor, principal advisor, and "Dear Friend," Lord Bute. He was a Scottish nobleman, a nephew of the Duke of Argyll, and a member of a strongly Hanoverian family. His political career was launched when he attached himself to the Prince of Wales in the late 1740s. After the death of Prince Frederick, Bute became a father-figure to Prince George. They exchanged letters daily, and Bute instructed the young heir in constitutional history and political principles. It was Bute who trained the patriot prince to hate "faction" and to resent the "bondage" into which the monarchy had supposedly fallen.

Already disliked by the new King, William Pitt quarreled bitterly with Bute over an impending war with Spain. The "Great Commoner," who had never lost sight of the goal of feasting on the wealth of the Indies, wanted to launch a preemptive strike against the Spanish empire. Bute, more reasonably, was convinced that the war with France must end soon, and wanted to maintain peace with Spain. Pitt angrily resigned in October 1761. Newcastle followed him eight months later, and Bute purged the administration of the Duke's "Old Corps" supporters, in a move felicitously described by one historian as "the Massacre of the Pelhamite Innocents." War with Spain, however, could not be avoided, and it made 1762 into another unexpected *annus mirabilis*. British expeditionary forces seized the French islands of Martinique and Grenada in the West Indies, the Cuban city of Havana, and Manila in the Philippines. These conquests were a little worrying to the Bute administration, because everyone knew that the French and Spanish would try to get them back. The prospect of an endless war might put the system of state finance under unbearable strain. Peace, therefore, was highly desirable, no matter how much Mr Pitt and his patriot supporters raged against it.

The Peace of Paris, signed on February 10, 1763 by representatives of Britain, France, and Spain, was a sensible solution to the problem of how to end the present war without causing international tensions that might lead to another war. For the sake of its American colonists, Britain was willing to take over French Canada, a possession it did not particularly covet. Much more desirable were the vast fishing grounds of the Grand Banks off Newfoundland. The French had seized Newfoundland late in the war, and although the British took it back, they were willing to concede fishing rights to their enemy in order to avoid further confrontations. The tiny islands of St Pierre and Miquelon off Newfoundland have been retained by France to this day. Minorca was restored to Britain, while France got back Guadeloupe, Martinique, and the slave fort at Gorée, but not Grenada or the Senegal forts. Manila was returned to Spain for a hefty ransom. In a bizarre exchange, Britain swopped Havana for Florida, while France further compensated Spain by handing over Louisiana. The French were allowed to trade in India but not to keep military forces there. Britain was permitted to cut logwood on the coast of Central America. Finally, the late George II would have been cheered at the news that the French were obliged to withdraw from his precious Hanover.

The Peace of Paris was a global settlement. Although it dealt extensively with commercial rights, at its heart was the assumption that territories around the world could be annexed or exchanged by European powers without taking the wishes of their inhabitants into account. This was not a new assumption, but it had never been applied on such a big scale, or to so many people. It seemed as if most of the world was being divided into spheres of European control. In this sense, the Peace of Paris marked a crucial step in the development of an imperialist mindset among British policy makers. From this point on, Britain's rulers would more or less take for granted their right to carve up the world for the benefit of their nation.

Nevertheless, the Peace was denounced in Britain by Pitt and his patriot followers, who saw it as a sell-out to the French. "Let us fancy a ministry devoted to the interest of France," one patriot writer speculated, "who rose to power, and gave back all the valuable conquests which England had made, at an immense expense of blood and treasure; and then let us ask, whether a Frenchman could have desired more? Whether he could even have hoped for so much? TWICE have the Whigs brought France to the brink of ruin; and TWICE has she been preserved by the Tories."[5] The last sentence implied that the Treaty of Utrecht foreshadowed the Peace of Paris, so that Bute and his cronies were just like the

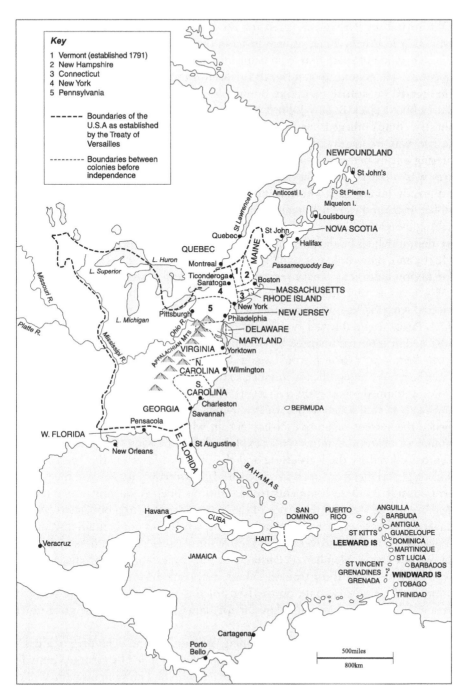

Map 6 *North America and the West Indies 1763–83. (Source: J. Steven Watson,* The Reign of George III, *Oxford, 1960, appendix.)*

Tories of Queen Anne's reign. It was a false accusation. Although the remaining "Old Tories" in Parliament voted for the Peace, they had nothing to do with fashioning it. As for Bute, he would have resented being stuck with any party label. This did not spare him from being lampooned in the patriot press as a Tory, a Jacobite, a Highland adventurer, and an arch-traitor. Popular caricatures showed him dressed in Scottish plaid like Bonnie Prince Charlie, or simply depicted him as a jackboot (Jack Boot = John, Earl of Bute), an apt symbol of his "despotic" ministry. Bute's alleged sexual liaison with Princess Augusta, King George's mother, was frequently alluded to, in graphically suggestive ways (a jackboot entering a frilly petticoat, for instance). The anti-Scottish element in these caricatures was often vicious. The Scots were pilloried as impoverished, self-serving, and greedy immigrants who had been granted an unjust monopoly on English public offices and were helping themselves to English wealth. This put in question the Anglo-Scottish Union, which was based on the creation of a single administrative unit, in which Englishmen or Scots could serve in any office.

In the end, Bute could not stand the pressure. The difficult passage of an unpopular tax on cider may have been the last straw, and he resigned in April 1763. "[M]y heart is very full whenever I think of that most unhappy moment," a dejected King George wrote to him.[6] The most celebrated patriot attack on Lord Bute's Peace was published two weeks later. It was written by John Wilkes and published in a journal financed by Pitt's brother-in-law, Lord Temple, entitled *The North Briton* (a "North Briton" was a derogatory term for a Scot). Number 45 of the journal – a significant number, calling to mind the Jacobite rebellion of 1745 – contained remarks on the resignation of the "insolent, incapable, despotic minister," as well as an attack on the King's speech from the throne that had opened the current session of Parliament, in which the signing of the Peace was announced. The anonymous writer explained that the King's speech "has always been considered by the legislature, and the public at large, as the *Speech of the Minister*," and therefore open to criticism.[7] Unfortunately for Wilkes, the government considered these comments to be seditious libel. A warrant was issued by the Secretary of State for the arrest of the author, printers, and publishers. As was usual in such cases, it was a general warrant, which did not contain any specific names. When it was discovered that John Wilkes was the author, he was arrested; but Wilkes was a Member of Parliament, and by established privilege an MP could only be arrested for treason, felony, or breach of the peace. The Court of Common Pleas released him on the basis of this privilege. Backed by powerful friends, Wilkes then brought a lawsuit for damages against all the government officers involved in his case.

The *North Briton* affair was becoming a cause for the defenders of English liberties, and a big headache for the new administration led by George Grenville, who happened to be Lord Temple's brother but who had no sympathy for Wilkes. The government decided to deal with the troublesome patriot by having him expelled from the House of Commons. A notorious rake, Wilkes had been a member of a club of male libertines, the Medmenham Monks, who had allegedly cavorted in mock rituals with prostitutes dressed up as nuns. For the amusement of the Monks, Wilkes had assisted in writing a pornographic poem, a parody of Pope's *Essay on Man* that contained the immortal lines, "life can little more supply / Than just a few good fucks, and then we die."[8] The Secretary of State, himself a well known libertine, read out the *Essay on Woman* in the House of Lords, amidst cries of horror and titters of amusement. Wilkes now faced a blasphemy charge, because the title page of the poem named a bishop as its editor. He fled to Paris, where his illegitimate daughter Polly was in school. The Commons expelled him, the courts found him guilty on both the seditious libel and the blasphemous libel charges, and when he failed to appear for sentencing, he was outlawed. The lawsuit for damages, however, continued in the courts, and Lord Chief Justice Camden finally ruled that general warrants could not be used, except in cases of treason. John Wilkes's supporters had won a major fight for liberty of the press. Their priapic hero, however, seemed to have wilted.

Troubles in America, 1764–1768

George Grenville had bigger fish to fry than John Wilkes during his two years as chief minister. A capable money manager and experienced Parliamentary politician, he was hampered from the first by the continuing influence of Lord Bute. Grenville threatened to resign if the King would not give him full confidence, to which the monarch reluctantly agreed. Bute officially left the political stage, although few people were willing to believe that he was not still manipulating the King. After George suffered a period of illness in 1765, he had a further misunderstanding with his chief minister, over a regency bill that would make arrangements for the continuation of government in case the monarch was incapacitated. George wanted his mother to become regent, but Grenville believed the gossip about her affair with Bute, and suspected that this was just another way of bringing the former favorite back into power.

The Grenville administration is chiefly known in America for the infamous Stamp Act of 1765. This was an attempt, made in the aftermath of Pontiac's rebellion, to compel American colonists to pay for their own frontier defense, by extending to them a duty on paper that already existed in Britain. Every piece of printed paper, from legal documents to playing cards, would be taxed and stamped by the British government. The amount to be raised was small, but the colonists were furious at what they saw as an illegal effort to tax them without the consent of their legislatures. The Virginia House of Burgesses passed angry resolutions rejecting any tax that was not passed by the representatives of the people. Riots against the stamp tax collectors broke out in several American towns, and at Boston, the governor's house was attacked by a mob. The protestors often displayed jackboots to show who they thought was really responsible for the outrageous tax. Upper class and middling men throughout the colonies organized societies opposed to it, calling themselves "The Sons of Liberty." Nine colonial legislatures sent delegates to a congress in New York, which drew up a declaration expounding the following principle: "That it is inseparably essential to the

Freedom of a People, and the undoubted right of Englishmen, that no taxes be imposed on them, but by their own Consent, given personally, or by their Representatives." The Massachusetts legislature went further in claiming that taxation by consent was founded in "the common Rights of Mankind," a breathtaking assertion.[9]

The level of resistance to the Stamp Act was unprecedented in the eighteenth-century British empire. The idea of "No Taxation without Representation" was startlingly new, and it challenged the idea of "virtual representation," by which those who could not vote were indirectly represented by legislators who sat for their county or town. The formation of a colonial congress, which could be viewed as an alternative to the British Parliament, was ominous. The fury of the Americans can only be understood as a reaction to a changing British political system, which the colonists knew about through newspaper accounts as well as through the reports of their agents or lobbyists at Westminster. The Stamp Act seemed to be part of a concerted assault on the liberty and prosperity of the colonies, accompanied as it was by two other pieces of obnoxious legislation: a new Sugar Act, which lowered the taxes included in the Molasses Act, but made them more enforceable by imposing a system of registration for cargoes; and a Currency Act that forbade the use of colonial paper money, or bills of credit, as legal tender. In light of these "despotic" measures, the fear that the British government had fallen into the hands of Tories and Jacobites seemed all too real to the Americans.

The reaction to the Stamp Act might have doomed Grenville's administration, but King George III was far less concerned about it than he was about the exclusion of Lord Bute. Ungrammatically, and in the tone of a resentful child, he wrote to his former tutor that Grenville's "ill humor does not astonish me that is the companion of his selfish disposition.... But thank God I have a friend [i.e. Bute] and that is what few Princes can boast of that except myself."[10] Finally, in a desperate bid to rid himself of Grenville, George accepted in June 1765 a ministry that would include the odious "faction" itself, the "Old Corps" led by the Duke of Newcastle and his younger protégé, the Marquess of Rockingham. The new ministry was cobbled together by the influence of the King's uncle, the Duke of Cumberland, who met with leading politicians at racing meetings. Cumberland's death in October left Rockingham in charge of the short-lived ministry. Its main achievement was to repeal the Stamp Act, but Parliament also passed a Declaratory Act asserting its "full power and authority to make laws and statutes of sufficient force and validity to bind the peoples of the colonies of *America*, subjects of the crown of *Great Britain*, in all cases whatsoever."[11] The Sugar Act was replaced by a low fixed duty on all imports of molasses. The government also tried to crack down on the American smuggling trade from Europe, and to encourage trade in the West Indies through creating free ports that could import goods from foreign colonies without charge.

Benjamin Franklin, residing in Britain as agent for the Pennsylvania legislature, thought the Declaratory Act was passed "merely to save Appearances," and was sure that "no future Ministry will ever attempt to tax us."[12] He was wrong on both accounts. It was a mistake to regard the Rockingham administration as taking a fundamentally different approach to the American colonies than its predecessor. Like the Grenville ministry, it wanted to bring the Americans into line with a new imperial commercial policy, whose object was to increase both the trade of the empire and the revenues derived from it. Slowly but surely, the Atlantic empire was being absorbed into an expanding British state. That change would soon require the creation of a Cabinet position dealing solely with colonial issues. The first Secretary of State for the colonies took office in December 1769.

Rockingham was gone by then. He and his friends did not last long in power, because the King did not like them much more than he liked Grenville. George had thought that the Stamp Act might be modified, but "the unhappy factions [i.e. the Whigs] that divide this Country would not permit this."[13] As might have been expected, George longed to bring Lord Bute's supporters back into the government, but the "Old Corps," who hated Bute, would not agree to this. Instead, they courted William Pitt, in hopes that the Whigs could be reunited. They did not grasp the extent to which Pitt, like the King himself, had turned his back on party politics. He had no wish to reconstitute a Whig administration; instead, he wanted to form one of his own, based purely on patriotism and "merit," or in other words, on devotion to Mr William Pitt. As a result, the last chance for Whig unity was lost. In July 1766, the King turned out his "Old Corps" ministers and asked Pitt to form a patriot ministry.

Things went badly for this administration from the first. Pitt was in poor health, suffering probably from depression, and he refused to lead in the House of Commons. Instead, he was elevated to the Lords as Earl of Chatham, which disgusted some of his former supporters. How could "the Great Commoner," who had so often declared himself to be opposed to personal rewards, accept such a distinction? Leadership of the ministry fell into the hands of younger men like Charles Townshend, the able but unpredictable Chancellor of the Exchequer, and the inexperienced Duke of Grafton, First Lord of the Treasury. Townshend revived the anger of the Americans by introducing the Revenue Act of 1767, establishing duties on the importation of glass, paint, lead, paper, and tea into the colonies. The purpose of the Revenue Act was to support a colonial fiscal and administrative bureaucracy, similar to that which existed in Great Britain. A commission of customs for all the colonies was to be set up at Boston, and four vice-admiralty courts, in which revenue cases were to be tried before a committee of judges (but no jury), were established.

Virtually no objections to the so-called Townshend Duties were heard from the opposition in Parliament, which shows how little dissension existed on colonial issues, but a boycott of British goods was immediately organized in the colonies. Townshend's premature death removed the chief backer of the duties, and in 1769 the Cabinet resolved to drop all of them except the one on tea. By that time, the government was losing popularity in Britain as well as in America, and was facing a huge embarrassment over the renewed affair of John Wilkes. Chatham's hoped-for ministry of patriots, now headed by Grafton, was vilified by many Britons as a corrupt faction of tyrannical Tories. How had this happened?

That Devil Wilkes, 1768–1770

John Wilkes cannot be personally blamed for most of the trouble. Like Henry Sacheverell in 1709–10, he merely exploited a deteriorating situation. The lack of clear direction in a wavering and disunited government was a major factor, but so too was the growth of a body of patriot opinion that was deeply suspicious of that government. Although it attracted some members of the elite, this radical patriotism took hold especially among urban shopkeepers and artisans, who thought that the whole system of imperial trade and the freedoms gained from the Glorious Revolution were in jeopardy. Wary of a king who seemed to be a throwback to the Stuarts, no longer willing to follow Pitt into an alliance with the forces of darkness, radical patriots in Britain and America rallied around an unlikely hero who they thought would protect liberty against her foes: the scandalous outlaw called by George III "that devil Wilkes."[14]

John Wilkes returned to London from exile in February 1768. Having received friendly hints from the administration, Wilkes was certain that he would not be arrested. He announced that he would run as a candidate in the general election of 1768, for the county of Middlesex, which contained the cities of London and Westminster. On the day of the poll, Wilkes's supporters marched down the Great West Road towards Brentford, where the voting was to take place, dressed up in blue ribbons and crying out "Wilkes and Liberty!" They drew the number 45 in chalk on every door they passed, to remember number 45 of the *North Briton*. Wilkes won the poll by over 400 votes, and a riot ensued. The windows of Lord Bute's London house were smashed, and genteel passers-by were forced to drink to "Wilkes and Liberty!" or have the numbers "4" and "5" inscribed on their shoes. Bonfires and dancing went on all night.

In a bold act of theater, designed to put his enemies on the defensive, the newly elected Wilkes promptly surrendered himself to the Court of King's Bench to be sentenced for his previous libels. Lord Chief Justice Mansfield presided over the court. As he could not claim Parliamentary privilege until he had been sworn in as an MP, Wilkes was ordered to be confined in the King's Bench Prison until his sentence was decided. While there, he received gifts from his supporters throughout England, many of them connected with the number 45. Buckles and buttons, coins and medals, punchbowls and snuffboxes bearing the blessed number were made in honor of the prisoner, along with a wig that had 45 curls and a corset, presented to Wilkes's daughter Polly, that had 45 pieces, 45 holes, and the number 45 marked on the stomach. In the coal port of Newcastle upon Tyne, 45 gentlemen drank 45 glasses of wine, with 45 fresh eggs in them, at 45 minutes past one. The purpose of all this good-humored celebration was not just amusement. Wilkes, the champion of merchants and tradesmen, had become part of the commercial culture of England – and of the colonies, too. From America, the Boston Sons of Liberty sent Wilkes two turtles, one of them weighing 45 pounds.

Meanwhile, outside the King's Bench Prison, huge crowds gathered every day to catch a glimpse of the patriot hero. The winter of 1768 had been harsh, and

John Wilkes Esq.

Drawn from the Life and Etch'd in Aquafortis by Will.ᵐ Hogarth.

Price 1 Shilling.   Publish'd according to Act of Parliament May y.ᵉ 10ᵗ.ʰ 1763.

Illustration 15   *William Hogarth meant to make fun of John Wilkes in this 1763 print, by emphasizing his cross-eyed stare and leering expression, but the image was quickly adopted by Wilkes's supporters in order to represent him as a man of the people. (William Hogarth, "John Wilkes, Esq.," 1763.)*

bread prices had risen, leaving many poor laborers in London complaining about their low wages. A worried ministry ordered troops to be sent to guard the prison. On May 10, 1768, hoping that the prisoner would be released for the new session of Parliament, a crowd of 15,000–20,000 people pressed up against the entrance to the jail. Somebody stuck a paper to the prison wall, bearing the lines "Venal judges & Minister combine / Wilkes & English Liberty to confine."[15] The soldiers pulled it down, the crowd threatened them, and the Riot Act was read twice. Angry voices were heard damning the King, the Parliament and the judges. The soldiers were ordered to fire into the crowd, killing five or six people and wounding 15. The protesters withdrew, carrying their dead, but for the next few days, mobs of weavers and coal heavers roamed the capital, breaking windows, attacking the houses of their employers, and beating up anybody who would not publicly pronounce the words "Wilkes and Liberty!" The respectable supporters of Wilkes, who were called "Wilkites," did not take part in this popular violence, but they defended it. "The licentiousness of a mob may be very alarming," wrote one Wilkite, "but any abuse of power in those who ought to be the guardians of liberty, appears to me to be infinitely more alarming."[16]

Wilkes was eventually sentenced on the libel charges to 22 months in prison and a heavy fine. He petitioned the House of Commons for redress, and was summoned to present his case, which he did with great fanfare and spirit. That the government was willing to give him this forum shows how nervous they were about him. At 3 a.m. on the morning of February 4, 1769, an exhausted House of Commons, having debated the Wilkes affair for hours, decided to expel him from its ranks. Before sleeping that morning, Wilkes wrote a letter to the electors of Middlesex. "If ministers can once usurp the power of declaring who *shall not* be your representative, the next step … is that of telling you whom you *shall* send to Parliament, and then the boasted Constitution of England will be entirely torn up by the roots."[17] Representation, the volatile issue raised by the Americans in the Stamp Act crisis, had become a Wilkite cause.

Wilkes was re-elected for Middlesex in the same month, without opposition. A shocked House of Commons voted that he was *incapable* of being elected, a personal disqualification that had never been made before. Wilkes was nevertheless elected a third time, and the House of Commons voted the election to be void. On the fourth attempt, in March, a government supporter came forward to oppose him, but Wilkes defeated him by 850 votes. The House of Commons declared the loser to be elected anyway. What further proof did the Americans need that the House of Commons itself, the defender of liberty against the Stuarts, had become corrupt and tyrannical? In fact, the House was just as much in favor of liberty as the men who controlled it were. In the next few months, however, their control began to crumble. Members of the opposition argued publicly in favor of Wilkes's election. As one of them put it, "the Constitution of Great Britain ought to be immortal, if any thing human can be made so; and the *main Pillar* which supports that Constitution, is the *Right* and *Freedom of Election*."[18] Outside Parliament, the Wilkites formed an association, the Society of Supporters of the Bill of Rights (SSBR), whose name harkened back to the famous document drawn up after the Glorious Revolution. Originally designed to pay off Wilkes's debts, the SSBR became an effective lobbying group, organizing dinners and drawing up petitions that called for the rights of voters to be respected. Seventeen counties and numerous towns, including Boston, sent petitions making such demands to the King, who ignored them all.

The anonymous newspaper writer "Junius," a supporter of Wilkes, addressed a fierce letter to George III in December 1769. The Irish, he wrote, "give you every day fresh marks of their resentment," while the Americans were "Looking forward to Independence." The king was not totally abandoned by his subjects, however, because "you have all the Jacobites, Nonjurors, Roman Catholics, and Tories of this country, and all Scotland without exception." These villains wanted George to act like a tyrant. Instead, Junius begged him to "Discard those little, personal resentments which have too long directed your public conduct," and tell his people that he would choose only ministers who possess their confidence. At present, the King was acting like a Stuart. "The name of Stuart, of itself," Junius wrote, "is only contemptible; – armed with the Sovereign authority, their principles are formidable. The Prince, who imitated their conduct, should be warned by their example."[19]

This was strong stuff, tantamount to a threat of insurrection. Meanwhile, the Wilkite petitioning campaign had gained the support of milder men, the "Old Corps" of Whigs in Parliament, led by Rockingham, who saw it as a means of undermining the Duke of Grafton's ministry. The tactic ultimately worked. In January 1770, as a new session of Parliament opened, William Pitt, Earl of Chatham, spoke resoundingly in the House of Lords against the exclusion of Wilkes. By the end of the month, the battered Duke of Grafton had resigned. "In your public character," "Junius" shot out at him, "you have injured every subject of the empire."[20] Grafton was replaced as chief minister by a more effective leader, the portly, hard-working Frederick, Lord North. From a Tory family, North sat in the House of Commons (his title was a "courtesy" given to the younger son of a lord). His fine oratory, calm temperament, and sense of humor would help him to manage both a tempestuous Parliament and a difficult King.

Wilkes was freed from prison in April 1770, and happy Wilkites celebrated by feasting, dancing, and setting off fireworks every 45 seconds. The patriot hero took up a position as alderman of London, to which he had been elected while in confinement. He had important friends in the government of the City, including the Lord Mayor, William Beckford. The Wilkites would continue to harass the ministry for the next four years. They were not merely gadflies, or anti-Scottish zealots, or muddle-headed imperialists. They were the first political movement in Britain since the Levellers of the 1640s to focus on the question of Parliamentary representation. Their conception of constitutional and legal rights revived and expanded on the ideas of the seventeenth-century Whigs. They also looked to the future in mobilizing opinion among the middling sort of Britons. Their biggest impact, however, may have been in the American colonies, where they helped to convince patriots that the House of Commons was itself an instrument of tyranny. The result would be a revolution.

14

The American Crisis, 1770–1784

Benjamin Franklin was gloomy about the situation of Great Britain in March 1770. "The Publick Affairs of this Nation are at present in great Disorder," he wrote:

Parties run very high, and have abus'd each other so thoroughly that there is not now left an unbespatter'd Character in the Kingdom of any Note or Importance … the Respect for Superiors, Trust in Parliament, and Regard to Government, is among the generality of the People totally lost; for even the King himself is treated in Publick Papers with a rude Freedom hitherto unexampled.[1]

Lord North's administration would create at least an appearance of stability, but things did not get any easier for King George III. The Americans rebelled, and for the first time in recent history, major politicians along with a portion of the British populace openly sympathized with the rebels. By the early 1780s, the Atlantic empire was falling apart, control over Ireland was deteriorating, and London itself was shaken by the worst riots ever seen in its history. What saved the British state from ruin was a combination of its own inherent strength and a partial return to the politics of Walpole's era, with an organized political party holding office. The main difference from the earlier period was that King George III himself had a major hand in shaping that party. The King who hated factions ultimately had to make one of his own in order to maintain control.

The American crisis is sometimes regarded as no more than a minor upset on the road towards global British power, but it was far more than that. An Atlantic empire based on commercial and cultural ties was lost, to be replaced by a South Asian empire in which the British were always conquerors and outsiders. The possibility of a trans-Atlantic union of English-speaking peoples, which Winston Churchill was still fondly dreaming of in the twentieth century, vanished forever. The loss of America also made a big difference within Britain itself. The "Old Corps" were not able to hold on to power after 1783, and the radical patriots failed to reform the political system. Their defeat was due in no small part to the view that they were endangering the British state by threatening the King. A conservative reaction against radical solutions would set in. It would last, with only a few interruptions, for almost five decades.

The Present Discontents, 1770–1775

In April 1770, Edmund Burke, an "Old Corps" MP, published a pamphlet entitled *Thoughts on the Present Discontents*. Born in Dublin, raised a Protestant but with a Catholic mother, Burke was an outsider in British politics. A complicated man and a deep thinker, he sought to place contemporary problems in the context of broader political theories. By seeking to govern without "faction," he argued, George III had tried to initiate "A scheme of perfection ... far beyond the visionary Republick of Plato." The essence of the King's scheme was "to draw *a line which should separate the Court from the Ministry*," so that "two systems of Administration were to be formed; one which should be in the real secret and confidence; the other merely ostensible, to perform the official and executory duties of Government." In this "double Cabinet" system, business would be done by the courtiers or "King's Friends," while the ministers merely executed their orders. As a result, "lawful Government is undone." George III should return administration to the hands of an "honourable connexion," to politicians "bound together by common opinions, common affections, and common interests." In short, the king should bring the "Old Corps" of Whigs back into power.[2]

Burke's analysis was exaggerated – there was no secret division between two Cabinets – but he was right in identifying the king's meddlesome intentions as the principal cause of political turmoil in Britain. The patriot views of George III, however, were not unique. Disgust for the corruption and manipulation of the "Old Corps" was a widely held opinion. Burke ignored this, just as he overlooked popular demands for reform of the Parliamentary system. A reply to Burke was written by the radical patriot Mrs Catharine Macaulay, author of a celebrated *History of England* and sister to the London alderman John Sawbridge, one of Wilkes's strongest supporters. Burke, she maintained, had rightly criticized the court, but had overlooked the "no less dangerous manoeuvres of Aristocratic faction and party, founded on and supported by the corrupt principle of self-interest." She deplored the rise, after the Glorious Revolution, of "this state faction, who called themselves whigs, but who in reality were as much the destructive, though the concealed enemies of public liberty" as the tyrannical Stuarts.[3]

Radical patriots like Catharine Macaulay tried to form a party of their own. Through the Society of Supporters of the Bill of Rights, they campaigned for annual elections to Parliament and the exclusion of officeholders or "placemen" from seats in the House of Commons. Early in 1771, radicals in London rallied behind the cause of free reporting of Parliamentary debates in newspapers. The government tried feebly to stop them, but the crowd was on their side. Lord North was mobbed in the streets; his hat was cut into pieces and distributed as mementos. Effigies of the chief ministers were ritually beheaded by a crowd outside

St James's Palace. Parliament reluctantly surrendered, and ever since its debates have been openly reported.

John Wilkes had spearheaded this campaign, but in general he seemed more interested in raising money to pay off his debts than in leading a radical party. Disillusioned by the selfish conduct of the patriot hero, two of Wilkes's strongest supporters, John Sawbridge and Reverend John Horne Tooke, left the SSBR in April 1771 to form their own organization, the Constitutional Society. This division did not undermine the popular appeal of the radicals, whose influence remained strong in London government throughout the 1770s, and who won about a dozen Parliamentary seats in the general elections of 1774.

Like the radical patriots in Britain, the American patriots did not cool off much after 1770. In South Carolina, the Wilkes affair never ended. The assembly voted to send £1500 to the SSBR; the governor ordered them to rescind it, and for five years no official business could be done in the colony. In Rhode Island, a customs sloop, the *Gaspée*, was set alight by local smugglers in 1772. When the British government set up a commission of inquiry to find out who had done it, several worried members of the Virginia House of Burgesses, including Thomas Jefferson, founded a Committee of Correspondence to keep an eye on what they saw as unwarranted interference in American affairs. It was soon imitated in other colonies. Another issue that caused great concern among the Americans was the threatened appointment of a Church of England bishop. Anglicans and non-Anglicans alike feared, without much reason, that religious uniformity was going to be forced on them by Britain.

Observing the scene from London, Benjamin Franklin was particularly worried by the billeting of 600 British soldiers at Boston: "Indiscretion on the part of their warmer People, or of the Soldiery, I am extreamly apprehensive may occasion a Tumult; and if Blood is once drawn, there is no foreseeing how far the Mischief may spread."[4] His words were prophetic. In March 1770, a riot by Boston townspeople against the military garrison ended with a volley of musket fire and five deaths. The Boston Massacre was of course compared by patriots to the St George's Fields Massacre of 1768, but in the American case a patriot lawyer, John Adams, successfully defended the commanding officer of the troops, who had apparently not given the order to fire. The Boston Massacre was commemorated annually thereafter (until it was replaced by July 4) with patriot orations that were issued as pamphlets. Two years after the shootings, the British government's decision to grant salaries from the crown to the governor, lieutenant governor, and judges of Massachusetts caused a furor in the colony. Patriots saw it as yet another attempt at royal control, and made bold claims that the Massachusetts assembly had the same rights as the British House of Commons in resisting abuses of the royal prerogative. Blame for "despotic" measures was gradually adhering to the King himself.

Chastened by past experience, the administration of Lord North did not at first take a strong line against the colonies. The Colonial Secretary, North's stepbrother the Earl of Dartmouth, was sympathetic to the Americans and did not wish to antagonize them. The attention of the chief minister was drawn more to the affairs of the East India Company than to those of the Americans. The anomaly of allowing a privately owned company to administer territorial possessions in India had begun to preoccupy the British government. Motivated on the one hand by a desire to impose central authority, on the other by a wish to draw government revenues from the Company – the same motivations that had created the disastrous American policy – the government sought to assert its control over the Company's directors and large shareholders, who formed the General Court of Proprietors. By an agreement of 1769 with the Grafton administration, the EIC was required to hand over £400,000 annually to the government, to keep its dividend, the amount of profit paid out to shareholders, at 12.5 percent, and to loan the rest of its profit to the state. However, a war with the Sultan of Mysore, combined with a devastating famine in Bengal and a reckless policy of raising dividends, sent Company stock spiraling downwards in 1771–2.

A select committee of the House of Commons was appointed to look into the affairs of the Company. Its chairman, John Burgoyne, was highly critical of the conduct of EIC officers who had enriched themselves in India. The outcome of the committee's work was the Regulating Act of 1773, which altered the structure of the EIC, raising the qualification for voting in the Court of Proprietors and extending the length of office of directors, from one to four years. For the first time, the Act gave the crown a direct hand in the governance of India, by allowing the King to nominate the Company's highest officers: a governor-general of Bengal, with authority over all Company territories, as well as a governing council and a supreme court to judge cases involving Britons. Unfortunately, the relationship of the governor-general to the ministers in Britain was not clearly defined. To help it out of its financial difficulties, the EIC was given a substantial loan by the government. Through a Tea Act of 1773, it was permitted to sell stocks of tea outside Britain, at a low fixed price and with the normal customs duties rescinded. The government encouraged sale of the Company's tea in the American colonies, where it stood to gain revenue from the remaining Townshend duty of 3 pence per pound. Even with this added tax, the EIC's product would be cheaper than the smuggled Dutch tea that most colonists drank.

The Americans thought otherwise. The dumping of £10,000 of EIC tea into Boston harbor in December 1773 by the local Committee of Correspondence, whose members may or may not have been dressed up as Indians, pushed Lord North and Dartmouth towards retaliatory measures in the first months of 1774. The Boston Port Act prohibited ships from loading or unloading goods in Boston harbor. A second Act gave the governor of Massachusetts authority to appoint all judges in the colony, while a third altered the colony's charter by allowing the British government to appoint the governor's council. Very little opposition was voiced to these "Intolerable Acts" in the British Parliament; on the contrary, North was criticized for being too easy on the Americans. King George was delighted: "perseverance and the meeting [of] difficulties with firmness," he wrote to North, "seem the only means of either with credit or success terminating public affairs."[5] North had indeed been firm with Boston, just as Walpole had been with Edinburgh after the Porteous Riot, but the result in both cases was added hostility.

Illustration 16 *A cartoon of May 1774 showing Lord North as "the Able Doctor," forcing America, a half-clad Indian woman, to swallow "the Bitter Draught" of East India Company tea. Lord Mansfield secures America's hands while another minister peers up her skirt. France and Spain, on the left, are both amazed, while on the right Lord Bute, dressed as a Highlander, looks on approvingly. Behind them, Britannia weeps at the shameful scene. ("The able Doctor, or America Swallowing the Bitter Draught," 1774. © American Antiquarian Society, Worcester, Massachusetts, USA, / The Bridgeman Art Library)*

North soon alienated American opinion further by the Quebec Act, which protected the Roman Catholic religion and French civil law in the newly conquered territory of New France, and extended the boundary of the colony to the Ohio River. Unlike the "Intolerable Acts," the Quebec Act *did* encounter fierce opposition, especially in the House of Lords, because it seemed to establish Catholicism in part of the empire.

The American patriots now moved swiftly towards open resistance. Spurred by Jefferson, the Committees of Correspondence from every colony except Georgia (none existed in Nova Scotia) sent delegates to a general congress in Philadelphia in September. British control began to break down. Dartmouth heard from South Carolina that the patriots "have raised an universal spirit of jealousy against Great Britain and of unanimity towards each other," while from Massachusetts the Secretary received reports of riots and predictions that "Civil government is near an end." From Virginia, where the colonists were clamoring to make war against Indians on the frontier, Governor Dunmore informed Lord Dartmouth that "the power of government … is entirely disregarded if not wholly overturned."[6] King George III himself was convinced that the colonies were in rebellion, and must be brought back to obedience: "the dye [*sic*] is now cast," he wrote to

Lord North, "the Colonies must either submit or triumph. I do not wish to come to severer measures, but we must not retreat."[7] Most of the members of the American Congress did not want to break ties with Great Britain, but on a local level, especially in New England, militia forces were preparing themselves for a fight. The commander in chief of the British forces in North America wrote desperately to Lord North that he did not have enough troops to defeat them. This may have convinced the chief minister to try conciliation early in 1775, by offering to remove all taxes if the Americans would accept that Parliament had the *right* to tax them.

Edmund Burke offered a more eloquent plan of conciliation in the House of Commons, proposing that the legislation to which the colonists had objected should be suspended, and that they should be asked instead to grant money to the crown. In this brilliant speech, Burke offered a famous definition of empire, "as distinguished from a single State or kingdom ... an Empire is the aggregate of many States, under one common head; whether this head be a monarch, or a presiding republick. It does, in such consititutions, frequently happen ... that the subordinate parts have many local privileges and immunities." Those privileges should be respected, because to oppose them would only push the provinces towards rebellion. "Will it not teach them that the Government, against which a claim of Liberty is tantamount to high-treason, is a Government to which submission is equivalent to Slavery?"[8] Burke was predicting the future British Commonwealth, a union of equal states, but he was not describing the eighteenth-century British empire, which was moving away from the old idea that every province had its own privileges, towards a more centrally organized structure.

The British government was beginning to think it was too late for conciliation anyway. In April 1775, the Massachusetts militia skirmished with British troops at Lexington, then gave them an unexpected drubbing at Concord. The following month, Ethan Allen and the Green Mountain Boys of Vermont seized the British garrison at Fort Ticonderoga, and the second Continental Congress met at Philadelphia. It ordered the defense of the colonies, and named George Washington of Virginia as commander of its forces. It then sent a last ditch request for peace to George III, offering him loyalty in exchange for a redress of all American grievances. The King refused to read the "Olive Branch Petition," declaring that his American subjects were now in rebellion. He was not quite correct. With the establishment of Congress as a legislative alternative to Parliament, the creation of a military force, and the first battles between colonists and British troops, an American revolution had begun.

Revolution in America, 1775–1782

Should the events of these years really be called a revolution? American independence, which was finally accepted by the Congress at Philadelphia on July 2, 1776, and promulgated two days later, was a revolutionary concept, because it involved not a return to a previous political state, but the creation of a new one.

Nobody was more aware of that than Thomas Paine, an English Quaker immigrant, former excise officer, and radical patriot, who was living in Philadelphia. In his influential pamphlet *Common Sense*, published in January 1776, Paine argued that the British constitution was fatally flawed by the "remains" of monarchical and aristocratic tyranny, which, "by being hereditary, are independent of the people; wherefore in a *constitutional sense* they contribute nothing towards the freedom of the state." For Paine, the goal of discarding the hereditary elements in government, and vesting authority in an elected legislature, was inseparable from the goal of independence. After all, Paine noted, "England consults the good of *this* country, no farther than it answers her *own* purpose," and England's purposes were tainted by the influence of monarchy and aristocracy.[9]

Paine's ideas were too radical for most of the delegates at Philadelphia. Benjamin Franklin signed the Declaration of Independence, not because he had suddenly become a republican at the age of 70, but because he could not see how the colonies might submit to Britain after so much discord and animosity. As he wrote on July 20 to Admiral Viscount Howe, the British naval commander, who had offered him a pardon:

It is impossible we should think of Submission to a Government, that has with the most wanton Barbarity and Cruelty, burnt our defenceless Towns in the midst of Winter, excited the Savages to massacre our Farmers, and our Slaves to murder their Masters.... These atrocious Injuries have extinguished every remaining Spark of Affection for that Parent Country we once held so dear.[10]

Franklin had already accepted that the United States of America must be a republic, with a democratic form of government. He had put his name on a Declaration of Independence, drafted chiefly by Thomas Jefferson, that not only enumerated the "atrocious Injuries" mentioned in his letter to Howe, but also asserted "that all men are created equal, that they are endowed by their Creator with certain unalienable Rights, that among these are Life, Liberty and the pursuit of Happiness." These were explosive principles. Like Paine and Jefferson, Franklin had become a revolutionary.

The American Revolution did not bring democracy to poor white men or women or black people. It did not free slaves, except those who fought for the American army, and only the future state of Vermont abolished slavery, beyond the age of 18. There was much truth in the English writer Samuel Johnson's mocking question, "how is it that we hear the loudest whelps for liberty among the drivers of negroes?"[11] Fear of slave revolts, and desire to seize Indian land, drove many into the patriot camp. The Revolution also failed to create social equality, whether between black and white, men and women, or rich merchants and the urban laborers who worked in the Boston dockyards. It did, however, create the republican framework in which enfranchisement would eventually, after many struggles, be achieved. It also promulgated a political language, centered on liberty and equality, that would inspire future generations to strive for them as a reality. In this sense, it was a real revolution.

The American Revolution's success was not inevitable. While estimates of how many people supported it are guesswork, it seems clear that only a minority of colonists were active patriots, even in radical Massachusetts. Loyalists, who stuck to Great Britain, were at least as numerous as patriots in the middle colonies and the south. Neutrals, or people reluctant to commit themselves, may have been the largest body of all. To whom were slaves and servants loyal? Early in the conflict, Lord Dunmore, governor of Virginia, made a proclamation that extended freedom to indentured servants and slaves of the rebels who joined the British forces. This offer, which did not include the slaves or servants of Loyalists, was repeated by British commanders in the southern colonies throughout the war, and it inspired up to 10,000 slaves, many of them women and children, to flee their masters and take refuge with the British army.

In the end, the Revolution was won by battles, not by popular support. The American militia gained a reputation for "Indian-style" fighting, consisting of ambushes and firing from behind trees or from the ground. The most important American victories, however, were fought between regular military units, using more or less conventional tactics. The American commander, George Washington, was not a great general by any means, but he was equal to the opposition, and his dogged persistence inspired a fervent personal loyalty among his troops, which no British commander of the war was able to match. On the British side, military efforts were hampered by several miscalculations. Lord North and his ministers misjudged the seriousness of the patriot military threat, the level of Loyalist support, and the difficulty of supplying armies across 3000 miles of ocean. The replacement of Lord Dartmouth as Colonial Secretary by a man with military experience, Lord George Germain, was supposed to assist the war effort, but Germain was hardly an uncontroversial figure – he had been court-martialed after the battle of Minden, for delay in drawing up his troops. While historians have praised Germain's strategic insights, he was not charismatic enough to carry his ministerial colleagues along with him, and he ultimately failed to retain America for the crown.

The Americans also made mistakes. Their first major offensive of the war was an act of aggression, cloaked as friendly assistance. Congress invaded Quebec, ostensibly to bring the blessings of legislative government to the *canadiens*, but in fact to seize the capital, a major port where British troops could be landed. Given the level of anti-Catholic rhetoric voiced by the American colonists, the refusal of most French-speaking inhabitants of the province to support the patriot army is not surprising. The city of Quebec was attacked in a blinding snowstorm on the last day of December 1775, but the assault failed. The British were soon to lose another important port that had cost them much trouble in the past. The Americans had besieged Boston since driving the British back from Concord. The British army attempted to break out in June 1775 by driving the Americans from Breed's Hill on the Charlestown peninsula, resulting in the bloody engagement known, incorrectly, as the battle of Bunker Hill. The siege continued. In January, General Washington ordered cannons, dragged down from Fort Ticonderoga, to be placed on Dorchester Heights, overlooking Boston. Seeing this, the astonished British commander asked to vacate the city in exchange for not destroying it.

The fall of Boston was a shock to the British government, which had now lost possession of all North American ports except Halifax and Quebec. A bold new strategy was adopted, calling for a three-pronged attack on the rebel forces. General Sir William Howe, brother of the Admiral, was to seize New York and clear the enemy from the Hudson Valley. A second army was to advance from Quebec, march south through the Champlain Valley and attack New England from the west. A third, smaller force was to drive the rebels out of the southern colonies, then move north to link up with Howe's army. None of this went as planned. Howe defeated Washington at the battle of Brooklyn Heights, forcing him out of New York City, but he failed to destroy the main rebel army. "Though his army is much dispirited from the late success of His Majesty's arms," Howe wrote to Lord George Germain, "yet I have not the smallest prospect of finishing the contest this campaign."[12] The Americans were losing hope nonetheless. "These are the times that try men's souls," mused Tom Paine. "Tyranny, like hell, is not easily conquered: yet we have this consolation with us, that the harder the conflict, the more glorious the triumph."[13] At the end of the year, Washington flung his famous coin across the Delaware River, threw his men after it, and surprised the so-called "Hessians" – German troops in British pay – at Trenton and Princeton. These were mere skirmishes, but the cautious Howe, twice bitten, chose to retreat across New Jersey.

The crucial year of war was 1777. Congress was divided and short of money, while the British government was becoming desperate for a major victory. Resurrecting the strategy of the previous year, General John Burgoyne – playwright, politician, and man about town – was ordered to march down from Quebec while Howe marched up from New York, trapping the rebel army between them. Unfortunately, no attempt was made to coordinate this grand strategy. Instead of moving north, Howe transported his army by sea to the south, landing in Chesapeake Bay. He defeated Washington at Brandywine Creek and Germantown, but once again did not destroy the rebels. The British triumphantly occupied Philadelphia, sending the Continental Congress scurrying off to western Pennsylvania. Then very bad news arrived. On his long, arduous march south from Quebec, "Gentleman Johnny" Burgoyne had overstretched his supply lines. Finally, at Saratoga in New York, Burgoyne had come up against a superior American force, which was led into battle by the energetic Benedict Arnold. The British dug into a redoubt, but the Americans stormed and seized it. Burgoyne surrendered, with his entire army of 6000 men.

Saratoga changed everything. Benjamin Franklin, who was in Paris negotiating assistance from the French, received a jubilant letter from a friend, asking "what Effect, my dear Sir, will it have upon the British Court and Nation? Will they think of sending another Army here? ... What Effect upon France and Spain? Can they hesitate a Moment, about acknowledging our Independance, entring into an Alliance with us; and protecting their own Trade to this Quarter?"[14] George III took the news calmly, while loyalists in the towns of Manchester and Liverpool agreed to raise two regiments for service in America. France saw its opportunity, and declared war in February 1778. Washington's army, spending a bitter winter at Valley Forge, was energized. Fearing a French naval attack, the British forces, now commanded by Sir Henry Clinton, withdrew from Philadelphia back to New York. Washington followed, sparring with them indecisively on a sweltering June day at the battle of Monmouth Courthouse in New Jersey, where dozens of men died of heat stroke. Rhode Island was abandoned by the British, and a French fleet blocked any attempt to invade the south. British forces had to be stationed in the West Indies to protect the sugar islands.

The situation of the British forces in 1779 was not promising. Clinton was bottled up at New York; virtually no other rebel territory lay in British hands. An attempt to outflank Washington along the Hudson resulted in a British defeat at Stony Point. Spain joined the war on the American side, and a Franco-Spanish invasion of Britain seemed a possibility. Luckily, both France and Spain became preoccupied with their own colonial objectives, the French in the West Indies, the Spanish in Florida. The temporary withdrawal of the French fleet allowed Clinton to send 4000 troops by sea to Charleston in South Carolina, where they over-whelmed a sizable American garrison and began a successful southern campaign. At Camden in August 1780, General Charles Cornwallis crushed a rebel army, inflicting the worst defeat the Americans suffered in the war. British forces over-ran the Carolinas, and Richmond, newly named capital of Virginia, was burned by Benedict Arnold, who had become a Loyalist after being denied promotion in the American army. Cornwallis, however, was unable to crush the remaining American militia forces in the Carolinas, which began to inflict small but signifi-cant defeats on his army. In the spring of 1781, Cornwallis moved north into Virginia, installing his army of about 7000 troops at Yorktown, not far from the original English colony at Jamestown. Here he awaited orders from New York.

Urged on by his French allies, Washington decided to engage Cornwallis. In a remarkably fast forced march, his army traveled from New York to Virginia in about a month. The French fleet had by then established control over Chesapeake Bay. Washington ordered a nighttime attack, with bayonets only, on two of the British redoubts around Yorktown. Free black troops from Rhode Island led one assault, taking the redoubt in ten minutes. The French army stormed the second redoubt. Unable to withdraw across turbulent waters in the York River, Cornwallis was forced to surrender. He pleaded illness so as not to appear at the capitulation ceremony on October 20. A British military band reportedly played "The World Turned Upside Down," a pointed reference to what was happening – even more so as the tune was that of a royalist song of the 1650s, "The King Shall Enjoy His Own Again." The world, however, would not be turned back upright, and the British king would never again enjoy dominion over the rebellious colonies.

King George III was not despondent. "I have no doubt," he wrote to Lord North, "when men are a little recovered of the shock felt by the bad news, ... that they will then find the necessity of carrying on the war, though the mode of it may require alterations."[15] His chief minister, however, was beginning to lose his nerve in the face of military setbacks, mounting costs, isolation abroad, and ever-louder criticism in Parliament. Money could be raised for the conflict only by offering inducements to investors, so that borrowing of about £91 million during the war actually raised the national debt by £115 million, to a staggering total of almost £240 million. Britain was now at war with France, Spain, and the Dutch. The West Indies were threatened by attack, as was British India, where the EIC had been involved in military operations against both the Maratha Confederacy and the Sultan of Mysore. Undermined by its own massive war expenditures, the Company was tottering financially, so that in 1781, when its charter came up for renewal, Lord North postponed the serious reforms that were urged on him by his ministerial colleagues, and the EIC charter was reissued on much the same terms as in 1773.

Yorktown was not simply bad news for Lord North: it unraveled his ministry. By January 1782, he had replaced Lord George Germain, and was giving out hints that he would prefer to continue the war against France and Spain, but not against the Americans. King George did not agree with him. In February, the opposition passed a motion in the House of Commons that called for an end to offensive operations in America. After barely surviving a second motion expressing no confidence in his administration, North was convinced that he must either resign or make peace with the Americans. King George refused to accept either option, and instead considered abdicating the throne. At this critical juncture, a group of independent backbench MPs informed the chief minister that they could no longer support him. North had depended on these men, not just for votes, but to bolster the prestige of his ministry, as they represented large county electorates. He now sent a letter to the king, explaining why he must resign: "The Parliament having altered their sentiments, and as their sentiments whether just or erroneous must ultimately prevail, Your Majesty … can lose no honour if you yield at length, as some of the most renowned and most glorious of your predecessors have done, to the opinion and wishes of the House of Commons."[16] The King reluctantly agreed, and North stepped down with a dignified speech on March 20. Sir Robert Walpole's ministry had expired in a similar fashion, but Walpole never made a lesson out of it to the King. By contrast, Lord North signaled to a reluctant George III, and to posterity, that the monarch *must* give way when the legislature opposed a chief minister. This was a respectable constitutional legacy for the man who had lost America.

The Crisis in Britain and Ireland, 1778–1782

The American Revolutionary war shook Britain and Ireland as well as the Atlantic empire. It caused consternation in the British public, because it was seen as a war between related peoples who shared the same basic values. It was hard to condemn the Americans when what they were asking for, at least initially, was no more than the "rights of free-born Englishmen." Considerable sympathy for them existed in the great trading towns of London, Bristol, and Liverpool, even if few Britons could accept the idea of their independence. Protestant Dissenters in many parts of England tended to side with them, like the Baptist preacher in Norwich who denounced the "hellish scheme" to force the Americans "to give up the best part of their birthright, I mean civil liberty."[17] In the first three years of the war, 11 English counties and 47 boroughs sent addresses or petitions to the crown concerning policy towards the Americans. The majority of these were addresses calling for coercive measures, which were encouraged by the ministry; but voters in seven counties and a number of towns sent petitions in favor of peace. In many cases, both a pro-coercion address and a peace petition were sent, which reveals a deep division among the electorate.

A motion to withdraw all troops from America was debated in the House of Lords in 1778 – it was during this debate that Lord Chatham, who favored American demands but strongly opposed their independence, suffered a fatal stroke. The radical press kept up a steady drumbeat of criticism of the war, and was joined by some independent voices. David Hartley, an MP, inventor, and friend of Benjamin Franklin, published a letter in 1778 to his constituents, condemning "The inflexible obstinacy of an Administration, who would hear no reason, and who ... has alienated your Colonies, and driven them into the arms of France."[18] Although Hartley lost his seat at Kingston-upon-Hull, his pamphlet went through seven editions. Opposition to the war should not be exaggerated – most Britons backed the government because they disliked rebels or feared the French – but it was unprecedented. Even the raucous politics of the early eighteenth century had not produced statements of solidarity with the enemy.

The war also complicated existing movements for reform in Britain and Ireland. These movements were not revolutionary, and they peaked at different times, so that it would be wrong to claim that they threatened to undermine the state, although they put extreme strain on the political system. The British reform movement arose partly from a growing religious diversity, within both the Church of England and the Dissenting denominations. New and often heterodox religious ideas had emerged, which the government did nothing to suppress. Some clergymen, both Anglicans and Dissenters, were attracted to the rationalist doctrines of Unitarianism. Doubting the Trinitarian beliefs of most Christian denominations, the Unitarians argued that God was a single person, and Jesus Christ a human being, at least while living on the earth. Among the Anglican Unitarians was the Reverend John Jebb, a Cambridge lecturer. In 1771, he joined a group of clergymen who met at the Feathers Tavern in London to write a petition objecting to the obligation of subscribing to the 39 Articles of the Church of England. The Feathers Tavern petition was presented to the House of Commons, where it was overwhelmingly rejected. Jebb would go on to become a leading figure in the Parliamentary reform movement. Another prominent Unitarian was Joseph Priestley, a Presbyterian minister, noted scientist, and correspondent of Benjamin Franklin. A strong supporter of the Americans, Priestley would also become a voice for Parliamentary reform in the 1780s.

Although it drew on religious beliefs, the reform movement had a secular organization. It was based on local clubs, like the debating societies that sprang up in most large British towns. They would meet regularly to discuss issues of the day, and they often admitted non-members to their debates. Their audiences consisted largely of men of the upper and professional middling sort, although some clubs, like the Robin Hood Society, were attended by shopkeepers and artisans, and in London there were at least four female debating societies, where only women could speak. The government tried to discourage these clubs by preventing them from meeting on Sundays, but otherwise little was done against them. The most radical societies wanted to extend the franchise to many more voters. They were enthused by a pamphlet published in 1776 by John Cartwright, a naval veteran and a major in the militia, provocatively entitled *Take Your Choice!* The choice was made clear on the title page: "Representation and Respect: Imposition and Contempt. Annual Parliaments and Liberty: Long Parliaments and Slavery." Major Cartwright added a further twist to a familiar argument: he favored universal suffrage. "All are by nature free; all are by nature equal," he maintained in words that sound as if they were borrowed directly from Thomas Jefferson. He continued to a conclusion that the Declaration of Independence never reached: "All the commons, therefore, have an equal right to vote in the elections of those who are to be the guardians of their lives and liberties."[19]

A more moderate reform position was presented by the Reverend Christopher Wyvill, an Anglican clergyman and landowner from Yorkshire. He advocated more frequent Parliaments, and the addition to the House of Commons of 100 Members for the counties, which were larger and less corrupt constituencies than the boroughs. Starting in Yorkshire, Wyvill organized associations of landowners and respectable middling folk, to promote his cause throughout England. He was particularly successful around London, where he received support, not always welcome, from the Rockingham Whigs. Wyvill wanted the Association Movement to remain independent, but he also needed allies in Parliament to promote his cause. Petitions for reform were sent to Parliament by associations in about half the counties in England. In March 1780, Wyvill organized a grand conference of delegates from the county associations, which must have looked to the government like a British version of the Continental Congress. Some local supporters thought Wyvill's demands did not go far enough. The radical Westminster Association, influenced by John Jebb, committed itself to equal electoral districts, universal male suffrage, the secret ballot, and salaries for MPs. Jebb and Major Cartwright founded the Society for Constitutional Information to publicize these objectives.

The Rockingham Whigs hoped to take advantage of the Association Movement in order to undermine Lord North's government, but they were more concerned with reining in royal influence than with Parliamentary reform. One of Rockingham's supporters, John Dunning, proposed an extraordinary resolution to the House of Commons in April 1780, stating that "the influence of the crown has increased, is increasing and ought to be diminished." To everyone's astonishment, the motion passed, indicating not just bad management on the part of the government but also the degree of mistrust of royal power that was felt in Parliament. Lord North quickly rallied his forces, and Dunning was unable to pass a further motion, calling for Parliament to remain in session until the complaints made in the Association Movement petitions had been addressed.

Historians have often commented on the lack of success of the Parliamentary reform societies of 1780. Their ultimate aims were not met, but in a very short time almost all the major ideas of Parliamentary reform had been articulated, and organizations created that would carry these ideas into the nineteenth century. To have achieved this during a war was remarkable. The reluctance of the government to crack down on the reformers, or to brand them as traitors, shows that there was apprehension about the possible consequences of such severity, as well as some sympathy for them even in government ranks. In spite of having to work within a system that was tightly controlled by vested interests, the reform movement had swiftly become a force in politics. This was demonstrated in the general elections held in October 1780, when reformers were elected to a small number of seats in the House of Commons. Charles James Fox, a Rockingham Whig and son of the devious Henry Fox, was chosen for Westminster with the support of the local Association.

By then, however, the reform movement had been damaged by the outbreak of the worst riots in British history. They were caused by a popular reaction *against* a religious reform that was supported by both the government and the opposition. In 1778, a Roman Catholic Relief Act was enacted by Parliament, which removed some of the penalties against Catholic priests in England, as well as allowing Catholics to buy land. In the following year, a similar bill was proposed for Scotland. The English Catholic community was small, but top-heavy with aristocrats and gentry. Scottish Catholics were concentrated in the Highlands, and Lord North wanted to increase army enlistments among them by offering them toleration. His intentions were stymied by the so-called Protestant Association, formed in Scotland by Presbyterian ministers to prevent passage of the Bill. The Association inspired riots against Catholics in Perth and Edinburgh in 1779. Its president, Lord George Gordon, a radical MP and son of a Scottish duke, led a march to the House of Commons on June 2, 1780, carrying a petition that called for repeal of the English Relief Act. Estimated at between 20,000 and 40,000 people, the marchers wore blue cockades, the token of the Wilkites, and carried banners with "NO POPERY" written on them. Politicians entering Parliament that morning were harangued by Lord George and manhandled by the crowd. They fearfully decided to postpone a vote on repeal. The Scottish Relief Bill was later dropped.

The crowd then went on a rampage. Catholic chapels and the houses of prominent Catholics were destroyed, as was Lord Chief Justice Mansfield's town house. Newgate prison was burned down, and troops were ordered out to defend the Bank of England. Fires and destruction continued through the night. "Sleep and rest were things not thought of," wrote one eyewitness, "the streets were swarming with people, and uproar, confusion, and terror reigned in every part."[20] A crowd set off to burn Mansfield's suburban house on Hampstead Heath, but the rioters were reportedly detained at an inn by the distribution of free beer, until soldiers dispersed them. For five days, the streets of London became a battleground, with troops firing repeatedly into the crowds. When the smoke cleared, 210 rioters were dead. Later, 75 more died of their wounds. The killing was done by the soldiers, not by the rioters, who harmed only property. Between 20 and 30 people were hanged for taking part in the riots. Lord George Gordon, however, was acquitted for his leading role in the disturbances, and went on to become, oddly enough, an Orthodox Jew.

The Burning & Plundering of NEWGATE & Setting the Felons at Liberty by the Mob.

Published 1st July 1780 by Fielding & Walker, Pater Noster Row.

Illustration 17 *The destruction of Newgate Prison during the Gordon Riots of June 1780. The prisoners are being set free by the mob, which includes some well dressed men and women carrying banners proclaiming "NO POPERY." ("The Burning & Plundering of Newgate & Setting of Felons at Liberty by the Mob," 1780. © City of London/Heritage-Images / Imagestate)*

The worst riots in the history of London deserve some explanation. At the time, French or American agitators were blamed for fomenting the trouble, which seems unlikely. Certainly, the riots reflected a violent strain of anti-Catholicism that was common among English and Scottish Protestants. They also expressed economic grievances, opposition to the war, and radical rhetoric. Some reformers chose to support the Protestant Association; others, including Wilkes, did not. The rioters themselves were not indiscriminate: they attacked wealthy targets, political figures, and symbols of oppression, like Newgate prison. The Protestant Association had clearly tapped into an enormous well of popular anger and resentment.

The patriot movement in Ireland grew out of similar popular sentiments, but it fostered religious cooperation rather than animosity. Inspired by the principles of

William Pitt, Protestant Irish patriots had called since the 1760s for legislative and economic independence from Britain. They were supported by a groundswell of opinion among the middling sort of people in the towns, a social group that included both Protestants and Catholics. Clubs, debating societies, and Masonic lodges flourished in Dublin, Belfast, and Cork, just as they did in London or Edinburgh. Some societies had patriot connections, like the Monks of the Screw, a Dublin club frequented by politicians. The great orator of the patriot movement was Henry Flood, a wealthy lawyer and minor literary figure. In 1768, Flood obtained the passage of an Act limiting the duration of the Irish Parliament, which had previously continued to sit throughout the life of a monarch – George II's Irish Parliament, in fact, had lasted 33 years. Flood wanted a limit of seven years, as in Britain, but the Privy Council altered this to eight, to his disgust.

The American Revolutionary War greatly strengthened the bargaining power of the Irish patriots. The withdrawal of British troops from Ireland for service in America made it necessary to organize local militia units, known as the Volunteers. Unlike every other official body in Ireland, membership in the Volunteers required no religious test, so Presbyterians and Catholics could serve alongside members of the official Church of Ireland. For the first time, patriots of all religions cooperated in a single enterprise. By 1779, the Volunteers had at least 40,000 members, drawn from the urban middling sort as well as the landed classes. They began to make political demands by supporting a patriot campaign for free trade with Britain. Facing a possible Franco-Spanish invasion, the British government conceded on the free trade issue, and gradually removed restrictions on Irish imports. British control over Ireland was wavering. The patriots in the Irish Parliament, whose main spokesman was the charismatic and hyperbolic orator Henry Grattan, were emboldened to claim that only an Irish legislature could make laws for Ireland. To gain allies, the patriots removed some legal restrictions on Catholics as well as the Test Act oath that excluded Presbyterians. When the Volunteers held an assembly of delegates at Dungannon in February 1782 – a national meeting that resembled both the Association Movement convention of 1780 and the Continental Congress – they endorsed a set of resolutions that included not only legislative independence but a relaxation of the penal laws against Catholics. With the resignation of Lord North in March, Ireland was in an uproar. How would the British government react?

Peace Abroad, Conflict at Home, 1782–1784

The answer to that question depended on which British politicians were in power. During the 21 confusing months after Lord North's resignation, no fewer than four administrations governed Britain, led by the Marquess of Rockingham (March to July 1782), the Earl of Shelburne (July 1782 to March 1783), Charles James Fox and Lord North (March to December 1783), and finally William Pitt the younger. These ministries were dominated by two separate groups, descended from the Whig factions of the 1750s: the Rockinghams or "Old Corps" and the patriot Whigs, led after the death of Lord Chatham by Shelburne and the younger Pitt. Both parties wanted peace, but Rockingham was prepared simply to accept American demands, while Shelburne sought to preserve a "special relationship" with the United States. Prospects for a favorable settlement had in fact improved in 1782. In the spring, Admiral Rodney had gained a decisive naval victory over the French fleet at the Battle of the Saints, which halted the French seizure of Caribbean islands. A Franco-Spanish attack on Gibraltar, using fire ships, was heroically repulsed in October. Although the war was clearly lost, Britain was no longer at the mercy of its enemies.

Unfortunately for government stability, the Rockingham administration was hated by George III, who planned from the first to replace it. For his part, Rockingham mistrusted the King, and on the advice of Burke and Fox he took some daring moves to restrict the monarchy during his brief tenure as chief minister. Useless offices in the royal household and redundant positions in administration were abolished, among them the Board of Trade, which had once been responsible for colonial policy. Parliament was given authority to examine and question the King's salary, the Civil List. Government contractors were declared ineligible from serving in the House of Commons, and revenue officers lost their votes in Parliamentary elections. Over time, these proved to be important changes that would reduce the much-feared influence of the crown and lead to a less corrupt administration. Meanwhile, the Northern and Southern Secretaries of State were converted into a Foreign Secretary and a Home Secretary.

Rockingham also addressed the demands of Irish patriots, which was all the more surprising in that he owned vast estates in Ireland and was a friend to many leading figures in the Ascendancy. He repealed the Declaratory Act of 1720 that had subordinated Ireland to legislation by the British Parliament. This did not immediately create legislative independence: the control exercised by the Privy Council had to be removed by the Irish Parliament, and a further Renunciation Act of 1783 was necessary to clarify British non-interference in Irish legislation. After these steps were achieved, however, the Parliament in Dublin was effectively able to pass its own legislation, which was subject only to royal approval. Not everyone agreed about what this meant. Henry Flood was skeptical about the consequences of the Declaratory Act repeal, which almost led him into a duel with his more optimistic colleague Henry Grattan. In the end, the Irish Parliament remained an unreformed Protestant institution, dominated by big landowners, while the lieutenant-governor, appointed by the crown, retained considerable power over Irish affairs. If legislative independence had been accompanied by Catholic emancipation and a thorough reform of Parliament, Ireland might have avoided union with Britain and another 130 years of civil strife.

The peace negotiations at Paris were concluded after Rockingham's premature death by his successor as chief minister, the young, idealistic Earl of Shelburne. The final settlement, signed in September 1783, was painful but not devastating to Britain. It gave Florida and Minorca to Spain, while France received the West Indian island of Tobago and the slave-trading forts in Senegal that had been lost in 1763, along with expanded fishing rights in the Grand Banks and trading rights in India. American independence was recognized, and the lands between the Ohio and Mississippi that had been granted to Quebec in 1774 were surrendered. This made practical sense, as American settlers were already flooding into them. More questionable was the British abandonment of the Loyalists, who were to receive no compensation for the loss of their property at the hands of the new American state governments. Between 80,000 and 100,000 Loyalists eventually fled north to Canada. The majority of them were small farmers of British ancestry, but they also included thousands of freed slaves and about 2000 Indians who had fought with the British. They settled in Quebec – whose francophone majority had to cope for the first time with a substantial English-speaking minority – as well as in Nova Scotia, Cape Breton, and the newly formed provinces of New Brunswick and Prince Edward Island. These immigrants represented the future of British North America, but the crown gave them little beyond the chance to resettle, along with the exalted title "United Empire Loyalists," bestowed in 1789 to recognize their sacrifices for the cause of imperial union.

As for the new United States, it would continue to maintain close trading and cultural links with Britain. The "more perfect union" formed by the states in 1787 was enshrined in a written constitution that borrowed many elements from British political thought: a balance of powers between executive, legislative, and judicial branches, an elected lower house, a patrician Senate that had some features of the House of Lords. In other respects, however, the new nation was very different from its motherland. It was a republic, based on an egalitarian rhetoric, even if Americans were not equal in practice. Its President had limited power and was not supposed to behave like a monarch (although several have). Its constitution was protected by a Supreme Court that claimed the authority to review the laws. The United States was a federal union, not a centralized one like Great Britain. The American Republic was imagined by minds trained in British legal and constitutional thought, but it was not simply a copy of the nation from which it had declared its independence.

Meanwhile, the treatment of the American Loyalists, as proposed in the preliminary articles of peace, helped to turn Parliament against the Shelburne administration. An inexperienced political manager, Shelburne was already under heavy fire from Charles James Fox, who wanted to replace him, and from Lord North. Fox was a talented but highly dissipated character, whose father had advanced his education by sending him off to brothels in Paris at a young age. George III despised him, just as he had also come to hate his former friend North, who had moved into opposition. Lord Shelburne took his defeats in the House of Commons on the peace preliminaries as a sign that he must resign, despite the King's stubborn insistence that he should ignore them. The chief ministers were beginning to accept the rules of responsible government. King George was not ready for this.

One can, however, feel sorry for George III in what he had to do next: stomach Fox and North as his advisors. Once again, he almost abdicated the throne, then changed his mind. The coalition, uniting a Whig reformer with the man held responsible by radicals for all the "tyrannical" measures of the 1770s, seemed unnatural to many. Together, Fox and North planned to carry out the reform of the East India Company that had been postponed in 1781. Their scheme would have given authority over Company affairs to a committee, named by the ministers and responsible to Parliament. The King was insulted by his exclusion from these arrangements, the EIC directors and shareholders were furious at losing their influence, and many political observers were horrified at what they saw as a naked grab for power by Fox and North. King George took the unheard of step of informing Members of the House of Lords that anybody who voted for the East India Bill was no friend of his. This panicked their Lordships, most of whom longed for some future office, and the Bill was defeated.

The King took the defeat as a vote of no confidence, and replaced the ministry in December 1783. William Pitt the younger, almost a boy at 24 years of age, and with no experience of office beyond a brief stint as Chancellor of the Exchequer under Shelburne, was chosen as chief minister. This was a reckless gamble on the part of the King, but it paid off. Fox and North were unpopular, and although they defeated Pitt's government in some early motions, their support in the House of Commons soon dwindled. An early general election was called for the spring of 1784. The King used every scrap of influence still at his disposal to make sure that Mr Pitt and his friends had a majority of seats in both Houses. Was it constitutional for him to act in this way – first betraying his own ministers, then maintaining in office a government that initially lacked a majority in the Commons? It was certainly not consistent with how many leading politicians perceived the constitution as operating in 1783, but Britain had few fixed constitutional rules, and if the King could get away with it, as he did, then it was sanctioned by success.

The new ministry was saved from immediate ruin by a general election that registered an upsurge of patriot sentiment among politicians and voters – not the radical patriotism of Wilkes and the Westminster Association, but a more conservative patriotism that looked to the monarchy as the foundation of the constitution. In election propaganda, George III was portrayed as the benign savior of his country from the republican designs of the shady Mr Fox. These were exaggerated views, but they expressed a common reaction to recent events. Many in the upper and middling ranks of society had no wish to put the crown, still reeling from the effects of defeat, in further danger by endorsing an administration that the King did not want. It was fortunate for George III that he found this unexpected backing for his actions, and even more fortunate that he had found William Pitt the younger, a politician whose patriot views seemed to mirror his own. Together, they would lead the country for almost 20 years, out of one international crisis and through a second, much more threatening one.

15

The Wealth of a Nation

If the political history of Britain from 1760 to 1783 reveals a nation in crisis, the economic history of these decades shows expansion in almost every direction. Economic historians used to write with breathless wonderment about the second half of the eighteenth century, describing it as a period of "Agricultural Revolution" and "Industrial Revolution." They were convinced that a "leap into sustained growth" happened after 1780, which created modern capitalism and altered every aspect of British economic life. Alas, such simple and straightforward ideas are no longer widely accepted. Few historians think of the agricultural and industrial changes of the late eighteenth century as revolutionary. They had long roots in the past; they did not happen suddenly; and their effects were uneven. Some aspects of the British economy *did* change in decisive ways between 1750 and 1800. Some had been changing for the previous two centuries. Some would not change for another fifty years or longer. We now know that the development of modern capitalism depends on local circumstances, so Great Britain no longer provides a standard model for other nations to follow. This does not mean that British economic history has lost its importance. In spite of all the qualifications and reservations expressed by historians, Britain remains the first nation on earth to develop both an agricultural system based on the pursuit of profit, and a manufacturing system dedicated to mass industrial production. Big transformations were happening in Britain in the late eighteenth century, even if we can no longer call them revolutionary.

How were they related to the spread of empire? Was British economic growth built on the backs of West Indian slaves and exploited peasants in Bengal? Not directly, perhaps: few of the profits made by sugar planters or East India traders were reinvested in British farming or industry. Instead, they tended to go back into overseas commerce. Nonetheless, the home market for consumer goods, which encouraged the expansion of British industries, had been gorged for decades on imports from the empire. The peasant farmers of India provided the cotton that supplied the fastest growing sector of the British textile industry. The importation of finished Indian calicoes (cotton cloth) had been barred since the early eighteenth century, a huge boon to the development of British fustians (mixed cotton–linen cloth). Clearly, the empire was a factor in British economic development.

Social historians have spent a great deal of time discussing whether the big transformations of the late eighteenth century benefited ordinary people or made their lives worse. In the long run, the answer may seem evident: Britons, and everybody who lives today in a developed industrial society, have a higher standard of living than their ancestors did in pre-industrial times, due in large part to the changes associated with what we call modern capitalism. However, life was not always made better by economic change. Valuable aspects may have been lost, such as control over how and when we work. A few people benefited from change much more than others, and conditions for some may have grown worse. Economic and social transformation on such a grand scale was not a uniform process. Nobody planned it out, and its effects were unpredictable. To simplify it by looking at "typical wage-earners" or "overall standards of living" may be misleading, although it is hard to avoid.

One point is clear: more Britons were around to experience change. When the first national census was taken in 1801, it found that about 10.5 million people were living in Great Britain. A century earlier, England, Wales, and Scotland had contained fewer than 7 million people. The rate of growth since 1750 has been estimated at 0.8 per cent, about double what it was in the first half of the century. Population growth occurred in rural as well as urban areas, and within most social groups. It was probably caused by a slightly earlier age of marriage, which resulted in more children. Infant mortality did not decline, and remained fearsomely high. If people were having more children, does this suggest that they were more optimistic about the future? Surely, laboring folk from the mid-eighteenth century onwards must have seen enhanced opportunity for themselves in economic change, or they would not have adapted to it with such rapidity. On the other hand, it is difficult to say whether their hopes of a better life were realized. Can we tell if they are being realized today?

Improving the Rural Landscape

Economic transformation was written onto the landscape, in both rural and urban areas. Changes in the physical environment reflected the priorities of those who owned property and the lifestyles of those who worked to survive in altered circumstances. As people in the past were often silent about how change affected them, the landscape itself often has to carry the weight of evidence.

The most important factor in the transformation of the British countryside, and one that has continued to the present, was the concentration of land in relatively few hands. In mid-eighteenth-century Britain, around 35 families, many of them aristocrats, possessed huge estates of 9000 acres or more. About 18,000 gentry and aristocratic families throughout the kingdom owned middle sized estates of 300 to 3000 acres. These two groups of mega- and medium owners can be considered the landed classes, the top of the social pyramid. Below them were about 210,000 freeholders, mostly English and Welsh yeoman farmers, who owned less than 300 acres. In the following 50 years, British landowners remained more or less stable in numbers, in spite of the dramatic growth in overall population. The large estates became bigger, while smaller ones shrank. The tendency of bigger landowners to buy up more land, and of smaller landowners to sell it, strengthened after 1750. Because land conferred status, the highest ranks of society were essentially frozen, apart from a few wealthy individuals who were able to purchase an estate. The limited size of the landed elite may have accelerated changes to the countryside. Within a small landowning class, alterations could be carried out quickly, consistently, and perhaps more ruthlessly, in reaction to market conditions.

Landowners were increasingly sensitive to the market. An example of this was the reversal of a long-term trend towards converting arable land, on which crops were grown, into pasture or grazing land for sheep and cattle. In the late eighteenth century, with the growth of population, the demand for wheat (which the British, confusingly, called corn) rose steadily, as did its price. The market for domestic wheat was particularly strong in wartime, when foreign imports were restricted. As a result, profit-minded landowners began to encourage their tenants to switch from pasturing or grazing to crop production, and in a few decades Britain became self-sufficient in wheat. Livestock farms did not wholly disappear, of course, especially in hilly areas, but they were often amalgamated and became larger. In Wiltshire, for example, the number of sheep farms declined by 12 percent from 1780 to 1830. Many fields in southern England or southeastern Scotland on which sheep graze today were planted with crops in the late eighteenth century.

The biggest physical transformation in late eighteenth-century Britain can still be seen from the air. Looking down on the British countryside, we can make out straight, even hedgerows dividing rectangular fields. In England and Wales, this is largely the result of Parliamentary enclosure since 1760. Unlike earlier forms of enclosing farm strips and common land, Parliamentary enclosure was carried out by an Act of the legislature, according to fixed rules. The land had to be surveyed, and the names of all proprietors determined. Each would receive a portion of the newly enclosed land, or would be compensated. The process was costly and time-consuming, but landowners saw it as comprehensive and fair, and the result had the weight of law behind it. A huge amount of land in England and Wales was enclosed in this way – more than 7 million acres between 1760 and 1815. That averages to about 125,000 acres every year, compared to about 7300 acres enclosed every year by Parliamentary Act between 1700 and 1760. In Scotland, common land or "commonties" could be divided by the Court of Sessions on the request of proprietors. About half a million Scottish acres were enclosed between 1720 and 1850. To consolidate the scattered farming strips known in Scotland as "runrig," application could be made to the county sheriff. By 1770, "runrig" was gone from the Scottish border regions and was disappearing in other Lowland areas as well.

The effects of Parliamentary enclosure in England and Wales were far-reaching. The central government became deeply involved in issues of local land use. The commissioners who were responsible for carrying out the enclosure had considerable powers, especially when it came to determining compensation. They could also build roads. Parliamentary enclosure often brought changes in road patterns, since landowners did not want old roads cutting across the new boundaries of their property. Turnpike or toll roads were being constructed at this time by private investors, and the smaller country roads that sprang up through enclosures were usually linked to them. Gradually, a network of road transport emerged, to connect even remote areas to markets. The tiny winding roads that crisscross the British countryside may frustrate foreign drivers today, but they were once the arteries that sustained agricultural change. The scattered farmhouses that still dot the British landscape were another consequence of enclosure. Once their land had been consolidated, few farmers wanted to continue to live in a village and commute to work; they preferred to reside on their farms.

Parliamentary enclosure also had some damaging environmental effects. Woodlands could be devastated. The commissioners were very effective in mapping wooded areas, determining who had rights to use them, and terminating those rights in one way or another, in favor of private owners. The new owners usually cut down the woods, although the cleared land often proved to be unprofitable, which was why it had been wooded in the first place. Wetlands and marshes were lost in a similar way. In southern England, the "inning" or filling in of enclosed wetlands and marshes by landowners completely altered coastal drainage patterns. Rivers became clogged up with silt from the newly drained land, which was frequently deposited in the harbors of small ports. The process was understood, but little was done to stop the landowners. Instead, costly projects for draining harbors might be undertaken, with limited results.

The straight hedgerows that can be seen surrounding many British fields today were another outcome of Parliamentary enclosure. They often replaced older hedgerows that were rendered obsolete by the remapping of land boundaries. About 200,000 miles of new hedges were planted in the century after 1750, the same amount as all the hedgerows planted in the previous 500 years! Ancient hedges tended to be mixed plantings, while Parliamentary enclosure hedges generally used one type of small tree as a barrier, such as hawthorns. The loss of diversity and the negative effects on wildlife were not much noticed at the time. Foxhunting gentlemen, however, preferred trees as boundary markers, since they could ride between them while chasing their prey.

The impact of enclosure on people's lives has long been debated. Landowners, of course, stood to profit mightily from it, as did big tenant farmers who were able to lease parts of the former commons. Small tenant farmers whose rights were bought out through a Parliamentary settlement would benefit initially, but they lost the use of the woodlands, grazing lands, and water that once formed part of the commons. We do not really know how many of them relied on those rights, but it may have been a substantial number. Landless laborers and "cottagers" who lived on tiny farm holdings certainly had the most to lose from enclosure of common lands, as it removed a source of economic independence and left them with little support beyond the meager wages paid for farm work. The very poor, in short, grew poorer. In many cases, however, rights to the commons had been eroded over time, which may explain why the final Acts of Parliamentary enclosure did not arouse more vociferous protest. To be sure, there were scattered incidents of violence and even some public complaints, like the petition sent in 1794 to the Duke of Buccleuch by some of his tenants in Northamptonshire: "We are convinced that the Benefit, if any, arising from the inclosure, will not be reciprocal, but entirely in your Grace's Favour; and considering the Amplitude of Your Possessions it cannot be an Object worthy of Your Grace's Notice to endeavour to encrease Your Grace's income at the expence of so many necessitated Persons."[1] Most "necessitated Persons," however, accepted what was happening to them without open comment, whatever they thought of it.

Enclosure, like other significant changes to the landscape, was often referred to as improvement by those who promoted it. This was hardly a new concept among landowners, although it took on broader connotations in the late eighteenth century. The impetus for improvement could be a desire to enhance profits, or it could be fashion, or simply peer pressure (at times, from genuine peers). Profit-oriented improvement sped up after 1750, in part because information about techniques and innovations was now so readily available through books and newspapers. Changes that would once have taken a generation to accomplish were carried out in the space of a few growing seasons. The effects of improvement may have been most dramatic in Scotland, where landlords were voracious readers of the literature of agricultural improvement, and acted on it with enthusiasm. By 1810, there were 21 societies for agricultural improvement in Scotland, compared to 38 in England and eight in Wales. In the Scottish Lowlands, landlords gradually put an end to the "farmtouns," where small farmers with communal or group rights to the land clustered around self-sufficient villages. They were replaced by individual tenancies and enclosed fields. In the Highlands, aristocratic landlords who no longer felt bound by the ties of clanship contemplated the wholesale removal of small tenant farmers or "cotters" to make room for big, pastoral estates. A few, like the Duke of Argyll, acted on such ideas by dispossessing tenants and planting fir trees.

A less disruptive aspect of late eighteenth-century improvement was stock-breeding. It was primarily undertaken for profit, although when we consider the striking portraits of prize bulls and sheep that were commissioned by landowners, we may wonder to what extent pride, competitiveness, and a certain aesthetic appreciation were also involved. Cattle were bred for weight and strength, sheep for the quality as well as quantity of their wool. The most famous stock-breeder of the late eighteenth century was a Leicestershire farmer, Robert Bakewell, whose portrait reveals that he had something of the physique of a prize bull himself. Careful breeding of horses had been done for centuries, so the practice was not unfamiliar to landed gentlemen who frequented race-courses and rode in fox hunts. As the success of stock-breeding depends on good nutrition and keeping animals alive over the winter months, the creation of multiple varieties of sheep and cattle in the late eighteenth century shows that livestock were better fed than in earlier centuries, when such efforts were hardly worth undertaking.

Improvements that depended on new methods or inventions were widely publicized in the eighteenth century, but they did not always catch on among farmers. The most famous innovator of the period was Jethro Tull, a lawyer who thought up a system of "pulverizing" or finely tilling the soil. Tull used a horse-drawn hoe to root out weeds, a redesigned plough to cut deeper furrows, and a seed-drill to plant seeds at regular intervals. Comparing his "New Husbandry" to the practices of old-fashioned farmers, Tull used a military metaphor: "Their Plants stand on the Ground in a confused Manner, like a Rabble, ours like a disciplin'd Army."[2] Tull's system, which he first publicized in 1733, added air and nutrients to soil, and avoided the use of manure, but it was not very successful with wheat and failed to impress most farmers. Nonetheless, his methods remained a topic of discussion throughout the century.

Some improvements that are identified with the eighteenth century really began much earlier and simply became more widespread, like the planting of turnips to add nutrients to soils. A myth emerged that ascribed the introduction of turnips to Viscount Townshend, Sir Robert Walpole's brother-in-law, who duly gained the nickname "Turnip" Townshend. He was said to have discovered the virtues of the lowly root while visiting Hanover with George I. In fact, almost no contemporary evidence links Townshend with turnips. By the end of the eighteenth century, however, many landlords, like the celebrated Thomas Coke of Norfolk, were eagerly pressing their tenants to make improvements, even writing up leases that required farmers to adopt innovative methods.

Another feature of late eighteenth-century improvement in the countryside was canals. These were usually financed by large landowners, who wanted to ship coal from the mines on their estates to local ports. The most famous canal builder was Francis Egerton, third Duke of Bridgewater, who employed "that wonderful self-instructed genius," the engineer James Brindley, to construct a canal from his coal mines at Worsley in Lancashire to the fast-growing city of Manchester, then asked him to build another one linking Manchester with the port of Liverpool. Beginning in 1761, the Manchester–Liverpool project took 15 years to complete, and cost the Duke a fortune, but it considerably lowered the cost of transport, not just of coal but of agricultural products as well. Its success set off a "canal mania" among landowners. "There is a period," gushed the Manchester writer John Aikin, "in which the mind of man, rouzed to attend to any particular subject, whether of art, science or regulation, is irresistibly impelled to proceed in its career; and the crisis was now arrived with respect to the internal communication between the different parts of this kingdom by means of navigable canals."[3] Before Bridgewater's canal, about 1000 miles of improved river and canal navigation had been built in Britain; in the 70 years after, about 3000 more miles were added. Total investment in canals reached £15 million between 1780 and 1815. This represented a massive mobilization of private capital, although canal-building also involved the state, as an Act of Parliament was necessary in order to construct canal works on other people's property. Still, as with turnpikes, there was very little state guidance or planning in the construction of canals, so that it would be an exaggeration to call the results a system. Canal-building companies used different widths and standards, making navigation more difficult than it had to be.

A different type of landscape improvement, dependent on fashion rather than profitability, altered the gardens that surrounded the houses of great landowners. In the seventeenth century, gardens had been laid out in the carefully controlled French fashion, with straight rows of box (a hedging plant) and a few carefully laid out flowers. Nature was not allowed to appear without restraint. By the early eighteenth century, English garden designers were breaking away from this model, by placing ornaments and miniature temples within more "natural" settings. The great English gardeners of the late eighteenth century, Lancelot "Capability" Brown and Humphrey Repton, sought to create environments in which nature could be appreciated in an apparently untouched and uncontrolled state. In fact, their gardens were meticulously planned, so as to emphasize classical concepts of natural beauty. They look like paintings or theatrical sets, with every element – trees, shrubs, hedges, ponds, neoclassical buildings – balanced and harmonized. The goal of changing nature so as to make it seem more "natural," and thus more aesthetically pleasing, became part of the eighteenth-century ideal of improvement. Uncontrolled nature, in the form of roaming deer and other animals, was kept out of gardens through a sloping, barely visible ditch, amusingly known as a ha-ha.

The appearance of great country houses changed as well, due to the neoclassical style popularized by the Scottish architect Robert Adam. Adam had visited Italy, where he saw the early excavations of the buried ancient town of Pompei. On his return, he began designing houses for the wealthy in Scotland and England, including Lord Mansfield's mansion on Hampstead Heath near London. By carefully reproducing Roman proportions, and by copying elaborate Roman interior decorations, Adam gave his clients the impression that they were living like the splendid aristocrats that they read about in classical literature. His later buildings were more varied, and included mock medieval castles. Distinctive and designed to be looked at, Adam's houses lent a picturesque grandeur to country estates.

However much we may admire their good taste in building, the landlords of the late eighteenth century have to be held accountable for the consequences of their actions. Were they good stewards of the rural environment? Their record seems mixed. On the one hand, they destroyed forests and marshlands, spoiled the fragile economy of common rights, and allowed huge piles of coal slag or refuse to accumulate around mining villages, where they did not have to look at it. On the other hand, they took care to preserve the productivity of the soil, and they encouraged the regular, well tended look that is still typical of the British countryside. In Scotland, they even planted trees. The marks of their good sense and their follies, their careful planning and their unbridled grasping, can be seen everywhere on the British landscape today. In a surprising number of cases, their descendants still own the land that they changed.

Rebuilding the Urban Landscape

The transformation of British towns in the late eighteenth century may seem less drastic than what was going on in the countryside. If you had strolled through a town in 1800, you might have noticed how many buildings, both public and private, had been built in earlier centuries. Amidst all the dirt and noise, improvements in town services might not immediately have struck you. It might also have surprised you to find that in most places the wealthy still lived in the center of town, with poor people in the suburbs – a tendency that was soon to be reversed. On the other hand, in only a few places would you have seen town walls or medieval military defenses, most of which had been demolished. Notable recent buildings might have caught your eye, and you would certainly have been aware of the number of taverns, coffeehouses, and shops that were open to customers. After a while, some deeper changes might have struck you.

First, urban areas had become bigger. The first national census in 1801 found that about one-third of the population in England and Wales was living in a town of 2500 inhabitants or larger, and one in five was living in a town of more than 10,000 people. The biggest city, London, with a massive population of 960,000, was home to about one in ten people in England and Wales. Scotland was only slightly less urbanized than England by 1800, with one in six Scots living in a town of at least 10,000 inhabitants. This represented a doubling of the urban percentage of the Scottish population since 1750, when less than 10 percent had lived in towns. While the English and Welsh were marching steadily into urban environments, the Scots were flying into them.

The biggest English provincial towns in 1700, Norwich and Bristol, were no longer the biggest towns in 1801. The cotton-importing and slave-trading port of Liverpool had grown to 88,000 people and was the second largest city in Britain. Nearby Manchester, center of cotton textile production, had a population of 84,000. The next biggest towns were Glasgow, the great tobacco port, and Edinburgh, with populations of about 83,000 and 82,000 respectively. No other Scottish towns compared with them in terms of population. Below these places in number of inhabitants were Birmingham (69,000), which lay at the heart of the iron-making region of the West Midlands; the southwestern English port of Bristol (64,000); and the wool-making town of Leeds in West Yorkshire (53,000). Carmarthen, the largest town in Wales, had 24,000 people, making it a medium sized market and port town. Evidently, commercial towns in industrial regions, and port towns that served those regions, were growing much faster than traditional market centers like Exeter or York.

In these growing urban environments, little was done to extend or enhance life for the mass of poorer inhabitants. Cities were still charnel houses for the poor, with much higher death rates than the countryside. In 1773, it was estimated that mortality rates in London stood at 46 deaths for every 1000 people, compared to 36 per 1000 in Liverpool or Manchester and 28 per 1000 in the countryside. Half of the burials in London were of children, a frightening statistic that did not substantially change throughout the eighteenth century. On the other hand, the mortality rate may have been decreasing in other British towns in the second half of the eighteenth century, which could account for some of their population growth. The notion that something might be done to relieve the everyday distress of the urban poor, beyond charity and the provisions of the Poor Laws, was not yet widespread, but some remarkable suggestions were made in this period. In 1767, the philanthropist Jonas Hanway succeeded in obtaining passage of a Parliamentary Act to protect infants who had been abandoned in London. It set up parish boards of supervisors that had the authority to send these babies into the countryside, to be fed by hired wet-nurses. Hanway estimated that it had saved 1500 lives every year.

The physical consequences of urban expansion were still limited. In most places, housing supply had not yet been overtaken by demand. The horrific slums known to Charles Dickens, where crowds of people huddled together in close, cramped, filthy tenements built around a central courtyard, were just beginning to appear in London by the end of the eighteenth century. Traditional housing for the poor was more spread out and varied; it was often found in cellars or attics or shanties built up against the sides of other buildings. It was rarely attractive, well built, or sanitary, but it was available, although many indigent people doubtless slept in the streets because they could not afford even the most rudimentary hovel. Strict segregation between the poor and the wealthy was not yet a feature of most British towns – instead, people of all social ranks lived in close proximity to one another. In London and Westminster, however, the process of segregation had begun in the mid-eighteenth century, with the construction of beautiful rows of town houses for the rich, set around leafy squares. The estates of Mayfair and Belgravia, still very fashionable addresses in London, were laid out in this way as planned residences for members of the elite who were spending the social season in the capital, away from their country manors.

A second important change in the urban landscapes of eighteenth-century Britain was the construction of new public buildings, for all sorts of purposes: government, commerce, worship, leisure. Numerous town halls were reconstructed or renovated in the latest architectural styles, as symbols of prosperity and civic pride. Hospitals for the sick and workhouses to lodge the indigent were designed by committees of concerned citizens. In practice, they were often little different from prisons, which were also built in increasing numbers. In the center of larger urban centers could be found new market halls, cloth halls, or commercial exchanges, where merchants met to do business. Rows of eighteenth-century shops can still be seen in many British towns, often fronted by a covered arcade or walkway so that polite shoppers did not have to get wet in the rain or dirty their feet in the mud and filth of the streets.

The churches did not miss out on this building boom. About 130 Anglican churches were constructed or reconstructed in the provincial towns of England and Wales in the eighteenth century, along with hundreds of Dissenting chapels. Many existing religious buildings went through smaller-scale renovations like the addition of galleries in order to accommodate more worshippers. London was supposed to have 50 new churches under a Tory-sponsored Parliamentary Act of 1711, although only a dozen of them were completed after the Whigs took power in 1714. Many London churches were renovated, and new churches appeared in fashionable suburbs. Yet by 1780 it was obvious that there were far from enough seats in churches and chapels to accommodate the growing populations of commercial cities and industrial towns.

On the profane side of the building boom can be counted the diverse leisure facilities for the elite and the middling sort that were created in the eighteenth century: assembly rooms where the polite classes could dance and hear concerts; pleasure gardens, like Vauxhall or Ranelagh just outside London, for strolling amidst "natural" landscapes and appreciating art or music; and provincial theaters where itinerant troupes of actors performed fashionable plays that had recently appeared in London. Spa towns like Bath grew up around such leisure facilities – and with 34,000 inhabitants, Bath was the thirteenth largest urban center in Britain by 1801. Bath became a sort of living architectural exhibit, a place where new building styles could be observed and admired. Its innovative edifices included the Circus and the Royal Crescent, residences for the wealthy that were designed to resemble monuments of the ancient world.

A third force for change in the urban landscape was improvement, which in the context of town life usually meant social services for the elite and middling sort of people. Improvement included public sanitation, like street sweeping or clearing of sewage, the provision of running water (sometimes, unfortunately, through lead pipes that tended to poison the customer), street lighting, and the maintenance of thoroughfares. From 1725 onwards, Parliament passed a series of 160 Acts creating local commissions whose purpose was to administer improvements in urban areas. Not all of the commissions were honest or effective, but together they were responsible for a shift in responsibility for public space in towns, away from the individual ratepayers and towards public bodies that were responsible to the civic authorities as well as to the central government.

The final type of change in the urban landscape involved the spread of industry. It might be thought that this was the most striking change of all, but in fact the physical impact of industrialization was far from overwhelming by 1800. You might have noticed factory buildings in towns and villages in the Midlands and the northwest, especially around the cotton producing center of Manchester. Factories were not just large workshops; they resembled big public buildings like hospitals or schools or prisons, and they contained hundreds of people – men, women, and children – who labored at specific tasks on a fixed schedule, with the aid of machinery. The first real factory was a silk-spinning mill constructed at Derby in 1702, but it was not until the advent of mechanized cotton spinning after 1770 that factories really became common. Still, by the end of the eighteenth century they were not widespread. One source counted 123 spinning mills in England and Wales in 1788, of which 41 were in Lancashire. Scotland had 19 spinning mills in 1788, most of them in the central area around Glasgow and Edinburgh. The environment inside factories was usually dreadful, due to constant noise, dangerous machines, and fibers floating in the air. Losing fingers or limbs in the machinery was common. Outside, the increased output of textiles encouraged the dyeing and bleaching industries, which dumped chemicals, especially chlorine, into local waters. Steam-powered factories used engines that burned coal, and issued billowing black clouds through huge smokestacks. The bad air of Manchester became notorious.

As factories were still fairly spread out, their noise and dust and smoke were not yet obnoxious to most people who did not work in them. A more shocking sight to contemporaries was the great iron forges of the West Midlands, central Scotland and South Wales, which belched out flame and smoke by day and night. A French visitor in 1784 compared the Carron workshops in Scotland, the largest ironworks anywhere in Britain, to both a natural wonder and a scene out of ancient mythology:

There is such a succession of these workshops that the outer air is quite hot; the night is so filled with fire and light that when from a distance we see, here a glowing mass of coal, there darting flames leaping from the blast furnaces, when we hear the heavy hammers striking the echoing anvils and the shrill whistling of the air pumps, we do not know whether we are looking at a volcano in eruption or have been miraculously transported to Vulcan's cave, where he and his cyclops are manufacturing lightning.[4]

The writer was impressed, but he never considered what it might be like to work every day in such an environment. What made these macabre scenes all the more strange was that they took place in what had recently been rural villages, now swollen to the size of small towns, but without any civic amenities. Merthyr Tydfil in South Wales was an example: once a tiny, isolated hamlet in a beautiful valley, its proximity to a coalfield brought it to the attention of the iron forge masters. By 1802 it was the site of 13 blast furnaces, employing several thousand men, but in social and cultural respects, it remained a small, remote Welsh village.

Another place of growing industrial wealth and increasing environmental devastation was the Potteries, a group of adjacent small towns in the West Midlands that are now collectively known as Stoke-on-Trent. Today, pottery-making does not evoke the image of big open pits and choking smoke, but this was what you would have encountered in the late eighteenth-century pottery towns. Clay was dug out of the pits, shaped into pots and plates and cups, then fired in large beehive-shaped kilns, which were of course fuelled by coal. The workers tended to live in close proximity to the kilns. The most famous and successful employer in the Potteries, Josiah Wedgwood, took some steps to address the awful conditions of life there. Wedgwood moved his main factory to nearby Etruria, where he funded a library and schools for his employees, and started a club to support them when they were sick. Wedgwood was one of several philanthropic employers of the late eighteenth century who attempted to address the problems of living in industrial towns. If their efforts were not always successful, it was in part because the changes which they were trying to address had been relatively rapid and overwhelming, leaving little time to figure out how to deal with them.

Not all features of the industrial landscape were bleak. In a village in eastern Shropshire, an area of coal mines, clay pits, and iron foundries, the iron master Abraham Darby III, a Quaker, paid for the construction of the first cast-iron bridge in the world. Opened for traffic in 1779, the Coalbrookdale bridge quickly became famous, and a hotel was opened nearby so that tourists could admire it.

View of the Iron Bridge over the River Severn, near Coalbrook-dale, Shropshire.

Published by Alexr Hogg Nº 16, in Paternoster Row.

Illustration 18   *The bridge at Coalbrookdale in the late eighteenth century, surrounded by industrial works. ("Coalbrookdale Bridge," engraving by T. F. Burney. © The Print Collector / Heritage-Images / Imagestate)*

The laced arc of gleaming metal is still beautiful to see, but its setting has changed back to greenery, and it is hard to remember today that it once stood beneath bare hillsides and belching smokestacks.

The overall effects of change in the landscape of British towns in the late eighteenth century were complex. The lives of the wealthy and middling classes were enhanced by new buildings, new opportunities for leisure, and civic improvements. In London and other large towns, the rich were separating their dwellings from the poor. As for laboring people, towns still offered higher wages and a better standard of living, but the conditions of existence were often unpromising. In industrial towns, laborers had to live in unhealthy and unpleasant environments, without the amenities of traditional village or town life, like markets, neighborhood taverns, nearby places of worship, or open spaces for recreation. You can still visit many of these early industrial spaces in Britain today, and judge for yourself whether the landscape there has fully recovered from the transformations of the late eighteenth century.

A Kingdom of Manufactures

The idea that Britain was suited by nature for manufacturing became entrenched in public consciousness as the American Revolutionary War drew to a close. As one writer put it in 1782:

The Kingdom of Great Britain, from its natural Situation, from the natural Productions, and from the natural Vigour and Activity both of Body and Mind of its Inhabitants, is particularly adapted to the Cultivation, Study, and Improvement of Manufactures ... [but] we have many powerful Rivals: Hence arise a Competition and an Emulation to excel in the Quality, or to render the different Manufactures of a lower Price at Foreign Markets.[5]

Whether or not this argument was a sort of psychological compensation for the loss of the war is debatable, but it was to have a profound effect on the future development of Britain and its empire. From the 1780s on, Britons saw themselves not just as a commercial people, but as the denizens of a manufacturing kingdom, whose mission was to dominate the markets of the world with inexpensive, mass-produced goods.

In part, this attitude was a reaction to increasing levels of production. A few numbers illustrate the point. Coal production rose between 1700 and 1800 from 2.5 million tons to over 10 million tons. The amount of cotton cloth woven in Britain increased from less than 5 million pounds weight before 1775 to 100 million pounds weight in 1815. Yorkshire broadcloths, which were made out of the long-haired, light wool known as worsted, also saw big increases in production, from less than 50,000 pieces per year before 1760, to 100,000 pieces in the 1770s and more than 400,000 in the first decade of the nineteenth century. The Scottish linen industry expanded from 2 million yards of cloth in 1727 to 12 million in 1768 and 19 million in 1808. In 1717, annual output of pig iron in Britain was about 20,000 tons; by 1788, it was 75,000 tons; and by 1806 it stood at a staggering 244,000 tons. These impressive figures may disguise as much as they reveal about the process of change over time. Coal production expanded pretty steadily, as did the weaving of Scottish linen. Pig iron output took off after 1750, cotton weaving after 1760. The rise in production of Yorkshire broadcloth began after 1760 as well, but it was not as steep as in the cotton industry. War years were boom times for the iron makers, especially at the Carron ironworks in Scotland, which supplied the British government, but they could be hard years in the textile industries, which depended on overseas trade. Not all forms of manufacturing were successful: the worsted cloth industry of East Anglia and the heavy woolen industry of the English West Country went into decline during this period.

One reason for the success of certain British manufactures was a gradual restructuring of the way people worked. The Scottish philosopher Adam Smith, in his great treatise *The Wealth of Nations*, published in 1776, summed up the basis of this reorganization as "the division of labor," meaning that workers performed separate and limited tasks, rather than trying to finish a whole product themselves. Smith's favorite example was pin-makers, who divided "a very trifling manufacture" among a variety of different workers: "One man draws out the wire, another straights it, a third cuts it, a fourth points it, a fifth grinds it at the top for receiving the head," and no fewer than three more men attach the head of the pin, making a total of 18 "distinct operations." By dividing their labor, ten men could make 48,000 pins a day. This was production on a mass scale, and it required regular working hours as well as supervision of labor. No longer could workers take Monday off or show up for work when they wished. Now they toiled six days a week, on set shifts that could reach 14 hours or more. They sat at benches rather than wandering around the workshop. They ate meals at their stations during short breaks, and they were watched throughout the working day by a supervisor. If they disobeyed rules, their wages were reduced. At the Etruria pottery, where "clocking-in" was first introduced, Josiah Wedgwood imposed a fine of 2 shillings on any worker who arrived late for work. This was what historians have called "industrial work discipline," and there can be little doubt that it was resented by workers.

We tend to attribute industrial change to another factor as well: machines. The late eighteenth century did see the advent of much new technology, but it usually developed in response to economic growth, rather than being the initial cause of growth. That, at least, was how Adam Smith saw it. He acknowledged that "everybody must be sensible how much labour is facilitated and abridged by the application of proper machinery." He was careful, however, to attribute the introduction of machines to the division of labour. "Men are much more likely to discover easier and readier methods of attaining any object," he wrote, "when the whole attention of their minds is directed towards that single object, than when it is dissipated among a great variety of things."[6] In other words, technology tended to develop in situations where labor was organized in a way that could adapt to it. Skilled artisans in small workshops, who fashioned an object from start to finish with their own hands and worked to their own schedules, might not need machines. By the eighteenth century, however, semi-skilled workers who specialized in carrying out a single part of the manufacturing process *did* need them, at least in the view of their employers. This provided a great incentive to inventors. Machines also required money for development and implementation, and patents to protect them from being copied without permission – factors that fell into place in the late eighteenth century, and resulted in a spate of significant technological changes.

Many of the machines introduced in the late eighteenth century had been invented earlier, and were simply reintroduced or redesigned. The steam engine, used to pump water out of coal mines, is a good example. Developed by Thomas Newcomen in the late seventeenth century, it made a limited impact on the mining industry before the Scottish engineer James Watt set out to improve it in 1763. Newcomen's engines lost energy over time because the movement of the piston cooled off the steam in the cylinder. Watt's first brainstorm was to separate an air-tight piston cylinder from the condenser where the steam was heated. He later added other small improvements, such as a governor or slide valve to control the engine's power. Watt patented his steam engine in 1769, by which time he had already met Matthew Boulton, owner of the Soho ironworks near Birmingham. Boulton was willing to manufacture and market Watt's engines. Employed first in coal mining, then in blowing blast furnaces in the iron industry, Watt's engines were eventually installed in flour mills, malt mills, stone mills that crushed materials used in pottery, and West Indian sugar refineries.

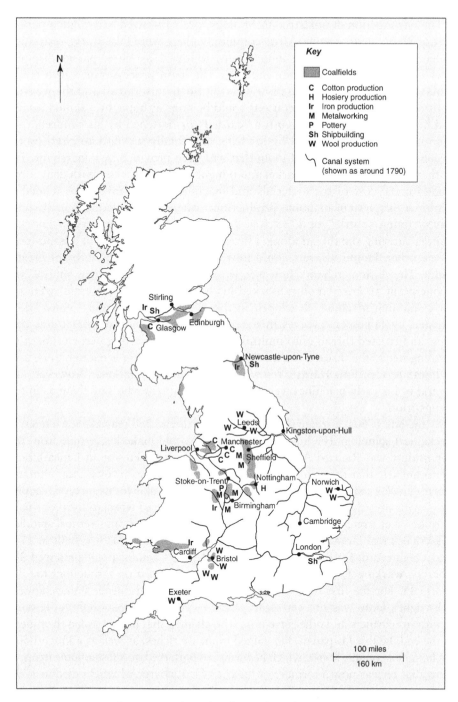

Map 7 *Mining, manufacturing, and canals in late eighteenth-century Britain. (Source: Eric Pawson,* The Early Industrial Revolution: Britain in the Eighteenth Century, *London, 1978, pp. 122, 148.)*

The introduction of industrial technology rarely followed as straight a path as that of Watt's steam engine. More commonly, there were false starts, resistance, stolen ideas, and competing innovations, followed by bitter patent disputes. This was the case in the cotton industry. The main processes in cotton textile production were the spinning of raw cotton fibers into thread and the weaving of thread into cloth. Both operations could be done at home by a skilled weaver and his family, with the raw cotton "carded" or flattened by his children, then spun into thread on a wheel by his wife, and finally woven into cloth by the weaver himself, using a hand-loom that had been provided by a merchant. The cloth was then carried to a market and bought by the merchant, with deductions made for the cost of the materials and machinery. Early inventions tended to reinforce this system of home production rather than undermine it. Richard Kay's "flying shuttle" of 1733 was a device that used hammers to knock a shuttle, carrying the thread along a fitted groove from one side of a hand-loom to the other. Home weavers could now work faster and on cloths of greater width. The cloth merchants, however, would not pay for Kay's new shuttle, and at one point an angry mob ransacked his house. Even less successful were the early spinning machines developed in the 1730s. The "spinning jenny," constructed by James Hargreaves in the 1760s, was a hand-powered frame that drew and twisted thread onto multiple spindles. The twisting was vital because it strengthened the thread. The machine was small and simple enough to be used in home production. Hargreaves was not much of a marketer, however, and several of his early machines were destroyed by rioters who saw them as unfair competition.

By the late 1760s, a severe shortage of cotton thread had reawakened interest in mechanical spinning. The business genius who would make his fortune from this opportunity was Richard Arkwright, a wig-maker from Preston in Lancashire. It seems unlikely that the water-frame spinning machine was his own idea, although Arkwright claimed that it was. He was certainly responsible for its success. It copied the designs of earlier machines, but used a water-powered wheel to turn four pairs of rollers that stretched the thread, which was then twisted onto vertical spindles. Arkwright's real innovation was to put this machine into a factory, built in 1771 near Cromford in Derbyshire. Within a decade, the Cromford mill employed 300 laborers, working 13-hour shifts. Production was carried on throughout the day and night. For the first time, cotton spinning had moved outside home industry. Arkwright's fame was not yet secure, however; he spent years fighting lawsuits against his partners and other inventors who claimed that he had stolen their ideas. In the end, he lost his patent, but gained immense riches, as well as a knighthood. He bought a country house, which he furnished with the latest fashionable items, to show that he was now a member of the elite. Sir Richard Arkwright died in 1792, leaving a fortune of half a million pounds. By then, however, a small farmer from Lancashire named Samuel Crompton had invented a superior spinning machine, known as the "jenny." It combined Arkwright's rollers with Hargreaves's moveable frame. A modest, reclusive man with no business ambitions, Crompton generously gave his invention to the public. By 1790, a Scottish manufacturer had figured out how to power it by a water-wheel, setting hundreds of spindles in motion.

From then on, cotton was spun on machines in factories, although it was still woven on hand-looms by skilled weavers, working at home. The factory workers were women and children, who could be employed for lower wages, while most of the home weavers were men. Child labor was common before the late eighteenth century, of course, but in factories, children were often expected to work the same long hours as adults, within a dangerous environment. Like children everywhere, they broke rules, and as a result were sometimes subjected to cruel punishments, such as suspension by their arms over the machinery. Adult female labor in factories may have had more positive consequences. It gave young women a chance for higher wages than they might find in other unskilled occupations, and enhanced their social status, although it was exhausting and damaging to health. Few older women chose to work in the mills. Factory labor was most attractive to women in northern England and central Scotland, where female home spinning was only a part-time occupation – thus, mechanized spinning offered a lucrative alternative. The dominance of women in the factory labor force was sometimes resented by male workers, because it drove down their wages. On the other hand, the spread of factories in northern England and central Scotland meant that wages for agricultural workers in those areas rose, due to the competition from industrial jobs.

It would be a mistake to suggest that British laborers engaged in manufacturing were suddenly converted into factory workers after 1770. The vast majority of them continued to work in small workshops with a dozen or so other employees, like those around Birmingham where small metal goods or "toys" were made; or they toiled away in their own homes, like the mostly female straw hat-makers who made the charming headgear that can be seen in portraits of upper class women of the 1770s and 1780s. The lines dividing different types of laborers were not strictly drawn. Many home weavers and coal miners, for example, still combined occasional industrial work with agricultural labor at harvest time. The lives of all workers would eventually be affected by work-discipline and mechanization, but the process of change was slow and variable.

It is also worth remembering how many people worked outside agriculture or manufacturing. The sailors who carried cargoes into every British port were men with highly specialized skills and a strong sense of occupational pride, who were nonetheless paid poorly and treated badly. Among them were many former agricultural laborers, and quite a few freed African slaves. In wartime, they were liable to be cornered in dingy alehouses by "press gangs" and forced into the Navy, where their nautical experience and valor provided Britain with a string of great naval victories. One of the largest groups of laborers in Britain was servants, ranging from the men and women who were charged with specific domestic tasks in the houses of the gentry and aristocracy, to the maids-of-all-work who cleaned and cooked in the houses of the middling sort, to the teenaged serving girls and boys in taverns and coffeehouses. Their employment was seldom secure, and they were often remunerated in food or lodging rather than money. The streets of British towns were crowded with vendors peddling wares of every sort, from old clothing to books to fruits and vegetables. Among them were many impoverished women who, after dark, joined the legions of prostitutes that could be found in London as well as in every port. Taken together, the labor of all these people, often held in little esteem then and since, contributed mightily to the commercial prosperity of the kingdom. Britain may have increasingly seen itself as the manufacturing center for the world, but the vitality of its economy depended on the ceaseless toil of millions of poor men and women who never saw the inside of a factory.

Part VI

Britain Against Revolution, 1783–1815

The reaction *in favor* of royal authority in 1783 was just as important as the reaction *against* a Catholic king in the Glorious Revolution of 1688. Both represented shifts in the balance of political opinion among property owners. The British state was set on a more conservative path after 1783, which it would maintain for 50 years. The preservation of order at home, and the extension of order into the Empire, became the chief priorities of successive conservative governments. The concept of order was broader and stricter than in Sir Robert Walpole's day: it encompassed social as well as political stability, and swift measures against those who threatened them.

Just as importantly, the disturbing legacy of the Glorious Revolution was finally laid to rest in conservative minds. The doctrine of resistance to the monarch in defense of constitutional rights, which had been weakly upheld by the Whigs and boldly trumpeted by radical patriots, was replaced among conservatives by a conviction that Britain was a nation where violent political upheavals were unnecessary. This did not mean a return to the Toryism of the early eighteenth century, because the Tories of that era had been shocked by the unsettling consequences of the Revolution of 1688. The conservatives of the 1780s felt that it had no unsettling consequences whatsoever. They were not opposed to every type of reform, but they were dead set against anything that, in their opinion, altered what they saw as a perfect constitution in Church and state.

The French Revolution horrified conservatives, because it raised again the possibility of republicanism and democracy. Radical groups, on the other hand, saw it as a replay of *their* version of the Glorious Revolution, another triumph for the right of resistance. They called out vigorously for fundamental reforms in favor of liberty and social justice, and were just as vigorously silenced by the government. In Ireland, radical patriots inspired a major rebellion. After its defeat, the most sweeping constitutional change that had been seen in that kingdom in over 600 years was instituted: namely, union with Great Britain. The British state itself was altered once again, although most British politicians declined to acknowledge that fact, and refused to give political rights to Ireland's Catholic majority.

If most of the British elite rejected revolution, did they also turn their backs on the rational ways of thinking that were associated with revolutionary change? Britain was the birthplace of the Enlightenment, and a haven for rational thought. By the late eighteenth century, however, reason was just as often enlisted in the defense of existing institutions as it was used to justify change. Critics of the establishment might draw on a countervailing trend towards individual sentiment or emotion, which would later become known as Romanticism. One of the most enduring legacies of this era was the concept of the British artist as a Romantic hero – almost always, a tragically emotional young man – at odds with the staid, conservative world around him.

16

The Nation Preserved

The royal coup that put William Pitt the younger into power at the end of 1783 was supported by many landed gentlemen and people of the middling sort throughout Britain. They were shaken by the consequences of the American Revolution, and alarmed by the possibility that Pitt's opponent Charles James Fox was marginalizing the monarchy, perhaps even aiming at a republic. As one government supporter put it during the elections of 1784, the real question was, "Whether is [*sic*] George III or Charles Fox to reign?"[1] By and large, the property-owning electorate preferred King George. Over the next decade, the fear of sudden change seemed to be justified, as France erupted into a violent revolution. Movements for Parliamentary reform resurfaced, with support among the lower and middling ranks. It was imagined that a revolution might even break out in Britain itself. When Pitt's government clamped down on the reformers, it again had the approval of a large proportion of the landed classes and many middling people. The conservative public opinion that had cemented Pitt's grip on power remained the moving force behind government until 1815. The resistance of the state to change was now seen by government supporters as its greatest virtue.

Mr Pitt Learns How to Govern, 1784–1789

William Pitt the younger seemed an unlikely figure to lead a ministry in the aftermath of the American crisis. At 24, he was inexperienced, although he was highly regarded as a speaker in Parliament. A younger son of the elder Pitt, he had studied at Cambridge, where he had not made many friends. He never married and had only one serious romantic attachment, in his late thirties. Reclusive and moody, Pitt took to drinking heavily with his close friend Henry Dundas, which did no good for his delicate health. In his personal opinions, Pitt was not an outright conservative. He believed in moderate Parliamentary reform and on three occasions, including once as chief minister, he presented reform bills to the House of

Commons, calling for the disenfranchisement of sparsely populated boroughs and votes for long-term tenants. All these bills were defeated. Over time, Pitt learned to be more cautious, both in catering to conservative public opinion, and in bowing to the desires of the King. "The friends of Mr Pitt," as his supporters were called, greatly admired him, but few would stand by him if the King turned against him. They were more concerned with preserving their own positions, or with protecting the monarchy from any fresh attacks. Yet they needed the personal leadership of the brilliant, calculating Pitt.

His long-time opponent was Charles James Fox. While contemporary prints depict Pitt as a cold, stick-thin figure with a pale, pinched, chinless face, Fox is shown as a fat, swarthy, stubble-chinned "man of the people." If nobody really knew Mr Pitt, everybody thought they knew Mr Fox. A gambler in politics as well as in private life, he lacked Pitt's controlled manner and deliberate purpose, but made up for it in passion and commitment. His reputation as a popular reformer was enhanced in the general elections of 1784, when he ran for Westminster, a constituency with a large electorate and a history of opposition to the government. It was also the city where Parliament itself met. Fox's successful election campaign was backed by the Prince of Wales, who hated his father, as all Hanoverian Princes of Wales were wont to do. Fox was also assisted by the beautiful Duchess of Devonshire – she reportedly won votes by giving out kisses to local butchers – and by an army of Irish chairmen, who when not carrying polite people around the streets in sedan-chairs, engaged in pitched battles with ministerial supporters. Pitt tried to have the election overturned in the House of Commons, but changed his mind when he realized the House was not with him. Fox would lead a force of about 200 "Old Whigs" in the Commons for the next 22 years. Although splinter groups remained common, the two-party system had returned, and it had an ideological basis, as the friends of Mr Fox proclaimed their adherence to traditional Whig principles of liberty and resistance, while the friends of Mr Pitt downplayed them.

In his first four years of office, Pitt undertook a number of important administrative changes that would have long-term consequences. Implementing the findings of a Parliamentary commission of accounts, he opened government contracts to public bidding, and tried to make public servants accept salaries rather than "fees," which were often essentially bribes. He gave Parliament supervisory control over parts of the King's yearly income, the Civil List, and ended extraordinary grants to the crown. The old system of self-interest and hidden influence was slowly giving way to the rules of a modern state bureaucracy.

Pitt's main tasks, however, were to restore British financial stability at home and prestige abroad. The first of these was a daunting goal, since the national debt in 1783 had reached £243 million, and the government was running a deficit of about £11 million on an annual expenditure of £24 million. Pitt tried everything to bring finances under control: he reduced expenditures, raised taxes, ran lotteries, and cracked down on the tea smugglers who were depriving the government of revenue. In one notorious incident in 1784, soldiers burned all the boats in the little port of Deal because so much smuggling was going on there. Pitt was sensible enough to realize that high customs duties benefited the smugglers. He reduced the duties on tea, which may have done more to discourage contraband than all his preventive measures. At the same time, he added or increased taxes on many other items: men's hats, ladies ribbons, male servants, gamekeepers, gloves, hackney coaches, carriages, pleasure horses, race horses, shooting licenses, pawn-brokers' licenses, window glass, bricks and tiles, candles, perfumes and powders, linens and calicoes, gold and silver plate, imported silk, imported gin, exported lead, letter postage, and retail shops. Some of these taxes, like the shop tax or a duty on coals, proved so unpopular they had to be repealed. Political writers complained about "The shameful profusion of Taxes," and worried about "the extreme Indigence of the Generality of the People, to bear the almost insupport-able Burden."[2] Yet bear it they did; and whatever the public thought of Pitt's taxes, they worked. In 1786, the government announced a £1 million surplus of revenue, which was placed in a sinking fund in order to reduce the national debt.

The even more lamentable financial condition of France at the end of the American Revolutionary War helped Pitt in foreign affairs. The French wanted to open up trade with Britain, which Pitt reluctantly agreed to do in a commercial treaty of 1786. He should have been more optimistic about the treaty, which enriched British manufacturers and French wine-growers. Hampered by massive debts, the French had no desire to enter into another war, even when the United Provinces were thrown into revolution in 1786. Dutch patriots deposed the Prince of Orange, whose determined wife summoned her brother, the King of Prussia, to crush the revolutionaries with his army. France did nothing to stop him, while Britain cheered him on. Four years later, Pitt's government pressured Spain into renouncing its claim to what is now Vancouver Island on the Pacific coast of North America. The French government again did nothing. In 1791, Pitt prepared for a war against Russia over seizure of a Turkish port on the Black Sea, but Parliament did not back him and he abandoned plans for a conflict. Clearly, in spite of the damaging defeat of 1783, Britain was still able to throw its weight around in global affairs, so long as the French were weak and the public was willing.

Pitt's imperial policies were much more coordinated and wide-ranging than those of his predecessors. He re-established the Board of Trade and created a six-member Board of Control for India. Dominated by Henry Dundas, the Board of Control effectively removed political affairs from the East India Company directorate. Seeking to expand Company trade with China, Pitt's government sent an embassy to the Emperor in 1791, which came away with few concessions, but was a big hit at the Chinese court, where Europeans were rarely seen. In the West Indies, Pitt enforced the Navigation Acts, forbidding direct trade with the new American republic. His agents conspired in vain with disgruntled politicians in Vermont and Kentucky, to keep those areas out of the United States. Legislatures were created in Lower and Upper Canada, corresponding to present-day Quebec and Ontario, in 1791. The government hoped that the two Canadas would pay for their own defense and that Upper Canada would develop into an English-speaking, Protestant territory. Pitt also proposed a customs union with Ireland, in exchange for the Irish Parliament taking responsibility for funding national defense, but the idea was condemned by British manufacturers, and was regarded with suspicion by Irish politicians. It went nowhere.

Pitt's energetic and controversial policy-making was largely successful in rescuing the British government from the doldrums into which it had fallen at the end of the American Revolutionary War. It did so, however, without directly addressing the issue of the King's role in politics, which had recently caused so much turmoil. Suddenly, in November 1788, royal authority became a burning question again, when the king began to suffer from delirium and serious delusions. He was put under the care of Reverend Dr Francis Willis, who used coercion, including a straitjacket and a restraining chair, to force the poor man back to his senses.

Meanwhile, a debate broke out in Parliament over whether the Prince of Wales should become regent. Prince George was hardly an exemplary character. Self-indulgent and dissolute, he had secretly married a Catholic woman, in violation of the Royal Marriages Act of 1772. If this union had been generally known, the Prince might have been barred from the throne. When George III became ill, Charles James Fox, who knew about the secret marriage, proposed that the Prince should at once become regent, with the full powers of a king, although Fox insisted, contradictorily, that this should be done through Act of Parliament, since "The Crown was hereditary, but the executive government was not." Pitt, by contrast, insisted that "the Prince of Wales had no more claim to hold the executive government of this country than any other subject whatsoever," and suggested limitations on his power as regent, including temporary restrictions on his ability to name political officers.[3] Both sides claimed to be acting in the true Whig spirit of the Glorious Revolution, and Pitt even boasted that he would "unwhig" Fox. Neither side was being entirely honest. The limitations on the regent's power were designed to keep Pitt's ministry in office. As for Fox's real aims, he summed them up in a letter to a friend: "at any rate, the Prince must be Regent, and of consequence the Ministry must change."[4]

He was wrong: the King recovered, and the Prince had to postpone his regency. What the debate had revealed was how much kingship had changed in the minds of politicians. Both sides spoke of it in terms of "executive power," as if monarchy were simply a component of government. With the exception of Edmund Burke, who argued that the Prince held full powers through hereditary right, nobody thought the heir should claim authority without Parliamentary approval. The attitude of the public, at least of those members of the public who supported the King, was somewhat different. They saw him as a symbol of the nation, not as a political figure. They warmed to his image as a faithful husband to Queen Charlotte and a loving father to a large family of 13 children. They loved to imagine him as simple "Farmer George," tending to his estate at Windsor or his garden at Kew. These portrayals were idealized. George had bad relations with his sons, and his sheltered life had little in common with that of an ordinary farmer. The royal image overwhelmed reality, not for the first or last time in the history of the British monarchy. The image remained beloved, and King George's recovery was celebrated in April 1789 with a magnificent St George's day service at St Paul's

Cathedral. Cheering crowds lined the streets as the royal carriage passed through the capital. Pitt was acclaimed, but Fox was hissed. The Bishop of London told the enormous congregation that they were there "for the dedication of a WHOLE PEOPLE, with their SOVEREIGN at their head, to their Almighty Protector, their common benefactor and deliverer."[5] The picture of a people harmoniously united under their King contrasts strongly with the suspicion of monarchy that was so widespread in the 1760s.

As events would show, the King still wanted to be the chief political player in Britain, not just a symbol or the benign "father of his people." Age and experience, however, seem to have taught him to be cautious in claiming what he regarded as his lawful authority. He was certainly wiser than his French counterpart, Louis XVI. Two months after the St Paul's service, the King of France was confronted by his subjects in a different way, when representatives to the Estates General at Versailles declared themselves to be a National Assembly, in defiance of the King. The French revolutionaries wanted Louis XVI to accept a largely symbolic position with restricted powers, but the King openly balked at being a figurehead, with disastrous consequences for the monarchy. His troubles would soon spill across the English Channel, and the same British King who had been so idolized by his people when his carriage passed in 1789 would have his carriage windows broken by them six years later.

The French Revolutionary Crisis in Britain

We do not know whether the Londoners who cheered the King in April 1789 were the same people who attacked him in October 1795. If they were, they may have been affected by two factors: the advent of a major war, which put enormous strains on Britain's economy, and agitation for reform by various clubs and societies. Historians have no sure way of judging how many Britons were truly committed to Parliamentary reform, but tens of thousands of middling and laboring people were mobilized by the reform societies. Some of these societies openly sympathized with the French Revolution. The complex circumstances that led to the downfall of the French monarchy did not exist in Britain, so that a British revolution was never likely. Nonetheless, the reform campaign was vociferous, and it stirred up an equally vociferous movement of support for "Church and King." Ideological and religious conflict, which had been simmering beneath the political system since the 1760s, suddenly boiled over. The government response was to suppress the reformers, which may paradoxically have increased the chances of covert sedition and insurrection.

Pitt's alienation from the reform movement came about gradually. It began with an attempt to repeal the Test and Corporation Acts. The Dissenting churches had changed markedly since the last repeal effort, in the 1730s. Many Presbyterians of the middling sort, like the scientist Joseph Priestley, had adopted Unitarian views, which were exempted from the Toleration Act. Conversely, Congregationalists and Baptists had been caught up in an evangelical revival movement that emphasized

Illustration 19 *In this cartoon by James Gillray, the Whig opposition is blamed, wrongly, for the attack on the King's coach in 1795. Charles James Fox is the figure with dark hair trying to open the carriage door; behind him stands the playwright and politician Thomas Sheridan. The driver of the coach is William Pitt the younger. (James Gillray, "The Republican Attack," 1795. © Courtesy of the Warden and Scholars of New College, Oxford, / The Bridgeman Art Library)*

a return to reliance on divine grace and predestination. Evangelical Dissenting congregations of all sorts had sprung up in the north and west of England, particularly in industrial centers where the Church of England did not have the resources to manage large increases in population. While Unitarians and evangelical Dissenters disagreed on basic theological issues, they could concur that the laws restricting their participation in political life should be removed.

The bishops of the Church of England disagreed, of course. Most of them were staunch High Churchmen, but even the evangelicals among them were wary of repealing the Test and Corporation Acts, on which Anglican dominance rested. Pitt's personal views may initially have been sympathetic to the Dissenters. He relied on the bishops to support him in the House of Lords, however, and he dutifully opposed the motions for repeal that were proposed in 1787, 1789, and 1790. His nemesis Charles James Fox stood with the Dissenters, who lost on every occasion. The popular poet Anna Laetitia Barbauld, a Presbyterian and supporter of repeal, was appalled by the failure of the last attempt, which she ascribed to the bishops raising the old cry of "the Church in danger." "*We* had too much reverence for your establishment to imagine that the structure was so loosely put together, or so much shaken by years, as that the removal of so slight a pin should endanger the whole fabric – or is the Test Act the *talisman*, that, when broken, the whole must fall to pieces like the magic palace of an enchanter?"[6] To some extent, it *was* the talisman, at least in a symbolic sense: when it broke in 1828, Parliamentary reform followed soon after.

Before the failure of the last repeal proposal, in November 1789, the London Revolution Society, a club of reformers, met to celebrate the 101st anniversary of the Glorious Revolution. Its president was the Whig Earl Stanhope, and the speaker on this auspicious evening was Reverend Richard Price, a Unitarian minister. Price stated that the Glorious Revolution had been concerned with the right to religious liberty and "the right to chuse our own governors; to cashier them for misconduct; and to frame a government for ourselves." Nevertheless, the Glorious Revolution "was an imperfect work." It did not extend toleration to Unitarians, or remove the Test and Corporation Acts, or remedy "The Inequality of Our Representation."[7] The recent Revolution in France, by contrast, had emancipated all religious groups, including Jews, and had promised equality to the people. The members of the club ended the evening by writing up a congratulatory address to the French National Assembly, which they hoped the British Parliament would imitate.

When Edmund Burke read the published version of Price's speech, he was outraged. Although he had previously favored the removal of religious restrictions, he was strongly opposed to repeal of the Test and Corporation Acts, and he had come to see the French Revolution as nothing more than the work of a violent mob. Burke's reply to Price, entitled *Reflections on the Revolution in France*, appeared in November 1790. Its impassioned and overwrought portrayal of the French Revolution as a string of "treasons, robberies, rapes, assassinations, slaughters, and burnings" was misleading, but prophetic, because after 1792 the republican government would in fact turn to a policy of terror in order to defeat its real and perceived enemies. Most telling was Burke's criticism of the revolutionaries for not respecting the past. "You began ill, by despising everything that belonged to you," he chided them. By contrast, the Glorious Revolution had preserved the British constitution. Burke envisaged government not as a sudden invention, but as "the offspring of convention," a binding agreement between past and present, "a partnership not only between those who are living, but those who are living, those who are dead, and those who are to be born."[8] He condemned democracy as individualism run wild, praised nobility of birth, and argued that all government rested on religion.

Conservatives were delighted by this performance, and 19,000 copies of the *Reflections* were sold by May 1791. Burke's friends, who had known him as a reformer and pro-American, were shocked and mystified. Tom Paine was one of them. His *Rights of Man* was a direct reply to Burke's *Reflections*. Paine's rhetoric was as overdone as Burke's, but he recognized the central theoretical point of his opponent's argument, and answered it: "Every age and generation must be as free to act for itself, *in all cases*, as the ages and generations which preceded it. The vanity and presumption of governing beyond the grave, is the most ridiculous and insolent of all tyrannies." Defending the French Declaration of the Rights of Man, Paine argued that civil rights were based on natural rights, which in turn were founded on the principle of human equality. Monarchy and aristocracy rested on ignorance, while "Government in a well-constituted republic, requires no belief from man beyond what his reason can give."[9] *Rights of Man* had a huge impact in Britain. Major John Cartwright's Society for Constitutional Information distributed over 100,000 copies of it to the reform societies. Paine followed it up with a second part in which he condemned the wasteful expenditure of corrupt governments like that of Britain, and suggested a scheme for using taxes to support the sick and indigent.

Paine's *Rights of Man* helped to inspire a remarkable work by a female journalist, Mary Wollstonecraft. *A Vindication of the Rights of Woman* (1792) was the first modern political statement of female equality. A former governess who mingled in Unitarian and reformist circles, Wollstonecraft believed that the subjection of women to men was just as irrational and tyrannical as divine right monarchy. "I love man as my fellow," she wrote, "but his scepter, real or usurped, extends not to me, unless the reason of an individual demands my homage; and even then the submission is to reason, and not to man."[10] If women were valued for rational thought rather than for chastity, and educated in moral principles rather than for frivolous pursuits, they would be better companions, mothers, and citizens. Wollstonecraft later visited France, married a fellow radical, William Godwin, and died in childbirth.

Wollstonecraft's ideas were utterly condemned by conservative reviewers, but they were seriously discussed by radical London debating societies, as were other topics pertaining to women. Voting rights for adult men, however, were at the head of the radical agenda in 1791–2. Paine's *Rights of Man* invigorated the reform clubs, like the Manchester Revolution Society or the Sheffield Constitutional Society, which recruited members among laboring men in industrial areas. In Scotland, at least 80 reform societies sprang up, and sent delegates to national conventions in 1792 and 1793. Early in 1792, the London Corresponding Society (LCS) was formed, with the purpose of keeping in touch with reform clubs throughout Britain. Its secretary was a Scottish-born shoemaker named Thomas Hardy. It welcomed members of all social ranks, and charged only a penny as a weekly subscription. Like other radical reform clubs, the LCS maintained links with the French revolutionary government, even after the declaration of a French republic in August 1792. A month after that dramatic upheaval, the LCS assured the French government that in Britain, "the reign of Ignorance, inseparable from that of Despotism, is vanishing ... Frenchmen you are already free, but Britons are preparing to be so."[11] These bold, incautious words predicted a British revolution.

The Whig party at first tried to take advantage of the formation of radical societies. A group of Whigs led by the young Charles Grey formed an Association of the Friends of the People and announced that a new reform bill would be presented to Parliament. Pitt's government pounced on them, by issuing a Royal Proclamation against Seditious Writings and Publications in May 1792. The Proclamation was not effective in discouraging the growth of radical newspapers, but it did scare the Whigs away from direct cooperation with the radical societies. Two years later, a number of conservative Whigs who opposed the French Revolution, including Edmund Burke, broke with Charles James Fox and joined the government.

The radical reformers also provoked violent reactions from conservative supporters outside Parliament. Learning of the formation of a Revolution Society around Birmingham, local clergymen and magistrates organized a pre-emptive strike in July 1791. An angry crowd of "Church and King" supporters ransacked Unitarian and Baptist chapels. In the middle of a game of backgammon, Joseph Priestley had to flee from his home, which was completely destroyed, along with his scientific instruments. Anti-Dissenting feeling was red-hot in the Birmingham area, as it had been in 1715 and 1750, when Jacobite-inspired mobs had carried out similar destruction. The conservative reaction found a further target in 1792–3, when Tom Paine was hanged in effigy in dozens of British towns. At the height of these incidents, the lawyer John Reeves organized the first meeting of the Association for the Preservation of Liberty and Property against Republicans and Levellers in November 1792. The long-winded name of the society harkened back to the Civil War era, when men of property had been horrified by the appearance of Levellers who called for all "free-born Englishmen" to be allowed to vote. Reeves was later put on trial, at the instigation of the Foxite Whigs, for asserting that the monarchy could function without the other branches of government. He was acquitted, but the incident shows the heightening of political rhetoric on both sides. On a less belligerent level, the evangelical writer Hannah More, the conservative answer to Mary Wollstonecraft, penned a series of *Cheap Repository Tracts*, advising laboring folk to be humble and obedient.

At first, William Pitt did little to assist the supporters of "Church and King." His attitude changed as France became a republic and radical attacks on monarchy became more frequent. The pressure on him to deal more harshly with the radicals was becoming intense, nowhere more so than in Scotland, where Lord Advocate Robert Dundas, brother of Pitt's friend Henry Dundas, was determined to crush them. Yet not much was done until France declared war on Britain on February 1, 1793, eleven days after the execution of the former King Louis XVI. While Pitt had not wanted war, now that revolutionary France had become Britain's enemy, he was willing to throw the full weight of the law against the reformers. The Scottish radical Thomas Muir, who had organized the first national reform convention, was prosecuted for sedition in August, and after a highly irregular trial was sentenced to 14 years of exile in Australia. Ironically, Muir had opposed the execution of Louis XVI. His arrest may have inspired the Scottish poet Robert Burns, who sided with reform although he worked as an exciseman, to pen the famous patriotic verses "Scots, wha hae wi' Wallace bled," which finish with the rousing lines, "Lay the proud usurpers low! / Tyrants fall in every foe! / LIBERTY'S in every blow! / Let us do, or die!!!"[12] Several other Scottish reformers were tried in the fall of 1793, and given sentences as heavy as Muir's.

The government had manipulated the trials of the Scottish radicals, but it would be more difficult to achieve this in England, where judges had less authority.

Spies and paid informers had gathered considerable evidence, much of it unreliable or invented, about the contacts of the LCS with France, and its plans for a national convention. The government started to arrest radicals in Manchester and London, including Thomas Hardy, the writer John Thelwall, and John Horne Tooke, who had supported John Wilkes back in 1770. *Habeas corpus* was suspended so as to make it easier to keep them in prison. They were accused of high treason, but their brilliant defense lawyer, Thomas Erskine, turned the trials into a fiasco for the prosecution. Aside from some indiscreet or intemperate remarks, the accused had done nothing to overthrow the British government. By the end of 1794, all of them had been acquitted.

This was a publicity disaster for the government, and a triumph for the system of trial by jury, which compares well with the summary justice being meted out by French revolutionary tribunals in the same year. The French situation was changing: in July 1794, the radical government in Paris, dominated by members of the Jacobin club, was overthrown by a political coup, and moderates again took charge of the Revolution. At the same time, the suspension of trade with France was causing considerable economic distress in Britain. In the summer of 1795, a grain scarcity in northern England brought hunger to the poor, and in radical Sheffield, food rioters clashed with troops. The LCS took advantage of the critical situation by organizing mass rallies on the outskirts of London, where addresses were drawn up demanding male suffrage, annual Parliaments and peace with France. The first, held in June 1795 in St George's Fields, site of the 1768 "massacre," drew more than 10,000 people; the second, which took place in October at Copenhagen House, Islington, may have been attended by 100,000. If the latter count was correct, this was probably the biggest public gathering for any purpose ever held in the British Isles up to that point in history.

Both meetings were peaceful, but the second was followed by an attack on the King's carriage as it drove to the opening of Parliament. The broken royal windows provoked a strong response from the government, in the form of the Treasonable Practices Act and the Seditious Meetings Act. The first Act widened the scope of treason to include "intimidating" the King or Parliament by act, writing, or speech. The second Act gave magistrates the authority to forbid public meetings and to close down unlicensed public lectures (except at Oxford and Cambridge Universities). The LCS protested that its aims were equal rights, not equalized property; that it sought "not to *overthrow*, but to *restore* and *realize*" the British constitution; and that it had always favored "Peaceful Reform, and not tumultary Revolt."[13] It made no difference: the Two Acts, as they were called, became law.

The Two Acts were vainly resisted by the Foxite Whigs as violations of the 1689 Declaration of Rights, and 94 petitions were presented against them to Parliament. In fact, the Acts were in the tradition of Whig measures like the Riot Act of 1716 or the Licensing Act of 1737, although their specific provisions were more restrictive than any legislation against political expression that had been passed since 1688. The redefinition of treason was particularly broad, and the powers given to magistrates were considerable. If the Two Acts had been rigorously enforced, they might have ended a political culture based on free speech and association, and brought about the British "Reign of Terror" that the radical reformers feared. However, they were seldom used. They did not have to be; the mere threat of them caused the LCS to stop holding mass meetings. It broke up into smaller units, while the debating societies either dissolved or turned to blander topics. In terms of fighting treason, however, the government may have made a mistake with the Two Acts, because they suspended public political activity and drove the most radical reformers underground, where they formed small, conspiratorial groups.

When mutinies broke out in the British Navy at Spithead and the Nore in May 1797, in protest against impressment, low pay, and bad food, the government was convinced that radical agents were involved. It is difficult to sort out the truth of the matter, but certainly a few of the leading mutineers had visions of a "Floating Republic" that would bring about social justice and democracy. The Spithead mutiny was settled with some concessions to the sailors. At the Nore, however, the delegates elected by the mutineers bickered with one another, and the Admiralty refused to deal with them. One by one, ships deserted the mutiny, which sputtered to an end. Several of its leaders were executed. It had been a great shock to the government, and to the King, who anxiously called for the death penalty for anyone who incited his armed forces to disobedience. Britain relied on its navy for protection, and in the war against revolutionary France, the British fleet would be vital to any hope of victory.

The Irish Rebellion and the Union

If the British sailors were disgruntled, it was in part because the war against France was not going well. In 1793, British forces had seized Toulon, the main French port on the Mediterranean, but a French counter-attack had forced them to evacuate it, under heavy fire from artillery commanded by a young officer, Napoleon Bonaparte. Some French islands in the Caribbean were captured, but at a terrible cost in lives, as yellow fever devastated the British troops. The Duke of York, second son of George III, led an expeditionary force into Belgium to support the Austrians against France. He ended up in retreat, and his army too had to be evacuated in the spring of 1795. This was the source of the children's rhyme "The grand old Duke of York, / He had 10,000 men. / He marched them up to the top of the hill, / And he marched them down again." It was not a bad characterization of the British war effort. By 1797, war finance was beginning to cause problems as well. To raise more money, the government had to offer a high discount to lenders, so that it added to the national debt almost twice as much money as it received in loans.

The defeat in Belgium broke up the first coalition against revolutionary France. Holland and Italy fell to French armies, and Spain chose to ally with France, which caused great consternation in Britain. In February 1797, the Spanish fleet set out from Cadiz to link up with the French navy, but Admiral John Jervis met and defeated them at Cape St Vincent. During the battle, under heavy fire, Commodore Horatio Nelson led boarding parties onto two Spanish ships, and captured them.

One week after this decisive victory, however, a minor French raid on the tiny Welsh village of Fishguard caused a panic in London, and a run on the Bank of England, with jittery investors demanding cash in exchange for notes. The rattled government authorized the Bank to suspend cash payments and issue a paper currency that was effectively no longer backed by gold. The result was a sudden rise in prices, although the damage that could be done by nervous investors was reduced.

The Fishguard raid was exceptional. The attention of France's military leaders was directed more to Ireland than to Britain in the late 1790s. The Irish government had faced considerable problems since legislative independence in 1782. If the Dublin Parliament were to represent the Irish population, Catholics would have to be allowed to vote and serve in it, which was not acceptable to the pillars of the Ascendancy. A Catholic Committee, consisting of urban merchants and shopkeepers, was organized to lobby Parliament for emancipation. The lord lieutenant, representing the British government, played a biased role in deciding the Catholic issue, because he relied on the influential Protestants who dominated the great offices of state. He sought to counter the influence of the Foxite Whigs, who had many friends in the Irish Parliament. Those friends had scuttled the negotiations for a commercial union with Britain in 1785, and had even declared the Prince of Wales as regent during the crisis of 1788–9.

Religious, political, and socio-economic issues intersected in complex ways in Ireland during the 1790s. In the countryside of the southwest and midlands, gangs of Catholic Whiteboys still carried out acts of revenge against landlords who raised rents. In the northern province of Ulster, where Catholics and Presbyterians competed for land and for employment in the growing linen industry, groups of Catholic "Defenders" and Protestant "Peep o' Day Boys" fought each other through bloody engagements, assassinations, and arson. The Defenders were organized like the Freemasons, with secret oaths and numbered lodges. More than 30 of them were killed by Peep o' Day Boys in the so-called "Battle of the Diamond" on September 21, 1795, which also resulted in the burning of hundreds of Catholic homes. That very evening, the victors in the fight founded their own Masonic-like organization, the Orange Order, named after William of Orange, the savior of Protestant Ireland in 1689. The Order was soon taken over by men of property, who used it to keep Ulster Catholics at the bottom of the social hierarchy.

Not all Protestants were inimical to Catholics. The secretary of the Catholic Committee was a young Protestant lawyer, Theobald Wolfe Tone, who had written against the remaining penal laws. In 1792, he set up a reform society known as the United Irishmen. Its members swore "to form a brotherhood of affection among Irishmen of every religious denomination, and ... to obtain an equal, full and adequate representation of all the people of Ireland."[14] The United Irishmen were particularly successful among the Presbyterian middling sort around Belfast, where they started their own newspaper, the *Northern Star*. Many Presbyterians resented their exclusion from political power, and sympathized with the goals of Scottish radicals.

Bowing to mounting political pressure for emancipation, the Irish Parliament in 1793 allowed Catholics to vote and serve in local offices, but not to sit in

Parliament or hold the highest political positions. In the following year, the appointment as lord lieutenant of Lord Fitzwilliam, a former Foxite Whig who had defected to the government, raised hopes of reform even higher. When Fitzwilliam made an agreement with Henry Grattan to support a bill allowing Catholics to serve in Parliament, however, he was sharply instructed by the government at Westminster that he should oppose it. Five days later, he was recalled by the King, and Grattan's bill went down to defeat. Evidently, legislative independence did not mean that Britain no longer interfered in Irish affairs. The sense of disappointment and disillusionment among the backers of Catholic emancipation was overwhelming.

At this critical juncture, the United Irishmen began to make plans for an armed uprising. In the north, they plotted with the Presbyterian militiamen of the Volunteer movement, while in the south, they approached the Defenders for assistance. Wolfe Tone was sent first to the United States, then to France in order to negotiate an invasion. An expedition carrying 15,000 French troops left for Ireland in December 1796. About half of them succeeded in reaching Bantry Bay in the southwest, but the weather was bad and in spite of Wolfe Tone's pleas, the French naval commanders would not allow a landing. The Irish government had already begun a crackdown on the radicals, suspending *habeas corpus*. Troops were sent into Ulster to eliminate the United Irishmen there, through a brutal campaign of house burnings, torture, floggings, and forced impressment into the navy. The conspirators still looked for help from abroad, possibly through a joint Franco-Dutch invasion, but the defeat by the Royal Navy of the Dutch fleet at Camperdown (Kamperduin) in October 1797 ended these hopes. Five months later, the government arrested most of the leaders of the United Irishmen in Dublin. The remaining plotters, including the renegade nobleman Lord Edward Fitzgerald, were thrown into despair, but they continued to lay plans for an uprising in May.

Four days before it was due to take place, the government apprehended Lord Edward, who was mortally wounded in the course of arrest. The uprising went ahead, but it was a disaster from the first. Only in County Wexford, south of Dublin, and in Ulster did it develop into a serious military threat to the government. The Wexford uprising was accompanied by considerable violence in the countryside, directed by Catholics against Protestant farmers, some of whom were burned alive in their own homes. The main force of the rebels, however, was recruited mostly in small towns. Its leaders were not exclusively Catholic, and the priest who commanded the Wexford rebels, Father John Murphy, was known for his good relations with local Protestants. The Ulster rebellion was commanded by a cotton manufacturer and a linen-draper, and was supported by about 10,000 Presbyterian artisans and men of the middling sort. Both the Wexford and Ulster rebels failed to take strategic points held by government troops, and were ultimately defeated. When the southern force was crushed by militia and British troops at Vinegar Hill in June, the rebellion was over. The aftermath was horrible. Summary executions were carried out by the government forces, houses were burned and the countryside was laid waste. Nobody was safe: even a former Member of Parliament, a landowner and a Protestant, was hanged by troops on

The Camp on Vinegar Hill

George Cruikshank

Illustration 20 *A British depiction of the Irish rebel camp at Vinegar Hill in 1798. This caricature by George Cruikshank illustrates the enduring British hostility to the Irish rebels. They are shown praying, shooting captives, and behaving like a radical mob. (George Cruikshank, "The Camp on Vinegar Hill, 1798." © Mary Evans Picture Library)*

the basis of flimsy evidence. This was similar to the vengeful military justice that had been handed out by the French revolutionaries in their own civil war.

Two months after the rebel surrender, the French finally landed about 1000 men in the isolated west of Ireland. They carried on a plucky campaign against a much bigger British force before surrendering. A second French detachment was sent to relieve them, but was captured by the Royal Navy. Wolfe Tone was among the prisoners. Before a court martial at Dublin, he asserted that "The great object of my life has been the independence of my country ... looking upon the connexion with England to have been her bane I have endeavoured by every means in my power to break that connexion; I have laboured in consequence to create a people in Ireland by raising three Millions of my Countrymen to the rank of Citizens."[15] Tone asked to be shot like a soldier, but when told he would be hanged instead, he cut his own throat with a razor. Often remembered today as an advocate of revolutionary violence, Tone was primarily a politician who sought democratic reform and cooperation between religious groups. He turned to insurrection as a last resort. It brought terrible retribution on him and on his countrymen.

The Irish rebellion hit the British government at a particularly sensitive time. On the same day as Lord Edward Fitzgerald's arrest, a French expedition under Napoleon Bonaparte left Toulon for Egypt. Its ultimate objective was to conquer the Middle East and march on to India, where the French had an ally in Sultan Tipu of Mysore. The goal was fantastically ambitious, but if it had succeeded, British trade would have been devastated. Admiral Nelson failed to catch up with the French invasion force as it crossed the Mediterranean, and Egypt quickly fell to Napoleon's army. The destruction of the invasion fleet by Nelson at the Battle of the Nile, however, meant that there was no retreat for the French. They finally surrendered to a British and Ottoman expeditionary force in 1801. Napoleon had by then fled back to France, where he overthrew the moderate republican government and made himself First Consul.

The British government's anxiety over the situation in Ireland and abroad was compounded by fears about "combinations" or secret associations at home. Under the strains of war, dearth, and high prices, economic conditions seriously worsened in the late 1790s, raising fears of starvation and fostering widespread discontent. The government responded by closing down the LCS in April 1798, and arresting its leaders. A secret committee of the House of Commons, drawing on rumors from informers, reported early in 1799 that it had found "the clearest proofs of a systematic design (long since adopted and acted upon by France, in conjunction with domestic traitors ...) to overturn the laws, constitution and government ... both in Great Britain and Ireland."[16] Magistrates in northern England began to complain about the spread of secret societies among textile workers. Again, the government reacted with repression, through the two Combination Acts of 1799 and 1800, which made all economic associations illegal, whether they involved laborers or employers. The Acts were to be imposed by a single magistrate, without a jury. Although the penalties spelled out in them were not severe, the Combination Acts clearly infringed on longstanding freedoms.

Faced by increasing difficulties, Pitt was turning in the direction of force and coercion, more strongly than any British government had done for over a century. In Ireland, he had a twofold solution: union and Catholic emancipation. The union was pushed through the Irish Parliament by Pitt's agent Viscount Castlereagh, using a combination of force, bribery, and promises of commercial prosperity. An impassioned last minute appeal against union by an ailing Henry Grattan had little effect. On January 1, 1801, the United Kingdom of Great Britain and Ireland came into existence. Ireland was given 100 seats in the House of Commons at Westminster, and 32 seats in the House of Lords – more than twice as many as Scotland. In spite of this apparent generosity, almost nobody regarded the two kingdoms as having become one nation, and the union was to be an unhappy one. It started off on the wrong foot when George III decided that he would not accept Catholic emancipation, and let it be known that anyone who supported it was no friend of his. The words were almost the same as those he had used to bring down the Fox–North coalition in 1783. Ever loyal, William Pitt offered his resignation, which was accepted in February 1801. Through a fit of pique, George III had lost the most capable chief minister who ever served him.

Conservatives Divided

The political history of the United Kingdom in the first decade and a half of the nineteenth century is not edifying. As in the 1760s, one ministry followed another in rapid succession. Pitt's replacement, Henry Addington, had served as Speaker of the House of Commons, but he was not really up to the task of leading a ministry. His main accomplishments were a short-lived treaty with France, and the extension of a recently introduced income tax to earnings of more than £150. Addington's ministry was opposed by Fox and by the former Foreign Secretary, William Grenville, son of the author of the Stamp Act. Pitt himself, however, held his fire until 1804. Once he decided to attack, the ministry rapidly collapsed. Because Fox was still odious to George III, Pitt took charge again as chief minister, at a critical moment in the war against France. An invasion was feared, and Napoleon was preparing to crown himself as Emperor of the French.

Britain was spared from invasion, but Napoleon went on to subdue most of Europe. In January 1806, a despondent William Pitt died, probably from cancer, leaving the King with no choice but to accept a "Ministry of All the Talents" that would include both Fox and Addington, now Lord Sidmouth, with William Grenville at its head. The one great achievement of the Talents was the abolition of the slave trade, on a motion made by Fox a few days before his own death. The biggest political mistake of the Talents was to raise again the vexed issue of Catholic emancipation. Forced to drop an attempt to allow Catholics and Dissenters to become generals in the army, Grenville bluntly told King George that his ministers claimed a right to advise him on future measures of Catholic relief. The King was infuriated by what he saw as bullying. "He considers the struggle as for his throne," reported Lord Chancellor Eldon, an anti-Catholic, "and he told me … that he must be the Protestant King of a Protestant Country, or no King."[17] The Ministry of All the Talents was turned out in March 1807 and replaced by a group of friends of the late Mr Pitt, who subsequently won a resounding electoral victory. Anti-Catholicism was still a winning issue in British politics.

Pitt's party, however, had broken in pieces after his death, and the anti-Catholic upsurge could not put it back together again, because its former members were fraught with personal rivalries, and not all were opposed to Catholic emancipation. As the Whigs favored peace with France, they were not likely to be taken back into the ministry, but they could still make trouble for the government. They forced the Duke of York to resign as commander-in-chief of the forces over a scandal involving his mistress, who sold military promotions for personal profit. The ministry gained stronger leadership by the end of 1809, when Spencer Perceval, a devout evangelical, became chief minister. "Little P," as he was called, declared that his loyalty was to the King alone and not to the revered memory of Mr Pitt. The Prince of Wales hated Perceval, and their relationship was worsened by George III's final attack of madness, or porphyria, at the end of 1810. The King would never recover, and spent his last decade in an agony of delirium, forcible restraint, and seclusion. He was separated from his family and treated with opium and straitjackets. He went blind and senile. The British public, long divided in its feelings for this controversial monarch, heard little about his sad fate.

Spencer Perceval responded to the King's descent into madness by proposing a regency bill virtually identical to that of 1788, putting tight restraints on the Prince's powers of patronage for the first year of his tenure. When the Prince and his brothers protested that these restraints were "perfectly unconstitutional, as they are contrary to, and subversive of, the principles which seated our family upon the throne of these realms," Perceval curtly replied that the ministers who had supported the similar regency bill of 1788–9 had received the "warmest acknowledgements" from George III for "their zealous concern for the honour and interests of his crown."[18] In other words, the crown mattered, not the Prince. "Prinny," as the Prince was known, sullenly gave in to "Little P."

Within a year, Perceval and Lord Eldon, government leader in the House of Lords, had convinced the Prince that they were indispensable to him. They even reinstated his brother, the Duke of York, as commander-in-chief. The Prince Regent's growing dislike of Catholic emancipation alienated him from his old friends the Whigs, and he heartily approved when the government suppressed an elected Irish Catholic Convention in 1811. Seeing that the ministers were firmly entrenched in power, opposition groups began to lay aside their differences and support the government. The anti-Catholic Sidmouth and the pro-Catholic Viscount Castlereagh both joined the grand conservative coalition. It continued to grow in strength even after the assassination in March 1812 of Spencer Perceval, who was stabbed by a bankrupt merchant in the lobby of the House of Commons. Perceval is the only prime minister in British history to have been assassinated, and he is usually remembered for nothing else, although he was the refounder of the conservative party. He also made banknotes into legal tender, a measure adopted in 1811 to help fund the war. Perceval's successor, Robert Jenkinson,

Earl of Liverpool, continued the policy of party reunification, bringing William Grenville and the brilliant orator George Canning back into the fold. Liverpool's task was made easier by the fact that the French empire was falling apart, the economy was improving, and the opposition was in disarray. As a result, the government could afford to postpone consideration of big, divisive issues.

One of them was Parliamentary reform, which had not disappeared. At first, the suppression of the reform societies had motivated some radicals to enter into violent conspiracies. Colonel Edward Despard, a United Irishman, former member of the LCS, and retired military officer, plotted to assassinate George III and overthrow the government with 4000 Irish supporters. His conspiracy was supposed to coincide with an uprising in Dublin, led by Robert Emmett. Despard, however, was betrayed, arrested, and executed in 1802, while Emmett led a hopeless attempt against Dublin Castle in July 1803 that resulted in utter failure. Sentenced to death for treason, he was the last person in the British Isles to suffer the full punishment of being hanged, drawn, and quartered.

The next phase of reform was quieter, and was marked by the abandonment of violence in favor of political organization. The strategy was initiated by the Westminster Committee, a group of veteran reformers that backed radical candidates in Parliamentary elections. The tailor Francis Place, a former leader of the LCS, was the most active member of the Committee. He found a champion in Sir Francis Burdett, a country gentleman from an "Old Tory" family who disliked Whigs of all varieties, but opposed the war with France and supported manhood suffrage. Burdett's victory in the 1807 election, against both Whig and conservative opposition, was a triumph of organization and a strong blow for independent voters. Burdett became a popular figure in the capital, almost a second John Wilkes. Another veteran reformer emerged from rustic retirement to found a new type of reform society. At the age of 72, Major John Cartwright, friend of American independence, started the first Hampden Club, named after John Hampden, who had resisted King Charles I's ship money tax. Dedicated to manhood suffrage, the club had over 150 branches in the north and Midlands of England by 1817.

The Midlands was troubled after 1811, not by reform clubs, but by violent protests in which workers destroyed the hand-powered knitting frames on which stockings were made. The chief grievance of these laborers was low wages, although they also objected to "cut-ups," cheap stockings cut out of material knit on a wide-framed machine, and sewn together. In Nottingham and other places, crowds of stocking-frame knitters attacked factories and smashed up the frames with sledgehammers. Their mythical leader was called "Ned Ludd," which gained them the nickname "Luddites." The government reacted by sending troops and seeking for "Ned Ludd," who probably never existed. Similar riots had happened many times in the past, and it was fear of radical political activity that caused the government to react so strongly. Most of the frame smashers did not have political goals, and they were more concerned with raising their incomes than with stopping the spread of machinery. They have left us the term "Luddite," which today is often used, misleadingly, to describe those who dislike computers or cell-phones.

The War against Napoleon

The government's main worry during these years was the continuing war with Napoleon's France. Historians have often compared it to the epic struggle with Hitler's Germany in the Second World War, although the differences were as great as the similarities. During both conflicts, Britain was under threat of invasion by a dictator who dominated Europe, and popular opinion was mobilized in defense of "King and Country." However, while peace with Nazi Germany was never seriously contemplated, a truce with Napoleonic France was a recurring option for British politicians. Unlike Hitler, the French Emperor had admirers in Parliament throughout the war. Finally, after the death of William Pitt the younger, no British chief minister could remotely compare with the dynamism and determination of Winston Churchill in the Second World War. The Napoleonic Wars were won without great leadership in Parliament.

The 1802 Treaty of Amiens was supposed to end the war forever. In fact, both sides knew it was only temporary, and continued to arm for a future conflict. As British tourists flocked to Paris, Napoleon strengthened his hold on the Netherlands and Italy, while Britain refused to vacate Malta in the Mediterranean. Meanwhile, the raising of 30,000 men for a reserve army and 450,000 volunteers in Britain and Ireland provided a formidable force for national defense. The volunteers were enthusiastic – one farmer declared that "If Buonyparte comes [I] will do anything to make him repent" – but they were also promised that they would not have to fight abroad.[19] Hostilities broke out again in the spring of 1804, and an invasion seemed imminent, as French troops massed on the coasts. Napoleon even considered using balloons to carry his men across the Channel. In the end, the invasion never happened, because the self-proclaimed Emperor decided to deal first with his Austrian and Russian enemies.

He also ordered Admiral Villeneuve, commanding the Toulon squadron, to link up with the Spanish fleet in order to block British attempts to reinforce Malta. Admiral Nelson caught up with Villeneuve on October 19, 1805, at Cape Trafalgar near Cadiz. Nelson sent his sailors into battle with the command "England expects that every man will do his duty" (interestingly, he did not mention the United Kingdom). Superior British ship-handling and gunnery led to a complete victory, with 19 French and Spanish ships captured or sunk (four more were taken a few days later). Yet the day was marred for Britain by the death of its greatest naval commander. As Nelson strode the quarterdeck of his flagship, HMS *Victory*, a musket ball entered his shoulder and shattered his spine. He expired in agony three hours later, after asking his flag captain to embrace him – "Kiss me, Hardy" – beseeching the nation to take care of his mistress, and thanking God that he had done his duty. The grief felt by the British public for its lost hero was tremendous. Old sailors wept and huge crowds appeared to watch as a procession of dignitaries escorted his coffin to St Paul's.

Worse news followed. In December 1805, Napoleon crushed the Russians and Austrians at Austerlitz. In the following year, he defeated the Prussians and

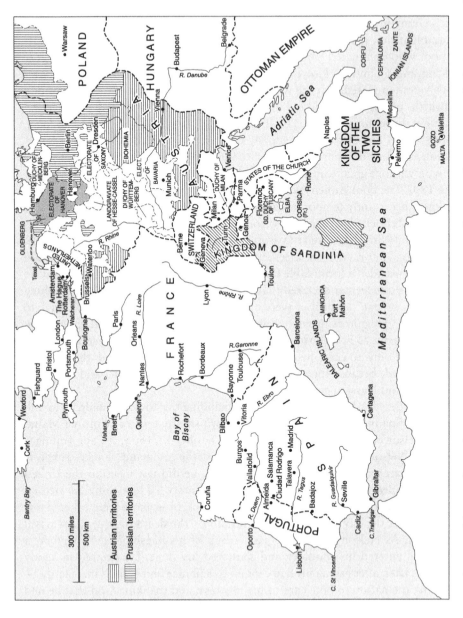

Map 8 *Europe at the start of the French Revolutionary Wars. (Source: J. Steven Watson, The Reign of George III, Oxford, 1960, appendix.)*

marched into Poland. From Berlin, he issued a decree blocking all European ports from trading with Britain. The British response was to forbid neutral ships from entering or leaving European ports without paying customs duties in Britain – essentially, a license to seize the shipping of non-combatant nations. Napoleon then decreed that France would confiscate any neutral ship stopping in Britain. This economic tit-for-tat hurt both sides, contributing to a severe economic recession in Britain that peaked in 1810–11. Meanwhile, Napoleon made a big strategic error in 1808 by invading his former ally Spain, and installing his brother Joseph as King. Britain sent an expeditionary force under Sir John Moore to assist the Spanish. Moore was chased back to Coruña by the French, and killed while his forces were being evacuated, but he kept his army intact. Under his successor, Sir Arthur Wellesley, later created Duke of Wellington, the British army in the Iberian peninsula would be a constant thorn in the side of the French Emperor.

Wellington, who had led troops in India and was derided as a "sepoy general" by Napoleon, was the first British commander to make a successful transition from the empire to a European command. Obsessed by discipline and training, he was a brilliant tactician, but limited as a strategic thinker, which made politicians in Britain doubt his abilities. Wellington's war was also costly in money and men. His first invasion of Spain in 1809 led to a bloody victory at Talavera. Lacking support from the Spanish, he retreated to Portugal, behind a heavily fortified position known as the lines of Torres Vedras. The French pursued him, but could not break through his defenses. They withdrew into Spain, where they faced a spreading popular resistance against them in the countryside (the word *guerilla*, or little war, was invented to describe this conflict). Advancing again in 1811 with a joint British, German, and Portuguese army, Wellington came up against the fortified cities of Badajoz and Ciudad Rodrigo, which he failed to capture. On his second attempt in the following year, he took Badajoz by storm, leading to heavy losses and a massacre of French troops. He went on to launch a daring attack on an over-extended French army at Salamanca, where a British cavalry charge broke three enemy divisions and captured a French regimental eagle, symbol of the Emperor. Wellington triumphantly entered Madrid. Again, however, his invasion failed when he was repulsed at Burgos and pushed back into Portugal.

By then, however, Napoleon had made the catastrophic decision to invade Russia. Defeated by the advance of winter, the Emperor had to retreat from Moscow, losing almost half a million men. As French troops were pulled out of Spain for service in central Europe, Wellington began his fourth and last invasion in the spring of 1813. This time, there would be no stopping him. Outmaneuvering his enemy, Wellington prevented a convergence of French forces and inflicted a severe defeat at Vitoria in northern Spain on an army commanded by Joseph Bonaparte himself. The French began to withdraw from Spain. The Iberian peninsula was no longer of much concern to Napoleon, who had been driven out of Germany and was preparing to defend France's borders against the Prussians, Austrians, and Russians. With the Peninsular War won, Wellington pursued the French across the Pyrenees mountains to Toulouse, where he fought a last action, successful but costly, four days after Napoleon had surrendered to the Allies.

The only other major British military intervention in Europe during these years was a disastrous expedition to Walcheren Island in the Netherlands in 1809, which resulted in 4000 deaths, largely due to malaria, typhus, and dysentery. Troops were also sent to the West Indies, where they died in great numbers. The War of 1812 with the United States involved British military units in the defense of Canada, but the Peninsular War was always given first priority.

Victory against Napoleon was made possible by the tenacity of British soldiers and sailors. The army was becoming more professional, thanks in part to the efforts of the controversial Duke of York. Although officers' commissions were bought, promotion by merit was the rule in wartime. Wellington called his men "the scum of the earth," but they were well trained and their morale was high. The Royal Navy was already a professional service; its crews were seasoned, and its officers worked their way up from lower to higher ranks. The lives of able seamen remained hard. Many were forcibly impressed, others served from boyhood until pensioned off, all had to put up with long voyages, monotonous work, floggings, and harrowing battles. Yet sailors came to expect a certain level of fair treatment, as well as ample victuals and strong drink, which preserved the harmony of a community on board ship.

One last effort was demanded of these men. In the spring of 1815, Napoleon escaped from exile and returned to France. The newly restored Bourbon King fled, and war began again. A hastily assembled French army marched north against the Allied forces stationed in Belgium. Wellington, commanding a combined army of British, Irish, Dutch-Belgian, and German troops, stationed his soldiers defensively around two walled farmhouses on a small hill near the village of Waterloo. On June 18, 1815, Napoleon faced the British general for the first time in battle. As heavy mud prevented effective use of his artillery, he sent waves of infantry to dislodge the Allies. Highlanders, British Guardsmen, and German troops halted the French advance. In the early afternoon, one of the farmhouses was taken by the French, but a massive cavalry charge failed to crack the Allied forces, which formed up in squares to repulse it. With the Prussian army arriving on his flank, Napoleon made one last throw of the dice, sending his Imperial Guard up the hill against the Allied lines. They were pushed back by the British Guards and Dutch regiments. The retreat became a rout, and the French army began to fall apart. Wellington waved his cocked hat, giving the signal for a general advance. Napoleon was finished, and the long wars against France were over.

How affected had the British people been by 22 years of war? A quarter million British soldiers and sailors lost their lives between 1793 and 1815. Over £1 billion was spent on war, and the national debt rose to almost £745 million. War aroused fervent patriotism; it mobilized vast human and financial resources; it caused widespread deprivation and near starvation among laboring people. Yet the last great war against France did not result in significant political changes in Britain. The conservative atmosphere established after the American Revolution endured for 15 years after Waterloo, before it was finally swept away by a tidal wave of reform.

17

Remaking the Empire

The first British empire was based on plunder and plantations. Its main goal was to make a profit for British commercial interests. The makers of the first empire had little desire to rule over foreign populations. Few of them were even concerned about spreading Christianity. They drove people who were not British or Protestant out of the territories that they claimed. When this was not feasible, as in the case of the Irish or the slaves brought to the New World, the settlers exploited their labor, passed laws to suppress them, and tried hard to ignore them. This began to change after 1763, when for the first time, Britons had to adjust to the idea of governing peoples who were not British, not Protestant, not even Christian. The conservative politicians who held power after the American Revolution were convinced that British rule was good for everyone, because it would introduce foreign peoples to the perfection of British justice and government. The evangelicals went further: they wanted British Protestantism to become the foundation of empire. Plunder was not forgotten, of course, although it took more respectable forms. The worst type of exploitation was eventually limited by the abolition of the slave trade. The new imperialism was remarkably successful, and the second British empire expanded in every direction. Strangely loved and fiercely hated, it developed distinct features in this period that would endure until it began to dissolve 150 years later.

Into the Pacific

The Pacific islands were the new found lands of late eighteenth-century imperialism. The British did not "discover" them, even from a European point of view. Most had been visited and charted by the Spanish or the Dutch, and before that, settled by native peoples, who were extraordinary navigators. The British, however, were the first to publicize their Pacific voyages widely, in scientific treatises and narrative accounts that caught the public imagination. This "opened up" the Pacific to

Europeans, just as a similar publicity had brought attention to the Americas two centuries earlier. In Australia, many of the mistakes and misdeeds of American colonization were to be replayed, with devastating results for indigenous peoples.

The great British explorer of the Pacific was Captain James Cook. The son of a farm laborer, Cook had worked his way up in the Royal Navy through his skills at mathematical surveying, by which information was gathered to make charts. In 1768, the Admiralty gave him command of a ship, HMS *Endeavour*, and sent him to the Pacific to observe the transit of the planet Venus over the face of the sun. The Royal Society hoped that this information could be used to measure the distance between the earth and the other planets. A rich young botanist, Joseph Banks, was to accompany Cook and make notes on the natural history of the Pacific islands. Before they set sail, Banks and Cook were given "Hints" by the president of the Royal Society regarding their conduct. They were to treat the native inhabitants with "patience and forebearance," avoid the shedding of blood, and remind themselves that the native peoples "are the natural, and in the strictest sense of the word, the legal possessors of the several Regions they inhabit."[1] These humane suggestions were belayed by Cook's second, sealed instructions from the Admiralty, which told him to seek out the fabled great Antarctic continent and take possession of it, hopefully with the consent of the natives. He never found it, but the *Endeavour*'s voyage to Tahiti, New Zealand, and the east coast of Australia would make him famous.

Cook was a careful and highly disciplined leader. He took precautions to avoid scurvy among his crew, and not a single man was lost to that dreadful disease. His ship was kept exceptionally clean. Like all naval commanders, he flogged his men for indiscipline, and he did not hesitate to flog Pacific islanders when they stole nails or bits of iron from his ship, but he was consistent and, by contemporary standards, fair in meting out punishments. For the most part, he kept the potential violence of his sailors against the native peoples under control. Although they were often treated like children, the islanders were viewed as noble and virtuous. When a Tahitian was shot dead in a dispute over a stolen musket, Joseph Banks "was highly displeased, saying, 'If we quarreled with those Indians, we should not agree with angels,' and he did what he could to accommodate the difference."[2] The sailors were mostly interested in obtaining the sexual favors of Tahitian women. Like all European expeditions, Cook's voyage left a trail of venereal diseases in its wake.

On his second expedition to the Pacific in 1772–5, Cook again searched for the southern continent. His ship *Resolution* skirted the fringes of Antarctica, a terrifying land of ice and snow. On board was a remarkable invention: a marine clock, copied from an original designed by the clockmaker John Harrison, showing the exact time at Greenwich. The marine clock, a breakthrough in navigation, was designed to allow the accurate measurement of longitude at sea. Cook carried it with him again on the *Resolution* during his third voyage, in 1778–9, when he explored the Pacific coast of North America, but failed to find a Northeast Passage to the Atlantic. Returning in disappointment to the Pacific islands, Cook's behavior towards the native peoples became increasingly violent and erratic. At Hawai'i, he was killed in a skirmish with islanders who were angry with him for flogging a chief. They may also have believed that he was the god Lono, returned to earth. To Britons, he was a different kind of god, the incarnation of enlightened, humane principles. His many admirers believed that the British empire was destined to spread these principles around the globe.

The voyages of Captain Cook have been seen as initiating a new kind of imperialism, based on a search for knowledge. Once gained, knowledge could be used to understand, but also to stereotype and dominate native peoples. Understanding, of course, was not a one-way system: native people learned about Europeans as well, although their exposure to the newcomers was usually determined by forces that were not under their control. A young Tahitian man named Omai, for example, traveled to Britain with Cook's second expedition, causing a sensation as a living example of a "noble savage." He managed to return to Tahiti with some remarkable tales to tell, but his countrymen made no plans to colonize Britain. They may have sensed that European colonial dominance was on the horizon. When it came, it was imposed in the traditional way, by firearms, not by botanical studies.

The first British attempt at settlement in the Pacific was made at Botany Bay in southeast Australia in 1788, although the colony soon moved to Port Jackson on Sydney Cove. The settlers were convicted criminals and their guards. The option of transporting British convicts to Virginia and the Carolinas had been removed by American independence. Not enough space for convicts existed in British prisons or in the "hulks," dismasted ships that were kept in the Thames, and it was found that prisoners could not long survive transportation to West Africa. At first, the convicts fared little better in New South Wales than in Africa, and died in droves from starvation and disease. It was not until the arrival of the "Second Fleet" in 1790 that the penal colony's survival was assured. By 1815, it numbered about 15,000 people, two-thirds of them men. The gender imbalance among European settlers in Australia would last until the 1880s.

Most of the first settlers were petty criminals, ordinary people who had stolen small amounts of property. They were joined in 1793 by Thomas Muir and a handful of exiled Scottish radicals, and, in the aftermath of the 1798 Irish rebellion, by over 600 United Irishmen. The Irish convicts were particularly badly treated and suffered a heavy mortality rate on the outward journey. They staged the first rebellion in the colony, near Sydney in 1804. It was crushed by government troops at a place later named "Vinegar Hill," after the Irish battleground of 1798. None of the convicts had easy lives. All were required to work as government laborers for a fixed period of time, and were liable to be flogged for breaking rules. After serving their time, they could purchase land and become small farmers. In the mid-1790s, passage to Australia was opened to free settlers as well, although the convicts outnumbered them for many decades.

The relations of the colonists with the Aboriginal peoples were fraught with violence and hostility from the first. While they sometimes admired the ability of Aborigines to live in such a difficult environment, the settlers were also eager to push them off their land, by force if necessary. The Aborigines mounted little resistance, in part because they did not regard the land as being owned by anyone, and so were not immediately aware of its having been lost. If the convicts were particularly brutal in dealing with native peoples, it may have been because they were despised by "respectable" folk themselves, and were eager to fashion Aborigines into a group inferior even to them. They were assisted by the spread of disease. As in North America, smallpox ravaged the natives, making British colonization easier. It was not, however, a welcoming land for the British. "I do not scruple to pronounce," whined the first lieutenant governor, "that in the whole world there is not a worse country. All that is contiguous to us is so very barren and forbidding that it may with truth be said that *here nature is reversed*; and if not so, she is nearly worn out."[3] The struggle to plant a European society on this island continent would be long and difficult.

All in all, the Pacific world offered little to the British in terms of plunder, except perhaps in the form of whales, which were avidly pursued by British whaling ships from one end of the ocean to the other. Whale oil, used in lamps, was a valuable commodity. Scientific exploration of the Pacific continued, with the encouragement of Sir Joseph Banks, president of the Royal Society after 1778. The most celebrated and ill-fated scientific voyage was that of HMS *Bounty*, dispatched to Tahiti in 1788 to pick up breadfruit plants, in hopes that they would provide cheap food for slaves in the West Indies. The captain of the *Bounty* was William Bligh, navigator of the *Resolution* on Captain Cook's final voyage. He may have flogged the men too wantonly, or he may just have sworn at them too much; in any case, he provoked a mutiny in April 1789. Bligh and 17 loyal crewmen were put in a 23-foot launch that they sailed for 3600 miles until they reached the Dutch colony at Timor. The mutineers returned to Tahiti, where most of them were eventually captured. Three were later hanged. Nine others, with twelve Tahitian women and six men, escaped in the *Bounty* to remote Pitcairn Island. There they tried to enslave the Tahitians, which resulted in a small-scale but savage racial war. By 1800, all but one of the mutineers was dead. He became an evangelical Christian, and the patriarch of a society that still exists on the island.

The final great British expedition of discovery in the Pacific was carried out by Captain George Vancouver in 1792–4. A veteran of Cook's last two voyages, Vancouver was sent to the west coast of North America to search for the Northeast Passage, which he was convinced did not exist, and to reclaim the land at Nootka Sound that had been occupied by Spain two years earlier. Vancouver surveyed the coasts of what is now British Columbia, satisfied himself that there was no Passage, and signed a convention with Spain that led to a mutual abandonment of Nootka Sound. The area was opened to whalers and fur-traders from all nations. After 1795, it was also opened to evangelical missionaries, who would make more of an impact on traditional island society than the whalers and explorers ever had.

As for the unfortunate William Bligh of *Bounty* fame, he went on to become governor of New South Wales, where his attempt to break up a local mafia, the so-called Rum Corps, led to a second mutiny against him in 1808. The Rum Corps, officially the New South Wales Corps, was a military unit that controlled supplies in the colony, and used rum as a form of currency. Bligh was arrested by his own troops, and exiled; when he tried to return to Sydney, he was locked up in prison for two years. The British government eventually re-established order under a new governor, but nobody was seriously punished for the rebellion. Evidently, New South Wales was developing as a frontier community, with its own sense of justice. To the convicts, the rum-trading militiamen, and the oppressed Aborigines of Australia, the idea of spreading British law and order in the Pacific must have seemed, at best, a bad joke.

Dominating India

The Pacific was the site of British imperial fantasies: India was the home of overwhelming realities. The British government in the late eighteenth century spent an enormous amount of time thinking about India. Every ten years, when the East India Company charter came up for renewal, it was carefully rewritten by the politicians, so as to reduce the Company's role as an independent trading entity and increase the government's control over Indian affairs. The governors-general sent to India in this period saw themselves not as Company representatives, but as agents of the British state. As such, they were not satisfied with the structure of the Company, the ways it raised revenues, or the unreliable influence that the Company exercised over Indian princes. Seeking order and stability, they reformed Company practices and annexed more and more territory to the EIC domains. By 1818, Britain had established an imperial dominion in India that rivaled the empire of the Mughals at its height.

The Indian empire was largely built by three remarkable men who served as governors-general of Bengal: Warren Hastings (governor, 1772–3; governor-general 1773–85), Charles, Earl Cornwallis (governor-general 1786–93 and 1805), and Richard Wellesley, created Marquess Wellesley (governor-general 1797–1805). Hastings was the last old-style Company official to administer British India. He was also the first governor of Bengal to be given authority over all Britain's possessions in the subcontinent. Like Clive, Hastings enriched himself through the proceeds of his office, and was often brutal in his dealings with Indian rulers. He bullied, cajoled, and bribed them. He sent troops to support friendly princes in wars that had little to do with British interests. When the Raja of Benares could not pay what Hastings demanded for the Company's military expenses, he was forcibly deposed. When two dowager princesses known as the Begums of Oudh (Awadh) refused to cough up money owed by their son and grandson to the Company, Hasting had their servants imprisoned in chains and starved. An Indian nobleman who had openly accused Hastings of bribery was ordered by the Calcutta Supreme Court to be put to death on an unrelated charge of forgery. Hastings may not have arranged the execution, but it benefited him, and it amounted to judicial murder, as forgery was not a capital offense in India.

Yet if he was high-handed in dealing with Indian princes and nobles, Hastings was also a reforming administrator. He created a revenue collection service, set up civil courts, and tried to stamp out private trading by Company officials. An admirer of Indian culture, who spoke Persian, Bengali, and Urdu, Hastings encouraged the study of Hindu law and of texts written in Sanskrit, the ancient language of India. He supported the founding of the Muslim College of Arabic Studies at Calcutta. While these may be regarded as forms of intellectual imperialism, designed to make educated Indians appreciate British rule, they also fostered a sense of collective pride among Bengalis in their own cultural heritage.

Hastings was undermined throughout his governor-generalship by an Executive Council that opposed him on crucial issues. His chief nemesis on the Council was Sir Philip Francis, with whom he once fought a duel. A man of strong opinions, Francis probably authored the radical letters of "Junius," but his ambition in later life was to replace Hastings as governor-general. Thwarted in this goal, he provided information to Edmund Burke that led to impeachment proceedings against Hastings in the British Parliament. Burke saw Hastings as a tyrant, a rebel against British policy, and a representative of the unbridled power of money. He feared that the next goal of the "men full of wealth" who had plundered India would be to corrupt Britain itself. "Our Liberty is as much in danger as our honour and our national Character," Burke warned. He argued that the empire was built not on profit or rapacity, but on the trust of local people in the "guardianship" of Britain. He was convinced "that if the British Empire is to be maintained, it is to be maintained by faith, that if the British Empire is to be propogated [*sic*], it is to be propogated by public faith, that if the British Empire falls, it will be through perfidy and violence."[4] Nobody had ever articulated the theoretical basis of empire so clearly or eloquently. Burke became obsessed with the Hastings impeachment, which dragged on for five years until the former governor-general was finally acquitted by the House of Lords in 1794.

By then, the governor-generalship had changed fundamentally. Lord Cornwallis, trying to save his reputation after the surrender at Yorktown, had agreed to take the position on the condition that he could overrule the Council. Once in India, he set about reforming the Company. He separated its trading personnel from those who handled tax revenues, and substituted fixed salaries for commissions, so as to make Company employees less likely to take bribes. This established a professional civil service in India, to carry out the orders of the government. Entry into it, however, was blocked to Indians. Unlike Hastings, Cornwallis had a low opinion of them. He deplored "the spirit of corruption that so highly prevails in native courts," and was particularly critical of "The pride and bigotry of the Mussulmen [i.e. Muslims]."[5] The Charter Act of 1793 restricted higher positions in Indian government to "covenanted" servants of the Company, meaning only Britons, since no Indian employees were "covenanted." After Cornwallis, the British in India were to be the rulers, and Indians were to be the ruled. The two groups gradually ceased to socialize regularly with one another, and intermarriage became rare. Yet loans from Indian merchants and bankers remained crucial to the financial security of the Company.

Moreover, tax revenues in Bengal continued to be raised by hereditary Indian landholders or *zamindars*. Before the Cornwallis administration, they had no title

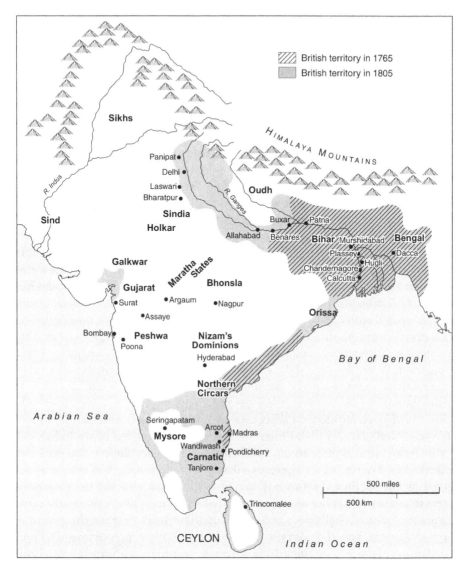

Map 9 *The growth of the British empire in India, 1765–1805. (Source: P. J. Marshall, ed.,*
The Oxford History of the British Empire, volume 2: The Eighteenth Century, *Oxford, 1998,*
p. 509.)

to their estates other than their claim to one-tenth of the revenues. The peasants
who farmed the land, and who had to hand over part of its produce as tax payments, often banded together to resist what they regarded as unjust demands
from the landholders. Cornwallis sought to regularize the revenue system through
a Permanent Settlement that was decreed in 1793. In language that would have
been familiar to improving British landlords, he described the Settlement as the
result of "humane and liberal sentiments … producing wealth and happiness to the
industrious and intelligent part of the individuals of this country."[6] The *zamindars*

lost their powers as local magistrates, but they were recognized as landowners, which gave them the ability to evict tenants. They were to turn over a fixed amount of revenue to the British collectors every year. These revenue demands, however, were very high, leading many old established families to sell their lands. The new owners included Indian merchants and bankers, grown rich from loans to the Company. They were often absentee landlords, with little regard for the concerns of the peasants. They raised rents and threw peasants who could not pay off the land. A kind of state-sponsored capitalism had been introduced to Indian agriculture. It squeezed the peasants in a way that was more reminiscent of Ireland than of Britain.

Through the civil service reforms and the Permanent Settlement, Cornwallis created a British-ruled state in India. It was modeled in part on the fiscal-military state at home, but it was more autocratic, with power firmly placed in the governor-general's hands, and more bureaucratic, with a professional salaried civil service that had not yet fully developed in Britain itself. The state saw itself as reformist, and it interfered more and more in Indian life. Yet nobody considered the formation of an Indian legislature, or even an advisory council. Such ideas would have been scoffed at as unworkable. The British-ruled state rested on a racial distinction between Britons and Indians, and it thrived on distinctions among Indians themselves – religious differences between Muslims and Hindus, as well as ethnic or linguistic differences, and differences of caste among the majority Hindu population. While the state did not create those differences, British policy served to accentuate them, to make them seem "natural," and to exploit them for British gain.

The third governor-general who created British India in this period was the Marquess Wellesley. An Irish Protestant landowner, he tended to see Indian politics in terms of a global struggle with the forces of revolution that had been unleashed by France. More aggressive than his predecessors, Wellesley was well served by his brother, the future Duke of Wellington, who led the Company's forces to victory in a series of major wars that left Britain as the dominant power in the subcontinent. Wellesley's two most important wars were fought against the state of Mysore and the Maratha Confederacy. With a predominantly Hindu population, Mysore was ruled by a tolerant, learned, and impetuous Muslim prince, Tipu Sultan, who longed to be the arbiter of South India. He had some advanced ideas, such as founding a local silk industry and even adding a rocket corps to his army. Governor-general Wellesley went to war against Tipu in 1798 after hearing that he had entered into negotiations with the French revolutionaries. The Sultan had even planted a tree of liberty on his island capital of Seringapatam (Srirangapatna)! An outraged Wellesley wrote to Tipu, expressing

the surprise and concern with which I perceived you disposed to involve yourself in all the ruinous consequences of a connection which threatens not only to subvert the foundations of friendship between you and the Company, but to introduce into the heart of your kingdom the principles of anarchy and confusion, to shake your own authority, to weaken the obedience of your subjects, and to destroy the religion which you revere.[7]

With the recent United Irish uprising on his mind, Wellesley was clearly worried by the potential impact of revolutionary principles in India. War followed, and Seringapatam was stormed by Company forces. Tipu, brave to the last, died defending the city's walls. He is now often seen as an Indian patriot, which is anachronistic as he fought for his family and state, not for an imagined India. Nonetheless, he was the last Indian ruler who could have stopped the British from dominating the subcontinent.

The Marathas were certainly not up to that task. They were a federation of Hindu princedoms in west central India that had once been a formidable power. By the late eighteenth century, they were bitterly divided by family rivalries. After challenging British power under Warren Hastings, they went back to squabbling among themselves. Wellesley picked them off one by one in 1803–5, aided by his brother Arthur's military talents and by his own diplomatic skills. During the Maratha War, a French-led army was expelled by the British from Delhi, and the Mughal Emperor was placed under the protection of the Company. From that point on, Britain not only had the mightiest military force in India, but could also claim legitimacy in ruling the former Mughal domains, because the Emperor was in its care. As for the Marathas, their power was broken, although it was not until 1818, after a third war with the British, that much of their territory was annexed by the Company, while the rest was broken up into princely states dependent on Britain.

Wellesley's bellicose policy had established British hegemony in India. It remained to be seen what the Company, and the British government, would do with it. The EIC Charter Act of 1813 pointed the way to the future. The sovereignty of the British monarch over the Company's territories was recognized, meaning that large parts of India were officially George III's domains. The Company lost its monopoly on Indian commerce, and the subcontinent was opened to free competition. The protection offered by the EIC to Indian exports was sacrificed, and private traders, in league with British manufacturers, drove up tariffs on Indian finished goods. As a result, the Indian cotton textile industry was ruined, to the benefit of Manchester. The 1813 Charter Act also admitted Christian missionaries into India for the first time, and an Anglican bishop was appointed. India was to be subjected to the British crown, dependent on British industry, and proselytized by British evangelicals. The heyday of John Company, of plunder and profit, was over. A new empire was born.

Saving British North America

The shift in the British government's attention from the Atlantic world to India and the Pacific after the American Revolutionary War was so marked that it is easy to forget that Britain still governed large parts of the Americas. In spite of the loss of the 13 colonies, British North America continued to grow and prosper, especially during the French wars. By 1806, the six colonies of British North America had a combined population of around 460,000. These colonies were ethnically, economically, and politically diverse. British administrators were nagged by the fear that they would follow in the path of the United States, towards republicanism and independence. In fact, they would develop their own distinct characteristics, as British, American, French, and indigenous cultures tugged them in different directions.

The Revolutionary and Napoleonic Wars marked the golden age of the Atlantic colonies. The oldest of them was Newfoundland, an island entirely dependent on cod fishing. Its 26,000 inhabitants in 1806 were divided between English Protestants and Irish Catholics, living in the town of St John's and in tiny, scattered fishing villages or "outports." Officially only a fishing station, Newfoundland had no legislature, and its governor was a naval officer. Before the 1740s, local justice was administered by a "fishing admiral," the captain of the first vessel to enter an outport every year. Justices of the peace gradually replaced them, and a Supreme Court was created in 1791, with the arch-conservative John Reeves as Chief Justice. During the ensuing wars against France, the island's economy experienced rapid expansion due to naval activity. The first newspaper was founded, and a movement for an elected assembly began.

Cape Breton Island, with a tiny population of 2500 Highland Scots, Acadians, and Loyalists, was the only other colony that lacked an assembly. By contrast, the remaining Atlantic colonies of Nova Scotia, New Brunswick, and Prince Edward Island had legislatures and governors, bickering constantly with one another. Nova Scotia contained 65,000 inhabitants in 1806, including Germans, Highland Scots, Loyalists, Acadians, and Micmac Indians. Thousands of black Loyalists had been settled there, but many moved on to Sierra Leone in West Africa because they were not given the land promised to them by the British government. The black population of Nova Scotia increased again during the war of 1812, when the Royal Navy brought hundreds of freed slaves to Halifax from the Chesapeake plantations. During the wars with France, Halifax became a boomtown. Naval ships crowded the port, and the Duke of Kent, Queen Victoria's father, lived there in splendor as commander of British forces in North America. The sailors and soldiers, however, made most of Halifax a very rough place, full of brothels and West Indian rum. The path that ran by the barracks was known as "Knock Him Down Street," because it was the site of so many fights and even murders.

New Brunswick was settled by Loyalists after the American Revolution. Its 35,000 inhabitants in 1806 were chiefly employed in the timber industry. Britain needed wood for building ships, especially after Napoleon closed down trade with the Baltic. By 1821, New Brunswick was exporting 400,000 tons of squared timber yearly, which is a lot of wood. A handful of great timber barons dominated colonial politics. Among those who found a fortune in the forests was Samuel Cunard of Halifax – he used the profits to create a famous steamship company. The prosperity caused by the French wars, however, did not much affect the 10,000 inhabitants of Prince Edward Island, the smallest in area of the British North American colonies. The island's tenant farmers, many of them Irish, fumed at the absentee proprietors of their land, and wanted them to forfeit their property through escheat to the crown. In 1809, the islanders formed the first organized

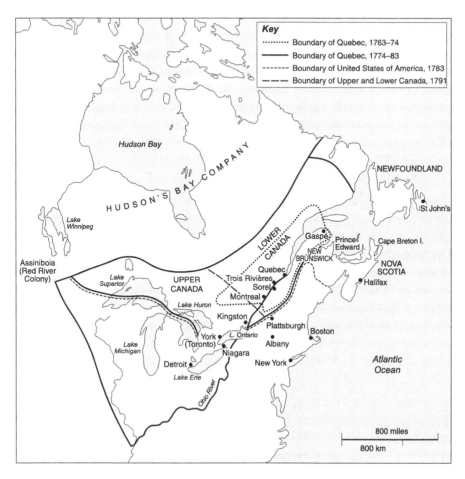

Map 10 *British North America, 1760–1815. (Source: P. J. Marshall, ed.,* The Oxford History of the British Empire, *volume 2: The Eighteenth Century,* Oxford, 1998, p. 373.)*

political party in British North America, called the Loyal Electors. Regarded as dangerous by the British government, it was soon suppressed.

The two larger colonies of Upper and Lower Canada were of limited strategic importance to Britain, but their people could cause far bigger problems than those of the Atlantic colonies. The chief issue in Lower Canada, or Quebec, was that most of the population, which numbered 250,000 in 1806, was made up of French-speaking Catholics with no inherent loyalty to the British crown. The problem among the 70,000 settlers who lived in Upper Canada was more subtle. Almost all of them were English-speaking Protestants, and the older settlers were Loyalists, but a second wave of Americans had moved there recently, looking for land. Many were Quakers or Congregationalists who resented the reservation of lands for the Anglican clergy in the colony. Influenced by the republicanism of their native country, the newer American immigrants were not regarded as reliable by the British government.

Upper and Lower Canada had been separated in 1791 in order to encourage British settlement in the former. They were given legislatures to placate the Loyalists and to teach the French Canadians, in Pitt the younger's words, "that the English laws were best."[8] The ultimate aim of the British government was to reduce or even eliminate the *canadiens*, the French Catholic population, but this did not go as planned. For a start, French Catholic families had a lot of babies. The British demand for wheat during the Napoleonic wars stimulated farming in Lower Canada, which meant better economic times and an incentive for tenant farmers to have more children. English-speaking fur traders from Montreal, however, began buying up the big estates or *seigneuries* that had been created under the French regime. This gave them a disproportionate economic influence. The so-called "English" merchants – in fact, most of them were Scots, and a few even spoke Gaelic – considered themselves to be loyal British subjects, and they saw to it that the first column commemorating Nelson's victory at Trafalgar was erected in Montreal in 1808. It is still there.

The English merchants sat on the governor's executive and legislative councils, but the Lower Canadian assembly was dominated by the *parti canadien*, the party of French-speaking Canadians. In 1806, it gained a public voice through the founding of a newspaper, *Le Canadien*, by a lawyer and assemblyman, Pierre-Stanislas Bédard. A warm admirer of the "balance" of the British constitution, Bédard attacked the "English party" for wrecking its chance of working in Lower Canada. Bédard assumed that in Britain, ministers were responsible to the legislature, which was not exactly the case. For publishing such radical views, Bédard was imprisoned and his newspaper closed down by government order in 1810. After a year in prison, this French Canadian version of John Wilkes was released in triumph.

The British government was worried about Lower Canada when war broke out with the United States in 1812, but in fact there was little sympathy for the Americans among the French population. Catholic priests leveled fierce attacks on the American republicans from the pulpit, advising their flocks that "our religion will be threatened by these enemies who are now threatening us, and who are without principles or morals."[9] At Châteauguay in 1813, an invading American force was soundly defeated by French Canadian militia. While they resented the "English party," the *canadiens* still looked to Britain as the protector of their rights.

The War of 1812 was fought mainly in Upper Canada. The ostensible cause of war was the British naval blockade of Napoleonic Europe, which led to American vessels being stopped, and British sailors who served on them being impressed into the Royal Navy. A more important cause was British support for the Indian nations that stood in the way of American expansion in the Great Lakes region. In particular, the British had backed the visionary Shawnee leader Tecumseh, who was driven out of Ohio by the Americans. Tecumseh fled to British territory, and would fight against the United States again in 1812. The Americans were not united, however, in declaring war on Britain, and the New England states were particularly opposed to the conflict.

The Americans attempted three invasions of Upper Canada, one in each year of the war. The first try went very badly for them. The British captured Detroit and threw back an American force at Queenston Heights near Niagara. In the following year, the Americans gained a decisive victory over the Royal Navy for control of Lake Erie – a shocking humiliation for the strongest navy on earth – and burned the town of York, the future Toronto. An invasion attempt across the Niagara frontier, however, was checked. The third and final American assault in 1814 culminated in a bloody, indecisive engagement at Lundy's Lane that resulted in more than 1600 casualties on both sides. British attempts to invade the United States were not much more successful. An incursion into New York was stopped by the American naval victory on Lake Champlain in 1814. A British expedition burned Washington in retaliation for the destruction of York, and sent First Lady Dolly Madison scurrying across the Potomac River, carrying with her a portrait of George Washington. As every American knows, "The Star-Spangled Banner" was written as Francis Scott Keyes watched the British bombard a fort outside Baltimore. The final disastrous British attack, at New Orleans in 1815, came after the Treaty of Ghent was signed, bringing the war to a close.

The War of 1812 ended in a draw, with no significant gains for either side. The real losers, in many ways, were the Great Lakes Indians, who were abandoned by the British and displaced by American settlers. The war was also shaped by political and religious divisions in Upper Canada. Local militiamen had flocked to defend the British cause, with the support of a Loyal and Patriotic Society, organized by the Anglican bishop. On the other hand, many recent settlers had remained neutral or had quietly rooted for the Americans. Fifteen American supporters were sentenced to hang at Ancaster in 1814, although seven of them were eventually deported instead. The tensions created by the war in Upper Canada would endure long after it was finished.

Vast territories lay to the west of Upper Canada. They were traversed by fur traders, belonging to the Hudson's Bay Company or to its rival, the Montreal-based North West Company. Most of the Nor'Westers, as they were called, were rugged Scottish merchants, and some were incredibly ambitious. In 1789, the Company sent Alexander Mackenzie and his wife, with a group of French Canadian and Indian guides, down an immense river that flowed into the frozen Arctic. Four years later, Mackenzie scrawled his name on a rock by the Pacific. Later journeys to the Pacific by Simon Fraser and David Thompson were also sponsored by the Nor'Westers. The fur trade companies, however, opposed settlement in the west, and tried to block Lord Selkirk's 1809 plan to bring Scottish immigrants to the Red River in what is now Manitoba. In the end, they failed, and settlers began to enter the prairies. Eventually, the British government would have to get involved in western matters, about which it cared little. No British politician was willing to consider independence for the remaining possessions in North America, but none wanted to worry much about them either. Their resources were important to Britain; their internal arrangements were not, so long as they followed an acceptable pattern. After 1815, however, the colonists would increasingly demand attention, with disturbing results.

Ending the Slave Trade

Although the degree of its involvement in colonial affairs was markedly different in North America, India, and the Pacific, the British government increasingly sought to impress on imperial administration what it saw as the values of the homeland: loyalty, hierarchy, respect for law, and a restrained conception of liberty. It certainly did not see British values as tending towards democracy, self-government, or extended rights for non-British peoples; instead, they were supposed to maintain order and ensure a continuing attachment to the mother country. The imposition of British values, however, could have unintended consequences. In particular, the moral imperatives of religious evangelicals began to infiltrate the government's economic and military objectives. Despite strong administrative resistance, the evangelical factor would have an enormous impact on the West Indies, through the campaign to abolish the slave trade.

The West Indian sugar plantations remained prosperous after the American Revolution, providing almost one-third of British colonial imports. Yet the islands continued to be death-traps for slaves. More than 2 million Africans had been transported to the British Caribbean by the early nineteenth century, but in 1810 the black population of the old colonies (not including those recently conquered from the French or Dutch) stood at about 540,000. A high death rate among slaves was one part of the reason for this; low fertility among female slaves was the other. African women worked for up to 12 hours each day cutting sugarcane, and like all slaves in the West Indies, they were malnourished. Poor nutrition delayed the age of menarche among slave women and limited their fertility. In addition, planters did not encourage the formation of nuclear families among slaves, although they developed nonetheless. The sexual exploitation of slave women by masters was endemic in the West Indies during the eighteenth century, as the diary of the planter Thomas Thistlewood unashamedly reveals.

Under these circumstances, a constant supply of slaves was still necessary to the West Indian plantations. Between 1795 and 1804, about 125,000 Africans were brought to the old colonies as slaves, and another 85,000 were shipped to the new colonies (Grenada, St Lucia, St Vincent, Trinidad, Tobago). This was big business. Slave-trading enriched the English ports of Liverpool and Bristol, and made huge fortunes for London merchants. Their big profits depended on vast human misery. Conditions in the slave ships remained horrendous, although they had been marginally improved since the previous century. Slaves were packed into the ships like sardines in a can, shackled and forced to lie in their own waste. The foul smell that emanated from slave ships was notorious. Their human cargo might be allowed up on deck once a day, but they were closely watched. Although frequent, slave rebellions on board ship were hardly ever successful. The punishment for a failed revolt was usually death. Jumping over the side of the ship was also common: 33 slaves from one vessel committed suicide in this way at St Christopher in 1737. Better food and fresher water, however, had lowered the death rate of slaves in the "middle passage," from 15 percent at the start of the eighteenth century to about half that level at its end.

The first explicit British calls for the end of slavery had been heard in the 1760s. They emanated not from radical groups, but from Granville Sharp, a London musician, former linen-draper, and evangelical Anglican whose brother was surgeon to King George III. After rescuing a slave who had been savagely beaten by his master, Sharp set himself to the study of the law, concluding that *"no right whatever* can be acquired to *the perpetual Service of a Man* without a *Contract*, and that such a *Contract* cannot be *implied*, unless the free Consent of both Parties is *implied* likewise, and clearly proved."[10] In practice, nobody could claim property in the person of another. These arguments were presented in 1772 to Lord Chief Justice Mansfield, in the case of James Somerset, a slave from Virginia who had escaped in London and been recaptured by his master. Unknown to the public, Mansfield's own household contained a young woman who was the illegitimate daughter of his nephew by a slave. The childless Lord Justice and his wife treated her as a member of their family. Whatever personal feelings he may have had regarding Somerset's case, however, were well hidden in the Lord Justice's careful verdict, which ruled simply that masters could not compel their slaves to leave England. His guarded admission that no longstanding body of English case law existed on the matter of slavery was taken by Sharp and his followers to mean that slavery did not legally exist in England. Six years later, the Court of Sessions in Edinburgh ruled outright that Scottish law could not support the existence of slavery.

In fact, there were few slaves anywhere in the British Isles, apart from those brought over temporarily from the West Indies by visiting masters. On the other hand, by the end of the American Revolutionary War, about 10,000 free black people lived in Britain. They included writers and hairdressers, servants and sailors, the majority living in poverty in London and other port towns. In 1785, a committee of well meaning white people, including Granville Sharp and the wealthy philanthropist Jonas Hanway, was organized with the intention of resettling black paupers, including those who had been sent to Nova Scotia after the American Revolution. They were to be taken to the West African coast at Sierra Leone. Today, the project may seem to us like racial cleansing or thinly veiled imperialism, but it was designed to bring about a black-ruled African Utopia to which freed slaves could go after emancipation. Sharp even tried to base the Sierra Leone government on that of the Anglo-Saxons, which he saw as a perfect democracy. The enterprise was never a big success. The settlers landed in the rainy season, when nothing would grow; they were attacked by indigenous peoples and bombarded by the French. White officials continued to govern the settlers, although for the first time anywhere, whites were tried before black juries. Sierra Leone became a crown colony in 1808, and by the mid-nineteenth century, about 70,000 former slaves had been resettled there, forming a colonial elite that would dominate until recent times.

The Committee for the Relief of the Black Poor was followed two years later by the creation of the Committee for Abolition of the African Slave Trade. Several of its dozen members were Quakers, who had been influenced by the recent rise of anti-slavery sentiment among American Friends. They were particularly affected by the horrific *Zong* incident of 1783, when 132 sick slaves in transit from Africa were thrown overboard and drowned as part of an attempted insurance fraud. The main fact-finder for the Committee was a young Anglican evangelical, Thomas Clarkson. His writings against slavery were very popular – the novelist Jane Austen claimed that she had been in love with them. Traveling to Bristol and Liverpool to make inquiries, Clarkson found out that sailors on slave ships were treated with extraordinary brutality and died in large numbers. One captain was in the habit of savagely beating his crew, as well as the slaves, with an artificial wooden hand. This evidence helped to undermine the assertion that the slave trade was an effective training ground for sailors in the Royal Navy.

Clarkson also turned to former slaves for information about the slave trade, including two men who wrote remarkable memoirs of their years in slavery. Ottobah Cugoano, born in what is now Ghana, was kidnapped into slavery, took part in a failed slave rebellion on board ship, and served for two years on a plantation in Grenada before his master brought him to England, where he was freed. His friend Olaudah Equiano claimed to be an Ibo from what is now Nigeria, although he may have been born in South Carolina. Equiano was sold to a Royal Navy officer, and served on naval ships during the Seven Years' War. He began to see himself as a patriotic British sailor, and was stunned when his master sold him. Industrious, literate, and an able businessman, Equiano earned enough money through private trade in the West Indies to buy his freedom. Journeying to England, he experienced a religious conversion and became a devout evangelical Christian. He was appointed supervisor of supplies for the Sierra Leone Company, but was fired after accusing a white officer of embezzling funds. His exciting memoirs contain snippets of real horror concerning slavery:

It was very common in several of the islands, particularly in St Kitts, for the slaves to be branded with the initial letters of their master's name, and a load of heavy iron hooks hung about their necks.... The iron muzzle, thumb-screws, &c. are so well known, as not to need a description, and were sometimes applied for the slightest faults. I have seen a negro beaten till some of his bones were broken, for only letting a pot boil over. It is not uncommon, after a flogging, to make slaves go on their knees, and thank their owners, and pray, or rather say, God bless them.[11]

This sort of chilling detail helped make Equiano's *Interesting Narrative* a bestseller.

The potter Josiah Wedgwood had a medal produced for the Committee for Abolition that became the icon of their movement. It showed a black man in chains, kneeling in prayer, under the inscription "Am I Not a Man and a Brother?" While the image has been described as paternalistic, it remains powerful, and was used to recruit widespread support for abolition. An engraved print of the *Brookes*, the Liverpool slave ship whose crowded conditions had been examined by a committee of the Privy Council, was also a big seller. By 1788, 103 petitions with tens of thousands of signatures had been sent to Parliament in favor of ending the slave trade. Later, a sugar boycott was initiated that caused hundreds of thousands of Britons to resist putting sweetener in their tea. Women, who could not sign Parliamentary petitions, were heavily involved in the boycott campaign. Sales of West Indian sugar dropped by a third in some parts of Britain, and sugar grown in South Asia was imported as a substitute.

In the spring of 1789, the case for abolition of the slave trade was presented to Parliament by William Wilberforce, MP for the port town of Kingston-upon-Hull and a prominent Anglican evangelical. He was at the center of a little circle of friends and relatives, all passionate Christians, who lived together in Clapham south of London, and made high-flying plans for purifying a wicked world. They condemned the drinking, swearing, gaming, sexual promiscuity, and Sabbath breaking that they saw, or thought they saw, all around them, and that they blamed on lack of religion. In his first great speech in favor of abolition, Wilberforce deplored the cruelty of the slave trade, but was careful not to argue for an end to slavery itself. He was typically self-deprecating in stating that "I mean not to accuse anyone but to take the shame upon myself, in common indeed with the whole Parliament of Great Britain, for having suffered this horrid trade to be carried on under our authority. We are all guilty."[12] His fellow MPs, heavily lobbied by the West Indian interest, did not share his feelings of shame. They voted to set up a further committee, and after it reported two years later, they soundly defeated abolition. To his eternal credit, Wilberforce did not give up; he tried again in 1792, when William Pitt himself spoke in favor of the cause. As in so many other respects, however, Pitt was ahead of his colleagues, especially Henry Dundas, who favored gradual abolition. The House of Lords rejected even that modest proposal. Still Wilberforce persisted, proposing abolition bills almost every year through the dire 1790s.

Unfortunately, the French Revolution divided and undermined the abolition movement. Clarkson visited France, where he conversed with revolutionary leaders who were in favor of abolition. Equiano joined the LCS. Wilberforce, on the other hand, stuck to the government, condemned the radicals, and voted for all the repressive legislation of the 1790s. A slave insurrection in the French colony of St Domingue changed some conservative minds about the practicality of preserving slavery. Jumping at the chance to expand its possessions in the Caribbean, the British government invaded St Domingue with 20,000 troops. About 12,000 of them died there, mostly of malaria and dysentery, and the mission turned into a fiasco. Renamed Haiti, St Domingue became the first independent republic with a black majority. A Maroon insurrection in Jamaica required another force of regular British troops to be dispatched to the islands; again, half of them never came back. Altogether, more than 45,000 British troops were buried in the West Indies between 1793 and 1801. Was sugar worth this cost?

In the first decade of the nineteenth century, the price of sugar went into decline. The French policy of seizing British ships led many Liverpool and Bristol slave traders to fly the American flag instead. Napoleon's reinstitution of slavery in France meant that British abolitionism began to seem patriotic. A new campaign was begun, attracting broad support. In 1806, with the Ministry of All the Talents in office, Wilberforce saw a chance to sink the slave trade by clothing it in unpatriotic colors. A bill was passed that prohibited Britons from participating in the slave trade with France or any foreign territory. This essentially ended two-thirds of the trade. The rest of it was abolished in the following year, after an overwhelming vote in Parliament that even George III, a supporter of the trade, could not ignore. When Wilberforce heard himself praised in the House of Commons in the final debate over abolition, he put his head in his hands and burst into tears. The House rose to its feet and applauded him – a rare act, and one that was officially forbidden, but Wilberforce deserved it.

In the British West Indies, over 800,000 Africans remained slaves. Their emancipation, which Wilberforce would continue to fight for, would take another 30 years. Yet the end of the slave trade was a major turning point. Britain backed it up with naval force, and wrote treaties with other nations that included abolition clauses. It became a central principle of British imperial policy. This was quite fitting. Most of the men and women who carried the abolition movement to victory were not opposed to the British empire; instead, they wanted it to be a moral and Christian force, not one based on cruelty and oppression. In the nineteenth century, evangelicalism was to be a powerful motivator in building a larger, stronger, more controlling British empire, with the spread of Christianity as one of its goals. Wilberforce was indeed a prophet: the effects of his proselytizing and moral rigor, which many find so hard to understand today, would purge and then strengthen the foundations of British rule.

18

Enlightened Culture

In intellectual, artistic, and cultural terms, the eighteenth century in Europe is often labeled the Age of Enlightenment. Although the Enlightenment took diverse forms, writers who saw themselves as part of it generally argued that individual human reason, rather than traditional, unexamined ideas or "superstitions," should guide moral decisions, social relations, and even religious beliefs. England had been home to two of the founders of enlightened thought, John Locke and Isaac Newton. Locke's philosophy of knowledge and Newton's physics had a profound impact on the Enlightenment throughout Europe. By the mid-eighteenth century, however, French writers known as *philosophes* had taken the ideas of Locke and Newton in new directions, towards a systematic critique of traditional customs and concepts. The rulers of Prussia, Austria, Russia, Sweden, and Spain would implement some of the ideas of the *philosophes* in governing their states, introducing toleration, a trained bureaucracy, and universal primary education. American revolutionaries like Thomas Jefferson and Benjamin Franklin would interpret enlightened ideas as republican and socially egalitarian. French revolutionaries would see themselves as acting on the principles of the *philosophes* by promoting liberty, equality, and fraternity. Did enlightened ideas develop in similar ways in England and Scotland?

The Scottish Enlightenment

Scotland experienced an Enlightenment that was similar in many respects to that of the rest of Europe or North America: that is, as a discernible movement in the realm of ideas, with significant social consequences. The reasons for the flourishing of enlightened thought in Scotland, and for its reaching far beyond a tiny circle of intellectuals, are not hard to discover. For a start, the Scots had a high level of education. After 1696, every parish was required to have a school, supported by a tax on land and supervised by the local presbytery. Education was not free, but the Kirk paid for the schooling of poor children. Boys usually stayed for about four years, girls for much less. They were taught reading, writing, arithmetic, and religion, which meant Presbyterian doctrines, along with a little Latin for the better students. In addition to the parish schools, there were grammar schools for the children of the respectable middling sort; new fee-paying or "adventure" schools that might teach boys bookkeeping and girls how to sew or spin; and charity schools, which in the Highlands were run by the Scottish Society for the Propagation of Christian Knowledge. The educational system tended to break down in large or isolated parishes. Nevertheless, by 1780 almost all Lowland children who lived in the countryside learned to read, as did a majority of town dwellers and Highlanders. Writing was a more difficult skill, but most Scottish students probably mastered it. In England, by contrast, literacy was highest in the towns, and not much more than half the population was able to read.

Scotland had five universities, supported by government endowments. All of them changed and expanded in the eighteenth century. Edinburgh University grew from 400 students to 1300, adding to its faculty four chairs in sciences, four in law, and a whole school of medicine. Locke's philosophy was taught at Scottish universities from the 1690s onward, and Newton's physics was introduced in the 1710s. Lectures were given in English, not Latin. The reputation of the Scottish universities for teaching sciences, mathematics, and medicine was second to none in Europe. In addition, several academies of learning were founded in Scottish towns in the late eighteenth century, to make higher education available to the urban middling sort who might not be able to afford the expense of a university. Anderson's Institution, initiated by a Glasgow science professor in 1796, offered courses in physics, chemistry, mathematics, botany, and agriculture to "young gentlemen designed for manufacture or commerce." It was also "the first regular institution in which the fair sex have been admitted to the temple of knowledge on the same footing as men."[1] About half the listeners in some popular science courses at the Institution were women.

The spread of Enlightenment at Scottish universities was made possible by the rise of the Moderate party of clergymen within the Kirk of Scotland. Until the mid-eighteenth century, the Kirk was not known for its tolerant views, and a minister had been suspended for heresy in Scotland as recently as 1729. However, a series of secessions by strict Calvinists between 1733 and 1761 left the Moderates in command of the General Assembly, the governing body of the Kirk. The Moderates believed in a broad, inclusive interpretation of Presbyterian doctrine. They also accepted lay patronage over parish appointments, while the Seceders maintained that parishioners had the right to choose a minister. Many of the Moderates had been educated at Glasgow University, where they had taken courses with Francis Hutcheson, a professor of philosophy who saw benevolence as the basis of morality, and rational inquiry as necessary for religion. By the mid-eighteenth century, about one in four ministers of the Kirk had studied at Glasgow.

The schools of philosophy and jurisprudence that emerged in the Scottish universities were in large part inspired by a reaction to the writings of the most famous skeptical philosopher in eighteenth-century Scotland, David Hume.

Although he spent much of his life abroad, and was refused chairs at both Edinburgh and Glasgow Universities, Hume was appointed keeper of the Edinburgh Advocates' Library in 1752, and served as secretary of the city's Philosophical Society. A thorough empiricist, Hume argued that "all the laws of nature, and all the operations of bodies without exception, are known only by experience." Everything that we believe is based on the habit of connecting different objects that we have experienced. Miracles cannot be proven from experience; therefore, Hume regarded them as improbable. He further noted that "the *Christian Religion* not only was at first attended with miracles, but even at this day cannot be believed by any reasonable person without one." For many readers, this statement amounted to a renunciation of Christianity. Hume also thought that justice was purely a matter of custom, based on what was socially useful. He did not take the same view of morality, however, as he accepted the concept of a basic moral sense. The habit of making moral distinctions "implies some sentiment, so universal and comprehensive as to extend to all mankind, and render the actions and conduct, even of the persons the most remote, an object of applause or censure."[2] Many readers were shocked by Hume, and when he died in 1776, they wanted to know whether he had accepted Christianity on his deathbed. He gave them no satisfaction.

Thomas Reid, professor of philosophy at Marischal College, University of Aberdeen, and a Presbyterian minister, respected Hume as "the greatest Metaphysician of the Age," but thought he had fallen into skepticism because he had put too much trust in sense experience and not paid enough attention to the operation of the human mind. Reid shared the view of Bishop George Berkeley, an early critic of Locke's empirical philosophy, who pointed out that sense experience does not correspond directly to the judgments we make about it. As Reid put it, "every operation of the senses, in its very nature, implies judgment or belief, as well as simple apprehension." Judgments "are the inspiration of the Almighty. ... They make up what is called the *common sense of mankind*."[3] In other words, knowledge based on experience was impossible without "common sense" or innate ideas, bestowed by nature.

Hume's skepticism about justice elicited replies from the Scottish judge Henry Home, Lord Kames, and from Adam Smith, professor of moral philosophy at Glasgow. Both maintained that justice arose from a moral sense that guided human relations, rather than from custom. The moral sense, Kames believed, could become the foundation for a tradition of legal justice. Adam Smith in *The Theory of the Moral Sentiments* (1759) emphasized the natural goodness of human beings:

man, who can subsist only in society, was fitted by nature to that situation for which he was made. All the members of human society stand in need of each other's assistance, and are likewise exposed to human injuries. Where the necessary assistance is reciprocally afforded from love, from gratitude, from friendship, and esteem, the society flourishes and is happy. All the different members of it are bound together by the agreeable bands of love and affection, and are, as it were, drawn to one common centre of mutual good offices.[4]

How different this happy picture of human society was from Thomas Hobbes's dark vision of brutish individuals banding together out of fear! For Smith, justice arose from the reactions stirred up in our innate moral sentiments by specific instances of crime or cruelty. Smith's confidence in human morality explains why, in the *Wealth of Nations*, he was willing to allow capitalist economic behavior to be guided by an "invisible hand." He was convinced that moral sentiments would protect the poor and the weak from exploitation, and that the betterment of each individual would serve social needs.

David Hume had a more positive influence on the historical writings of the Scottish Enlightenment, which were fixated with the idea of progress. Hume's *History of England* (1754–62) identified the rise of liberty and civility with the "Germanic" virtues of the English, and depicted the Scots as barbarians who were raised to civilization only by contact with England. A similar interpretation pervaded the voluminous historical writings of Reverend William Robertson, principal of Edinburgh University, moderator of the General Assembly of the Scottish Kirk, and leader of the Moderate Presbyterian party. Although his *History of Scotland* shows some sympathy for important figures in the nation's past, its general thesis was that the Scots were barbarous and needed to be united with the English in order for Scottish society to progress. Robertson's other historical works, including an unfinished *History of America*, are characterized by a scorn for barbarians like the American Indians. The major Scottish dissenter from this prevalent historical viewpoint was Adam Ferguson, professor at Edinburgh and former chaplain to a Highland Regiment. Like the *philosophe* Jean-Jacques Rousseau, Ferguson believed that the virtue and energy of "primitive" peoples could provide a better defense of liberty and independence than was found in more developed societies, where virtue was weakened by luxury, leading to despotic government.

Scottish intellectual life was beset by increasing differences of opinion by the end of the eighteenth century. During the French Revolution, the Moderate establishment stood firmly behind Henry Dundas, the government's Scottish manager, and rejected revolutionary change. Nonetheless, some leading intellectual figures, like Thomas Reid, supported radical reform. The Scottish Enlightenment split in fragments. It would have an enduring influence, however, in the English-speaking colonies of British North America, where the majority of learned persons for the next century were Scots, and in the emerging United States. Scottish university graduates and admirers of the Scottish philosophers would carry enlightened ideas of education, morality, jurisprudence, capitalism, and history into the new Republic, with far-reaching effects. In many important respects, from its acceptance of innate goodness to its belief in progress, the culture of the United States today is a product of the Scottish Enlightenment.

Searching for the English Enlightenment

Defining the Enlightenment in England is more complicated than in Scotland. Given the pervasive influence of Newton and Locke, one could easily make the argument that almost every aspect of English intellectual life in the eighteenth century was enlightened, and leave it at that. Unfortunately, such an approach does not go very far in explaining what most educated people actually believed. Nor does it help us to understand the marked cultural differences among the English – why some turned to religious evangelicalism, whose premises were explicitly anti-rational, while others adopted radical, unorthodox ideas that were highly controversial.

The impact of the Enlightenment in England was affected by the weakness of formal educational institutions. Unlike those in Scotland, the English universities did not produce a group of professional intellectuals who exercised cultural influence on a national level. Oxford and Cambridge were in a sorry state of decline. Since the mid-seventeenth century, their enrollments had shrunk and their students had become more socially exclusive. In 1759, only 182 freshmen entered Oxford, the lowest number since 1500. Dissenters could not take degrees at either university. Both Oxford and Cambridge contained learned and hard-working scholars, but they were more likely to be immersed in Anglo-Saxon grammar than in science. Cambridge was more Whig than Oxford, more welcoming to the ideas of Locke and Newton, and perhaps less intellectually sleepy, but it would be difficult to argue that it provided an enlightened environment.

Evidently, we have to look towards alternative educational institutions, like the Dissenting Academies, to find the English Enlightenment. Even here, we should not expect to find a unified, dynamic force for change. Many of the roughly 35 Academies founded since 1689 for the education of Dissenters offered a mathematical or scientific curriculum, but by the end of the eighteenth century they were turning increasingly into denominational training schools for ministers. Private clubs and societies could also provide outlets for rational ideas, but they existed mainly as places to socialize. Even the leading national institution for knowledge, the Royal Society, was more a gentleman's club than a nerve-center of scientific research. With a few notable exceptions, like Benjamin Franklin's experiments on electricity, the activities that it encouraged did not make much of a contribution to the history of science. As president after 1778, Sir Joseph Banks would try to make the Royal Society more relevant, but his efforts turned mainly in the direction of global research expeditions, rather than experimental science.

A brighter source of enlightenment was the Lunar Society of Birmingham, founded around 1765 by a group of inventors, manufacturers, and intellectuals who lived in the English Midlands. The Lunar men included the improver of the steam-engine, James Watt, the ironmaster Matthew Boulton, the pottery manufacturer Josiah Wedgwood, the chemist Joseph Priestley, and the botanist Erasmus Darwin, whose theories on the evolution of plants and animals later influenced his grandson, Charles Darwin. The purpose of the Society was to promote useful inventions and to discuss natural philosophy. The conversations at its meetings ranged from minerals and metals to balloons and steam-powered vehicles. The Society backed Priestley's experiments with "dephlogisticated air" until it was proven that "phlogiston," the substance that supposedly made things burn, did not exist, and that Priestley's glass vessels were actually filled with oxygen.

Illustration 21   *A flatulent explosion takes place in this satirical representation by James Gillray of a lecture at the Royal Institution in 1802. Humphry Davy is the young man on the right, behind the table. (James Gillray, "New Discoveries in PNEUMATICKS!" 1802. © The Print Collector / Heritage-Images / Imagestate)*

Opponents of slavery and supporters of female education, the Lunar Society members represented the practical, reforming side of the English Enlightenment. Many of them were Dissenters and radicals, however, which eventually landed them in trouble. Priestley's Birmingham house was destroyed by a mob in 1791, and Darwin was attacked in print as a supporter of the French Revolution. Facing such hostility, the Society gradually stopped meeting.

The scientific work of the Lunar men, although not their radical politics, was picked up after 1799 by the Royal Institution, a private research organization in London. Among its founders was Henry Cavendish, the shy and eccentric discoverer of hydrogen, which he called "inflammable air." The Royal Institution offered courses of scientific lectures to the public. The most popular presenter was the chemist Sir Humphry Davy, an exuberant Cornishman who experimented with acids, isolated sodium and potassium, and invented a safety lamp for miners. Davy's chemical assistant was Michael Faraday, a man of humble origins and member of a small Calvinist sect. Faraday would become the most famous scientist in nineteenth-century Britain for his discovery of electromagnetic induction, on which both power generators and modern field theory are based.

The literary Enlightenment is very difficult to locate in England, as can be illustrated through the career of a highly influential writer, Samuel Johnson, who died in 1784. He was best known for compiling the first reliable dictionary of the

English language and for writing a voluminous series of *Lives of the Poets*. Some of the most enlightened minds in England met at his literary club. Yet Johnson avoided the language of liberty, natural rights, or human progress that is associated with the Enlightenment. His opinions, recorded for posterity by his admirer and biographer, James Boswell, were often more witty than reasonable. Intensely religious, Johnson held strongly to Anglican orthodoxy, including belief in miracles, although he made friends with many who were outside the Church of England. He generally opposed political change, and when he wanted to make an impression, he might even express Jacobite views. He dismissed the Scottish Enlightenment as derivative, telling Boswell, who was a Scot, "Sir, ... you have learnt a little from us, and you think yourselves very great men." While he seemed to favor the downtrodden, he maintained that "mankind are happier in a state of inequality and subordination."[5] Johnson was a modern writer in coming to terms with the world through the power of his own mind, but he probably would have treated with abuse any attempt to label him as a writer of the Enlightenment.

Yet some writers welcomed such an identification, because they sought a Europe-wide reputation. The best known of them was the historian Edward Gibbon. The offspring of a Tory family, he secretly converted to Catholicism in his youth, was sent to Switzerland for re-education, and ended up a critic of all religion. His decision to write a history of the decline and fall of the Roman Empire was inspired by the sublime experience of "musing in the Church of the Zoccolanti or Franciscan friars, while they were singing Vespers in the Temple of Jupiter in the ruins of the Capitol."[6] In composing his great work, Gibbon combined careful scholarship with a dose of Hume's skepticism and the irony of Voltaire. He admired the Romans, but was critical of their imperial urges. On the other hand, he refused to glamorize the barbarians as "noble savages." In Gibbon's view, Christianity had undermined the Roman Empire and brought on a "dark age" of superstition and ignorance. His own doubts about the divinity of Christ can be detected in statements about how Romans saw the principle of divine unity "defaced by the wild enthusiasm, and annihilated by the airy speculations of the new sectaries [i.e. Christians]."[7] Not surprisingly, the *Decline and Fall* was immediately attacked as anti-Christian. Gibbon defended his scholarly accuracy and stuck to his interpretation. He greeted the French Revolution with approval, but later changed his mind, deciding that he agreed with Edmund Burke's condemnation of it. As Burke held the irreligion of the *philosophes* to be largely responsible for the horrors of the Revolution, Gibbon may have been preparing to renounce some of his own enlightened views, but he died before this happened.

Gibbon was part of an international Enlightenment. Other enlightened writers belonged to a more specifically English context, based on Newtonian science and unorthodox religious ideas. One of them was David Hartley (father of the MP mentioned in Chapter 15), a doctor and musician who in 1749 proposed that human knowledge is generated by vibrations of the nervous system in response to sensations. The self is nothing more than the location for these vibrations, which are associated by the mind to form ideas. Hartley's materialist explanation of knowledge, however, was harnessed to a mystical desire for self-annihilation and union with God. This aspect of his thinking was rejected by his admirer Joseph Priestley. He used Hartley's materialist psychology to disprove the notion of a soul, which Priestley saw as a pagan addition to Christian doctrines. Only the body was resurrected at the end of time, according to Priestley, not the imaginary soul. God would reward everyone with eternal happiness, rather than punishing some in retribution for sin.

Priestley's belief in a benevolent God led him to argue that, on earth, "the happiness of the whole community is the ultimate aim of government."[8] This idea would greatly influence the lawyer and philosopher Jeremy Bentham, who in 1789 published a work espousing what he called "the principle of utility." He defined it as "that principle which approves or disapproves of every action whatsoever, according to the tendency which it appears to have to augment or diminish the happiness of the party whose interest is in question."[9] By happiness, Bentham meant the sensation of pleasure and the avoidance of pain. As a lawyer, he was particularly interested in the pain inflicted by criminal punishments, which in his view should be proportional to the crime in order to be effective. Bentham's concept of proportionality was radical, even if he was not particularly merciful in his suggestions for how malefactors might be punished. He proposed building a prison, called a "Panopticon," with cells constructed around a central viewing station, where an inspector could constantly watch the prisoners without being seen. No wonder Bentham is sometimes regarded as the prophet of the totalitarian states of the twentieth century! His intentions, however, were always to increase human happiness, not to impose new restraints on individuals.

The utilitarian dream of endlessly increasing human happiness was challenged in 1798 by Thomas Malthus, an Anglican clergyman and professor of political economy at Haileybury, a college for training EIC officials. Malthus calculated that while food supply crept upward arithmetically, population soared geometrically. Since happy people were more likely to breed, any increase in human happiness would inevitably lead to a scarcity of food, high prices, and economic ruin. It was evident to Malthus that "the actual distresses of some of the lower classes, by which they are prevented from giving the proper food and attention to their children, act as a positive check to the natural increase of population."[10] In short, the misery of the multitude was necessary to preserve the general welfare of society. A less enlightened idea could hardly be imagined, although Malthus used reason to prove it. To be sure, his reasoning may seem faulty in the light of modern productivity, and he gives poor people little credit for limiting the size of their families. Nevertheless, Malthus was a pioneer of the "dismal science" of economics, which his close friend David Ricardo, son of a Dutch-Jewish financier, would lead in different directions in the early nineteenth century. Ricardo developed theories of rent, wages, and value that shaped later economic thought.

Although Ricardo ended up a political reformer, the conclusions of his mentor Malthus were praised by conservatives, who saw them as an irrefutable answer to reforming notions. As for Gibbon, Hartley, Priestley, and Bentham, they were certainly widely admired, but they were just as widely condemned by those who saw them as dangerous radicals or unbelievers. The majority of English readers preferred less controversial opinions. Were they therefore less enlightened? Most English men and women of the upper classes and the middling sort remained firm believers in the orthodox doctrines of Christianity. They based their morality on the Bible and the laws of the land, and they countenanced no skeptical views about religion, politics, or society. They might be interested in new fields of study like archaeology, botany, or fossils, but none of these threatened their essential beliefs. Many were attracted to the philosophy of Reverend William Paley, Anglican archdeacon of Carlisle, who argued that Christian theology could be observed everywhere in the natural world, because nature, like a watch, appeared to be an artifact, created by a divine artisan. This was as rational a concept as most English readers were willing to entertain. Whether or not such readers should be called enlightened remains a matter for debate.

The Cult of Sentiment

The Enlightenment was not just about individual reason; it was also concerned with individual sentiments, which Adam Smith, like Jean-Jacques Rousseau, held to be the only sound basis for morality. The British public did not have to wait for Smith or Rousseau to inform them of the importance of feelings or emotions. They were already highly attuned to sentiment, which had been a major theme in British culture since the 1730s. With roots in religious thought, it had moved into the realm of secular writings, where it fell under the influence of the Enlightenment. By 1800, the cult of sentiment had left a mark in all aspects of the arts in Britain, stronger in many respects than the legacy of enlightened reason.

We might trace the beginning of the English obsession with sentiment to a religious treatise, William Law's *Serious Call to a Devout and Serious Life*, which first appeared in 1728. Law was a Nonjuring clergyman and a Jacobite, who could not hold a benefice in the Church of England. He served briefly as tutor to Edward Gibbon, whose views he failed utterly to mold, and later lived in the household of Gibbon's spinster aunt. Scandalized by what he saw as the lax religious devotion of an impious society, Law urged Anglicans to accept a rigorous piety that stemmed from heartfelt emotions. He warned that "unless our heart and passions are eagerly bent upon the work of our salvation; unless holy fears animate our endeavours, and keep our consciences strict and tender about every part of our duty, ... we shall in all probability fall into a state of negligence."[11] Law's plea for a religion rooted in feeling was later adopted by his friend John Wesley as the central message of Methodist evangelicalism.

Within a few years, the emphasis on feeling had been taken up by secular writers like Samuel Richardson. A devout man who made a living as a printer, Richardson wrote novels with clear moral purposes. The beleaguered heroines in Richardson's *Pamela* and *Clarissa* express their conflicting sentiments in letters addressed to intimate friends. Every incident that they relate is reflected in a lens of personal feeling. Consider, for example, Clarissa's comment on seeking a meeting with her seducer, Lovelace:

This man has *more terror at seeing me, than I can have at seeing him*! How can that be? If he had half as much, he would not wish to see me! His motive *love*! Yes indeed! Love of himself! He knows no other; for love, that deserves the name, seeks the satisfaction of the beloved object more than its own. Weighed in this scale, what a profanation is this man guilty of![12]

The profusion of exclamation points certainly heightens the emotional impact! Feelings of terror and love would of course have been familiar to any reader of evangelical religious literature, although they are found here in a worldly context.

Richardson was mocked by his rival, Henry Fielding, whose own novels tended towards satire, but he became an enormously successful writer, especially among women readers. He was among the first of many eighteenth-century novelists who would use sentiment or feeling in presenting a modern moral story. Oliver Goldsmith would repeat Richardson's success in *The Vicar of Wakefield* (1766), whose central character is a naive and benevolent minister of the Church of England. Later, Fanny Burney would reaffirm the centrality of female experience in the sentimental novel through her popular works, beginning with *Evelina* (1778), in which a secluded young woman learns about the world. In Burney's writings, the religious undertones of sentimentalism were largely replaced by a concern with proper social behavior. Chastity, however, remained a central issue, the mark of a respectable woman's virtue and her ticket to a successful marriage.

Over time, themes derived from enlightened philosophy began to infiltrate the literature of sentiment. The popular *Tristram Shandy* (1759–67) by Laurence Sterne, a clergyman in the north of England, was an experimental, comical version of the sentimental novel, in which the narrator's most fleeting and intimate thoughts or feelings are presented without a continuous story line or much sense of purpose, moral or otherwise. It combines Richardson with the psychology of David Hartley. The reader's own emotions are stirred by direct appeals from the author, as well as by tricks of composition like empty chapters and unfinished sentences. Sterne's work inspired Henry Mackenzie, a Scottish attorney, to write *The Man of Feeling* (1771), which must contain more scenes of men crying their eyes out than any other novel in the English language. For Mackenzie, tears were the watery signs of an innate moral sentiment, an idea he may have derived from Adam Smith.

Sentiment had an impact on the visual arts as well, especially portrait painting. Before the mid-eighteenth century, portraits were intended to show a likeness and to cause the viewer to think about the attributes of the subject. The cult of sentiment, however, encouraged portrait painters to appeal to the emotions of the audience by revealing some aspect of the subject – a facial expression, a hand gesture, a piece of clothing – that would cause a reaction to be felt. Joshua Reynolds, the most successful painter of the late eighteenth century, was a master of this subtle art of evoking an emotional response. His subjects are often shown in classical or formal poses, but with instantly recognizable traits that cause us to think that we know that person's individual character, not by rational reflection but through a sudden feeling of recognition. Reynolds's chief competitor in the field of portrait-painting, Thomas Gainsborough, carried the process a stage further by using dynamic brush-strokes that convey emotion through the paint itself.

People of taste might try to incorporate the cult of sentiment into their personal behavior. The journals of James Boswell, the son of a Scottish laird, record "my thoughts on different subjects at different times, the whims that may seize me and the sallies of my luxuriant imagination."[13] He chronicled his attempts to find a purpose in life, along with his conversations, love affairs, and frequent dalliances with prostitutes. He made a Grand Tour of continental Europe, meeting Voltaire and Rousseau and becoming a passionate admirer of Pasquale Paoli, the charismatic leader of a peasant rebellion in Corsica. On his return to England, Boswell appeared in Corsican costume at a fancy-dress ball, which made him famous. He attached himself to Samuel Johnson, who became a benign substitute for his own abusive father, and traveled with him to the remote islands of northwest Scotland. After his mentor's death, Boswell immortalized him in an admiring biography. We know more about Boswell's thoughts, whims, and imagination than about any other figure of the late eighteenth century.

By the 1770s, the "man of feeling" was well known enough to be the object of satire, notably in the 1775 play *The Rivals* by Richard Brinsley Sheridan, who later became a Whig politician. Like the vain "Macaroni" who dressed up in outlandishly fashionable clothes, and was lampooned in countless graphic prints of the period, the "man of feeling" was perceived as unmanly, because he tormented himself about everything. In Jane Austen's novels, which were in part a reaction against the sentimental genre, the heroes are sensitive, but not to the point of showing their emotions openly, while the heroines tend to be sensible and down-to-earth. This may explain why Austen's works did not sell very well until the twentieth century. The vogue for sentiment in popular fiction writing would continue in Britain throughout the nineteenth century, although male characters became more commanding, and female characters more passive.

Even in the late eighteenth century, there was a manly side to sentimentalism, associated with patriotic feelings. Boswell was passionately attached to Scotland, in spite of the frequent teasing of Johnson, who had a low opinion of the Scots. His patriot pride was emotional rather than political; it arose from a strong nostalgia for his homeland, not from a wish for Scottish independence. Sentimental patriotism invigorated late eighteenth-century writing in both Scotland and Wales. The ancient literatures of both nations were reinvented, although those who were responsible claimed that they were merely being rediscovered. Iolo Morganwg (Edward Williams), a stonemason from Glamorgan in South Wales, wrote Welsh poetry in the style of the ancient bards, which he passed off as genuine. A tireless promoter of supposed traditions that he had in fact dreamed up himself, Morganwg organized the first Gorsedd or festival of bardic poetry, which was held, oddly enough, outside London in 1792. Morganwg was also responsible for inspiring the national Eisteddfod, a celebration of Welsh culture that is still held annually. His counterpart in Scotland was the writer James Macpherson, who claimed to have discovered the works of the ancient Celtic bard Ossian, which in fact he had composed from surviving fragments. A more authentic writer of patriotic Scots verse, expressed in a Lowland dialect, was Robert Burns. He lived up to a prophecy he made in 1789:

> Ye'll soon hae poets o' the Scottish nation,
> Will gar [make] Fame blaw until her trumpet crack,
> And warsle [wrestle] Time, and lay him on his back![14]

Burns mixed nostalgic Jacobitism with enlightened and revolutionary principles. Of humble origins, he was adopted by the literary elite of Edinburgh. Since his early death in 1796 he has become an icon of national identity to Scots throughout the world.

By the late eighteenth century, the cult of sentiment was firmly established as a feature of British culture. Yet it had strayed far from its religious origins, and had been partly secularized by the influence of enlightened thought. For many readers, it was more a form of personal expression than a pathway to revelation or higher truths. Like the rationalism of the Enlightenment, it could be enlisted in support of the existing order, through appeals to patriotic emotions, affection for the King, or attachment to religion. The Romantic poets would attempt to raise sentiment back up to the level of the universal, the eternal, the sublime, and make it something it had never been before: dangerous.

The Romantic Revolt

Romanticism is a term that has many meanings, but we will use it to refer to a cultural movement that arose in the late eighteenth century, in opposition to strict rationalism. It drew on the cult of sentiment and on the philosophy of Rousseau, but it was most concerned with interpreting human emotion in non-material or non-scientific terms, as the outpouring of the spirit or the soul. For the Romantics, feelings connect us with the divine, which they understood as a higher state of being. Their religious and philosophical beliefs were unorthodox, and most of them were critics of the existing social order, which they saw as chaining an inherent desire for liberty.

Some of the intellectual roots of Romanticism can be found in Edmund Burke's *Enquiry into the Sublime and Beautiful*, published in 1757, before he became a politician. Drawing on David Hartley's theory of human psychology, Burke proposed that what we find beautiful causes pleasure to the senses, while the sublime causes us fear or terror. Burke described the sublime as an overwhelming natural force that suspends reason and draws out the deepest emotions:

The passion caused by the great and sublime in nature, when those causes operate most powerfully, is Astonishment; and astonishment is that state of the soul, in which all its motions are suspended, with some degree of horror. In this case the mind is so entirely filled with its object, that it cannot entertain any other, nor by consequence reason with that object which employs it. Hence arises the great power of the sublime, that far from being produced by them, it anticipates our reasonings, and hurries us on by an irresistible force.[15]

Burke's idea of the sublime would have suggested a religious connection in the minds of his readers, who knew the biblical saying, that fear of God was the beginning of wisdom.

Terror and fear were essential elements in the Gothic novels of the late eighteenth century, so called because they evoked the "superstitious" and "barbarous" feelings associated with the Middle Ages, and were usually set in medieval monasteries, castles, or dungeons. The earliest of them was *The Castle of Otranto* (1764), written by Horace Walpole, son of the late chief minister, Sir Robert. Horace Walpole designed his own Gothic fantasy house at Strawberry Hill near London. Also set in a mysterious castle was Anne Radcliffe's *The Mysteries of Udolpho* (1794), whose overwrought scenes of ghostly horror and overly imaginative heroine were satirized by Jane Austen in *Northanger Abbey*. Supernatural occurrences in the novels of Walpole and Radcliffe turn out to be false, but those that appear in William Beckford's Gothic writings are presented as real. Beckford was the wayward son and namesake of a powerful West Indian planter and ally of John Wilkes. The central figure in Beckford's novel *Vathek* (1786), written when he was only 22 years old, is an Arabian prince who summons up spirits, sacrifices babies, gains the ability to kill with a single glance, and ends up waiting for eternal torment in an underground hell. Beckford's own behavior was not nearly so bad, although he scandalized polite society when he was caught having sex with another young gentleman. He built himself a grand house, Fonthill Abbey, that expressed his wild imagination.

A different precursor of Romanticism was visionary or prophetic literature. Popular belief in biblical prophecies had never disappeared in Britain, in spite of the influence of enlightened rationalism. The spread of evangelicalism revived prophetic writings, which were given a further boost by the disasters of the American Revolutionary War. The troubled 1790s saw the rise of two major prophetic figures: Richard Brothers, a former sailor who called himself "Nephew of the Almighty," and Joanna Southcott, a farmer's daughter and domestic servant, who published accounts of her visionary dreams and in 1802 declared that she was about to give birth to the Son of God (sadly, this did not happen). Both gained considerable followings. The most notable literary figure who wrote visionary works was William Blake, a London printer, engraver, and poet. His mind filled with occult philosophy and radical politics, Blake regularly communicated with spirits. His early poetry was sentimental but full of brilliant imagery. His later writings were epic fantasies in which symbolic figures act out contemporary events on a cosmic stage. Here, for example, are the first lines of his unfinished poem on the French Revolution, printed in 1791:

The dead brood over Europe, the cloud and vision descends over chearful France,
O cloud well appointed! Sick, sick, the Prince on his couch, wreath'd in dim
And appalling mist, his strong hand outstretch'd, from his shoulder down the bone
Runs aching cold into the scepter, too heavy for mortal grasp, no more
To be swayed by visible hand, nor in cruelty bruise the mild flourishing mountains.[16]

The Revolution in France, which Blake fervently supported, becomes in this poem much more than a historical event: it is an episode in a universal myth.

Strictly speaking, the Romantic movement in literature stems from the partnership of two young poets, Samuel Taylor Coleridge and William Wordsworth, who in 1798 published a collection of poems, entitled *Lyrical Ballads*. Both men were supporters of the French Revolution, and Coleridge had wanted to start a commune based on the radical theories of William Godwin. *Lyrical Ballads* contained Coleridge's strange poem "The Rime of the Ancient Mariner," about a sailor who is cursed for shooting an albatross, and achieves redemption only after having a vision of divine creation. Depressive, addicted to opium, and fascinated by German Idealist philosophy, young Coleridge was a wild and unpredictable character, but he grew more conservative with age. "I have accordingly snapped my squeaking baby trumpet of sedition," he wrote as early as 1796, "and have hung up its fragments in the chamber of Penitences."[17] After recovering from a mental breakdown in 1814, Coleridge turned his back on his former radicalism, and soon ceased writing new poetry. His later philosophical works stress the importance of religious belief and the need for a "clerisy" or educated class of clergy, scholars, and artists who should guide the nation.

Wordworth's career was less dramatic. Orphaned at 13, he lived for most of his life with his beloved sister Dorothy, whose journals provided him with many of the subjects for his poetry. An admirer of Tom Paine, he spent a year with a mistress in revolutionary France. He later wrote emotionally of that hopeful time:

> Bliss was it in that dawn to be alive,
> But to be young was very Heaven! O times,
> In which the meagre, stale, forbidding ways
> Of custom, law, and statute, took at once
> The attraction of a country in romance![18]

By 1802, when he visited France again during the Peace of Amiens, he had changed his mind. France had fallen under the sway of Napoleon, and Wordsworth had become an English patriot: "Europe is yet in bonds; but let that pass, / Thought for another moment. Thou art free, / My Country!"[19] Wordsworth married in the same year, residing for the rest of his long life at Grasmere in the remote Lake District of northwest England. Dorothy remained in his household, but he broke up with Coleridge after 1810. By the end of the Napoleonic Wars, he was a supporter of the conservative government. Although he continued to write poetry, most of it did not match his early work. For Wordsworth as for Coleridge, the French Revolution was a crucial moment of contact with the beautiful and the sublime, the joyful and the terrifying. After they had renounced it, they never encountered the same experience again.

Their increasing conservatism was a great disappointment to the second generation of Romantic poets – Lord Byron, Percy Bysshe Shelley, and John Keats. All three men held radical opinions and led short lives, the first two very turbulent and exciting ones. Byron gained immense popularity through poems like "Childe

Harolde" and "Manfred," about lonely outcasts who have been unjustly shunned by society. Like the Emperor Napoleon, or Satan in John Milton's epic *Paradise Lost*, the Byronic hero possesses a demonic energy along with a flawed grandeur. Byron lived as if he were a character from his own works. Shunned by respectable society for separating from his wife, notorious for his sexual escapades, he left Britain for continental Europe, tried to start a revolution in Italy, and died in 1824 of rheumatic fever, while taking part in a Greek uprising against the Turks.

His friend Shelley, whose family were wealthy landowners, gained his own notoriety in 1811 when he published, at the age of 19, the first open declaration of atheism to appear in Britain. As heaven was just a dream, Shelley exhorted human beings to build a worldly paradise: "Oh happy Earth! reality of Heaven! / ... Thou consummation of all mortal hope!"[20] The government put him under surveillance for distributing tracts that called for dissolution of the union with Ireland. Shelley eloped in 1814 with Mary, the teenaged daughter of William Godwin and Mary Wollstonecraft. As Shelley was already married, this created a complicated set of personal relationships that lasted until his first wife drowned herself. At Geneva in 1816, while staying with Lord Byron (who had fathered a child by her half-sister), Mary Shelley began writing her novel *Frankenstein*, in which a scientist seeks to become a god-like creator of life, but instead constructs a tragic monster. After 1818, the Shelleys lived in Italy, where Percy continued to write poems in favor of revolutionary change, and where he was drowned in a boating accident in 1822.

John Keats, the only one of the trio who came from a middling background, had a quieter life. He gave up a medical career to devote himself to poetry, living mostly in the northern suburbs of London. His radical sympathies led to attacks on his work from the conservative press that wounded but did not kill him (although Byron meanly suggested that they had). During a visit to Rome, where he did not try to start a revolution, Keats died of tuberculosis in 1821. He was a consummate poetic craftsman, and his verses contain more pleasure than terror, or in Burke's terms, more beauty than sublimity. As he put it in one of his most famous poems, "Beauty is truth, truth beauty, – that is all / Ye know on earth, and all ye need to know."[21] Wordsworth was shocked by Keats's paganism, an audacious position to take in an age of evangelical Christianity.

Poetic Romanticism constituted a rebellion against accepted forms and beliefs. Before it was tamed by the deaths of younger poets, or the growing conservatism of older ones, it constituted a challenge to existing British culture, and to British society. It argued for the primacy of individual feeling against social convention, glorified raw, unbridled nature over the values of politeness or civility, and endowed the imagination of the artist with powers that resembled those of a god. It had a visual counterpart in the remarkable landscape paintings of J. M. W. Turner, with their lofty, empyrean points of view and hazy, dreamlike evocations of nature. The Romantics are now so familiar to us, and so accepted as great artists, that their rebelliousness is easy to ignore, but this may simply show to what extent they were, in their own way, successful revolutionaries.

Part VII

A New Order Begins, 1815–1837

The history of the British state had rarely been tranquil. It was created after 1688 for two main purposes: to protect the Protestant Succession, and to win wars against France. By 1815, after many vicissitudes, those goals had been achieved, and the state was beginning to lose its focus. Large segments of the British public were demanding change. Protestant Dissenters continued to seethe at the Test and Corporation Acts. Irish Catholics clamored for political emancipation. Middling and laboring men wanted the vote. The reformers were thwarted again and again, yet they stubbornly refused to disappear. By delaying the day of reckoning, conservatives would blunt its eventual impact, but they would not succeed in avoiding it.

By the 1820s, the British state had developed a political dynamic that was straining its conservative character. To preserve national prestige, economic prosperity, the supremacy of the landed classes, and the relatively open system of British government, while avoiding revolution, politicians were pushed towards making concessions to groups that were not directly included in the existing system. Some political leaders gave ground reluctantly. Others accepted that preserving the integrity of government might require greater flexibility on major issues. The state slowly began to accommodate itself to new social and economic realities, especially industrialization and the enhanced economic clout of the middling sort. After 1827, piecemeal change was overwhelmed by a flood of innovation. A reformed British state emerged, with the Whigs at its head. It was based on the principle that active reform could have beneficial consequences, not just in addressing social issues, but in maintaining the stability of government. Although it was not a totally new state, and not yet a democracy, its assumptions were different from those that had previously prevailed. It reflected a social system in which the old, fixed hierarchy of orders seemed to have given way to a new, more volatile social structure based on the concept of class.

The transformation of the old British state had consequences for the empire, where settler populations had begun to make demands similar to those heard from excluded groups in Britain. Successive British governments would do their best to resist colonial pressures for reform, but would finally have to give in to them in order to keep the empire whole. In India, however, the British state changed only in the scope of its activities. It remained an autocratic entity that imposed reform from above, without taking the views of Indians much into consideration. Direct criticism of the empire from within its own bureaucratic structure would take decades to develop. The reformed British state – the liberal state of the nineteenth century – would concede limited autonomy to the settler colonies, but it would subject India and Africa to even greater intrusions.

19

The State Reformed

At the conclusion of the Napoleonic Wars, the British government was in the hands of conservatives who had little desire to revisit divisive political issues, namely Parliamentary reform, Catholic emancipation, and repeal of the Test and Corporation Acts. For five years after 1815, they held firm against intense popular pressure for an extended franchise, by relying on the continued opposition to radical change of many among the upper and middling sort of people. The resurgence of reform, however, revealed deep differences of opinion within the government itself. The shaken conservatives began to move towards change on a number of fronts, although not on the franchise question. What finally pushed the Parliamentary reform agenda forward after 1830 was a combination of renewed popular unrest, growing conflict among conservatives, and an unusual degree of united resolve among the opposition. The Whigs who came back into power in 1830 would disappoint the radical reformers in the end, but they would inaugurate a half-century of rapid change that would culminate in a wider franchise, an interventionist government, and an almost secular Parliament: in short, a liberal state.

The Unreformed System

The government in 1815 was a coalition of various conservative factions, headed by Lord Liverpool in the House of Lords and by Viscount Castlereagh in the House of Commons (as an Irish peer, Castlereagh did not have a seat in the House of Lords by right and could be elected to the lower chamber). Government supporters did not call themselves conservatives, a term that came into vogue about 25 years later, and many of them did not like the label Tories either, as it bore bad old associations and was used mainly by their enemies. If asked to identify themselves, they might have used the vague expression "friends of Mr Pitt." This meant that they wanted to preserve what they saw as Pitt's legacy. Ultimately, the

Liverpool government stood for maintaining the existing constitution in Church and state, which is why it is not misleading to call it conservative.

The ruler whom the ministers served was not much of a role-model. The Prince Regent was lazy, fat, self-indulgent, an alcoholic, and a bigamist. Secretly married to a Catholic with whom he lived until 1803, George entered into a second, public marriage in 1795 with Princess Caroline of Brunswick. He found her so unattractive at their first meeting that he immediately called for a brandy to fortify him. After the birth of their only child, Princess Charlotte, George unceremoniously abandoned his Protestant wife and returned to his Catholic one. Treated with cruelty and indignity by her boorish husband, who denied her access to their daughter after 1812, Princess Caroline left Britain to live in Italy. On the more positive side, Prince George was a dedicated collector of art and builder of the fascinating, if bizarre, Royal Pavilion at Brighton, which resembles the palace of an Indian maharajah. Like his father, the Prince had strong ideas about his own authority, but he was so unpopular that he was not usually able to implement them. He retained the power to name ministers, who governed through the collective body known as the Cabinet. Although Prince George may have felt that the Cabinet was responsible to him, in fact it depended on the support of Parliament.

That legislative body had not seen much structural change since 1660. The government of Great Britain and Ireland had remained firmly in the hands of the landed classes. The House of Lords was still a bastion of inherited privilege. It had expanded under William Pitt, from 189 members in 1780 to 269 in 1800, but almost all the new peers had previous family connections with the aristocracy. By 1815, the peerage as a whole was richer than it had ever been, on account of strict settlements, consolidation of land, enclosure, mining, high corn prices, investment in government securities, and the holding of public office. The culture of the peerage was arguably more uniform as well. Apart from the Scottish peers, all the voting members of the House of Lords were Anglicans. Almost three-quarters of them had attended one of the four great public (i.e. private) schools (Eton, Harrow, Westminster, and Winchester), by contrast with the early eighteenth century, when most aristocratic children were educated at home. Two-thirds of the peerage had been to Oxford or Cambridge, and most took a Grand Tour of Europe after university, at least when peace made this possible. Throughout their lives, aristocrats were surrounded by dependants, from needy relatives to the armies of servants who waited on them in their great country houses, from the tenant farmers and farm laborers who came to them, hat in hand, to beg for favors, to the tradesmen who brought fashionable goods to their great London mansions, hoping they would buy. They were at the top of what the radical Willliam Cobbett called "a chain of dependence running through the whole nation, which, though not everywhere seen, is everywhere felt."[1] The political power of the aristocracy lasted for another century. Their social power only faded after the First World War, and their cultural power has not yet entirely dissipated.

Yet already in 1815, some thought that the House of Lords was less important than the House of Commons. "Nobody cares a damn for the House of Lords," the Duke of Wellington bluntly observed, adding "the House of Commons is everything in England."[2] The 658 seats in the House of Commons contained merchants, industrialists, financiers, and lawyers, but they were dominated by landed gentlemen. The gentry often had the same educational and cultural background as the aristocracy, and many of them were just as rich – all that set them apart was the lack of an aristocratic title. MPs in the Commons were elected by a small number of voters, numbering perhaps half a million in the whole United Kingdom in 1831, out of a total population of more than 24 million (16.5 million in Great Britain, 7.8 million in Ireland). In Scotland, a mere 4000 voters chose the whole national delegation to the Commons. Voters in county elections had to possess 40 shillings of freehold land or more, but every borough had its own franchise. Some decayed boroughs consisted of empty fields or sparsely inhabited seacoasts, with almost no voters, while in others, only the municipal corporation, consisting of a handful of town officers, could vote. It was estimated in 1827 that the holders of 276 seats in the House of Commons had simply been nominated by landed patrons, and elected without any contest taking place. Eight influential peers were said to control 51 seats in the lower house. Meanwhile, the growing industrial towns of Birmingham, Manchester, Leeds, and Sheffield had no borough representation at all. Yet the House of Commons claimed to represent the nation, and in fact its members were careful to take note of public opinion, at least among the landed elite and the respectable middling sort of people.

The financial and administrative agencies of the state had been growing throughout the eighteenth century, especially the revenue services – Customs, Excise, Stamps, and Taxes – which employed 20,000 people. The supply departments of the army and navy numbered around 4000, but this does not include the large number of dockyard workers, or the private contractors who provided uniforms, weapons, food, and drink for Britain's soldiers and sailors. On the other hand, the chief agency of domestic administration, the Home Office, employed only 17 people, and the Colonial Office only 14. The government was not yet run by professional civil servants, but it was already one that depended on a bureaucracy of revenue collectors.

The welfare of ordinary Britons was handled by local government, whose structure had hardly changed at all since the seventeenth century. In England, justices of the peace handled almost all local business, from criminal trials to civil suits, the upkeep of roads and bridges to the appointment of local officers such as constables and overseers of the poor. In spite of frequent complaints about their declining social status, most JPs continued to be landed gentlemen, or in towns, leading merchants. They were joined on the bench by a substantial number of Anglican clergymen – 10 percent of all JPs – who had a zeal for secular administration. Only a minority of justices did any substantial work, but those who did were often very busy. A group of JPs, meeting in the Berkshire village of Speen in 1795 during a period of major food shortages, came up with a system of poor relief that subsidized the wages of agricultural laborers up to the level of subsistence, as determined by the price of a loaf of bread and the size of the laborer's family. This became known as the Speenhamland system. It operated mainly in the southeast of England, although William Pitt tried in vain to have it made national. While it saved laborers from starving, it also encouraged employers to keep wages low.

The Speenhamland system may not have been satisfactory over time, but it was innovative, and it shows that local government in the countryside was able to respond to an emergency. The situation was different in the towns, where local government was often ineffective or non-existent. Manchester, with 140,000 inhabitants in 1831, was still officially a manor, governed by a medieval body called a court-leet. Many other towns were run by antiquated, oligarchic corporations that existed mostly to benefit the families that had run them for generations. To make up for these shortcomings, and to provide the improvements that town dwellers increasingly demanded, Parliament had set up special commissions for water, lighting, paving, the regulation of markets, etc. Light generated by coal gas was first used by an inventor in a Cornish mining village in 1792, and soon commissions were set up to install and maintain gas street lamps in British towns. London had 40,000 gas street lamps by 1823, lighting 213 thoroughfares. The nineteenth century was born under the yellowish, ethereal glow of gas light. Evidently, special commissions could be efficient in carrying out improvements, and they drew many people of the middling sort into the business of local administration. Most commissions were not directly responsible to the public, however, and it was not uncommon for them to strive mainly for the financial benefit of the commissioners themselves.

An even more complex patchwork of ancient survivals and modern expedients existed in Scotland. In the rural Lowlands, local government, including poor relief and education, was mostly handled through the parish. Under the lay patronage system of the eighteenth century, "heritors" or landlords who held church patronage had an increasing role in parish affairs. The Church courts or Kirk sessions were still active, imposing fines and minor punishments on blasphemers, drunkards, and fornicators. To move from parish to parish in the Lowlands, one might still need a "testificat" or certificate of good behavior from a parish clergyman. In spite of the abolition of heritable jurisdictions, barons' courts still met, in which the landlord sat as judge and could impose rent collection on his tenants. Scottish town corporations were just as oligarchic and poorly run as English ones. Glasgow did not have a commission for "police" or improvement until 1800. Edinburgh had no street lights in the Old Town, and its finances were so ineptly managed that it had to declare bankruptcy in 1833. In spite of the presence of its Town Guard and the fact that so many lawyers lived there, the Scottish capital was known as an unruly place, and saw at least eight major outbreaks of riot between 1740 and 1791.

Irish government was beset by more basic contradictions. Irish Parliamentary representation had been partly reformed by the 1800 Act of Union, which abolished the smallest and most easily controlled boroughs in the kingdom – their patrons were actually compensated for the loss. The real problem with Irish representation, of course, was that while Catholic property owners were allowed to vote, they could not hold a Parliamentary seat or any political office. Added to this was the anomaly of Ireland's separate executive. The lord lieutenant, head-quartered at Dublin Castle, continued to be the agent of British government policy in Ireland, giving the impression that this was a colony rather than an integrated part of the United Kingdom. Local administration was organized on the English model, but again, Catholics could not serve as JPs. The local authorities were unable to control violence in the Irish countryside, whether from Catholic or Presbyterian gangs.

Surveying the British system of government in 1815, we might conclude that it needed reform at every level. This was not how most of the governing elite saw it. They believed that they were living under the most excellent constitution that had ever been devised. While radicals criticized it as a "deformed and destructive system," its defenders marveled that it showed "not merely no symptom of irretrievable decay, but a more expansive energy."[3] The landed classes had no intention of changing a set of arrangements that had, after all, made them powerful and kept them rich. Many among the middling sort of people were equally supportive of the constitution, because it staved off lower class revolution. Of course, there were many other middling people who had grievances against it, for religious or social or political reasons. We have no way of knowing what the majority of people thought of the British constitution, because nobody bothered to ask. The political system had not broken down since the 1640s, but that may not reveal much about it. Until the 1780s, no other European constitution had collapsed, either. By 1815, only the French and the Dutch had gone through genuine revolutions. Nobody could be absolutely certain that Britain was not next.

The Radical Revival, 1815–1821

One way to ensure that neither Britain nor any other country would experience a revolution was to prevent another major international war. This was the goal of the Congress of Vienna, the grand international gathering that attempted to restore the security of Europe in 1815. As Foreign Secretary, Castlereagh represented Britain at the Congress, although Wellington later took his place. Wisely, the delegates decided not to punish France for causing more than two decades of bloodshed. Britain received some French islands in the Caribbean, along with other conquests: Malta, Trinidad, Demerara, Ceylon (now Sri Lanka), and the Cape of Good Hope, the last three ceded by the Dutch. Hanover became a kingdom within a German Confederation that replaced the old Holy Roman Empire. The most short-sighted aspect of the Congress of Vienna was its refusal to consider the importance of national sentiments, which were linked in the minds of the delegates with revolution. Its most solid achievement was in establishing a peace that lasted through most of Europe until 1914. This was done by international cooperation, and was supposed to be safeguarded through regular conferences, four of which were held down to 1822. The tsar of Russia, however, tried to use the conferences to provide support for an active counter-revolutionary policy. The realistic Castlereagh, worried about how this would play with the British public, refused to assist him. On the other hand, the Foreign Secretary would offer no aid to the Spanish American revolutionaries in their struggle for independence, either.

In domestic policy, Lord Liverpool's government sought to avoid unrest by guaranteeing a stable food supply. Its means of accomplishing this, however, was the infamous Corn Law of 1815, which turned out to be a highly unpopular piece of legislation. The grain farmers of Britain and Ireland had experienced bumper harvests in 1812 and 1813, causing prices to fall. To raise the price of wheat again, they had cut back on production, encouraging merchants to import grain. The government planned to fix the supply of wheat by legislating that no imports could enter the country unless the price rose above a supposedly fair level of 80 shillings per quarter-hundredweight. Landowners were delighted, but manufacturing towns petitioned against the law, on the grounds that it would keep the price of grain high. Riots against the law broke out in London, Edinburgh, and other places. While the economist Thomas Malthus defended the Corn Laws, his disciple David Ricardo, an advocate of free trade, condemned them. The government had in fact created a seriously divisive social issue, pitting farmers against industrial workers and town dwellers.

Economic conditions worsened after the war, aggravating the effects of the Corn Law. Post-war deflation of prices meant that manufacturers began to reduce their labor force. It was a bad time for 300,000 discharged soldiers and sailors to be released onto the job market. Many of them could not find employment. The harvests of 1816 and 1817 were poor, and grain prices began to rise towards the 80 shilling level. Food riots broke out in southeast England in 1816, and Luddite attacks against machinery soon revived in the Midlands. Meanwhile, taxes on consumption, which should have been reduced after the war, remained high, because the House of Commons had voted down the income tax, against the wishes of the government. The financial situation was dire: more than £50 million had to be raised annually to cover the national debt and war pensions, and the budget ran into annual deficits of up to £13 million. To many people, it seemed as if the profligacy and corruption of the Liverpool administration was ruining the country. There might be a simple answer: Parliamentary reform.

After 1815, the mass meeting emerged again as an instrument of radical agitation. Because they were reminiscent of the French Revolution, huge gatherings caused great concern to the government. The first mass reform meeting in London since 1795 took place at Spa Fields, Islington, in December 1816. It was organized by the eccentric Society of Spencean Philanthropists, the disciples of a radical named Thomas Spence, who had died two years previously. Spence had argued that parishes should own all land and resources communally, renting out the rights to use them and dividing the proceeds between social services and quarterly payments to every man, woman, and child. Among the followers of this early form of socialism was Arthur Thistlewood, a former soldier and farmer. According to a government spy, Thistlewood planned to turn the meeting in Spa Fields into a riot, during which the Spenceans would seize the Tower of London and the Bank of England. This improbable conspiracy was not what attracted 10,000 people to the meeting; they came to hear Henry "Orator" Hunt, a gentleman farmer and electrifying speaker, who addressed them from out of the window of a public house. He had already thrilled large crowds in Birmingham, Nottingham, and several northern industrial towns. Hunt always wore a white top hat, signifying the purity of his cause, as he called for universal male suffrage and annual Parliaments. Local magistrates decided to suppress the Spa Fields meeting. A constable was stabbed, and Thistlewood was arrested along with three other Spenceans. A jury, however, rejected the government spy's testimony, which resulted in all the Philanthropists being released.

The threat of insurrection seemed to multiply rapidly in the following three years. In part, this was because the government relied on paid informers, who justified themselves by revealing grand conspiracies that often had little basis in reality. In part, it was because of government overreaction to minor incidents. In January 1817, the Prince Regent opened Parliament with a speech in which he hoped that both Houses "would feel a just indignation at the attempts which had been made to take advantage of the distresses of the country for the purpose of exciting a spirit of sedition and violence."[4] On his way back to his residence at Carlton House, the windows of the Prince's carriage were shot out by an air gun. An outraged Parliament decided to suspend *habeas corpus*, allowing radicals to be kept in jail without trial. In this tense situation, reformers in Manchester decided to organize a march to London by 4000–5000 textile workers, to carry a petition for reform to the Prince Regent. It was a cold spring, and because they carried blankets to keep them warm, they were called "Blanketeers." Samuel Bamford, a radical weaver from Lancashire, left a description of them: "A few were decently clothed, and well appointed for the journey; many were covered only by rags which admitted the cold wind, and were already damped by a gentle but chilling rain."[5] They do not sound much like an insurrectionary force, but in numbers and purpose they seemed threatening to the authorities. The Riot Act was read before they even left Manchester, and most of them did not get very far.

In June 1817, an actual uprising took place around the village of Pentridge in Derbyshire. It was led by Jeremiah Brandreth, an unemployed stocking maker from neighboring Nottinghamshire, where most of the Luddite attacks had taken place. About 300 laborers joined him, and another couple of hundred rose up in South Yorkshire. One of the rebels confessed that "He believed the day and hour were fixed when the whole nation was expected to rise; and before the middle of the week, he believed there would be hundreds of thousands in arms … there were men appointed all over the nation."[6] Brandreth himself thought that the Hampden Clubs, which were peaceful reform associations, were going to support his uprising. In fact, the unfortunate man had more or less been duped into starting the rebellion by a government spy, and his little army of insurgents was quickly dispersed by soldiers. This did not save Brandreth from execution. He and two other leaders of the Pentridge Rising were hanged and beheaded for high treason – they were spared the horrible sentence of drawing and quartering. Fourteen other rebels were transported to Australia. The poet Shelley wrote a eulogy for the executed men, comparing their deaths to that of Princess Charlotte, the heir to the throne, who died in childbirth around the same time.

He was not alone in mourning what he saw as the "murder" of British liberty. Cheap periodicals from the radical press were spreading the same message to a mass audience. "Not only a great majority," wrote Thomas Wooler, editor of a radical newspaper called *The Black Dwarf*, "but the REAL whole of society, sees that its interests have been grossly betrayed; that a vile administration is resorting to absolute tyranny, to screen its prodigality, its peculation ... and its imbecility of complexion."[7] Blasphemous and sometimes pornographic, the radical press held the government directly responsible for the economic misery of the nation. Conservatives soon began to clamp down on it. Prosecutions for writing or publishing seditious libels were initiated by private bodies, like the Society for the Suppression of Vice, an evangelical organization supported by William Wilberforce. Between 1817 and 1821, no fewer than 131 accusations of seditious libel were brought against the press. William Cobbett, a former conservative who wrote the radical journal *The Political Register*, fled to the United States. Wooler was arrested and acquitted, although he later spent 18 months in prison for inciting discontent. Legal repression that depended on jury trials, however, proved no more effective than in the 1790s, because juries were reluctant to convict printers and publishers.

By 1819, supporters of the government were genuinely afraid of the possibility of a revolution. Their fear explains what happened in St Peter's Fields, Manchester, on August 16. A mass gathering had been organized there in favor of Parliamentary reform. Preparations were very elaborate, as Samuel Bamford recalled:

First were selected twelve of the most comely and decent-looking youths, who were placed in two rows of six each, with each a branch of laurel held presented in his hand, as a token of amity and peace, – then followed the men of several districts in fives, – then the band of music, an excellent one, – then the colours; a blue one of silk, with inscriptions in golden letters, "UNITY AND STRENGTH." "LIBERTY AND FRATERNITY." A green one of silk, with golden letters, "PARLIAMENTS ANNUAL." "SUFFRAGE UNIVERSAL"; and betwixt them on a staff, a handsome cap of crimson velvet, with a tuft of laurel, and the cap tastefully braided with the word, LIBERTAS, in front.[8]

Evidently, this meeting was designed to show off both the strength and the respectability of a community-based reform movement.

About 50,000 people crowded into St Peter's Fields, where "Orator" Hunt was to speak. The Manchester magistrates were convinced that the crowd was armed and dangerous – in fact, some of them were carrying pikes. The local yeomanry, a militia cavalry unit, were ordered to arrest Hunt, which they did by charging into the crowd – their horses may have panicked – and cutting a bloody path through it with their sabers. Although Bamford tried to persuade people to stand fast, the field cleared in ten minutes. The results were horrific: 18 people were killed and more than 500 injured, including 100 women. The government unsuccessfully tried to suppress published accounts of what became known as the Peterloo Massacre, a mocking reference to the recent battle of Waterloo. Peterloo remained an embarrassment to the local authorities for a long time. Even today, only a small plaque marks the site of the killings.

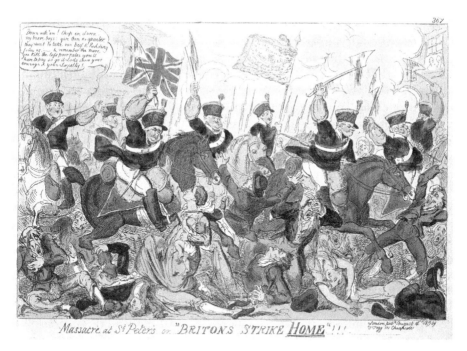

Illustration 22 *The Peterloo Massacre as imagined by a contemporary cartoonist, probably Robert or George Cruikshank. The Yeoman Cavalry are shown as grim, well fed soldiers with axes, hacking down raggedly dressed men, women, and children. (Robert or George Cruikshank, "Massacre at St Peters or 'Britons Strike Home'!!!" 1819. © British Museum, London, UK, / The Bridgeman Art Library)*

Although it was followed by many petitions and protests, Peterloo temporarily ended the mass movement for Parliamentary reform. Hunt was sent to jail for two and a half years, while Bamford and others received lesser sentences. The high-strung Lord Liverpool was inclined to blame what had happened at Manchester on the influence of the French Revolution, which had "directed the attention of the lower orders of the community, and those immediately above them, to political considerations," and had "shaken all respect for established authority and ancient institutions."[9] By the end of the year, Parliament had passed the Six Acts, concocted mainly by the Home Secretary, Lord Sidmouth. They outlawed military-style drilling, allowed magistrates to search any property or person for arms, prohibited meetings of more than 50 people without a magistrate's consent, reduced delays in trials for misdemeanors, imposed stronger punishments on blasphemous or seditious publications, and made journals that published opinions rather than news liable to the stamp tax. The wisdom of passing these measures seemed to be proven in February 1820, when constables stormed a hayloft in Cato Street, London, and arrested several Spencean Philanthropists, including the hapless Arthur Thistlewood. They were accused of plotting to assassinate the Cabinet and ignite a general insurrection. A government spy was involved, as usual, and it is impossible to sort out how much truth lay behind the Cato Street

Conspiracy. For once, a jury accepted the guilt of the plotters. Thistlewood, who had killed a constable in the course of arrest, was hanged, along with four others.

The Six Acts put the price of radical newspapers out of the reach of laboring people, and the threat of military force ended the period of mass mobilization. In other respects, however, the Six Acts proved ineffective, because no organized police force existed to enforce them. Military drilling by radical groups continued. In the spring of 1820, angry textile workers appeared in arms near Falkirk in Scotland and in West Yorkshire. A gradually improving economy would discourage such incidents. Anti-government sentiment, however, remained strong in many parts of the country, as was loudly demonstrated by the enthusiastic public support shown for the claims of the abused Queen Caroline. This extraordinary affair was highly embarrassing for the crown and the administration. After the death of sad, mad George III in January 1820, the Prince Regent became King George IV. He immediately showed his deep feelings towards his estranged wife by asking that her name be left out of Anglican prayers for the monarch. An infuriated Caroline insisted on her rights as Queen, refused the separation settlement offered by the government, and returned to London, where she was greeted by cheering crowds. She moved into the house of a radical alderman. Unwillingly, the Liverpool administration had to initiate a royal divorce, through a bill of pains and penalties presented to the House of Lords.

The divorce proceedings turned into a disaster for the government, and a new occasion for mass political mobilization. The Queen was idolized by the common people of London, who turned out in droves to see her. Women saw her as an icon of female suffering at the hands of callous men. Radical newspapers represented her as a model of womanly virtue, mistreated and abandoned by her cruel husband. Reformers toasted her name along with that of Henry Hunt. She received addresses from places throughout Britain, including one from the workers of Manchester, who told her that "The same power which scourged us is oppressing you ... your Majesty's enemies ... are also the enemies of the rights and liberties of the whole People."[10] A petition supporting the Queen and calling on the King to dismiss his ministers arrived from Edinburgh, with an astonishing 17,000 signatures on it.

Desperately, the government presented eye-witness testimony of the Queen cavorting with an Italian lover, but it changed nobody's mind, as the King's behavior was known to be worse. The bill of pains and penalties passed the House of Lords by only nine votes, and the government, sensing defeat in the House of Commons, abandoned it. The Whigs had supported the popular cause in the Queen Caroline affair, and for once they had stood firm. The abandonment of the divorce was celebrated with bonfires in which effigies of the chief witnesses against the Queen were burned. Yet Caroline's triumph was short-lived. When George IV was crowned in a lavish ceremony in July 1821, the Queen was not invited. She arrived at Westminster Abbey and demanded entrance, only to be turned away. Three weeks later, she died of an inflammation of the bowels. Radicals hijacked her funeral cortege and directed it through central London, past huge crowds of mourners.

The Queen Caroline affair was not inconsequential. It taught the Whigs that the opinions of laboring people really mattered. It showed the reformers that, if they worked with a Parliamentary party, they might obtain results. It emphasized to the government how easily a majority might be lost. As for George IV, while he would never be popular, after the trial he was at least accepted by the public as filling the necessary role of monarch. A courtier was pleased to record that the King had been greeted with only a few cries of "the Queen!" while visiting the theater for the first time after the divorce proceedings were dropped. Nevertheless, one wonders how he felt when a man in the theater gallery cried out to him, "Where's your wife, Georgy?"[11]

Conservative Reform, 1821–1830

The period that followed the Queen Caroline affair is sometimes represented as marking a shift in government policy, towards limited reform. This may be misleading. The conservative coalition had always included groups that were in favor of some reform or other. Lord Liverpool himself had spoken in favor of free trade in 1820. Even in the years of repression, the government had been willing to sanction reformist legislation, as long as it did not menace the ruling elite and was not very sweeping. In 1819, through the efforts of Sir Robert Peel, a Lancashire cotton manufacturer and conservative politician, a Factory Act had been passed that restricted child labor in cotton mills to 12 hours a day (not including meal times), and prohibited the employment of children under the age of nine. Although the Act was unenforceable, because no inspectors were appointed to make it work, it was an important step in asserting the government's responsibility for working conditions.

What made the period after 1820 different was that reform-minded ministers in Liverpool's government were able to carry through projects that previously might not have had much chance of success. Although they would have denied it, this revealed the impact of radical agitation on the conservative coalition. The upsurge of radicalism convinced those who had resisted specific changes that they might now be necessary, if for no other reason than to prevent the Whigs from achieving further Parliamentary victories. What the conservatives would not consider, however, was the main demand of the radicals: namely, a broadening of the Parliamentary franchise.

The chief factor that allowed conservative reform in the 1820s was the return of financial stability. This was achieved in part by readopting the gold standard, which had been abandoned during the wars against France. The paper money that the government had issued in wartime could now be exchanged for a new gold coin, the sovereign. A boom in trade and manufacturing in the early 1820s finally brought the national budget into a surplus, and allowed the government to reduce some of the heavy duties on consumer items. It also encouraged the first moves towards free trade. As President of the Board of Trade, William Huskisson reduced tariffs on imported goods, while giving preference to trade with the colonies. A more liberal attitude was also adopted towards trade unions. The Combination Acts of 1799, which had prohibited the formation of unions, were removed in 1824, because it was feared that restrictions on association were actually encouraging an underground labor movement. Incidents of violence among laborers, however, caused a nervous government to restore restrictions on union organization in 1825. By preventing unions from inflicting harm on employers, and making breach of contract by workers into a criminal offense, the new legislation effectively blocked the use of strike action.

Perhaps the most ardent conservative reformer of the 1820s was the Home Secretary Robert Peel, son of the industrialist who had sponsored the first Factory Act. A strong Protestant and opponent of Catholic emancipation, Peel was also an energetic and imaginative administrator. He reduced the number of crimes punishable by death, a change that had long been called for by Whig legal critics. In practice, capital punishment had often been commuted to a lesser sentence, and Peel was motivated by a desire for efficiency, not leniency, but at least he saw to it that nobody would hang for many petty infractions of the law. The average number of executions in England and Wales declined, from 108 per year in the period 1817–21 to 61 per year in 1822–6. If the face of English law was still fearsome, it was at least less random in its use of violence.

The conservative politician who benefited most from the shift towards reform was George Canning, who came from an Irish Protestant family. Canning was a brilliant speaker in the House of Commons, and a gifted writer. He helped the novelist Sir Walter Scott to found *The Quarterly Review*, a conservative literary journal that was set up in response to the Whig *Edinburgh Review*. Canning's support for Catholic emancipation, and his prickly relations with other conservative leaders, meant that he was often out of office. Then in 1822, the morose and depressive Foreign Secretary, Viscount Castlereagh, cut his own throat with a razor. Canning took his place, and set about altering certain aspects of British foreign policy. While he did not fundamentally change Castlereagh's priorities, Canning was much more willing to put aside the conservative dislike for republican governments. His aggressive advancement of British interests throughout the world, combined with a reluctance to become involved in European conflicts, would mark British foreign policy for the rest of the nineteenth century.

Canning separated Britain further from the reactionary aims of Russia, which were designed to choke off any chance of further revolution. Seeking to expand British influence in South and Central America, he recognized the new republics of Buenos Aires (Argentina), Colombia, and Mexico, as well as the Brazilian declaration of independence from Portugal. These were shrewd and far-sighted moves, as the new regimes would become heavily dependent on British manufactured goods, while providing Britain with raw materials and food. When the Greeks rose up against Turkish occupation, however, Canning was reluctant to assist them openly, as the Russian tsar asked him to do. He joked that the autocratic tsar would learn that "the Greeks are after all rebels, and not worthy [of] the sympathy of a legitimate Government."[12] He negotiated a protocol with the Ottoman Sultan to obtain limited self-government for Greece. In 1828, after

Canning's death, a combined English, French, and Russian fleet destroyed the Turkish navy at Navarino Bay, insuring Greek independence.

Canning was clearly the man to succeed Lord Liverpool, who suffered from serious hypertension. Struck by a cerebral hemorrhage in February 1827, Liverpool had to be replaced as chief minister. George IV asked Canning to form a government, but insisted that it include a majority of anti-Catholics. However, several anti-Catholic politicians, including Robert Peel, declined to serve in it. Canning was forced to ask Whigs to join his ministry, which brought them into power for the first time since 1807. Their leader, Earl Grey (the same man who gave his name to Earl Grey tea), refused to join the coalition, snobbishly remarking that Canning was not qualified to serve as chief minister because his mother had been an actress. (It may be remembered that Grey had once founded a club known as the Friends of the People.) The noble lord's opposition made little difference, since Canning died of a liver inflammation in August. An interim ministry lasted until January 1828 – the King replaced it before Parliament even met. He then asked the Duke of Wellington to form a government.

Wellington was renowned as a war hero, but he could also claim considerable political experience, so he was not an absurd choice for chief minister. His views were generally more cautious than Canning's, but he was not known as an anti-Catholic – in fact, he had almost no personal religious views at all. While his aim was to reconstruct Liverpool's conservative coalition, he agreed with Robert Peel that "the country could not be governed upon any exclusive principles … it was impossible to narrow our views to the mere personal opinions that might be held by political men, but … we must carry them much further."[13] In spite of opposition from landowners in the House of Lords, Wellington was able to enact one of Lord Liverpool's last policies, by passing a revised Corn Law whose "sliding scale" of prices and duties took some account of free trade principles. Imports of grain would be admitted, subject to a duty, when the price of domestic wheat reached 60 shillings per quarter-hundredweight. The duty would decrease up to 72 shillings a quarter, at which point grain would be admitted freely into the country. The "sliding scale" would remain in place until the Corn Laws were fully repealed, and free trade instituted, in 1846.

Robert Peel was restored by Wellington to the Home Office, where he busied himself creating a Metropolitan Police Force for London. Its constables were nicknamed "Bobbies" in his honor, and the name has stuck ever since. Several friends of George Canning were also reappointed by the Duke, but they soon quarreled with him and left the ministry. While he was a great leader of soldiers, Wellington was not much of a team captain in political terms. His government was weak and divided, and it would be forced into abject surrender on two fundamental issues: the repeal of the Test and Corporation Acts and Catholic Emancipation.

The first happened with astonishing swiftness. A lobbying campaign by a United Committee of Dissenting groups had begun in 1827. It represented a much greater percentage of the population than had been the case during the last repeal campaign in the late 1780s. Evangelical revivals among Congregationalists and Baptists, the formation of a separate Methodist denomination after the death of

John Wesley, and the failure of the Church of England in ministering to the expanding populations of urban districts had led to a dramatic growth in the number of Protestant Dissenters. By 1828, about 30 percent of Britons were Protestants who worshipped outside the Anglican Church. When the Whig Lord John Russell presented a motion for repeal of the Test and Corporation Acts to the House of Commons, the conservatives were not prepared to mount a strong response to it. The motion passed easily, although the bishops made sure that the ensuing bill repealing the Acts limited political rights to Christians. While the British state was not secularized, it took a step in that direction.

Catholic emancipation was not so easily won. After all, anti-Catholicism had been the foundation of the British state after the Glorious Revolution. The Gordon Riots were not forgotten; nor had fears of Irish radicalism dissipated since the rebellion of 1798. To overcome these factors, a moderate Catholic Association had been organized in Ireland to lobby for repeal. Under the leadership of a charismatic lawyer and small landowner, Daniel O'Connell, it began to organize mass meetings in the Irish countryside, offering associate membership to farmers for the small amount of one penny. In January 1828, over a million people appeared at 1600 parish meetings held by the Association, to endorse resolutions calling for emancipation. The government could not ignore this massive display of support. Five months later, O'Connell was elected as MP for County Clare, although as a Catholic he could not take his seat in the Commons. Wellington, who had grown up in Ireland, began to fear an insurrection. Although O'Connell was a moderate, and an admirer of Henry Grattan, more radical forces might emerge if emancipation were denied. In the spring of 1829, the anti-Catholic Robert Peel reluctantly shepherded through Parliament a bill allowing Catholics to hold all political offices in the United Kingdom, except those representing the crown. The franchise requirement in Irish county elections, however, was to be raised from 40 shillings to £10, which effectively took the vote away from most Catholic farmers. The Roman Catholic Church was given no institutional recognition. It was a peevish, small-minded bill, but it was enough: the Protestant state had fallen.

Conservatives throughout Britain felt betrayed. Their leaders had broken faith with the Glorious Revolution and the Hanoverian Succession. In June 1830, the reigning representative of the Hanoverian dynasty, the unloved and enormously fat King George IV, died. "Certainly nobody ever was less regretted than the late king," wrote one observer, "and the breath was hardly out of his body before the press burst forth in full cry against him, and raked up all his vices, follies and misdeeds, which were numerous and glaring enough."[14] An election had to be held. Another bulwark of the old British state – the unreformed Parliament – was about to come crashing down.

The Great Reform Act

The downfall of the old system was not inevitable. It could have been resisted in the early 1830s as it had been in the 1810s. To defeat the advocates of reform, however, the conservatives would have been obliged to resort to severely repressive tactics that might have altered the system in a different direction, perhaps towards a government backed by military force. Since the landed and middling classes had often benefited from the responsiveness of Parliament to public opinion, they had no desire to jettison it in favor of a more authoritarian regime. Besides, there was nobody to play the autocrat – certainly not the new King, William IV, another wayward son of George III, a genial, bumbling, and opinionated former sailor who had fathered a brood of illegitimate children by a well known actress.

Yet the unreformed system, however weak it had become, did not go gently to its rest. It had to be forced into the grave. This was done by a combination of adroit political maneuvering by the Whig party and constant pressure by the radical reformers outside Parliament. The elections of 1830 strengthened the Whigs, especially in the north of England, but did not give them an outright majority of seats in the House of Commons. Only the accidental death of William Huskisson made it impossible for Wellington to patch together a coalition with reform-minded conservatives. While examining the tracks a little too closely, Huskisson was run over by a steam train at the opening of the Liverpool–Manchester railway. His followers soon joined the Whigs in forming a new government. Earl Grey became chief minister, and the driver of a political steam train that would flatten the unreformed system – but not without a struggle.

The bill for Parliamentary reform presented by Lord John Russell in March 1831 was not just a Whig political gambit. It was a response to mounting public agitation. At the end of 1829, a Birmingham banker named Thomas Attwood had founded a movement, the Political Union, whose aim was to obtain peaceful reform. Similar groups had appeared throughout England, including the Metropolitan Union, organized in London by Daniel O'Connell and Henry Hunt. More radical reformers were holding nightly meetings at the Blackfriars Rotunda in London, addressing large crowds with speeches in favor of universal male suffrage. From the Rotunda lectures emerged the National Union of the Working Classes and Others (exactly what "Others" meant was not specified). "We are the people," declared a supporter of the NUWC, "our business is with the people, and to transact it properly, we must take it into our own hands."[15] When he rose to speak in favor of a reform bill in the House of Commons, Russell knew that this sort of rhetoric was frightening his conservative colleagues with the possibility of radical change. What he offered them was a moderate solution. Every borough in England and Wales was to have a uniform franchise requirement, based on ownership of £10 of property. Over 100 "rotten" boroughs with few or no electors were to be disenfranchised, or were to lose one of their two MPs. The unrepresented cities were to receive representation, while scores of county seats were to be added to the House. Thomas Babington Macaulay, a Whig who would later become the most famous of English historians, spoke these cautious words in favor of the bill: "I am opposed to Universal Suffrage because I think that it would produce a destructive revolution. I support this plan because I am sure that it is our best security against a revolution."[16]

The struggle to pass a reform bill lasted more than a year. The initial bill passed a second reading in the Commons by only one vote, and the government was

The Champions of **Reform** destroying the **Monster** of **Corruption**

Illustration 23 *In a cartoon of March 1831, King William IV looks on as "the Champions of Reform," led by Earl Grey, who is armed with a sword, strike down "the Monster of Corruption." Among the monster's heads are Sir Robert Peel (at the top) and the Duke of Wellington (second from the top). Reform did not happen quite as easily as this. ("The Champions of Reform Destroying the Monster of Corruption," 1831. © The Trustees of the British Museum)*

subsequently defeated on a hostile amendment. Grey asked the King for a new election, in order to strengthen his majority. His subsequent electoral success not only demonstrated the popularity of reform, but also illustrated a peculiar feature of the old system, which gave a strong advantage in general elections to a sitting ministry. A second reform bill easily passed the House of Commons, but the House of Lords voted it down in October. Supporters of reform reacted with anger and violence. Riots broke out in cities throughout England. In London, the house of the Duke of Wellington was attacked by a mob. Nottingham Castle was burned down. At Bristol, more than 100 buildings were torched, including the Customs House, the Lord Mayor's Mansion House and the Palace of the bishop, who had voted against reform. Troops were ordered to suppress the Bristol crowd, and more than 400 people were killed or wounded – the numbers have never been precisely known, because nobody in authority wanted to count them. Worried by the violence, the reformer Francis Place organized a National Political Union, with 6000 members, to counter the radical NUWC and encourage working class support for the Whig bill.

When a third version was presented to the House of Commons late in the year, King William agreed that he would create new peers to facilitate its passage through the House of Lords. This was not unprecedented: Queen Anne had done the same for Robert Harley in 1711, in order to secure passage of the Treaty of Utrecht. The moment of truth came, however, and the King flinched. He refused to create the new peers, so Grey resigned. Replying to the King with a slap in the face, the House of Commons voted in support of the outgoing ministers. Nobody knew it then, but the political authority of the Hanoverian monarchy had just suffered an irreparable blow. In May, King William asked the Duke of Wellington to form a government. As Wellington had been telling friends that reform "must lead to the total extinction of the power and property of this country," to choose him as chief minister was to announce that the reform bill was effectively dead.[17] Again, the public reacted, this time more peacefully. Attwood denounced the new government before crowds of up to 200,000 people at Birmingham. Francis Place set off a financial crisis by asking supporters of reform to cash in their securities at the Bank of England (his motto was "To stop the Duke, go for gold"). This was the point at which an autocracy might have emerged, perhaps a military regime under the Duke of Wellington. Conversely, there might have been a revolution. Neither happened, because few people really desired either option. After three days of trying to form a government, Wellington advised the King to recall Lord Grey, who was given a promise that new peers would be created. The House of Lords decided not to challenge him, and passed the bill. It was signed by the King on June 7, 1832, and became law.

The Great Reform Act, as it was known, disenfranchised 56 small English boroughs and reduced 31 others by one member (the small southwestern town of Weymouth had elected four MPs and lost two of them). Forty-one towns, including Manchester, Birmingham, Leeds, and Sheffield, gained representation, adding 63 new borough MPs to the House of Commons. Sixty-two new county seats were also created, either by adding a third member to existing counties or by subdividing larger counties. Wales added three county representatives and two for new boroughs. A separate Reform Act for Scotland, passed in July, created eight new burgh seats and regrouped the smaller burghs, while an Irish Reform Act in August added five new MPs. In all parts of the United Kingdom, a £10 voting franchise was to apply, but it included leasehold and other types of tenancies as well as freehold property. In general, middling men in towns throughout the United Kingdom could now vote, as could most farmers in Britain, but not those in Ireland, where holdings were smaller. Few members of the working classes could meet the £10 voting requirement. Depending on which estimates one uses, the electorate may have grown by 80 percent in England and Wales, from 366,000 to 653,000. In Scotland, it leaped from 4500 to 65,000, and even in Ireland, it increased from less than 50,000 to 90,000. This was not a democratic reform, and it is probable that a higher percentage of adult males in England and Wales could vote in 1700 than in 1833. Nevertheless, the Act represented a move towards democracy, because for the first time, the principle of representation by population had been acknowledged by Parliament.

The Whigs, who had defended their bill with admirable courage, were convinced that it would be the last reform of its kind. They were wrong. Further reform bills followed in 1867 and 1884, enfranchising artisans, urban workers, and rural laborers. It was not until 1918, however, that all adult males and women over 30 were given the vote, not until 1928 that the franchise was equalized for men and women. At that point, Britain became a democratic state. Corruption was not wiped out by the Reform Act, either. In some places, it became worse, as the ties of social deference declined and parties began to supply funds for local electioneering. Small boroughs were not eliminated, and continued to be manipulated by rich patrons. Nor did the Reform Act break the dominance of the landed classes in British politics. Although their numbers declined in the House of Commons, they continued to provide a majority of MPs for most of the nineteenth century. The House of Lords lost prestige through the fight over reform, but kept its veto power over legislation until 1911, and was not substantially reformed until the 1990s.

In spite of its shortcomings, the Great Reform Act was a momentous change. It put in question everything that had to do with the British constitution, including local government. Parliamentary reform was duly followed by Municipal Corporations Acts, two for the Scottish burghs in 1833, followed by one for England and Wales in 1835. These important Acts established elected corporations, based on a uniform £10 franchise, in all of the old borough towns of Great Britain. Urban areas that were not yet boroughs were allowed to petition for incorporation, which the major industrial cities promptly did. In some places, long-established oligarchies were broken overnight. The new town governments were not necessarily less corrupt or more efficient, but they were at least responsible to a broader electorate.

Although they had no clear plan, the Whigs were laying the foundations for a reformed British state. It had a symbolic birth when Parliament burned down in 1834, to be replaced by the building that stands today. The chief characteristics of the new state were active intervention in social problems, the extension of individual liberty, and an acceptance of minority religious views that verged at times on secularism. The Whigs addressed the nation's social problems with bureaucratic solutions, based on utilitarian principles. Emphasis was laid on efficiency and low cost, rather than humanitarianism. An 1833 Factory Act limited child labor to nine hours a day, backing the restriction up with a squad of inspectors. The Poor Law Amendment Act of 1834 instituted a uniform national system, designed to keep the indigent from starving while avoiding heavy expenses for ratepayers. "Outdoor" relief or payments to the able-bodied, as in the Speenhamland system, were abandoned in favor of "indoor" relief or workhouses, where men, women, and children were separated and required to perform menial labor. In every parish or union of parishes, the property owners who paid the poor rate were to elect a Board of Guardians to supervise the workhouse, levy the rates, and report to a national Poor Law Commission. The New Poor Law, as it was called, was a masterpiece of administrative logic that was heartily detested by the poor, and disliked by many ratepayers of the middling sort who saw it as removing their influence over local affairs.

If the Whigs believed in social engineering, they were also staunch defenders of liberty of conscience. Protestant Dissenters were allowed to marry in their own chapels, and the non-denominational University of London was chartered. From 1837, registers of births, marriages, and deaths were to be kept by the state rather than by parish churches. Church tithes on land, previously calculated as a percentage of produce, were commuted into money payments, but the issue of whether non-Anglicans should have to pay taxes to the Church of England would continue to rankle. The perception that the Whigs were hostile to the Church generated a strong reaction, called the Oxford Movement, whose clerical supporters defended traditional doctrines and denounced Whig reform as "national apostasy." The Oxford Tractarians, who published a series of religious pamphlets called *Tracts for the Times*, were horrified when the government abolished ten Anglican bishoprics in Ireland and tried to appropriate their revenues to state purposes. To them, it was evidence that the Church was once more in danger.

The Whig commitment to individual liberty was strong enough to bring about the abolition of slavery in most of the colonies. Yet they did nothing to improve the lives of freed slaves. Liberty, for the Whigs, meant freedom from illegitimate restraint, not from destitution. Liberal policy, moreover, did not rule out coercion when the interests of the state were threatened. The government dealt harshly, for example, with the problem of Irish law and order, responding to rural unrest with a coercion act that suspended *habeas corpus* and imposed martial law. In some respects, the reformed British state was not very different from its predecessor.

The Whig government was led until July 1834 by Earl Grey, who resigned after becoming depressed by Cabinet dissension. His successor was Viscount Melbourne, a former supporter of Canning. Gruff, cynical, and ruthless, Melbourne enjoyed a rakish reputation. The King soon tried to be rid of him, asking Sir Robert Peel (who had inherited his father's title in 1830) to form a ministry. Peel responded to the task with typical energy, issuing the first statement of conservative party doctrine, the Tamworth Manifesto. To save his beloved Church of England from further losses, he set up an Ecclesiastical Commission to plan its reorganization. A general election did not give Peel a majority, however, and he resigned in 1835, putting Melbourne back in office at the head of an alliance of Whigs, radicals, and Irish MPs. This was the last time in British history that a monarch would attempt to replace an obnoxious ministry that still had a majority in the House of Commons. The trick had worked for George III in 1783, 1801, and 1807, but failed for his son because royal influence could no longer insure success. King William complained that Melbourne was turning him into a mere cipher. Monarchs would gradually learn to play that role with better grace.

On June 20, 1837, King William IV died at Windsor Castle. He was remembered by one political insider, a bit unkindly, as "something of a blackguard and something more of a buffoon. It is but fair to his memory at the same time to say that he was a good-natured, kind hearted, and well-meaning man and he always acted an honourable and straitforward, if not always a sound and discreet, part."[18] His successor was his 19-year-old niece, Princess Victoria. Her birth had been due to the premature death of Princess Charlotte in 1817, which had caused Victoria's worried father, the Duke of Kent, to marry quickly in order to propagate the royal lineage. Victoria came to the throne as a representative of the House of Brunswick, but as a woman she could not succeed to the throne of Hanover, so the Hanoverian monarchy effectively ended with her uncle. The close partnership, amounting to complicity, between the King and his ministers, which had been the hallmark of British government under the first two Georges, and again from 1783 to 1812, had been dissolved by the inept sons of George III. William IV was the last king to attempt an exertion of his own prerogative against the wishes of the House of Commons. His failures in 1832 and 1835 were decisive. In any case, as a young woman, Victoria was treated differently from her predecessors. Melbourne was paternal to her, Peel a bit of a bully. The Queen outlasted both of them, and in 64 years of rule, she learned to demand deference from her chief ministers. In spite of her jealous guardianship of royal prerogatives, however, she would never behave in the autocratic manner of her grandfather and uncles. In this as in so many respects, the British state of the eighteenth century had given way to a new and more liberal regime.

20

A Class Society

Visitors to Britain from other countries are often struck by how frequently the subject of class division comes up in conversation. Britain's class system may or may not be more rigid or pervasive than that of any other country, but it is more talked about, even today. This fixation can be attributed partly to the survival of an aristocracy, partly to the development of a strong working class identity, but it also has to do with the length of time that class has been an accepted term of social analysis in Britain. The language of class began to catch on among Britons in the early nineteenth century, and it stuck.

Has it ever been the best description of reality? This is hard to determine. Before industrialization, nobody thought in terms of classes: instead, society was divided by inherited status, wealth, and occupation into a variety of social groups. The sum total of these groups was a hierarchy, and everybody knew where they stood in it. If we think of class as nothing more than a general way of describing the hierarchical ranking of social groups, then the term might be applied to almost any period of British history. By the early nineteenth century, however, people were starting to think of British society in terms of three classes, designated as upper, middle, and working, or landlords, capitalists, and laborers. Decades before Karl Marx, many social commentators believed that these classes were engaged in a struggle for dominance with one another, a struggle that had been set off by capitalism. This may not have been a very precise description of how society was structured, or of how it operated. The upper class was divided between aristocrats, gentry, and very wealthy business or banking families. The middle class encompassed everyone from merchants and industrialists to doctors, lawyers, farmers, and tradesmen. The working class included industrial laborers, farm workers, unskilled laborers of all varieties, as well as servants. The lines separating these classes were not always clear. People did not necessarily identify with the class to which they supposedly belonged, and they did not always feel resentment towards others because of class. It may be better to use a terminology of upper *classes*, middle *classes*, and working *classes* to express some of the diversity within each.

We can make too much of class. The economist John Stuart Mill warned about this as early as 1834, when he noted how British commentators "revolve in their eternal circle of landlords, capitalists and labourers, until they seem to think of the distinction of society in these three classes, as if it were one of God's ordinances, not man's, and as little under human control as the division of day and night."[1] We should think twice, however, before throwing out the whole idea of class. First, we should remember that class had some reality to Britons in the past, or it would not have remained a part of their ordinary vocabulary for so long. Second, Britons in the early nineteenth century *did* often act in unison with one another because they felt a common tie of class, whatever that may have meant to them. It is easy to find problems with the concept of class as a tool of historical explanation, but if we discard it altogether, we will have to ignore a great deal of British experience over the past two centuries.

Culture Wars?

One way of understanding class in Britain is as a cultural formation. A person is upper class because he or she acts and thinks a certain way, prefers certain ways of dressing, eating, socializing, etc. Culture is not random; it tends to convey specific messages about social groups. At the same time, it is not perfectly predictable or fixed – it changes over time, it can have individualized aspects, and not every expression of culture conveys the same message. We can certainly identify a culture of the upper classes in early nineteenth-century Britain. Middle class culture may be more difficult to separate, but historians have argued that it was taking on distinct features by the 1830s. Was a cultural conflict developing between the two classes?

If so, it was not an equal contest. Before the 1830s, the upper classes were able to dominate the private and the public social spaces of British culture, without serious competition from any other group. They partied, played, made love, and married within a sphere that was exclusive, although not totally closed. Readers of Jane Austen are familiar with the endless round of dances, dinners, and visits in splendid carriages that characterized the life of the upper classes in the countryside. Guests of the middle classes might be invited, but they were expected to observe social distinctions and not act above their station. Austen made gentle fun of the snobbery of her heroine Emma Woodhouse, who remarks with disapproval on a ball held by a wealthy family "of low origin, in trade, and only moderately genteel … [They] were very respectable, in their way, but ought to be taught that it was not for them to arrange the terms on which the superior families would visit them."[2] Emma's attitude was doubtless familiar to Austen's readers.

Many diversions of the upper classes were restricted to the wealthy and well connected. Peers and gentlemen reveled in the blood sports of fox hunting and pheasant shooting, which were legally permitted to landowners alone. They flocked to racecourses throughout England, where huge sums were won and lost on sleek-limbed horses. They might spend time with their families at Bath, which retained its position as a center for polite amusements and matchmaking, although the middling sort were gradually invading it. The coastal town of Brighton, enlivened by the presence of the Prince Regent, was another favorite resort for the upper classes. There, they could bathe, fully clothed, in sea water, which was regarded as beneficial for health.

The London season, with its plays and balls and spectacular parties, continued to be a magnet for the upper classes. A highly prized possession for a fashionable young man or woman was a voucher of admission to the weekly ball at Almack's, a suite of assembly rooms in St James's. Gentlemen had to wear knee breeches, and the Duke of Wellington himself was once turned out of the club for appearing in trousers. Another spot to see and be seen was the pleasure gardens at Vauxhall, a place the Prince Regent loved. Vauxhall was famous for elaborate illuminations, generated by gas lamps installed in the trees. The victory at Waterloo was celebrated with a dazzling display of 20,000 lights. The upper classes went to Vauxhall to show off their fashionably tight coats, low-cut dresses, and enormous hats, as well as to eat wafer-thin ham in exclusive supper boxes, while they watched fireworks or Indian jugglers or balloons ascending in the air. Vauxhall's entrance price was far too high for laboring people, but the middle classes regularly packed the place with up to 15,000 gawking visitors. However, the owners went bankrupt in 1840, and while the gardens reopened, they never attracted so fashionable a crowd. A chronicler later recalled of Vauxhall in the Regency period that "the evening costume of the company was elegant: head-dresses of flowers and feathers were seen in the promenade, and the entire place sparkled as did no other place of public amusement. But low prices brought low company."[3] Low company was one thing the upper classes could not tolerate. When the prices at Almack's went down after 1835, the elite simply stopped attending.

Gradually after 1830, the upper classes withdrew from many public spaces in London. The capital's rapid growth in size and wealth had brought with it a loss of exclusivity. In addition, public attention to upper class behavior was no longer welcomed, as it brought too much criticism. Private gentlemen's clubs, on the other hand, were thriving, because they offered upper class men an opportunity to drink and converse with others of the same background and social standing, without being observed by the public. Boodle's, White's, and Brooks's were the most celebrated clubs – the first even gave its name to a faction of landowners that staunchly upheld the Corn Laws. Later clubs, like Crockford's, were essentially gambling halls for the elite, where their passion for betting would not be noticed by their social inferiors. The growing desire for privacy among the upper classes, and their increasing aversion to public criticism, also affected the practice of dueling. Fighting duels in defense of honor remained common during the Regency period, although the practice was widely condemned. Viscount Castlereagh faced off in a duel against his rival George Canning in 1809, and the Duke of Wellington fought a duel as late as 1829. By the 1830s, however, dueling had become rare, except among army officers, and it was no longer dishonorable for a gentleman to refuse to fight one. This represented a significant cultural change, as the maintenance of honor by violence had once been a prerogative of the upper classes.

The sex lives of the elite had also attracted much negative comment during the Regency. Sexual antics among high born or wealthy men were nothing new, but

Illustration 24   *An evening at Vauxhall Gardens in 1820, from the illustrations by Robert and George Cruikshanks to Life in London by Pierce Egan. The book chronicles the adventures of two young men, Tom and Jerry, who move between high and low social circles in the capital. (Robert and George Cruikshank, "Tom, Jerry and Logic Making the Most of an Evening at Vauxhall Gardens," 1820. © Private Collection, The Stapleton Collection / The Bridgeman Art Library)*

they had never been as widely publicized as in the period after 1815. When the high-priced courtesan Harriette Wilson published her memoirs in 1825, it caused a sensation because she dared to name her many aristocratic lovers. They included the Duke of Wellington, whom she described, unflatteringly, as resembling a rat-catcher. Wilson offered to leave the names of her clients out of her book for a fee, to which Wellington is supposed to have replied, "Publish, and be damned." Wilson's memoirs went through no fewer than 30 editions. The cold breeze of respectability that blew through the 1830s made upper class men more careful to keep their sex lives out of the glare of publicity.

If the aristocracy and gentry were curbing their cultural exuberance, they were also losing some of their role in artistic production. Patronage of painters, sculptors, and architects had formerly been an upper class preserve, but changes had occurred in the visual arts. Painters were acting more independently. Those who objected to the tightly controlled elitism of the Royal Academy had formed their own societies. They could make a living from diverse sources, including print-making and exhibitions, without relying too much on high-born patrons. The two most notable English painters of the early nineteenth century, John Constable and J. M. W. Turner, were both Royal Academicians, who concentrated on idealized depictions of nature. Neither of them painted portraits, the bread-and-butter of high society artists. Constable sold few paintings – he lived off his wife's inheritance, and by giving lectures to artistic and scientific associations. Although he was a staunch conservative who deplored the Reform Act, Constable had no close ties to political figures. For his part, Turner depended intermittently on aristocratic patrons, but he also sold works to middle class industrialists, and he became famous by publicly exhibiting his large commemorative paintings, showing subjects like the battle of Trafalgar or the burning of Parliament. The great architect of the period, Sir John Soane, attracted few private clients. He mostly designed public buildings in London, including the Bank of England. After his death in 1837, he left his London house and its bizarre collections of artifacts to the nation, as a museum to be appreciated by all.

The market for literary works was wider than that for paintings or buildings, and British writers had already separated themselves from upper class patronage. Novelists remained fascinated with the upper classes, but tended to present them in ways that were appealing to middle class readers. Sir Walter Scott's series of *Waverley* novels, for example, were nostalgic evocations of Scottish history, full of brave knights and noble lairds. The American writer James Fenimore Cooper, who knew Scott, thought that "The bias of his feelings, his prejudices, I might almost say of his nature, is deference to hereditary rank."[4] Scott's sense of deference was on full display in 1822, when he was master of ceremonies during King George IV's magnificent state visit to Edinburgh. He virtually reinvented traditional Scottish culture, leading to one Scotsman's complaint that the novelist "has ridiculously made us appear to be a nation of Highlanders, and the bagpipe and the tartan are the order of the day."[5] Scott lived like an ancient laird on his estate at Abbotsford. Yet however idealized their depictions of the Scottish aristocracy may have been, Scott's novels were also exciting romances that sold to a broad public, and could be found on the bookshelves of many middle class homes.

Other writers of the period took a humorous view of the foibles of the upper classes. The heroines in Jane Austen novels are invariably connected to landed society, although occasionally, like Elizabeth Bennet in *Pride and Prejudice*, they are related to members of the middle classes, and their status is often in jeopardy due to inheritance laws that favor male heirs. Austen lightly mocked aristocratic pretense, and in her writings, high birth does not guarantee good character. Similarly, the novelist Maria Edgeworth satirized the Protestant landed elite of Ireland in books like *Castle Rackrent*, although she did so from the point of view of a woman who herself managed a decaying Irish estate. One of the few thoroughly middle class authors in Britain was Charles Dickens, whose first big success, the 1837 novel *Pickwick Papers*, dealt with the travels and adventures of a naive but lovable retired businessman, Samuel Pickwick. Dickens's heroes hardly ever represented the landed classes. This would have been unthinkable for a novelist of the eighteenth century.

The cultural leadership of the upper classes was starting to waver in the early nineteenth century. As it did, many observers began to note how the middle classes, a term that came into vogue around 1820, were beginning to push socially and politically against the landed elite that they had so long admired and imitated. This view was widely voiced in the debates about reform that raged from 1815 until the 1830s. Whig publicists even claimed that the middle classes had gained a moral superiority over the aristocracy and gentry, which entitled them to a part in government. In 1818, Sir James Mackintosh, a lawyer, historian, and Whig MP, wrote in the *Edinburgh Review* that "If we were compelled to confine all elective influence to one order, we must indeed vest it in the middling classes; both because they possess the largest share of sense and virtue, and because they have the most numerous connexions of interest with the other parts of society."[6] The idea that the middle ranks of society were morally superior to the aristocracy was an old one, but it was given new vitality after 1815, when the scandalous behavior of many leading members of the landed classes became notorious.

The perceived virtue and respectability of the middle classes was linked to evangelical Protestantism. Of course, there were pious and moral Christians among the upper classes, but evangelicalism had not made great headway among them. Insofar as we can identify a separate middle class culture in the early nineteenth century, it was to a large extent an evangelical culture, whether within the Church of England or outside it. The Anglican evangelical movement was estimated to include about 1000 clergymen in the early nineteenth century. Meanwhile, evangelical Dissent was expanding rapidly. The number of new licenses taken out for Dissenting chapels in England and Wales doubled in 1795–1808 as compared to the previous 20 years, and by 1811 Dissenting places of worship outnumbered Anglican ones by more than 1000. The Methodists became a separate religious denomination, under the authoritarian leadership of Reverend Jabez Bunting. Determined to make Methodism more socially acceptable, Bunting abandoned revivalism by itinerant preachers in favor of a settled, trained, and regularly ordained ministry. This strategy was highly successful in middle class areas, where worshippers wanted their minister to be called "Reverend" and to have the same status as an Anglican priest. A conservative stalwart as well as a paragon of middle class evangelical respectability, it is not surprising that Bunting was nicknamed "the Methodist Pope."

Within the middle classes, the group that was most often seen as being in conflict with the landed elite was the manufacturers. In the north of England and the Lowlands of Scotland, industrialization had created a group of local entrepreneurs – bankers and merchants as well as industrialists – whose culture was more or less distinct from that of the upper classes. Dissenters or Separatist Presbyterians in religion, they did not socialize with the landed elite or long for the lifestyles of the gentry. They saw hard work as the basis of their wealth, and took considerable satisfaction in their own success. The editor of the *Leeds Mercury*, the local newspaper of a northern industrial town, boasted in 1821 that "Never in any country beneath the sun, was an order of men more estimable and valuable, more praised and praiseworthy."[7] Within their provincial communities, these bankers, merchants, and manufacturers exercised considerable influence, even if they seldom ran for election to Parliament. They dominated civic improvement commissions and were active in moral causes like the temperance movement, which was directed against strong drink. The offspring of highly successful middle class families might be educated in public schools, conform to the Church of England, buy landed estates, and separate themselves from business, but relatively few reached this level of wealth and prestige.

On a local level, the middle classes were crucial to cultural promotion. The attorney and banker William Roscoe, for example, strove to make his native Liverpool into a center of high culture. A Unitarian and a strong opponent of the slave trade, Roscoe became a notable poet, art historian, and collector of paintings. For a time, he lived like a gentleman on a country estate, but when his bank failed and he was financially ruined, Roscoe moved to a smaller house in town, where he continued to promote the arts. In 1817, he helped to found a Royal Institution for adult education in Liverpool. Roscoe imagined in his poems "some industrious man, whose prudent mind, / To business is in earlier years inclin'd," but who "quits the chace" when older, and finally "Feels genuine taste." Such men were raising Liverpool to cultural greatness, so that "The ARTS have chosen here their blest retreat."[8] While Roscoe's efforts were exceptional, similar stories of the advancement of culture by middle class patrons can be found throughout Britain.

The middle classes were also having a big impact on the culture of consumption. Although they still tended to imitate the tastes of their social superiors, they were consuming on such a large scale that they were overtaking the upper classes as the main market for luxury goods. The increasing size and range of shops in the early nineteenth century is a sign of this change. Huge shopping emporia could be found in London by the 1820s, selling everything from lighting to books – the "Temple of the Muses" was a bookshop so big that a coach and six horses could be driven around its circular sales counter. Another example of the growing significance of a middle class buying public is provided by Staffordshire pottery. In the eighteenth century, Josiah Wedgwood's dinner wares had been aimed at upper class clients. He kept his prices high, and prided himself on fine services produced for Queen Charlotte or the Empress of Russia. By the early nineteenth century, the Wedgwood Company and other producers of high-end ceramics were facing a host of low-end competitors in the pottery towns of Staffordshire, who made cheap copies of their designs for a middle class audience. Some of these nameless factories were producing semi-original works of their own, including the famous Staffordshire figurines that adorned many Victorian mantelpieces. Slowly, the high-end makers began to offer lower-priced items. While refined taste continued to be associated with the upper classes, it was the marketability of such taste among the middle classes that made profits for the pottery industry.

It may be an exaggeration to imagine a "culture clash" between the upper and middle classes in the early nineteenth century. Tensions existed, especially over free trade or Parliamentary reform, but in general the middle classes were far less concerned about overturning the elite than they were about separating themselves from those who were lower down on the social scale. A middle class exodus to the suburbs of British cities began in the early nineteenth century. Urban centers were increasingly left to the poor, or in the case of London, were divided between extremely wealthy, upper class districts and destitute slums. The social distance between London's West End and East End was, and remains, a glaring illustration of class stratification in modern Britain. The middle classes of the capital would move further and further away from the city center in the course of the nineteenth century, as omnibuses, railways, and finally the Underground (the subway system) allowed them to commute to work. The raw mixture of social groups that seethes through Hogarth's depictions of mid-eighteenth-century London had now become a faint, disreputable memory.

Workers, Trade Unions, and Socialism

The most striking social development of the early nineteenth century was a growing awareness among industrial laborers that they belonged to a separate and distinct group. Until the 1820s, they usually referred to themselves in general terms as "Workers" or as "the Artisans, Mechanicks and Labouring Classes," but the expression "working classes" had become widespread by 1831, when it appeared in the literature of numerous Parliamentary reform organizations. Whether laborers of all types, men as well as women, skilled as well as unskilled, should be counted in the working classes, or whether it included only male "mechanics" who worked in factories, depended on the context in which the term was used.

Most industrial workers continued to toil in their own homes, or in workshops. They were paid rates for each piece of material that they produced, rather than straightforward wages. The piece-rates fluctuated a great deal depending on the ups and downs of the economy. The effects of bad economic times were passed on to workers rather than absorbed by their bosses. In the 1820s, for example, metal workers in Birmingham were expected to give a discount on their products to employers, because trade conditions were poor. Rent on equipment and the cost of raw materials were deducted from piece-rates, so that a Nottingham frame-work knitter earning 13 shillings and 6 pence per week in 1811 might end up with 4 shillings less because of the cost of coal, candles, frame rental, etc. Half the factory workers in Britain were paid piece-rates, and were subject to various types of deductions. Skilled male factory workers in the cotton industry earned relatively good wages, up to almost 23 shillings a week. Far lower wages were paid to women, who earned less than 10 shillings weekly, and to children under 11, who might take home a couple of shillings (girls were usually given a penny more than boys, to encourage them to stay in the factory). Older workers were offered much lower wages than those in their thirties. Variations in industrial wages were extreme, so it is hard to make generalizations about standards of living based on earnings. However, for the majority of workers, living close to the edge of poverty, the bad economic years – 1816, 1819, 1826–7, 1830–1 – were devastating.

The most hard-hit trades in a recession were those that could not count on steady, long-term employment, and those in which wages were falling. The saddest example of both was the handloom weavers, who worked at home for piece-rates.

In the late eighteenth century, the growth in the textile industry due to factory-based spinning had caused the numbers of hand-loom weavers to swell, and their incomes to rise, so that many of them were earning 25 shillings a week. Employers hired more and more of them, driving down piece-rates. By 1831, there were over 250,000 handloom weavers in Britain, but their wages were tumbling, and competition from factory weaving was about to ruin them. Unable to compete with cheaper, factory-woven products, handloom weavers saw their wages fall in the 1830s to the starvation level of 5 shillings a week or less. They gained the nickname "poverty knockers." The reformer Richard Oastler wanted to rescue them by fixing their wages in 1834. When asked by a Parliamentary select committee if, by doing so, he was prepared to put an end to the freedom of labor, Oastler replied that "I would put an end to the freedom to murder, and ... to any thing which prevents the poor man from getting a good living by fair and reasonable work."[9] The bill for a minimum wage failed due to opposition from employers, however, and over the next two decades, the number of handloom weavers fell by 90 percent.

Housing for laboring people had never been particularly good, but in the industrial districts of the early nineteenth century, it was beginning to deteriorate badly. The causes were simple: as industry grew, more and more people were living in cramped conditions, without basic conveniences. The coal-miners of northeast England increased in numbers from 12,000 in 1800 to 33,000 in 1844. Houses for the pitmen were provided by mine owners in villages near the mines, but they were so badly built that one observer described them as "on the whole the worst and dearest of which any large specimens can be found in England." This was ascribed to "the high number of men in one room, the smallness of the ground plot on which a great number of houses are thrust, the want of water, the absence of privies, and the frequent placing of one house on top of another."[10] Urban lodging for industrial workers often followed the same pattern. In Manchester and Birmingham, laboring people were crammed into tenements built around a central courtyard, with a gutter down the middle to carry out waste and sewage. These places were perfect breeding-grounds for disease, especially cholera, which ravaged the industrial districts of England in 1831–2. Almost 700 people died of cholera in one metal-working town, Bilston near Birmingham. Even in normal times, life expectancy in the slums of industrial cities was low. In 1840, almost 60 percent of working class children born in Manchester died under the age of five.

Did the harsh life experiences of working people in industrial areas create a sense of class solidarity? Perhaps, but outward expressions of class awareness usually required additional factors: namely, ideas that could organize and mobilize large numbers of people. The most important of these ideas in the early nineteenth century were trade unionism, socialism, and respectability. Trade unions originated in the eighteenth century as clubs or friendly societies, springing up mainly among textile workers. Their chief purpose was to limit the number of apprentices who could join a trade, so that wages would not be forced down by a growing number of hands. The government was not sympathetic to them. The Combination Acts of 1799 and 1800 outlawed any union of workers in restraint of trade, and in 1814 the Elizabethan statute requiring apprenticeships in skilled trades was repealed by Parliament. These measures would propel large numbers of skilled workers into illegal unionism, in order to protect their trades against unskilled competition. Friendly societies continued to exist legally after 1800, but their unionizing activities were mostly secret, as they were liable to prosecution. The repeal of the Combination Acts in 1824 led to a sudden upsurge in trade union organization. Between 1829 and 1832, national unions were formed for the spinners, potters, and builders. Membership was restricted to men, who paid into a central fund that would support them with small weekly payments when they went on strike. The male spinners encouraged women to form their own union, but this would not happen for many years.

The concept of a general union of all trades was promoted by the radical supporters of Robert Owen. He was not a laborer; on the contrary, he was a wealthy cotton manufacturer of Welsh origins who had turned his mill at New Lanark in Scotland into a model of philanthropy, with decent housing, medical care, and provisions for workers' education. Owen dreamed of founding cooperative communities where everyone would be equal and everything would be shared. His ideas were called socialist or communist, terms which did not have very precise meanings in the early nineteenth century. Owen founded cooperative societies to sell goods, versions of which still exist throughout Britain and America. The object of his socialism was, in the words of *The Poor Man's Guardian*, a newspaper that supported him, "the sublimest that can be conceived, namely – to establish for the productive classes a complete dominion over the fruits of their own industry."[11] In other words, socialism would restore to the worker the full value of his or her labor, part of which was now "stolen" by the employer as profit. Owen did not believe in class conflict, however; he actually wanted workers and employers to collaborate in forming "national companies of production," which would "exchange their products with each another upon a principle of equitable exchange of labour for a fair equal value of labour."[12]

In 1833 at London, Owen and his followers formed a Grand National Consolidated Trade Union to promote these goals. It was organized on the pattern of Freemasonry, with local lodges, grand lodges, and a Grand Council of Delegates elected by the central committees of the lodges. Viewed with suspicion by the existing trade unions, the GNCTU was not very successful, but it would play a part in the formation of the London Working Men's Association in 1837. Out of that society came the People's Charter, a document demanding universal suffrage, equal electoral districts, annual Parliaments, and a secret ballot. The Chartist movement of 1837–48 tried three times to persuade Parliament to pass the People's Charter, failing on each attempt. Chartism became the largest working class organization that had yet been seen in Britain.

Owenite socialism was often derided by later radicals, including Karl Marx, as "utopian," muddle-headed, and too moderate. Yet it possessed a remarkable vitality. Idealistic in tone and vague in its practical aims, it attracted a social mixture of skilled artisans, factory workers, middle class feminists who sought equality for women, and even a few evangelicals who founded a "Communist Church." Owen himself was intellectually restless, and he ended up believing in Spiritualism, a final expression of his longing for a perfect world. Throughout his career, Owen consistently upheld the inherent goodness of human beings, which he thought would lead them to choose equality and collaboration over exploitation and conflict.

The third idea that helped to form working class solidarity was respectability, meaning behavior consistent with conventional moral and religious principles. It was not an inherently radical idea, and it has often been overlooked by those who want to emphasize the revolutionary potential of the working classes. Yet the leaders of working class movements were often just as concerned with it as they were with trade union organization or socialism. Respectability was a recurring theme in the autobiography of Francis Place, the radical tailor of London. The district in which he grew up, he recalled, contained "much that was low vulgar and dissolute. … Want of Chastity in the girls was common, and was hardly a matter of reproach." Fifty years later, Place was pleased to record, this had all changed. "Scarcely can any lads … now be found who are either thieves or low blackguards. … Want of Chastity … is as rare as it was common. In nothing has the change for the better been greater than in the moral conduct and the increase of knowledge … amongst this class of persons."[13] Place was a skilled artisan, not an industrial worker, but similar attitudes were spreading among workers in industrial districts, particularly those who belonged to trade unions.

Methodism contributed greatly to the growing working class preoccupation with respectability. Laboring folk often joined splinter movements that were not part of the mainstream Methodist connection, like the Primitive Methodists. They upheld a strict moral code that condemned swearing, drunkenness, and fornication. They were also strongly opposed to rowdy games and pastimes. It was observed in 1840 that "in the manufacturing districts, where the Methodists have gained most influence … they have helped to expel an immense quantity of dog-fighting, cock-fighting, bull-baiting, badger-baiting and such blackguard amusements."[14] For generations, clergymen and moralists of the upper and middling classes had tried to stamp out these violent but popular recreations, in vain. Dog-fights and bull-baiting began to die out when a segment of the working classes turned against them.

Francis Place connected respectability with education. The spread of working class education had come about largely through the efforts of the churches and of middle class philanthropists. Church of England Sunday Schools, which became widespread in the late eighteenth century, stressed basic literacy along with a message of piety, morality, and obedience to social superiors. More innovative was the system devised by the Quaker educational reformer Joseph Lancaster, which used older pupils, or monitors, to educate and discipline their juniors. Lancaster gained the admiration of King George III and several prominent politicians, although he was accused by High Church Anglicans of having stolen the ideas of a Church of England clergyman, Andrew Bell. Both Lancaster and Bell wanted working class boys and girls to become loyal subjects, morally upright Christians, and uncomplaining laborers, not trade unionists or socialists. Once literacy was achieved, however, there was no way to predict what its consequences would be.

Illustration 25   *Another illustration by the Cruikshanks from Pierce Egan,* Life in London, *this time depicting a working class tavern. Notice the black sailors. With its brawls and gambling, heavy drinking and prostitution, Francis Place would certainly not have judged it to be respectable. (Tom and Jerry "Masquerading it" among the Cadgers in the "Back Slums" © Topfoto)*

Religion, education, and morality were supposed to set the respectable working class family apart from what was seen as a "dangerous" underclass of drunkards, criminals, and prostitutes. The common denominators of grinding poverty and crowded living conditions, however, meant that rough and respectable culture were never entirely separate. Besides, respectability was not a secure state: the Methodist saint of today could be the fallen sinner of tomorrow. Yet while his soul might always be in danger, the working class man who kept to the straight and narrow path felt no inferiority to the upper class libertine. By claiming moral rectitude, in fact, a working man or woman could sometimes gain the courage to stand up to those above them. Respectability can be criticized as an attempt to tame the radical impulses of the workers by forcing them to imitate the values of the middle classes, but it should also be recognized as an effort on the part of working people to assert their own equality with those who ruled their lives.

Rural Rides

Few social theorists of the nineteenth century believed that rural laborers formed a class. They were too isolated from one another, too diverse in their experiences, too lacking in access to the ideas that could give them a sense of class awareness or solidarity. In the early nineteenth century, however, many rural laborers responded to economic hardship in much the same way as industrial workers: that is, they protested and began to organize. Because their efforts largely failed, their condition was ignored by radical leaders who felt that the future belonged to industry.

One radical who did not ignore them was William Cobbett, the most widely read radical journalist of his day. A farmer himself, Cobbett made a series of journeys through southeastern England in the early 1820s, which he wrote about in a book entitled *Rural Rides*. Cobbett was an obsessive and slightly paranoid individual, who blamed all the nation's woes on the "Pitt system" that benefited "tax-eaters," that is, government officials. He railed against stock-jobbers, Jews, and Quakers. As a direct observer of agricultural change, however, Cobbett could be insightful. He noted that a good deal of enclosure was "misapplied" to waste lands that could not easily be improved, and he bemoaned "a great dilapidation and constant pulling down or falling down of houses" in the countryside. He witnessed terrible poverty in several of the counties through which he rode. "Why do not farmers now *feed* and *lodge* their work-people, as they did formerly?" he asked rhetorically. "Because they cannot keep them *upon so little* as they give them in wages." Convicts and slaves, Cobbett claimed, ate better than English laborers, who were "thin, ragged, shivering, dejected mortals, such as never were seen in any other country upon earth." At less than £23 a year, a farm laborer did not earn even half of what Cobbett thought was needed to supply bread, bacon, and beer to a family, let alone pay the rent. "Monstrous state of things!" he exclaimed.[15] Most laboring families did not starve – to stay alive, they grew their own produce on garden plots. Their condition was nonetheless dire.

The gradual disappearance of smallholdings was one cause of rural poverty. The 1830s would later be remembered as the last period when small-scale, independent farmers could be found in many English villages. Enclosure may at first have benefited them, but over time they were not able to compete with the enlarged and improved farms of the bigger tenants or the landlords. A second cause of poverty was the decline of home spinning, a traditional way for rural women to supplement the family income. Home spinning collapsed everywhere as factory spinning expanded in northern England, leaving southern women without alternative employment. Meanwhile, rents were rising constantly, while rural wages, which had increased up to around 1810, were falling sharply thereafter. Many laborers were employed for only part of the year, and when out of work, depended on the poor rates for survival. The situation was generally worse in the south of England than in the north, where the lure of industry kept the wages of rural laborers higher. It seems shocking that, in the most prosperous nation on earth, the largest single group of laborers would be kept in such a state of destitution.

Along with economic privation came the disintegration of rural communities. The social and cultural bonds that had linked landlords, farmers, and laborers were falling apart in many villages. One sign of this was the decline of customary rights like gleaning, which allowed the poor to pick up stubble after a field of grain had been harvested. Another sign was the disappearance of village celebrations such as morris dancing or the harvest home, when employers and workers shared a big meal at the close of the harvest. Some customs died out more slowly.

"Lifting" or "heaving" took place around Easter in the English north and Midlands. Men would lift women into the air on one day; women would lift men the next. Clergymen and landowners were regularly seized and lifted, often against their will. By allowing a brief reversal of sexual and social roles, such rituals contributed to the harmony of the rural community. As they faded, so did a sense of social integration.

Farm laborers periodically reacted to the decline of their economic security with anonymous threatening letters or isolated acts of violence. In the last two months of 1830, individual protests welled up into a remarkable movement that caused hundreds of incidents throughout southern England. Laborers met to demand higher wages, lower rents, and reduction of the tithes paid to the Church of England. They attacked, verbally and physically, farmers, landowners, overseers of the poor, JPs, and parish ministers. They set fire to hay-ricks and destroyed threshing machines, which separated grains from stalks by passing them through rollers. Threatening letters were dispatched, bearing the signature of the mysterious "Captain Swing," a rural cousin of Ned Ludd. "This is to acquaint you," one of them read, "that if your thrashing Machines are not destroyed by you directly we shall commence our labours / signed on behalf of the whole / Swing." Another was more blunt and poetic: "Revenge for thee is on the Wing, / From thy determined Capt. Swing." The threshing machines, which were not very efficient, may have been symbolic targets of an anger that was mainly caused by poverty and worsening economic times. "Our complaint is that we have not a suficient maint[en]ance to suport our famleys," wrote one group of laborers in Sussex.[16] The disturbances were suppressed by troops. Nineteen men were hanged, and almost 500 convicted rioters, including two women, were transported to Australia.

The Swing riots were followed by the first attempt to organize farm workers into a trade union. George Loveless, a Methodist lay preacher, founded the Friendly Society of Agricultural Labourers at Tolpuddle, Dorset in 1833. Their main grievance was low wages. To join the union, workers had to pass through an initiation ceremony, probably borrowed from Freemasonry, that included swearing an oath. A spy soon betrayed them, and six members of the Society were condemned to transportation under an Act against "unlawful oaths." Other trade unions campaigned in support of the Tolpuddle "martyrs," which led the Whig government to speed up their transportation. Soon repenting, it issued a pardon to the men in 1838. The next concerted attempt to unionize farm laborers came in the 1870s. The failure to introduce trade unions among them suggests that rural workers did not share the same economic or political attitudes as their industrial counterparts, but it does not mean that they felt no solidarity with one another.

The English system of agriculture was established in the Lowlands of Scotland before 1830, but there as in the north of England, the presence of industry kept wages relatively high. In the Highlands, however, commercial farming was tearing up the fabric of rural society. As Highland landowners converted from cattle raising to sheep farming, the extensive grazing lands that had been open to members of the clan were broken up into sheep-raising estates. The clansmen and their families were evicted in what became known as the Highland Clearances. Smallholdings called "crofts" were established for them on the coasts, where they raised potatoes and gathered kelp or seaweed, used in manufacturing soap and glass. On the Sutherland estate, between 6000 and 10,000 people were relocated to crofting settlements between 1807 and 1821. The crofters, however, did not have enough land to support themselves, and had to hire out their labor to the landowners, for at least 200 days a year according to one estimate. The old bonds of Highland lordship were broken, and the proud clansmen became rural laborers, living in extreme poverty and dependence. When the potato blight fell on them in the 1840s, some would starve to death.

The potato also became the basis of Irish peasant agriculture in the early nineteenth century. The smallest tenants or "cottiers," living in mud huts on tiny plots of land with no security of tenure, proliferated in the western parts of the island. They were sustained by potatoes, which could grow even in damp, peaty soils. In Ulster and around Dublin, by contrast, a wheat farming system of the English type had developed, with a hierarchy of landlords, farmers, and farm laborers. Irish wheat farming prospered in the early nineteenth century, as did textile production, and the island's population steadily rose from around five million in 1800 to more than eight million in 1841. By then, however, the cotton and wool industries were teetering due to English competition, and only the linen trade of Ulster continued to thrive. English demand for Irish wheat remained strong, but this meant that food was removed from local markets. Meanwhile, the smallest holdings were continually subdivided as the families of cottiers grew. After all, was it not obvious that even a minuscule plot of soggy land could grow potatoes? The conditions for a horrendous disaster – the Irish potato famine of 1845–9 – were being laid. Human mistakes and inhumane responses would make it one of the worst tragedies in European history.

Were smallholders inevitably doomed by the advance of agrarian capitalism? In other developing parts of the world, small proprietors did not always suffer the same grim fate that befell them in the British Isles. Because land in Britain was concentrated in the hands of relatively few owners with absolute property rights, however, the farming system changed radically in ways that crushed smallholders. Before the introduction of mechanized techniques, agricultural improvement often depended on smallholders being forced into an expanding workforce of poorly paid farm laborers. The government did nothing to relieve small proprietors of the burdens of tithes and taxes. In a less aristocratic society, or under a more democratic government, they might have been better protected. The problem for smallholders may not have been that British agriculture was modernized; instead, British society may not have been modernized fast enough.

Gender, Family, and Domesticity

Social class shaped, and was shaped by, relations between men and women, parents and children. Class divisions were rooted in family practices, and in turn, gender roles and household structures differed according to class. During the early nineteenth century, a middle class ideal of the perfect household – with a patriarchal father, a mother devoted to her offspring, and children raised to be moral and obedient – seeped through all social classes, with various results for masculine and feminine roles.

Among the upper classes, masculinity was traditionally connected with the duties of lordship, as well as with habits like dueling, blood sports, and service in the military. By the 1830s, lordship was in decline, dueling and blood sports were under attack by moralists, ladies took part in fox hunting, and there was no new war on the horizon. Traditional upper class manliness began to seem rather old-fashioned and out of place. One answer to this was to reinvent tradition. A movement to restore knightly chivalry began in these years, inspired in part by the novels of Sir Walter Scott. It would culminate in recreations of jousting tournaments and the building of huge country houses that resembled medieval castles. If the aristocrat could not be a real knight on horseback, he could at least imitate the valor and piety of his ancestors. Public schools for upper class boys, which were reformed in the early nineteenth century, inculcated doctrines of "muscular Christianity" through strict discipline, daily chapel services, and an emphasis on organized sports.

Upper class women could not hope to gain much freedom from reviving the values of the Middle Ages. During the Regency period, however, a few examples of unbridled female sexual behavior had provoked a strong moral reaction against women who flaunted convention. After 1820, the frivolity of the Regency was rejected by writers on female manners and conduct, in favor of strict chastity, religious piety, and submission to fathers or husbands. By the 1830s, James Fenimore Cooper found Englishwomen of the elite classes to be "punctiliously polite" and with "less nature about them" than Americans. "All their conduct is rigidly regulated," he noted.[17] Yet he admired them as wives and mothers. The raising of virtuous children had in fact become the chief goal of the upper class wife. Paradoxically, few spent much time interacting with their offspring, who were actually raised by governesses. Discipline was left to fathers, and it tended to be physical. Flogging children for misbehavior was an acceptable practice. Upper class boys continued to be beaten mercilessly at school, for every type of infraction. No wonder many of them developed a sadomasochistic delight in flogging, which was referred to in Europe as "the English vice."

Arranged marriages were becoming less common among the upper classes. Instead, spouses were chosen through a complicated series of social contacts, personal interactions, fact-gathering interviews, and consultations with family members, a process familiar to any reader of Jane Austen's novels. Mutual attraction was still regarded as a poor basis for a secure marriage, but Austen was sardonic about how this stricture was applied: "When any two young people take it into their heads to marry, they are pretty sure by perseverance to carry their point, be they ever so poor, or ever so imprudent, or ever so little likely to be necessary to each other's ultimate comfort."[18] She was exaggerating. Not many members of the upper classes married for love alone, or ended up with "unsuitable" spouses. Money, property, and titles remained powerful means of attraction in the process of finding a partner.

While personal happiness was increasingly pointed to as a goal of upper class marriage, nothing was done to change the physical abuse of married women. It is impossible to guess at the extent of wife-beating in the upper classes, but the unpleasant subject was raised in the celebrated trials of Caroline Norton. A poet and close friend of the Whig leader Lord Melbourne, Norton was married to an abusive Tory barrister whose brother was a peer. A particularly harsh beating caused her to miscarry her fourth child. After leaving her husband in 1836, she lost everything to him: her money, her clothing, her letters, and her children. As a woman, she had no legal existence separate from that of her husband, and she could not sue him for divorce, although her husband took an unsuccessful legal action against her friend Melbourne for alleged adultery. Using a male pseudonym, Caroline Norton wrote pamphlets calling for changes in the law, underlining the "strange and appalling fact" that "no degree of tyranny or brutality, nor the most gross and open infidelity on the part of the husband, is understood to bar his power to take his children from his wife."[19] In 1839, Parliament passed an Act allowing women to sue for custody of young children. Reform of the laws governing divorce and married women's property, however, would take decades longer.

Middle class masculinity differed from that of the upper classes in its general aversion to violence. Men of the middle classes did not engage in duels or ride to hounds, and evangelical religion filled many of them with a horror of blood sports. Middle class opinion encouraged the Whig government to pass a Cruelty to Animals Act in 1835 that outlawed many popular blood sports, although fox hunting, the beloved pastime of the upper classes, remained exempt until the early twenty-first century. Manliness among the middle classes consisted mainly of leadership within the family and success in one's business or occupation. According to the writers of conduct books, the authority of the middle class husband and father was not to be challenged, because it rested on the strongest foundations. "There cannot, indeed, be a sight more uncouth," stated the female author of an advice manual for young women in 1815, "than that of a man and his wife struggling for power; for where it ought to be invested [i.e. in the man], nature, reason and scripture concur to declare."[20] Men were expected to exercise discipline over their households, by reason if possible, by force if necessary. Wife-beating in middle class families is hard to discover, but it was certainly not unknown, and the flogging of children was common. Yet the warmth of evangelical piety in middle class families often gave a strong glow to marital love. The men and women of the middle classes married for affection and companionship, which were idealized in the poetry and novels that they read. Of course, a sound financial basis could serve to strengthen emotional ties, and marital connections remained important in building a business.

Femininity among the middle classes was focused on the domestic scene of household management and the raising of children. A middle class woman's place was not in the world outside, but within the confines of the home. The physical tasks of cooking and cleaning were performed by servants in most middle class households, but the mistress of the house was expected to make sure that everything ran smoothly and that order was maintained. Motherhood placed her in a role that was exalted as saintly or angelic by contemporary writers. Like the Virgin Mary, the middle class mother was seen as utterly detached from sexuality. Chaste before marriage, she accepted sex within marriage as necessary for procreation. This glorification of mothers had cultural roots in sentimental literature and religious evangelicalism, but the ideal did not necessarily carry over into practice. Private diaries and medical literature suggest that middle class women were not as uninterested in sex as advice manuals thought they should be. As for female withdrawal from the public sphere, this too was not absolute. Involvement in business affairs by wives may have been less common among the middle classes in the nineteenth century than it had been earlier, but women often assisted in the entrepreneurial efforts of their husbands. It was considered shocking for a respectable woman to take an active part in the daily routine of business, just as it would have been shocking for her to vote or preach or take part in any other public activity. Yet there were some women, usually widows, who loaned money or owned enterprises, and many women who ran shops.

In contrast to the middle classes, masculinity among the urban laboring classes was traditionally associated with violent sports, such as bare-fisted boxing, cudgeling or the free-for-all game of stoolball. The British soldiers who withstood murderous volleys of musket and cannon fire in Spain and at Waterloo had been molded by such brutal concepts of what it meant to be a man. Male apprentices in urban areas were particularly notorious for heavy drinking, aggressive sexuality, and youthful bravado. Francis Place remembered with some embarrassment how as a young apprentice he had frequented Cock and Hen Clubs, gatherings held at alehouses that lined the Thames, where "The amusements were drinking – smoking – swearing – and singing flashy songs ... the boys and girls paired off by degree 'till by twelve o'clock none remained."[21] He did not need to explain what happened next.

Young women of the urban laboring classes mixed freely with men, worked for wages, and were not always shunned by their communities for experiencing sexual relations before marriage. Informal unions remained common among laboring folk, and separation from a spouse was not treated as scandalous. A London woman asked a magistrate for a separation in 1801 because "in the absence of her husband, which frequently happened for some considerable time, she did very well, and got forward, but whenever he returned, he beat her, spent her money, and threatened her life."[22] Her case may be contrasted with that of Caroline Norton, who could not obtain a legal divorce from her violent husband. The working class wife probably obtained her separation, but this should not lead us to conclude that it was always easy for women of the laboring classes to escape from a bad marriage. Wife-beating was at least as widespread among laboring families as among other sections of the population, and extreme violence by working class husbands might even be prosecuted in the courts.

By the early nineteenth century, the influence of evangelicalism and the rise of respectability were making deep inroads into the working class understanding of gender, especially in industrial areas. Apprenticeship declined, unemployment became a typical affliction, and women began to compete with men for jobs in industry. The perception that working class masculinity was threatened led some to adopt the domestic ideals of the middle classes, which made the husband into a sober, peaceable, patriarchal lord and relegated wives to the private sphere of child-rearing and household chores. The advocates of working class domesticity placed a particularly high value on female chastity. Francis Place was preoccupied by the subject, writing that while sex before marriage was common in his youth, by the 1830s "A tradesmans daughter that would misconduct herself [by having sexual relations before marriage] would be abandoned by her companions, and probably by her parents."[23] He thoroughly approved of this treatment, as he identified lack of chastity with the savage manners of bygone days.

Families that lived in poverty, however, often found it impossible to maintain the values of domesticity, because women and children had to work outside the home, and households were subjected to periodic disruptions. Clergymen and middle class observers frequently decried the drunkenness and wife-beating that they linked with family life among the poor, and were horrified by the persistence of loose sexual morality. One shocked visitor to the coal mines of northern England recorded how "These gloomy and loathsome caverns are made the scenes of the most bestial debauchery. If a man and a woman meet in them, and are excited by passion at the moment, they indulge in it."[24] This may have been a middle class fantasy, but the young women employed in coal mines, usually to haul carts of ore, were probably less fixated on chastity than the tradesman's daughter of Francis Place's imagination. Through the New Poor Law of 1834, the government gave working class women reason to ponder the consequences of sex. Before the 1830s, if an unmarried woman bore a child, she could identify its father before a magistrate, who had the authority to compel the father to contribute to its support, so that it would not become dependent on the poor rates. If the father did not wish to be fined, the parish would pay for the couple to be married. The New Poor Law, however, obliged unmarried mothers to move into workhouses, and required nothing at all from fathers. Punishing the mother was seen by reformers as just, for as one Whig politician put it, "though want of chastity was a crime, a sin in a man, it was still greater in a woman, whose error corrupted society at its very root."[25] The so-called "bastardy clause" was bitterly resented by the poor, but did little to reduce the level of illegitimate births.

Rural laboring families shared many of the problems of urban workers. Older concepts of gender may have lasted longer in the countryside than in the town, and middle class ideals of domesticity may have spread more slowly. In many villages, the parish church or the Methodist chapel exerted a strong influence on the behavior of laboring people, but this did not prevent a rise in illegitimate births, the continuing popularity of cohabitation (nicknamed "living tally"), or the persistence of practices that were hardly in accordance with strict religious beliefs. The rural custom of the "wife sale," a kind of plebeian divorce ceremony, was one such survival. By her own consent, a wife was brought to market by her husband, wearing a halter, and was auctioned off to the highest bidder – almost always her lover, who had agreed beforehand to make a bid. The practice demonstrates the independence of rural folk from legal strictures, but it also shows how much humiliation a woman in the countryside might have to endure in order to free herself from an unwanted husband.

A few female radicals in the 1830s and 1840s advocated equality between the sexes and the abolition of patriarchal family relations. Most of these early feminists came from middle class backgrounds, but they adhered to the socialism of Robert Owen and tried to preach to working class audiences. They were deeply opposed to the values of domesticity, and critical of evangelical piety. "The efforts woman makes to emancipate herself from domestic thralldom and the slavery of superstition," one of them stated in 1842, "are ... chilled and depressed by priestly power and the tyranny of custom."[26] Through the Owenite feminists, alternative ways of thinking about gender were emerging in the early nineteenth century, but they did not make a big dent on the advance of the ideals of domesticity, which would characterize the Victorian family. For better or worse, we are still wedded to versions of those ideals today.

21

Imperial Portraits

The British empire in 1815 was one of the largest and most far-flung empires ever seen in history. It included fur-trading posts strung across the vast North American interior; the wheat-fields of Upper and Lower Canada; the Atlantic Maritime colonies with their bustling little ports; a glistening string of sugar islands in the Caribbean; the Cape of Good Hope at the tip of southern Africa; vast territories, encompassing many diverse peoples, in southern, central, and northeast India; and the convict settlement in Australia. Like Spain in previous centuries, however, Britain claimed far more territory around the globe than it was able to govern. Built through trade wars and the initiatives of local settlers or officials, the British empire was not a single, unified structure. Although attempts were made in the early nineteenth century to give it more coherence, it remained an amalgamation of diverse territories. The circumstances of each colony were different, and together they produced various challenges for Britain.

Two examples of the growing complexity of the British empire in the early nineteenth century are Singapore and the Cape Colony. Both were annexed by Britain as a result of rivalry with the Dutch. Singapore, however, was one man's imperial project. When territory taken from the Dutch in Southeast Asia (now Indonesia and Malaya) was given back after 1814, some British merchants and officials were disgusted. Among them was Sir Stamford Raffles, who had briefly governed the colony of Java. Seeking to block the Dutch from re-establishing commercial control, Raffles signed an agreement with a local Malay chieftain to create a trading post on the Singapore River. He then intervened in a civil war between two brothers, both of whom claimed to be sultan of the area. Raffles's candidate won, and obligingly confirmed British rights to the Singapore trading post in 1819. It took another five years before a treaty with the Dutch and a new agreement with the sultan confirmed the cession of Singapore Island to the East India Company. Meanwhile, the reforming Raffles had abolished slavery there and set up a college for the Malay elite. The EIC directors were far from delighted: claiming that he owed the Company money, they drove him into bankruptcy.

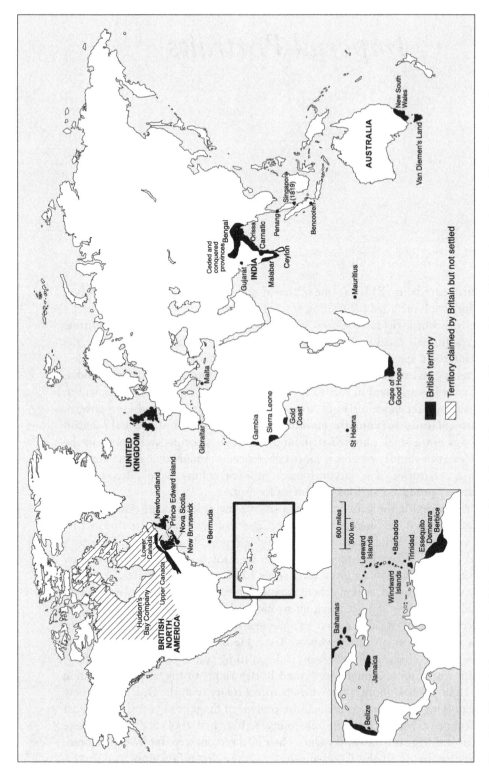

Map 11 *The British empire in 1815. (Source: P. J. Marshall, ed., The Oxford History of the British Empire, volume 2: The Eighteenth Century, Oxford, 1998, p. 6.)*

He died, a bitter man, in 1826. Singapore would not have existed without him. Lying along the trade route from China to India, it became one of the most prosperous of British colonies.

The Cape Colony, by contrast, was regarded by the British government as a point of considerable strategic value, because it was on the vital sea passage to India. Seized by a British military force in 1795, it was returned to the Dutch in 1802, then taken again in 1806. With its capital at Cape Town, the colony contained 16,000 Dutch immigrants and about as many slaves. Some of the slaves were from Malaya, while others were Africans imported into the colony. The local Khoikhoi people worked as "servants" to the Dutch. Their children were all indentured as laborers for 25 years to Dutch farmers or "Boers." Stern Calvinists in religion, the Boers raised grapes to make wine and pastured sheep or cattle. The British did not at first interfere much with the Cape Colony. They allowed Dutch law and local government to continue. While they outlawed the slave trade, they upheld slavery and "apprenticeship," as servitude was euphemistically called. They even strengthened existing laws that required Khoikhoi to carry a pass if they wished to travel from one place to another. Anyone caught without a pass could be immediately enslaved. In the 1820s, this hands-off policy began to change. British settlers arrived, and with them came evangelical missionaries who wanted to convert the Khoikoi to Christianity. The missionaries obtained a removal of the pass laws in 1828. Tensions with the Boers increased as Dutch local government was abolished and English became the language of the courts. The abolition of slavery within most of the British empire outraged the Boers, who had come to believe that their racial dominance was sanctioned by God. Between 1836 and 1840, about 7000 Boer pioneers or *Voortrekkers* left the Cape Colony for the interior of South Africa, seizing native land in order to set up their own tiny, independent republics.

Singapore was a quirky example of individual effort leading to huge commercial success, without much government involvement. The Cape Colony had a much more complicated history, rooted in international conflict. Once its authority was established there, Britain became embroiled in the ethnic and racial issues that divided the colony. In both places, imperial government has to be understood with reference to local situations, not simply as a force that was imposed from outside. The impact of imperial initiatives, like the abolition of slavery, depended on what was going on within the colony. This would continually frustrate reform-minded policy makers in Britain, who wanted to implement simple, uniform solutions to colonial issues. Their ideas were often viewed as misguided or authoritarian in the colonies, and might be resisted by force.

The British public was not very interested in the complexity of the empire. For ordinary Britons, overseas possessions were signs of prestige and power, rewards for the long years of war against France and Spain. They provided a vast market for British goods, as well as places where ordinary Britons could settle and prosper through trade or farming. The confident, energetic British national identity of the nineteenth century rested in large part on the extent and prosperity of the empire. Few doubted that Britain deserved to rule so many domains. The evangelical missionaries popularized the notion that God had chosen the British peoples to spread Christianity, and with it the benefits of civilization, around the globe. How this might affect the Cree or the Khoikhoi or the Aboriginals was not a matter of great concern – these exotic peoples were alien to the British, and were treated by them with considerable disdain. As for the settler colonies, Britons continued to regard them simply as little bits of the homeland, transplanted abroad. The realities of life in Canada or Australia, which transformed the settlers and created new identities, were not much appreciated by the British public.

The rest of this chapter tries to make sense of the British empire of the early nineteenth century by examining some of the individuals who lived in it and shaped its destiny. These brief sketches are devoted to people who were born in, or who emigrated to, British colonies in North America, the West Indies, South Asia, and the Pacific. They may not be entirely typical examples, but their diverse experiences reveal much about how the British empire affected people around the world in the early nineteenth century.

The Patriot: Louis-Joseph Papineau

Like the Cape Colony, Lower Canada (modern Quebec) was a British possession containing a European settler population that was mostly non-British. The French-speaking Catholic inhabitants of Lower Canada, or *canadiens*, viewed the British government as necessary, because it protected them from their enemies, the Americans; but they resented British attempts to govern them through a narrow oligarchy of English-speaking Protestant merchants, rather than through the elected legislature. The leader of the popular or *patriote* party in the Lower Canadian assembly during the 1820s and 1830s was the brilliant orator Louis-Joseph Papineau. He was not himself a man of the people – he was one of the *seigneurs* or manorial lords who owned big landed estates that dated back to the French regime. Papineau was not so different from the landowners who dominated the Whig party in Britain, and in fact he felt a strong affinity with them, as well as a great respect for the British constitution.

Papineau summed up his view of the British empire in a speech made in 1834 and printed in the *patriote* newspaper *La Minerve* (*The Minerva*). "The motives of our attachment to the metropolis [i.e. Britain]," he explained,

are found above all in the powerful protection that she offers us against external aggressions [i.e. the United States]. [They are also found in] the advantageous outlet that she offers to our products by a reciprocally useful exchange. It is with this aim that she must multiply her colonial possessions, not to plant in them aristocratic institutions, if they are not acceptable. That which will give the most content to the people will attach them more to England.[1]

He sounds very much like an American patriot of the 1760s, arguing that the empire can only be preserved if the King and Parliament heed the voice of the colonial legislatures. Yet Papineau was a nationalist as well as a patriot. He wanted to preserve the language, law, religion, and culture of the *peuple cana-dien*, the French-speaking Canadian people, which included the old system of landowning.

In the 1830s, that system was in crisis. Lower Canada was facing economic problems similar to, although less serious than, those that would hit Ireland in the 1840s. The wheat boom of the Napoleonic Wars had come to an end, leaving a hugely increased population and a declining agriculture. On many Lower Canadian farms, potato cultivation was adopted to feed large families. Young men and women often had to migrate to the logging camps or to Montreal in order to make a living. Much of the best farmland in the colony, however, had been laid out by the government in American-style townships and offered to new immigrants from Britain. This embittered many *canadien* farmers. For the first time, unemployment became a serious problem in the countryside, and the prospect of food shortages loomed.

Papineau's answer to the economic crisis was to shift power away from the nominated executive council, towards the legislature. After gaining a huge elec-toral victory in 1834, the *patriotes* drew up a series of 92 demands which they presented to the British government. Most of the demands were for long-established Parliamentary rights, like legislative control over finances, but they also called for an elected executive council, a degree of democracy that did not yet exist in Britain. The British Parliament rejected Papineau's resolutions, and instead allowed the governor to raise taxes without the consent of the assembly, threaten-ing coercion if further trouble ensued. At this point, Papineau was caught between his eager followers and the intransigence of the British Whigs. He began to hold mass rallies, imitating those of Daniel O'Connell in Ireland, where he whipped up anger against Britain. His followers declared that they were "ready to help Papineau overthrow the English government and give Canada an independent government like the American government."[2] Still, Papineau held off from open resistance until the British tried to arrest him. Finally, in November 1837, a few thousand armed *patriotes* rose in rebellion in the countryside around Montreal. Their forces were defeated by British troops, and their leaders, including Papineau, fled to the United States. Some exiled *patriotes* invaded Lower Canada from the USA in 1838, but this attempt was again crushed. Twelve rebels were executed, and 58 were sent to Australia.

The rebellion of 1837 was condemned by the Roman Catholic Church, and it attracted little support in the larger towns of Lower Canada. The British govern-ment, however, was alarmed enough to send a leading Whig politician, Lord Durham, to report on the situation in the Canadas. He concluded that "respon-sible government" or control by the legislature should be conceded, but he also recommended that French Canadians be assimilated through a forced union with the English-speaking colonies. Although the two Canadas were united in 1841, it took another five years of political struggle before "responsible government" was won. Far from being assimilated, French-speaking politicians became a powerful force in the united Canadian legislature. In 1867, a largely self-governing federation of British North American colonies (excluding Newfoundland) was created, and British troops finally withdrew from the continent. Meanwhile, Papineau had returned to his native land, where he lived until 1871. He opposed both the Canadian Union and Confederation, calling instead for annexation to the United States. Ironically, the rebellion he had raised in 1837 had helped to push Britain and the Canadas towards a new imperial structure that resembled a partnership of separate states. That structure would eventually set a pattern for transforming the British empire into a Commonwealth of nations. The survival of French culture within North America, however, remains a continuing struggle.

The Emigrant: Catherine Parr Traill

Political unrest was widespread in British North America in the 1830s, just as it was in Britain. In Prince Edward Island, an Escheat Party was formed, calling for redistribution of land to tenant farmers. At Halifax, the radical journalist Joseph Howe excoriated the corruption of the local merchant oligarchy in his newspaper, *The Novascotian*. Upper Canada was shaken by partisan struggles. The main source of political and social tension there was between pro-British Anglican loyalists and American or Scottish settlers, many of them from Dissenting Protestant groups. The radical reformer William Lyon Mackenzie, a fiery newspaper publisher and first mayor of the city of Toronto, vigorously attacked the "tyranny" of the lieutenant-governor and his councilors, as well as the favoritism shown by them towards the Church of England. An agricultural depression in the mid-1830s increased the popularity of the reformist message. In December 1837, after news arrived of the Lower Canadian rebellion, Mackenzie tried to set off an uprising in Toronto, but his motley gang of supporters was dispersed by loyalist militia. Mackenzie fled to the United States, where he organized several armed raids into Upper Canada in 1838.

Catherine Parr Traill, a recent British immigrant who had settled in the backwoods at Lakefield near Peterborough, took the loyalist side in the 1837 Rebellion. Her husband served in the militia against the rebels. Catherine Parr Traill came from a remarkable literary family. Born Catherine Strickland, she was the daughter of an English gentleman whose early death required his children to seek their own fortunes. Her eldest sisters, Eliza and Agnes, became popular historians. Her younger sister, Susanna, wrote patriotic songs, children's books, and works for the Anti-Slavery League, before marrying a Scottish military officer, John Moodie, and emigrating to Upper Canada. Catherine, who had already published several books for young readers, married Moodie's friend and fellow officer, Thomas Traill, and left England to join her sister. Her book *The Backwoods of Canada*, published in 1836, was the first full-length account of life on the Canadian frontier.

In the thirty years after 1815, about 730,000 emigrants from the British Isles settled in the North American colonies. Two-thirds of them emigrated after 1830. Almost half were Irish, and a disproportionate number were Scots. Like the Traills and Moodies, the majority paid for their own passage. A few were brought over by government assistance programs, or by local organizations like the Petworth Emigration Committee, which transported 1800 rural laborers and their families from southeast England after the Captain Swing riots of 1830. Private land companies, among them the Canada Company, settled numerous British emigrants, particularly Highland Scots, on tracts of land purchased from the crown. Most emigrants traveled across the Atlantic in steerage, where they were overcrowded, underfed, and susceptible to disease. Cholera epidemics ravaged emigrant ships in the 1830s, and Catherine Parr Traill witnessed the effects of one when her own vessel reached Montreal in 1832.

Traill's impressions of Canada reveal a growing awareness that British North America was not simply a primitive reproduction of the home country. When she first arrived in Upper Canada in 1832, the hilly countryside reminded her of Gloucestershire, but it lacked "the charm with which civilization has so eminently adorned that fine county. ... Here the bold forests of oak, beech, maple, and basswood, with now and then a dark pine, cover the hills, only enlivened by an occasional settlement, with its log house and zig-zag fences of split timber." The fences particularly offended her, and she longed for "the rich English hedge-rows." She understood, however, that wood fences were more practical. "Matters of taste appear to be little regarded," she lamented.[3] Traill quickly adapted herself to the new country. Although she was of gentry stock, she came to realize that "The poor gentleman of delicate or refined habits" was the worst type of immigrant; the best, by contrast, were "the poor hard-working sober labourers, who have industrious habits, a large family to provide for, and a laudable horror of the workhouse and parish overseers." As for the ideal settler's wife, she "should be active, industrious, ingenious, cheerful, not above putting her hand to whatever is necessary to be done in her household." Melancholy women who pine for the homeland "deaden the energies of their husbands and brothers by constant and useless repining."[4] Pioneer life brought about a sort of rough and ready equality between classes and even between men and women, but it did not erase the importance of hierarchy in Traill's mind. As a person of genteel breeding, she disliked the "disagreeable manner and affectation of equality" that she noticed among "the inferior sort of Irish and Scotch," although she was more willing to accept the informality and democratic customs of "native Americans."[5]

Traill held strong Anglican religious beliefs, in contrast to her sister Susanna Moodie, who attended Dissenting chapels and later became a Spiritualist. Both women spent time among the local Ojibwa Indians (whom they called Chippewa), and Traill noted with satisfaction that conversion to Christianity had erased "the traits of cunning and warlike ferocity that previously marked this singular people. ... Certain it is that the introduction of the Christian religion is the first greatest step to civilization and improvement." Traill was also aware that Indians were declining in numbers, although she accepted this as inevitable. "The race is slowly passing away from the face of the earth," she observed with some regret.[6] Years later, in her classic memoir entitled *Roughing It in the Bush*, Susanna Moodie would write about native peoples with considerable sympathy, but her sister's attitude – condescending, without being overtly hostile – was probably more common among British settlers.

Catherine Parr Traill never returned to Britain. During the course of her long life, she published several more books, including a notable study of Canadian botany. She became the matriarch of a large family, dying in 1899 at the age of 97. Although she probably thought of herself as British until the day she died, Traill was already showing signs of a more independent, less polite North American identity as early as the 1830s. As she quickly realized, she could not simply live as a transplanted Briton in a place that was so different from her native land. At the same time, she was reluctant to give up her background and become wholly Canadian. The delicate balance between adaptation to a new environment and attachment to the old homeland, between North American equality and British gentility, between nature and culture, would continue to complicate English Canadian identity throughout the nineteenth century, and beyond.

The Freed Slave: Mary Prince

Just before she married and left England for Canada in 1831, Susanna Strickland was asked by her friends in the Anti-Slavery League to write down the life story of a former West Indian slave, Mary Prince. This was part of the campaign that would lead to the Abolition of Slavery Act of 1833. Mary Prince's remarkable story is a stark reminder that slavery remained a brutally exploitative and highly profitable system, right up to the end. It is also one of very few records of the experiences of a female slave. Although her narrative was undoubtedly changed by her evangelical benefactors to serve their purposes, it retains strong marks of her own voice.

Mary Prince was born into slavery in Bermuda in 1788. She was sold three times, twice by private agreement and once at a slave market, where she was "surrounded by strange men, who examined and handled me in the same manner that a butcher would a calf or a lamb he was about to purchase."[7] She worked mostly as a domestic slave, although for ten years she toiled in the horrific salt ponds of the Turks Islands. Mary Prince was frequently beaten by her masters and mistresses, and she witnessed terrible cruelties meted out as punishments to slaves. She describes the whipping of a pregnant fellow slave who had let a cow get loose. "My master flew into a terrible passion, and ordered the poor creature to be stripped quite naked, and to be tied up to a tree in the yard. He then flogged her as hard as he could lick, both with the whip and cow skin, till she was all over streaming with blood. He rested, and then beat her again and again. Her shrieks were terrible."[8] The child was still-born and the woman died soon after. Prince does not directly refer to sexual abuse, but she hints at it in recounting how one of her masters would order her to bathe him. She called him "a very indecent man ... with no shame for his servants, no shame for his own flesh."[9]

On the island of Antigua, Mary Prince began to attend a Moravian chapel. An evangelical Church with central European origins, the Moravians allowed slaves to join their community. A Moravian minister married Mary Prince to a black freeman who worked as a cooper, but she was not allowed by her master to live with him. Having saved money through taking in washing, selling coffee and yams, and even trading hogs, Mary Prince wanted to purchase her freedom, but her master refused this as well. Instead, he brought her to England with him. Once there, she was confronted by a dilemma. "I knew that I was free in England, but I did not know where to go, or how to get my living; and therefore, I did not like to leave the house."[10] Her master, accusing her of laziness, actually threatened to throw her out. Finally, in August 1828, she was offered shelter by some Moravian missionaries, and left her master and mistress. A few months later, she was directed to the Anti-Slavery Society. Although she was free in England, her master would not agree to recognize her freedom legally in the West Indies, which meant that she could not return to her husband. Mary Prince concluded her narrative by wondering "how English people can go out into the West Indies and act in such a beastly manner … they forget God and all feeling of shame." Answering the defenders of slavery, who argued that slaves did not really want to be free, she asserted that "they put a cloak about the truth. It is not so. All slaves want to be free – to be free is very sweet."[11]

Within a few years, they would all be declared free: but freedom was not as sweet as they had hoped. Few of them were to be as fortunate as Mary Prince in finding immediate liberation and employment. Abolition was not granted easily. It came in the wake of a last major revolt on Jamaica in 1831–2, in which 60,000 slaves, inspired by the Baptist preacher Sam Sharpe, rose up against their masters in order to claim freedom. Plantations were torched and 14 whites were killed before the rebellion was savagely repressed. About 540 black people died. Sam Sharpe was hanged, still declaring on the gallows that slavery was immoral. If he had lived, would he have been satisfied with the way West Indian slavery was finally ended? We do not know what Mary Prince would have thought of it, as she disappeared from history shortly before it took place.

The Abolition of Slavery Act of 1833 represented a great victory for the dying William Wilberforce and his Parliamentary allies, but it was designed to be gradual, and was full of special provisions as well as exceptions. The Act ended slavery in the West Indies in August 1834, four months later in the Cape Colony of South Africa. The territories of the EIC, however, were exempted, and slavery was not outlawed in India until 1860. In the West African colony of Sierra Leone, slavery lasted until 1928. Under the provisions of the 1833 Act, West Indian slave owners were compensated in the amount of £20 million, an enormous sum. The bishop of Exeter received a handsome £12,700 for the 665 human beings he owned. No compensation was offered to the slaves. Instead, they were to become apprenticed laborers for a period of six years, and their children could be bound by indentures that would last up to the age of 21. If they worked in agriculture on the property of their former owners, apprentices were tied to the land and were forbidden to move without the permission of their masters. No apprentice was allowed to leave the colony in which he or she had been a slave. To be sure, apprentices could purchase their freedom. Nonetheless, the new system was not very different from slavery, and it shows how important to the prosperity of the Empire the forced labor of blacks was still held to be. Bermuda and Antigua opted for immediate emancipation, but Jamaica and the other islands adopted apprenticeship.

The abolitionists did not give up in 1833. They recognized the shortcomings of the Abolition Act, and they continued to lobby for an end to apprenticeship. The government ultimately gave in to the pressure, declaring full emancipation from August 1, 1838. The dawn of freedom was greeted with parades, church services, and public rejoicings throughout the British Caribbean. About 750,000 people were freed. For most of them, the future would bring growing poverty and economic distress, as Britain gradually withdrew its investment in the West Indies. Yet no matter how hard their condition may have been, and still is, Mary Prince was doubtless correct in claiming that to be free was very sweet.

The Philosopher: Rammohan Roy

About a month after the passage of the Abolition of Slavery Act in 1833, a Bengali man died of meningitis in Bristol, England, at the age of 61. His name was Rammohan Roy, and he was one of the most significant figures in Indian intellectual history. Like Louis-Joseph Papineau, he was a landowner of high status, who became an ardent reformer. Born a Kuhlin Brahman, one of the highest ranking castes in Bengali society, Roy left his family estates to become a moneylender in Calcutta. He later held various positions in the revenue and judicial services of the EIC, although as an Indian he could not hope to rise very high in the Company ranks. He also studied religious writings – not only those of his own faith, Hinduism (a term he actually invented), but also those of Buddhism, Islam, and Christianity. Based on his reading of Hindu scriptures, he renounced the veneration of images and argued that different deities were manifestations of a single God. He saw this as the potential basis for a universal religion.

Rammohan Roy stood at the centre of a reformist circle that included both Bengalis and Britons. Together with his friends and supporters, he created a public culture in Bengal that was partly indigenous, partly modeled on that of Great Britain. They founded newspapers and journals in which Roy's ideas were promulgated. They started a debating club, the Atmiya Sabha or Friendly Society, and in 1828 they formed the Brahmo Samaj, a religious association whose goal was to promote Hindu monotheism. Passionately interested in education, Roy participated in setting up institutions of higher learning in Calcutta, including the Vedanta College, where students were instructed in a mixture of European and Indian knowledge. He sought to make British rule more responsive to Bengali public opinion.

During the 1820s, Roy devoted himself to the cause of women's rights. He argued against polygamy, in favor of female inheritance, and above all for the abolition of *sati*, the practice by which widows burned themselves on the funeral pyres of their late husbands. Roy's criticism of *sati* was based on his own researches into traditional Hindu law. He praised "the interest and care which our ancient legislators took in the promotion of the comfort and care of the female part of the community," compared with modern laws that had led "to their complete privation, directly or indirectly, of most of those objects that render life agreeable."[12] Roy was enough of a social observer to notice that many women committed *sati* because they were pressured by their husband's relatives, who did not want to share inheritances with them. His opinions on *sati* were controversial, not just among his fellow Hindus, but also among the British. In the early nineteenth century, Governor-general Wellesley had deplored widow burning, but he was unwilling to do anything about it. Roy addressed Governor-general William Bentinck on the subject, in terms that deliberately flattered the British. He urged Bentinck to put an end to a "system of female destruction ... admirably suited to the selfish and servile disposition of the populace." He appealed to the governor-general's sense of "justice and humanity" in dealing with a practice "so incompatible with the principles of British rule."[13] In 1829, Bentinck declared *sati* to be illegal, and it gradually disappeared.

The abolition of *sati* was an important step for the EIC, which had previously sought not to interfere in social or cultural issues. It had been pushed in an interventionist direction not just by Rammohan Roy, but by local administrators, evangelical missionaries, and bureaucrats in the East India Office in London. Among the latter was James Mill, who had written an influential *History of British India* in 1817 before being named chief examiner of correspondence for the Company. Mill's background and views were entirely different from Rammohan Roy's. The son of a Scottish shoemaker and small landholder, Mill was educated at the University of Edinburgh in the principles of the Enlightenment. He moved to London, where he became a friend of the utilitarian philosopher Jeremy Bentham and the economist David Ricardo. Mill, who never went to India and was not able to read any Indian languages, convinced himself that the people of India were barbarous, and had to be raised to civilization by the British. He described the Hindu population in grotesque terms, as indolent, feeble-minded, immoral, and avaricious. "There is a state of barbarity and rudeness," Mill wrote, "which implies, perhaps, a weakness of mind too great to be capable of perceiving ... the benefits of labour. This, however, is a state beyond which the Hindus have long passed."[14] Clearly, he had no knowledge of the frenetic Hindu capitalism that thrived in Calcutta. As for the treatment of women, Mill was convinced that "A state of dependence more strict and humiliating than that which is ordained for the weaker sex among the Hindus cannot easily be conceived."[15] Mill believed that ancient Hindu laws conferred no rights at all on women. Like Rammohan Roy, however, he deplored the "barbarous sacrifice" of widow-burning.[16]

Because he shared some of their aims, Rammohan Roy might be seen as the accomplice of James Mill and the evangelical missionaries in their efforts to "civilize" India. Yet Roy always maintained that Indians were a civilized people whose laws and customs had been corrupted by centuries of foreign domination. He wanted Indians to take a more active part in their own government. He adopted a cautious, practical approach, advising the British government in 1831 that "by gradually introducing the natives" into the EIC departments of revenue and justice, they "may become attached to the present system of government, so that it may become consolidated, and maintain itself by the influence of the intelligent and respectable classes of the inhabitants, and by the general good will of the people."[17] His ultimate aim was to put India on the same constitutional path as Canada, which meant that Britain must grant basic legal rights and increased self-government.

Roy was in a difficult position in asking for political reforms. With no Indian legislature from which he could make demands, he was left with little choice but to launch personal appeals to the governor-general, the British Parliament, and even the King. He considered running for a seat in the House of Commons in order to give himself a platform, but this never happened. If he had been elected, he might have run into the Whig politician Thomas Babington Macaulay, whose opinions about Indians were similar to those of James Mill. In 1834, Macaulay resigned his seat in Parliament and took up a position on the new Supreme Council for India. After spending less than a year there, he wrote an influential "Minute on Indian Education," advising Governor-general Bentinck not to spend any more money on Indian colleges that taught in Sanskrit or Arabic. Instead, the Indian elite should be instructed in English only. Although he knew no Asian languages, Macaulay asserted that "a single shelf of a good European library was worth the whole native literature of India and Arabia … all the historical information that has been collected from all the books written in the Sanscrit language is less valuable than what may be found in the most paltry abridgements used in preparatory schools in England."[18] Macaulay was not entirely prejudiced against Indians: he advocated an end to censorship of the Indian press, and pressed for legal reforms that would make Britons and Indians equal under the law. Rammohan Roy would have welcomed these changes, even if Macaulay's other views might have distressed him.

Roy did not live to read Macaulay's "Minute." He was in England on a diplomatic mission on behalf of the Mughal Emperor when he died suddenly in 1833. The British India of which he dreamed, with a civil service open to Indians and a limited degree of self-government, would emerge very gradually in the early twentieth century. Britain was never prepared, however, to allow India to become another Canada. It had too much at stake in the commercial exploitation of the South Asian subcontinent to permit self-rule. As a result, the only path that was open to Indian nationalists was complete independence, which was at last achieved in 1947. With his great admiration for Britain, Rammohan Roy might have seen independence as regrettable, if necessary. He might have been even more saddened that his concept of the Supreme Being did not become the basis for religious unity in the new India, or in the world.

The Memsahibs

Women – Indian, Eurasian, and British – provided an important perspective on British rule in early nineteenth-century India. Issues that affected Indian women, like *sati*, were widely discussed, and frequent comparisons were made between the status of women in India and Britain. Unfortunately, not much attention was given to the group of Indian women whose lives were most directly affected by the British presence, the wives and mistresses of British officers and administrators. Marriages between British men and high-ranking Indian women still occurred, and the offspring of such unions might enjoy the mother's social status in Indian society – the son of Colonel William Gardiner and his Indian wife, for example, married the niece of the Mughal Emperor. Irregular unions, however, were far more common. The Eurasian children born from these unions lived in an unstable world between Indian and British society. They often dressed like Europeans, but they were not accepted as Britons in either a social or a legal sense.

We know much more about the British women who lived in India in the early nineteenth century, because some of them left written accounts of their experiences. They did not come to settle permanently; instead, they saw India either as travelers or as the wives of officials, merchants, and soldiers. A few, like Anna Harriette Leonowens, heroine of the twentieth-century musical *Anna and the King of Siam*, grew up in India because their parents were not wealthy enough to send them back to Britain for education. Most, however, stayed for only a few years. The majority of British women in India were married to ordinary soldiers, but those who wrote memoirs tended to be of higher status. They were usually surrounded by a legion of servants: Frances Parks and her husband, an EIC official in Allahabad, had 57 of them, plus a dozen extra bearers for traveling in hot weather. This was many times the number of domestics that a middle class family would have had in Britain. Their Indian servants referred to British women as "*memsahibs*" or mistresses, and the name has stuck. Because their presence discouraged relations between British men and Indian women, and because they transplanted British ideas of respectability and domesticity to the subcontinent, the *memsahibs* gave the British community in India a greater sense of separation from the majority population. On the other hand, they were not usually involved in the daily business of asserting British dominance, which was left mainly to men, and their writings sometimes give us a more thoughtful, nuanced, or sympathetic view of India than is found among male authors.

This does not mean that British women failed to share the cultural or religious presuppositions of British men. Mary Martha Sherwood, a clergyman's daughter who lived in India between 1806 and 1816, was horrified by almost everything she saw there. As an evangelical Christian, she was particularly concerned that there had been "few if any attempts to awaken our heathen fellow-subjects from the horrible darkness of the most corrupt and abominable superstitions." She blamed Hinduism and Islam, "those abominable creeds," for all the "symptoms of misery and degradation in the natives of India." The wearing of loincloths by men and children particularly disturbed her, because it seemed "indecent." On the other hand, she was not a racist, and genuinely believed that Christianity would raise all Indians to a condition of "personal decency" and "cheerful contentment."[19]

Some British women were enchanted by India. "How much there is to delight the eye in this bright, this beautiful world!" enthused Frances Parks, who lived in

India for 24 years, from the 1820s to the 1840s. "Roaming about with a good tent and a good Arab [horse], one might be happy for ever in India." She was fascinated, as so many Britons were, by the *zenana* or women's quarters, in which upper class Indian women lived in seclusion from men. This was an aristocratic Muslim custom that had been imitated by wealthy Hindus. Parks was thrilled when she was first given entrance to a *zenana*, and was charmed by the beauty and grace of her young hostess. She also noted, however, that women in the *zenana* "generally forget their learning, when they grow up, or they neglect it." They had very little to keep them busy or amused, other than taking opium pills to ward off colds, and engaging in gossip: "never was any place so full of intrigue, scandal, or chit-chat." She admired the independence of one elderly Hindu lady, the widow of a Maratha prince, to whom she complained about the restrictive customs of her native land. "We spoke of the severity of the laws of England with respect to married women," Parks recorded, "how completely by law they are the slaves of their husbands, and how little hope there is of redress." The legal enslavement of English married women, Parks concluded, created "one perpetual sati, or burning of the heart." She was also critical of the cultural insensitivity of her British compatriots, some of whom organized dance parties at the Taj Mahal.[20]

Female memoirs of life in India were often concerned with correcting the misconceptions that had been created by previous, mostly male, writers. Anna Harriette Leonowens opined that the average Hindu woman "is by no means as degraded as is so frequently represented by travelers, who are apt to mistake the common street-woman with whom they are brought in to contact for the wife and mother of an ordinary Hindoo home."[21] Emma Roberts, a writer and journalist who lived in India from 1828 to 1833, praised "The highly civilized state of the country, and the courteous manners of all classes of the people," words that directly contradicted James Mill. Roberts thought Indian servants tended to be extraordinarily honest, in spite of complaints from some British residents. She suggested that "persons who have come out young and inexperienced to India, and who, in too many instances, entertain a prejudice against the colour of those with whom they are surrounded, are apt to fancy excellencies and perfections in servants at home, which only exists in their own imaginations." She feared that her countrymen, those "proud and disdainful islanders ... usually contrive to make themselves hated wherever they go."[22] These comments, of course, tell us as much about British attitudes, and British society, as they do about India.

Perhaps the most extraordinary thought recorded by a British woman in early nineteenth-century India was written down by the Honorable Emily Eden, sister of George Eden, Earl of Auckland, who was governor-general from 1835 to 1841. It might be thought that Emily Eden would be the sort of "proud and disdainful" upper class Briton of whom Emma Roberts despaired, but in fact she was a sensitive observer of Indian life, and she grasped a point few men of her nation wished to accept, that the British empire would not last for ever. On one occasion, while contemplating the ruins of an Indian town, she speculated about a time 2000 years in the future, when "some black Governor-General of England will be marching through its southern provinces, and will go and look at some ruins, and doubt whether London ever was a large town ... and his sister will write to her [friend] at New Delhi, and complain of the cold, ... and how the natives wear bonnets, and then, of course, mention that she wants to go home."[23]

Passages to Australia

Further from Britain even than India was the settler colony at New South Wales in southeast Australia. Although prisoners continued to be transported there, by the 1830s it was changing into a colony of free British settlers and emancipated convicts, in some respects similar to Upper Canada. Yet it continued to be administered by two councils nominated by the governor, without an assembly. Social mobility in Australia was restricted by lack of access to land. As a result, most immigrants became laborers, and a version of the British class system gradually developed. The absence of a powerful neighbor like the United States had a profound impact on Australia, increasing a sense of isolation and, at first, a dependence on Britain. Unlike Upper Canadians, who adopted a North American accent that originated in Nova Scotia, Australians continued to speak with a British-style accent, based on that of working class Londoners.

Between 1810 and 1821, considerable efforts had been made by Governor Lachlan Macquarie to transform New South Wales from a rugged penal settlement into a regular colony. He built 265 new public buildings, including several schools, and encouraged "emancipists" or former convicts to take up positions in Australian society. Macquarie was opposed by the "exclusives," an elite of wealthy free settlers, and was eventually recalled to Britain after the publication of an unfavorable report on his activities. The "exclusives" continued to dominate the governor's councils, countering calls for an assembly from "emancipists" and trying to censor an emerging opposition press. Plans to set aside land for the Church of England, however, had to be abandoned because the colony already contained such a mixture of religions. In 1835, the Australian Patriotic Association, backed by influential "emancipists," was founded to lobby for representative government. A partially elected legislative council, based on a restricted franchise, was granted to New South Wales in 1843; the newer colonies of Van Dieman's Land (Tasmania, founded 1825), Western Australia (1829), and South Australia (1836) would have to wait until 1850 for even this limited reform.

The lack of an assembly did not bother Peter Cunningham, a naval surgeon who published an influential book on New South Wales in 1827. In his view, Australia was preferable to Canada for British emigrants because settlement was near the coasts and the winters were mild; besides, in North America "the settler is necessitated to perform most of his field labour himself (or with the aid of his family)," while in Australia, "labourers are plentiful."[24] He meant convict laborers, who were treated in some ways like slaves. They lived together in huts, worked from dawn to dusk, and could be whipped by order of a magistrate for laziness or disobedience. About 42,000 convicts were whipped in New South Wales between 1830 and 1837, receiving an average sentence of 45 lashes. Cunningham thought the transportation of convicts to be an excellent form of colonization for the mother country, "because in this way you make the *unproductive* portion of her population *productive*, by converting those who were formerly her pests into useful auxiliaries to increase her wealth and strength." As for the Aboriginals, Cunningham described them as beggars, thieves, and murderers, existing "at the very zero of civilization" due to a lack of environmental challenges. Evidently, he had never tried to survive in the bush.[25]

Cunningham's book was aimed at better-off migrants, who could invest up to £1200 in an Australian farm. By contrast, Edward Gibbon Wakefield argued for a much broader emigration of British laboring people, with government assistance. By keeping the price of land high, Wakefield advised, the government could compensate itself for the costs of assisted emigration. If more labor were needed, Chinese peasants could be admitted. Edward Gibbon Wakefield was a curious character. He had served time in Newgate Prison for trying to elope with a 15-year-old heiress, so he may have felt some empathy with transported convicts. A Whig in politics, he served as Lord Durham's secretary after the 1837 Canadian rebellions. His chief goal was to make the idea of a global empire more attractive to the British public. Through assisted emigration, Wakefield hoped, "the mother country and the colony would become partners in a new trade – the creation of happy human beings." This was a utopian vision, although it gave rise to several practical schemes.[26]

Wakefield helped to inspire a wave of government-assisted British emigration to Australia. Between 1832 and 1842, about 70,000 immigrants arrived in New South Wales alone, their passage largely paid by agencies supported by the Colonial Office. As Wakefield had advised, the price of land in Australia had been fixed at a high level of 5 shillings per acre in 1831, rising to £1 in 1842. Consequently, most newcomers were not able to purchase property, and instead became farm laborers. This did not discourage them from leaving Britain, because the wages of free laborers were comparatively high in Australia. They suffered terribly on the long journey to the South Pacific, which could take three to five months. Crammed into tight quarters, with limited washing and toilet facilities, they were fed on biscuits, beef or pork, rice, oatmeal, and raisins, with water or tea to drink. The poorest passengers, used to eating far less than this at home, found the ship's fare sumptuous, but most complained about it. The ship's medical officer played a crucial role in distributing food supplies and maintaining sanitation. Disease claimed a heavy toll among children, who were often weakened by malnutrition because they did not like the food. A loss of one child in twenty was not uncommon. Ellen Moger, who tragically lost three children, including a baby, on a voyage to Australia in 1839, wrote "I firmly believe that the dear children would have lived, and much sickness been spared, had we experienced proper attention from our Doctor and been provided with a little natural nourishment."[27] The bodies of her children were buried at sea.

On arrival, the immigrants quickly found employment as laborers. Hugh Watson from Leith in Scotland emigrated to Adelaide, South Australia, in 1839, and was soon working as a shepherd. He earned £1 a week, about twice the wages he might have made in his homeland, but with food and lodging added. His wife earned another £1 a week taking in washing. Watson was ecstatic. "Any person may begin work the next day he comes to land," he advised his parents, adding "I think no man can starve here as the poor immigrants at New York did when they arrived there in poverty." He was particularly amazed that no game laws restricted hunting to landowners: "Every man here has freedom to shoot what he pleases." He thought this was "the most beautiful country I ever saw; the trees are always green here and our winter is nearly over."[28] Not everybody was as content as Hugh Watson; some immigrants wanted land at lower prices. They spilled over the fixed colonial boundaries and became "squatters," raising cattle and sheep on land that had no legal proprietor. Aboriginal peoples might continue to live there, unaware that their traditional rights to the land were in jeopardy. By 1836, the government had agreed to sell licenses to squatters, and within four years there were 673 licensed "squatting stations" on the borders of New South Wales. The squatters, however, could not manage their large farms without the help of convict laborers. Some of these laborers ran away, to become "bushrangers" or cattle rustlers.

Australia was a land of strong social contrasts. While bushrangers roamed the outback, a fashionable elite could be found in Sydney, holding balls and grand dinners, subscribing to musical concerts, and imitating the etiquette of the British upper classes. They regarded convicts with trepidation and shunned the company of "emancipists." Fears of democracy and republicanism spread among the Australian social elite in the 1820s, and would return to haunt them in the Gold Rush days of the 1850s. The social divisions that emerged in the early nineteenth century continued to have a deep effect on the future of the island continent. Class would become a more important issue in Australia than in any other settler colony. Meanwhile, the possibility that Australia might become a republic, and sever its remaining ties to Great Britain, would resurface periodically down to the present day.

As had happened in British North America, the British settler colonies in the South Pacific were developing along their own paths, in ways that the government of the home country had not planned or foreseen. Already by the late 1830s, it was evident that the different parts of the British empire had little in common, other than diversity and conflict. A single imperial strategy, whether aimed at civilizing or evangelizing or simply exploiting the resources of the colonies, was increasingly unfeasible. In the end, imperial government itself became extremely difficult, presenting Britain with the option of withdrawal or expending further resources on seemingly insoluble problems. In the settler colonies, withdrawal was not particularly difficult, but in India and Africa it was to have traumatic consequences for British prestige and for a British national identity that had become intimately bound up with the goals of imperialism.

Conclusion

The past may resemble a constantly moving river in which nothing really begins or ends, but historians eventually have to moor their imaginary boats and consider where they think they have traveled. The main themes of this book – the rise of a British state, the importance of patriotism, the spread of an empire, and the transition to an industrial society – need to be restated again and linked together chronologically, to illustrate their structure and implications. They reveal a complex picture of a nation that pioneered what it meant to be modern. At the heart of that picture is politics.

Party Politics

England in the late seventeenth century was a kingdom with a relatively strong central government, a thriving commerce and a population bitterly divided by religion. Scotland was a smaller, poorer, and less powerful kingdom with similar religious problems. The English colonies in the New World were of growing economic importance, but they did not constitute an organized empire. England's potential as a regional and global power was hampered by internal political and doctrinal conflicts that had caused a series of Civil Wars in the mid-seventeenth century. The stability of the English state, comprising the fiscal and administrative operations of government, was undermined by continuing confrontations between the crown and Parliament. Political parties, with clear ideological positions, competed furiously with one another for control of the legislature.

What was needed to avoid continuing violent upheavals was a partnership between the ruler and the parties. This was the main result of the Glorious Revolution of 1688. Monarchs who depended on Parliament for their titles became more reliant on party support in order to govern. Partisan struggles between Whigs and Tories remained lively, but they were now played out within the confines of a national legislature whose existence was more or less continuous.

The parties sought mass support, but they did not usually turn to rebellion when deprived of office. They became intertwined with elite sociability and depended on the circulation of ideas through a commercialized press.

Historians have often laid emphasis on constitutional change in the late seventeenth century rather than on political conflict. They have argued that the English constitution was fundamentally altered by the Glorious Revolution of 1688, bringing about a new era of Parliamentary sovereignty. This book has taken a different approach, suggesting that the Revolution institutionalized the legislature, diminished political violence, and weakened the legitimacy of the monarch, but did not make Parliament sovereign. The Revolution also led to limited toleration of diverse religious views and a less controlled press. Without political competition, it is unlikely that these changes could have been brought about, or would have survived.

The Creation of a British State

Faced after 1689 with the challenge of war against France, England's political leaders created a much more powerful and effective state. Its main objectives were the raising of money through taxes or loans and the expansion of military and naval forces. The security of the state made it necessary to absorb Scotland into a British union in 1707, a move that was resented by many Scots. Although both the Whig and Tory parties participated in shaping the British state, the Whigs became its main defenders, because they were most committed to winning the war against France and to bringing about the Hanoverian Succession. After 1714, the Whigs excluded their Tory opponents from holding power for almost fifty years, by associating them with opposition to the Hanoverian monarchy. During those decades, the Whigs continued to follow the fiscal and administrative strategies that had been laid down in the earlier wars against France. They also preserved the Protestant religious foundations of the state, from which the monarchy derived its legitimacy.

It would be misleading to suggest that the British state was all-powerful, or that its administrative apparatus was highly developed. Nevertheless, it had an increasing impact on everyday life in Britain. Legal and traditional rights were defended by popular opinion, sometimes through riots, and politicians were careful not to tamper with them, because they might rely on them if turned out of office. The marketplace for ideas was open, but was not without limits, especially regarding expressions of treason or blasphemy.

The Development of a Commercial Society

Britain continued to be ruled after 1688 by those who owned land, the aristocracy and gentry. Because it depended so heavily on investment by merchants and bankers, however, the British state became closely intertwined with commerce.

This increased the already important role of trade in the deliberations of government. It also encouraged the development of a commercial society. By the mid-eighteenth century, the British saw themselves as a people who depended on overseas commerce.

With the increase of prosperity after the end of the first round of wars against France, the upper classes and middling sort of people began to purchase consumer goods on a level that had not been seen before. This stimulated overseas imports, especially from the empire, as well as internal production. With new wealth came new investment in public structures and the building of private houses for the upper classes and middling sort, which changed the appearance of British towns. Commercialization, as this process has been called, was a complex cultural and economic phenomenon, encouraged by the more open political, social, and religious life of eighteenth-century Britain. It did not undermine the elite; instead, changes in fashion and taste tended to bolster the leadership of the landed classes. As consumers, women enjoyed more economic clout, but their social and legal status did not change. Eventually, the worldliness of commercial society helped to generate a religious reaction in evangelicalism. Commercial ideals, however, permeated British culture throughout the eighteenth century. They elevated individual sentiments, which in turn helped to elevate the political feeling called patriotism.

The Rise of Patriotism

From the 1750s onward, the dominant political ideology of British commercial society was patriotism. Its purpose was to support the aims of the state, but it could easily turn into criticism of government policy. Patriots often complained that ministers had not been energetic enough in promoting British commercial interests around the globe, or in protecting the traditional rights of Britons. A radical brand of patriotism fired up the British public during the mid-century wars against France, and later generated powerful movements for reform of the political system. In the American colonies, radical patriotism provided the ideological basis for a revolution against British rule. After the defeat in America and amidst a rising patriot challenge in Ireland, however, the British reform movement was checked by a conservative patriotism that looked to the King as the guarantor of stability and national unity. From 1783 until 1830, conservative patriotism would dominate the government of Great Britain.

Whether conservative or radical, patriotism assumed that every member of society had a stake in the nation. For the radicals, this meant that more people should be given a vote for representatives in Parliament, and that members of minority religious groups should be allowed to serve in public offices without restrictions. Some radicals went so far as to advocate voting rights for all adult men. To the conservatives, by contrast, democracy meant anarchy. They wanted Britons of all social ranks to accept the priority of national unity under the existing form of government. In religious terms, the overriding concern of conservative patriots was to preserve the established Churches as the basis of the state's legitimacy.

The New Empire

The rise of conservative patriotism after 1783 made the British empire into a focal point of national consciousness. The loss of the American colonies had brought an end to the possibility of a unified British Atlantic world based on commerce. The reconstructed empire was global, and was founded as much on strategic considerations as on trade. The British government attempted to direct it with a firmer hand. Greater control was established over the East India Company, and the foundations of a reconstituted British North America were laid. A vigorous policy of territorial expansion followed, in India, Africa, and the South Pacific. The wars against Revolutionary and Napoleonic France led to further British military commitments around the world. Ireland, always an anomaly within the empire, became part of an expanded United Kingdom.

By the early nineteenth century, the British empire had overcome all challengers in order to dominate large parts of the globe, from Canada to Australia, the Cape of Good Hope to India. The abolition of slavery in 1833 seemed to herald a new moral purpose for the empire. Evangelical missionaries already saw Britain's overseas territories as a vast recruiting ground for Christianity. In reality, however, it was already proving impossible to govern Britain's disparate possessions as if they were parts of one united entity. The Canadians were demanding more self-government; the Dutch-speaking South Africans were resentful of British rule; the Australians were moving beyond colonial frontiers. While India appeared to be a perfect laboratory for British ideas, and a perfect market for British goods, its governors had limited understanding of the societies over which they ruled, and little appreciation of the growing desire among Indians for self-determination.

Economic Transformation

Meanwhile, the commercial expansion of the eighteenth century helped to accelerate a series of profound economic changes within Britain. They included an intensified pursuit of agricultural profits by landowners, the development of bigger workshops and factories, the adoption of new techniques of production, including machinery, and the broader use of unskilled or semi-skilled labor in manufacturing. None of these changes emerged with revolutionary speed, but cumulatively, they comprised a thorough transformation of economic life, towards modern capitalism. In the countryside, small landholders disappeared, enclosures proliferated, and the wealth of landlords came to depend on the toil of impoverished agricultural laborers. In villages and small towns, women and children were increasingly employed in large-scale manufacturing, including cotton spinning mills. Skilled tradesmen found it harder and harder to compete with lower paid laborers who carried out specific stages of manufacturing in large workshops. Industrial development began to have an impact on village and town environments, through pollution and overcrowding. As people streamed into manufacturing centers, housing conditions deteriorated, as did the cultural amenities available to laboring folk.

These changes would contribute to the emergence of class divisions. Groups that were defined by their status, type of work, and cultural experiences began to think of themselves as having common interests that were distinct from those of other groups. Ideals of respectability and domesticity cut across social lines, but were adopted differently according to class. To be sure, class divisions may not have fully reflected the complexity of existence, but as a means of summing up social relations and social aspirations, they became of central significance in British life.

The Emergence of a Liberal State

By the 1820s, the premise of British national unity was becoming difficult to maintain. Britain was once again severely fragmented by social, economic, religious, and political cleavages. The absorption of Ireland into the United Kingdom in 1801 made it harder to understand exactly what "the nation" meant. Change in the state itself began to seem inevitable. The conservative government set off an era of reform by removing religious restrictions and opening the state to Dissenters and Catholics. The Whigs went further in the Reform Act of 1832, by altering the basis of the system of representation, so that it reflected population rather than land. This did not bring democracy, but it inaugurated changes that would soon enfranchise most of the male population.

The reformed British state was not entirely different from the old, but its premises had been rethought. The safeguarding of Protestantism and financial solvency were no longer its overriding ambitions. It embraced broader administrative aims and interfered more directly in the lives of those over whom it ruled. It was motivated by enlightened ideas of utility, as well as by evangelical morality. Gradually, traditional rights were extended or redefined. Even the legal status of women became a subject for discussion by reformers. While no major politician of the 1830s followed a utopian vision of social improvement, most of them subscribed to a liberal concept of progress that would supposedly lead the nation towards a better future for all.

Was This Modernity?

Should Britain in 1837 be called a modern society? To address this question, we should recognize that there is no single prototype of modernity. To be modern can mean many different things, although it can generally be understood as conformity to the major changes that have been associated with the past three centuries of world history. By the late eighteenth century, Britain had pioneered many of those changes: a competitive political system, a fiscally stable state, a commercial society, patriotism, global imperialism, industrialization, wage labor, opposition to slavery, social and political reform. It may have lagged behind in other areas that are associated with modernity, such as democracy or social and gender equality. It also lacked, happily enough, many of the means of repression and control that can be called modern, although they might often be found within the domains of the British empire. While no other country in Europe would imitate Britain's development precisely, almost all would try to apply aspects of British experience to their own situations. The settler colonies of the empire shared many aspects of British society and culture, some of which were transplanted into non-settler colonies as well. Before the rise of the United States as a global power, no nation had so profound an impact on what it meant to be modern as Great Britain.

The British state that has been studied in this book left an enormous and complicated legacy to the modern world, especially to countries that once formed part of its empire. In its settler colonies, Britain allowed representative institutions to spread, along with the rule of law, commercial values, and a broadly tolerant culture. The British legacy had a negative side as well, as the persistence of racial and social distinctions showed. In the non-settler colonies, Britain governed more autocratically. Even the positive aspects of the British legacy were not always freely bestowed. Britain rarely wanted to encourage self-government, economic autonomy, freedom, or equality in any of its colonies: these things were fought for by colonial peoples, not given by the colonizers. Nevertheless, the struggles of British history, from the Civil Wars to the Glorious Revolution to the reform movements, provided examples for colonial peoples to follow, and political languages with which to express their demands. Activists in Ireland and India, Canada and Australia, would draw on Britain's conflicted past in asserting the rights of their own people, just as the American revolutionaries did in the 1770s. Conservative politicians in the empire could look to British history too, for models of patriotic statesmanship and change without violent revolution. Today, the British empire is dead, and is not greatly missed, except by eccentrics and extreme nationalists. In many respects, it has been succeeded by the more informal imperial influence of Britain's rebellious eighteenth-century offspring, the United States. What legacy will America leave to the world? You will have to answer that question yourselves.

Notes

Chapter 2

1 Thomas More, *Utopia*, ed. David Wootton (Indianapolis, 1999), p. 66.
2 J[ohn]. W[orlidge]., *Systema Agriculturae, The Mystery of Husbandry Discovered* (London, 1669), p. 10.
3 Ibid., p. 16.
4 Andrew Yarranton, *The Improvement Improved, By A Second Edition Of The Great Improvement of Lands by Clover: Or, The Wonderful Advantage by, and right management of Clover* (London, 1663), pp. xi–xii.
5 John Evelyn, *Sylva, Or, A Discourse of Forest-Trees, And the Propagation of Timber in His Majesties Dominions* (London, 1664), p. 2.
6 Celia Fiennes, *Through England on a Side Saddle in the Time of William and Mary* (London, 1888), p. 207.
7 Ibid., p. 208.
8 Quoted in Keith Wrightson, *Earthly Necessities: Economic Lives in Early Modern Britain* (New Haven, CT, 2000), p. 171.
9 G. W. Groos, ed. and trans., *The Diary of Baron Waldstein, A Traveller in Elizabethan England* (London, 1981), pp. 33, 35.
10 Fiennes, *Through England on a Side Saddle*, p. 122.

Chapter 3

1 Quoted in Felicity Heal and Clive Holmes, *The Gentry in England and Wales, 1500–1700* (Stanford, CA, 1994), p. 7.
2 Quoted in Susan E. Whyman, *Sociability and Power in Late-Stuart England: The Cultural World of the Verneys, 1660–1720* (Oxford, 1999), p. 41.
3 Henry Smith, *A Preparative to Marriage*, in N. H. Keeble, ed., *The Cultural Identity of Seventeeenth-Century Woman* (London and New York, 1994), p. 149.
4 "Sir Anthony Ashley Cooper on His Wife Margaret, 1649," in Ralph Houlbrooke, ed., *English Family Life, 1576–1716* (Oxford, 1988), pp. 169–70.

5   Quoted in David Harris Sacks, *The Widening Gate: Bristol and the Atlantic Economy, 1450–1700* (Berkeley and Los Angeles, 1991), p. 61.

6   Robert Latham, ed., *The Shorter Pepys* (Berkeley and Los Angeles, 1985), pp. 183, 323.

7   Latham, ed., *The Shorter Pepys*, pp. 560, 597.

8   John Dryden, "Annus Mirabilis," verse 260, lines 1036–40, in Earl Miner, ed., *Selected Poetry and Prose of John Dryden* (New York, 1969), p. 165.

9   John Milton, *Paradise Lost*, ed. Alaistair Fowler (2nd edn, Harlow, 1998), p. 132, book II, lines 477–9.

10 Andrew Marvell, "Further Advice to a Painter," in George deF. Lord, ed., *Poems on Affairs of State, Volume I: 1660–1678* (New Haven, CT, 1963), p. 164, lines 3–4.

11 Celia Fiennes, *Through England on a Side Saddle in the Time of William and Mary* (London, 1888), p. 113.

12 Quoted in Ronald Hutton, *The Rise and Fall of Merry England: The Ritual Year, 1400–1700* (Oxford, 1994), p. 225.

Part II Introduction

1   John Bowle, ed., *The Diary of John Evelyn* (Oxford, 1965), p. 368.

Chapter 4

1   John Oldham, "Satires on the Jesuits," in Elias F. Mengel Jr, ed., *Poems on Affairs of State, Volume II: 1678–1681* (New Haven, CT, 1965), p. 26, lines 123–8.

2   "Presentment of the Grand Jury of Ossulston," quoted in Tim Harris, *London Crowds in the Reign of Charles II: Propaganda and Politics from the Restoration until the Exclusion Crisis* (Cambridge, 1987), pp. 143–4.

3   Quoted in Tim Harris, *Politics under the Later Stuarts: Party Conflict in a Divided Society, 1660–1715* (London, 1993), p. 104.

4   Quoted in Brian Cowan, *The Social Life of Coffee: The Emergence of the British Coffeehouse* (New Haven, CT, 2006), p. 212.

Chapter 5

1   "A New Ballad," in Elias F. Mengel Jr, ed., *Poems on Affairs of State, Volume II: 1678–1681* (New Haven, CT, 1965), p. 177, lines 21–5.

2   Quoted in Ronald Hutton, *Charles II: King of England, Scotland and Ireland* (Oxford, 1989), p. 346.

3   John Bowle, ed., *The Diary of John Evelyn* (Oxford, 1965), p. 290.

4   [Anon.], *Vox Patriae: Or, the Resentments and Indignation, of the Free-born Subjects of England, Against Popery, Arbitrary Government, the Duke of York, or Any Popish Successor* (London, 1681), p. i.

5   Thomas Stackhouse, ed., *Bishop Burnet's History of His Own Times* (London, 1906), p. 220.

6   Quoted in Tim Harris, *Revolution: The Great Crisis of the British Monarchy, 1685–1720* (London, 2006), p. 69.

7 Quoted in John Miller, *James II: A Study in Kingship* (London, 1989), p. 156.

8 J. P. Kenyon, ed., *The Stuart Constitution: Documents and Commentary* (Cambridge, 1966), pp. 410–11.

9 The quotes in this paragraph are from George Hilton Jones, *Convergent Forces: Immediate Causes of the Revolution of 1688 in England* (Ames, IA, 1990), pp. 12, 14.

10 John Locke, *A Letter Concerning Toleration*, ed. James H. Tully (Indianapolis, 1983), pp. 28, 39.

11 [Richard Claridge], *A Defence of the Present Government under King William and Queen Mary* (London, 1689), p. 5.

12 *The New Oath Examined, and found Guilty* ([London], [1689]).

13 Quoted in Harris, *Revolution*, p. 392.

Chapter 6

1 Richard Ligon, *A True and Exact History of the Island of Barbadoes* (London, 1673), p. 43.

2 Quoted in Richard Dunn, *Sugar and Slaves: The Rise of the Planter Class in the English West Indies, 1624–1713* (New York, 1973), p. 323.

3 Ligon, *True and Exact History*, pp. 47, 53.

4 Quoted in Dunn, *Sugar and Slaves*, p. 239.

5 Ligon, *True and Exact History*, p. 51.

6 Quoted in Edmund Morgan, *American Slavery, American Freedom: The Ordeal of Colonial Virginia* (New York, 1975), p. 312.

7 Increase Mather, *A Brief Relation of the State of New England* (London, 1689), p. 18.

8 T. Aubrey, *The Sea-Surgeon, or the Guinea Man's Vade Mecum* (London, 1729), pp. 121, 132.

Chapter 7

1 George Savile, Marquess of Halifax, quoted in J. R. Western, *Monarchy and Revolution: The English State in the 1680s* (London, 1972), p. 381.

2 Bishop Burnet, *A History of His Own Times*, ed. Thomas Stackhouse (London, 1906), p. 299.

3 Quoted in Edward Gregg, *Queen Anne* (London, 1984), p. 152.

4 Richard Steele, *Memoirs of the Life of the most noble Thomas, late Marquess of Wharton*, quoted in G. S. Holmes and W. A. Speck, eds, *The Divided Society: Parties and Politics in England, 1694–1716* (New York, 1968), p. 157.

5 Quoted in G. A. Cranfield, *The Press and Society, from Caxton to Northcliffe* (London, 1978), pp. 38–9.

6 *The High Church Address to Dr Henry Sacheverell* (London, 1710), p. 8, quoted in William Gibson, *Enlightenment Prelate: Benjamin Hoadly, 1676–1761* (Cambridge, 2004), p. 114.

7 *The Flying Post*, no. 3294, November 6–8, 1712, quoted in Geoffrey Holmes, *British Politics in the Age of Anne* (2nd edn, London and Ronceverte, 1987), p. 23.

8 [John Trenchard], *An Argument, Shewing, that a Standing Army Is inconsistent with A Free Government, And absolutely destructive to the Constitution of the English Monarchy* (London, 1697), p. 14.

9 [Henry Hall?], "Upon the King's Return from Flanders," in William J. Cameron, ed., *Poems on Affairs of State, Volume V: 1688–1697* (New Haven, CT, 1971), p. 455.

10 William Shippen, "Faction Display'd," in Frank H. Ellis, ed., *Poems on Affairs of State, Volume VI: 1697–1704* (New Haven, CT, 1970), p. 651, lines 9–12.

11 Sir Humphrey Mackworth, *Peace at Home: Or, A Vindication Of the Proceedings of the Honourable the House of Commons on the Bill for Preventing Danger from Occasional Conformity* (London, 1703), p. 2.

12 Quoted in David Chandler, *Marlborough as Military Commander* (London, 1973), p. 150.

13 Andrew Fletcher, *Political Writings*, ed. John Robertson (Cambridge, 1997), p. 132.

14 *A Letter Concerning Trade, from Several Scots-Gentlemen that are Merchants in England, To their Country-Men that are Merchants in Scotland* ([Edinburgh], [1706]), pp. 14–15.

Chapter 8

1 Henry Sacheverell, *The Perils of False Brethren, both in Church, and State* (2nd edn, London, 1709), p. 5.

2 Quoted in Geoffrey Holmes, *The Trial of Dr Sacheverell* (London, 1973), p. 144.

3 [Jonathan Swift], *The Conduct of the Allies, And of the Late Ministry, in the Beginning and Carrying On the Present War* (Edinburgh, 1712), p. 56.

4 Beatrice Curtis Brown, ed., *The Letters and Diplomatic Instructions of Queen Anne* (London, 1935), p. 403.

5 Harold Williams, ed., *The Correspondence of Jonathan Swift* (5 vols, Oxford, 1963–5), vol. 2, p. 101.

6 [Francis Atterbury], *English Advice to the Freeholders of England* (1714), pp. 6, 26, 30.

7 Quoted in Hannah Smith, *Georgian Monarchy: Politics and Culture, 1714–1760* (Cambridge, 2006), p. 27.

8 A. B. Grosart, ed., *The Towneley Manuscripts: English Jacobite Ballads, Songs and Satires, &c.* (Manchester, 1877), p. 7.

9 Quoted in Daniel Szechi, *1715: The Great Jacobite Rebellion* (New Haven, CT, 2006), p. 154.

10 [John Trenchard and Thomas Gordon], *Cato's Letters*, ed. Ronald Hamowy (2 vols, Indianapolis, 1995), vol. 1, p. 155, no. 21, March 18, 1720.

11 Thomas Hobbes, *Leviathan*, ed. Richard Tuck (Cambridge, 1996), p. 124.

12 John Locke, *Two Treatises of Government*, ed. Peter Laslett (Cambridge, 1988), pp. 350–1, 353.

13 [George I], *At the Court of St. James's, the 22th [sic] of September 1714. Present, the King's Most Excellent Majesty in Council* (London, 1714).

Chapter 9

1 Mary Astell, *Some Reflections upon Marriage* (London, 1703), p. 97.
2 Jeremy Collier, *A Short View of the Immorality, and Profaneness, of the English Stage* (London, 1698), p. 2.
3 John Dryden, "To My Honour'd Kinsman," in Earl Miner, ed., *Selected Poetry and Prose of John Dryden* (New York, 1969), p. 528, lines 1–4.
4 Alexander Pope, "The Rape of the Lock," in Aubrey Williams, ed., *Poetry and Prose of Alexander Pope* (Boston, 1969), p. 96, canto IV, lines 175–6.
5 Pope, "An Essay on Man," in ibid., p. 131, epistle II, lines 1–2; p. 157, epistle IV, line 394.
6 Jonathan Swift, *Gulliver's Travels*, ed. Paul Turner (Oxford, 1998), p. 288.
7 Ibid., p. 287.
8 Daniel Defoe, *Robinson Crusoe*, ed. Michael Shinagel (New York, 1994), pp. 64–5.
9 Joseph Addison and Richard Steele, *The Spectator*, ed. C. Gregory Smith (4 vols, London, 1958), vol. 2, p. 401, no. 302, February 15, 1712.
10 Ibid., vol. 1, p. 472, no. 156, August 29, 1711.
11 Allan Ramsay, *The Gentle Shepherd: A Scots Pastoral Comedy* (Edinburgh, 1725), p. 2, act I, scene 1.
12 Addison and Steele, *Spectator*, vol. 1, p. 56, no. 18, March 21, 1711.
13 Robert Boyle, *The Sceptical Chymist* (London, 1661), "Praeface Introductory," p. [vi].
14 Sir Isaac Newton, *The Mathematical Principles of Natural Philosophy*, trans. Andrew Motte (2 vols, London, 1729), vol. 1, "Author's Preface," p. [iv].
15 John Locke, *An Essay Concerning Human Understanding*, ed. Roger Woolhouse (Harmondsworth, 1997), book II, ch. 1, p. 109.

Chapter 10

1 Quoted in W. A. Speck, *Stability and Strife: England 1714–1760* (London, 1977), p. 228.
2 William Coxe, *Memoirs of the Life and Administration of Sir Robert Walpole* (3 vols, London, 1798), vol. 1, p. 757.
3 Romney Sedgwick, ed., *Lord Hervey's Memoirs* (abridged and revised edn, London, 1963), pp. 1, 6.
4 Ibid., pp. 247, 260.
5 Cambridge University Library, Cholmondeley (Houghton) Manuscripts, 65/54a.
6 Historical Manuscripts Commission, *Report on the Manuscripts of Lord Polwarth* (5 vols, London, 1911–61), vol. 5, p. 201.
7 Jonathan Swift, "A Letter to the Whole People of Ireland" in *The Drapier's Letters and Other Works*, ed. Herbert Davis (Oxford, 1941), p. 63.
8 Quoted in S. J. Connolly, *Religion, Law and Power: The Making of Protestant Ireland, 1660–1760* (Oxford, 1992), p. 239.
9 Coxe, *Memoirs of Walpole*, vol. 2, p. 263.
10 Sedgwick, ed., *Lord Hervey's Memoirs*, p. 65.
11 Alexander Pope, "The Dunciad, Part IV," in Aubrey Williams, ed., *Poetry and Prose of Alexander Pope* (Boston, 1969), p. 376, lines 601–4.
12 "Caleb D'Anvers" [Henry St John, Viscount Bolingbroke], *A Dissertation upon Parties* (3rd edn, London, 1735), pp. 108–9.

13 *The Craftsman*, no. 355, April 21, 1733.

14 Sedgwick, ed., *Memoirs of Lord Hervey*, p. 154.

15 Quoted in A. J. Henderson, *London and the National Government, 1721–1742* (Durham, NC, 1945), p. 183.

16 Quoted in B. W. Hill, *Sir Robert Walpole, "Sole and Prime Minister"* (London, 1989), p. 207.

17 *A Full Collection of All the Proclamations and Orders published by the Authority of Charles, Prince of Wales* ([Glasgow], [1745]), p. 10.

18 Samuel Haward, *Zeal and Loyalty Recommended, In a Sermon Preach'd at Poole in Dorsetshire, On Occasion of the Present Unnatural Rebellion, December 1st, 1745* (2nd edn, London, 1746), p. 10.

19 Henry Fielding, *The History of Tom Jones, A Foundling*, ed. Fredson Bowers (Middletown, CT, 1975), book 12, ch. 7, p. 647.

20 From the draft of a speech to be made after his accession, in Aubrey Newman, ed., "Leicester House Politics, 1750–1760: From the Papers of John, Second Earl of Egmont," *Camden Miscellany, 23*, Camden Society Publications, 4th Series, 7 (1969), pp. 119–20.

21 Quoted in Frank Felsenstein, *Anti-Semitic Stereotypes: A Paradigm of Otherness in English Popular Culture, 1660–1830* (Baltimore, 1995), pp. 205–6.

22 James, Earl Waldegrave, "Memoirs of 1754–1757," in J. C. D. Clark, ed., *The Memoirs and Speeches of James, 2nd Earl Waldegrave* (Cambridge, 1988), p. 155.

23 Quoted in Nicholas Rogers, *Whigs and Cities: Popular Politics in the Age of Walpole and Pitt* (Oxford, 1989), pp. 95–6.

24 [Anonymous], *All is Out – or, Admiral Byng* (London, [1756]).

25 William Pitt, *Letters written by the late Earl of Chatham to his Nephew Thomas Pitt, Esq. (afterwards Lord Camelford) then at Cambridge* (5th edn, London, 1805), p. 73.

26 *The Monitor*, no. 108, August 13, 1757, p. 647.

27 Quoted in John B. Owen, *The Eighteenth Century, 1714–1815* (New York, 1974), p. 87.

28 Horace Walpole, *Memoirs and Portraits*, ed. Matthew Hodgart (New York, 1963), p. 77.

29 Quoted in Andrew Charlesworth, ed., *An Atlas of Rural Protest in Britain, 1548–1900* (Philadelphia, 1983), p. 126.

30 Quoted in Bruce Lenman, *The Jacobite Clans of the Great Glen* (London, 1984), p. 194.

31 *The Monitor*, no. 276, November 1, 1760, p. 1670.

32 Philip Dormer-Stanhope, Earl of Chesterfield, *Lord Chesterfield's Worldly Wisdom: Selections from his Letters and Characters*, ed. George Birkbeck Hill (Oxford, 1891), p. 185.

33 Quoted in Jeremy Black, *George III: America's Last King* (New Haven, CT, 2006), p. 44.

34 Romney Sedgwick, *Letters from George III to Lord Bute, 1756–1766* (London, 1939), p. 18.

Chapter 11

1 Henry St. John, Viscount Bolingbroke, *A Letter to Sir William Windham, etc.* (London, 1753), pp. 27–8.

2 Daniel Defoe, *A Tour through England and Wales* (2 vols, London, 1959), vol. 1, p. 336.

3 Quoted in J. V. Beckett, *The Aristocracy in England, 1660–1914* (Oxford, 1986), p. 83.

4 Defoe, *Tour through England and Wales*, vol. 2, p. 34.

5 Quoted in John Smail, *The Origins of Middle Class Culture: Halifax, Yorkshire, 1660–1780* (Ithaca, NY, 1994), p. 204.

6 Henry St John, Viscount Bolingbroke, "On Luxury," in *A Collection of Political Tracts* (London, 1748), pp. 73, 76.

7 Bernard Mandeville, *The Fable of the Bees, or Prviate Vices, Publick Benefits*, ed. F. B. Kaye (2 vols, Indianapolis, 1988), vol. 1, p. 123.

8 Defoe, *Tour through England and Wales*, vol. 1, p. 260; vol. 2, pp. 80, 213.

9 Ibid., vol. 2, p. 251.

10 Henry Fielding, *An Enquiry into the Causes of the Late Increase of Robbers* (Dublin, 1751), p. 1, 3.

11 Henry Fielding, *A True State of the Case of Bosavern Penlez* (London, 1749), p. 52.

12 Quoted in John R. Gillis, *For Better, For Worse: British Marriages, 1600 to the Present* (Oxford, 1985), p. 94.

13 Daniel Rowland, *Eight Sermons Upon Practical Subjects* (2nd edn, London, [1774]), p. 60.

14 George Whitefield, *The Nature and Necessity of our NEW BIRTH in Christ Jesus, in Order to Salvation. A Sermon Preached in the Church of St Mary Radcliffe in Bristol* (London, 1737), p. 2.

15 John Wesley, *Advice to the People Called Methodists* ([Newcastle upon Tyne], 1745), p. 5.

16 Quoted in John Kent, *Wesley and the Wesleyans: Religion in Eighteenth-Century Britain* (Cambridge, 2002), p. 34.

17 Daniel Rowland, *Three Sermons Upon Practical Subjects* (London, 1778), p. 77.

Chapter 12

1 "A True Antigallican," *Britain, Strike Home. A Poem. Humbly Inscribed to Every Briton* (London, 1754), pp. 6, 7, 9.

2 Captain Cope, *A New History of the East-Indies* (London, 1754), p. iii.

3 William Burke, *An Account of the European Settlements in America* (2 vols., London, 1757), vol. 2, pp. 119, 122.

4 Quoted in Mavis C. Campbell, *The Maroons of Jamaica, 1655–1796: A History of Resistance, Collaboration and Betrayal* (Granby, MA, 1988), pp. 127–8.

5 Quoted in Bernard Bailyn, *The Origins of American Politics* (New York, 1967), p. 126.

6 Jonathan Edwards, "The Distinguishing Marks of a Work of the Spirit," in Alan Heimert and Perry Miller, eds., *The Great Awakening: Documents Illustrating the Crisis and Its Consequences* (Indianapolis, 1967), pp. 205, 212.

7 Quoted in Richard Bushman, *The Refinement of America: Persons, Houses, Cities* (New York, 1992), p. 39.

8 Benjamin Franklin, *Reflexions on Courtship and Marriage: In Two Letters to a Friend* (Philadelphia and Edinburgh, 1750), p. 16.

9 Quoted in Fred Anderson, *Crucible of War: The Seven Years' War and the Fate of Empire in British North America, 1754–1766* (New York, 2000), p. 38.

10 Samuel Cooper, *A Sermon Preached before His Excellency Thomas Pownall, Esq; Captain-General and Governor in Chief, The Honorable His Majesty's Council and House of Representatives, of the Province of the Massachusetts-Bay in New-England, October 16th, 1759. Upon Occasion of the Success of His Majesty's Arms in the Reduction of Quebec* (Boston, [1759]), p. 53.

11 John Campbell, *Memoirs of the Revolution in Bengal* (London, 1764), pp. 119, 121.

12 Peter Quenell, ed., *Memoirs of William Hickey* (London, 1984), p. 234.

Chapter 13

1 James Boswell, *The Life of Johnson*, ed. Christopher Hibbert (Harmondsworth, 1979), p. 182, April 1775.

2 John Carswell and Lewis Arnold Dralle, eds, *The Political Journal of George Bubb Dodington* (Oxford, 1965), p. 387.

3 Ibid., p. 50.

4 Quoted in John Brooke, *King George III* (London, 1972), p. 485.

5 *A Select Collection of the Most Interesting Letters on the Government, Liberty and Constitution of England; which have appear'd in the different News-papers, from the elevation of Lord Bute, to the Death of the Earl of Egremont* (2nd edn, 3 vols, London, 1763), vol. 1, p. 15.

6 Romney Sedgwick, ed., *Letters of George III to Lord Bute* (London, 1939), p. 212.

7 [John Wilkes], *The North Briton* (2nd edn, 3 vols, Dublin, 1763), vol. 2, p. 228, no. 45, April 23, 1763.

8 Quoted in Peter Wagner, *Eros Revived: Erotica of the Enlightenment in England and America* (London, 1988), p. 54.

9 Edmund Morgan, ed., *Prologue to Revolution: Sources and Documents on the Stamp Act Crisis, 1765–1766* (New York, 1973), pp. 56, 63.

10 Sedgwick, ed., *Letters from George III to Lord Bute*, p. 233.

11 "The Declaratory Act," in Morgan, ed., *Prologue to Revolution*, p. 155.

12 Leonard W. Labaree et al., eds, *The Papers of Benjamin Franklin* (38 vols, New Haven, CT, 1959–), vol. 13, p. 186.

13 Quoted in G. M. Ditchfield, *George III: An Essay in Monarchy* (London, 2002), p. 122.

14 Quoted in Arthur H. Cash, *John Wilkes: The Scandalous Father of Civil Liberty* (New Haven, CT, 2006), p. 4.

15 Quoted in George Rudé, *Paris and London in the Eighteenth Century: Studies in Popular Protest* (New York, 1971), p. 234.

16 *English Liberty Established: Or, The most material Circumstances relative to John Wilkes, Esq; Member of Parliament for the County of Middlesex* (London, 1768), p. 16.

17 Quoted in Cash, *John Wilkes*, p. 248.

18 [Sir William Meredith], *The Question Stated: Whether the Freeholders of Middlesex Lost their Right, by Voting for Mr Wilkes at the Last Election?* (London, 1769), p. 72.

19 C. W. Everett, ed., *The Letters of Junius* (London, 1927), pp. 135–48, letter 35, December 19, 1769.

20 Ibid., p. 149, letter 36, February 14, 1770.

Chapter 14

1 Leonard W. Labaree et al., eds, *The Papers of Benjamin Franklin* (38 vols, New Haven, CT, 1959–), vol. 17, p. 114.

2 Edmund Burke, *Thoughts on the Cause of the Present Discontents*, in Paul Langford, ed., *The Writings and Speeches of Edmund Burke, Volume 2: Party, Parliament, and the American Crisis, 1766–1774* (Oxford, 1981), pp. 260–1, 265, 313, 315.

3 Catharine Macaulay, *Observations on a Pamphlet, entitled, Thoughts on the Cause of the Present Discontents* (4th edn, London, 1770), pp. 7, 17.

4 Labaree et al., eds, *Papers of Benjamin Franklin*, vol. 16, p. 10.

5 W. Bodham Donne, ed., *The Correspondence of King George the Third with Lord North from 1768 to 1783* (2 vols, London, 1867), vol. 1, p. 184.

6 K. G. Davies, ed., *Documents of the American Revolution, 1770–1783* (21 vols, Dublin, 1972–81), vol. 8, pp. 153, 181, 266.

7 Donne, ed., *Correspondence of George III with Lord North*, vol. 1, p. 202.

8 Edmund Burke, "Speech on Conciliation with America," in W. M. Elofson and John A. Woods, eds, *The Writings and Speeches of Edmund Burke, Volume 3* (Oxford, 1996), pp. 132–3.

9 Thomas Paine, *Common Sense*, in *Rights of Man, Common Sense and Other Political Writings*, ed. Mark Philp (Oxford, 1995), pp. 8, 30.

10 Labaree et al., eds, *Papers of Benjamin Franklin*, vol. 22, p. 519.

11 Samuel Johnson, *Taxation no Tyranny*, in *Political Writings*, ed. Donald J. Greene (Indianapolis, 2000), p. 454.

12 Davies, ed., *Documents of the American Revolution*, vol 12, p. 232.

13 Thomas Paine, *The American Crisis, No. 1*, in *Rights of Man*, ed. Philp, p. 63.

14 Labaree et al., eds, *Papers of Benjamin Franklin*, vol. 25, p. 104.

15 Donne, ed., *Correspondence of King George III with Lord North*, vol. 2, p. 393.

16 Quoted in Peter D. G. Thomas, *Lord North* (London, 1976), p. 132.

17 Quoted in James E. Bradley, *Religion, Revolution and English Radicalism: Nonconformity in Eighteenth-Century Politics and Society* (Cambridge, 1990), p. 153.

18 David Hartley, *Letters on the American War* ([London], [1778]), p. 1.

19 John Cartwright, *Take Your Choice!* (London, 1776), pp. 21–2.

20 Thomas Holcroft, *A Plain and Succinct Narrative of the Late Riots and Disturbances in the Cities of London and Westminster, and Borough of Southwark* (London, 1780), p. 33.

Chapter 15

1 Quoted in J. M. Neeson, *Commoners: Common Right, Enclosure and Social Change in England, 1700–1820* (Cambridge, 1993), p. 268.

2 Jethro Tull, *The Horse-Hoeing Husbandry: Or, An Essay On the Principles of Tillage and Vegetation* (London, 1733), p. 129.

3 John Aikin, *A Description of the Country from Thirty to Forty Miles Around Manchester* (London, [1795]), pp. 112, 116–17.

4 Quoted in Paul Mantoux, *The Industrial Revolution in the Eighteenth Century* (revised edn, Chicago and London, 1961, 1983), p. 306.

5 [Anonymous], *The Case of Mr Richard Arkwright and Co.* ([London], [1782]), p. 1.

6 Adam Smith, *An Inquiry into the Nature and Causes of the Wealth of Nations*, ed. W. B. Todd (2 vols, Indianapolis, 1981), vol. 1, pp. 14–15, 19–20.

Chapter 16

1 Quoted in John Brooke, *George III* (London, 1972), p. 413.

2 [Anonymous], *New Taxes Unnecessary! A Plan for Paying the National Debt, Without Levying any Tax, or Borrowing Any Money* (Southwark, [1784]), p. 1.

3 [Anonymous], *Fox against Fox!!! Or Political Blossoms of the Right Hon. Charles James Fox* (London, 1788), pp. 68, 69.

4 Lord John Russell, ed., *Memorials and Correspondence of Charles James Fox* (2 vols., Philadelphia, 1853), vol. 2, p. 244.

5 Quoted in Nigel Aston, "St Paul's and the Public Culture of Eighteenth-Century Britain," in Derek Keene, Arthur Burns and Andrew Saint, eds, *St Paul's: The Cathedral Church of London, 604–2004* (New Haven, CT, 2004), p. 369.

6 Anna Laetitia Barbauld, *An Address to the Opposers of the Repeal of the Test and Corporation Acts* (4th edn, London, 1790), pp. 7–8.

7 Richard Price, *A Discourse on the Love of Our Country* (London, 1790), pp. 34, 35, 39.

8 Edmund Burke, *Reflections on the Revolution in France*, in L. G. Mitchell, ed., *The Writings and Speeches of Edmund Burke, Volume 8: The French Revolution, 1790–1794* (Oxford, 1989), pp. 86, 90, 147.

9 Thomas Paine, *Rights of Man* (1791), in *Rights of Man, Common Sense and Other Political Writings*, ed. Mark Philp (Oxford, 1995), pp. 91–2, 190.

10 Mary Wollstonecraft, *Vindication of the Rights of Woman*, ed. Miriam Brody Kramnick (Harmondsworth, 1982), p. 121.

11 Quoted in Albert Goodwin, *The Friends of Liberty: The English Democratic Movement in the Age of the French Revolution* (London, 1979), p. 255.

12 Robert Burns, "Bruce's Address to his Army at Bannockburn," in *The Poetical Works of Robert Burns* (London, 1911), p. 324.

13 [John Ashley], *To the Parliament and People of Great Britain, An Explicit Declaration of the Principles and Views of the London Corresponding Society* (London, 1795), pp. 2–3.

14 "The declaration, resolution and constitutions of the society of United Irishmen, 1797," in Edmund Curtis and R. B. McDowell, eds, *Irish Historical Documents, 1172–1922* (New York, 1968), p. 240.

15 Quoted in Marianne Elliott, *Wolfe Tone: Prophet of Irish Independence* (New Haven, CT, 1989), pp. 392–3.

16 Quoted in Goodwin, *Friends of Liberty*, p. 452.

17 Horace Twiss, *The Public and Private Life of Lord Chancellor Eldon, with Selections from His Correspondence* (3 vols, London, 1844), vol. 2, p. 34.

18 Spencer Walpole, *The Life of the Right Honourable Spencer Perceval* (2 vols, London, 1874), vol. 2, pp. 170, 171.

19 Linda Colley, *Britons: Forging the Nation, 1707–1837* (New Haven, CT, 1992), p. 308.

Chapter 17

1 Quoted in Anne Salmond, *The Trial of the Cannibal Dog: The Remarkable Story of Captain Cook's Encounters in the South Seas* (New Haven, CT, 2003), p. 57.
2 Sydney Parkinson, *A Journal of a Voyage to the South Seas, in His Majesty's Ship the Endeavour* (London, 1784), p. 15.
3 Quoted in Robert Hughes, *The Fatal Shore* (New York, 1986), p. 95.
4 Speeches of 7 May 1789 and 5 June 1794, in P. J. Marshall, ed., *The Writings and Speeches of Edmund Burke, vol. 7: India: The Hastings Trial, 1789–1794* (Oxford, 2000), pp. 63, 392–3.
5 Charles Ross, ed., *Correspondence of Charles, First Marquis Cornwallis* (3 vols, London, 1859), vol. 1, pp. 385, 547–8.
6 Ibid., vol. 1, p. 546.
7 Robert Rouiere Pierce, *Memoirs and Correspondence of the Most Noble Richard Marquess Wellesley* (3 vols, London, 1846), vol. 1, p. 213.
8 Quoted in John Ehrman, *The Younger Pitt: The Years of Acclaim* (London, 1969), p. 370.
9 Quoted in Fernand Ouellet, *Lower Canada, 1791–1840: Social Change and Nationalism*, trans. Patricia Claxton (Toronto, 1980), p. 101.
10 Granville Sharp, *An Appendix to the Representation (Printed in the Year 1769) of the Injustice and Dangerous Tendency of Tolerating Slavery, or of Admitting the least Claim of Private Property in the Persons of Men in England* (London, 1772), p. 6.
11 Olaudah Equiano, *The Interesting Narrative and Other Writings*, ed. Vincent Carretta (Harmondsworth, 1995), p. 107.
12 Quoted in John Pollock, *Wilberforce* (New York, 1977), p. 89.

Chapter 18

1 Thomas Garnett, *Observations on a Tour Through the Highlands and Part of the Western Isles of Scotland* (2 vols, London, 1800), vol. 2, pp. 201, 202.
2 David Hume, *Enquiries Concerning Human Understanding and Concerning the Principles of Morals*, eds. L. A. Selby-Bigge and P. H. Nidditch (3rd edn, London, 1989), pp. 29, 131, 272, paras 25, 101, 221.
3 Thomas Reid, *An Inquiry into the Human Mind on the Principles of Common Sense*, ed. Derek R. Brookes (Edinburgh, 1997), pp. 215, 257.
4 Adam Smith, *The Theory of the Moral Sentiments*, eds D. D. Raphael and A. L. Macfie (Indianapolis, 1984), p. 85.
5 James Boswell, *The Life of Johnson*, ed. Christopher Hibbert (Harmondsworth, 1981), pp. 138, 164.
6 Edward Gibbon, *Memoirs of My Life* (Harmondsworth, 1984), p. 143.
7 Edward Gibbon, *The History of the Decline and Fall of the Roman Empire* (6 vols, London, 1776–88), vol. 1, p. 525.
8 Joseph Priestley, *An Essay on the First Principles of Government; and on the Nature of Political, Civil, and Religious Liberty* (London, 1768), p. 64.
9 Jeremy Bentham, *An Introduction to the Principles of Morals and Legislation*, eds J. H. Burns and H. L. A. Hart (London, 1970), p. 12.

10 Thomas Malthus, *An Essay on the Principle of Population and A Summary View of the Principle of Population*, ed. Anthony Flew (Harmondsworth, 1976), p. 89.

11 William Law, *A Serious Call to a Serious and Devout Life* (London and New York, 1940), pp. 23–4.

12 Samuel Richardson, *Clarissa, or, The History of a Young Lady* (4 vols, London, Melbourne and Toronto, 1962), vol. 1, p. 325.

13 James Boswell, *Boswell's London Journal, 1762–1763*, ed. Frederick A. Pottle (New York, 1950), p. 39.

14 Burns, "Scot's Prologue," in *The Poetical Works of Robert Burns* (London, 1911), p. 211.

15 Edmund Burke, *A Philosophical Enquiry into the Origins of Our Ideas of the Sublime and the Beautiful*, in T. O. McLoughlin and James T. Boulton, eds, *The Writings and Speeches of Edmund Burke, Volume 1: The Early Writings* (Oxford, 1997), p. 230.

16 William Blake, "The French Revolution," in Geoffrey Keynes, ed., *Poetry and Prose of William Blake* (London, 1946), p. 166.

17 Quoted in Richard Holmes, *Coleridge: Early Visions* (New York, 1989), p. 116.

18 William Wordsworth, "The Prelude (1850 edn)," in Thomas Hutchinson, ed., *Wordsworth: Poetical Works* (London, 1974), p. 570, book 11, lines 108–12.

19 Wordsworth, "Poems Dedicated to National Independence and Liberty," in ibid., p. 243, no. 10, lines 9–11.

20 Percy Bysshe Shelley, "Queen Mab," in Donald H. Reiman and Sharon B. Powers, eds, *Shelley's Poetry and Prose* (New York, 1977), p. 63, canto 9, lines 1, 4.

21 John Keats, "Ode on a Grecian Urn," in John Barnard, ed., *John Keats: The Complete Poems* (3rd edn, Harmondsworth, 1988), p. 346, lines 49–50.

Chapter 19

1 Quoted in John Cannon, *Aristocratic Century: The Peerage of Eighteenth-Century England* (Cambridge, 1984), p. 169.

2 John Gore, ed., *The Creevey Papers* (London, 1963), p. 165.

3 T. B. Oldfield and Henry Hallam, quoted in H. J. Hanham, ed., *The Nineteenth Century Constitution* (Cambridge, 1969), p. 6.

4 Cited in Robert Duke Yonge, *The Life and Administration of Robert Banks, Second Earl of Liverpool* (3 vols, London, 1868), vol. 2, p. 289.

5 Samuel Bamford, *Passages in the Life of a Radical* (Oxford, 1984), p. 31.

6 Quoted in E. P. Thompson, *The Making of the English Working Class* (Harmondsworth, 1968), p. 724.

7 *The Black Dwarf*, April 16, 1817, in G. D. H. Cole and A. W. Filson, eds, *British Working Class Movements: Selected Documents 1789–1875* (London, 1965), p. 146.

8 Bamford, *Passages*, p. 146.

9 Quoted in Yonge, *Life and Administration of Robert Banks*, vol. 2, p. 431.

10 Quoted in Nicholas Rogers, *Crowds, Culture and Politics in Georgian Britain* (Oxford, 1998), p. 256.

11 Roger Fulford, ed., *The Greville Memoirs* (London, 1963), p. 1.

12 Edward J. Stapleton, ed., *Some Official Correspondence of George Canning* (2 vols, London, 1887), vol. 2, p. 28.

13 W. T. Haly, ed., *The Opinions of Sir Robert Peel, Expressed in Parliament and in Public* (London, 1843), p. 9.

14 Fulford, ed., *Greville Memoirs*, p. 27.

15 William Benbow, "The Grand National Holiday," in Cole and Filson, eds, *British Working Class Movements*, p. 230.

16 Speech of March 2, 1831, in Sydney W. Jackman, ed., *The English Reform Tradition, 1790–1810* (Englewood Cliffs, NJ, 1965), p. 55.

17 Quoted in John Cannon, *Parliamentary Reform, 1640–1832* (Cambridge, 1972), p. 260.

18 Fulford, ed., *Greville Memoirs*, p. 121.

Chapter 20

1   Quoted in David Cannadine, *The Rise and Fall of Class in Britain* (New York, 1999), p. 82.

2   Jane Austen, *Emma*, ed. Ronald Blythe (Harmondsworth, 1981), pp. 217–18.

3   Quoted in Venetia Murray, *An Elegant Madness: High Society in Regency England* (Harmondsworth, 1998), p. 108.

4   James Fenimore Cooper, *Gleanings in Europe: England*, eds Donald A. Ringe and Kenneth W. Stagges (Albany, NY, 1982), p. 121.

5   John Gore, ed., *The Creevey Papers* (London, 1963), p. 180.

6   Quoted in Dror Wahrman, *Imagining the Middle Class: The Political Representation of Class in Britain, c.1780–1840* (Cambridge, 1999), p. 248.

7   Quoted in Harold Perkin, *The Origins of Modern English Society* (London and Henley, 1969), p. 230.

8   William Roscoe, "Mount Pleasant," in George Chandler, *William Roscoe of Liverpool, 1753–1831* (London, 1953), p. 334.

9   Quoted in E. P. Thompson, *The Making of the English Working Class* (Harmondsworth, 1968), p. 329.

10 Quoted in John Rule, *The Labouring Classes in Early Industrial England, 1750–1850* (London and New York, 1986), p. 86.

11 Quoted in Barbara Taylor, *Eve and the New Jerusalem: Socialism and Feminism in the Nineteenth Century* (New York, 1983), p. 87.

12 "The Owenite Program," in Cole and Filson, eds, *British Working Class Documents*, p. 271.

13 Mary Thale, ed., *The Autobiography of Francis Place (1771–1854)* (Cambridge, 1972), p. 73.

14 Quoted in Robert W. Malcolmson, *Popular Recreations in English Society, 1700–1850* (Cambridge, 1973), p. 106.

15 William Cobbett, *Rural Rides* (London, 1958), pp. 43, 219, 256, 306.

16 Quoted in Eric Hobsbawm and George Rudé, *Captain Swing: A Social History of the Great English Agricultural Uprising of 1830* (New York, 1968), pp. 119, 204–5.

17 Cooper, *England*, p. 188.

18 Jane Austen, *Persuasion*, ed. D. W. Harding (Harmondsworth, 1965), p. 250.

19 "Pearce Stevenson" [Caroline Norton], *A Plain Letter to the Lord Chancellor on the Infant Custody Bill* (London, 1839), pp. 4–5.

20 Quoted in Leonore Davidoff and Catherine Hall, *Family Fortunes: Men and Women of the English Middle Class, 1780–1850* (London, 1987), p. 174.

21 Thale, ed., *Autobiography of Francis Place*, p. 77.

22 Quoted in Anna Clark, *The Struggle for the Breeches: Gender and the Making of the British Working Class* (Berkeley and Los Angeles, 1995), p. 78.

23 Thale, ed., *Autobiography of Francis Place*, p. 81.

24 Quoted in Elie Halévy, *A History of the English People in the Nineteenth Century, Volume 1: England in 1815*, trans. E. I. Watkin and D. A. Barker (London, 1970), p. 263.

25 Quoted in John R. Gillis, *For Better, For Worse: British Marriages, 1600 to the Present* (Oxford, 1985), p. 239.

26 Quoted in Taylor, *Eve and the New Jerusalem*, p. 147.

Chapter 21

1 "Discours de Papineau sur la première résolution," in Fernand Ouellet, ed., *Papineau* (2nd edn, Quebec, 1970), p. 54.

2 Quoted in Fernand Ouellet, *Lower Canada 1791–1840: Social Change and Nationalism*, trans. Patricia Claxton (Toronto, 1980), p. 289.

3 Catherine Parr Traill, *The Backwoods of Canada: Being Letters from the Wife of an Emigrant Officer, Illustrative of the Domestic Economy of British America* (3rd edn, London, 1838), p. 56.

4 Ibid., pp. 176, 177, 181.

5 Ibid., p. 83.

6 Ibid., pp. 63, 220.

7 Mary Prince, *The History of Mary Prince, A West Indian Slave*, ed. Sara Salih (Harmondsworth, 2000), pp. 11.

8 Ibid., p. 15.

9 Ibid., p. 24.

10 Ibid., p. 33.

11 Ibid., pp. 37–8.

12 Rammohan Roy, "Brief Remarks Concerning Modern Encroachments on the Ancient Rights of Females," in Bruce Carlisle Robertson, ed., *The Essential Writings of Raja Rammohan Roy* (Delhi, 1999), p. 147.

13 Ibid., pp. 163–4.

14 James Mill, *The History of British India*, ed. H. H. Wilson (5 vols, London, 1848), vol. 1, pp. 480–1.

15 Ibid., vol. 1, p. 447.

16 Ibid., vol. 1, pp. 417–18.

17 Roy, *Essential Writings*, pp. 224–5.

18 Thomas Babington Macaulay, "Minute on Indian Education," in G. O. Trevelyan, *The Competition Wallah* (2nd edn, London, 1866), p. 322.

19 Mary Martha Sherwood, in Indira Ghose, ed., *Memsahibs Abroad: Writings by Women Travellers in Nineteenth Century India* (Delhi, 1998), pp. 42–3, 88–9.

20 Frances Parks, in ibid., pp. 113, 162, 168–9.

21 Anna Harriette Leonowens, in ibid., pp. 180–1.

22 Emma Roberts, in ibid., pp. 112, 189, 283.

23 Emily Eden, in ibid., p. 116.

24 Peter Cunningham, *Two Years in New South Wales* (London, 1827), vol. 1, p. 7.

25 Ibid., vol. 2, pp. 45–6, 119, 210.

26 "Robert Gouger" [i.e. Edward Gibbon Wakefield], *A Letter from Sydney, The Principal Town of Australasia* (London, 1829), p. 196.

27 Quoted in Robin Haines, *Life and Death in the Age of Sail: The Passage to Australia* (Sydney, 2003), p. 103.

28 Quoted in ibid., pp. 119–21.

Bibliography

This list of secondary sources includes only books, most of them printed in the past 30 years. Articles that have appeared in scholarly journals are not included, but students should not ignore them. Among the most important journals that publish articles in British history are *Past and Present*, *The Historical Journal*, *The Journal of British Studies*, *The English Historical Review*, *The Scottish Historical Review*, *The Welsh History Review*, and *History*. Many other specialized journals exist, covering specific areas of study (for example, social, economic, or gender history), regions (the Midlands, the North, etc.) and time periods. All of the major nations that were once part of the British empire have their own historical journals. Articles can be found through the online library service known as *Historical Abstracts*, through indexes to individual journals (which are often available online), or through searching journal databases like JSTOR, to which many research libraries subscribe.

Primary sources – that is, contemporary writings and materials – can be tracked down through the notes and bibliographies found in secondary works. If you lack direct access to primary sources in British history, you might seek out a library that subscribes to a digitized collection. Two major databases of digitized primary materials exist for this period: *Early English Books Online* from Chadwyck Healey and *Eighteenth-Century Collections Online* from Gale. Each of them contains more than 125,000 digitized books. Some sources are available online without paying a subscription, including the important and expanding collection entitled *British History Online*, found at http://www.british-history.ac.uk. Another free online database is the *Proceedings of the Old Bailey*, the chief court in London, which can be found at http://www.oldbaileyonline.org. A number of free digitized sources are gradually becoming available through BOPCRIS (the British Official Publications Collaborative Reader Information Services at the University of Southampton), the Oxford Digital Library Project, and various projects at the British Library, although access to some of them may be restricted.

If you are researching the biography of an individual, you should begin with the *Oxford Dictionary of National Biography*, which is available online in many research libraries. If the person you are researching was a Member of the House of Commons, you should consult the series of volumes known as *The History of Parliament*, which contains information on individuals, constituencies, and elections. For the period covered by this book, *The History of Parliament* is divided into five parts: 1660–90 (edited by Basil Duke Henning), 1690–1714 (edited by Eveline Cruickshanks), 1714–54 (edited by Romney Sedgwick), 1754–90 (edited by Sir Lewis Namier and John Brooke) and 1790–1820 (edited by R. G. Thorne).

Many memoirs, journals, and letters for this period have been issued in multivolume editions. Some of the most important are the *Memoirs* of John, Lord Hervey, for the reign of George II (edited by Romney Sedgwick); Horace Walpole's enormous correspondence (edited by W. S. Lewis); Horace Walpole's *Memoirs* of the reigns of George II and George III; James Boswell's journals, covering the period 1762 to 1795; the correspondence of Edmund Burke; the diaries and journals of Frances (Fanny) Burney, later Madame D'Arblay; and the *Memoirs* of Charles Greville for the reigns of George IV and William IV.

If you are lucky enough to have the opportunity to do some research in England or Wales, you should first consult the online catalogue of national archives at http://www.nationalarchives.gov.uk. An equivalent catalogue of Scottish archives is at http://www.scan.org.uk.

Great Britain and Ireland

Textboooks, Surveys, and Companions

England, Wales, and Scotland

Bucholz, Robert, and Key, Newton. *Early Modern England, 1485–1714*. Oxford, 2004.

Christie, Ian. *Wars and Revolutions: English History 1760–1815*. London, 1982.

Davies, John. *A History of Wales*. Harmondsworth, 2007.

Devine, T. M. *The Scottish Nation: A History, 1700–2000*. Harmondsworth, 1999.

Dickinson, H. T., ed. *A Companion to Eighteenth-Century Britain*. Oxford, 2002.

Hilton, Boyd. *A Mad, Bad and Dangerous People? England 1783–1846*. Oxford, 2006.

Holmes, Geoffrey. *The Making of a Great Power: Late Stuart and Early Georgian Britain, 1660–1722*. London, 1993.

Holmes, Geoffrey, and Szechi, Daniel. *The Age of Oligarchy: Pre-Industrial Britain, 1722–1783*. London, 1993.

Hoppit, Julian. *A Land of Liberty? England, 1689–1727*. Oxford, 2000.

Jenkins, Geraint. *The Foundations of Modern Wales, 1642–1780*. Oxford, 1987.

Jones, J. R. *Country and Court: England, 1658–1714*. London, 1978.

Kearney, Hugh. *The British Isles: A History of Four Nations*. Cambridge, 2006.

Kishlansky, Mark. *A Monarchy Transformed: Britain 1603–1714*. London, 1996.

Langford, Paul. *A Polite and Commercial People: England 1727–1788*. Oxford, 1989.

Lenman, Bruce. *Integration and Enlightenment: Scotland, 1746–1832*. Edinburgh, 1992.

O'Gorman, Frank. *The Long Eighteenth Century: British Political and Social History, 1688–1832*. New York, 1997.

Owen, John B. *The Eighteenth Century, 1714–1815*. New York, 1974.

Prest, Wilfrid. *Albion Ascendant: English History, 1660–1815*. Oxford, 1998.

Speck, W. S. *Stability and Strife: England, 1714–1760*. London, 1977.

Smout, T. C. *A History of the Scottish People, 1560–1830*. London, 1969.

Webb, R. K. *Modern England*. New York, 1980.

Ireland

Connolly, S. J., ed. *The Oxford Companion to Irish History.* Oxford, 1998.

Foster, R. F. *Modern Ireland.* Harmondsworth, 1990.

Cullen, L. B. *The Emergence of Modern Ireland.* London, 1981.

Moody, T. W., Martin, F. X., and Byrne, F. J., eds. *A New History of Ireland.* 9 volumes, Oxford, 1976–90.

Politics and Government, 1660–1714

England and Wales

Black, Jeremy. *A System of Ambition? British Foreign Policy, 1660–1793.* Stroud, 2000.

Brewer, John. *The Sinews of Power: War, Money and the English State, 1688–1783.* New York, 1989.

Bucholz, R. O. *The Augustan Court: Queen Anne and the Decline of Court Culture.* Stanford, CA, 1993.

DeKrey, Gary Stuart. *A Fractured Society: The Politics of London in the First Age of Party, 1688–1719.* Oxford, 1985.

Dickinson, H. T. *Bolingbroke.* London, 1975.

Dickinson, H. T. *Liberty and Property: Political Ideology in Eighteenth-Century Britain.* London, 1977.

Downie, J. A. *Robert Harley and the Press: Propaganda and Public Opinion in the Age of Swift and Defoe.* Cambridge, 1977.

Gregg, Edward. *Queen Anne.* London, 1984.

Harris, Tim. *Politics under the Later Stuarts: Party Conflict in a Divided Society, 1660–1715.* London, 1993.

Harris, Tim. *Restoration: Charles II and His Kingdoms, 1660–1685.* London, 2005.

Harris, Tim. *Revolution: The Great Crisis of the British Monarchy, 1685–1720.* London, 2006.

Holmes, Geoffrey. *British Politics in the Age of Anne.* London, 1987.

Holmes, Geoffrey. *The Trial of Dr Sacheverell.* London, 1973.

Horwitz, Henry. *Parliament, Policy and Politics in the Reign of William III.* Manchester, 1977.

Hutton, Ronald. *Charles II, King of England, Scotland and Ireland.* Oxford, 1989.

Hutton, Ronald. *The Restoration: A Political and Religious History of England and Wales, 1658–1667* (Oxford, 1985).

Kenyon, John. *Revolution Politics: The Politics of Party, 1689–1720.* Cambridge, 1977.

Langford, Paul. *Public Life and the Propertied Englishman, 1689–1798.* Oxford, 1992.

Lenman, Bruce. *The Jacobite Risings in Britain, 1689–1746.* London, 1981.

Miller, John. *James II: A Study in Kingship.* London, 1989.

Monod, Paul Kléber. *Jacobitism and the English People, 1688–1788.* Cambridge, 1989.

Pincus, Steven C. A. *Protestantism and Patriotism: Ideologies and the Making of English Foreign Policy, 1650–1688.* Cambridge, 1996.

Schwoerer, Lois, ed. *The Revolution of 1688–1689: Changing Perspectives.* Cambridge, 1992.

Speck, W. A. *Reluctant Revolutionaries: Englishmen and the Revolution of 1688.* Oxford, 1989.

Speck, W. A. *Tory and Whig: The Struggle in the Constituencies, 1701–1715*. London, 1970.

Stone, Lawrence, ed. *An Imperial State at War: Britain from 1689 to 1815*. New York, 1994.

Szechi, Daniel. *The Jacobites: Britain and Europe, 1688–1788*. Manchester, 1994.

Weil, Rachel. *Political Passions: Gender, the Family and Political Argument in England, 1680–1714*. Manchester, 2000.

Scotland and the Union

Devine, T. M. *Scotland and the Union, 1707–2007*. Edinburgh, 2008.

Ferguson, William. *Scotland's Relations with England: A Survey to 1707*. Edinburgh, 1977.

Grant, Alexander, and Stringer, Keith J., eds. *Uniting the Kingdom? The Making of British History*. London, 1995.

Riley, P. W. J. *King William III and the Scottish Politicians*. Edinburgh, 1979.

Riley, P. W. J. *The Union of England and Scotland. A Study of Anglo-Scottish Politics in the Eighteenth Century*. Manchester, 1978.

Robertson, John, ed. *A Union for Empire: Political Thought and the British Union of 1707*. Cambridge, 1995.

Szechi, Daniel. *1715: The Great Jacobite Rebellion*. New Haven, CT, 2006.

Ireland

Bartlett, Tim, and Hayton, David, eds. *Penal Era and Golden Age: Essays in Irish History, 1690–1800*. Belfast, 1979.

Connolly, S. J. *Religion, Law and Power: The Making of Protestant Ireland, 1660–1760*. Oxford, 1992.

James, Francis G. *Ireland in the Empire: A History of Ireland from the Williamite Wars to the Eve of the American Revolution*. Cambridge, MA, 1973.

O'Ciardha, Eamonn. *Ireland and the Jacobite Cause, 1685–1766: A Fatal Attachment*. Dublin, 2004.

Simms, J. G. *Jacobite Ireland*. Dublin, 2000.

Politics and Government, 1714–1760

Great Britain

Black, Jeremy. *King George II: Puppet of the Politicians?* Exeter, 2007.

Black, Jeremy. *Pitt the Elder*. Cambridge, 1992.

Black, Jeremy, ed. *Britain in the Age of Walpole*. New York, 1984.

Browning, Reed. *The Duke of Newcastle*. New Haven, CT, 1975.

Browning, Reed. *Political and Constitutional Ideas of the Court Whigs*. Baton Rouge, LA, 1982.

Colley, Linda. *Britons: Forging the Nation, 1707–1837*. New Haven, CT, 1992.

Colley, Linda. *In Defiance of Oligarchy: The Tory Party 1714–60*. Cambridge, 1982.

Cruickshanks, Eveline. *Political Untouchables: The Tories and the '45*. London, 1975.

Cruickshanks, Eveline, and Erskine-Hill, Howard. *The Atterbury Plot*. London, 2004.

Dickinson, H. T. *The Politics of the People in Eighteenth-Century Britain*. New York, 1995.

Gerrard, Christine. *The Patriot Opposition to Walpole: Politics, Poetry and National Myth, 1725–42*. Oxford, 1994.

Hatton, Ragnhild. *George I, Elector and King*. London, 1978.

Hill, B. W. *Sir Robert Walpole: "Sole and Prime Minister."* London, 1989.

Langford, Paul. *The Excise Crisis: Society and Politics in the Age of Walpole*. Oxford, 1975.

McLynn, Frank. *Charles Edward Stuart: A Tragedy in Many Acts*. London, 1988.

Pittock, Murray. *The Myth of the Jacobite Clans*. Edinburgh, 1995.

Plumb, J. H. *Sir Robert Walpole*. 2 volumes, London, 1956–61.

Smith, Hannah. *Georgian Monarchy: Politics and Culture, 1714–1760*. Cambridge, 2006.

Rogers, Nicholas. *Crowds, Culture and Politics in Georgian Britain*. Oxford, 1998.

Rogers, Nicholas. *Whigs and Cities: Popular Politics in the Age of Walpole and Pitt*. Oxford, 1989.

Wilson, Kathleen. *The Sense of the People: Politics, Culture and Imperialism in England, 1715–1785*. Cambridge, 1995.

Ireland

Hill, Jacqueline R. *From Patriots to Unionists: Dublin Civic Politics and Irish Protestant Patriotism, 1660–1840*. Oxford, 1997.

McNally, Patrick. *Parties, Patriots and Undertakers: Parliamentary Politics in Early Hanoverian Ireland*. Dublin, 1997.

Mahoney, Robert. *Jonathan Swift: The Irish Identity*. New Haven, CT, 1995.

Politics and Government, 1760–1801

Great Britain

Barker, Hannah. *Newspapers, Politics and Public Opinion in Late Eighteenth-Century England*. Oxford, 1998.

Black, Jeremy. *George III: America's Last King*. New Haven, CT, 2006.

Brewer, John. *Party Ideology and Popular Politics at the Accession of George III*. Cambridge, 1976.

Brooke, John. *King George III*. London, 1972.

Cash, Arthur C. *John Wilkes: The Scandalous Father of Civil Liberty*. New Haven, CT, 2006.

Christie, Ian. *Stress and Stability in Late Eighteenth-Century Britain*. Oxford, 1984.

Conway, Stephen. *The British Isles and the War of American Independence*. Cambridge, 2000.

Cookson, J. E. *The British Armed Nation, 1793–1815*. Oxford, 1997.

Dickinson, H. T. *British Radicalism and the French Revolution, 1789–1815*. Oxford, 1985.

Ditchfield, G. M. *George III: An Essay in Monarchy*. London, 2003.

Ehrman, John. *The Younger Pitt*. 3 volumes, London, 1969–96.

Epstein, James. *Radical Expression: Political Language, Ritual and Symbol in England, 1790–1850*. New York, 1994.

Goodwin, Albert. *The Friends of Liberty: The English Democratic Movement in the Age of the French Revolution*. London, 1979.

Gould, Eliga H. *The Persistence of Empire: British Political Culture in the Age of the American Revolution*. Chapel Hill, NC, 2000.

McCalman, Iain. *Radical Underworld: Prophets, Revolutionaries and Pornographers in London, 1795–1840*. Oxford, 1993.

Morris, Marilyn. *The British Monarchy and the French Revolution*. New Haven, CT, 1998.

Namier, Sir Lewis. *Crossroads of Power: Essays on Eighteenth-Century England*. London, 1962.

Philp, Mark, ed. *The French Revolution and British Popular Politics*. Cambridge, 2004.

Rudé, George. *Wilkes and Liberty: A Social Study of 1763 to 1774*. Oxford, 1962.

Sack, James J. *From Jacobite to Conservative: Reaction and Orthodoxy in Britain, c.1760–1832*. Cambridge, 1993.

Thomas, Peter D. G. *Lord North*. London, 1976.

Ireland

Bartlett, Thomas, Dickson, David, Keogh, Daire, and Whelan, Kevin. *1798: A Bicentennial Perspective*. Dublin, 2003.

Elliott, Marianne. *Partners in Revolution: The United Irishmen and France*. New Haven, CT, 1982.

Elliott, Marianne. *Robert Emmett: The Making of a Legend*. London, 2003.

Elliott, Marianne. *Wolfe Tone: Prophet of Irish Independence*. New Haven, CT, 1992.

Smyth, Jim. *The Men of No Property: Irish Radicals and Popular Politics in the Late Eighteenth Century*. London, 1992.

Politics and Government, 1801–1837

Brock, Michael. *The Great Reform Act*. London, 1973.

Burns, Arthur, and Innes, Joanna, eds. *Rethinking the Age of Reform, 1780–1850*. Cambridge, 2003.

Clark, Anna. *Scandal: The Sexual Politics of the British Constitution*. Princeton, NJ, 2004.

Evans, Eric. *The Great Reform Act of 1832*. London, 1994.

Gash, Norman. *Lord Liverpool*. Cambridge, MA, 1985.

Gash, Norman. *Mr Secretary Peel: The Life of Sir Robert Peel to 1830*. London, 1985.

Gilmartin, Kevin. *Print Politics: The Press and Radical Opposition in Early Nineteenth-Century England*. Cambridge, 1996.

Hilton, Boyd. *Corn, Cash, Commerce: The Economic Policies of the Tory Governments, 1815–30*. Oxford, 1977.

Hinde, Wendy. *Catholic Emancipation: A Shake to Men's Minds*. Oxford, 1992.

Jupp, Peter. *British Politics on the Eve of Reform: The Duke of Wellington's Administration, 1828–30*. Basingstoke, 1997.

Lopatin, Nancy. *Political Unions, Popular Politics and the Great Reform Act of 1832*. Basingstoke, 1999.

Macdonagh, Oliver. *The Emancipist: Daniel O'Connell, 1830–1847*. New York, 1987.

Macdonagh, Oliver. *The Hereditary Bondsman: Daniel O'Connell, 1775–1829*. New York, 1988.

Mandler, Peter. *Aristocratic Government in the Age of Reform: Whigs and Liberals, 1830–1852.* Oxford, 1990.

Semmel, Stuart. *Napoleon and the British.* New Haven, CT, 2004.

Smith, E. A. *George IV.* New Haven, CT, 1999.

Smith, E. A. *Lord Grey, 1764–1845.* Oxford, 1990.

Vernon, James. *Politics and the People: A Study in English Political Culture, c.1815–1867.* Cambridge, 1992.

Religion

Bossy, John. *The English Catholic Community, 1570–1850.* London, 1975.

Bradley, James E. *Religion, Revolution and English Radicalism: Nonconformity in Eighteenth-Century Politics and Society.* Cambridge, 1990.

Clark, J. C. D. *English Society, 1660–1832: Religion, Ideology and Society during the Ancien Régime.* Cambridge, 2000.

Claydon, Tony. *William III and the Godly Revolution.* Cambridge, 1996.

Claydon, Tony, and McBride, Ian, eds. *Protestantism and National Identity: Britain and Ireland c.1650– c.1850.* Cambridge, 1998.

Fagan, Patrick. *Catholics in a Protestant Country: The Papist Constituency in Eighteenth-Century Dublin.* Dublin, 1998.

Felsenstein, Frank. *Anti-Semitic Stereotypes: A Paradigm of Otherness in English Popular Culture, 1660–1830.* Baltimore, 1995.

Gilbert, A. D. *Religion and Society in Industrial England: Church, Chapel and Social Change, 1740–1900.* London, 1976.

Gwynn, Robin D. *Huguenot Heritage: The History and Contribution of the Huguenots in Britain.* London, 1985.

Haydon, Colin. *Anti-Catholicism in Eighteenth-Century England.* Manchester, 1993.

Hempton, David. *Religion and Political Culture in Great Britain and Ireland: From the Glorious Revolution to the Decline of Empire.* Cambridge, 1996.

Hempton, David. *The Religion of the People: Methodism and Popular Religion, c.1750–1900.* London, 1996.

Hempton, David, and Hill, Myrtle. *Evangelical Protestantism in Ulster Society, 1740–1890.* London, 1992.

Hilton, Boyd. *The Age of Atonement. The Influence of Evangelicalism on Social and Economic Thought, 1785–1865.* Oxford, 1992.

Jacob, W. M. *Lay People and Religion in the Early Eighteenth Century.* Cambridge, 1996.

Jones, David Ceri. *Glorious Work in the World: Welsh Methodism and the International Evangelical Revival, 1735–1750.* Cardiff, 2004.

Katz, David S. *The Jews in the History of England, 1485–1850.* Oxford, 1994.

Kent, John. *Wesley and the Wesleyans.* Cambridge, 2002.

Rack, Henry. *Reasonable Enthusiast: John Wesley and the Rise of Methodism.* Peterborough, 2002.

Rivers, Isabel. *Reason, Grace and Sentiment: A Study of the Language of Religion and Ethics in England, 1660–1780.* Cambridge, 1991.

Rupp, E. G. *Religion in England, 1688–1791.* Oxford, 1986.

Shaw, Jane. *Miracles in Enlightenment England.* New Haven, CT, 2006.

Smith, Mark. *Religion in Industrial Society: Oldham and Saddleworth, 1740–1865.* Oxford, 1994.

Valenze, Deborah. *Prophetic Sons and Daughters: Female Preaching and Popular Religion in Industrial England*. Princeton, NJ, 1985.

Walsh, John, Haydon, Colin, and Taylor, Stephen, eds. *The Church of England, c.1689–c.1833. From Toleration to Tractarianism*. Cambridge, 1993.

Ward, W. R. *The Protestant Evangelical Awakening*. London, 1992.

Watts, Michael R. *The Dissenters: From the Reformation to the French Revolution*. Oxford, 1978.

Watts, Michael R. *The Dissenters: The Expansion of Evangelical Nonconformity, 1791–1859*. Oxford, 1995.

Social Relations: Ranks, Occupations, Racial Minorities

Beckett, J. V. *The Aristocracy in England, 1660–1914*. Oxford, 1986.

Cannon, John. *Aristocratic Century: The Peerage of Eighteenth-Century England*. Cambridge, 1984.

Devine, T. M., and Mitchison, Rosalind. *People and Society in Scotland, volume 1: 1760–1830*. Edinburgh, 1988.

Earle, Peter. *The Making of the English Middle Class. Business, Society and Family Life in London, 1660–1730*. Berkeley, CA, 1989.

Gerzina, Gretchen. *Black London: Life before Emancipation*. New Brunswick, NJ, 1995.

Hancock, David. *Citizens of the World: London Merchants and the Integration of the British Atlantic Community, 1735–1785*. Cambridge, 1995.

Hill, Bridget. *Servants: English Domestics in the Eighteenth Century*. Oxford, 1996.

Hitchcock, Tim. *Chronicling Poverty: The Voices and Strategies of the English Poor, 1640–1840*. Basingstoke, 1997.

Holmes, Geoffrey. *Augustan England: Professions, State and Society, 1680–1830*. London, 1982.

Houston, R. A., and Whyte, I. D., eds. *Scottish Society, 1500–1800*. Cambridge, 1989.

Howell, David W. *Patriarchs and Parasites: The Gentry of South-West Wales in the Eighteenth Century*. Cardiff, 1986.

Howell, David W. *The Rural Poor in Eighteenth-Century Wales*. Cardiff, 2000.

Hunt, Margaret. *The Middling Sort: Commerce, Gender and the Family in England, 1680–1780*. Berkeley, CA, 1996.

Jenkins, Philip. *The Making of a Ruling Class: The Glamorgan Gentry, 1640–1790*. Cambridge, 1983.

Mingay, G. E. *English Landed Society in the Eighteenth Century*. London, 1963.

Myers, Norma. *Reconstructing the Black Past: Blacks in Britain 1780–1830*. London, 1996.

Neeson, J. M. *Commoners: Common Right, Enclosure and Social Change in England, 1700–1820*. Cambridge, 1993.

Perkin, Harold J. *The Origins of Modern English Society, 1780–1880*. London, 1969.

Porter, Roy. *English Society in the Eighteenth Century*. London, 1990.

Rediker, Marcus. *Between the Devil and the Deep Blue Sea: Merchant Seamen, Pirates and the Anglo-American Maritime World, 1700–1750*. Cambridge, 1987.

Rodger, N. A. M. *The Wooden World: An Anatomy of the Georgian Navy*. Annapolis, MD, 1986.

Rosenheim, James. *The Emergence of a Ruling Order: England 1650–1750*. London, 1998.

Rule, John. *The Labouring Classes in Early Industrial England, 1750–1850*. London, 1986.

Sharpe, J. A. *Early Modern England: A Social History, 1550–1760*. London, 1997.

Smail, John. *The Origins of Middle-Class Culture. Halifax, Yorkshire, 1660–1780*. Ithaca, NY, 1994.

Snell, K. D. M. *Annals of the Labouring Poor: Social Change and Agrarian England, 1660–1900*. Cambridge, 1985.

Stone, Lawrence, and Stone, Jeanne C. Fawtier. *An Open Elite? England, 1540–1880*. Oxford, 1986.

Thompson, E. P. *The Making of the English Working Class*. Harmondsworth, 1970.

Wahrman, Dror. *Imagining the Middle Class: The Political Representation of Class in Britain, 1780–1840*. Cambridge, 1995.

Whyman, Susan. *Sociability and Power in Late-Stuart England. The Cultural Worlds of the Verneys, 1660–1720*. Oxford, 1999.

Gender, the Family, and Sexuality

Barker, Hannah, and Chailus, Elaine, eds. *Gender in Eighteenth-Century England*. New York, 1997.

Barker, Hannah, and Chailus, Elaine, eds. *Women's History, 1700–1850: An Introduction*. London, 2005.

Clark, Anna. *The Struggle for the Breeches: Gender and the Making of the British Working Class*. Berkeley, CA, 1997.

Davidoff, Leonore, and Hall, Catherine. *Family Fortunes: Men and Women of the English Middle Class, 1780–1850*. London, 1987.

Fletcher, Anthony. *Gender, Sex and Subordination in England, 1500–1800*. New Haven, CT, 1995.

Gillis, John. *For Better, For Worse: British Marriages, 1600 to the Present*. Oxford, 1985.

Hill, Bridget. *Women Alone: Spinsters in England, 1660–1850*. New Haven, CT, 2001.

Hitchcock, Tim. *English Sexualities, 1700–1800*. Basingstoke, 1997.

Leneman, Leah, and Mitchison, Rosalind. *Sin in the City: Sexuality and Social Control in Urban Scotland, 1660–1780*. Dalkeith, 2001.

Mendelson, Sara, and Crawford, Patricia. *Women in Early Modern England*. Oxford, 1998.

O'Dowd, Mary. *A History of Women in Ireland, 1500–1800*. Harlow, 2005.

Porter, Roy, and Hall, Lesley. *The Facts of Life: The Creation of Sexual Knowledge in Britain, 1650–1950*. New Haven, CT, 1995.

Shoemaker, Robert B. *Gender in English Society 1650–1850*. London, 1998.

Stone, Lawrence. *The Family, Sex and Marriage in England, 1500–1800*. Harmondsworth, 1979.

Stone, Lawrence. *Uncertain Unions: Marriage in England, 1660–1753*. Oxford, 1992.

Vickery, Amanda. *The Gentleman's Daughter: Women's Lives in Georgian England*. New Haven, CT, 1998.

Cultural Practices

Barker, Hannah. *Newspapers, Politics and English Society, 1695–1855*. London, 1999.

Barnard, Toby. *Making the Grand Figure: Lives and Possessions in Ireland, 1660–1770*. New Haven, CT, 2004.

Black, Jeremy. *Italy and the Grand Tour*. New Haven, CT, 2003.

Bostridge, Ian. *Witchcraft and its Transformations, c.1650–1750*. Oxford, 1997.

Brewer, John, and Staves, Susan, eds. *Early Modern Conceptions of Property*. London, 1995.

Clark, Peter. *The English Alehouse: A Social History, 1200–1830*. Harlow, 1983.

Cowan, Brian. *The Social Life of Coffee: The Emergence of the British Coffeehouse*. New Haven, CT, 2005.

Cranfield, G. A. *The Press and Society from Caxton to Northcliffe*. London, 1978.

Gatrell, V. A. C. *City of Laughter: Sex and Satire in Eighteenth-Century London*. New York, 2006.

Davies, Owen. *Witchcraft, Magic and Culture, 1736–1951*. Manchester, 1999.

Girouard, Mark. *Life in the English Country House*. New Haven, CT, 1978.

Hobsbawm, E. A., and Ranger, T. O., eds. *The Invention of Tradition*. Oxford, 1983.

Houston, R. A. *Scottish Literacy and Scottish Identity, 1600–1800*. Cambridge, 1985.

Hutton, Ronald. *The Rise and Fall of Merry England: The Ritual Year, 1400–1700*. Oxford, 1994.

McDowell, Paula. *The Women of Grub Street: Press, Politics and Gender in the London Literary Marketplace, 1678–1730*. Oxford, 1998.

McKendrick, Neil, Brewer, John, and Plumb, J. H. *The Birth of a Consumer Society: The Commercialization of Eighteenth-Century England*. London, 1982.

Malcolmson, Robert W. *Popular Recreations in English Society, 1700–1850*. Cambridge, 1973.

Mandler, Peter, *The Fall and Rise of the Stately Home*. New Haven, CT, 1999.

Raven, James. *Judging New Wealth: Popular Publishing and Responses to Commerce in England, 1750–1800*. Oxford, 1992.

Ribeiro, Aileen. *The Art of Dress: Fashion in England and France, 1750–1820*. New Haven, CT, 1995.

Styles, John. *The Dress of the People: Everyday Fashion in Eighteenth-Century England*. New Haven, CT, 2008.

Thompson, E. P. *Customs in Common: Studies in Traditional Popular Culture*. New York, 1991.

Tranter, N. L. *Sport, Economy and Society in Britain: 1750–1914*. Cambridge, 1998.

Underdown, David. *Start of Play: Cricket and Culture in Eighteenth-Century England*. London, 2000.

Wahrman, Dror. *The Making of the Modern Self: Identity and Culture in Eighteenth-Century England*. New Haven, CT, 2004.

Town Life

Borsay, Peter. *The English Urban Renaissance: Culture and Society in the Provincial Town, 1660–1770*. Oxford, 1989.

Chalklin, C. W. *The Rise of the English Town, 1650–1850*. Cambridge, 2001.

Clark, Peter, ed. *The Transformation of English Provincial Towns*. London, 1984.

Corfield, P. J. *The Impact of English Towns, 1700–1800*. Oxford, 1982.

Estabrook, Carl B. *Urbane and Rustic England: Cultural Ties and Social Spheres in the Provinces, 1660–1780*. Manchester, 1998.

Hitchcock, Tim. *Down and Out in Eighteenth-Century London*. Hambledon, 2005.

Houston, R. A. *Social Change in the Age of Enlightenment: Edinburgh, 1660–1760*. Oxford, 1994.

Monod, Paul Kléber. *The Murder of Mr Grebell: Madness and Civility in an English Town*. New Haven, CT, 2003.

Porter, Roy. *London: A Social History*. Cambridge, MA, 1995.

Rudé, George. *Hanoverian London, 1714–1808*. Berkeley, CA, 1971.

Sweet, Rosemary. *The Writing of Urban Histories in Eighteenth-Century England*. Oxford, 1997.

Sweet, Rosemary. *The English Town, 1680–1840*. New York, 1999.

Waller, Philip, ed. *The English Urban Landscape*. Oxford, 2000.

Social Problems and Policies

Poverty and Disease

Andrews, Donna T. *Philanthropy and Police: London Charity in the Eighteenth Century*. Princeton, NJ, 1990.

Barry, Jonathan, and Jones, Colin, eds. *Medicine and Charity before the Welfare State*. London, 1994.

Boyer, George. *An Economic History of the English Poor Law, 1750–1850*. Cambridge, 1990.

Davison, Lee, Hitchcock, Tim, Keirn, Tim, and Shoemaker, R. B., eds. *Stilling the Grumbling Hive: The Response to Social and Economic Problems in England, 1689–1750*. Basingstoke, 1992.

Cunningham, Hugh, and Innes, Joanna, eds. *Charity, Philanthropy and Reform from the 1690s to 1850*. Basingstoke, 1998.

Fideler, Paul. *Social Welfare in Pre-Industrial England. The Old Poor Law Tradition*. Basingstoke, 2006.

Porter, Roy. *Disease, Medicine and Society in England, 1550–1860*. Cambridge, 1995.

Porter, Roy. *Mind-Forg'd Manacles: A History of Madness in England from the Restoration to the Regency*. London, 1990.

Scull, Andrew. *The Most Solitary of Afflictions: Madness and Society in Britain, 1700–1900*. New Haven, CT, 1993.

Crime and Disorder

Andrews, Donna T., and McGowan, Randy. *The Perreaus and Mrs Rudd: Forgery and Betrayal in Eighteenth-Century London*. Berkeley, CA, 2001.

Beattie, J. M. *Crime and the Courts in England, 1660–1800*. Princeton, NJ, 1986.

Beattie, J. M. *Policing and Punishment in London, 1660–1750*. Oxford, 2001.

Emsley, Clive. *Crime and Society in England, 1750–1900*. Harlow, 1987.

Gatrell, V. A. C. *The Hanging Tree: Execution and the English People, 1770–1868*. Oxford, 1994.

Hay, Douglas, Linebaugh, Peter, Rule, John G., Thompson, E. P., and Winslow, Cal. *Albion's Fatal Tree: Crime and Society in Eighteenth-Century England*. New York, 1975.

King, Peter. *Crime, Justice and Discretion in England, 1740–1820*. Oxford, 2000.

Landau, Norma. *The Justices of the Peace, 1679–1760*. Berkeley, CA, 1984.

Landau, Norma, ed. *Law, Crime and English Society, 1660–1830*. Cambridge, 2002.

Linebaugh, Peter. *The London Hanged: Crime and Civil Society in the Eighteenth Century*. Harmondsworth, 1991.

Sharpe, J. A. *Crime in Early Modern England, 1550–1750*. Harlow, 1984.

Shoemaker, R. B. *The London Mob: Violence and Disorder in Eighteenth-Century England*. Hambledon, 2004.

Styles, John, and Brewer, John, eds. *An Ungovernable People: The English and Their Law in the Seventeenth and Eighteenth Centuries*. New Brunswick, NJ, 1980.

Thompson, E. P. *Whigs and Hunters: The Origins of the Black Act*. New York, 1975.

Economic Life

Barker, Hannah. *The Business of Women: Female Enterprise and Urban Development in Northern England, 1760–1830*. Oxford, 2006.

Berg, Maxine. *The Age of Manufactures: Industry, Work and Innovation in Britain, 1700–1820*. London, 1985.

Berg, Maxine. *Luxury and Pleasure in Eighteenth-Century Britain*. Oxford, 2005.

Berg, Maxine, and Clifford, Helen, eds. *Consumers and Luxury: Consumer Culture in Europe, 1650–1850*. Manchester, 1999.

Berg, Maxine, Hudson, Pat, and Sonenscher, Michael, eds. *Manufacture in Town and Country before the Factory*. Cambridge, 1983.

Chambers, J. D., and Mingay, G. E. *The Agricultural Revolution, 1660–1780*. London, 1975.

Cullen, L. B. *An Economic History of Ireland since 1660*. London, 1972.

Daunton, M. J. *Progress and Poverty: An Economic and Social History of Britain, 1700–1850*. Oxford, 1995.

Deane, Phyllis. *The First Industrial Revolution*. Cambridge, 1979.

Devine, T. M. *The Transformation of Rural Scotland: Social Change and the Agrarian Economy, 1660–1815*. Edinburgh, 1994.

Floud, Roderick, and McCloskey, Deirdre, eds. *The Economic History of Britain since 1700, volume 1: 1700–1860*. Cambridge, 1994.

Holderness, B. A. *Pre-Industrial England: Economy and Society, 1500–1750*. London, 1976.

Holderness, B. A., and Turner, Michael. *Land, Labour and Agriculture, 1700–1920*. Hambledon, 1990.

Houston, R. A. *The Population History of Britain and Ireland, 1500–1750*. Cambridge, 1995.

Kowalewski-Wallace, Elizabeth. *Consuming Subjects: Women, Shopping and Business in the Eighteenth Century*. New York, 1997.

Mokyr, Joel. *The British Industrial Revolution: An Economic Perspective*. Boulder, CO, 1998.

Pawson, Eric. *The Early Industrial Revolution: Britain in the Eighteenth Century*. London, 1978.

Smout, T. C. *Nature Contested: Environmental History in Scotland and Northern Ireland since 1600*. Edinburgh, 2000.

Thirsk, Joan, ed. *The English Rural Landscape*. Oxford, 2000.

Tranter, N. L. *Population and Society, 1750–1940*. Harlow, 1985.

Valenze, Deborah. *The First Industrial Woman*. Oxford, 1995.

Weatherhill, Lorna. *Consumer Behaviour and Material Culture in Britain, 1660–1760*. London, 1988.

Wrightson, Keith. *Earthly Necessities: Economic Lives in Early Modern Britain*. New Haven, CT, 2000.

Intellectual Life

Trends in Thought and Culture

Barker-Benfield, G. J. *The Culture of Sensibility: Sex and Society in Eighteenth-Century Britain.* Chicago, 1992.

Brewer, John. *The Pleasures of the Imagination: English Culture in the Eighteenth Century.* London, 1997.

Broadie, Alexander, ed. *The Cambridge Companion to the Scottish Enlightenment.* Cambridge, 2003.

Kidd, Colin. *Subverting Scotland's Past: Scottish Whig Historians and the creation of an Anglo-English Identity, 1689–c.1830.* Cambridge, 1993.

Kidd, Colin. *British Identities Before Nationalism: Ethnicity and Nationhood in the Atlantic World, 1600–1800.* Cambridge, 1999.

Klein, Lawrence. E. *Shaftesbury and the Culture of Politeness.* Cambridge, 1994.

Newman, Gerald. *The Rise of English Nationalism: A Cultural History, 1740–1830.* New York, 1987.

Pittock, Murray G. A. *The Invention of Scotland: The Stuart Myth and the Scottish Identity, 1638 to the Present.* London, 1991.

Porter, Roy. *The Creation of the Modern World: The Untold Story of the English Enlightenment.* New York, 2000.

Sher, Richard B. *Church and University in the Scottish Enlightenment: The Moderate Literati of Edinburgh.* Princeton, NJ, 1985.

Sher, Richard B. *The Enlightenment and the Book: Scottish Authors and Their Publishers in Eighteenth-Century Britain.* Chicago, 2006.

Sloan, Kim, with Burnett, Andrew, eds. *Enlightenment: Discovering the World in the Eighteenth Century.* London, 2003.

Literature, Philosophy, Science, Music

Backsheider, Paula. *Daniel Defoe: His Life.* Baltimore, 1989.

Battestin, Martin, and Battestin, Ruth R. *Henry Fielding: A Life.* London, 1989.

Bentley, G. E. *The Stranger from Paradise: A Biography of William Blake.* New Haven, CT, 2001.

Clark, J. C. D. *Samuel Johnson: Literature, Religion and English Cultural Politics from the Restoration to Romanticism.* Cambridge, 1994.

Dinwiddy, J. R. *Bentham.* Ed. William Twining. Stanford, CA, 2004.

Erskine-Hill, Howard. *Poetry of Opposition and Revolution, Dryden to Wordsworth.* Oxford, 1996.

Higgins, Ian. *Swift's Politics: A Study in Disaffection.* Cambridge, 1994.

Holmes, Richard. *Coleridge.* 2 volumes, New York, 1990–9.

Hudson, Nicholas. *Samuel Johnson and the Making of Modern England.* Cambridge, 2003.

Jones, Peter, ed. *Philosophy and Science in the Scottish Enlightenment.* Edinburgh, 1988.

Keymer, Tom, and Mee, Jon. *The Cambridge Companion to English Literature, 1740 to 1830.* Cambridge, 2004.

Mee, John. *Dangerous Enthusiasm: William Blake and the Culture of Radicalism in the 1790s.* Oxford, 1992.

Pocock, J. G. A. *Virtue, Commerce and History: Essays on Political Thought and History.* Cambridge, 1985.

Pocock, J. G. A. *Barbarism and Religion.* 4 volumes, 2001–8.

Rivers, Isabel, and Wykes, David L., eds. *Joseph Priestley: Scientist, Philosopher and Theologian.* Oxford, 2008.

Robertson, John. *The Scottish Enlightenment and the Militia Issue.* Edinburgh, 1985.

Smith, Ruth. *Handel's Oratorios and Eighteenth-Century Thought.* Cambridge, 1995.

Uglow, Jenny. *The Lunar Men.* London, 2002.

Weinbrot, Howard D. *Britannia's Issue: The Rise of British Literature from Dryden to Ossian.* Cambridge, 1993.

Westfall, Richard. *Never at Rest: A Biography of Isaac Newton.* Cambridge, 1980.

Winch, Donald. *Riches and Poverty: An Intellectual History of Political Economy in Britain, 1750–1834.* Cambridge, 1996.

Womersley, David. *Gibbon and the "Watchmen of the Holy City": The Historian and his Reputation, 1776–1815.* Oxford, 2002.

Painting, Architecture, Visual Arts

Barrell, John. *The Political Theory of Painting from Reynolds to Hazlitt.* New Haven, CT, 1986.

Curl, James Steven. *Georgian Architecture.* London, 2002.

Darley, Gillian. *John Soane, An Accidental Romantic.* New Haven, CT, 1999.

Donald, Diana. *The Age of Caricature: Satirical Prints in the Reign of George III.* New Haven, CT, 1996.

Hamilton, James. *Turner.* New York, 2007.

Harris, John. *The Palladian Revival: Lord Burlington, His Villa and Garden at Chiswick.* New Haven, CT, 1994.

Jardine, Lisa. *On a Grander Scale: The Outstanding Career of Sir Christopher Wren.* London, 2002.

Macmillan, Duncan. *Painting in Scotland: The Golden Age.* Oxford, 1986.

Paulson, Ronald. *Hogarth.* 3 volumes, New Brunswick, NJ, 1991.

Pears, Iain. *The Discovery of Painting: The Growth of Interest in the Arts in England, 1680–1768.* New Haven, CT, 1988.

Scott, Jonathan. *The Pleasures of Antiquity; British Collectors of Greece and Rome.* New Haven, CT, 2003.

Solkin, David H. *Painting for Money: The Visual Arts and the Public Sphere in Eighteenth-Century England.* New Haven, CT, 1992.

Summerson, John, and Colvin, Howard. *Georgian London.* New Haven, CT, 2003.

Uglow, Jenny. *Hogarth: A Life and a World.* New York, 1997.

Worsley, Giles. *Classical Architecture in Britain: The Heroic Age.* New Haven, CT, 1995.

The British Empire

Empire as Concept and Reality

Armitage, David. *The Ideological Origins of the British Empire.* Cambridge, 2000.

Beinart, William, and Hughes, Lotte, eds. *The Oxford History of the British Empire Companion: Environment and Empire.* Oxford, 2007.

Bowen, H. V. *Elites, Enterprise and the Making of the British Overseas Empire, 1688–1775*. New York, 1995.

Canny, Nicholas, ed. *The Oxford History of the British Empire, Volume 1: The Origins of Empire*. Oxford, 1998.

Colley, Linda. *Captives: Britain, Empire and the World, 1600–1850*. New York, 2004.

Colley, Linda. *The Ordeal of Elizabeth Marsh: A Woman in World History*. New York, 2007.

Etherington, Norman, ed. *The Oxford History of the British Empire Companion: Missions and Empire*. Oxford, 2008.

Levine, Philippa. *The British Empire: Sunrise to Sunset*. London, 2007.

Levine, Philippa, ed., *The Oxford History of the British Empire Companion: Gender and Empire*. Oxford, 2004.

Marshall, P. J. *The Making and Unmaking of Empires: Britain, India and America, c.1750–1783*. Oxford, 2005.

Marshall, P. J., ed. *The Oxford History of the British Empire, Volume 2: The Eighteenth Century*. Oxford, 1998.

Miller, David Philip, and Reill, Peter Hanns, eds. *Visions of Empire: Voyages, Botany and Representations of Nature*. Cambridge, 1996.

Porter, Andrew, ed. *The Oxford History of the British Empire, Volume 3: The Nineteenth Century*. Oxford, 1998.

Ritchie, Robert C. *Captain Kidd and the War against the Pirates*. Cambridge, MA, 1986.

Wilson, Kathleen. *The Island Race: Englishness, Empire and Gender in the Eighteenth Century*. London, 2003.

Wilson, Kathleen, ed. *The New Imperial History: Culture, Identity and Modernity in Britain and the Empire, 1660–1840*. Cambridge, 2004.

India

Barrow, Ian. *Making History, Drawing Territory: British Mapping in India, c.1765–1920*. New Delhi, 2003.

Bayly, C. A. *Indian Society and the Making of the British Empire*. Cambridge, 1988.

Bowen, H. V., Lincoln, Margarette, and Rigby, Nigel, eds. *The Worlds of the East India Company*. Woodbridge, Suffolk, 2002.

Dirks, Nicholas B. *The Scandal of Empire: India and the Creation of Imperial Britain*. Cambridge, MA, 2006.

Fisher, Michael. *The First Indian Author in English: Dean Mahomet (1759–1851) in India, Ireland and England*. New York, 1996.

Keay, John. *The Honourable Company: A History of the English East India Company*. New York, 1993.

Lawson, Philip. *The East India Company: A History*. London, 1993.

Majeed, Javed. *Ungoverned Imaginings: John Mill's "The History of British India" and Orientalism*. Oxford, 1992.

Marshall, P. J. *The Impeachment of Warren Hastings*. Oxford, 1965.

Raza, Rosemary. *In Their Own Words: British Women Writers and India, 1740–1857*. New Delhi, 2006.

Stokes, Eric. *The English Utilitarians and India*. Oxford, 1989.

Sundar, Pushpa. *Patrons and Philistines: Arts and the State in British India, 1773–1947*. New Delhi, 1995.

North America

The American Colonies to 1783

Anderson, Fred. *Crucible of War: The Seven Years' War and the Fate of Empire in British North America, 1754–1766*. New York, 2000.

Armitage, David, and Braddick, Michael J., eds. *The British Atlantic World, 1500–1800*. Basingstoke, 2002.

Bailyn, Bernard. *The Peopling of British North America*. New York, 1986.

Bailyn, Bernard, with DeWolfe, Barbara. *Voyagers to the West: A Passage in the Peopling of British America on the Eve of the Revolution*. New York, 1986.

Bailyn, Bernard, and Morgan, Philip, eds. *Strangers Within the Realm: Cultural Margins of the First British Empire*. Chapel Hill, NC, 1991.

Breen, T. H. *The Marketplace of Revolution: How Consumer Culture Shaped American Independence*. New York, 2004.

Gould, Eliga H., and Onuf, Peter, eds. *Empire and Nation: The American Revolution in the Atlantic World*. Baltimore, 2005.

Greene, Jack P. *Peripheries and Center: Constitutional Development in the Extended Polities of the British Empire and the United States, 1607–1788*. Athens, GA, 1986.

Greene, Jack P. *Pursuits of Happiness: The Social Development of Early Modern British Colonies and the Formation of American Culture*. Chapel Hill, NC, 1988.

Kidd, Colin. *The Forging of Race: Race and Scripture in the Protestant Atlantic World, 1600–2000*. Cambridge, 2006.

Mancke, Elizabeth, and Shammas, Carol, eds. *The Creation of the British Atlantic World*. Baltimore, 2007.

Olwell, Robert, and Tully, Allan, eds. *Cultures and Identities in Colonial British America*. Baltimore, 2006.

Pole, J. R. *Political Representation in England and the Origins of the American Republic*. New York, 1966.

Sher, Richard B., and Smitten, David, eds. *Scotland and America in the Age of the Enlightenment*. Princeton, NJ, 1990.

Steele, Ian K. *The English Atlantic: An Exploration of Communication and Community*. Oxford, 1986.

Canada

Buckner, Philip, ed. *The Oxford History of the British Empire Companion: Canada and the British Empire*. Oxford, 2008.

Bumsted, J. M. *The Peoples of Canada: A Pre-Confederation History*. Don Mills, Ontario, 2003.

Craig, Gerald M. *Upper Canada: The Formative Years, 1784–1841*. Toronto, 1963.

Errington, Elizabeth Jane. *Emigrant Worlds and Transatlantic Communities: Migration to Upper Canada in the First Half of the Nineteenth Century*. Montreal, 2007.

Errington, Elizabeth Jane. *Wives and Mothers, Schoolmistresses and Scullery Maids: Working Women in Upper Canada, 1791–1840*. Montreal, 1995.

Greer, Alan. *The Patriots and the People: The Rebellion of 1837 in Rural Lower Canada*. Toronto, 1993.

Lawson, Philip. *The Imperial Challenge: Quebec and Britain in the Age of the American Revolution*. Montreal, 1990.

Ouellet, Fernand. *Lower Canada, 1791–1840: Social Change and Nationalism*. Trans. Patricia Claxton. Toronto, 1980.

Rawlyk, George A. *The Canada Fire: Radical Evangelicalism in British North America, 1775–1812*. Kingston, 1994.

Walker, James. *The Black Loyalists: The Search for a Promised Land in Nova Scotia and Sierra Leone, 1783–1870*. New York, 1976.

Wilton, Carol. *Popular Politics and Political Culture in Upper Canada, 1800–1850*. Montreal, 2000.

Winks, Robin. *The Blacks in Canada: A History*. Montreal, 1971.

The Caribbean

Amussen, Susan. *Caribbean Exchanges: Slavery and the Transformation of English Society, 1640–1700*. Chapel Hill, NC, 2007.

Beckles, Hilary. *Natural Rebels: A History of Enslaved Black Women in Barbados*. New Brunswick, NJ, 1989.

Beckles, Hilary. *A History of Barbados*. Cambridge, 1990.

Bush, Barbara. *Slave Women in Caribbean Society, 1650–1838*. Bloomington, IN, 1990.

Campbell, Mavis C. *The Maroons of Jamaica, 1655–1796*. Granby, MA, 1988.

Carrington, Selwyn H. H. *The Sugar Industry and the Abolition of the Slave Trade, 1775–1807*. Gainesville, FL, 2002.

Craton, Michael. *Testing the Chains: Resistance to Slavery in the British West Indies*. Ithaca, NY, 1982.

Dunn, Richard. *Sugar and Slaves: The Rise of the Planter Class in the English West Indies, 1624–1713*. Chapel Hill, NC, 1972.

Hall, Douglas. *In Miserable Slavery: Thomas Thistlewood in Jamaica, 1750–86*. Kingston, 1999.

Smith, S. D. *Slavery, Capital and Gentry Capitalism in the British Atlantic*. Cambridge, 2007.

The Slave Trade and Anti-Slavery

Braidwood, Stephen J. *Black Poor and White Philanthropists: London's Blacks and the Foundation of the Sierra Leone Settlement, 1786–1791*. Liverpool, 1994.

Davis, David Brion. *The Problem of Slavery in the Age of the American Revolution*. Ithaca, NY, 1973.

Eltis, David. *Economic Growth and the Ending of the Transatlantic Slave Trade*. Oxford, 1987.

Hochschild, Adam. *Bury the Chains: Prophets and Rebels in the Fight to Free an Empire's Slaves*. New York, 2005.

Jennings, Judith. *The Business of Abolishing the African Slave Trade, 1783–1807*. London, 1997.

Oldfield, J. R. *Popular Politics and British Anti-Slavery. The Mobilization of Public Opinion against the Slave Trade, 1787–1807*. London, 1998.

Pollock, John. *Wilberforce*. New York, 1977.

Schama, Simon. *Rough Crossings: Britain, the Slaves and the American Revolution*. London, 2005.

Turley, David. *The Culture of English Anti-Slavery, 1780–1860*. London, 1991.

Walvin, James. *England, Slaves and Freedom, 1776–1838*. Jackson, MS, 1986.

Walvin, James. *Black Ivory: A History of British Slavery*. Oxford, 2001.

The Pacific

Beaglehole, J. C. *The Life of Captain James Cook*. Stanford, CA, 1974.

Day, David. *Claiming a Continent: A New History of Australia*. Sydney, 2005.

Dening, Greg. *Mr Bligh's Bad Language: Passion, Power and Theatre on the Bounty*. Cambridge, 1992.

Haines, Robin. *Life and Death in the Age of Sail: The Passage to Australia*. Sydney, 2003.

Hughes, Robert. *The Fatal Shore*. New York, 1987.

Rudé, George. *Protest and Punishment: The Story of the Social and Political Protesters Transported to Australia, 1788–1868*. London, 1978.

Salmond, Anne. *The Trial of the Cannibal Dog: The Remarkable Story of Captain Cook's Encounters in the South Seas*. New Haven, CT, 2003.

Shaw, A. G. L. *The Story of Australia*. London, 1972.

Shaw, A. G. L. *Convicts and the Colonies*. Melbourne, 1977.

Index